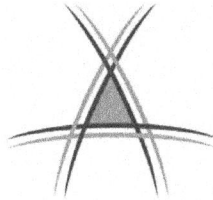

ASCENT
CENTER FOR TECHNICAL KNOWLEDGE

Autodesk® Revit® 2015 Architecture Fundamentals

Student Guide - Metric

Revision 2.0
July 2014

AUTODESK.
Authorized Author

AUTODESK.
Official Training Guide

CONTINUING EDUCATION AIA®

ASCENT - Center for Technical Knowledge®
Autodesk® Revit® 2015
Architecture Fundamentals - Metric
Revision 2.0

Prepared and produced by:

ASCENT Center for Technical Knowledge
630 Peter Jefferson Parkway, Suite 175
Charlottesville, VA 22911

866-527-2368
www.ascented.com

ASCENT - Center for Technical Knowledge is a division of RAND Worldwide Inc., providing custom developed knowledge products and services for leading engineering software applications. ASCENT is focused on specializing in the creation of education programs that incorporate the best of classroom learning and technology-based training offerings.

We welcome any comments you may have regarding this training manual, or any of our products. To contact us please email: feedback@ASCENTed.com.

Table of Contents

Preface

The Autodesk® Revit® software is a powerful Building Information Modeling (BIM) program that works the way architects think. The program streamlines the design process through the use of a central 3D model, where changes made in one view update across all views and on the printable sheets. This training guide is designed to teach you the Autodesk Revit functionality as you would work with it throughout the design process. You begin by learning about the user interface and basic drawing, editing, and viewing tools. Then you learn design development tools including how to model walls, doors, windows, floors, ceilings, stairs and more. Finally, you learn the processes that take the model into the construction documentation phase.

Since building projects themselves tend to be extremely complex, the Autodesk Revit software is also complex. The objective of the *Autodesk Revit 2015 Architecture Fundamentals* training guide is to enable students to create full 3D architectural project models and set them up in working drawings. This training guide focuses on basic tools that the majority of students need to work with the Autodesk Revit software.

The topics in this training guide include the following:

- Understand the purpose of Building Information Management (BIM) and how it is applied in the Autodesk Revit software.

- Navigating the Autodesk Revit workspace and interface.

- Working with the basic drawing and editing tools.

- Creating Levels and Grids as datum elements for the model.

- Creating a 3D building model with walls, curtain walls, windows, and doors.

- Adding floors, ceilings, and roofs to the building model.

- Creating component-based and custom stairs.

- Adding component features, such as furniture and equipment.

- Setting up sheets for plotting with text, dimensions, details, tags, and schedules.

- Creating details.

Icon Reference Chart

The following icons are used throughout this training guide to help you to quickly and easily find helpful information.

	Indicates the Learning Objectives that are covered in the current chapter or section of the training guide.
Enhanced in 2015	Indicates items that have been enhanced in the Autodesk Revit 2015 Architecture software.
New in 2015	Indicates items that are new in the Autodesk Revit 2015 Architecture software.
	Indicates items that are included to assist you in preparing for the Autodesk Revit 2015 Architecture Certified Professional exam.
	Indicates items that are included to assist you in preparing for the Autodesk Revit 2015 Architecture Certified User exam.

Appendix C includes a list of the Autodesk Certification topics and objectives for the Autodesk Revit software. References to content in this training guide have been included to assist you in preparing for both the User and Professional certification exams.

Students and Educators can Access Free Autodesk Software and Resources

Autodesk challenges you to get started with free educational licenses for professional software and creativity apps used by millions of architects, engineers, designers, and hobbyists today. Bring Autodesk software into your classroom, studio, or workshop to learn, teach, and explore real-world design challenges the way professionals do.

Get started today - register at the Autodesk Education Community and download one of the many Autodesk software applications available.

Visit www.autodesk.com/joinedu/

Free products are subject to the terms and conditions of the end-user license and services agreement that accompanies the software. The software is for personal use for education purposes and is not intended for classroom or lab use.

Class Files

To download the Class Files that are required for this training guide, use the following steps:

1. Type the ftp address shown at the bottom of the page into the address bar of your internet browser. If you are using an ASCENT ebook you can select the link instead. The ftp address must be typed exactly as shown.

Address bar

ftp://ftp.ascented.com/cware/lagopus.zip

File   Edit   View   Favorites   Tools   Help

2. Press <Enter> and follow the instructions to download the zip file that contains the Class Files.

3. The zip file contains an .exe file that you need to extract. To extract the files, double-click on the .exe file and follow the instructions to unzip the file. Once unzipped, a Class Files folder is automatically added to the C:\ drive on your computer.

Do not change the location in which the Class Files folder is created. Doing so can prevent the practices in the training guide from working correctly.

ftp://ftp.ascented.com/cware/lagopus.zip

Setting Up the Interface

The Autodesk® Building Design Suite version of the Autodesk® Revit® software is designed to be used with all building disciplines but the interface can be modified to suit each user's need. In this topic you learn how to modify the discipline-specific interface that is used in this training guide.

Discipline Specific Interface

The Autodesk Revit software has three disciplines: Architecture, Structure, and MEP (Mechanical, Electrical, and Plumbing, which is also know as Systems). When using the Autodesk Building Design Suite, all of the tools for these disciplines are installed in one copy of the software. By default, all of the tools, templates, and sample files are available, as shown in Figure 1. Most users only need access to their specific set of tools and the interface can be customized to suit those needs.

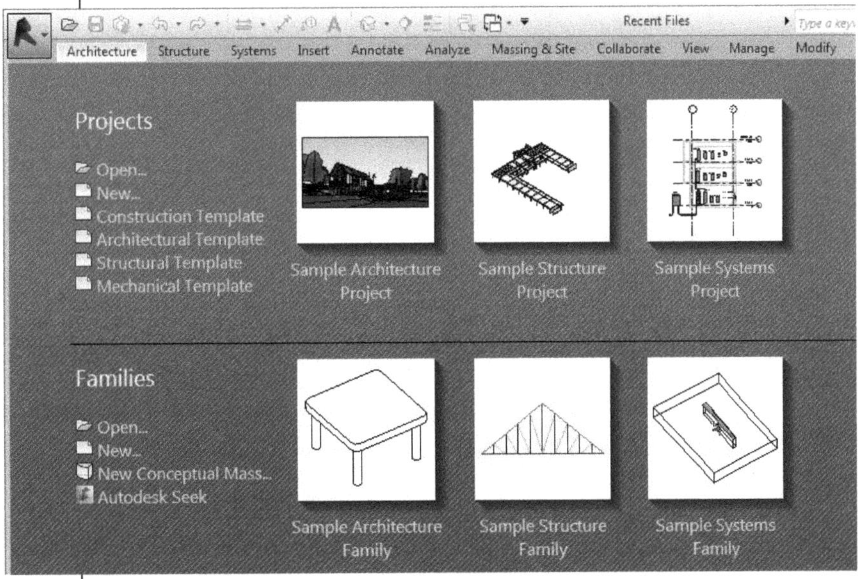

Figure 1

- The following steps describe how to set up the suite-based software to match the layout of the discipline-specific software. If you are using the discipline-specific software you do not need to make any changes.

- This training guide is based on the Autodesk Revit interface. If you are using Autodesk Revit Architecture, there might be a few differences in the number of tabs.

Setup the Autodesk Revit Interface by Discipline

1. In the upper left corner of the screen, expand  (Application Menu) and click  Options .
2. In the Options dialog box, in the left pane, select **User Interface**.
3. In the *Configure* area, under *Tools and analyses* (as shown in Figure 2), clear all of options that you do not want to use.

You are not deleting these tools, just removing them from the current user interface.

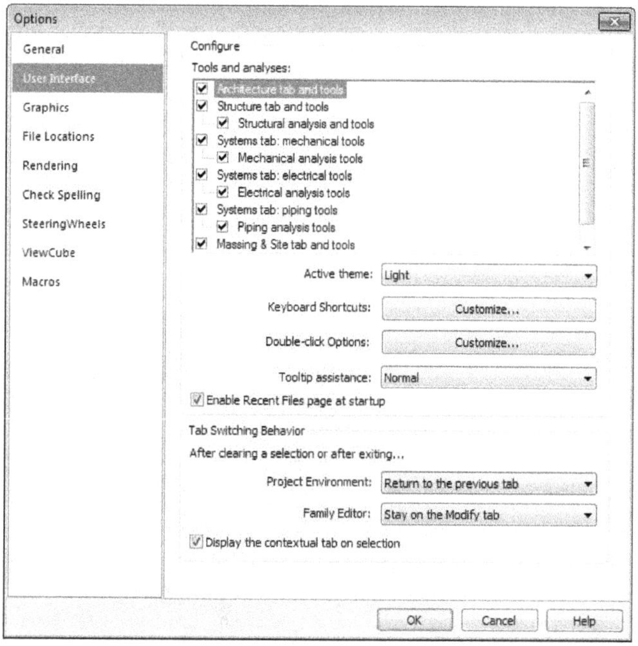

Figure 2

- To match the Autodesk Revit Architecture interface, select only the following options:

  - *Architecture* tab and tools
  - *Structure* tab and tools (but not Structural analysis and tools)
  - *Massing and Site* tab and tools
  - Energy analysis and tools

4. You can also specify which templates display when starting a new project. In the left pane, select **File Locations**.

5. In the right pane (as shown in Figure 3), select and order the templates that you want to display. Typically, these are set up by the company.

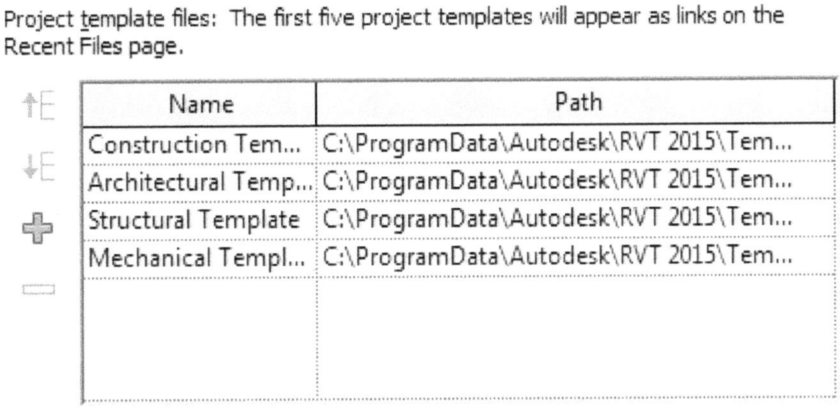

Project template files: The first five project templates will appear as links on the Recent Files page.

Name	Path
Construction Tem...	C:\ProgramData\Autodesk\RVT 2015\Tem...
Architectural Temp...	C:\ProgramData\Autodesk\RVT 2015\Tem...
Structural Template	C:\ProgramData\Autodesk\RVT 2015\Tem...
Mechanical Templ...	C:\ProgramData\Autodesk\RVT 2015\Tem...

Figure 3

- To match the Autodesk Revit Architecture interface, select **Architectural Template** and move it to the top of the list. Remove the **Structural Template** and **Mechanical Template**.

6. Click OK. The interface and template locations update for this installation of the software.

- You might also need to move the tabs to a different order. To do so, select the tab, hold down <Ctrl> and drag the tab to the new location.

    - To match the Autodesk Revit Architecture interface you do not need to modify the tab locations.

Introduction to BIM and Autodesk Revit

This training guide is divided into three phases: Introduction to BIM and Autodesk Revit, Design Development, and Construction Documents. The first phase provides an overview of using Building Information Modeling with the Autodesk® Revit® software, how to use the Autodesk Revit interface and viewing tools, and basic drawing and editing tools.

The first phase covers the following topics:

- Introduction to BIM and Autodesk Revit

- Basic Drawing and Modify Tools

- Setting Up Levels and Grids

Chapter 1

Introduction to BIM and Autodesk Revit

In this chapter you learn about Building Information Modeling (BIM) and how it is used in the Autodesk® Revit® software. You investigate the software interface and terminology, learn how to start projects, and work with the viewing commands including zoom controls, 3D isometric, and perspective views.

This chapter contains the following topics:

- **Building Information Modeling**
- **Overview of the Interface**
- **Standard Terminology**
- **Starting Projects**
- **Viewing Commands**

1.1 Building Information Modeling

Learning Objective

- Describe the concept of Building Information Modeling and its workflow in relation to the Autodesk Revit software.

Building Information Modeling (BIM) is an approach to the entire building life cycle. The BIM process supports the ability to coordinate, update, and share design data with team members throughout the design, construction, and management phases of a building's life.

The Autodesk Revit software is a *Parametric Building Modeler*, and is an important part of the BIM process. *Parametric* means you can establish a relationship between two building elements; when one element changes the other element changes as well. *Building* signifies that this software is designed for working with buildings, as opposed to gears or roads. *Modeler* signifies how a project is built in a single file around the building model (as shown on the left in Figure 1–1). All views, such as plans (as shown on the right in Figure 1–1), elevations, sections, details, schedules, as well as all design sheets printed for construction documents, are automatically generated based on the model.

When a change is made anywhere in the model, all of the views update automatically. For example, if you add an element in a plan view, it displays in the related section view and in schedules (if applicable).

Figure 1–1

- The Autodesk® Revit® software includes tools for architectural, mechanical, electrical, plumbing, and structural design.

- It is important that everyone works in the same version and build of the software.

Workflow and BIM

BIM has changed the process of how a building is designed. The Autodesk Revit software is a true BIM product in that it is much more than a drafting software. By creating complete models and associated views of those models, the software takes much of the tediousness out of producing a building design.

In the traditional design process, plans create the basis for the model, from which you then create sections and elevations, as shown in Figure 1–2. Construction Documents (CDs) can then be created. In this workflow, changes are made at the plan level and then coordinated with other documents in the set.

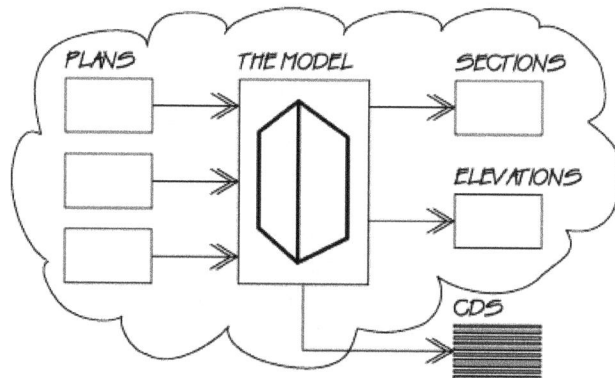

Figure 1–2

In the BIM, the design process revolves around the model, as shown in Figure 1–3. Plans, elevations, and sections are simply 2D versions of the 3D model. Changes made in one view automatically update in all views. Even Construction Documents update automatically with callout tags in sync with the sheet numbers. This is called bidirectional associativity.

*The elements that you create in the software are **smart** elements that know they are walls, windows, doors, or stairs. Because they are smart elements, they display properly in plan, elevation, or 3D views. This ensures that drawings are coordinated across the project because the same model generates all of the necessary views.*

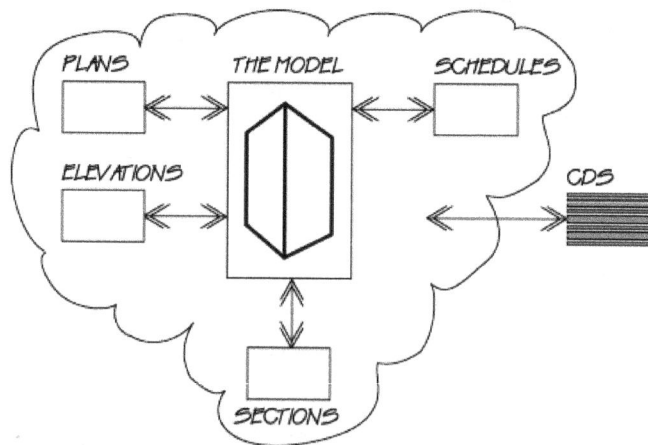

Figure 1–3

Views and Sheets

In the traditional workflow, the most time-consuming part of the project is the construction documents. With BIM, the base views of those documents (i.e., floor plans, ceiling plans, elevations, sections, and schedules) are produced automatically and update as the model is updated, saving hours of work. The views are then placed on sheets that form the construction document set.

For example, a floor plan is duplicated to create a Life Safety Plan. In the new view, certain categories of elements are turned off (such as grids and section marks) while furniture elements are set to halftone. Annotation is added as required. The plan is then placed on a sheet, as shown in Figure 1–4.

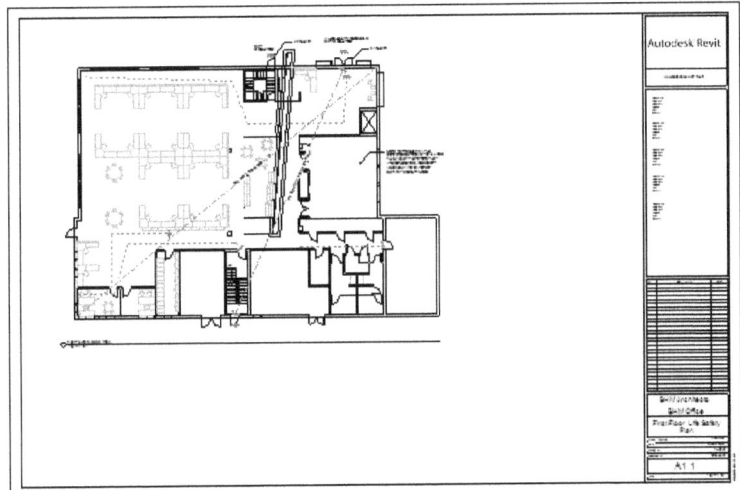

Figure 1–4

- Work can continue on a view and is automatically updated on the sheet.

- Annotating views in the preliminary design phase is often not required. You might be able to wait until you are further along in the project.

1.2 Overview of the Interface

Autodesk Certification Topics & Objectives

Pro.   User

User Interface

- Identify primary parts of the User Interface (UI)   ✓
- Use the Project Browser   ✓   ✓
- Change the view scale   ✓

Learning Objective

- Navigate the graphic user interface.

The Autodesk Revit interface is designed for intuitive and efficient access to commands and views. It includes the Ribbon, Quick Access Toolbar, Application Menu, Navigation Bar, and Status Bar, which are common to the Autodesk® software. It also includes tools that are specific to the Autodesk Revit software, including the Properties palette, Project Browser, and View Control Bar. The interface is shown in Figure 1–5.

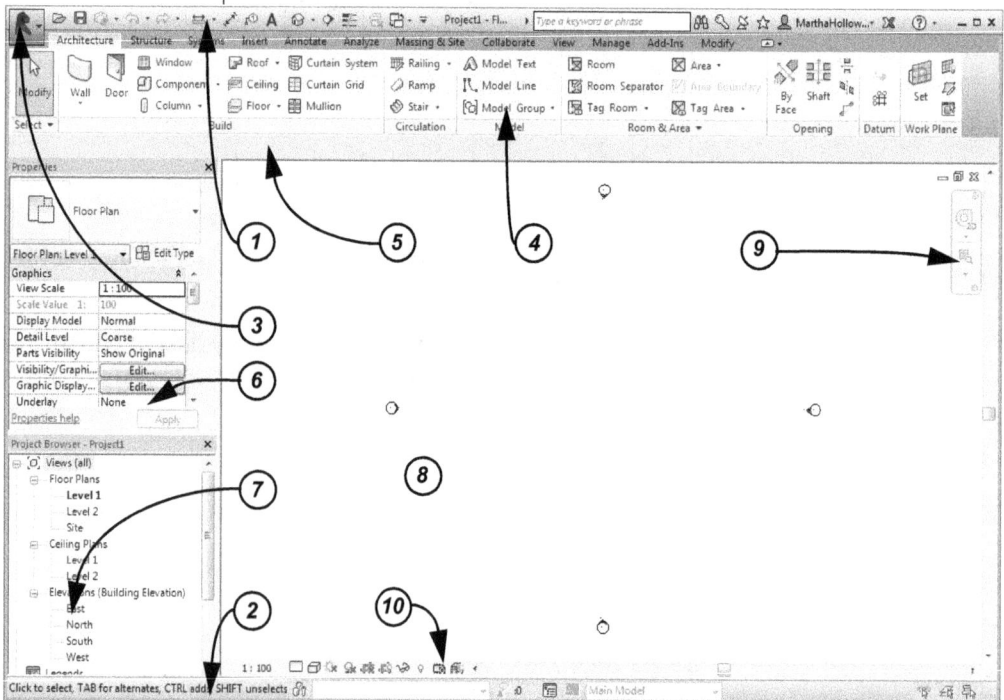

Figure 1–5

1. Quick Access Toolbar	6. Properties Palette
2. Status Bar	7. Project Browser
3. Application Menu	8. View Window
4. Ribbon	9. Navigation Bar
5. Options Bar	10. View Control Bar

1. Quick Access Toolbar

The Quick Access Toolbar provides access to commonly used commands, such as **Open**, **Save**, **Undo** and **Redo**, **Dimension**, and **3D View**, as shown in Figure 1–6.

Figure 1–6

* The Quick Access Toolbar is easily customizable. Select the arrow at the end of the toolbar. You can choose from the list of commands or click **Customize Quick Access Toolbar** to bring up a dialog box where you can modify the location of the tools on the toolbar as shown in Figure 1–7.

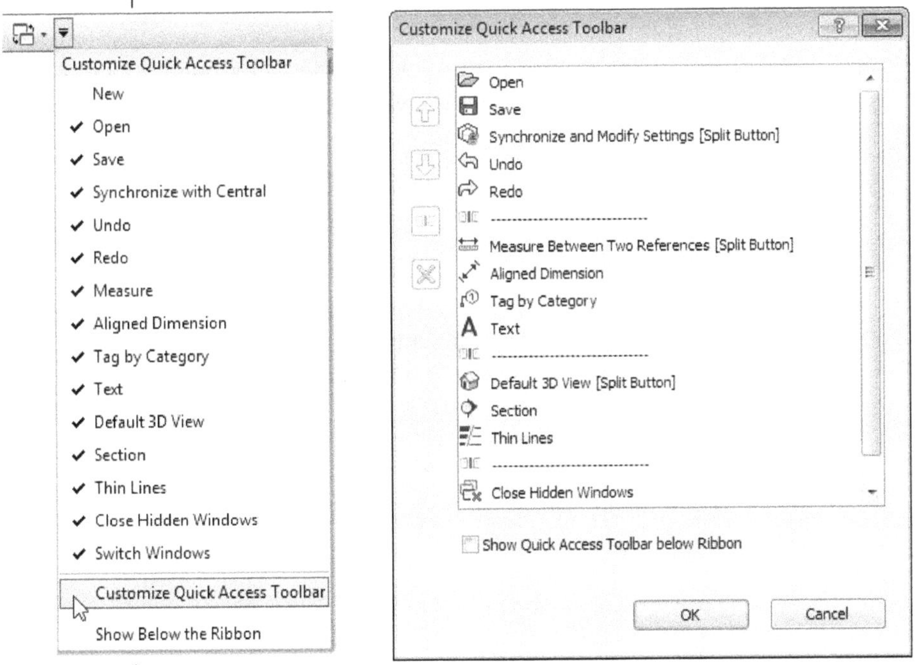

Figure 1–7

- You can also customize it by adding commands from any of the Ribbon tabs. Right-click on the command in the Ribbon and select **Add to Quick Access Toolbar** as shown in Figure 1–8.

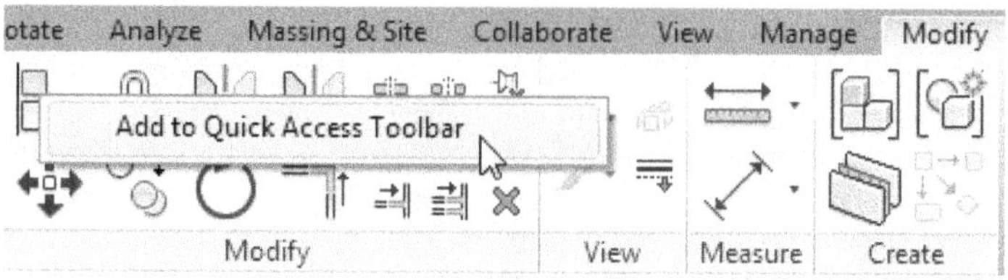

Figure 1–8

The other end of the Quick Access Toolbar hosts the InfoCenter, which enables you to quickly search for help on the web, as shown in Figure 1–9. You can specify which Help documents to search and collapse or expand the *Search* field to save screen space. You can also sign into the Autodesk 360 service to access additional on-line services.

You can collapse or expand the Search field to save screen space.

Figure 1–9

2. Status Bar

The Status Bar provides information about the current process, such as the next step for a command, as shown in Figure 1–10.

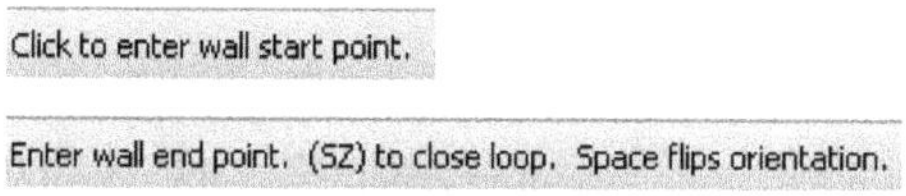

Figure 1–10

- Other options in the Status Bar are related to Worksets and Design Options (advanced tools) as well as selection methods and filters.

Enhanced in 2015

Hint: Right-click Menus

Right-click menus help you to work smoothly and efficiently by enabling you to quickly access required commands. These menus provide access to basic viewing commands, recently used commands, and the available Browsers, as shown in Figure 1–11. Additional options vary depending on the element or command that you are using.

Figure 1–11

3. Application Menu

The Application Menu provides access to file commands, settings, and documents, as shown in Figure 1–12. Hover the cursor over a command to display a list of additional tools.

If you click the primary icon, rather than the arrow, it starts the default command.

Figure 1–12

- At the bottom of the menu, click Options to open the Options dialog box or click Exit Revit to exit the software.

How To: Recent Drawings

To display a list of recently used documents, click 🗐 (Recent Documents) in the Application menu. The documents can be reordered as shown in Figure 1–13.

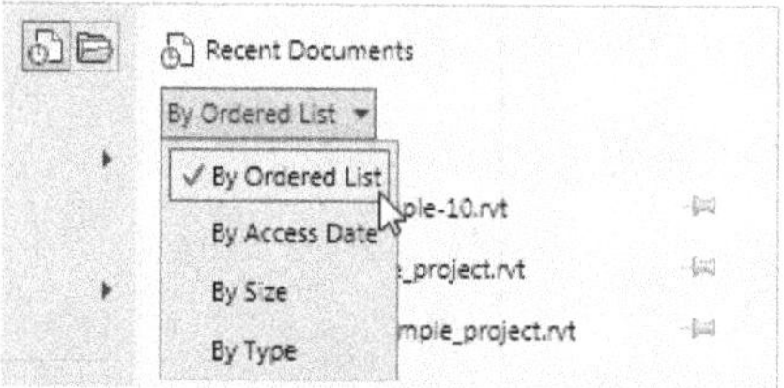

Figure 1–13

- Click ⊨ (Pin) next to a document name to keep it available, even if more documents are opened than can be displayed. It displays with the push pin tacked in (⚲).

How To: Open Drawings

To display a list of open documents and views, click

🗁 (Open Documents). The list displays the open documents and each view that is open, as shown in Figure 1–14.

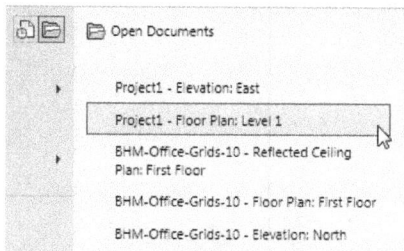

You can use the Open Documents list to change between views.

Figure 1–14

- Click ⬜ (Close) to close the current project.

- When you expand 🗁 (Open) there is an option

(🗁 (Sample Files)), which opens a folder containing the sample files supplied with the software.

4. Ribbon

The Ribbon contains tools in a series of tabs and panels as shown in Figure 1–15. Selecting a tab displays a group of related panels. The panels contain a variety of tools, grouped by function.

Figure 1–15

When you start a command that creates new elements or you select an element, the Ribbon displays the *Modify | contextual* tab. This contains general editing commands and command specific tools at the end of the tab, as shown in Figure 1–16.

Figure 1–16

- When you hover over a tool on the Ribbon, tooltips display the tool's name and a short description. If you continue hovering over the tool, a graphic displays (and sometimes a video), as shown in Figure 1–17.

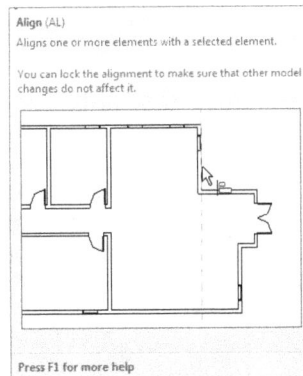

Figure 1–17

- Many commands have shortcut keys. For example, press <A> and then press <L> for **Align** or press <M> and then press <V> for **Move**. They are listed next to the name of the command in the tooltips. Do not press <Enter> to execute shortcuts.

- The order in which the Ribbon tabs are displayed can be modified. Select the tab, hold down <Ctrl>, and drag it to a new location. The location is remembered when you restart the software.

- Any panel can be dragged by its title into the drawing area to become a floating panel. Click the **Return Panels to Ribbon** button as shown in Figure 1–18 to replace the panel.

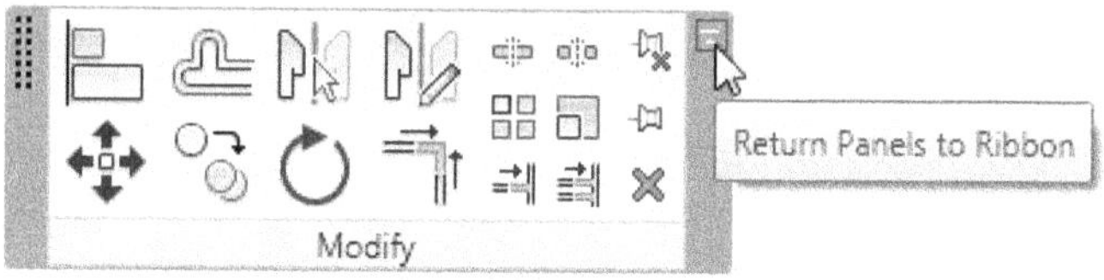

Figure 1–18

Hint: You are always in a command when using the Autodesk Revit software.

When you are finished working with a tool, you typically default back to the **Modify** command. To end a command, use one of the following methods:

- In any Ribbon tab, click (Modify).
- Press <Esc> once or twice to revert to **Modify**.
- Right-click and select **Cancel...** once or twice.
- Start another command.

5. Options Bar

The Options Bar displays options that are related to the selected command or element. For example, when the **Rotate** command is active it displays options for rotating the selected elements, as shown at the top in Figure 1–19. When the **Place Dimensions** command is active it displays dimension related options, as shown at the bottom in Figure 1–19.

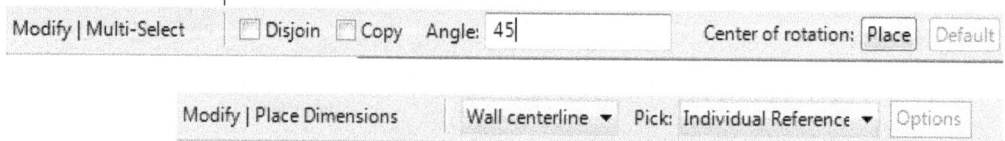

Figure 1–19

6. Properties Palette

In the Properties palette you can make extensive modifications to views and elements. If nothing is selected and you are not in a command, the Properties palette displays options for the current view, as shown on the left in Figure 1–20. If a command or element is selected, it displays options for the associated element, as shown on the right in Figure 1–20.

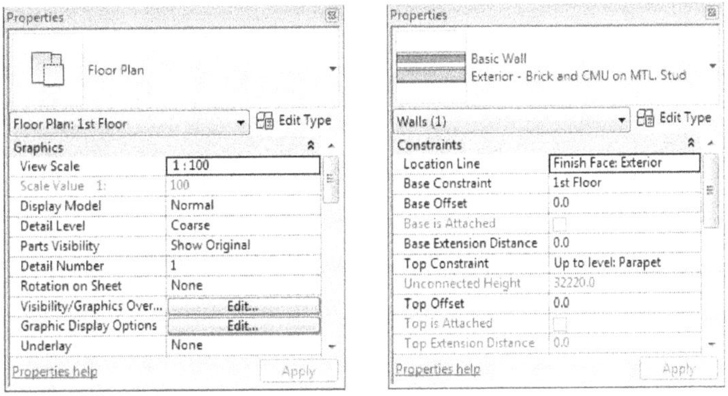

Figure 1–20

*   Items that are grayed out are read-only.

*   The Properties palette is usually kept open while working on a project to easily permit modifications at any time. It can be placed on a second monitor as well as floated, resized, and docked on top of the Project Browser or other dockable palettes.

*   If the Properties palette and other palettes are docked on top of each other, the tabs are displayed at the bottom of the combined palette, as shown in Figure 1–21. Click the tab to display its associated panel.

Figure 1–21

- If the Properties palette does not display, click

  ▦ (Properties) in the *Modify* tab>Properties panel, or press
  <P> twice.

- You can also access the user interface options by selecting

  the *View* tab>Windows panel, expanding 🔲 (User
  Interface), and selecting an option.

- When multiple elements are selected, you can filter the
  elements selected in the Properties palette using the
  drop-down list, as shown in Figure 1–22.

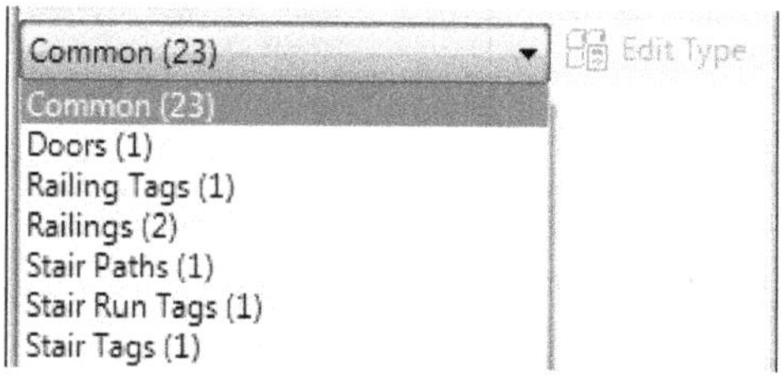

Common (23) ▼	🔲 Edit Type
Common (23)	
Doors (1)	
Railing Tags (1)	
Railings (2)	
Stair Paths (1)	
Stair Run Tags (1)	
Stair Tags (1)	

Figure 1–22

- When you start a command or select an element, you can set
  the element type in the Type Selector as shown in
  Figure 1–23.

*Right-click on the Type
Selector to add it to the
Quick Access Toolbar
and/or to the Ribbon
Modify tab.*

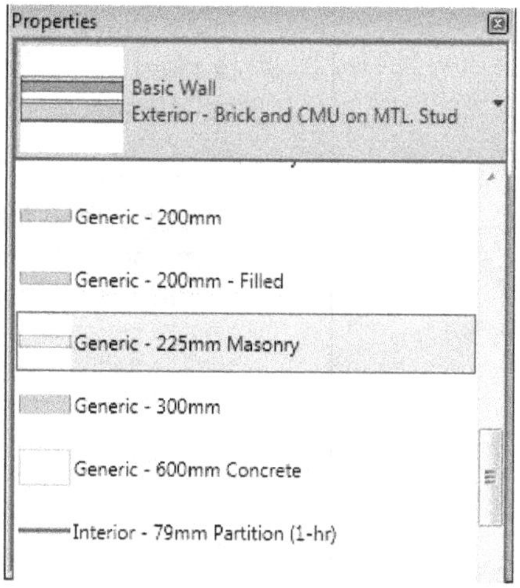

Properties

Basic Wall
Exterior - Brick and CMU on MTL. Stud

Generic - 200mm

Generic - 200mm - Filled

Generic - 225mm Masonry

Generic - 300mm

Generic - 600mm Concrete

Interior - 79mm Partition (1-hr)

Figure 1–23

Hint: Type Properties

Type Properties are parameters that are common to all of the elements in a specific family. When a single type of element is selected, click ⊞ (Edit Type) in Properties to open the Type Properties dialog box, as shown in Figure 1–24.

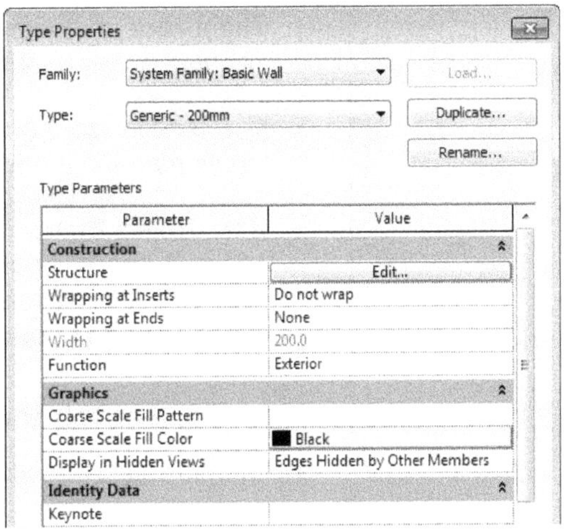

Figure 1–24

7. Project Browser

The Project Browser lists the views that can be opened in the software as shown in Figure 1–25. This includes all views of the model in which you are working and any additional views that you create, such as floor plans, ceiling plans, 3D views, elevations, sections, etc. It also includes views of schedules, legends, sheets (for plotting), groups, and Autodesk Revit Links.

The Project Browser displays the name of the active project.

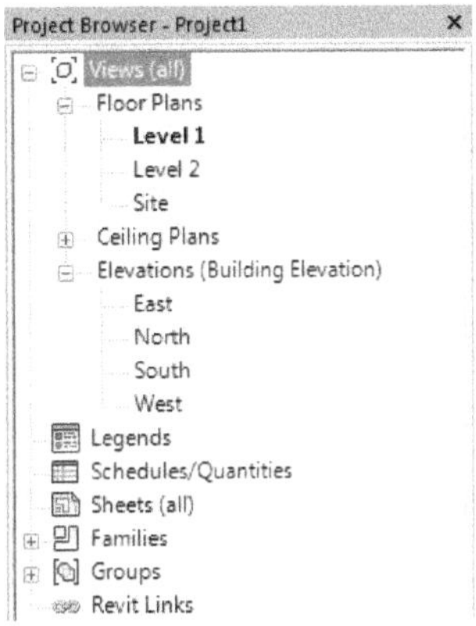

Figure 1–25

- Double-click on an item in the list to open the associated view.

- To display the views associated with a view type, click ⊞ (Expand) next to the section name. To hide the views in the section, click ⊟ (Contract).

- Right-click on a view and select **Rename** or press <F2> to rename a view in the Project Browser.

- If you no longer need a view, you can remove it. Right-click on its name in the Project Browser and select **Delete**.

- The Project Browser can be floated, resized, docked on top of the Properties palette, and customized. If the Properties palette and the Project Browser are docked on top of each other, use the appropriate tab to display the required panel.

How To: Search the Project Browser

1. In the Project Browser, right-click on the top level Views node as shown in Figure 1–26.

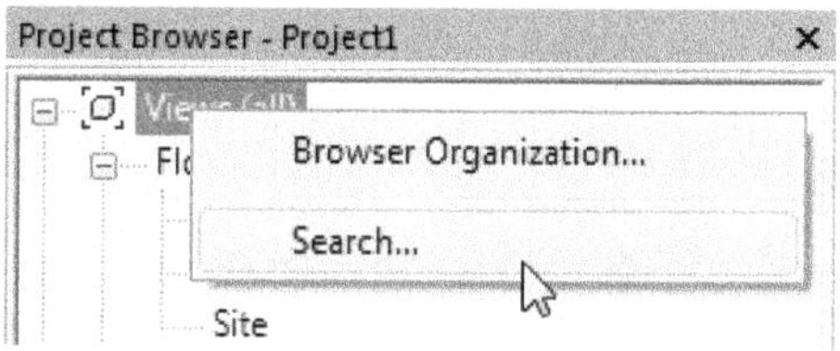

Figure 1–26

2. In the Search in Project Browser dialog box, type the words that you want to find (as shown on the left in Figure 1–27), and click Next .

3. In the Project Browser, the first instance of that search displays as shown on the right in Figure 1–27.

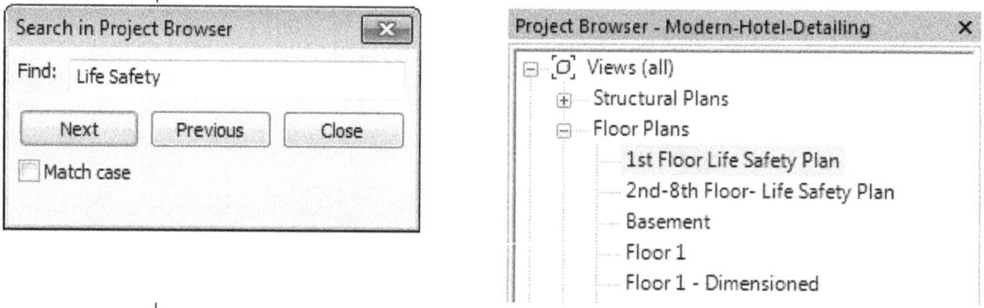

Figure 1–27

4. Continue using [Next] and [Previous] to move through the list.

5. Click [Close] when you are done.

8. View Window

Each view of a project opens in its own window, as shown in Figure 1–28. Each view displays a Navigation Bar (for quick access to viewing tools) and the View Control Bar.

In 3D views you can also use the ViewCube to rotate the view.

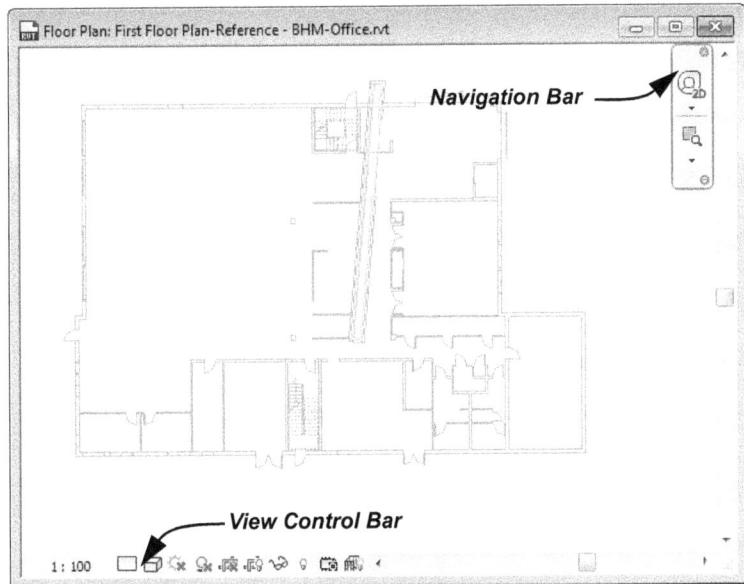

Figure 1–28

- Each view of a project opens in its own window. You can use the Project Browser or press <Ctrl>+<Tab> to cycle through the open views.

- If you have multiple views open you can select a view by name. In the Quick Access Toolbar or *View* tab>Windows panel, expand 🗔 (Switch Windows) and select from the list.

- If you have more than one view open, click 🗗 (Cascade) or 🗗 (Tile) in the *View* tab>Windows panel to arrange them in the selected order on the screen. You can also use the shortcut keys by pressing <W> and then pressing <C> for **Cascade** or pressing <W> and then pressing <T> for **Tile**.

9. Navigation Bar

The Navigation Bar enables you to access various viewing commands, as shown in Figure 1–29.

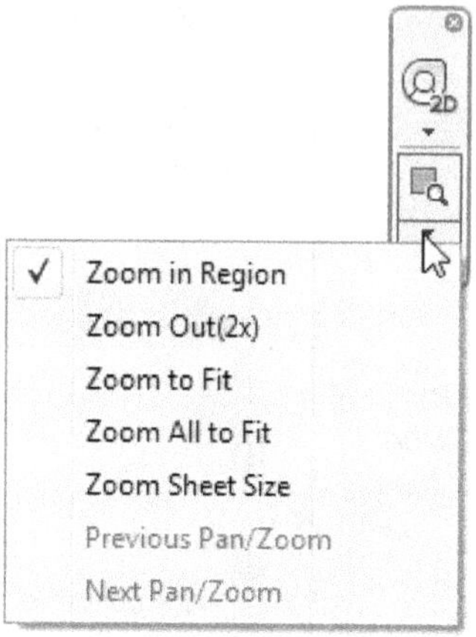

Figure 1–29

10. View Control Bar

The View Control Bar (shown in Figure 1–30), displays at the bottom of each view window. It controls aspects of that view, such as the scale and detail level. It also includes tools that display parts of the view and hide or isolate elements in the view.

Figure 1–30

1.3 Standard Terminology

Learning Objective

- Use typical terms and concepts found in the software.

As you start working with BIM based software, you should know the typical terms used to describe items in the Autodesk Revit software. There are several types of elements, as shown in Figure 1–31, and described in the following table.

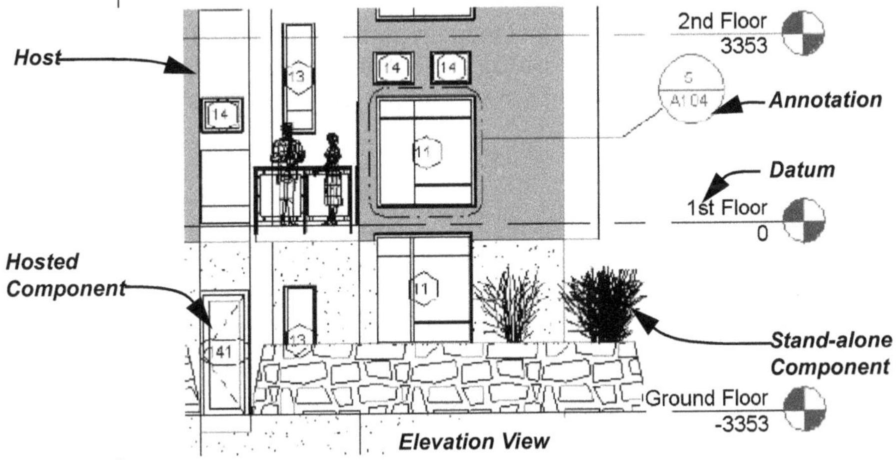

Figure 1–31

Host	*Built-in-place* construction elements (such as floors, walls, roofs, ceilings, stairs, and ramps). They can stand alone in the project.
Components	Elements that need to be attached to host elements (such as doors, windows, and railings), as well as stand-alone items (such as furniture and equipment).
Views	Enables you to display and manipulate the project. For example, you can view and work in floor plans, ceiling plans, elevations, sections, schedules, and 3D views. You can change a design from any view. All views are stored in the project.
Datum	Elements that define the project context. These include levels for the floors, column grids, and reference planes that help you draw.
Annotation	2D elements that are placed in views to define the information drawn in the project. These include dimensions, text, tags, and symbols. The view scale controls their size.

Property Types

There are two types of properties for most elements in the software:

- **Instance Properties:** Parameters that can be set for the individual element you are drawing or modifying. They display in the Properties palette.

- **Type Properties:** Control options for all elements of the same type. If you modify these parameters, all elements of the selected type change.

Instance properties display in the Properties palette, which can be toggled on/off in the *Modify* tab>Properties panel (as shown in Figure 1–32), or by typing the shortcut **PP**.

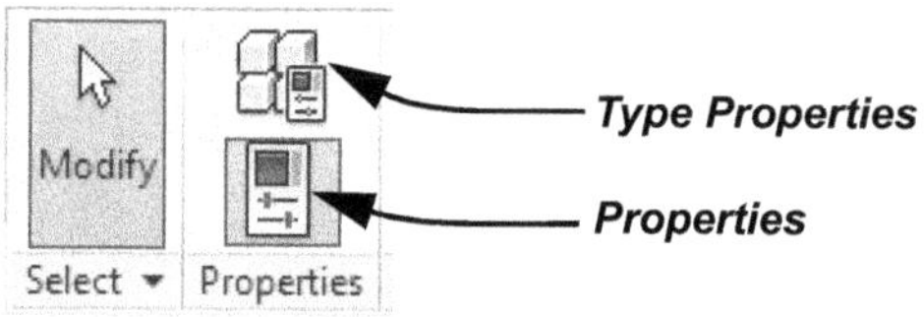

Figure 1–32

- To display the type properties, click (Edit Type) in Properties, to open the Type Properties dialog box, as shown in Figure 1–33. Any changes you make in the Type Properties dialog box impact all instances of the type in the project.

The parameters shown in the dialog boxes vary according to the type of element selected.

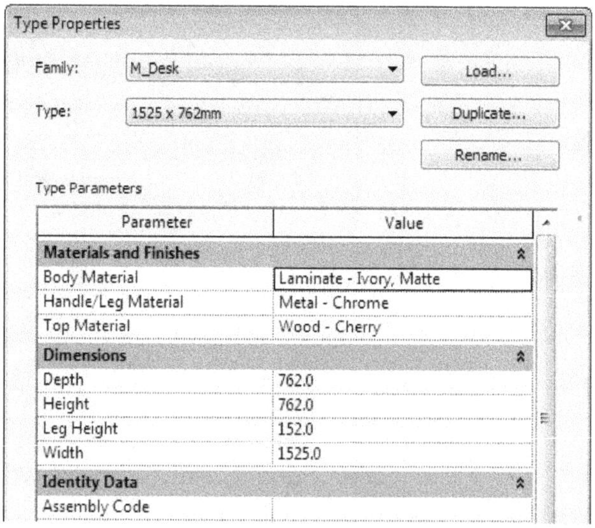

Figure 1–33

1.4 Starting Projects

Autodesk Certification Topics & Objectives

Pro.   User

User Interface

- Identify file types   ✓

Learning Objectives

- Open and save existing projects.
- Start new projects using templates.

File operations to open existing files, create new files from a template, and save files in the Autodesk Revit software are found in the Application Menu, as shown in Figure 1–34.

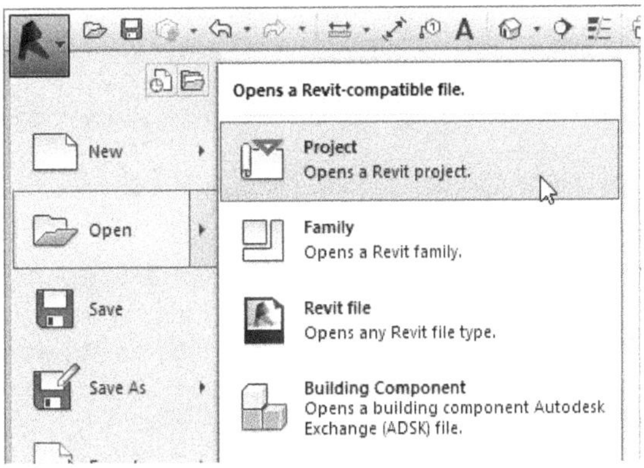

Figure 1–34

There are three main file types:

- **Project files (.rvt):** Your primary drawing files. This is where you do the majority of your work in the building model with views and sheets. They are initially based on template files.

- **Family files (.rfa):** Separate components that can be inserted in a project. For example, the Single Flush and Double Glass door families include a variety of door sizes, and the Desk family includes a number of desk sizes and styles. Title block and Annotation Symbol files are special types of family files.

- **Template files (.rte):** Designed to hold standard information and settings for creating new project files. The software includes several templates for residential, commercial, and structural projects. You can also create custom templates.

Opening Projects

To open an existing project, in the Quick Access Toolbar or Application Menu click [📂] (Open), or press <Ctrl>+<O>. The Open dialog box opens (as shown in Figure 1–35), in which you can navigate to the required folder and select a project file.

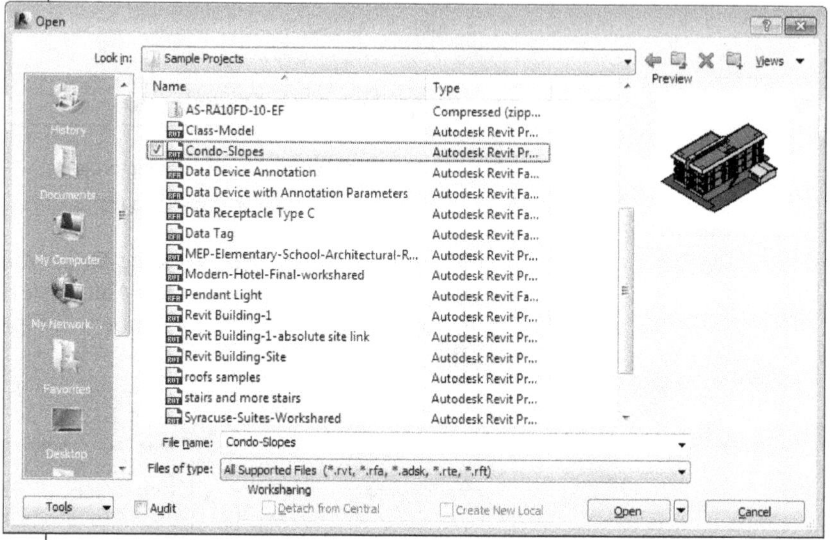

Figure 1–35

- When you first open the Autodesk Revit software, the Startup Screen displays, showing lists of recently used projects and family files as shown in Figure 1–36. This screen also displays if you close all projects.

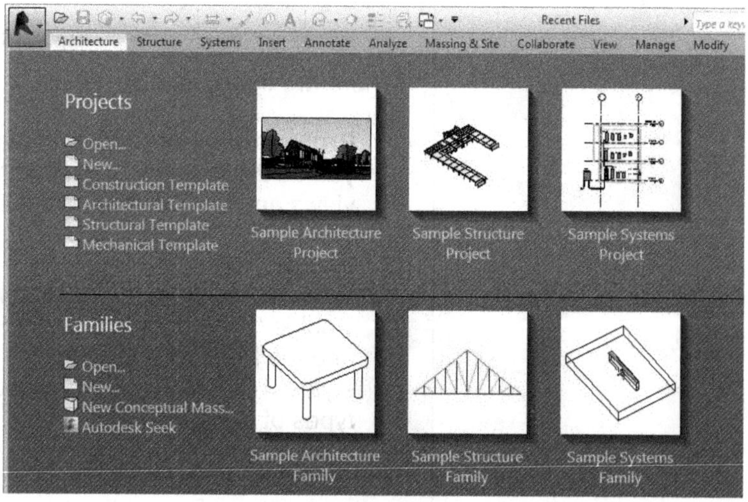

Figure 1–36

- You can select the picture of a recently opened project or use one of the options on the left to open or start a new project using the default templates.

Hint: Opening Workset-Related Files

Worksets are used when the project becomes large enough for multiple people to work on it at the same time. At this point, the project manager creates a central file with multiple worksets (such as element interiors, building shell, and site) that are used by the project team members.

When you open a workset related file it creates a new local file on your computer as shown in Figure 1–37. Do not work in the main central file.

Figure 1–37

Starting New Projects

New projects are based on a template file. The template file includes preset levels, views, and some families, such as wall styles and text styles. Check with your BIM Manager about which template you need to use for your projects. Your company might have more than one based on the types of building that you are designing.

How To: Start a New Project

1. In the Application Menu, expand ⬜ (New) and click ⬛ (Project) (as shown in Figure 1–38), or press <Ctrl>+<N>.

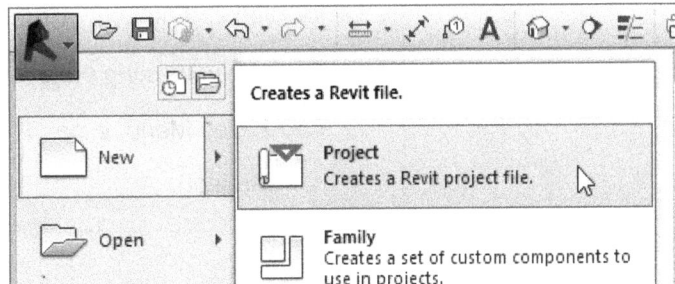

Figure 1–38

The list of Template files is set in the Options dialog box in the File Locations pane. It might vary depending on the installed product and company standards.

2. In the New Project dialog box (shown in Figure 1–39), select the template that you want to use and click [OK].

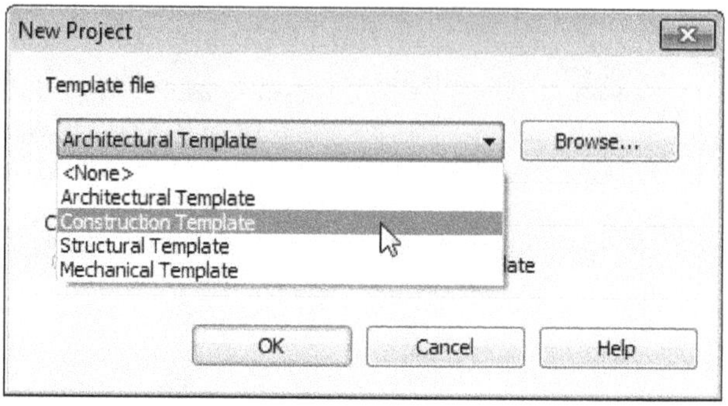

Figure 1–39

- You can select from a list of templates if they have been set up by your BIM Manager.

- You can add ◻ (New) to the Quick Access Toolbar. At the end of the Quick Access Toolbar, click ▼ (Customize Quick Access Toolbar) and select **New**, as shown in Figure 1–40.

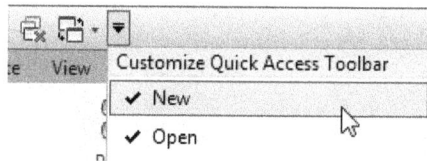

Figure 1–40

Saving Projects

Saving your project frequently is a good idea. In the Quick Access Toolbar or Application Menu click 🖫 (Save), or press <Ctrl>+<S> to save your project. If the project has not yet been saved, the Save As dialog box opens, where you can specify a file location and name.

- To save an existing project with a new name, in the Application Menu, expand 🖫 (Save As) and click 🗋 (Project).

- If you have not saved in a set amount of time, the software opens the Project Not Saved Recently alert box, as shown in Figure 1–41. Select **Save the project**. If you want to set reminder intervals or not save at this time, select the other options.

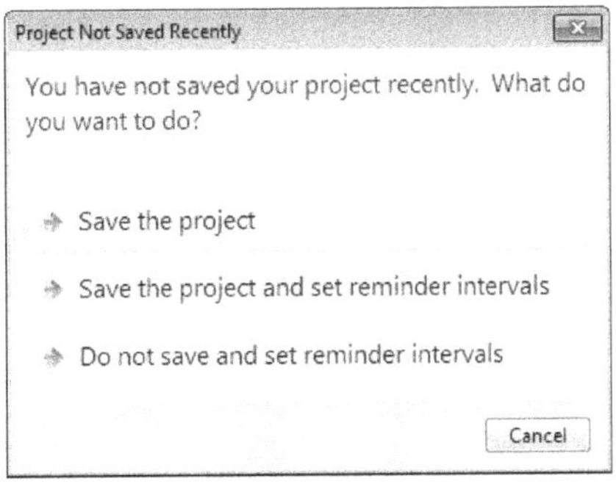

Figure 1–41

- You can set the *Save Reminder interval* to **15** or **30 minutes**, **1**, **2**, or **4 hours**, or to have **No reminders** display. In the Application Menu, click [Options] to open the Options dialog box. In the left pane, select **General** and set the interval as shown in Figure 1–42.

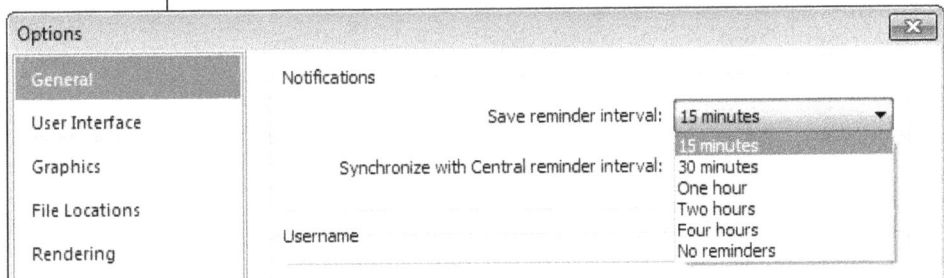

Figure 1–42

Saving Backup Copies

By default, the software saves a backup copy of a project file when you save the project. Backup copies are numbered incrementally (e.g., **My Project.0001.rvt**, **My Project.0002.rvt**, etc.) and are saved in the same folder as the original file. In the Save As dialog box, click [Options...] to control how many backup copies are saved. The default number is three backups. If you exceed this number, the software deletes the oldest backup file.

Hint: Saving Workset-Related Projects

If you use worksets in your project, you need to save the project locally and to the central file. It is recommended to save the local file frequently, just like any other file, and save to the central file every hour or so.

To synchronize your changes with the main file, in the Quick Access Toolbar expand (Synchronize and Modify Settings) and click (Synchronize Now). After you save to the central file, save the file locally again.

At the end of the day, or when you are finished with the current session, use (Synchronize and Modify Settings) to relinquish the files you have been working on to the central file.

1.5 Viewing Commands

Learning Objectives

- Manipulate 2D and 3D views by zooming and panning.
- Create 3D Isometric and Perspective views.
- Set the Visual Style of a view.

Zoom commands are crucial to working efficiently in most drawing programs and the Autodesk Revit software is no exception. Once in a view, you can use the Zoom controls to navigate within it. You can zoom in and out and pan in any view. There are also special tools for viewing in 3D.

Zooming and Panning

Using The Mouse to Zoom and Pan

Use the mouse wheel (as shown in Figure 1–43) as the main method of moving around the drawing.

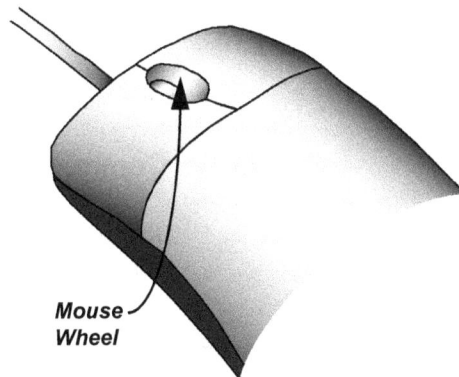

Mouse Wheel

Figure 1–43

- Scroll the wheel on the mouse up to zoom in and down to zoom out.

- Hold down the wheel and move the mouse to pan.

- Double-click on the wheel to zoom to the extents of the drawing.

- In a 3D view, hold down <Shift> and the mouse wheel and move the mouse to rotate around the model.

Zoom Controls

A number of additional zoom methods enable you to control the screen display. **Zoom** and **Pan** can be performed at any time while using other commands.

- You can access the **Zoom** commands in the Navigation Bar in the upper right corner of the view (as shown in Figure 1–44). You can also access them from most right-click menus and by typing the shortcut commands.

*(2D Wheel) provides cursor-specific access to **Zoom** and **Pan**.*

✓	Zoom in Region
	Zoom Out(2x)
	Zoom to Fit
	Zoom All to Fit
	Zoom Sheet Size
	Previous Pan/Zoom
	Next Pan/Zoom

Figure 1–44

Zoom Commands

	Zoom In Region (ZR)	Zooms into a region that you define. Drag the cursor or select two points to define the rectangular area you want to zoom into. This is the default command.
	Zoom Out(2x) (ZO)	Zooms out to half the current magnification around the center of the elements.
	Zoom To Fit (ZF or ZE)	Zooms out so that the entire contents of the project only display on the screen in the current view.
	Zoom All To Fit (ZA)	Zooms out so that the entire contents of the project display on the screen in all open views.
	Zoom Sheet Size (ZS)	Zooms in or out in relation to the sheet size.
N/A	**Previous Pan/Zoom (ZP)**	Steps back one **Zoom** command.
N/A	**Next Pan/Zoom**	Steps forward one **Zoom** command if you have done a **Previous Pan/Zoom**.

Viewing in 3D

*There are two types of 3D views: isometric views created by the **3D View** command and perspective views created by the **Camera** command.*

Even if you started a project entirely in plan views, you can quickly create 3D views of the model, as shown in Figure 1–45.

Figure 1–45

Working in 3D views helps you visualize the project and position some of the elements correctly. You can create and modify elements in 3D views just as in plan views.

- Once you have created a 3D view, you can save it and easily return to it.

How To: Create and Save a 3D Isometric View

1. In the Quick Access Toolbar or *View* tab>Create panel, click
   (Default 3D View). The default 3D Southeast isometric view opens, as shown in Figure 1–46.

Figure 1–46

You can spin the view to a different angle using the mouse wheel or the middle button of a three-button mouse. Hold down <Shift> as you press the wheel or middle button and drag the cursor.

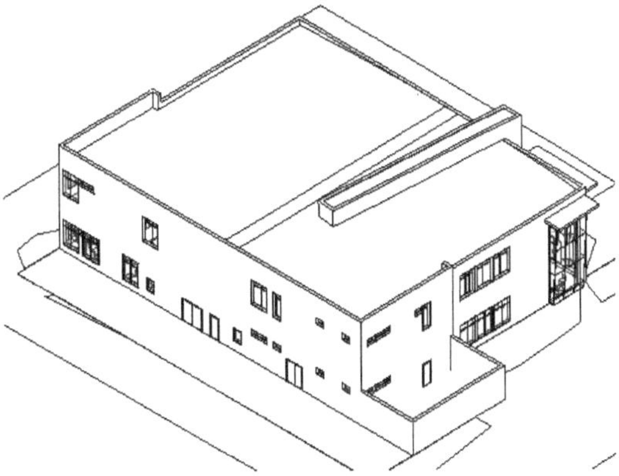

2. Modify the view to display the building from other directions.
3. In the Project Browser, right-click on the {3D} view and select **Rename...**.

You can also rename perspective views.

4. Type a new name in the Rename View dialog box, as shown in Figure 1–47, and click [OK] .

Figure 1–47

- When changes to the default 3D view are saved and you start another default 3D view, it displays the Southeast isometric view once again. If you modified the default 3D view but did not save it to a new name, the **Default 3D View** command opens the view in the last orientation you specified.

How To: Create a Perspective View

1. Switch to a Floor Plan view.
2. In the Quick Access Toolbar or *View* tab>Create panel, expand ⬠ (Default 3D View) and click ◉ (Camera).
3. Place the camera on the view.
4. Point the camera in the direction in which you want it to shoot by placing the target on the view, as shown in Figure 1–48.

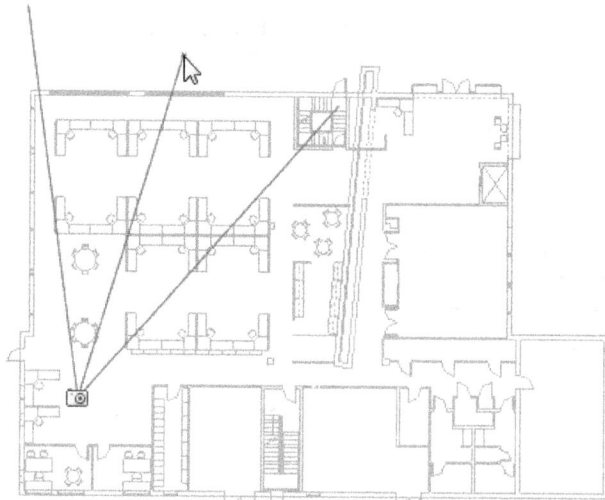

Figure 1–48

Use the round controls to modify the display size of the view and press <Shift> + the mouse wheel to change the view.

A new view is displayed, as shown in Figure 1–49.

Figure 1–49

- You can further modify a view by adding shadows, as shown in Figure 1–50. In the View Control Bar, toggle 💡 (Shadows Off) and ⚪ (Shadows On). Shadows display in any model view, not just in the 3D views.

Figure 1–50

Hint: Using the ViewCube

The ViewCube provides visual clues as to where you are in a 3D view. It helps you move around the model with quick access to specific views (such as top, front, and right), as well as corner and directional views, as shown in Figure 1–51.

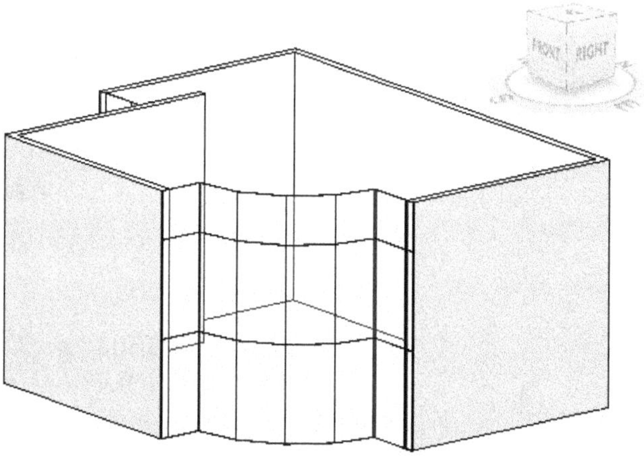

Figure 1–51

Move the cursor over any face of the ViewCube to highlight it. Once a face is highlighted, you can select it to reorient the model. You can also click and drag on the ViewCube to rotate the box, which rotates the model.

- 🏠 (Home) displays when you roll the cursor over the ViewCube. Click it to return to the view defined as **Home**. To change the Home view, set the view as you want it, right-click on the ViewCube, and select **Set Current View as Home**.

- The ViewCube is available in isometric and perspective views.

Visual Styles

Any view can have a visual style applied. The **Visual Style** options found in the View Control Bar (as shown in Figure 1–52), specify the shading of the building model. These options apply to plan, elevation, section, and 3D views.

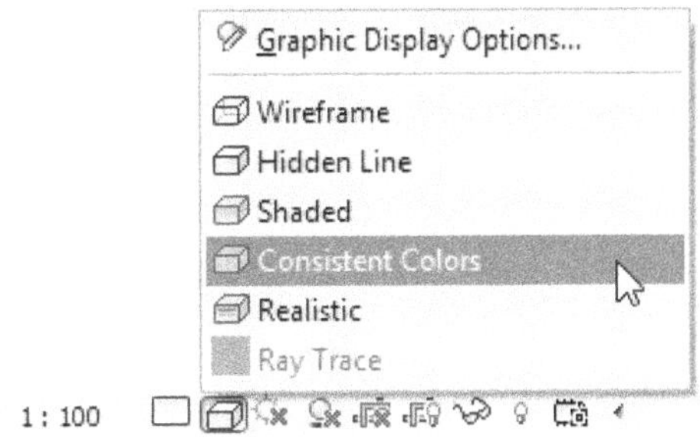

Figure 1–52

The **Wireframe** visual style displays the lines and edges that make up elements, but hides the surfaces. This can be useful when you are dealing with complex intersections.

The **Hidden Line** visual style displays the lines, edges, and surfaces of the elements, but it does not display any colors. This is the most common visual style to use while working on a design.

The **Shaded** and **Consistent Colors** visual styles give you a sense of the materials, including transparent glass, as shown in Figure 1–53.

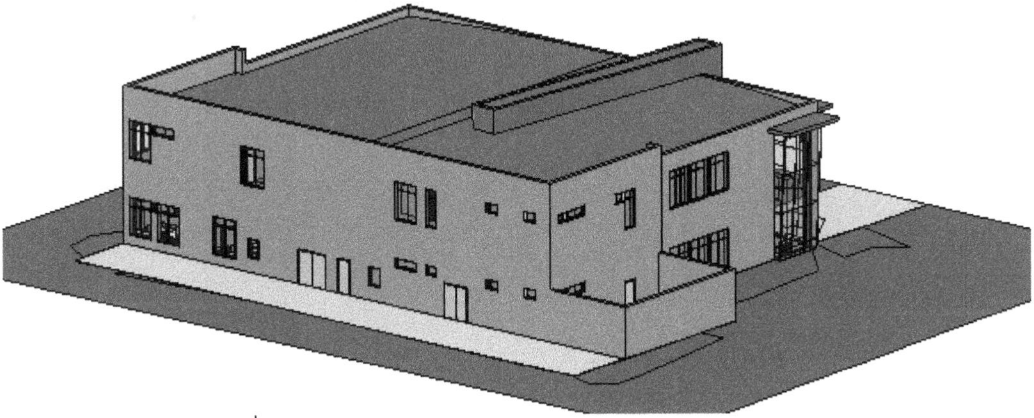

Figure 1–53

- The **Realistic** visual style displays what is shown when you render the view, including RPC (Rich Photographic Content) components and artificial lights. It takes a lot of computer power to execute this visual style. Therefore, it is better to use the other visual styles most of the time as you are working.

- The **Ray Trace** visual style is useful if you have created a 3D view that you want to render. It gradually moves from draft resolution to photorealistic. You can stop the process at any time.

Hint: Rendering

Rendering is a powerful tool in BIM which enables you to display a photorealistic view of the model you are working on, such as the example shown in Figure 1–54. This can be used to help clients and designers to understand a building's design in better detail.

Figure 1–54

- In the View Control Bar, click (Show Rendering Dialog) to set up the options. **Show Rendering Dialog** is only available in 3D views.

Practice 1a

Open and Review a Project

Learning Objectives

- Navigate the graphic user interface.
- Manipulate 2D and 3D views by zooming and panning.
- Create 3D Isometric and Perspective views.
- Set the Visual Style of a view.

Estimated time for completion: 15 minutes

In this practice you will open a project file and view each of the various areas in the interface. You will investigate elements, commands, and their options. You will also open views through the Project Browser and view the model in 3D, as shown in Figure 1–55.

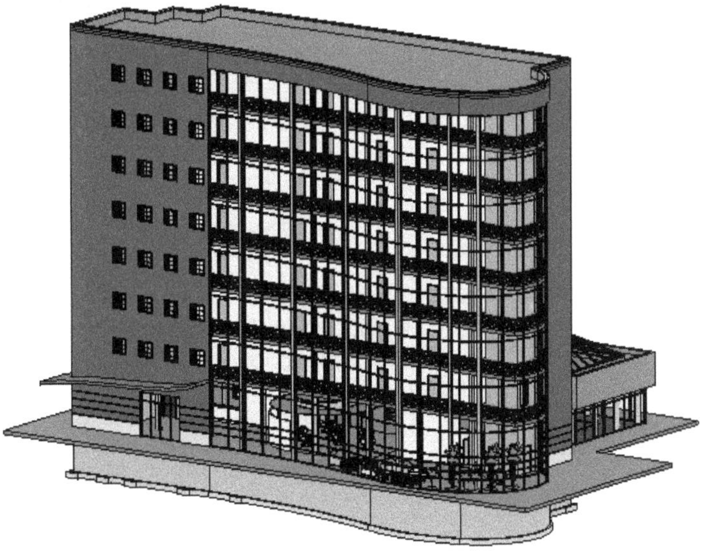

Figure 1–55

Task 1 - Explore the interface.

1. In the Application Menu, expand ☐ (Open) and click ☐ (Project).

2. In the Open dialog box, select **Modern-Hotel-Final-M.rvt**. It is found in your class folder and is a version of the main project you will work on throughout the training guide.

3. Click [Open]. The 3D view of the modern hotel building opens in the drawing window.

If the Project Browser and Properties palette are docked over each other, use the Project Browser tab at the bottom to display it.

4. In the Project Browser, expand the *Floor Plans* node. Double-click on **Floor 1** to open it. This view is referred to as **Floor Plans: Floor 1**.

5. Take time to review the floor plan to get acquainted with it.

6. Review the various parts of the screen.

7. In the drawing window, hover the cursor over one of the doors. A tooltip displays describing the element, as shown in Figure 1–56.

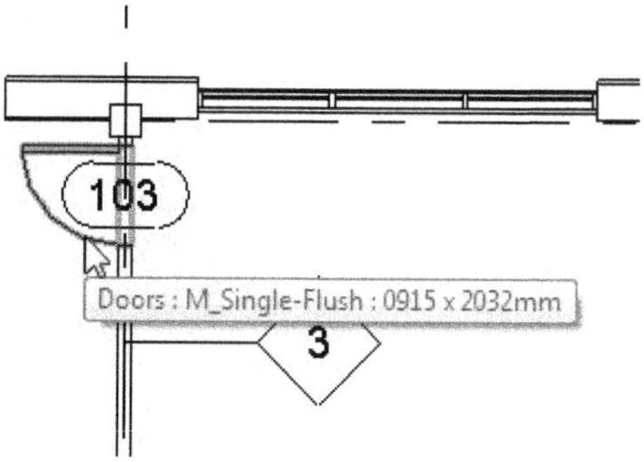

Figure 1–56

8. Hover the cursor over another element to display its description.

9. Select a door. The Ribbon changes to the *Modify | Doors* tab.

10. Click in an empty space to release the selection.

11. Hold down <Ctrl> and select several elements of different types. The Ribbon changes to the *Modify | Multi-Select* tab.

12. Click in an empty space to release the selection set.

13. In the *Architecture* tab>Build panel, click (Wall). The Ribbon changes to the *Modify | Place Wall* tab and at the end of the Ribbon, the Draw panel is displayed. It contains tools that enable you to create walls. The rest of the Ribbon displays the same tools that are found on the *Modify* tab.

14. In the Select panel, click (Modify) to return to the main Ribbon.

15. In the *Architecture* tab>Build panel, click 🚪 (Door). The Ribbon changes to the *Modify | Place Door* tab and displays the options and tools you can use to create doors.

16. In the Select panel, click ⌖ (Modify) to return to the main Ribbon.

Task 2 - Look at views.

You might need to widen the Project Browser to display the full names of the views.

1. In the Project Browser, verify that the *Floor Plans* node is open. Double-click on the **Floor 1 - Furniture Plan** view.

2. The basic floor plan displays with the furniture, but without the annotations that were displayed in the **Floor 1** view. Open the **1st Floor Life Safety Plan** view by double-clicking on it.

3. The walls and furniture display, but the furniture is grayed out and red lines describing important life safety information display.

*This view is referred to as **Elevations (Building Elevation): East** view.*

4. In the Project Browser, scroll down and expand *Elevations (Building Elevation)*. Double-click on the **East** elevation to open the view.

5. Expand *Sections (Building Section)* and double-click on the **East-West Section** to open it.

6. At the bottom of the drawing window, in the View Control Bar, click 🗗 (Visual Style) and select **Shaded**. The elements in the section are now easier to read.

7. In the Project Browser, scroll down to the *Sheets (all)* node and expand the node.

8. View several of the sheets. Some have views already applied, (e.g., **A2.3 - 2nd-8th Floor Plan (Typical)** as shown in Figure 1–57).

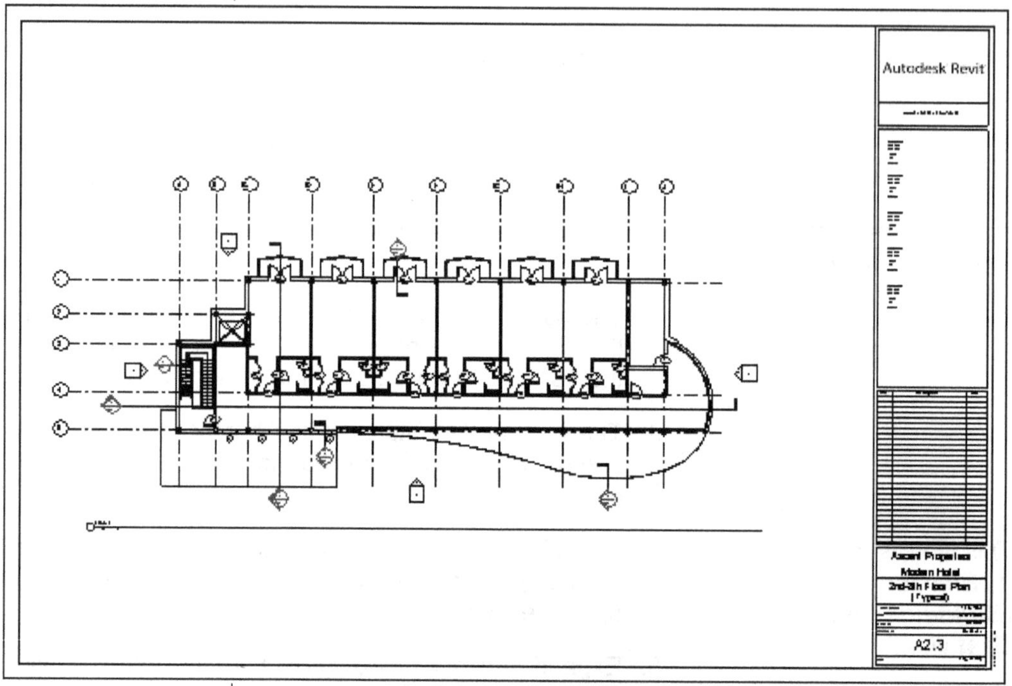

Figure 1–57

9. Which sheet displays the view that you just set to **Shaded**?

Task 3 - Practice viewing tools.

1. Return to the **Floor Plans: Floor 1** view.

2. In the Navigation Bar, click [icon] and select **Zoom In Region** or type **ZR**. Zoom in on one of the stairs.

3. Pan to another part of the building by holding and dragging the middle mouse button or wheel. Alternatively, you can use the 2D Wheel in the Navigation Bar.

4. Double-click on the mouse wheel to zoom out to fit the extents of the view.

5. In the Quick Access Toolbar, click ▣ (3D View) to open the default 3D view, as shown in Figure 1–58.

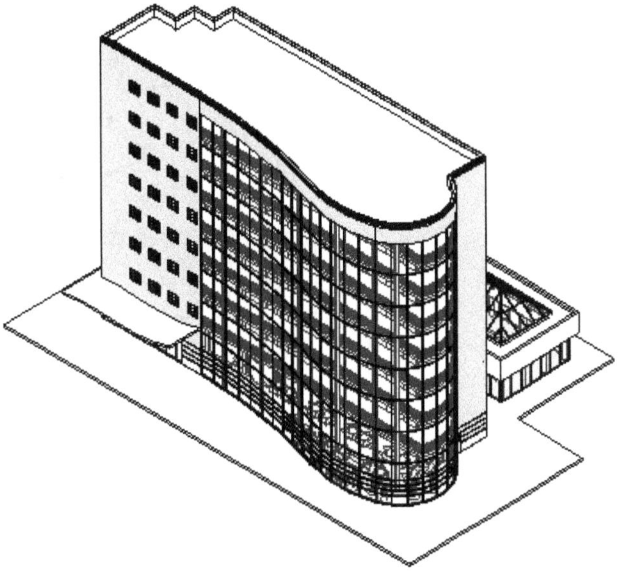

Figure 1–58

6. Hold down <Shift> and use the middle mouse button or wheel to rotate the model in the 3D view.

7. In the View Control Bar, change the *Visual Style* to ▱ (Shaded). Then try ▱ (Consistent Colors). Which one works best when you view the back of the building?

8. Use the ViewCube to find a view that you want to use.

9. In the Project Browser, expand *3D Views* and right-click on the {3D} view and select **Rename**. Enter the view name in the dialog box.

10. Review the other 3D views that have already been created.

11. Press <<Ctrl>+<Tab> to cycle through the open views.

12. In the Quick Access Toolbar, expand ▱ (Switch Windows) and select the **Modern-Hotel-Final-M.rvt - Floor Plan: Floor 1** view.

13. In the Quick Access Toolbar, click ▱ (Close Hidden Windows). This closes all of the other windows except the one in which you are working.

14. In the Quick Access Toolbar, expand ⬚ (Default 3D View) and click ⬚ (Camera).

15. Click the first point near the Lobby room name and click the second point (target) outside the building, as shown in Figure 1–59.

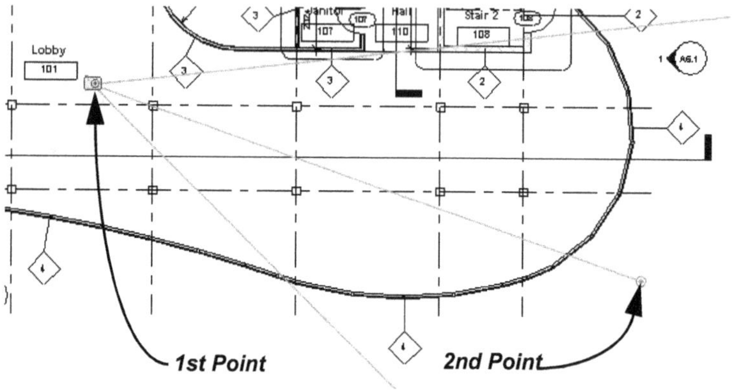

1st Point   **2nd Point**

Figure 1–59

16. The furniture and planters display even though they did not display in the floor plan view.

This file is not set up to work with Raytrace.

17. In the View Control Bar, set the *Visual Style* to ⬚ (Realistic).

18. In the Project Browser, right-click on the new camera view and select **Rename...** In the Rename View dialog box, type **Lobby Seating Area** and click ⬚ OK ⬚.

19. In the Quick Access Toolbar, click ⬚ (Save) to save the project.

20. In the Application Menu, click ⬚ (Close), or type <Ctrl>+<F4>. This closes the entire project.

Chapter Review Questions

1. When you create a project in the Autodesk Revit software, do you draw in 3D (as shown on the left in Figure 1–60) or 2D (as shown on the right in Figure 1–60)?

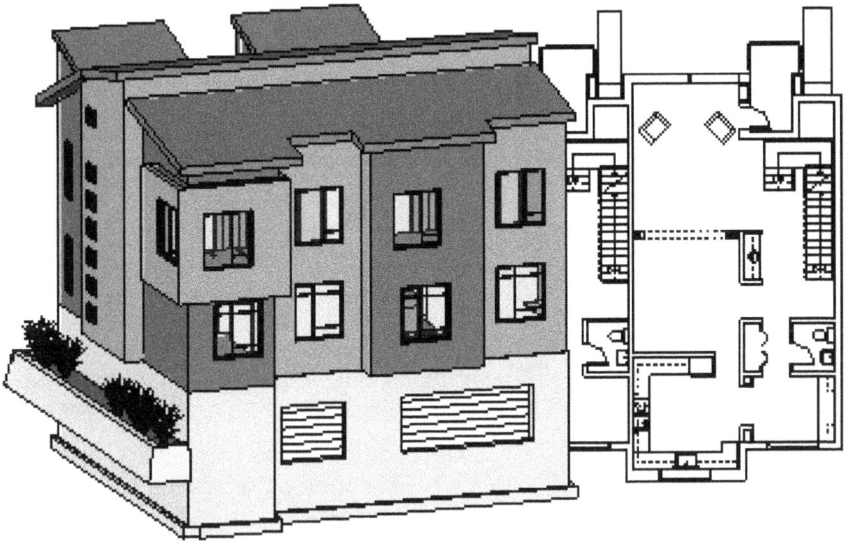

Figure 1–60

   a. You draw in 2D in plan views and in 3D in non-plan views.

   b. You model in 3D almost all of the time, even when you are using what looks like a flat view.

   c. You draw in 2D or 3D depending on how you toggle the 2D/3D control.

   d. You draw in 2D in plan and section views and model in 3D in isometric views.

2. What is the purpose of the Project Browser?

   a. It enables you to browse through the building project, similar to a walk through.

   b. It is the interface for managing all of the files that are needed to create the complete architectural model of the building.

   c. It manages multiple Autodesk Revit projects as an alternative to using Windows Explorer.

   d. It is used to access and manage the views of the project.

3. Which part(s) of the interface changes according to the command you are using? (Select all that apply.)

    a. Ribbon

    b. View Control Bar

    c. Options Bar

    d. Properties Palette

4. The difference between Type Properties and Properties (the Ribbon location is shown in Figure 1–61) is...

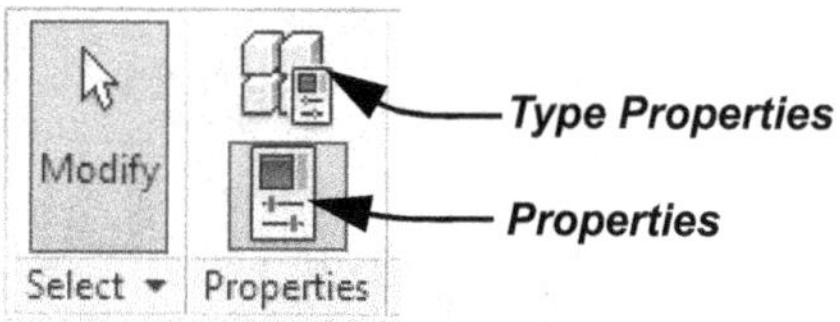

Figure 1–61

    a. Properties stores parameters that apply to the selected individual element(s). Type Properties stores parameters that impact every element of the same type in the project.

    b. Properties stores the location parameters of an element. Type Properties stores the size and identity parameters of an element.

    c. Properties only stores parameters of the view. Type Properties stores parameters of model components.

5. When you start a new project, how do you specify the base information in the new file?

    a. Transfer the base information from an existing project.

    b. Select the right template for the task.

    c. The Autodesk Revit software automatically extracts the base information from imported or linked file(s).

6. What is the main difference between a view made using (3D View) and a view made using (Camera)?

    a. Use **3D View** for exterior views and **Camera** for interiors.

    b. **3D View** creates a static image and a **Camera** view is live and always updated.

    c. **3D View** is isometric and a **Camera** view is perspective.

    d. **3D View** is used for the overall building and a **Camera** view is used for looking in tight spaces.

Command Summary

Button	Command	Location
General Tools		
	Modify	• **Quick Access Toolbar** • **Ribbon:** All tabs>Select panel • **Shortcut:** <M> and <D>
	New	• **Quick Access Toolbar** (Optional) • **Application Menu** • **Shortcut:** <Ctrl>+<N>
	Open	• **Quick Access Toolbar** • **Application Menu** • **Shortcut:** <Ctrl>+<O>
	Open Documents	• **Application Menu**
	Properties	• **Ribbon:** *Modify* tab>Properties panel • **Shortcut:** <P> and <P>
	Recent Documents	• **Application Menu**
	Save	• **Quick Access Toolbar** • **Application Menu** • **Shortcut:** <Ctrl>+<S>
	Synchronize and Modify Settings	• **Quick Access Toolbar**
	Synchronize Now/	• **Quick Access Toolbar**>expand Synchronize and Modify Settings
	Type Properties	• **Ribbon:** *Modify* tab>Properties panel • **Properties Palette**
Viewing Tools		
	Camera	• **Quick Access Toolbar**> Expand Default 3D View • **Ribbon:** *View* tab>Create panel> expand Default 3D View
	Default 3D View	• **Quick Access Toolbar** • **Ribbon:** *View* tab>Create panel
	Home	• **ViewCube**
N/A	**Next Pan/Zoom**	• **Navigation Bar** • **Right-click Menu**
N/A	**Previous Pan/Zoom**	• **Navigation Bar** • **Right-click Menu** • **Shortcut:** <Z> and <P>

☉ ☉	**Shadows On/Off**	• **View Control Bar**
	Zoom All to Fit	• **Navigation Bar** • **Shortcut:** <Z> and <A>
	Zoom In Region	• **Navigation Bar** • **Right-click Menu** • **Shortcut:** <Z> and <R>
	Zoom Out 2x	• **Navigation Bar** • **Right-click Menu** • **Shortcut:** <Z> and <O>
	Zoom Sheet Size	• **Navigation Bar** • **Shortcut:** <Z> and <S>
	Zoom to Fit	• **Navigation Bar** • **Right-click Menu** • **Shortcut:** <Z> and <F>, <Z> and <E>
	Show Rendering Dialog/ Render	• **View Control Bar** • **Ribbon:** *View* tab>Graphics panel • **Shortcut:** <R> and <R>

Visual Styles

	Consistent Colors	• **View Control Bar**:
	Hidden Line	• **View Control Bar** • **Shortcut:** <H> and <L>
	Ray Trace	• **View Control Bar**:
	Realistic	• **View Control Bar**
	Shaded	• **View Control Bar** • **Shortcut:** <S> and <D>
	Wireframe	• **View Control Bar** • **Shortcut:** <W> and <F>

Chapter 2

Basic Drawing and Modify Tools

In this chapter you learn how to use the basic drawing and modify tools that apply to almost all types of elements. These tools include alignment lines, temporary dimensions, snaps, and the Properties palette. You learn how to select elements for editing and how to move, copy, rotate, mirror, and array them. You also learn to align, split, trim, extend, and offset elements.

This chapter contains the following topics:

- **Using General Drawing Tools**
- **Editing Elements**
- **Working with Basic Modify Tools**
- **Working with Additional Modify Tools**

2.1 Using General Drawing Tools

Learning Objectives

- Use contextual Ribbon tabs, the Options Bar and Properties as you draw and modify.
- Draw elements using draw and pick tools.
- Use drawing aids including alignment lines, temporary dimensions and snaps.

When you start a command, the contextual Ribbon tab, Options Bar, and Properties palette enable you to set up features for each new element you are placing in the project. As you are drawing, several features called *drawing aids* display, as shown in Figure 2–1. They help you to create designs quickly and accurately.

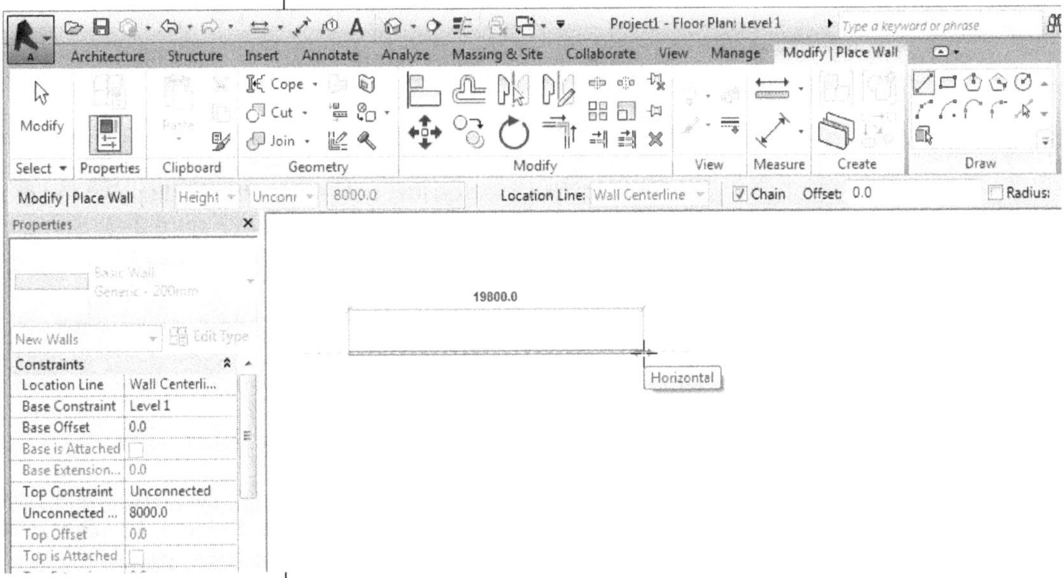

Figure 2–1

Contextual Ribbon

When you select a command or an element in the model, the Modify tab displays with additional contextual tools. For example, when you start the ⬚ (Wall) command, the *Modify | Place Wall* tab displays, as shown in Figure 2–2.

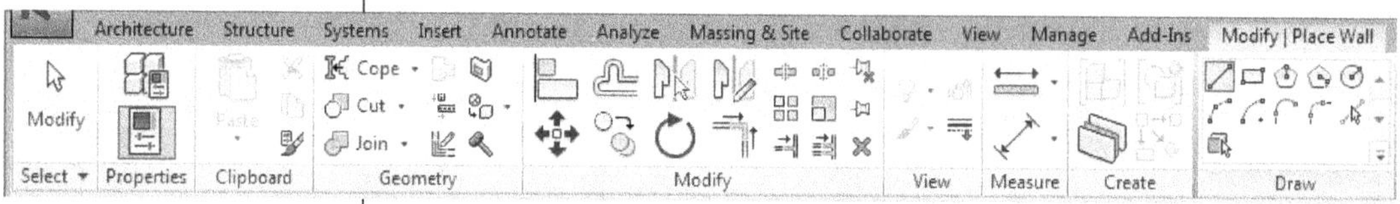

Figure 2–2

- The standard Modify tools are always displayed to the left in the ribbon, while the contextual tools are displayed to the right with a green panel title.

- To finish a command and return to the standard ribbon tabs at any time, in the *Select* panel, click ↳ (Modify).

Options Bar

The Options Bar, located just below the ribbon, displays the most used options for the element, as shown in Figure 2–3. Some of these options are also found in the Properties palette.

Figure 2–3

Properties Palette

The Properties palette displays the current element's family and type in the *Type Selector*. Click the Type Selector to expand the list of available families and types. In the lower part of the properties palette you can modify parameters for the selected object, as shown in Figure 2–4.

Some parameters are only available when you are editing an element. These parameters are grayed out when you are creating an element.

Figure 2–4

- Changes in the palette do not take effect until you click Apply or move the cursor away from the palette.

- The Properties palette can be floated and moved around the interface. You can also dock it on top of other browsers and then switch between them using the tabs at the bottom of the palette, as shown in Figure 2–5.

To dock the palette, drag the titlebar over the titlebar of the other browser.

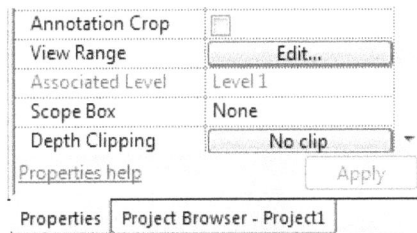

Figure 2–5

The Properties palette can be toggled on and off using the following methods:

- Right-click and select **Properties** in the contextual menu.

- In the *Modify* tab>Properties panel click (Properties).

- In the *View* tab, expand (User Interface), and select **Properties**.

- Use the shortcut by pressing <P> twice.

Draw Tools

Linear elements include walls, lines, detail lines, and sketches for floors, ceilings, roofs, stairs, ramps and railings.

Many elements in Autodesk® Revit® are linear elements, such as the walls shown in Figure 2–6. They are drawn using the tools on the *Draw* panel in the contextual Ribbon that displays when you start the related command. The available tools vary according to the element being drawn.

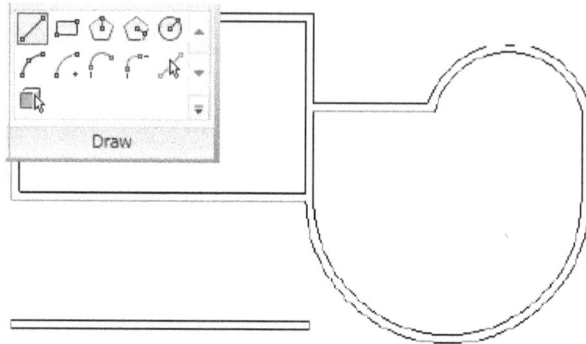

Figure 2–6

- Two styles of tools are available: one where you *draw* the element using a geometric form, and another where you *pick* an existing element (such as a line, face, or wall) as the basis for the new element's geometry.

How To: Draw Linear Elements

1. Start the command you want to use, such as ⌓ (Wall).
2. In the contextual tab>Draw panel, select a drawing tool, such as ╱ (Line), as shown in Figure 2–7. Select points to define the elements using other drawing aids, such as temporary dimensions, alignment lines, and snaps.

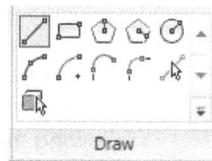

You can change from one Draw tool shape in the middle of a command.

Figure 2–7

▣ (Pick Face) is used with conceptual mass elements and is only available in a 3D view.

- Use ⚲ (Pick Lines) to create an element by selecting an existing wall, line or edge. This is often used with an offset distance to add the element a specified distance away from the selected element.

3. Finish the command. You can click ⍟ (Modify), press <Esc> twice, or right-click and select **Cancel** twice.

Draw Tools

⟋	**Line**	Draws a straight linear element defined by the first and last points. If Chain is enabled, you can continue selecting end points for multiple segments.
⬓	**Rectangle**	Draws four linear elements defined from two opposing corner points. You can adjust the dimensions after selecting both points.
⬠	**Inscribed Polygon**	Draws a polygon inscribed in a hypothetical circle with the number of sides specified in the Options Bar.
⬠	**Circumscribed Polygon**	Draws a polygon circumscribed around a hypothetical circle with the number of sides specified in the Options Bar.
◯	**Circle**	Draws a circular linear element defined by a center point and radius.
⌒	**Start-End-Radius Arc**	Draws a curved linear element defined by a start, end, and radius of the arc. The outside dimension shown is the included angle of the arc. The inside dimension is the radius.
⌒	**Center-ends Arc**	Draws a curved linear element defined by a center, radius, and included angle. The selected point of the radius also defines the start point of the arc.
⌒	**Tangent End Arc**	Draws a curved linear element tangent to another element. Select an end point for the first point, but do not select the intersection of two or more elements. Then select a second point based on the included angle of the arc.
⌒	**Fillet Arc**	Draws a curved linear element defined by two other linear elements and a radius. Because it is difficult to select the correct radius by clicking, this command automatically moves to edit mode. Select the dimension and then modify the radius of the fillet.
⋏	**Spline**	Draws a curved linear element based on selected points. The curve does not actually touch the points (Model and Detail Lines only).
⬭	**Ellipse**	Draws an ellipse from a primary and secondary axis (Model and Detail Lines only).
⌒	**Partial Ellipse**	Draws only one side of the ellipse, like an arc. A partial ellipse also has a primary and secondary axis (Model and Detail Lines only).

Pick Tools

⟋	**Pick Lines**	Use this option to select existing linear elements in the project. This is useful when you start the project from an imported 2D drawing.
▦	**Pick Face**	Use this option to select the face of a 3D massing element (walls and 3D views only).
▤	**Pick Walls**	Use this option to select an existing wall in the project to be the basis for a new sketch line (floors, ceilings, etc.).

Draw Options

When you are in Drawing mode, several options display in the Options Bar, as shown in Figure 2–8.

☑ Chain   Offset: 0.0   ☐ Radius: 1000.0

Figure 2–8

- The **Chain** option controls how many segments are drawn in one process. If it is not selected, the **Line** and **Arc** tools only draw one segment at a time. If it is selected, you can continue drawing segments until you select the command again.

- The *Offset* field enables you to enter values to draw the linear elements at a specified distance from the selected points.

- When using a radial draw tool, you can select the **Radius** option and add a radius in the edit field.

- To draw angled lines, move the cursor to the desired angle shown by the temporary dimensions, and type the distance value. The angle increments shown vary depending on how far in or out the view is zoomed.

Different options display according to the type of element that is selected, or the command that is active.

Drawing Aids

As soon as you start drawing in the software, three drawing aids display: *alignment lines*, *temporary dimensions*, and *snaps*. These are available with most drawing and many modification commands.

Alignment Lines

Dashed *alignment lines* display as soon as you select your first point, as shown in Figure 2–9. They help keep lines horizontal, vertical, or at a specified angle. They also line up with the implied intersections of walls and other elements.

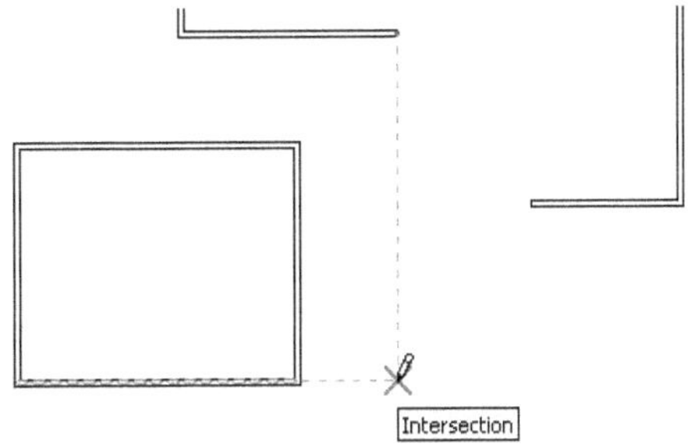

Figure 2–9

- Hold down <Shift> to force the alignments to be orthogonal (90 degree angles only).

Temporary Dimensions

Along with alignment lines, *temporary dimensions* display as you draw to help place linear elements at the correct length, angle and location, as shown in Figure 2–10.

You can type in the dimension, move the cursor until you see the dimension you want, or place the element and then modify the dimension as required.

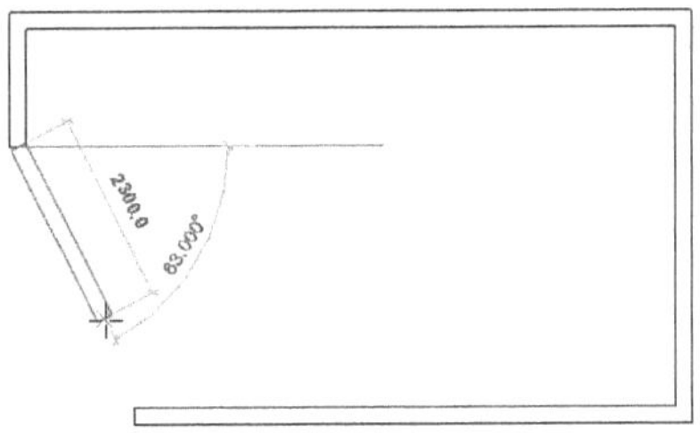

Figure 2–10

- For Metric measurements, the software defaults to millimeters. For example, if you type **4**, it assumes you mean 4mm. To indicate meters, type **M** after the distance.

- The increments displayed for temporary dimensions change as you zoom in or out on the elements. These *dimension snap* increments are for both linear and angular dimensions, and can be set in the Snaps dialog box.

Dimensions are a powerful tool to help create and annotate the model.

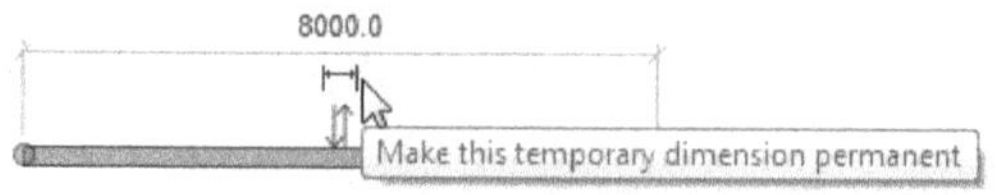

- Temporary dimensions disappear as soon as you finish drawing linear elements. If you want to make them permanent, select the control shown in Figure 2–11.

Figure 2–11

- The size of the temporary dimensions, in pixels, can be set in the Options dialog box on the *Graphics* tab.

Snaps

Snaps are key points that help you reference existing elements to exact points when drawing, as shown in Figure 2–12.

Figure 2–12

They include *Endpoints, Midpoints, Nearest, Work Plane Grid, Quadrants, Intersections, Centers, Perpendicular, Tangents*, and *Points.* When you move the cursor over an element, the **Snap** symbol displays. Each snap location type displays with a different symbol.

- To modify the snap settings, in the *Manage* tab>Settings

  panel, click 🧲 (Snaps). This opens the Snaps dialog box, where you can set which snap points are active, as well as the snap distances (for dimension and angular increments). It also displays the keyboard shortcuts for each snap, which you can use to override the automatic snapping.

> **Hint: Snap Overrides**
>
> You can use shortcut key combinations (displayed in the Snaps dialog box) or right-click and select **Snap Overrides** to temporarily override snap settings. Temporary overrides only affect a single pick but can be very helpful when there are snaps nearby other than the one you want to use.

Reference Planes

As you develop designs in Autodesk Revit, there are times when you need lines that don't print to help you define certain locations. You can draw *reference planes* (displayed as dashed green lines) and snap elements to then whenever you need to line up elements. For example, the lighting fixtures in the reflected ceiling plan shown in Figure 2–13 are aligned using reference planes.

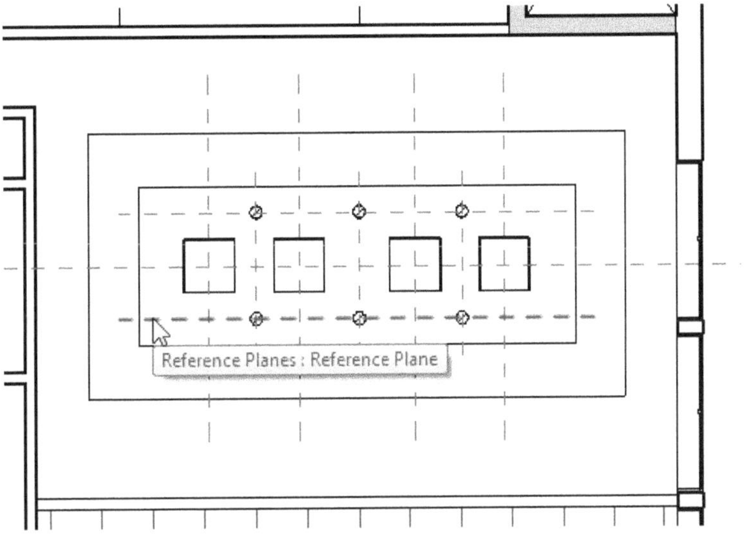

Reference Planes : Reference Plane

Figure 2–13

- Reference lines display in associated views because they are infinite planes, and not just lines. However, reference planes do not display in 3D views.

How To: Sketch with Reference Planes

1. In the *Architecture* tab>Work Plane panel, click ⬚ (Ref Plane) or use the shortcut by pressing <R> and then pressing <P>.
2. In the *Modify | Place Reference Plane* tab>Draw panel, click
   ╱ (Line) or ⬚ (Pick Lines).

   - For ╱ (Line), select two points that define the reference plane.

   - For ⬚ (Pick Lines), select any linear element and a reference plane is created that matches the length of that element.

- In the Options Bar, the Offset field enables you to enter values to draw the reference plane at a specified distance from a selected point. For example, set *Offset* to 3000mm and select the end points of an existing wall to create a reference plane 3000mm away. You can also use *Offset* with **Pick Lines**.

3. When you have created all of the required reference planes, end the command by clicking ↖ (Modify) or by using one of the other options.

- To change the length of a reference plane, drag the circle at either end.

- You can name reference planes to keep track of their purpose. This also enables you to use a reference plane as a work plane when creating or placing other elements in the project. Select the reference plane and in the Properties palette, in the *Identity Data* area, enter a name, as shown in Figure 2–14.

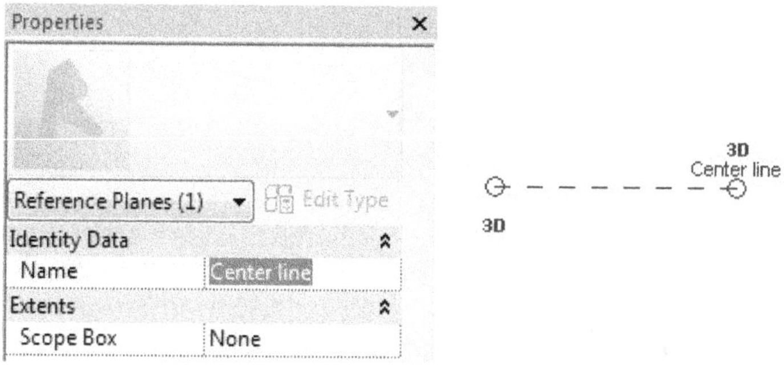

Figure 2–14

2.2 Editing Elements

Learning Objectives

- Select elements to modify.
- Modify elements using the Ribbon, Properties, temporary dimensions, and controls.
- Filter selection sets.

Building design projects typically involve extensive changes to the positions of walls, doors, and other elements. The Autodesk Revit software was designed to make such changes quickly and efficiently. When you select an element there are a number of ways to change it, as shown in Figure 2–15:

When you hover the cursor over an element, a tooltip displays its family and type.

- *Controls* enable you to drag, flip, lock, and rotate the element.
- *Temporary dimensions* enable you to change the element's dimensions.
- Modify commands and element-specific tools display in the contextual tab in the Ribbon.
- The Properties palette displays the Type Selector and associated parameters.

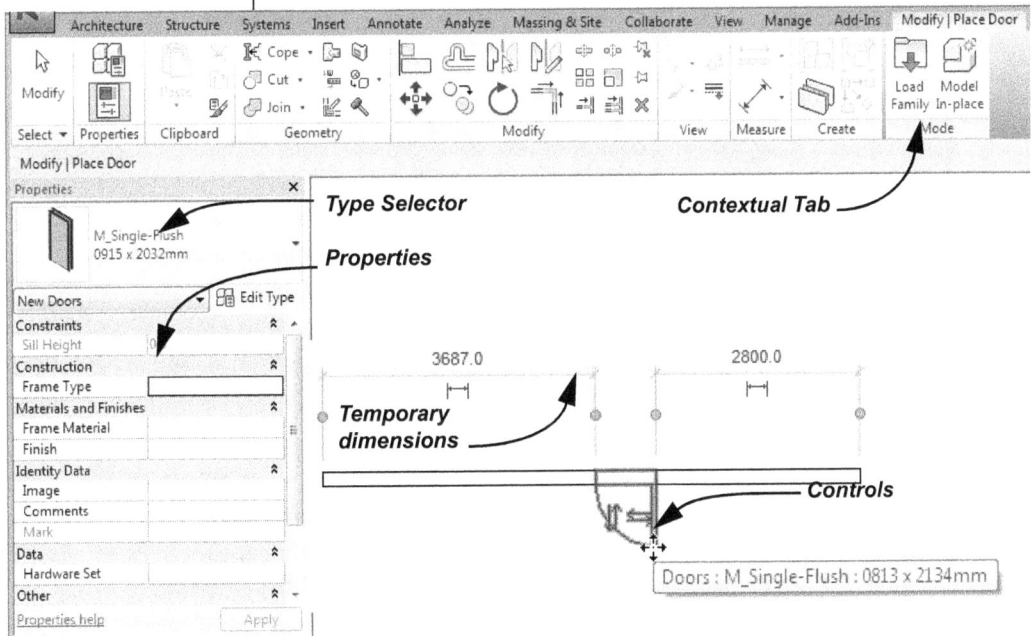

Figure 2–15

- To delete an element, select it and press <Delete>, right-click and select **Delete**, or in the Modify panel, click ✖ (Delete).

- When working with temporary dimensions, the default location of the dimension line might not be where you need it to be. You can click on the circular control to move the witness line to another part of the element (such as a different layer in a multilayer wall), or drag it to a new element. In the example shown on the left in Figure 2–16, the dimension is from the center of the left wall to the selected wall. To change the dimension so that it touches the grid line, drag the circular control (also called the witness line) so that it touches the grid line, as shown on the right in Figure 2–16.

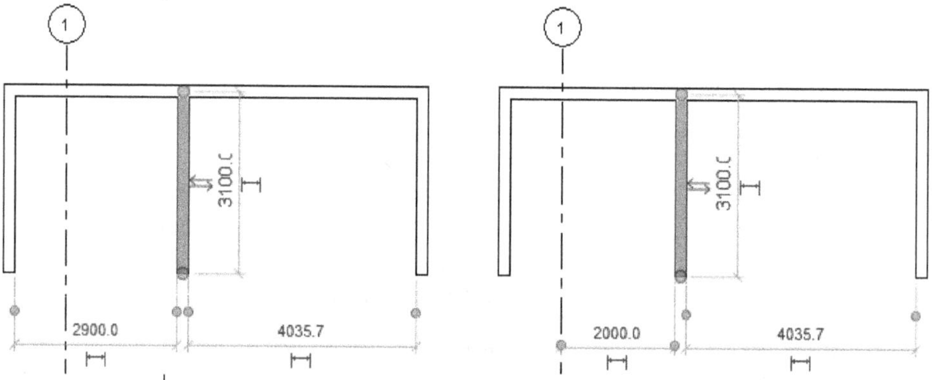

Figure 2–16

- The new location of a temporary dimension for an element is remembered as long as you are in the same session of the software.

Hint: Nudge

Nudge enables you to move an element in short increments. When an element is selected, you can press one of the four arrow keys to move the element in that direction. The distance the element moves depends on how far in or out you are zoomed. This is very useful with annotation elements.

Selecting Elements

You can select elements in several ways:

- To select a single element, place the cursor on the edge of the element and click to select.

- To add another element to a selection set, hold down <Ctrl> and select another item.

- To remove an element from a selection set, hold down
  <Shift> and select the element.

- If you click and drag the cursor to *window* around elements,
  you have two selection options, as shown in Figure 2–17. If
  you drag from left to right, you only select the elements
  completely inside the window. If you drag from right to left,
  you select elements both inside and crossing the window.

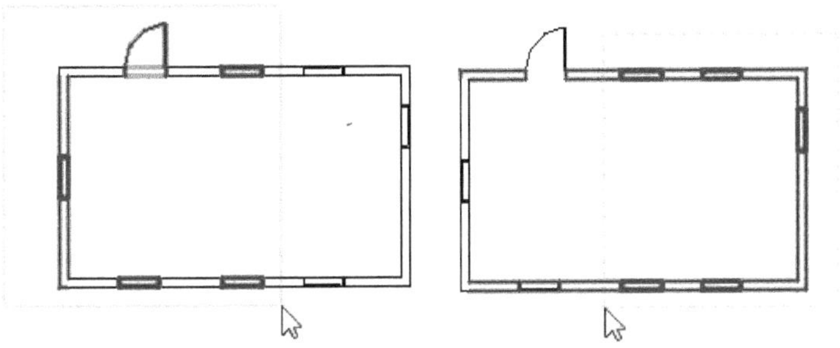

Figure 2–17

- If several elements are on or near each other, press <Tab> to
  cycle through them before you click. If there are elements
  that might be linked to each other, such as walls that are
  connected, pressing <Tab> selects the chain of elements.

- Press <Ctrl>+<Left Arrow> to reselect the previous selection
  set. You can also right-click in the drawing window with
  nothing selected and select **Select Previous**.

- To select all elements of a specific type, right-click on an
  element and select **Select All Instances>Visible in View** or
  In Entire Project, as shown in Figure 2–18.

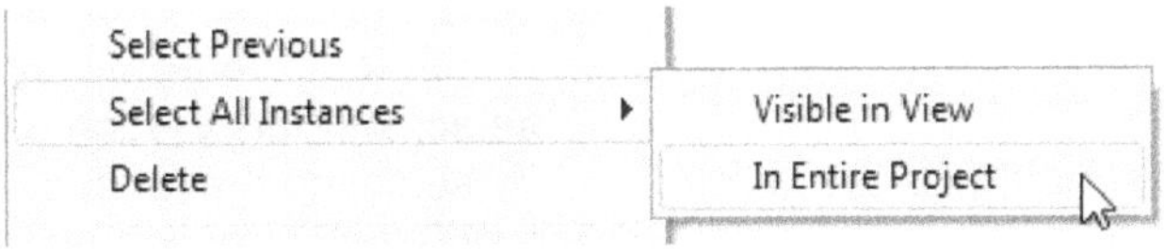

Figure 2–18

Hint: Selection Options

You can control how the software selects specific elements in a project by toggling them on and off on Status Bar, or in any Ribbon tab expand the *Select* panel's title as shown in Figure 2–19.

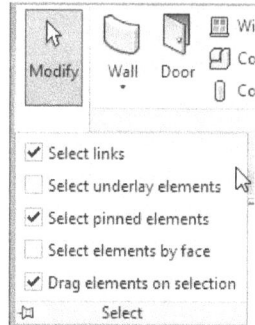

Figure 2–19

- **Select links:** When toggled on, you can selected linked drawings or Autodesk Revit models. When it is toggled off you cannot select them when using **Modify** or **Move**.

- **Select underlay elements:** When toggled on, you can select underlay elements. When toggled off, you cannot select them when using **Modify** or **Move**.

- **Select pinned elements:** When toggled on, you can selected pinned elements. When toggled off, you cannot select them when using **Modify** or **Move**.

- **Select elements by face:** When toggled on you can select elements (such as the floors or walls in an elevation) by selecting the interior face or selecting an edge. When toggled off, you can only select elements by selecting an edge.

- **Drag elements on selection:** When toggled on, you can hover over an element, select it, and drag it to a new location. When toggled off, the Crossing or Box select mode starts when you press and drag, even if you are on top of an element. Once elements have been selected they can still be dragged to a new location.

Selecting Multiple Elements

When multiple element types are selected, the *Multi-Select* contextual tab opens in the Ribbon, as shown in Figure 2–20. This gives you access to all of the Modify tools, as well as the **Filter** command.

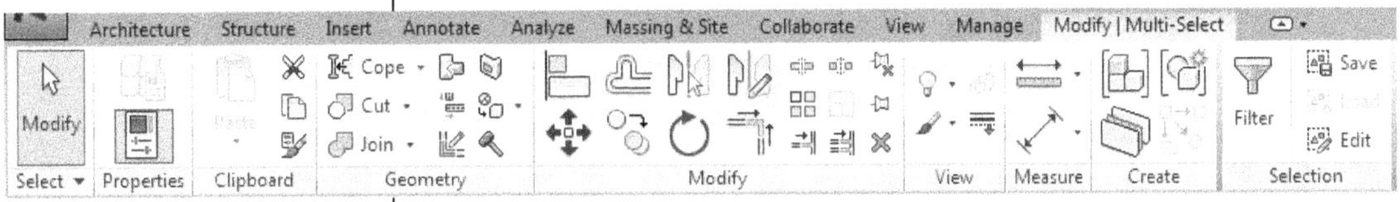

Figure 2–20

- The Properties palette displays tools that are common to all element types if they are available. You can also select just one type and make modifications, as shown in Figure 2–21.

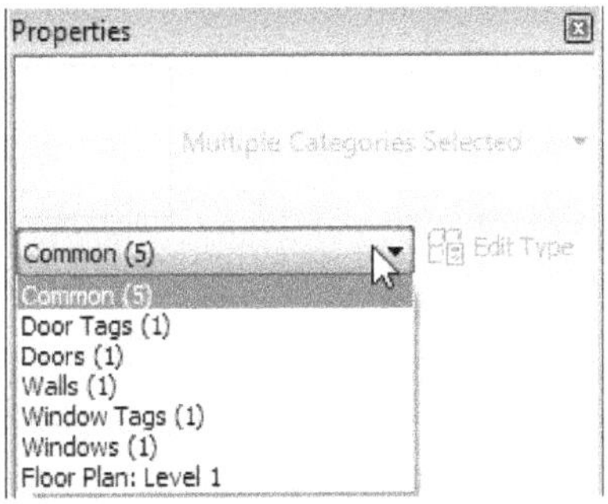

Figure 2–21

Filtering Selection Sets

The **Filter** command enables you to specify the types of elements to select. For example, you might only want to select columns, as shown in Figure 2–22.

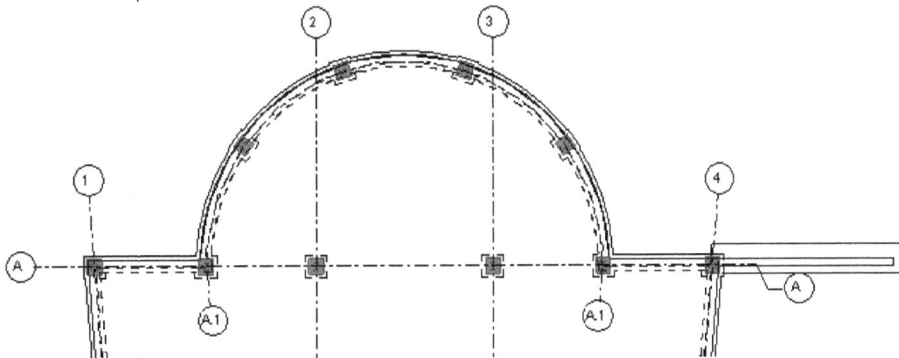

Figure 2–22

How To: Filter a Selection Set

1. Select everything in the required area.
2. in the *Modify | Multi-Select* tab>Selection panel, or in the Status Bar, click ⍚ (Filter). The Filter dialog box opens, as shown in Figure 2–23.

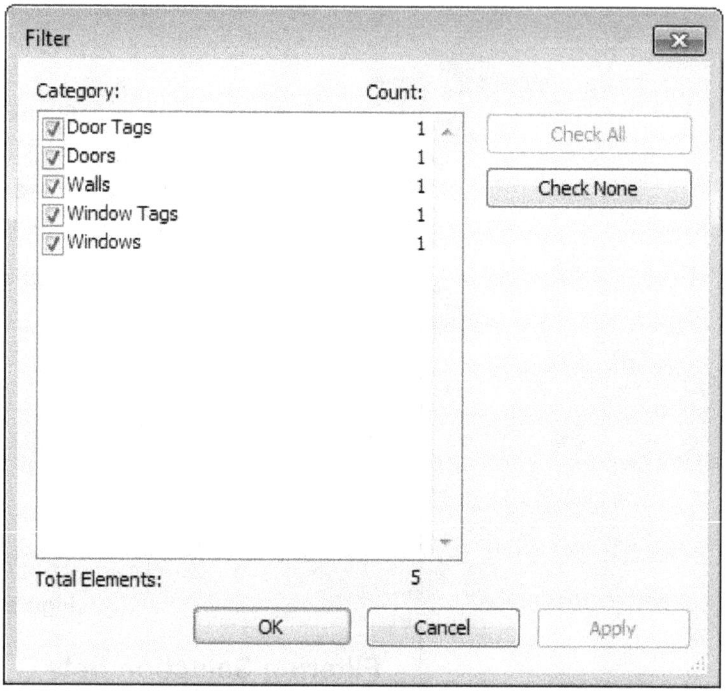

The Filter dialog box displays all types of elements in the original selection.

Figure 2–23

3. Click [Check None] to clear all of the options and then select the element types that you want included in the selection.

4. Click [OK]. The selection set is now limited to the elements you specified.

- In the Status Bar, the number of elements selected displays beside the Filter icon, as shown in Figure 2–24. You can also see the number of selected elements in the Properties palette.

Figure 2–24

Practice 2a

Draw and Modify Elements

Learning Objectives

- Create walls using draw tools and drawing aids.
- Add and modify a door.

Estimated time for completion: 10 minutes

In this practice you will use the **Wall** command along with Draw tools and drawing aids, such as temporary dimensions and snaps. You will use the **Modify** command and modify the walls using grips, temporary dimensions, the Type Selector, and Properties. You will add a door and modify it using temporary dimensions and controls. The completed drawing is shown in Figure 2–25.

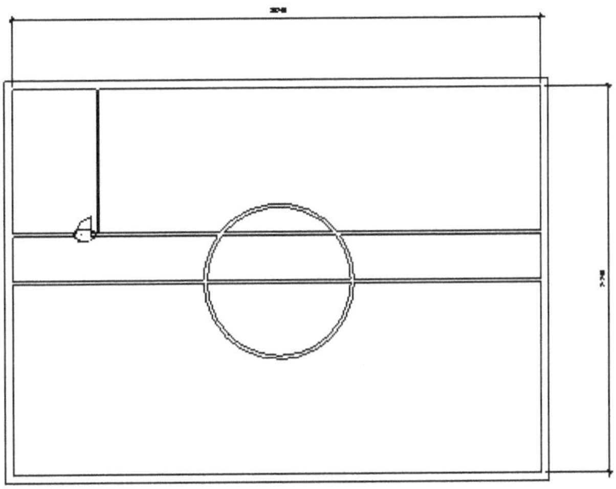

Figure 2–25

Task 1 - Draw and modify walls.

1. In the Application Menu, click ☐ (New)> ⬛ (Project).

2. In the New Project dialog box, select **Architectural Template** in the Template file drop-down list, and click ⬛ OK ⬛ .

3. In the Quick Access Toolbar, click ⬛ (Save). When prompted, name the project **Simple Building.rvt**.

4. In the *Architecture* tab>Build panel, click ☐ (Wall).

---

5. In the *Modify | Place Wall* tab>Draw panel, click

    ▭ (Rectangle) and draw a rectangle approximately **30500mm x 21500mm.** You do not have to be precise because you can change the dimensions later.

6. Note that the dimensions are temporary. Select the vertical dimension text and type **21500**, as shown in Figure 2–26. Press <Enter>.

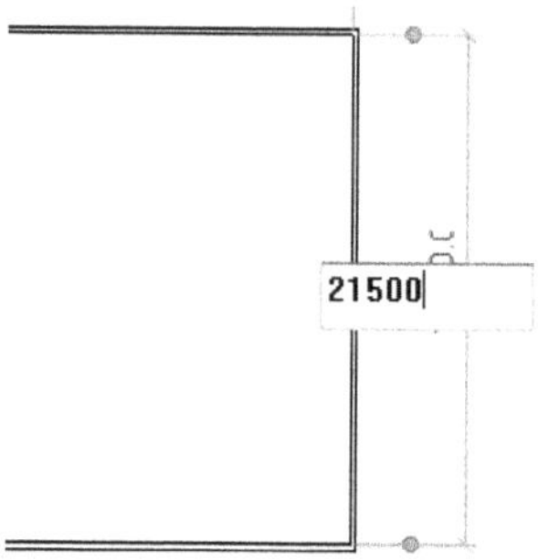

Figure 2–26

7. The dimensions are still displayed as temporary. Click the dimension controls of both the dimensions to make them permanent, as shown in Figure 2–27.

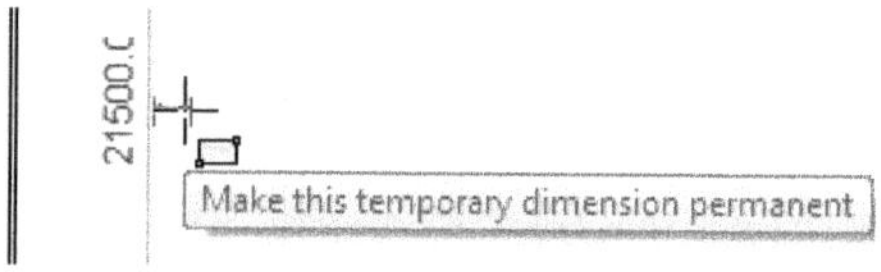

Figure 2–27

- You will change the horizontal wall dimension using the permanent dimension.

8. In the Select panel, click ⮑ (Modify). (You can also use one of the other methods to switch to **Modify,** including using the shortcut by pressing <M> and pressing <D>, pressing <Esc> once or twice, or by right-clicking and selecting **Cancel** once or twice.)

9. Select either vertical wall. The horizontal dimension becomes active (changes to blue). Click the dimension text and type **30500**, as shown in Figure 2–28.

Figure 2–28

10. Click in an empty space to end the selection. You are still in the **Modify** command.

11. In the *Architecture* tab>Build panel, click ⬭ (Wall). In the Draw panel, verify that ✐ (Line) is selected. Draw a wall horizontally from midpoint to midpoint of the vertical walls.

12. Draw another horizontal wall **2500mm** above the middle horizontal wall. You can use temporary dimensions or the *Offset* field to do this.

13. Draw a vertical wall exactly 5000mm from the left wall, as shown in Figure 2–29.

If the temporary dimension is reading the face of the wall, continue to click on the control until it correctly identifies the center of the wall.

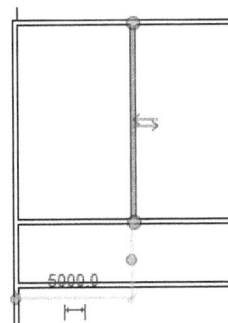

Figure 2–29

14. In the Draw panel, click ⊘ (Circle) and draw a **4200mm** radius circular wall at the midpoint of the lower interior horizontal wall, as shown in Figure 2–30.

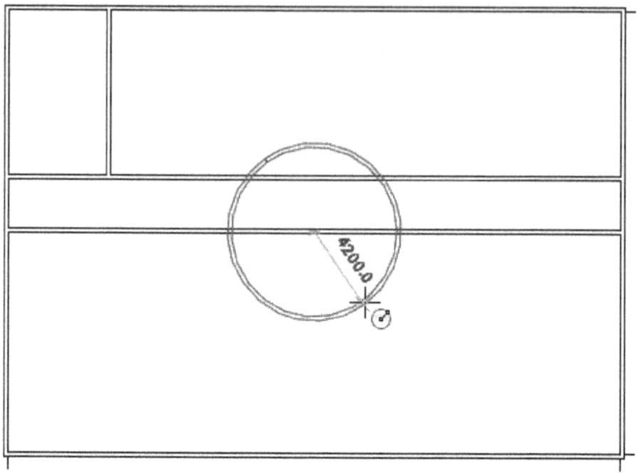

Figure 2–30

15. Click ⬉ (Modify) to finish the command.

16. Hover the cursor over one of the outside walls, press <Tab> to highlight the chain of outside walls, and click to select the walls.

17. In the Type Selector, select **Basic Wall: Exterior - Block on Mtl. Stud**, as shown in Figure 2–31. The thickness of the outside walls change.

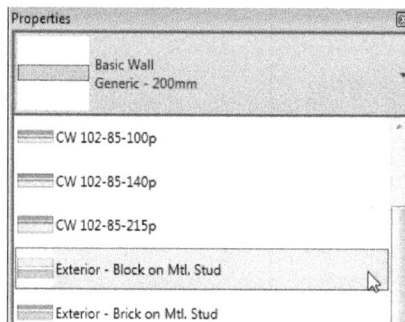

Figure 2–31

18. Click in empty space to release the selection.

19. Select the vertical interior wall and change it to one of the small interior partition styles.

20. Click in an empty space to release the selection.

Task 2 - Add and modify a door.

1. Zoom in on the room in the upper left corner.

2. In the *Architecture* tab>Build panel, click ▯ (Door).

3. In the *Modify | Place Door* tab>Tag panel, click ▯① (Tag on Placement) if it is not already selected.

4. Place a door anywhere along the wall in the hallway.

5. Click ▷ (Modify) to finish the command.

6. Select the door. Use temporary dimensions to move it so that it is **300mm**from the right interior vertical wall. If required, use controls to flip the door so that it swings into the room, as shown in Figure 2–32.

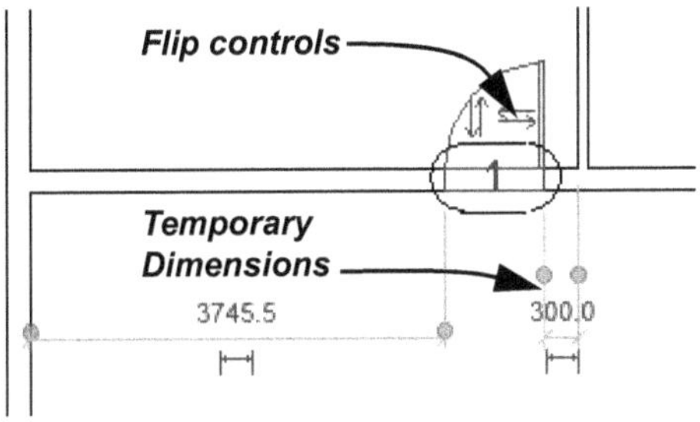

Figure 2–32

7. Type **ZE** to zoom out to the full view.

8. Save the project.

2.3 Working with Basic Modify Tools

Learning Objectives

- Move and copy elements.
- Rotate elements around the center or an origin.
- Mirror elements by picking an axis or by drawing an axis.
- Create Linear and Radial Arrays of elements.

The Autodesk Revit software contains controls and temporary dimensions that enable you to edit elements. Additional modifying tools can be used with individual elements or any selection of elements. They are found in the *Modify* tab>Modify panel, as shown in Figure 2–33, and in contextual tabs.

Figure 2–33

- The **Move**, **Copy**, **Rotate**, **Mirror**, and **Array** commands are covered in this topic. Other tools are covered later.

- For most modify commands, you can either select the elements and start the command, or start the command, select the elements, and press <Enter> to finish the selection and move to the next step in the command.

Moving and Copying Elements

The **Move** and **Copy** commands enable you to select the element(s) and move or copy them from one place to another. You can use alignment lines, temporary dimensions, and snaps to help place the elements, as shown in Figure 2–34.

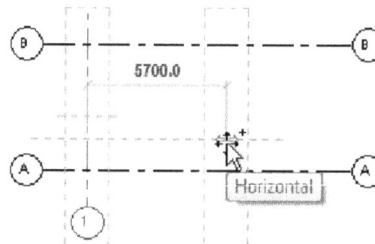

Figure 2–34

How To: Move or Copy Elements

1. Select the elements you want to move or copy.

*You can also use the shortcut for the **Move** command by pressing <M> and pressing <V>, or for the **Copy** command by pressing <C> and pressing <O>.*

2. In the Modify panel, click ✛ (Move) or ⟳ (Copy). A boundary box displays around the selected elements.
3. Select a move start point on or near the element.
4. Select a second point. Use alignment lines and temporary dimensions to help place the elements.
5. When you are finished, you can start another modify command using the elements that remain selected, or switch back to **Modify** to end the command.

- If you start the **Move** command and hold down <Ctrl>, the elements are copied.

Move/Copy Elements

The **Move** and **Copy** commands have several options that display in the Options Bar, as shown in Figure 2–35.

☐ Constrain ☐ Disjoin ☐ Multiple

Figure 2–35

Constrain	Restricts the movement of the cursor to horizontal or vertical, or along the axis of an item that is at an angle. This keeps you from selecting a point at an angle by mistake. **Constrain** is off by default.
Disjoin (Move only)	Breaks any connections between the elements being moved and other elements. If **Disjoin** is on, the elements move separately. If it is off, the connected elements also move or stretch. **Disjoin** is off by default.
Multiple (Copy only)	Enables you to make multiple copies of one selection. **Multiple** is off by default.

- These commands only work within the current view, not between views or projects. To copy between views or projects, use 🗐 (Copy to Clipboard) and 📋 (Paste).

Enhanced in 2015

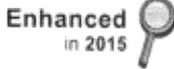

Hint: Pinning Elements

If you do not want elements to be moved, you can pin them in place, as shown in Figure 2–36. Select the elements and in the

Modify tab, in the Modify panel, click ⊡ (Pin). Pinned elements can be copied, but not moved. If you try to delete a pinned element, a warning dialog displays reminding you that you must unpin the element before the command can be started.

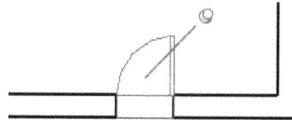

Figure 2–36

Select the element and click ⊡ₓ (Unpin) or use the shortcut by pressing <U> and pressing <P> to free it.

Rotating Elements

The **Rotate** command enables you to rotate selected elements around a center point or origin. You can use alignment lines, temporary dimensions, and snaps to help specify the center of rotation and the angle. You can also create copies of the element as it is being rotated.

How To: Rotate Elements

1. Select the element(s) you want to rotate.

2. In the Modify panel, click ⟲ (Rotate) or use the shortcut by pressing <R> and pressing <O>.

3. The center of rotation is automatically set to the center of the element or group of elements, as shown on the left in Figure 2–37. To change the center of rotation, as shown on the right in Figure 2–37, use the following:

   • Drag the ⟲ (Center of Rotation) control to a new point.

   • In the Options Bar, next to **Center of rotation**, click [Place] and use snaps to move it to a new location.

   • Press the <Spacebar> to select the center of rotation and click to move it to a new location.

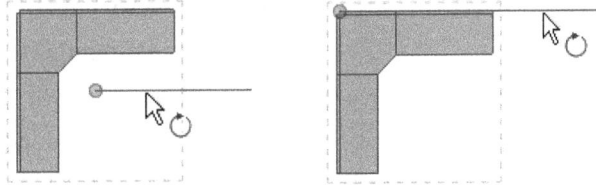

Figure 2–37

- To start the **Rotate** command with an automatic prompt to select the center of rotation, select the elements first and type **R3**.

4. In the Options Bar, specify if you want to make a Copy (select **Copy** option), type an angle in the *Angle* field (as shown in Figure 2–38), and press <Enter>. You can also specify the angle on screen.

*To specify the angle on screen, select a point for the **rotate start ray** (the reference line for the rotation angle). Then select a second point, using the temporary dimension to help you set the angle.*

Figure 2–38

5. The rotated element(s) remain highlighted, enabling you to start another command, or return to **Modify** to finish.

- The **Disjoin** option breaks any connections between the elements being rotated and other elements. If **Disjoin** is on (selected), the elements rotate separately. If it is off (cleared), the connected elements also move or stretch. **Disjoin** is off by default.

Mirroring Elements

The **Mirror** command enables you to mirror elements about an axis defined by a selected element, as shown in Figure 2–39, or by selected points.

Figure 2–39

How To: Mirror Elements

1. Select the element(s) to mirror.
2. In the Modify panel, select the method you want to use:

   - Click ⌷ (Mirror - Pick Axis) or use the shortcut by pressing <M> twice. This prompts you to select an element as the **Axis of Reflection** (mirror line).

   - Click ⌷ (Mirror - Draw Axis) or use the shortcut by pressing <D> and pressing <M>. This prompts you to select two points to define the axis about which the elements mirror.

3. The new mirrored element(s) remain highlighted, enabling you to start another command, or return to **Modify** to finish.

   - By default, the original elements that were mirrored remain. To delete the original elements, clear the **Copy** option in the Options Bar.

Hint: Scale

The Autodesk Revit software is designed with full-size elements. Therefore, not much can be scaled. However, you can use ⌷ (Scale) in reference planes, images, and imported files from other programs.

Creating Linear and Radial Arrays

A linear array creates a straight line pattern of elements, while a radial array creates a circular pattern around a center point.

The **Array** command creates multiple copies of selected elements in a linear or radial pattern, as shown in Figure 2–40. For example, you can array a row of columns to create a row of evenly spaced columns on a grid, or array a row of parking spaces. The arrayed elements can be grouped or placed as separate elements.

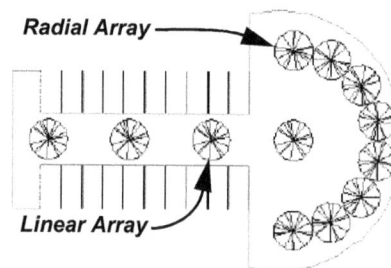

Figure 2–40

How To: Create a Linear Array

1. Select the element(s) to array.
2. In the Modify panel, click ⬚⬚ (Array).
3. In the Options Bar, click ⬚ (Linear).
4. Specify the other options as required.
5. Select a start point and an end point to set the spacing and direction of the array. The array is displayed.
6. If the **Group and Associate** option is selected, you are prompted again for the number of items, as shown in Figure 2–41. Type a new number or click on the screen to finish the command.

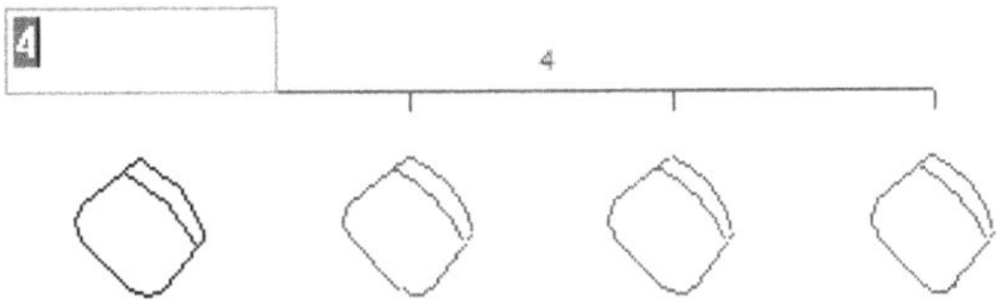

Figure 2–41

- To make a linear array in two directions, you need to array one direction first, select the arrayed elements, and then array them again in the other direction.

Array Options

In the Options Bar, set up the **Array** options for **Linear Array** (top of Figure 2–42) or **Radial Array** (bottom of Figure 2–42).

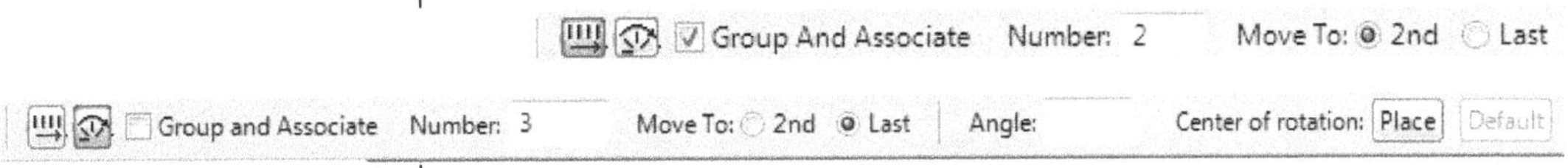

Figure 2–42

Group and Associate	Creates an array group element out of all arrayed elements. Groups can be selected by selecting any elements in the group.
Number	Specifies how many instances you want in the array.
Move To:	**2nd** specifies the distance or angle between the center points of the two elements.
	Last specifies the overall distance or angle of the entire array.
Constrain	Restricts the direction of the array to only vertical or horizontal (Linear only).

Angle	Specifies the angle (Radial only).
Center of rotation	Specifies a location for the origin about which the elements rotate (Radial only).

How To: Create a Radial Array

1. Select the element(s) to array.

2. In the Modify panel, click ⬚⬚ (Array).

3. In the Options Bar, click 🔲 (Radial).

4. Drag ⟲ (Center of Rotation) or use [Place] to the move the center of rotation to the appropriate location, as shown in Figure 2–43.

*Remember to set the **Center of Rotation** control first, because it is easy to forget to move it before specifying the angle.*

Figure 2–43

5. Specify the other options as required.
6. In the Options Bar, type an angle and press <Enter>, or specify the rotation angle by selecting points on the screen.

Modifying Array Groups

When you select an element in an array that has been grouped, you can change the number of instances in the array, as shown in Figure 2–44. For radial arrays you can also modify the distance to the center.

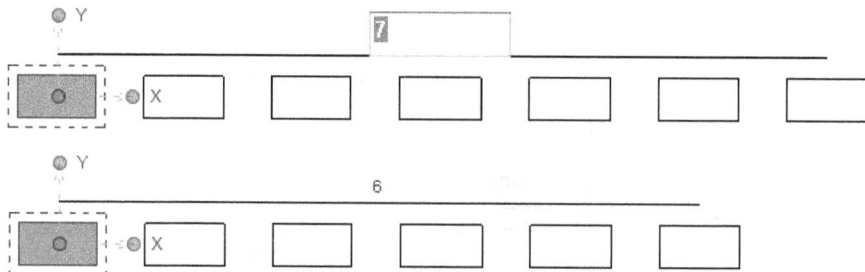

Figure 2–44

- Dashed lines surround the element(s) in a group, and the XY control lets you move the origin point of the group

If you move one of the elements within the array group, the other elements move in response based on the distance and/or angle, as shown in Figure 2–45

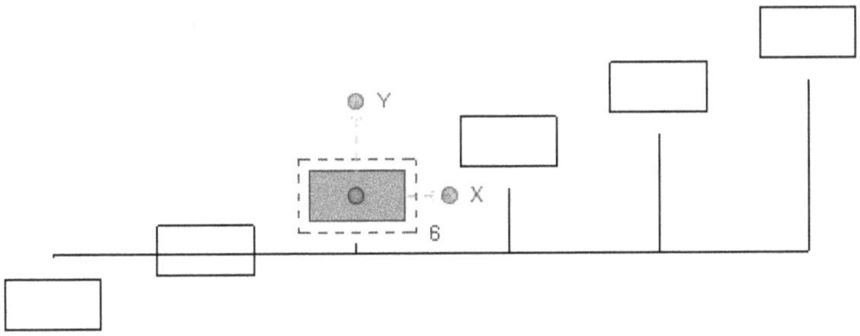

Figure 2–45

- To remove the array constraint on the group, select all of the elements in the array group and, in the *Modify* contextual tab>Group panel, click ⌗ (Ungroup).

- If you select an individual element in an array and click ⌗ (Ungroup), the element you selected is removed from the array, while the rest of the elements remain in the array group.

- You can use ▽ (Filter) to ensure that you are selecting only **Model Groups**.

Practice 2b

Work with Basic Modify Tools

Learning Objectives

- Copy walls to create a series of offices and mirror a door for the last office.
- Add and array desks around a circular wall.
- Add, rotate, and array a pair of columns across the front of the building.

Estimated time for completion: 15 minutes

In this practice you will use **Move**, **Copy**, **Mirror**, **Copy** and **Array** to modify and add elements to a simple building, as shown in Figure 2–46.

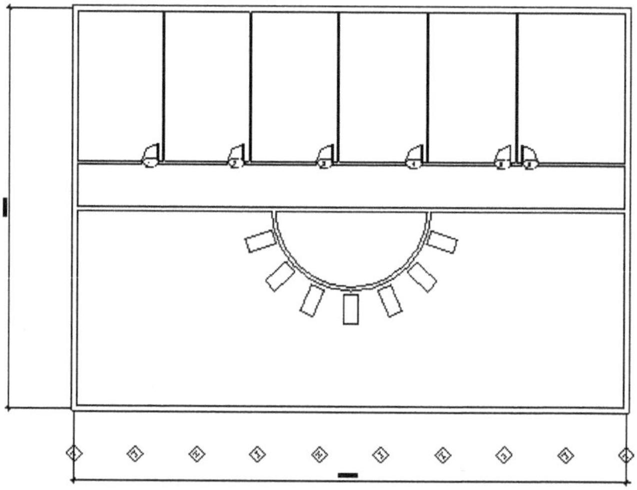

Figure 2–46

Task 1 - Modify walls and doors.

1. Open the project **Simple-Building-1-M.rvt** from your class folder.

2. Select the top arc of the circular wall.

3. In the Modify panel, click ✖ (Delete). The walls that the circular wall crossed are automatically cleaned up.

*Remember that you can also press <Delete>, or right-click and select **Delete**.*

4. Select the vertical interior wall, door, and door tag. Hold down <Ctrl> to select more than one element, or use a selection window.

5. In the Modify panel, click ⌖ (Copy).

6. In the Options Bar, select the **Constrain** and **Multiple** options. The **Constrain** option forces the cursor to move only horizontally or vertically.

7. Select the start point and the end point, as shown in Figure 2–47. The wall, door, and door tag are copied to the right and the door tag displays 2.

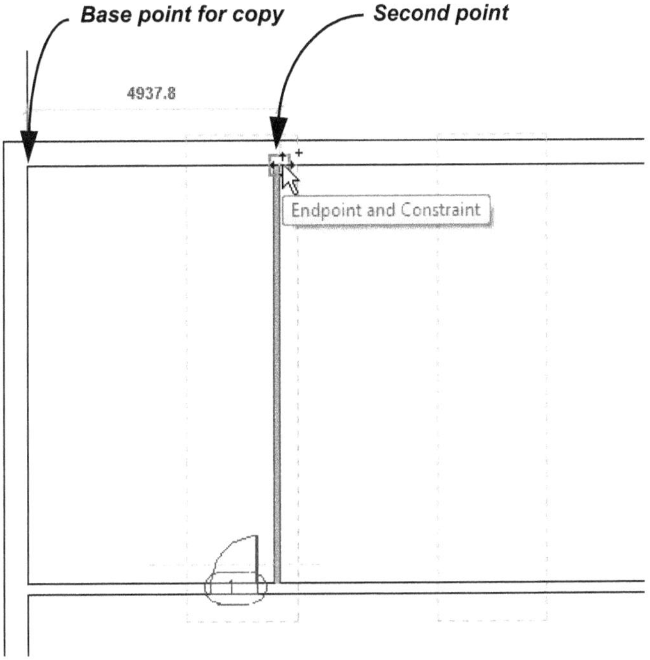

Base point for copy   *Second point*

4937.8

Endpoint and Constraint

Figure 2–47

8. The new elements are still selected and you can continue to copy them. Use similar start and end points for the additional copies. The final layout is shown in Figure 2–48.

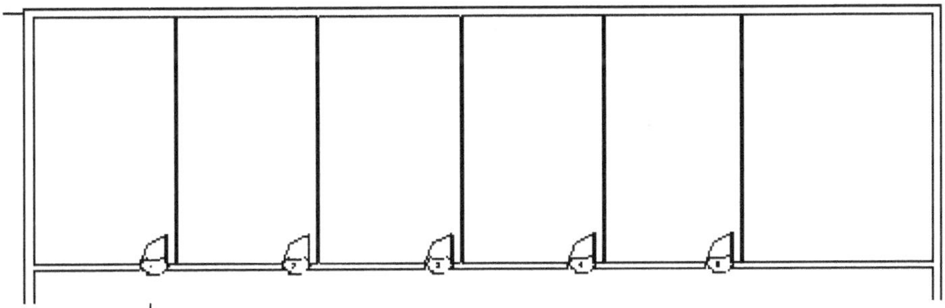

Figure 2–48

9. Finish the command by returning to **Modify**.

10. Zoom in on the room to the far right.

11. Select door #5 and the associated door tag.

12. In the Modify panel, click ⬚ (Mirror - Pick Axis), or use the shortcut by pressing <M> twice. In the Options Bar, ensure that **Copy** is selected.

13. Select the vertical wall between the rooms as the mirror axis. An alignment line displays along the center of the wall. Place the new door, as shown in Figure 2–49.

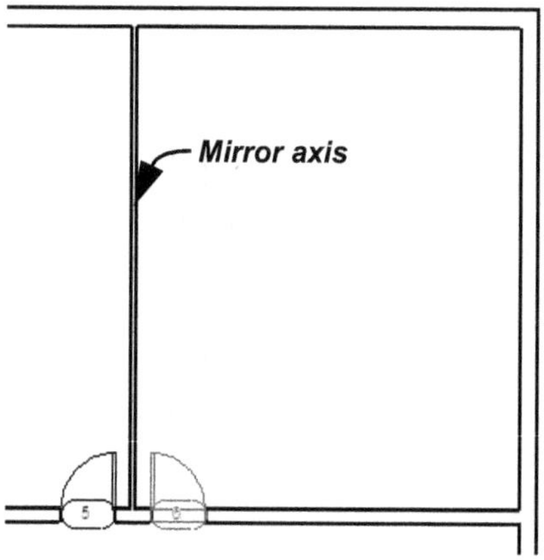

Mirror axis

Figure 2–49

14. Click in empty space to release the selection.

Task 2 - Add reference planes and use them to place a component.

---

1. In the *Architecture* tab>Work plane panel, click ⬚ (Ref Plane).

2. Draw two reference planes, as shown in Figure 2–50. The vertical one starts at the midpoint of the wall. You can place the horizontal plane anywhere, and then use temporary dimensions to place it more exactly.)

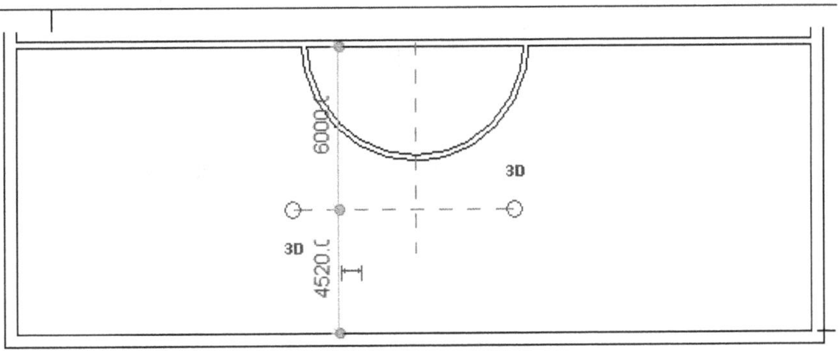

Figure 2–50

3. In the *Architecture* tab>Build panel, click ⬚ (Component).

4. In the Properties palette, in the Type Selector, verify that **M_Desk: 1525 x 762mm** is selected, as shown in Figure 2–51.

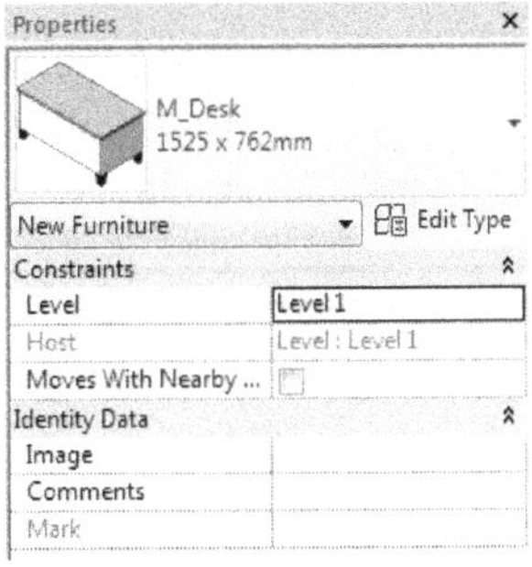

Figure 2–51

5. As you move the cursor you can see that the desk is horizontal. Press <Spacebar> to rotate the desk 90 degrees.

6. Place the desk at the intersection of the two reference planes, as shown in Figure 2–52. Zoom in as required to ensure that you are connected to the reference planes, and not to any other alignment lines.

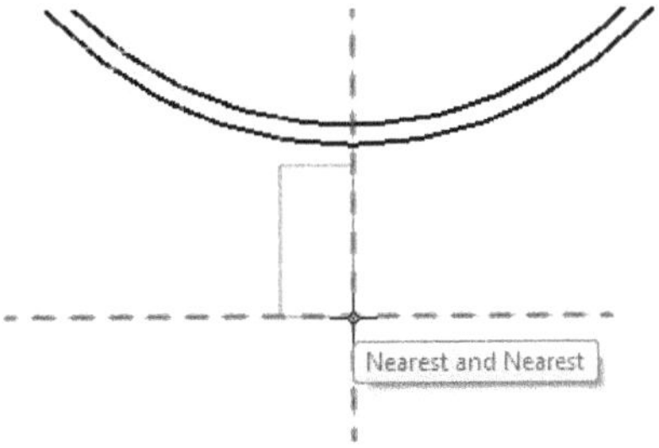

Nearest and Nearest

Figure 2–52

7. Click ⌕ (Modify) and select the desk you just placed.

8. In the Modify panel, click ✛ (Move). Select the start point of the move as the vertical alignment line of the desk, and the end point as the vertical reference plane.

9. Save the project.

Task 3 - Create a Radial Array.

---

1. Select the desk.

2. In the Modify panel, click ⊞ (Array).

3. In the Options Bar, click 🔄 (Radial). Clear the **Group and associate** option, set the *Number* field to 15, and set the *Move to:* field to **2nd.**

4. Drag the center of rotation from the center of the desk to the midpoint of the wall, as shown in Figure 2–53

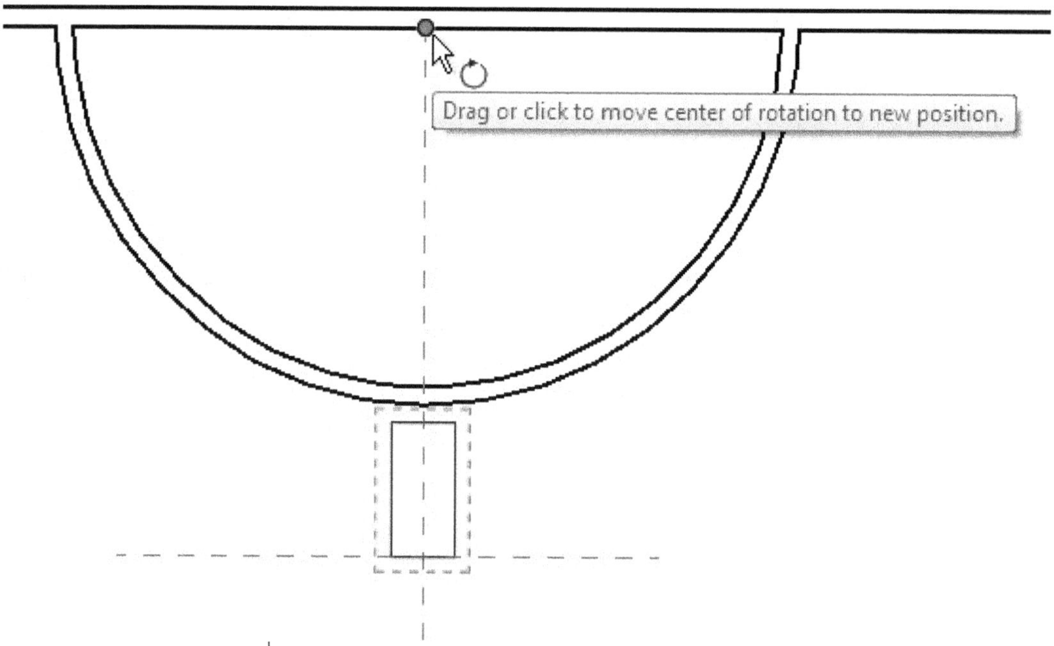

Drag or click to move center of rotation to new position.

Figure 2–53

5. Return to the Options Bar and set the *Angle* to **360**. The array displays as shown in Figure 2–54.

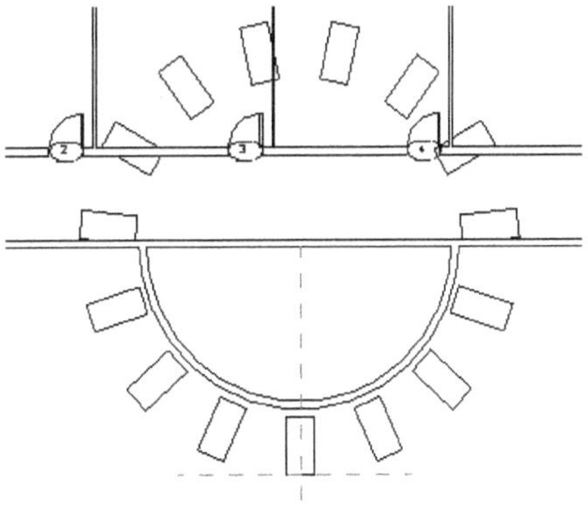

Sometimes it is easier to create more elements then you need, and then delete the ones that are not required, as is done in this example.

Figure 2–54

6. Delete all of the desks that are outside of the room that has the original desk.

7. Delete the reference planes. These are no longer needed, and deleting them ensures they do not display in other views.

8. Zoom out to display the entire view.

Task 4 - Add columns.

1. In the *Architecture* tab>Build panel, expand ⬙ (Column), and click ⬙ (Column: Architectural).

2. In the Type Selector, verify that **M_Rectangular Column: 457 x 457mm** is selected.

3. Using alignment lines and temporary dimensions, place the column on the front left of the building, as shown in Figure 2–55.

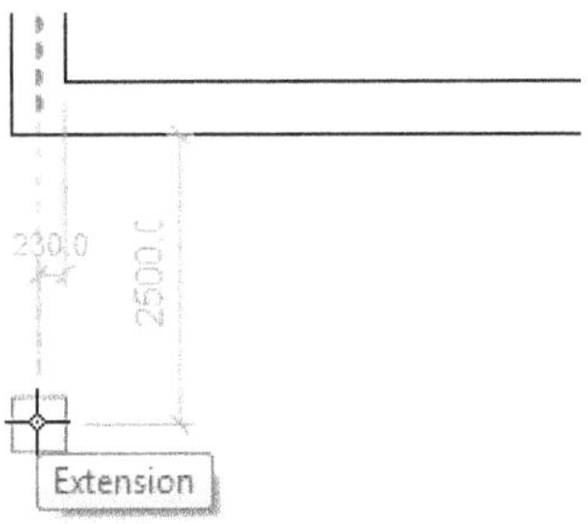

Figure 2–55

4. In the *Architecture* tab>Build panel, expand ☐ (Column), and click ☐ (Structural Column).

5. In the Type Selector, verify that **UC-Universal Column - Column: 305x305x97UC** is selected.

6. In the Options Bar, set the **Height** to **Level 2**, as shown in Figure 2–56.

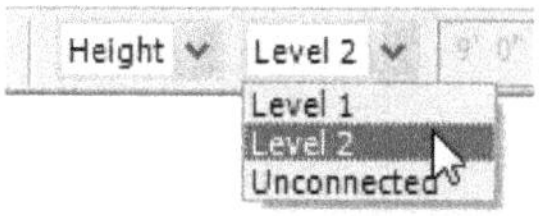

Figure 2–56

7. Place the structural column at the center of the architectural column using the **Midpoint and Extension** snaps, as shown in Figure 2–57.

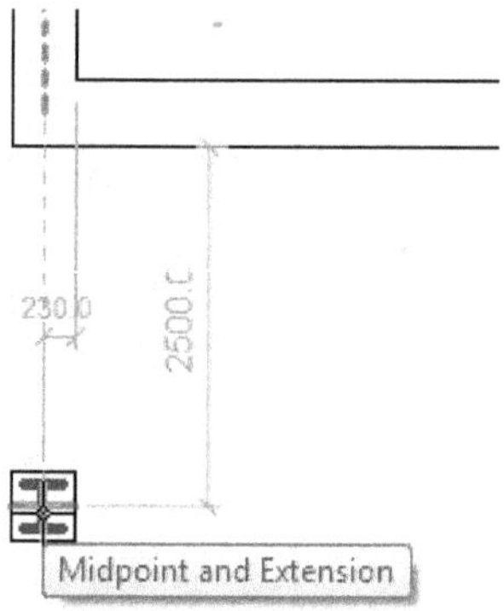

Figure 2–57

8. Save the project.

Task 5 - Rotate and Array the columns.

1. Click ☐ (Modify) and select the two columns.

2. In the *Modify | Multi-Select* tab>Modify panel, click ○ (Rotate).

3. For the start ray, click horizontally, as shown on the left in Figure 2–58.

4. Move the ray line until you see the temporary dimension 45.000, as shown on the right in Figure 2–58.

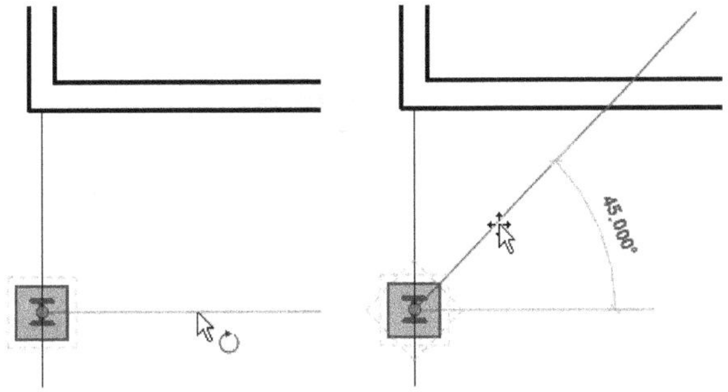

Figure 2–58

5. With the two columns still selected, in the *Modify |*

Multi-Select tab>Modify panel, click ⊞ (Array).

6. In the Options Bar, click 📶 (Linear), clear **Group and Associate**, set the *Number* to **10**, and set *Move To:* to **Last**.

7. For the start point, click the midpoint of the columns. For the endpoint of the array, select the **Horizontal and Extension** of the center of the far right wall as shown in Figure 2–59.

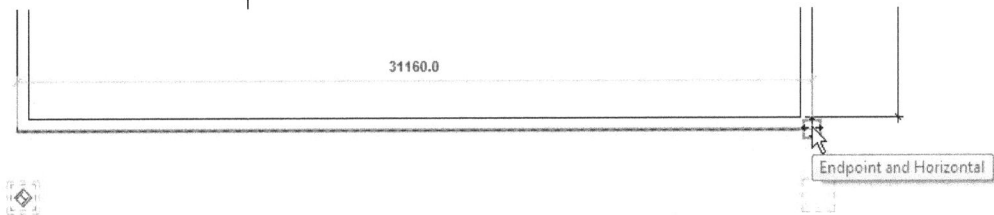

31160.0

Endpoint and Horizontal

Figure 2–59

8. Zoom out to display the entire building.

9. The columns are arrayed evenly across the front of the building as shown in Figure 2–60.

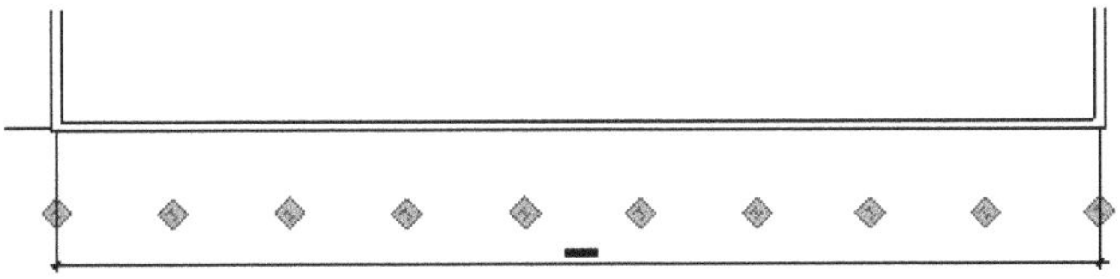

Figure 2–60

10. Save the project.

2.4 Working with Additional Modify Tools

Autodesk Certification Topics & Objectives

Pro.   **User**

Elements

- Trim objects ✓

Learning Objective

- Use modify tools to align, split, trim, and offset walls and other elements.

As you work on a project, some additional tools on the *Modify* tab>Modify panel, as shown in Figure 2–61, can help you with placing, modifying, and constraining elements. **Align** can be used with a variety of elements, while **Split Element**, **Trim/Extend**, and **Offset** can only be used with linear elements.

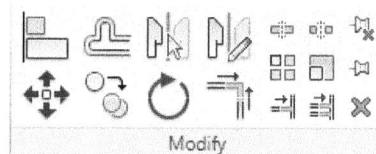

Figure 2–61

Aligning Elements

The **Align** command enables you to line up one element with another, as shown in Figure 2–62. Most Autodesk Revit elements can be aligned. For example, you can line up the tops of windows with the top of a door, or line up furniture with a wall.

First Pick ——   *Second Pick*

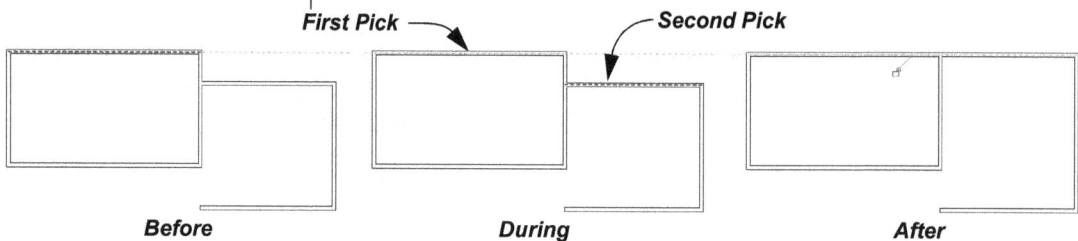

Before   *During*   *After*

Figure 2–62

How To: Align Elements

1. In the *Modify* tab>Modify panel, click (Align) or use the shortcut by pressing <A> and then pressing <L>.
2. Select a line or point on the element that is going to remain stationary. For walls, press <Tab> to select the correct wall face.
3. Select a line or point on the element to be aligned. The second element moves into alignment with the first one.

- The **Align** command works in both plan and elevation views.

- The **Align** command also works in 3D views. Ensure you select the correct component of the elements to align. For example, to line up two windows vertically select the side of the frame of each window. Zoom in if needed.

- You can lock alignments so that the elements move together if either one is moved. Once you have created the alignment, a padlock is displayed. Click on the padlock to lock it, as shown in Figure 2–63.

Locking elements enlarges the size of the project file, so use this option carefully.

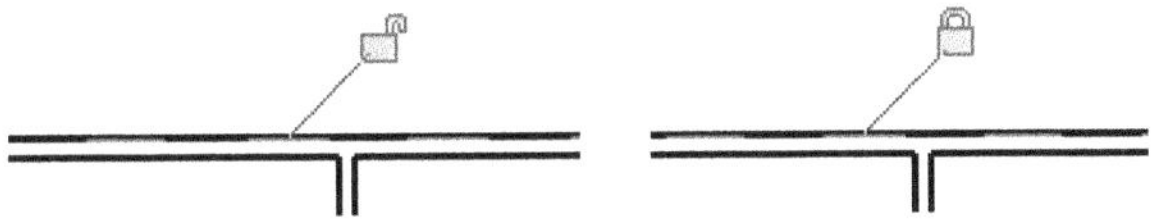

Figure 2–63

- Select the **Multiple Alignment** option to select multiple elements to align with the first element, as shown in Figure 2–64. You can also hold down <Ctrl> to make multiple alignments.

- For walls, you can specify if you want the command to prefer **Wall centerlines**, **Wall faces**, **Center of core**, or **Faces of core**, as shown in Figure 2–64. The core refers to the structural members of a wall as opposed to facing materials, such as sheetrock.

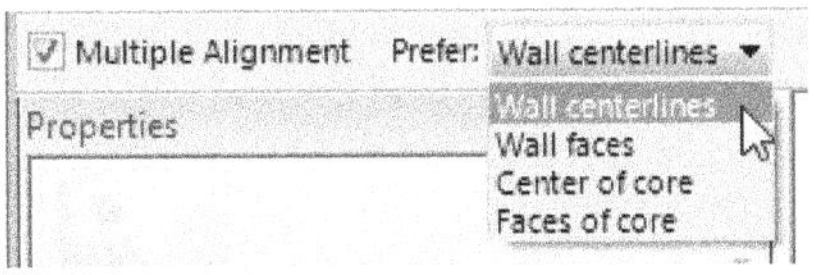

Figure 2–64

Splitting Linear Elements

The **Split** Element command enables you to break a linear element at a specific point. You can use alignment lines, snaps, and temporary dimensions to help place the split point. After you have split the linear element, you can use other editing commands to modify the two parts, or change the type of one part, as shown with walls in Figure 2–65.

You can split walls in plan, elevation or 3D views.

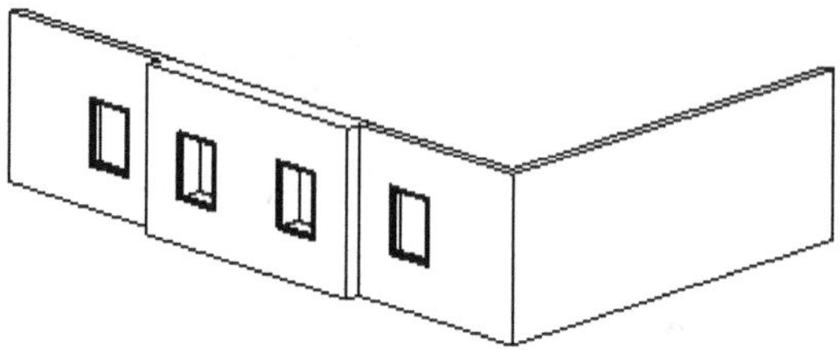

Figure 2–65

*   There are two commands: ⊹ (Split Element) and ⊹ (Split with Gap).

How To: Split Linear Elements

1. In the *Modify* tab>Modify panel, click ⊹ (Split Element) or use the shortcut by pressing <S> and pressing <L>.
2. In the Options Bar, select or clear the **Delete Inner Segment** option.
3. Move the cursor to the point you want to split and select the point.
4. Repeat for any additional split locations.
5. Modify the elements that were split, as required.

*   The **Delete Inner Segment** option is used when you select two split points along a linear element. When the option is selected, the segment between the two split points is automatically removed.

*   ⊹ (Split with Gap) splits the linear element at the point you select (as shown in Figure 2–66), but also creates a *Joint Gap* specified in the Options Bar.

This command is typically used with structural precast slabs.

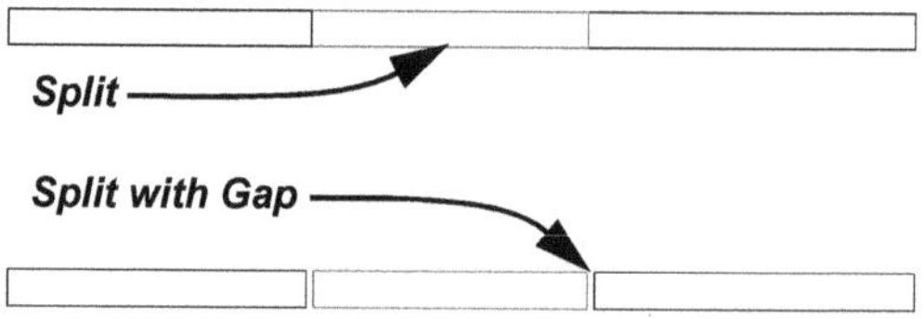

Figure 2–66

Trimming and Extending

There are three trim/extend methods that you can use with linear elements: **Trim/Extend to Corner**, **Trim/Extend Single Element**, and **Trim/Extend Multiple Elements**.

- When selecting elements to trim, click the part of the element that you want to keep. The opposite part of the line is then trimmed.

How To: Trim/Extend to Corner

1. In the *Modify* tab>Modify panel, click ⇶ (Trim/Extend to Corner) or use the shortcut by pressing <T> and pressing <R>.
2. Select the first linear element on the side you want to keep.
3. Select the second linear element on the side you want to keep, as shown in Figure 2–67.

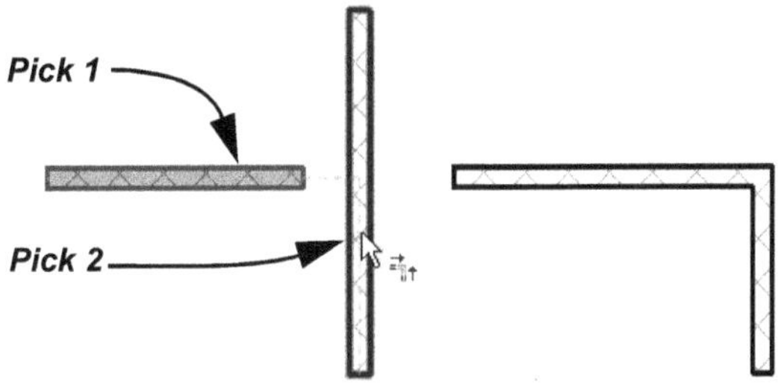

Figure 2–67

How To: Trim/Extend a Single Element

1. In the *Modify* tab>Modify panel, click ⇉ (Trim/Extend Single Element).
2. Select the cutting or boundary edge.
3. Select the linear element to be trimmed or extended, as shown in Figure 2–68.

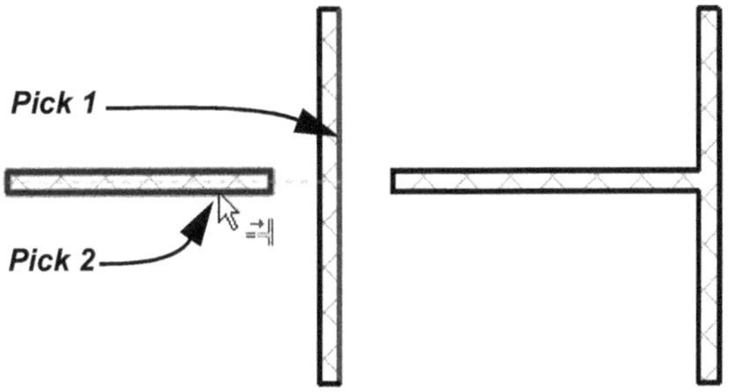

Figure 2–68

How To: Trim/Extend Multiple Elements

1. In the *Modify* tab>Modify panel, click ⬚ (Trim/Extend Multiple Elements).
2. Select the cutting or boundary edge.
3. Select the linear elements that you want to trim or extend by selecting one at a time, or by using a crossing window, as shown in Figure 2–69. For trimming, select the side you want to keep.

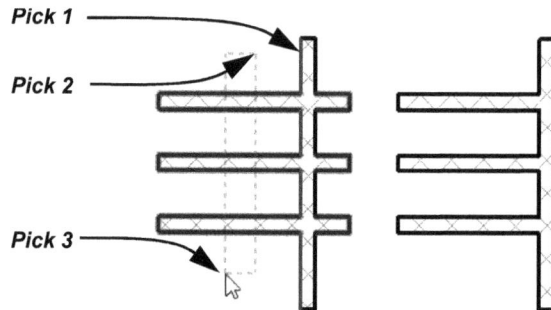

Enhanced in 2015

Pick 1
Pick 2
Pick 3

Figure 2–69

- You can click in an empty space to clear the selection and select another cutting edge or boundary.

Offsetting Elements

The **Offset** command is an easy way of creating parallel copies of linear elements at a specified distance, as shown in Figure 2–70. Walls, beams, braces, and lines are among the elements that can be offset.

Figure 2–70

- If you offset a wall that has a door or window embedded in it, the elements are copied with the offset wall.

The offset distance can be set by typing the distance (**Numerical** method shown in Figure 2–71) or by selecting points on the screen (**Graphical** method).

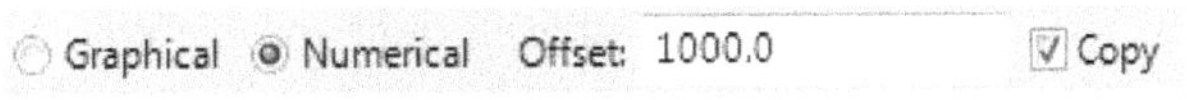

○ Graphical ◉ Numerical   Offset: 1000.0   ☑ Copy

Figure 2–71

How To: Offset using the Numerical Method

*The **Copy** option (which is on by default) makes a copy of the element being offset. If this option is not selected, the **Offset** command moves the element the set offset distance.*

1. In the *Modify* tab>Modify panel, click ⬚ (Offset) or use the shortcut by pressing <O> and pressing <F>.
2. In the Options Bar, select the **Numerical** option.
3. In the Options Bar, type the desired distance in the *Offset* field.
4. Move the cursor over the element you want to offset. A dashed line previews the offset location. Move the cursor to flip the sides, as required.
5. Click to create the offset.
6. Repeat Steps 4 and 5 to offset other elements by the same distance, or to change the distance for another offset.
- With the **Numerical** option, you can select multiple connected linear elements for offsetting. Hover the cursor over an element and press <Tab> until the other related elements are highlighted. Select the element to offset all of the elements at the same time.

How To: Offset using the Graphical Method

1. Start the **Offset** command.
2. In the Options Bar, select the **Graphical** option.
3. Select the linear element to offset.
4. Select two points that define the distance of the offset and which side to apply it. You can type an override in the temporary dimension for the second point.

- Most linear elements connected at a corner automatically trim or extend to meet at the offset distance, as shown in Figure 2–72.

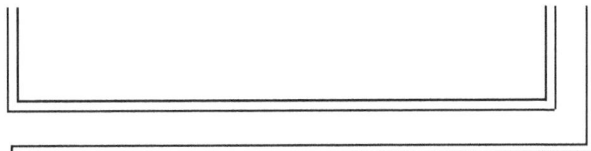

Figure 2–72

Hint: Hiding Elements in Views

As you are working, you can hide individual elements or entire categories of elements to clarify the display. They remain hidden until you display them again. Hidden elements do not print.

- Select the element(s) you want to hide, right-click and select **Hide in view>Elements** or **Hide in view>Category**.

- The **Elements** option hides only the elements that you selected, while the **Category** option hides all elements in that category. For example, you can select one grid line and use **Hide in view>Category** to hide all of the grid lines.

- To display the elements or category again, in the View Control Bar, click 🔲 (Reveal Hidden Elements). The border and all hidden elements are displayed in magenta, while visible elements in the view are grayed out, as shown in Figure 2–73. Select the hidden elements you want to restore, right-click, and select **Unhide in View>Elements** or **Unhide in View>Category** or in the *Modify* | contextual tab> Reveal Hidden Elements panel click 🔲 (Unhide Element) or 🔲 (Unhide Category).

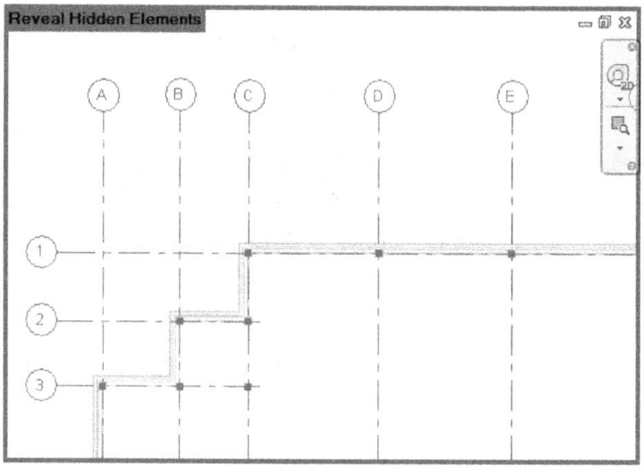

Figure 2–73

When you are finished, in the View Control Bar, click 🔲 (Close Reveal Hidden Elements) or, in the *Modify* | contextual tab> Reveal Hidden Elements panel click ☒ (Toggle Reveal Hidden Elements Mode).

Practice 2c

Work with Additional Modify Tools

Learning Objective

- Use the Modify tools: Align, Split, Trim/Extend, and Offset.

Estimated time for completion: 10 minutes

In this practice you will use the **Align**, **Split**, **Trim/Extend**, and **Offset** commands to modify the simple building shown in Figure 2–74.

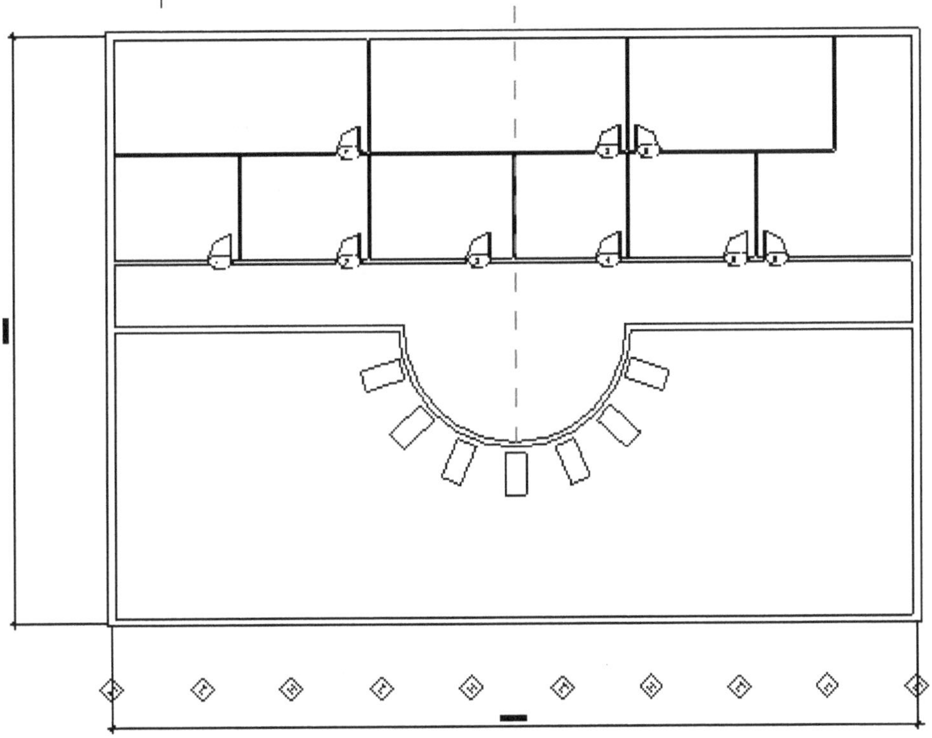

Figure 2–74

Task 1 - Split and Remove Walls

1. Open the project **Simple-Building-2-M.rvt,** found in your class folder.

2. In the *Modify* tab>Modify panel click ⊕ (Split Element).

3. In the Options Bar, select **Delete Inner Segment**.

4. Click on the horizontal wall where it intersects with the curved wall at both ends. The wall segment between these points is removed, as shown in Figure 2–75.

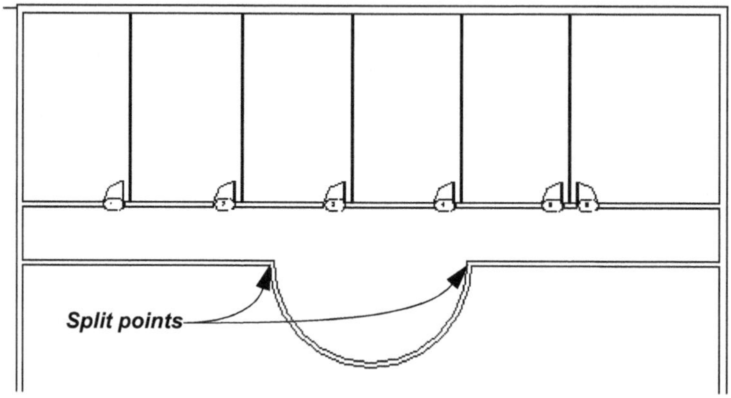

Figure 2–75

5. Click (Modify) to finish.

Task 2 - Offset and Trim Walls

1. In the *Modify* tab> Modify panel click (Offset).

2. In the Options Bar set the *Offset* to **4250mm** and ensure that **Copy** is selected.

3. Select the top horizontal wall while ensuring that the dashed alignment line displays inside the building, as shown in Figure 2–76.

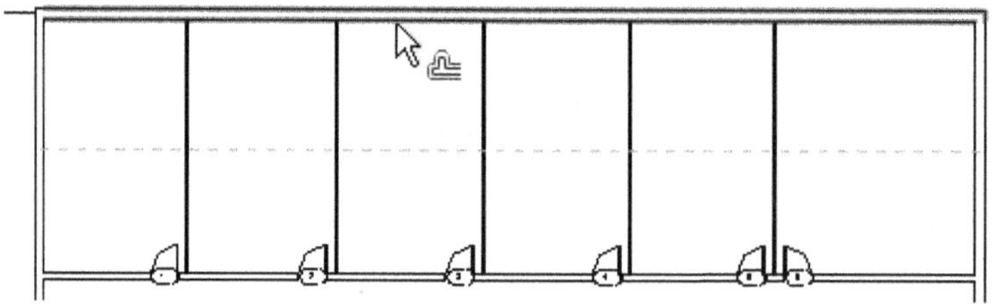

Figure 2–76

4. With **Offset** still active, change the *Offset* to **3000mm** and offset the last vertical interior wall to the right, as shown in Figure 2–77.

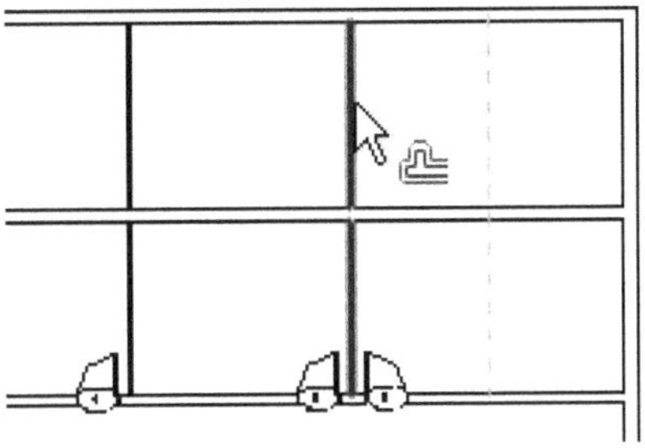

Figure 2–77

5. Click   (Modify) and select the new horizontal wall that was created from the exterior wall. Change the wall to **Basic Wall: Interior - 138mm Partition (1-hr).** The layout of the new walls should display as shown in Figure 2–78.

The vertical wall does not need to be changed because it was offset from an interior wall.

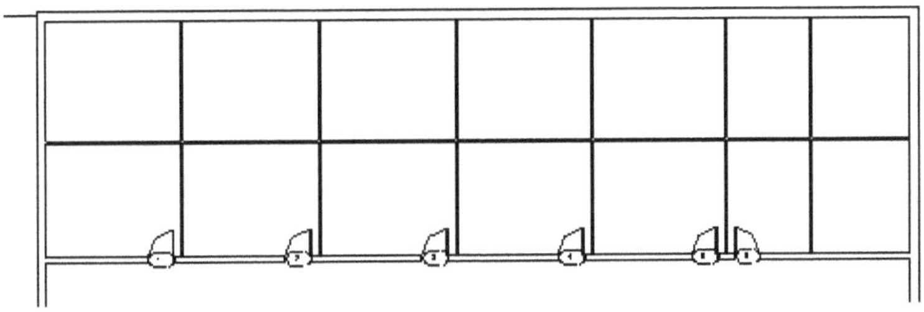

Figure 2–78

6. In the *Modify* tab>Modify panel, click   (Trim/Extend Multiple Elements).

7. Select the new horizontal wall as the element to trim against.

8. Select every other wall BELOW the new wall. (Remember, you select the elements that you want to keep.) The walls should display as shown in Figure 2–79.

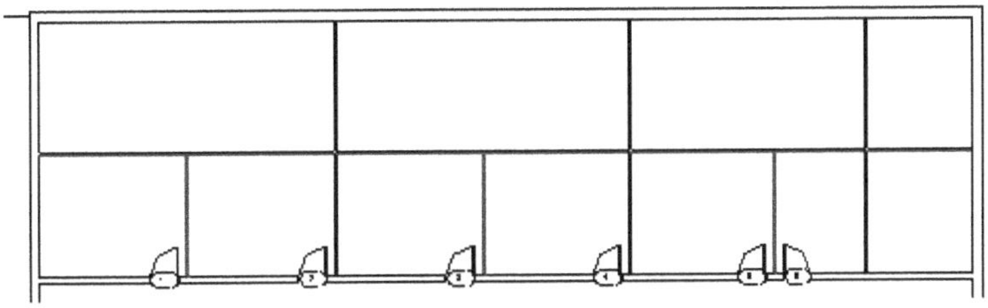

Figure 2–79

9. In the *Modify* tab>Modify panel click ⭲ (Trim/Extend to corner) and select the two walls to trim as shown in Figure 2–80.

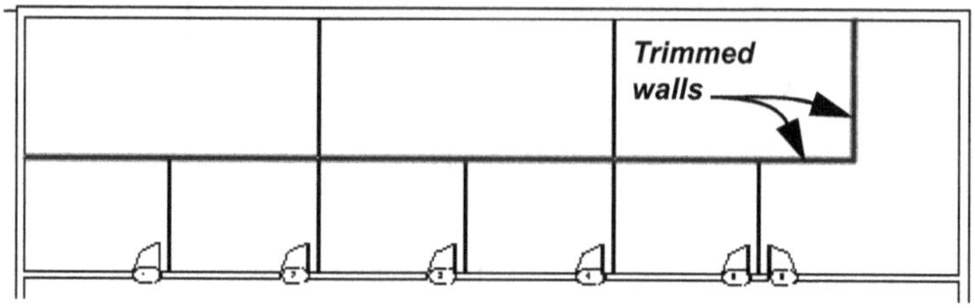

Figure 2–80

10. Add doors into the new rooms.

11. Save the project.

Task 3 - Align Walls.

1. In the *Architecture* tab>Work Plane panel click ✐ (Ref Plane).

2. Draw a reference plane vertically up from the midpoint of the curved wall, as shown in Figure 2–81.

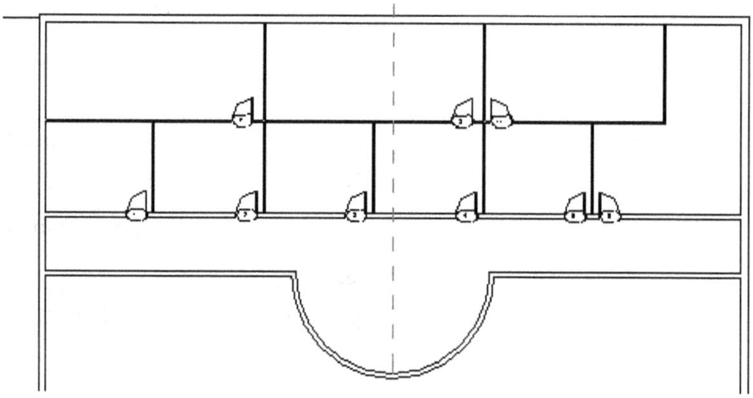

Figure 2–81

3. In the *Modify* tab>Modify panel, click ⊡ (Align).

4. Select the reference plane, and then the wall to the left. The wall should line up with the reference plane.

5. Save and close the project.

Chapter Review Questions

1. What is the purpose of an alignment line?

   a. Displays when the new element you are placing or drawing is aligned with the grid system.

   b. Indicates that the new element you are placing or drawing is aligned with an existing object.

   c. Displays when the new element you are placing or drawing is aligned with a selected tracking point.

   d. Indicates that the new element is aligned with true north rather than project north.

2. When you are drawing (not editing) a linear element, how do you edit the temporary dimension, as that shown in Figure 2–82?

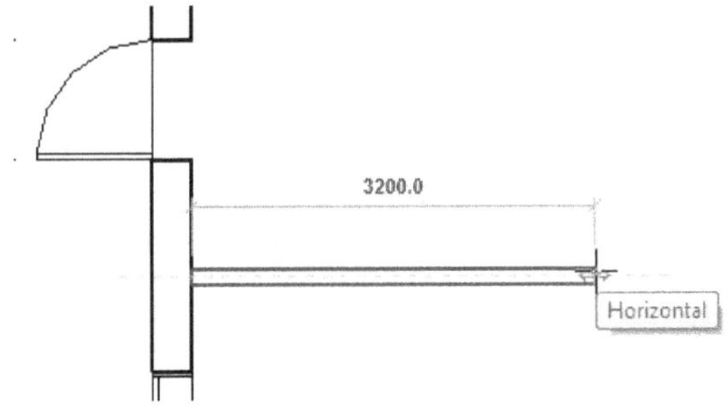

Figure 2–82

   a. Select the temporary dimension and enter a new value.

   b. Type a new value and press <Enter>.

   c. Type a new value in the Distance/Length box in the Options Bar and press <Enter>.

3. How do you select all door types, but no other elements in a view?

   a. In the Project Browser, select the *Door* category.

   b. Select one door, right-click and select **Select All Instances>Visible in View**.

   c. Select all of the objects in the view and use ▽ (Filter) to clear the other categories.

   d. Select one door, and click ⬛ (Select Multiple) in the Ribbon.

4. What are the two methods for starting ⊹ (Move) or
   ⟲ (Copy)?

   a. Start the command first and then select the objects, or
      select the objects and then start the command.

   b. Start the command from the *Modify* tab, or select the
      object and then select **Move** or **Copy** from the right-click
      menu.

   c. Start the command from the *Modify* tab, or select the
      objects and select **Auto-Move**.

   d. Use the **Move/Copy** command or **Cut/Copy** and **Paste**
      using the Clipboard.

5. Where do you change the wall type for a selected wall, as
   shown in Figure 2–83?

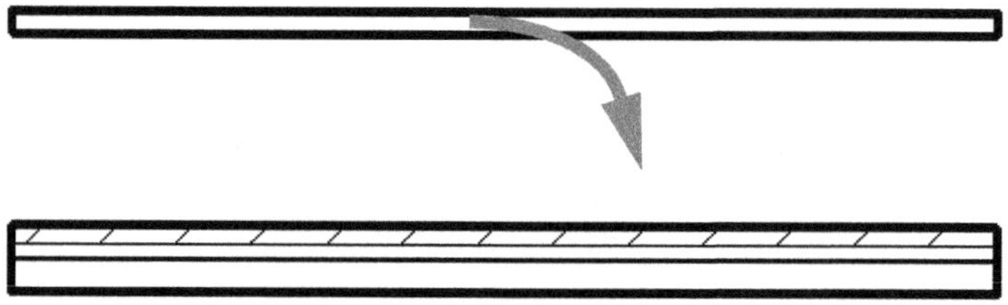

Figure 2–83

   a. In the *Modify | Walls* tab> Properties panel, click
      ⊞ (Type Properties) and select a new wall type in the
      dialog box.

   b. In the Options Bar, click `Change Element Type ▾`.

   c. Select the dynamic control next to the selected wall and
      select a new type in the drop-down list.

   d. In Properties, select a new type in the Type Selector
      drop-down list.

6. Both ⟳ (Rotate) and ⊞ (Array) with ⬧ (Radial) have a center of rotation that defaults to the center of the element or group of elements you have selected. How do you move the center of rotation to another point as shown in Figure 2–84? (Select all that apply.)

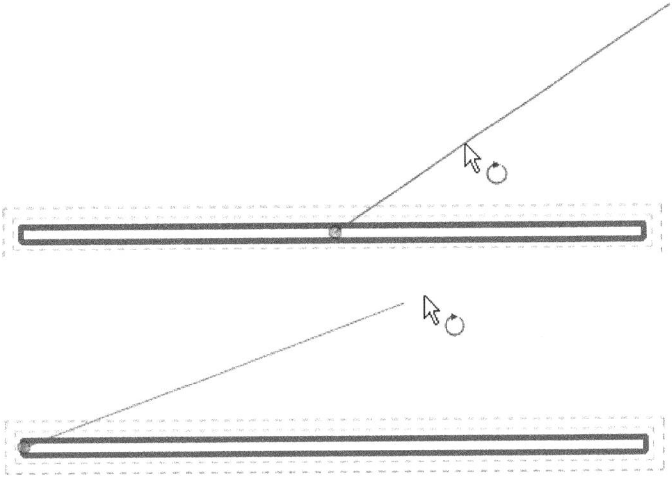

Figure 2–84

a. Select the center of rotation and drag it to a new location.

b. In the Options Bar, click Place and select the new point.

c. In the *Modify* tab> Placement panel, click ⊙ (Center) and select the new point.

d. Right-click and select **Snap Overrides>Centers** and select the new point.

7. Which command would you use to remove part of a wall?

a. ⊹ (Split Element)

b. ⬚ (Wall Joins)

c. ⬚ (Cut Geometry)

d. ⬚ (Demolish)

8. Which of the following are ways in which you can create additional parallel walls, as shown in Figure 2–85? (Select all that apply.)

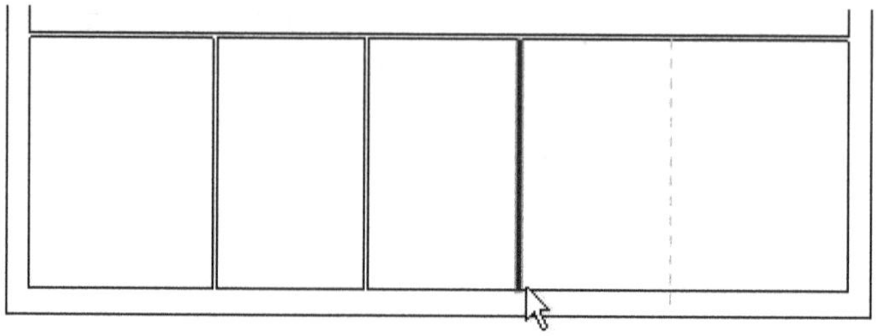

Figure 2–85

  a. Select an existing wall, right-click and select **Create Offset**.

  b. Use the **Offset** tool in the *Modify* tab.

  c. Select an existing wall, hold down <Ctrl> and drag the wall to a new location.

  d. Use the **Wall** tool and set an offset in the Options Bar.

9. Which command do you use if you want two walls that are not touching to come together, as shown in Figure 2–86?

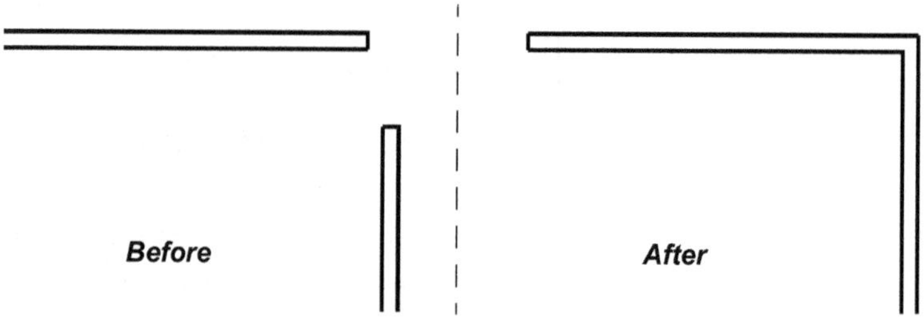

Before   *After*

Figure 2–86

  a. (Edit Wall Joins)

  b. (Trim/Extend to Corner)

  c. (Join Geometry)

  d. (Edit Profile)

Command Summary

Button	Command	Location
Draw Tools		
	Line	• **Ribbon:** *Modify	(various linear elements)* tab>Draw panel
	Rectangle	• **Ribbon:** *Modify	(various linear elements)* tab>Draw panel
	Inscribed Polygon	• **Ribbon:** *Modify	(various linear elements)* tab>Draw panel
	Circumscribed Polygon	• **Ribbon:** *Modify	(various linear elements)* tab>Draw panel
	Circle	• **Ribbon:** *Modify	(various linear elements)* tab>Draw panel
	Start-End-Radius Arc	• **Ribbon:** *Modify	(various linear elements)* tab>Draw panel
	Center-ends Arc	• **Ribbon:** *Modify	(various linear elements)* tab>Draw panel
	Tangent End Arc	• **Ribbon:** *Modify	(various linear elements)* tab>Draw panel
	Fillet Arc	• **Ribbon:** *Modify	(various linear elements)* tab>Draw panel
	Spline	• **Ribbon:** *Modify	Place Lines, Place Detail Lines, and various boundary sketches*>Draw panel
	Ellipse	• **Ribbon:** *Modify	Place Lines, Place Detail Lines, and various boundary sketches*>Draw panel
	Ellipse Arc	• **Ribbon:** *Modify	Place Lines, Place Detail Lines, and various boundary sketches*>Draw panel
	Pick Lines	• **Ribbon:** *Modify	(various linear elements)* tab>Draw panel
	Pick Faces	• **Ribbon:** *Modify	Place Wall*> Draw panel
	Pick Walls	• **Ribbon:** *Modify	(various boundary sketches)*>Draw panel
Modify Tools		
	Align	• **Ribbon:** *Modify* tab>Modify panel • **Shortcut:** <A> and <L>
	Array	• **Ribbon:** *Modify* tab>Modify panel • **Shortcut:** <A> and <R>
	Copy	• **Ribbon:** *Modify* tab>Modify panel • **Shortcut:** <C> and <O>
	Copy to Clipboard	• **Ribbon:** *Modify* tab>Clipboard panel • **Shortcut:** <Ctrl>+<C>

	Delete	• **Ribbon:** *Modify* tab>Modify panel • **Shortcut:** <D> and <E>
	Mirror - Draw Axis	• **Ribbon:** *Modify* tab>Modify panel • **Shortcut:** <D> and <M>
	Mirror - Pick Axis	• **Ribbon:** *Modify* tab>Modify panel • **Shortcut:** <M> and <M>
	Move	• **Ribbon:** *Modify* tab>Modify panel • **Shortcut:** <M> and <V>
	Offset	• **Ribbon:** *Modify* tab>Modify panel • **Shortcut:** <O> and <F>
	Paste	• **Ribbon:** *Modify* tab>Clipboard panel • **Shortcut:** <Ctrl>+<V>
	Pin	• **Ribbon:** *Modify* tab>Modify panel • **Shortcut:** <P> and <N>
	Rotate	• **Ribbon:** *Modify* tab>Modify panel • **Shortcut:** <R> and <O>
	Scale	• **Ribbon:** *Modify* tab>Modify panel • **Shortcut:** <R> and <E>
	Split Element	• **Ribbon:** *Modify* tab>Modify panel • **Shortcut:** <S> and <L>
	Split with Gap	• **Ribbon:** *Modify* tab>Modify panel
	Trim/Extend to Corner	• **Ribbon:** *Modify* tab>Modify panel • **Shortcut:** <T> and <R>
	Trim/Extend Multiple Elements	• **Ribbon:** *Modify* tab>Modify panel
	Trim/Extend Single Element	• **Ribbon:** *Modify* tab>Modify panel
	Unpin	• **Ribbon:** *Modify* tab>Modify panel • **Shortcut:** <U> and <P>

Select Tools

	Drag elements on selection	• **Ribbon:** All tabs>Expanded Select panel • **Status Bar**
	Filter	• **Ribbon:** *Modify	Multi-Select* tab>Filter panel>Filter • **Status Bar**
	Select Elements By Face	• **Ribbon:** All tabs>Expanded Select panel • **Status Bar**
	Select Links	• **Ribbon:** All tabs>Expanded Select panel • **Status Bar**

	Select Pinned Elements	• **Ribbon:** All tabs>Expanded Select panel
		• **Status Bar**
	Select Underlay Elements	• **Ribbon:** All tabs>Expanded Select panel
		• **Status Bar**
	Selection Sets: Add to Selection	• **Ribbon:** *Edit Selection Set* tab>Edit Selection panel
	Selection Sets: Load	• **Ribbon:** *Modify	Multi-Select* tab>Selection panel or *Manage* tab>Selection panel
	Selection Sets: Edit	• **Ribbon:** *Modify	Multi-Select* tab>Selection panel or *Manage* tab>Selection panel
	Selection Sets: Remove from Selection	• **Ribbon:** *Edit Selection Set* tab>Edit Selection panel
	Selection Sets: Save	• **Ribbon:** *Modify	Multi-Select* tab>Selection panel or *Manage* tab>Selection panel

Chapter 3

Setting Up Levels and Grids

In this chapter you learn about levels that define vertical heights, grids, and specify locations for columns. You also learn how to import CAD files and use them as a basis for constructing a project.

This chapter contains the following topics:

- **Setting Up Levels**
- **Linking and Importing CAD Files**
- **Creating Structural Grids**
- **Adding Columns**

3.1 Setting Up Levels

Autodesk Certification Topics & Objectives

Pro.   User

Views

- Use levels   ✓   ✓

Learning Objectives

- Add and modify levels.
- Create Plan Views from levels.

Levels define stories and other vertical heights (such as a roof or the top of a parapet), as shown in Figure 3–1. The default template includes two levels, but you can define as many levels in a project as required. They can go down (for basements) as well as up.

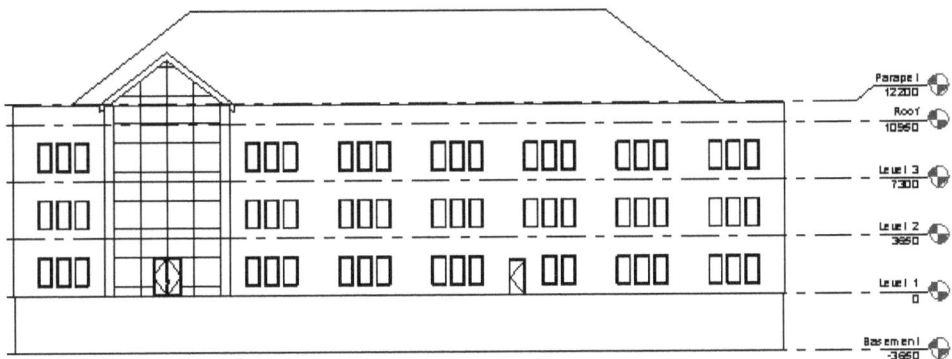

Figure 3–1

- You must be in an elevation or section view to define levels.

- Once you constrain an element to a level it moves with the level when the level is changed.

How To: Create Levels

1. Open an elevation or section view.

2. In the *Architecture* tab>Datum panel, click (Level), or type **LL**.
3. In the Type Selector, set the Level Head type if needed.

*To end a command, press <Esc>, or right-click and select **Cancel**, or click (Modify) or another command.*

4. In the *Modify | Place Level* tab>Draw panel, click either (Pick Lines) to select an element or (Line) to draw a level.
5. Continue adding levels as required.
6. Press <Esc> or select another command to finish.

- Level names are automatically incremented as you place them. You can rename levels in Properties or by double-clicking on the name.

- To use (Pick Lines), in the Options Bar, specify an *Offset* and select the level above or below to place the new level, as shown in Figure 3–2.

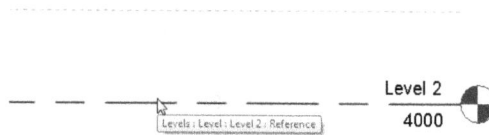

This is the fastest way of creating multiple levels.

Level 2
4000

Levels : Level : Level 2 : Reference

Figure 3–2

- To use (Line), align the cursor with the left end point of the existing level for the level's start point. A temporary dimension displays from that level. Select a point at the desired distance from the existing level or type a value. Drag the level line to the right until it lines up with the bubble on the existing level, and click to set the level end point, as shown in Figure 3–3.

You can draw the level lines from left to right or right to left.

3048
Extension
Level 2
3048
Level 1
0

Level 3
6096 Extension
Level 2
3048
Level 1
0

Figure 3–3

- You can also use (Copy) to duplicate level lines. The level names are incremented but a plan view is not created.

Modifying Levels

You can change levels using standard controls, temporary dimensions, and lock tools, as shown in Figure 3–4. You can also make changes to the level name and height by clicking on the information in the level element or in Properties.

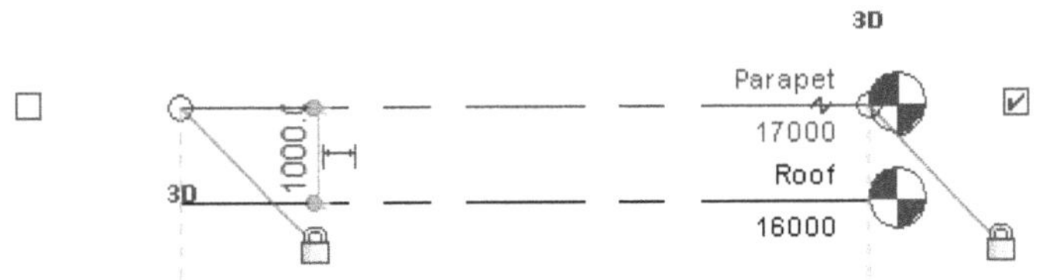

Figure 3–4

Elements, such as walls and columns can be referenced to a level height. Changing that height affects the entire model.

- ☑ ☐ (Hide / Show Bubble) displays on either end of the level line and toggles the level head symbol and level information on or off.

- 2D 3D (Switch to 3D / 2D extents) controls whether any movement or adjustment to the level line is reflected in other views (3D) or only affects the current view.

- 🔒 🔓 (Create or remove a length or alignment constraint) controls whether the level is locked in alignment with the other levels. If it is locked, the blue dashed alignment line displays. When a level element is stretched, all of the other levels stretch as well. This helps to maintain conventional drafting standards. If it is unlocked, the level stretches independent of the other levels.

- ⊙ (Modify the level by dragging its model end) at each end of the datum enables you to drag the level head to a new location. The vertical dashed line indicates if the end is locked to other levels.

- The temporary dimensions between the levels can be edited and changed to permanent dimensions. Click ⊢⊣ (Make this temporary dimension permanent) to keep the dimension displayed. You can still modify the increment by selecting the level. The permanent dimension temporarily turns blue, enabling you to edit the value.

- Click ⌇ (Add Elbow) to add a jog to the level line as shown in Figure 3–5. Drag the blue sizing handles to new locations as required. This is a view-specific change.

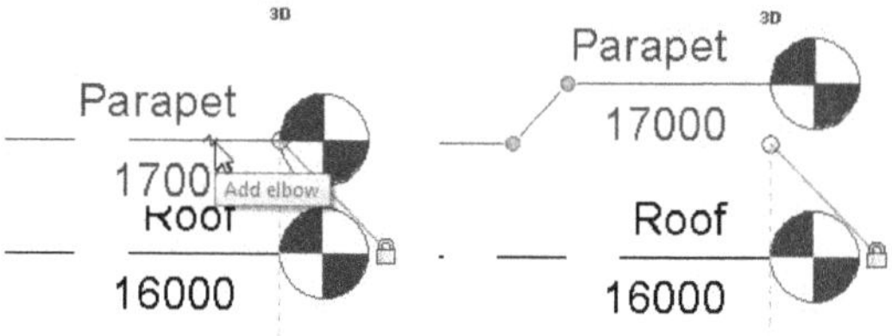

Parapet
1700 Add elbow
Roof
16000

Parapet
17000
Roof
16000

Figure 3–5

Renaming Levels

You can rename a level by double-clicking on the name next to the level head or by selecting the level and modifying the *Name* in Properties.

- If you rename a Level, an alert box opens, prompting you to rename the corresponding views as shown in Figure 3–6. Click [Yes]. The view is also renamed in the Project Browser.

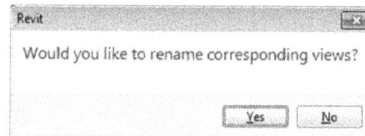

Revit
Would you like to rename corresponding views?
[Yes]   [No]

Figure 3–6

Hint: Copying Levels and Grids from other projects

Levels and grid lines can be added by drawing over existing levels or grids in an imported or linked CAD. It can also be copied and monitored from a linked Autodesk® Revit® file. Some projects might require both methods.

Creating Plan Views

When you place a level, a **Floor Plan** view and a **Reflected Ceiling Plan** view for that level are automatically created if the **Make Plan View** option is selected in the Options Bar, as shown in Figure 3–7. If you do not want plan views to be created, clear the option.

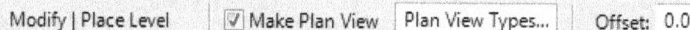

Modify | Place Level   ☑ Make Plan View   Plan View Types...   Offset: 0.0

Figure 3–7

Typically, you do not need to create plan views for levels that specify data, such as the top of a storefront window or the top of a parapet.

- Click Plan View Types... to specify which plan views to create. The standard views are **Ceiling Plan** and **Floor Plan**.

- You can determine whether a plan view is created for a level, by the color of the level head. Level heads with views are blue (such as Level 1 and Level 2 in Figure 3–8), and level heads without views are black (such as Level 3 in Figure 3–8).

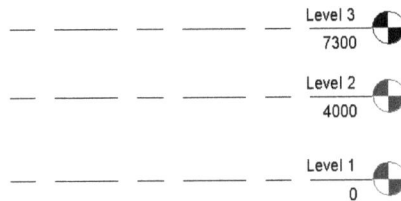

Figure 3–8

- If you have copied levels or otherwise chosen not to add a plan view when adding levels, you can create plan views and reflected ceiling plan views to match the levels.

How To: Create Plan and Reflected Ceiling Plan Views

1. In the *View* tab>Create panel, expand ⬚ (Plan Views) and click ⬚ (Floor Plan) or ⬚ (Reflected Ceiling Plan).
2. In the New Plan (or New RCP) dialog box (shown in Figure 3–9), select the levels for which you want to create plan views.

Hold down <Ctrl> to select more than one level.

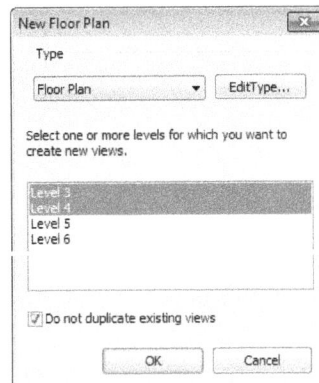

Figure 3–9

3. Click OK .

Practice 3a

Set Up Levels

Learning Objective

- Add and modify levels.

Estimated time for completion: 10 minutes

In this practice you will set up the levels needed in the Modern Hotel project, including the floors, the top of the footing, and the parapet, as shown in Figure 3–10.

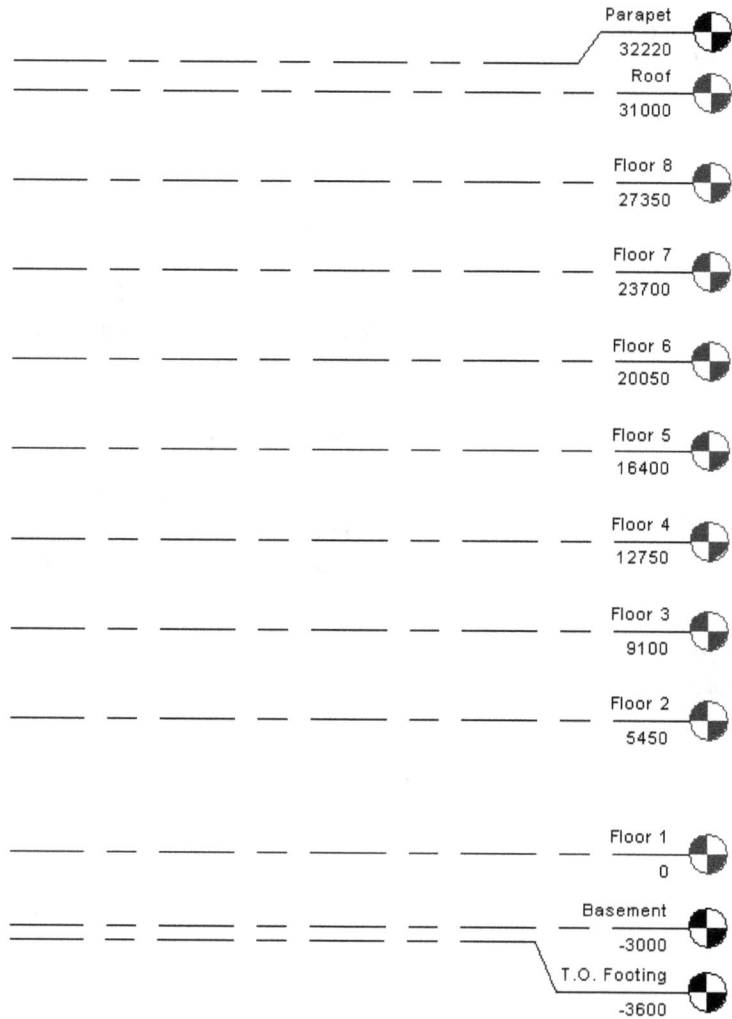

The scale used in Figure 3–10 has been modified for printing clarity.

Parapet	32220
Roof	31000
Floor 8	27350
Floor 7	23700
Floor 6	20050
Floor 5	16400
Floor 4	12750
Floor 3	9100
Floor 2	5450
Floor 1	0
Basement	-3000
T.O. Footing	-3600

Figure 3–10

Task 1 - Add and Modify Levels.

1. Open the project **Modern-Hotel-Start-M.rvt** from your class folder.

2. Open the **Elevations (Building Elevation): North** view.

3. The project has two existing levels named **Level 1** and **Level 2**. These were defined in the template.

4. Zoom in on the level names.

5. Double-click on the name Level 1 and rename it as **Floor 1** as shown in Figure 3–11. Press <Enter>.

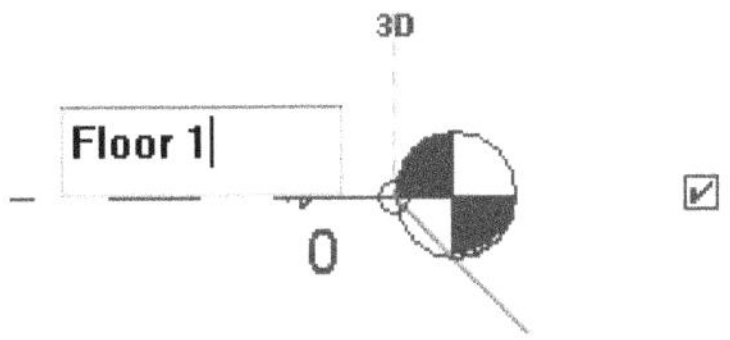

3D

Floor 1|

0

Figure 3–11

6. Click [Yes] (press <Enter> or type **Y**) when prompted to rename the corresponding views.

7. Repeat the process and rename *Level 2* as **Floor 2**. Double-click on the height of Floor 2 (4000mm) and change it to **5450mm**.

8. In the *Architecture* tab>Datum panel, click (Level).

9. In the *Modify | Place Level* tab>Draw panel, click (Pick Lines). In the Options Bar, set the *Offset* to **3650mm**.

10. Hover the cursor over the level line of **Floor 2** and move the cursor slightly upward so that the offset level line is displayed above the **Floor 2** level. Click to create the new level **Floor 3**.

11. Create additional levels until there are a total of eight levels above Floor 1 (up to Floor 9).

12. Rename *Floor 9* as **Roof**. (Rename the corresponding views.)

13. In the Options Bar, clear the **Make Plan View** option and set the *Offset* to **1220mm**. Create one additional level above the highest level, **Roof**. This level does not need a plan view.

14. Rename the top level as **Parapet**, as shown in Figure 3–12.

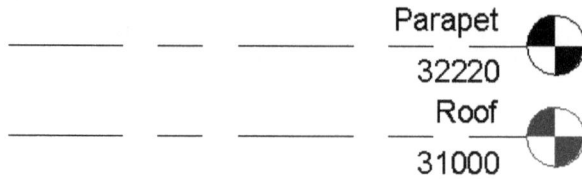

$$\begin{array}{c} \text{Parapet} \\ \overline{32220} \end{array}$$

$$\begin{array}{c} \text{Roof} \\ \overline{31000} \end{array}$$

Figure 3–12

15. Add two levels below **Floor 1**. Name them **Basement** and **T.O. Footing** and set the heights as shown in Figure 3–13. You can modify the levels using the controls as required.

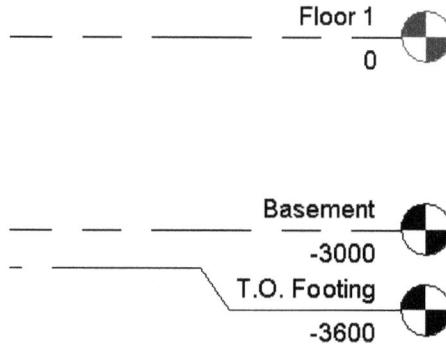

$$\begin{array}{c} \text{Floor 1} \\ 0 \end{array}$$

$$\begin{array}{c} \text{Basement} \\ -3000 \end{array}$$

$$\begin{array}{c} \text{T.O. Footing} \\ -3600 \end{array}$$

Figure 3–13

16. Zoom out to display the entire project.

17. Save the project.

3.2 Linking and Importing CAD Files

Autodesk Certification Topics & Objectives

Pro.   User

Collaboration

- Import DWG and image files ✓

Learning Objective

- Link and import CAD files.

While not specifically a datum element, linked or imported files can help you to establish information. For example, the designer might lay out a floor plan using the standard 2D AutoCAD® software, and you need to incorporate that information into your building model. In addition, many renovation projects start with existing 2D drawings. Instead of redrawing from scratch, import or link the CAD file, as shown in Figure 3–14, and trace over it in the Autodesk Revit software.

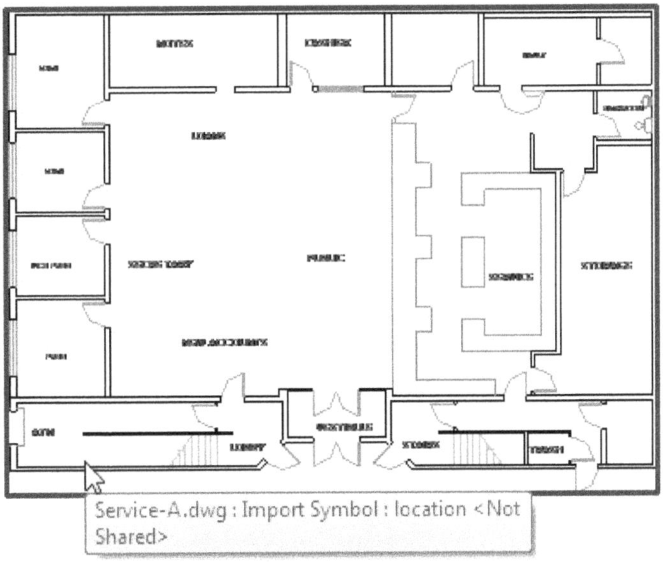

Service-A.dwg : Import Symbol : location <Not Shared>

Figure 3–14

- CAD files that can be imported or linked include AutoCAD DWG and DXF, Microstation DGN, ACIS SAT, and Sketchup SKP files.

Importing vs. Linking

CAD files can be imported or linked. The process for importing and linking is similar, but the outcome is different.

Imported and linked files behave in a similar manner in the project.

- **Imported files:** Become part of the project and are not connected to the original file. Use them if you know that the original drawing is not going to change.

- **Linked files:** Become part of the project but are still connected to the original file. Use them if you expect the original drawing to change. The link is automatically updated when you open the project.

How To: Link or Import a CAD File

1. Open the view into which you want to link or import the file.
   - For a 2D file, this should be a 2D view. For a 3D file, open a 3D view.

2. In the *Insert* tab>Link panel, click 🗋 (Link CAD), or in the *Insert* tab>Import panel, click 🗋 (Import CAD).

3. In the Link CAD Formats or Import CAD Formats dialog box (shown in Figure 3–15), select the file that you want to import.

The dialog box for Link CAD Formats and Import CAD Formats is the same.

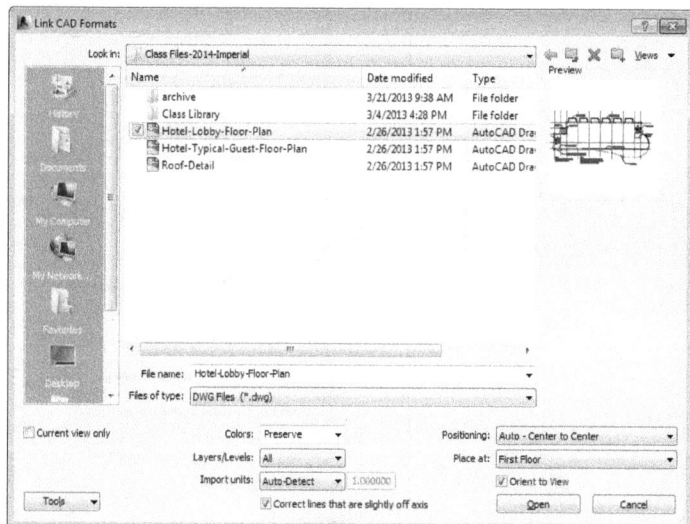

Figure 3–15

- Select a file type in the **Files of Type** drop-down list to limit the files that are displayed.

4. Set the other options as shown in Figure 3–16.

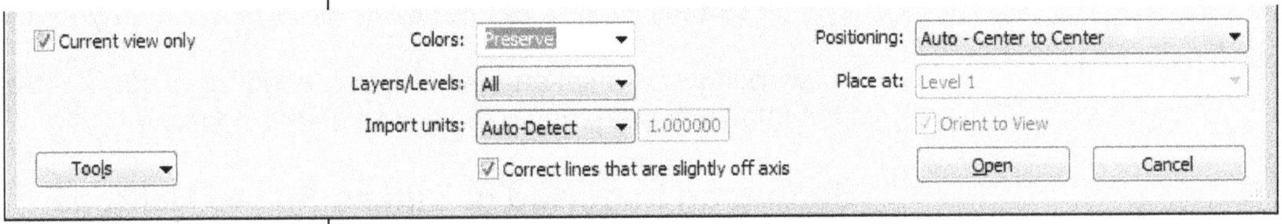

Figure 3–16

5. Click [Open] .

Link and Import Options

Current view only	Determine whether the CAD file is placed in every view, or only in the current view. This is especially useful if you are working with a 2D floor plan that you only need to have in one view.
Colors	Specify the color settings. Typical Autodesk Revit projects are mainly black and white. However, other software frequently uses color. You can **Invert** the original colors, **Preserve** them, or change everything to **Black and White**.
Layers	Indicates which CAD layers are going to be brought into the model. Select how you want layers to be imported: **All**, **Visible**, or **Specify...**.
Import units	Select the units of the original file, as required. **Auto-Detect** works in most cases.
Correct Lines...	If lines in a CAD file are off axis by less than 0.1 degree selecting this option straightens them. It is selected by default.
Positioning	Specify how you want the imported file to be positioned in the current project: **Auto-Center to Center**, **Auto-Origin to Origin**, **Manual-Origin**, **Manual-Base Point**, or **Manual-Center**.
Place at	Select a level in which to place the imported file. If you selected **Current view only**, this option is grayed out.

- Once the imported or linked file is in the project, you can move it as one element using standard modify tools.

- If you do not want to move an imported or linked element by mistake, select the instance and in the *Modify* tab>Modify panel, click ⊷ (Pin).

- To prevent pinned elements from being selected, toggle off

  ⬚ (Select Pinned Elements) in the Status Bar. If you are

  working with a linked element, you can toggle off ⬚ (Select Links) without pinning the linked element first.

Setting an Imported or Linked File to Halftone

To help determine the difference between your model elements and the linked or imported file, you can override the visibility graphics of the linked or imported file and set it to halftone as shown in Figure 3–17.

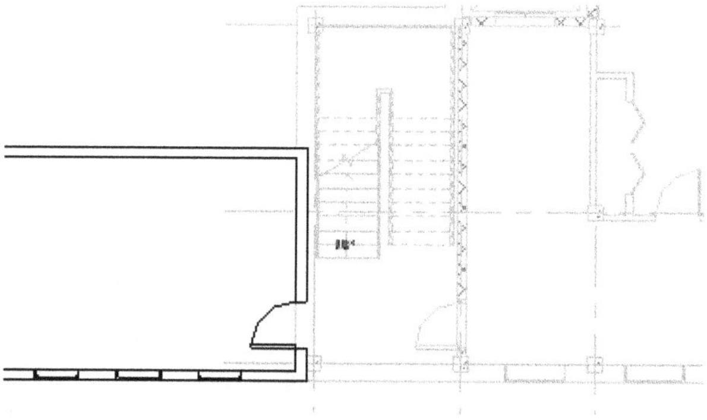

Figure 3–17

How To: Set an Element Halftone

1. Select the imported file.
2. Right-click and select **Override Graphics in View>By Element...**.
3. In the View Specific Element Graphics dialog box, select **Halftone**, as shown in Figure 3–18.

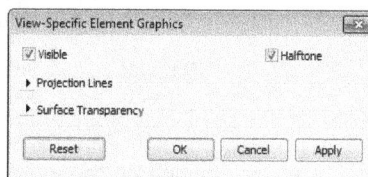

Figure 3–18

4. Click ⬚ OK ⬚.

3.3 Creating Structural Grids

Autodesk Certification Topics & Objectives

Pro.   User

Modeling

- Use grids   ✓

Learning Objective

- Add and modify structural grid lines.

Another important item to set up early in a project is the structural grid, as shown in Figure 3–19. For example, if you are designing a warehouse, you can have a standard structural grid that undergirds the design and indicates how to space the bays for the storage system. Grids are the basis for architectural and structural column locations.

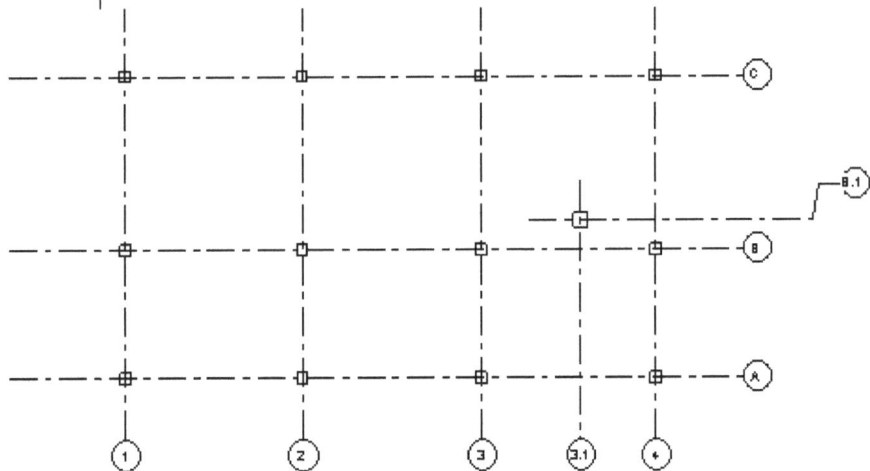

Figure 3–19

Adding Grids

Grids can be placed at any time in the design process. Each line or arc in a grid is a separate entity and can be placed, moved, and modified individually. The grid type defines the line style and size of the bubble, which is automatically inserted at one end of the line.

How To: Create a Structural Grid

1. In the *Architecture* tab>Datum panel, click ⊞ (Grid).
2. In the *Modify | Place Grid* tab>Draw panel, select the method of creating the grid line. You can click ╱ (Line), ╭ (Start-End-Radius Arc), ⌒ (Center-ends Arc), or ⚲ (Pick Lines). You can also create multi-segment grids.
3. In the Options Bar, set the *Offset* if required.
4. Continue adding grid lines as required.

How To: Create Multi-Segment Grids

1. In the *Architecture* tab>Datum panel, click ⊞ (Grid).
2. In the *Modify | Place Grid* tab>Draw panel, click ↳ (Multi-Segment).
3. In the *Modify | Edit Sketch* tab>Draw panel, use the tools to sketch the grid.
4. Click ✔ (Finish Edit Mode). The new grid displays as shown in Figure 3–20.

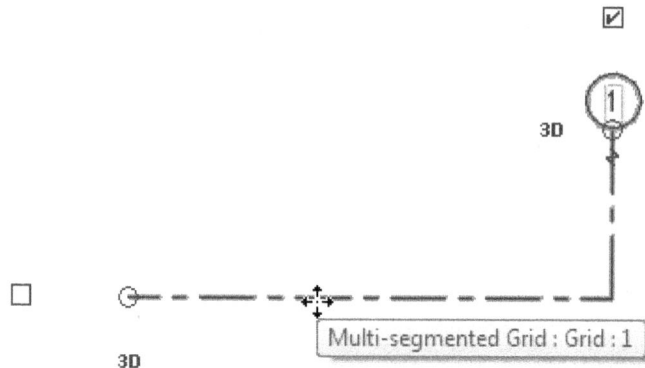

Figure 3–20

Modifying Grid Lines

As with other elements, you can modify grid lines and columns in a variety of ways, such as using shape handles, temporary dimensions, and locks, as shown in Figure 3–21. You can also modify the Properties.

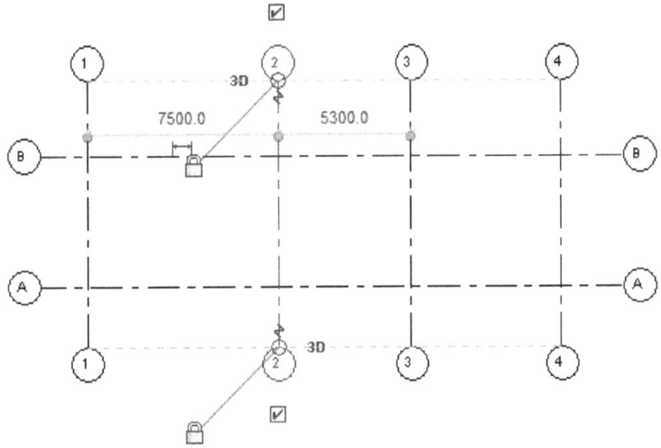

Figure 3–21

Once a grid line has been placed, you can modify it in the following ways:

- With temporary dimensions, you can adjust the distance between the grid lines and other nearby elements, such as walls.

- The small boxes at either end of the line control the bubble display. Place a check in the box to display the bubble at that end.

- Shape handles (unfilled circles) at each end of the line control its length. Drag a circle to adjust the length.

- If the lines are the same length, alignment lines and padlocks are displayed. When the padlocks are locked, modifying the length of one grid line modifies all of the lines. Unlock off the padlock to adjust the length of a single line.

- To modify a grid number, double-click on the number in the bubble. An edit field displays and you can type the new number. Grid numbers can be numbers, letters, or a combination of the two.

- Select the **Add elbow** control when the bubbles are too close together. Extra blue circles display, which enable you to move the bubble away from the other lines.

Hint: Creating a Gap in Grid Lines

If you do not want the grid line to display across the entire model, create a gap in the grid lines by changing the **Grid type** to **Grid: 6.5mm Bubble Custom Gap** or **Grid: 6.5mm Bubble Gap**. Then select the grid and move the additional solid circle control that displays near each end of the grid line to the appropriate location, as shown in Figure 3–22.

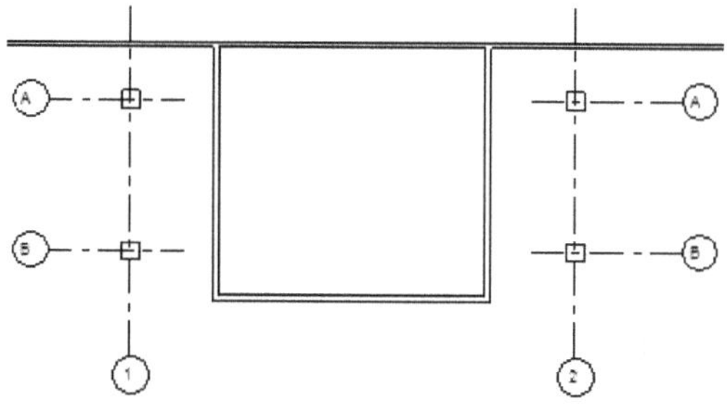

Figure 3–22

- If you want to place a bubble at both ends of a grid line by default, you need to edit the Grid type. In Properties, click ▦ (Edit Type). In the Type Properties dialog box, select **Plan View Symbols End 1 (Default)**. Click [OK] twice to update the type used in the project, as shown in Figure 3–23.

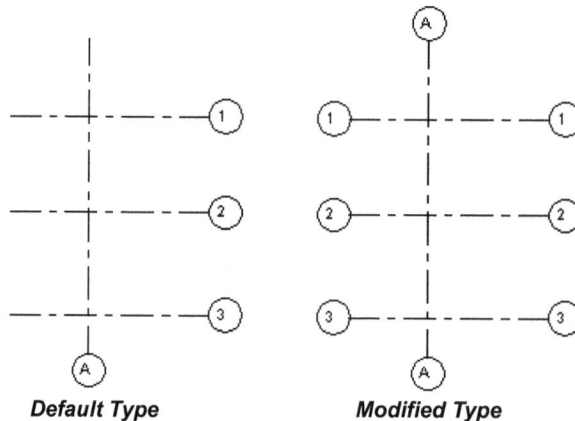

Default Type   *Modified Type*

Figure 3–23

3.4 Adding Columns

Learning Objective

- Add architectural and structural columns.

The Autodesk Revit software includes two commands for adding columns: one for standard columns and one for structural columns. Standard columns can be viewed as placeholders or decorative elements, as shown in Figure 3–24, while structural columns include more precise information related to industry standards.

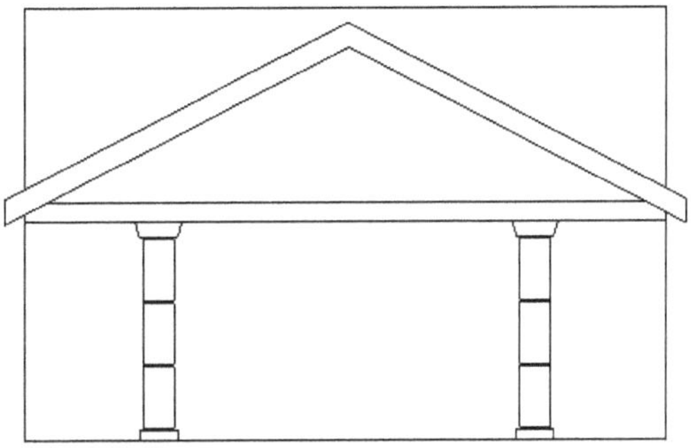

Figure 3–24

How To: Add Columns

1. In the *Architecture* tab>Build panel, expand ⬚ (Column) and click either ⬚ (Column: Architectural) or ⬚ (Structural Column). The Structural Column is always the default.
2. In the Type Selector, select the column you want to use, as shown in Figure 3–25.

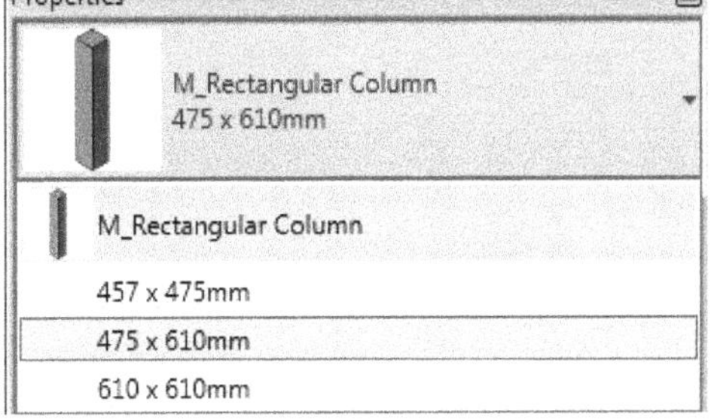

Figure 3–25

3. In the Options Bar, set the *Height* (or *Depth*) for the column. You can select a level (as shown in Figure 3–26), or select **Unconnected** to specify a height.

Architectural columns typically go from the level you are on up to another level or to a specific height. Structural columns are typically set from the level you are on down to another level or to a specific depth.

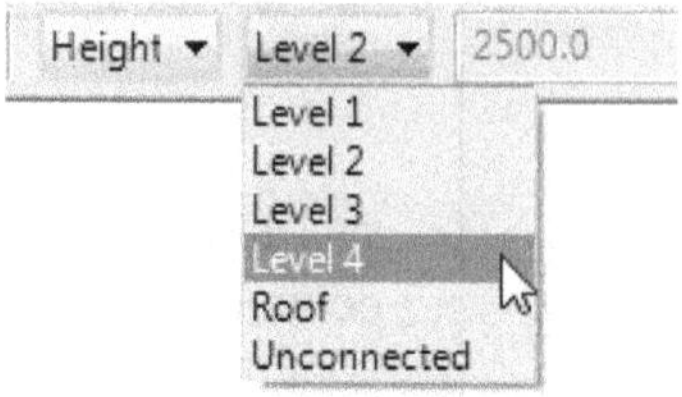

Figure 3–26

4. If you select the **Rotate after placement** option, you are prompted for a rotation angle after you select the insertion point for the column.
5. Place the column as required. It snaps to grid lines and walls. You can also place a column in empty space as a free instance unconnected to any grid lines.
6. Continue placing columns as required.

- If you are working with structural columns, you have two additional options in the *Modify | Place Structural Column* tab>Multiple panel:

  - To place columns at the intersection of grid lines, click

    (At Grids) and select the grid lines. Columns will only be placed at the intersections of the selected grid lines.

  - To place structural columns wherever you have an

    architectural column, click (At Columns) and select the columns. The structural columns are placed at the center of the architectural columns, as shown in Figure 3–27.

Figure 3–27

- A column placed in a wall is automatically cleaned up. If the wall has a hatch pattern, it also fills the architectural column area, as shown in Figure 3–28. Structural columns remain separate even if they are the same material as the surrounding walls.

Figure 3–28

- To access additional column styles, in the *Modify | Place Column* tab>Model panel, click ⬇ (Load Family). In the Load Family dialog box, navigate to the *Columns* folder in the software's Library, as shown in Figure 3–29.

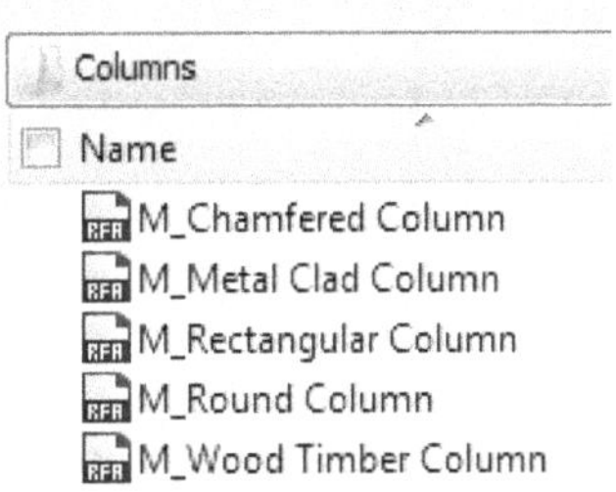

Figure 3–29

- Structural columns are divided into folders by material type in the *Structural>Columns* folder. They include *Concrete*, *Precast Concrete*, *Steel*, and *Wood*.

Modifying Columns

You can modify columns using Properties, the Type Selector, the Options Bar, and the *Modify | Column* tab tools, as shown in Figure 3–30.

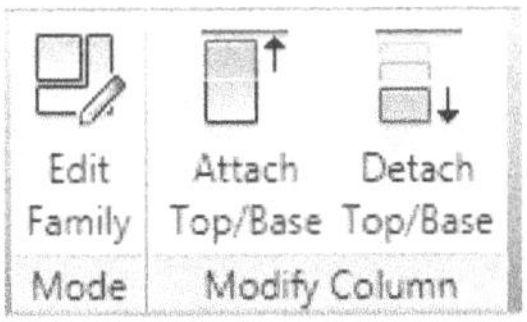

Figure 3–30

- Along with the standard modifying commands (such as **Move** and **Rotate**), you can ⬆ (Attach) or ⬇ (Detach) a column's top and base to floors, ceilings, roofs, reference planes, and structural framing.

- By default, columns move with nearby grids. This connects the column to the grid without absolutely locking it. However, you can still move it independently. When you select a column to modify, you can turn this option off by clearing the **Move With Grids** option in the Options Bar or in the Properties of selected columns.

- In Properties, you can change the *Base Level* and *Top Level*, as well as the offsets from these levels and several other options, as shown in Figure 3–31.

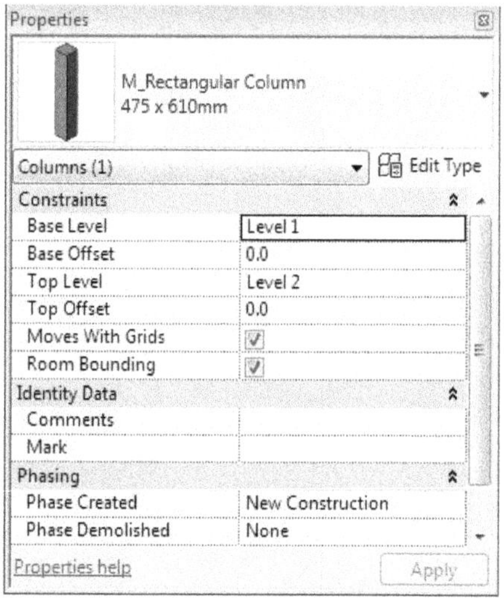

Structural columns have additional parameters.

Figure 3–31

- Deleting a grid line or wall does not delete the columns placed on them.

Practice 3b

Add Structural Grids and Columns

Learning Objectives

- Link a CAD file.
- Add and modify structural grid lines.
- Add architectural and structural columns.

Estimated time for completion: 15 minutes

In this practice you will import floor plans from the AutoCAD software and use it as a base layout for the first floor lobby and for a typical guest floor. You will then add grid lines using information in the imported file and add structural columns to the grid, as shown in Figure 3–32.

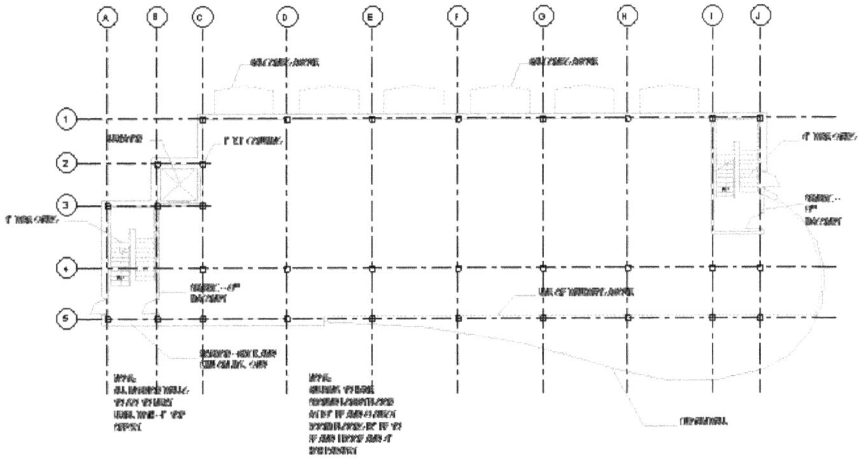

Figure 3–32

Task 1 - Import a CAD file.

1. Open the project **Modern-Hotel-Grids-M.rvt** from your class folder.

2. Open the **Floor Plans: Floor 1** view.

3. In the *Insert* tab>Link panel, click 🗎 (Link CAD).

4. In the Link CAD Formats dialog box, select the file **Hotel-Lobby-Floor-Plan-M.dwg**.

5. Set the following options:

- Current view only: Select this option
- Colors: **Black and White**
- Layers: **All**
- Import Units: **Auto-Detect**
- Positioning: **Auto-Origin to Origin**

6. Click [Open]. The linked file is placed in the project on the **Floor Plans: Floor 1** view.

7. Select the linked file. It is all in one element and pinned in place because it was imported origin to origin.

8. Right-click and select **Override Graphics in View>By Element**.

9. In the View-Specific Element Graphics dialog box, select **Halftone**.

10. Click [OK].

11. Click in empty space to release the selection. The linked file displays in halftone with columns and grids, as shown in Figure 3–33.

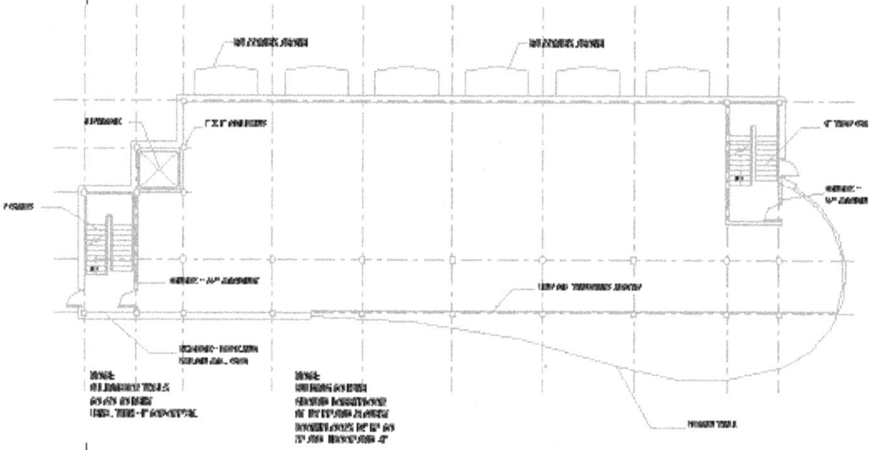

Figure 3–33

12. Move the existing elevation markers so that they surround the floor plan.

13. Open the **Floor Plans: Floor 2** view.

14. Link the CAD file **Hotel-Typical-Guest-Floor-Plan-M.dwg** using the options that were used for **Floor 1**.

15. Override the graphics and set the imported file to halftone.

16. Save the project.

Task 2 - Create structural grids.

1. Open the **Floor Plans: Floor 1** view.

2. In the *Architecture* tab>Datum panel, click ⊞ (Grid).

3. In the *Modify | Place Grid* tab>Draw panel, click ⟋ (Pick Lines).

4. Select the first vertical grid line on the left of the linked file. Click inside the bubble, type **A**, and press <Enter>.

5. Continue selecting the vertical grid lines displayed in the imported file. The letters automatically increment.

6. Click the first horizontal grid line and change the letter in the bubble to **1**.

7. Continue selecting the horizontal grid lines. The numbers automatically increment.

8. Return to the **Modify** command.

9. Check the lengths of all grid lines. Modify the length by dragging the ends if required. The final drawing is shown in Figure 3–34.

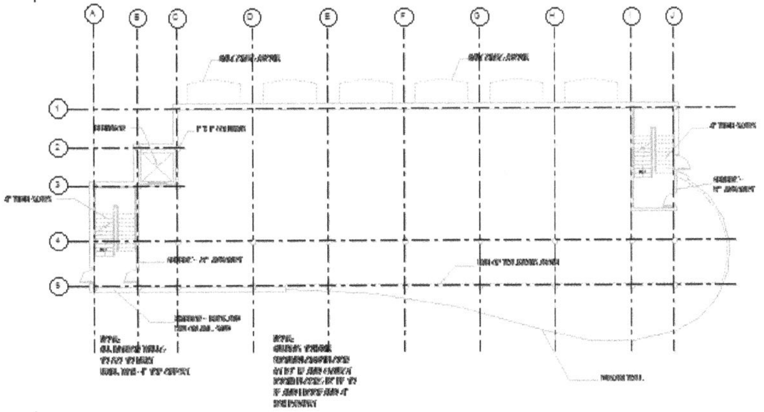

Figure 3–34

10. Save the project.

Task 3 - Add columns.

1. In the *Architecture* tab>Build panel, click ⬚ (Structural Column).

2. In the Type Selector, select **M_Concrete-Square-Column: 300 x 300mm**.

Verify that Height (not Depth) is selected in the Options Bar.

3. In the Options Bar, set the *Height* to **Floor 2**.

4. In the *Modify | Place Structural Column* tab>Multiple panel, click ⬚ (At Grids).

5. Hold down <Ctrl> and select all of the horizontal and vertical grid lines in the project. In the *Modify | Place Structural Column>At Grid Intersection* tab>Multiple panel, click ✓ (Finish).

6. Return to the **Modify** command.

7. Delete the columns at **A1**, **A2**, and **B1**, as well as **A4** and **B4**, as shown in Figure 3–35.

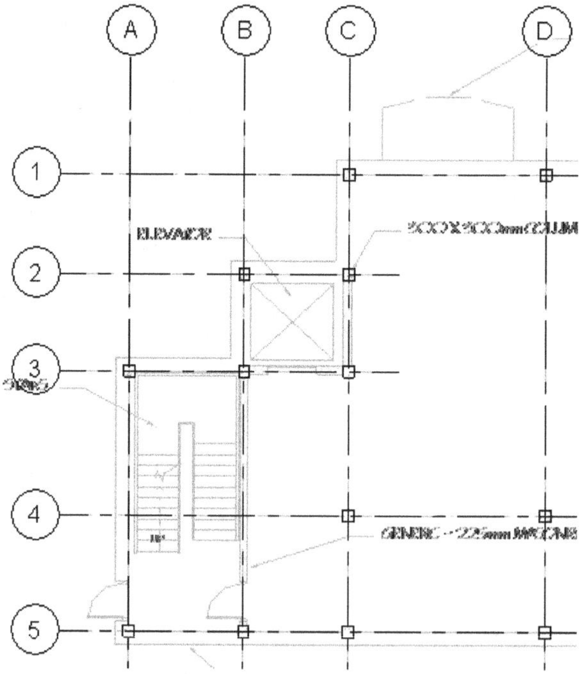

Figure 3–35

8. In the Quick Access Toolbar, click ⌂ (3D View). The columns are only set to the height of the 2nd floor (Floor 2), as shown in Figure 3–36.

The linked file does not display in the 3D view because it was only linked to the plan view.

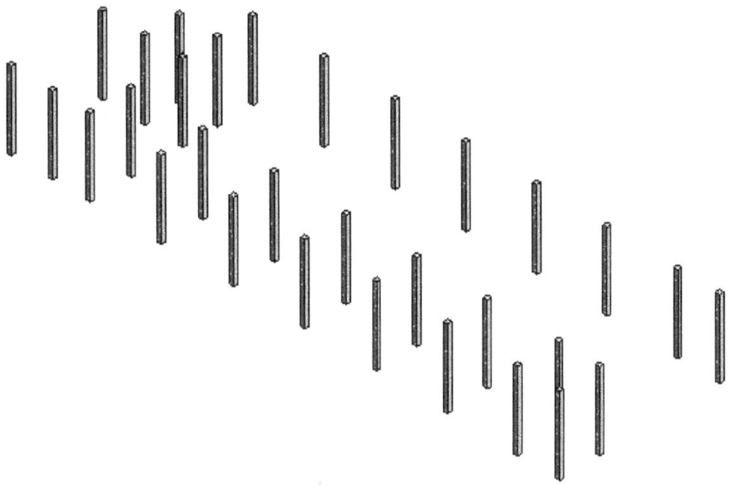

Figure 3–36

9. Select all of the columns. You can select one column, then right-click and select **Select All Instances>Visible in View**.

10. In Properties, in the *Constraints* area, change the *Base Level* to **T.O. Footing** and the *Top Level* to **Roof**. The columns now extend from the top of the footing to the roof.

11. Click in space to release the selection.

12. View several different floor plan views to verify the columns display.

13. Return to the **Floor Plans: Floor 1** view.

14. Save the project.

*Type **ZA** to zoom out in the view if needed.*

Chapter Review Questions

1. What type of view do you need to be in to add a level to your project?

   a. Any non-plan view.

   b. As this is done using a dialog box, the view does not matter.

   c. Any view except for 3D.

   d. Any section or elevation view.

2. How do you add a level name and target to both ends of a level line, as shown in Figure 3–37?

Figure 3–37

   a. Select the level line and ensure that the control box at both ends is checked.

   b. Select the level line and change the *Type* to **Dual Targets**.

   c. Select the level line, click the **Add Target** button in the Ribbon, and click the end to which you want to add a target.

   d. In the Manage Datum dialog box, select a level type that has a name and target at both ends.

3. Which of the following types of CAD formats can you import into the Autodesk Revit software? (Select all that apply.)

   a. DWG

   b. XLS

   c. SAT

   d. DGN

4. How do you line up grid lines that might be different lengths, as shown in Figure 3–38?

Figure 3–38

a. Use ⇥ (Trim/Extend Multiple Elements) to line them up with a common reference line.

b. Select the grid line and drag its model end to line up with the other grid lines.

c. Select the grid line, right-click and select **Auto-Align**.

d. In Properties, change the *Length* and then use ✛ (Move) to get them into position.

5. Where can columns (whose command access is shown in Figure 3–39) be placed?

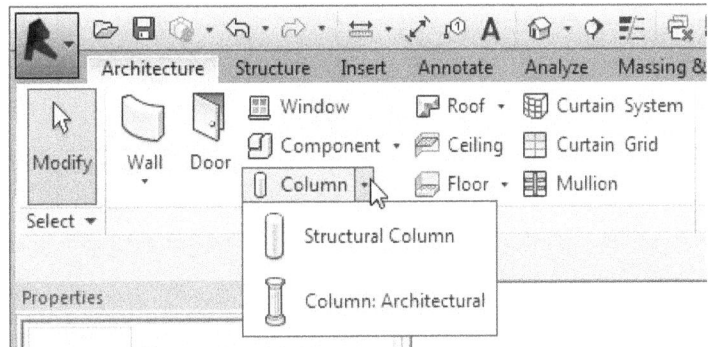

Figure 3–39

a. Columns can only be placed on grids.

b. Architectural columns can be placed anywhere, but structural columns can only be placed on grids.

c. Both types of columns can be placed wherever you want.

d. Grid-based column types must be placed on the grid, but free-standing column types can be placed anywhere.

Command Summary

Button	Command	Location
	At Columns	• **Ribbon:** *Modify	Place Structural Column* tab>Multiple panel>At Columns
	At Grids	• **Ribbon:** *Modify	Place Structural Column* tab>Multiple panel>At Grids
	Column	• **Ribbon:** *Architecture* tab>Build panel>Column
	Column> Architectural	• **Ribbon:** *Architecture* tab>Build panel>Column>Column: Architectural
	Column> Structural	• **Ribbon:** *Architecture* tab>Build panel>Column>Structural Column
	Grid	• **Ribbon:** *Architecture* tab>Datum panel>Grid • Shortcut: GR
	Import CAD	• **Ribbon:** *Insert* tab>Import panel> Import CAD
	Level	• **Ribbon:** *Architecture* tab>Datum panel>Level • Shortcut: LL
	Link CAD	• **Ribbon:** *Insert* tab>Link panel> Link CAD
	Multi-Segment (Grid)	• **Ribbon:** *Modify	Place Grid* tab>Draw panel>Multi-Segment

Design Development Phase

The second phase of this training guide focuses on teaching you how to use the tools available in the Autodesk® Revit® software to create the design model.

The second phase covers the following topics:

- Modeling Walls
- Working with Doors and Windows
- Working with Curtain Walls
- Working with Views
- Adding Components
- Modeling Floors
- Modeling Ceilings
- Modeling Roofs
- Vertical Circulation

Chapter 4

Modeling Walls

In this chapter you learn how to model and modify walls. You learn how to alter existing walls by using controls, dynamic and permanent dimensions, and wall joins, or by changing wall types, You also learn how to modify a wall's instance and type properties.

This chapter contains the following topics:

- **Modeling Walls**
- **Modifying Walls**

4.1 Modeling Walls

Autodesk Certification Topics & Objectives

Pro.   User

Elements

- Create and modify walls   ✓

⊘ Learning Objectives

- Model walls.
- Specify the wall type.
- Set the Height and Location Line of the walls.

Walls in the Autodesk® Revit® software are more than just two lines on a plan. They are full 3D elements that show height, thickness, and materials, among other things. As with most elements in the software, you can select from a list of types and set additional options, such as the *Height* and *Location Line*.

- *Wall types* enable you to use different styles for various needs. For example, Figure 4–1 shows exterior walls with block and brick, corridor walls of block (for a higher fire rating), and interior partitions.

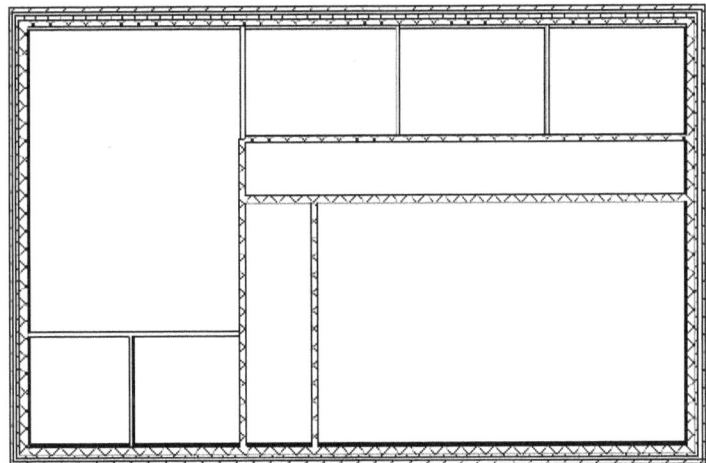

Figure 4–1

- To display the hatching in the walls, the *Detail Level* of the view must be set to **Medium** or **Fine**. You can set the *Detail Level* in the View Control Bar, as shown in Figure 4–2.

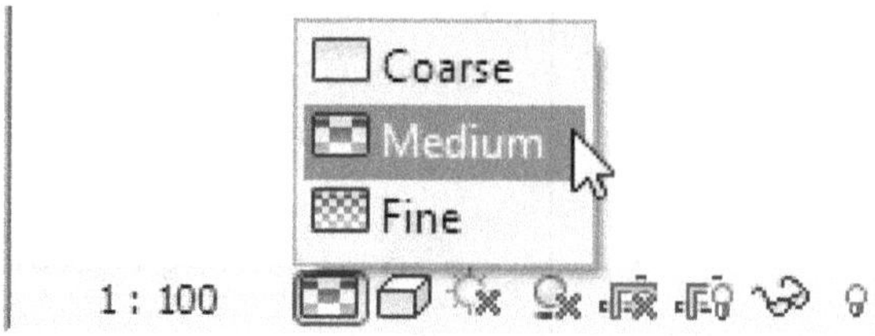

Figure 4–2

How To: Model a Wall

1. In the *Architecture* tab>Build panel, click ⬡ (Wall) or type the shortcut **WA**.
2. In the Type Selector, select a wall type as shown in Figure 4–3.

Basic curtain walls are added using this command. Select a curtain wall type in the Type Selector.

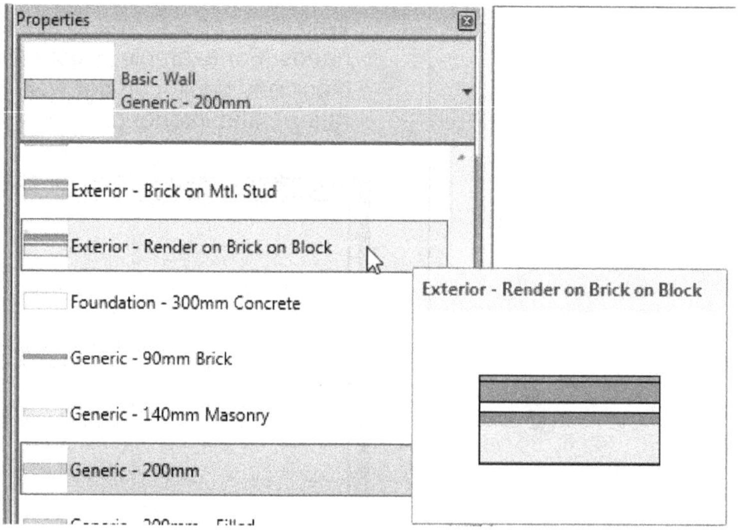

Figure 4–3

3. In the *Modify | Place Wall* tab>Draw panel, select one of the following options to create the wall:

✎	**Sketching Options**	Set to **Line** by default. The other sketching options include **Rectangle**, **Inscribed Polygon**, **Circumscribed Polygon**, **Circle**, **Start-End-Radius Arc**, **Center-ends Arc**, **Tangent End Arc**, and **Fillet Arc**.

↖	**Pick Lines**	Creates walls based on existing lines in the project.
🖱	**Pick Faces**	Creates walls based on existing faces of 3D Massing elements and generic models.

4. In the Options Bar, set the *Height* of the walls. It can be set to an **Unconnected** height or to the height of a level, as shown in Figure 4–4.

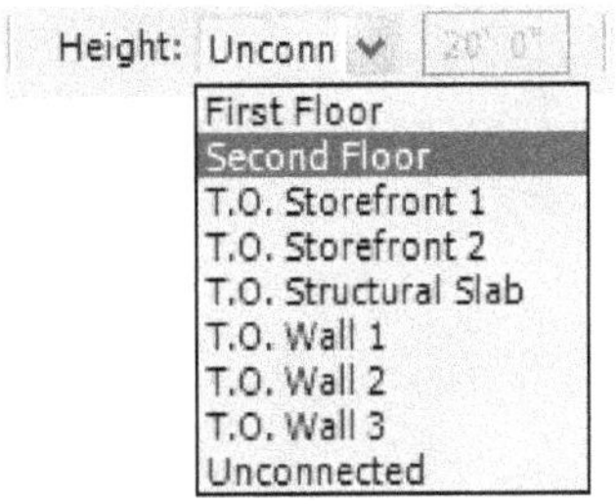

Height: Unconn ▾ 20' 0"

First Floor
Second Floor
T.O. Storefront 1
T.O. Storefront 2
T.O. Structural Slab
T.O. Wall 1
T.O. Wall 2
T.O. Wall 3
Unconnected

Figure 4–4

5. Set the *Location Line* for the justification of the wall as you draw. Options include **Wall Centerline** (as shown in Figure 4–5), **Core Centerline**, **Finish Face: Exterior**, **Finish Face: Interior**, **Core Face: Exterior**, and **Core Face: Interior**.

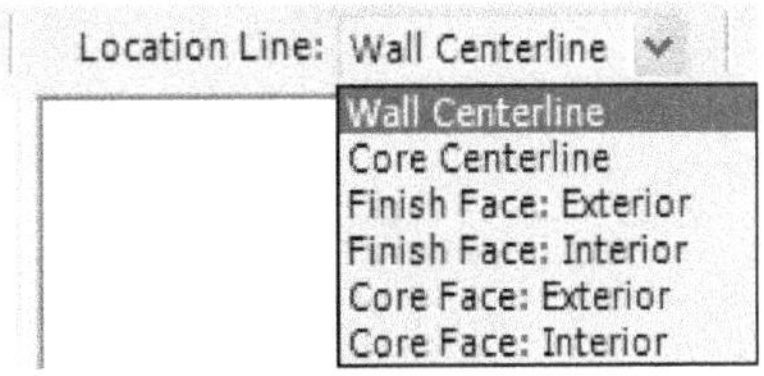

Location Line: Wall Centerline ▾

Wall Centerline
Core Centerline
Finish Face: Exterior
Finish Face: Interior
Core Face: Exterior
Core Face: Interior

Figure 4–5

6. In the Options Bar, three more options are available. They are described in the table below.

Chain	Selected by default. Enables you to draw multiple walls that are joined.
Offset	When **Pick Lines** is selected, enables you to enter the distance at which a new wall is created from an existing wall.
Radius	Enables you to add a radius to a wall. Used with the **Rectangle**, **Circle**, **Arc**, and **Polygon** options.

Press the <Spacebar> to switch the orientation of the wall while drawing it (flip inside/outside for compound walls with different materials). You can also do this after the walls are created.

7. Select points to draw the walls.
   - Alignment lines help you draw straight lines at the appropriate angles.
   - Temporary dimensions enable you to set the wall length.
   - Snap to specific points on walls and to other elements.
8. Press <Esc> to finish the group of walls if using the **Chain** option. This enables you to continue in the **Wall** command so you can draw more walls.
9. Return to the **Modify** command to completely finish the command.

4.2 Modifying Walls

Autodesk Certification Topics & Objectives

Pro.   User

Elements

• Create and modify walls   ✓

Learning Objectives

- Change wall types.
- Modify walls with controls and dynamic dimensions.
- Add permanent dimensions.
- Modify wall joins.
- Modify wall instance and type properties.

The Autodesk Revit software provides several methods of modifying walls. You can change the type of wall, use controls to modify the wall orientation, use dynamic and fixed dimensions to change the length of a wall (as shown in Figure 4–6), and modify wall joins. You can also change the wall properties for selected instances or for an entire wall type.

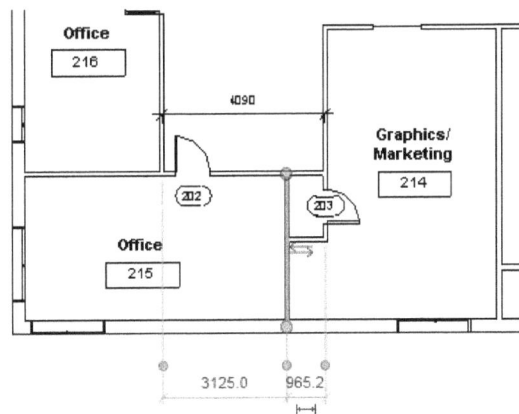

Figure 4–6

• If you are working in a 3D view and have zoomed in to a location in which the wall edges are not displayed, you can select the wall face instead of the edges. To enable this feature, in the Status Bar, toggle on 🖱️ (Select elements by face).

Changing the Wall Type

When you select a single element or several elements of the same type (e.g., several walls), you can change their style in the Type Selector, as shown in Figure 4–7.

Many wall types include materials, such as brick, masonry, and drywall.

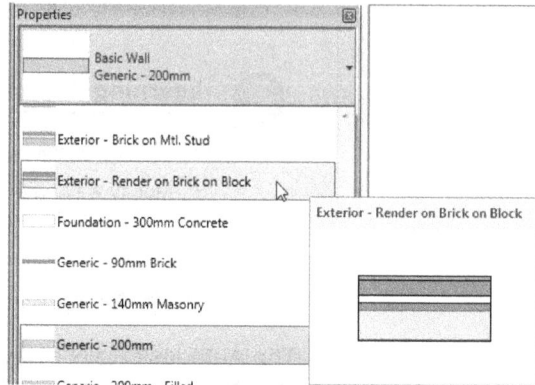

Properties

Basic Wall
Generic - 200mm

Exterior - Brick on Mtl. Stud

Exterior - Render on Brick on Block

Foundation - 300mm Concrete

Generic - 90mm Brick

Generic - 140mm Masonry

Generic - 200mm

Exterior - Render on Brick on Block

Figure 4–7

Controls for Walls

Controls for walls include **Drag wall end** (circles at each end of the wall) and **Change wall's orientation** (flip arrows). Dynamic Dimensions controls include **Move witness line** (circles on dimension extension lines) and **Make this temporary dimension permanent** (dimension icon), as shown in Figure 4–8.

Changing the wall orientation is most important for walls with different materials on either side. For example, when drawing a block and brick wall, you might have put the brick on the inside by mistake.

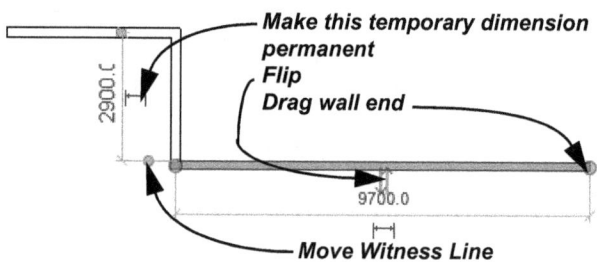

Make this temporary dimension permanent
Flip
Drag wall end

2900.0

9700.0

Move Witness Line

Figure 4–8

- When dragging a *wall end*, dynamic dimensions are displayed that can help you estimate the point at which to stop. Snaps are also available if you get close to another element.

- Select the **Flip** arrows or press the <Spacebar> to flip the orientation. The wall flips about the location line.

Dynamic Dimensions and Walls

When you select a wall, dynamic dimensions display, that enable you to change its length and position as shown in Figure 4–9.

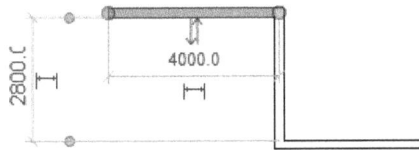

Figure 4–9

- To change a dimension, click on the dimension text and type the new distance in the edit field.

- Dynamic dimensions automatically link to the closest wall ends of nearby walls. To change which end the dimension works with, you can drag the blue circle to move the *witness line* to a new point. You can also click on the control to toggle between justifications within the wall.

- If you want a permanent dimension in place of the dynamic dimension, click ⊢⊣.

How To: Add Permanent Dimensions

1. In the Quick Access Toolbar, or in the *Annotate* tab>Dimension panel, or the *Modify* tab>Measure panel, click

    ⟋ (Aligned Dimension).
2. Select the first element to dimension.
3. Select the rest of the elements in order, as shown in Figure 4–10.

Permanent dimensions also provide you with additional temporary dimensions when you are modifying elements.

Figure 4–10

- When you finish placing a string of dimensions, you can modify them so that they display an equal distance apart, as shown in Figure 4–11. Click ^{EQ} (Toggle Dimension Equality) to turn it on or off.

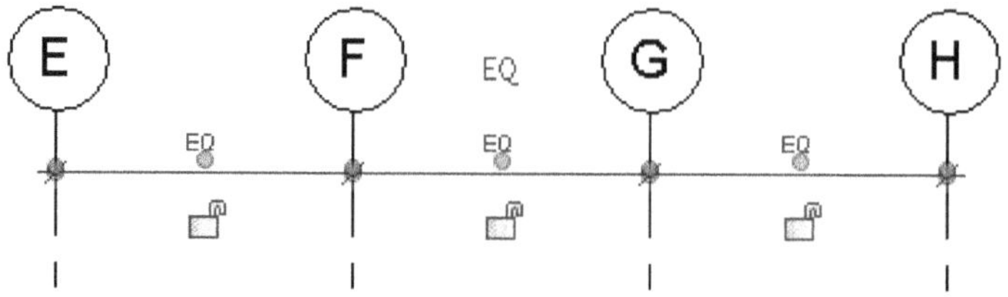

If you delete a dimension set to EQ, the elements remain an equal distance apart.

Figure 4–11

Wall Joins

The software automatically joins walls when they come together at an intersection, as shown on the left in Figure 4–12. However, there are times when you do not want the walls to clean up, such as when one fire-rated wall butts into another, as shown on the right in Figure 4–12.

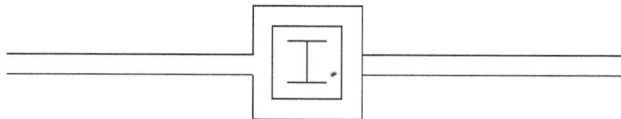

Figure 4–12

- To change how a wall joins to another wall, right-click on the control at the end of the wall and select **Disallow Join**, as shown on the left in Figure 4–13. Once the end is not joined, you can drag it to the appropriate location, as shown on the right in Figure 4–13.

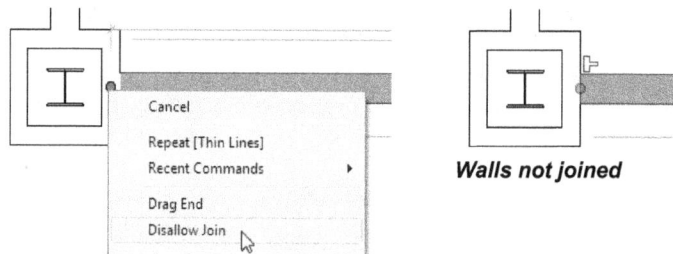

Figure 4–13

- To rejoin the walls, click ⌐ (Allow Join) or right-click on the end control and select Allow Join. Manually drag the wall back to where you want it to touch the target wall.

Wall Openings

You can add openings in walls that are not windows or doors by using the **Wall Opening** tool. This creates rectangular openings for both straight and curved walls, as shown in Figure 4–14.

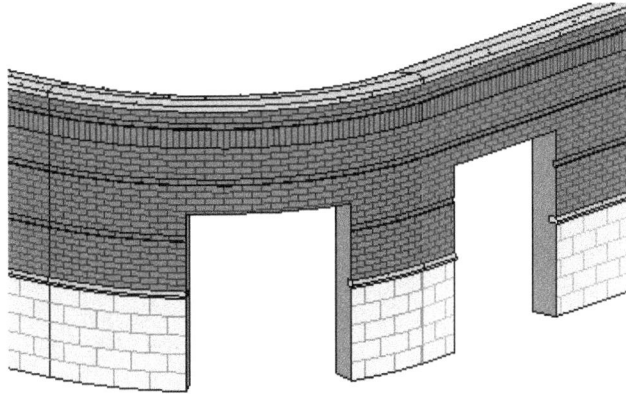

Figure 4–14

How To: Add Wall Openings

1. Open an elevation, section, or 3D view.

2. In the *Architecture* tab>Openings panel click ⊓ (Wall Opening).
3. Select the wall.
4. Pick two points on the wall that determine the opening size.

- You can use temporary dimensions to size the opening.

Modifying Wall Properties

Wall properties are separated into several categories, as shown in Figure 4–15. The primary area is *Constraints*, which includes the *Location Line, Base* and *Top Constraint[s], Offsets,* and *Room Bounding* properties. The other available areas include *Structural, Dimensions, Identity Data,* and *Phasing*.

These properties are Instance Properties. They only impact the selected instances of a wall, not all walls of the same type.

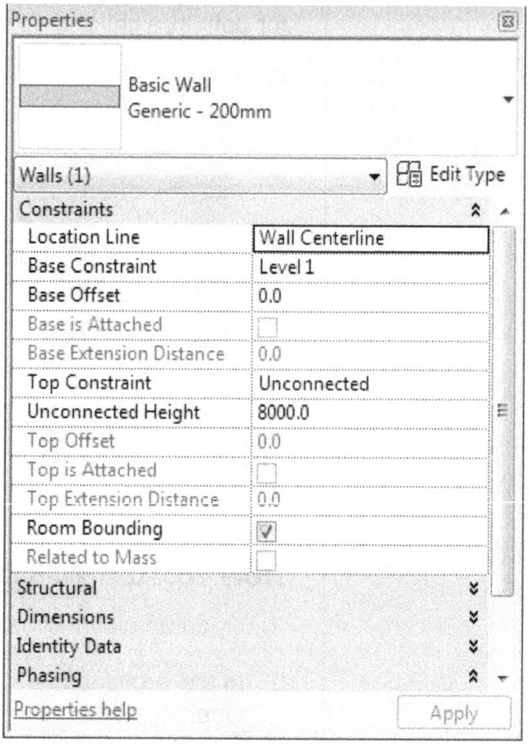

Figure 4–15

- Two categories that are found on all elements, not just walls, are *Identity Data* and *Phasing*.

Modifying Wall Type Properties

Type Properties, as shown in Figure 4–16, contain the parameters that control every instance of a wall type. Most of the time, you do not need to modify these. However, they can be helpful when you are ready to assign information, such as keynotes that can be used in a schedule.

- With a wall selected, in the Properties palette, click

   ⊞ (Edit Type) or in the *Modify | Walls* tab>Properties panel,

   click ⊞ (Type Properties).

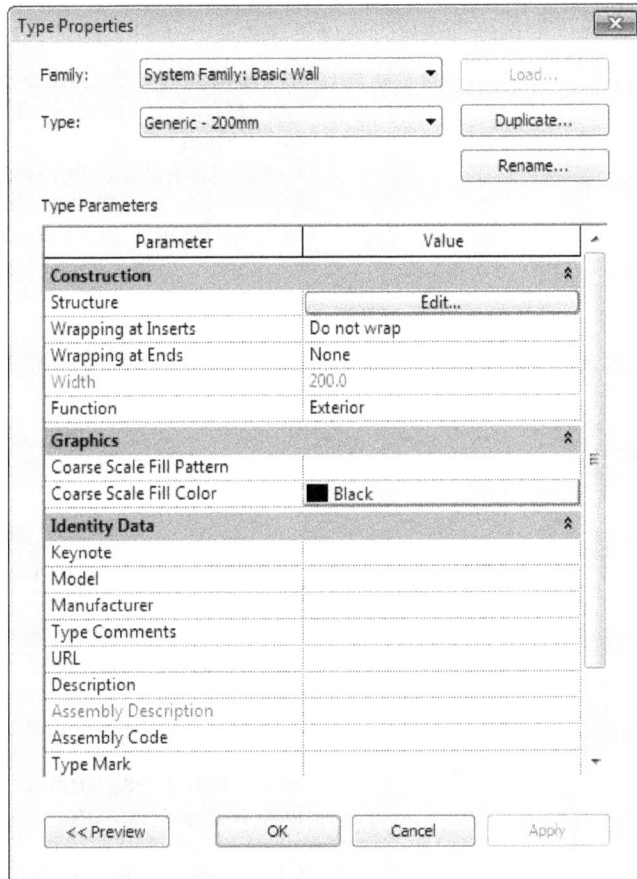

Figure 4–16

- You can use the Type Properties dialog box to create new wall types or edit existing ones.

Hint: Matching Properties

You can select an existing wall and use it to assign the wall type and instance properties to other walls by using the **Match Type** command. This command also works with all elements that have types.

1. In the *Modify* tab>Clipboard panel, click ✏️ (Match Type) or type **MA**. The cursor changes to an arrow with a clean paintbrush.
2. Select the source element that you want all of the others to match. The paintbrush changes to look as if it has been dipped in black paint as shown in Figure 4–17.

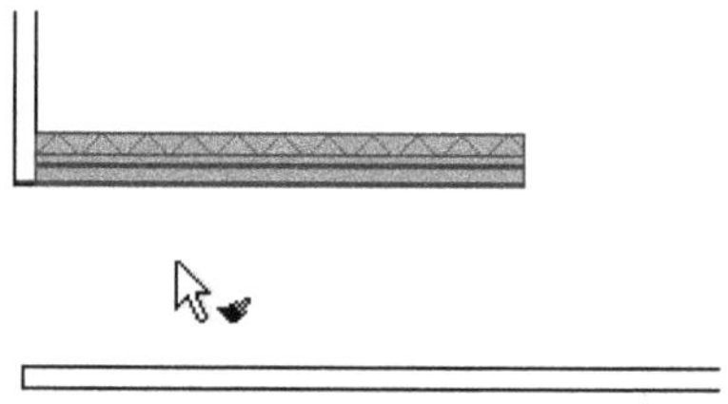

Figure 4–17

3. To select more than one element, in the *Modify | Match Type* tab>Multiple panel, click 🔲 (Select Multiple). You can then use windows, crossings, <Ctrl>, and <Shift> to create a selection set of elements to change.
4. Select the elements that you want to change. For multiple selections, press <Enter> or click ✓ (Finish) to apply the type to the selection.

- Click in an empty space in the project to empty the brush so that you can repeat the command with a different element.

- Elements to be matched must be of the same type (e.g., all walls, all doors, etc.).

Practice 4a

Model the Exterior Shell

Learning Objectives

- Trace over walls in an imported DWG file.
- Add curtain walls.
- Modify wall joins.

Estimated time for completion: 20 minutes

In this practice you will add exterior walls, including a curtain wall, to create the exterior shell of the project. You will use an imported file to help establish the location of the walls. You will then add a parapet wall over the curtain wall. The completed model is shown in Figure 4–18.

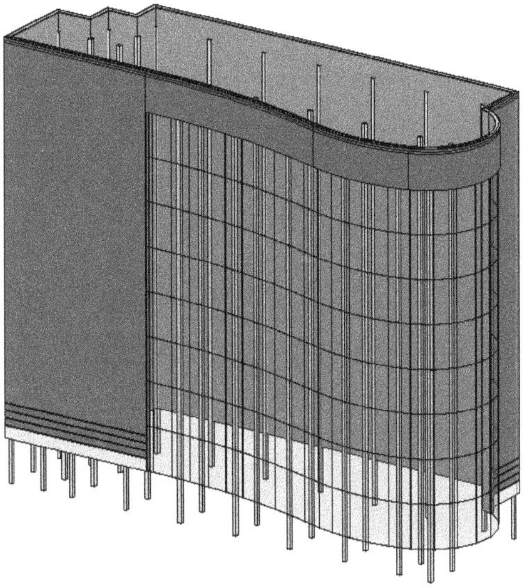

Figure 4–18

Task 1 - Add walls by picking lines.

1. Open the project **Modern-Hotel-Walls-M.rvt** from your class folder.

2. Verify that you are in the **Floor Plans: Floor 1** view.

3. In the View Control Bar, set the *Detail Level* to ▨ (Medium). Doing so enables the multiple layers of the wall that is going to be added to be displayed.

4. In the *Architecture* tab>Build panel, click ⬚ (Wall).

5. In the Type Selector, select **Basic Wall: Exterior - Brick and CMU on MTL. Stud**.

6. In the Options Bar, set the *Height* to **Parapet** and the *Location Line* to **Finish Face: Exterior**. Verify that the **Chain** option is selected. In Properties, verify that both *Base Offset* and *Top Offset* are set to **0.0**.

7. In the Draw panel, click ⚮ (Pick Lines).

8. Select one of the exterior walls in the imported file, as shown in Figure 4–19. Ensure the dashed line displays inside the wall. This wall is a compound wall and you want the brick to display on the outside.

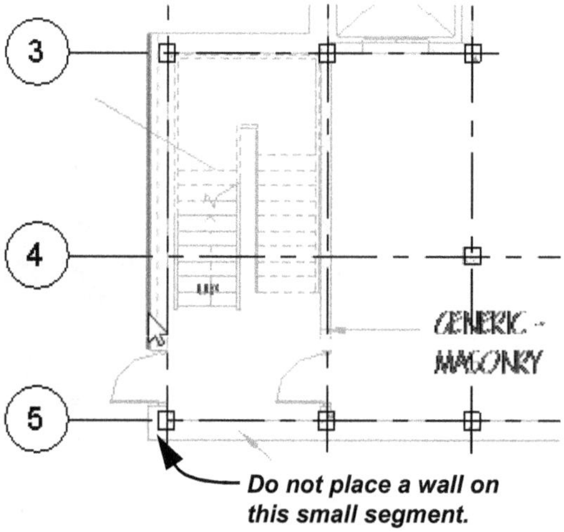

Do not place a wall on
this small segment.

Figure 4–19

9. Continue selecting lines around the exterior of the building. Do not select the curved curtain wall lines.

   - Use ↰ (Flip) to change the wall's orientation if the stucco side of the wall is not on the outside.

10. Return to the **Modify** command.

11. At the door openings on either end of the building, do not add walls on either side of the door. Instead, use the **Drag Wall End** control, as shown in Figure 4–20, to lengthen the wall across the opening. The intersections should clean up automatically.

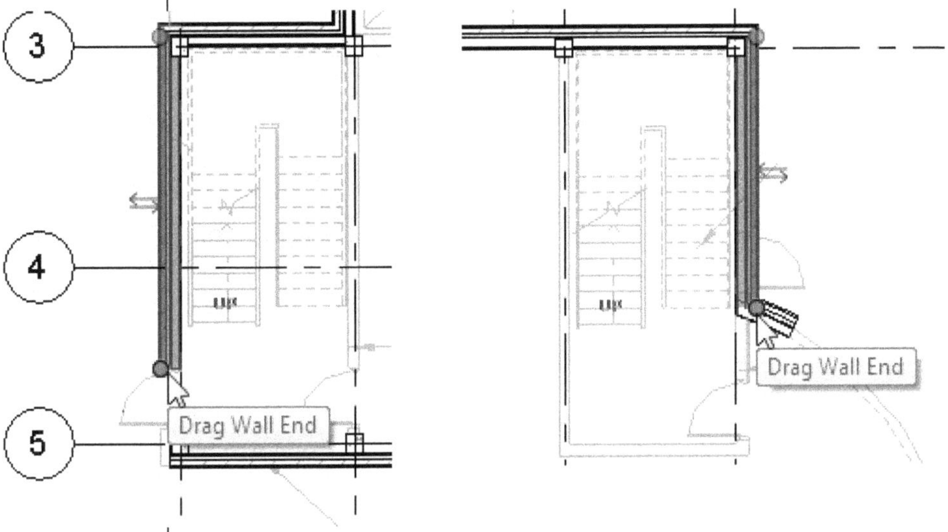

Figure 4–20

12. Save the project.

Task 2 - Add basic curtain walls.

---

1. Click ⬜ (Wall).

2. In the Type Selector, select **Curtain Wall: Exterior Glazing**. In the Options Bar, set the *Height* to **Roof**. In Properties, set the *Top Offset* to (negative) **-1850mm**. This places the top of the curtain wall below the roof level.

3. Use ⬆ (Pick Lines) and select the three curved lines.

4. In the Quick Access Toolbar, click 📦 (3D View).

The columns are hidden to make this graphic more readable.

5. In the View Control Bar, set the *Visual Style* to

   ⬦ (Consistent Colors). The curtain wall does not extend to the top of the parapet, as shown in Figure 4–21.

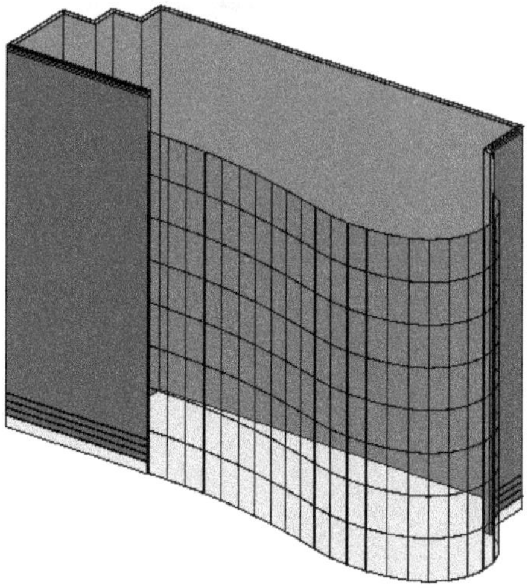

Figure 4–21

Task 3 - Add a parapet.

1. Open the **Floor Plans: Roof** view.

2. In the View Control Bar, set the *Detail Level* to ▨ (Medium) to display the layers of the walls.

3. Select the small curved piece of wall at the northeast corner of the building on Column Line J. Right-click on the right end point grip and select **Disallow Join,** as shown in Figure 4–22.

Some walls, when they try to automatically clean up, cause problems. Disallowing a join can resolve the issue.

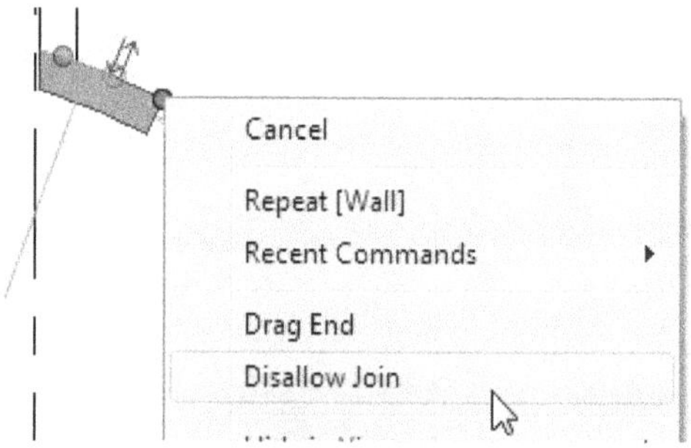

Figure 4–22

4. Repeat the process again on the other wall that connects to the curtain wall near the intersection of Grid D5.

5. Start the **Wall** command.

6. In the Type Selector, select **Basic Wall: Exterior - Brick on MTL. Stud - parapet**. The alert, shown in Figure 4–23, displays because the software remembered the last settings of the properties.

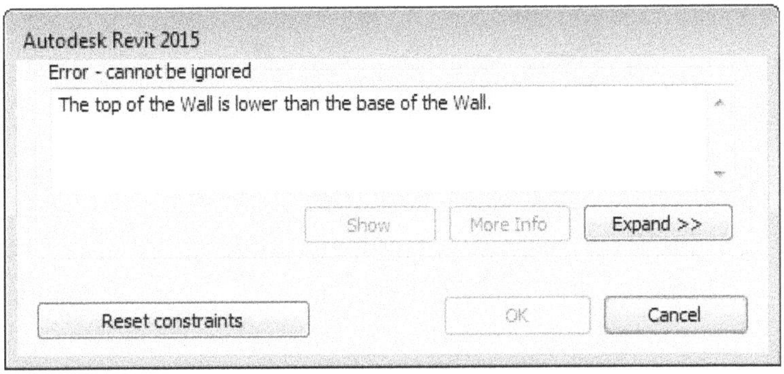

Autodesk Revit 2015

Error - cannot be ignored

The top of the Wall is lower than the base of the Wall.

Show　　　More Info　　　Expand >>

Reset constraints　　　　　OK　　　Cancel

Figure 4–23

7. Click [Reset constraints]. All of the properties are reset.

8. Select the **Basic Wall: Exterior - Brick on MTL. Stud - parapet** again and set the following properties:

- Base Constraint: **Roof**
- Base Offset: (negative) **-1850mm**
- Top Constraint: **Up to level: Parapet**
- Top Offset: **0.0**

9. In the Draw panel, click ⬚ (Pick Lines). Move the cursor over the middle curved curtain wall and press <Tab> until the curtain wall reference displays as shown in Figure 4–24 and then click to place the wall.

Ensure that you are selecting the main line of the curtain wall or a grid line and not one of the curtain wall panels.

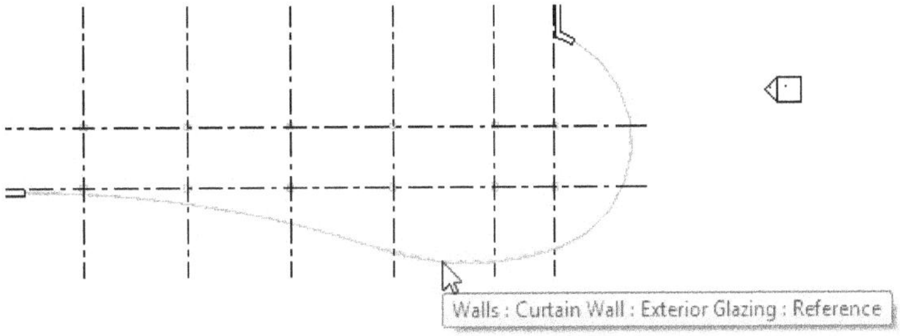

Walls : Curtain Wall : Exterior Glazing : Reference

Figure 4–24

10. In the *Modify | Place Wall* tab>Draw panel, click

   ⌒ (Start-End-Radius Arc).

11. Select the points in the order shown in Figure 4–25. Ensure that you select the endpoints before selecting the tangent point on the arc.

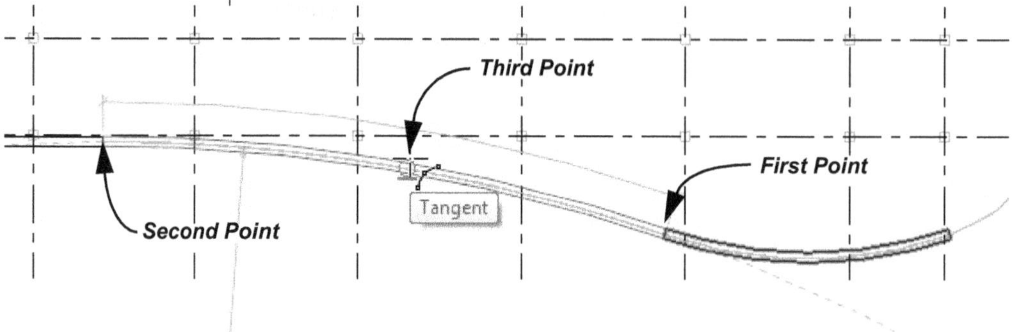

Third Point

First Point

Tangent

Second Point

Figure 4–25

- Creating the wall this way solves some issues because the center line of the curtain wall is at a slight offset from the main wall.
- If a warning displays about a wall sweep you can ignore it.

12. Repeat the process in a similar manner for the other part of the arc, starting with the endpoint of the small wall, and then the endpoint of the curved wall, and finally the tangent point.

13. Return to the **Modify** command.

14. Type **ZA** to display the full floor plan.

15. Return to the 3D view. The new parapet wall over the curtain wall displays as shown in Figure 4–26.

The columns are hidden to clarify the image.

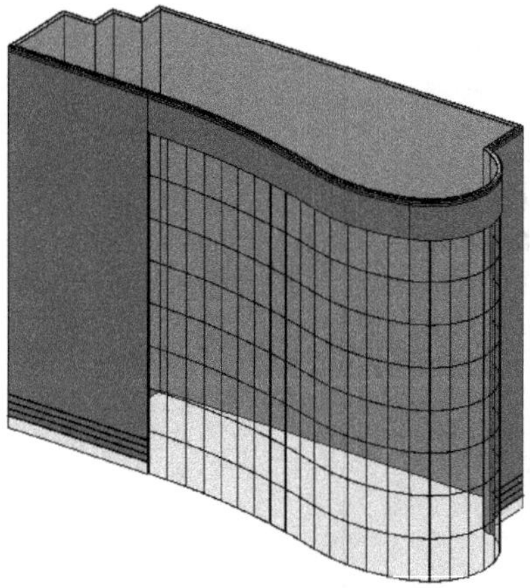

Figure 4–26

16. Save the project.

Practice 4b | # Add Interior Walls

![learning objectives icon] **Learning Objectives**

- Draw interior walls.
- Align and lock walls to other walls.
- Add a partial height wall.
- Use modify tools including **Align**, **Offset**, **Trim/Extend**, **Copy**, and **Mirror** to create walls.

Estimated time for completion: 20-30 minutes

In this practice you will add interior walls to the first floor plan, as shown in Figure 4–27, and use **Offset**, **Split Element**, **Trim**, and **Align** to help create them. As an optional task, you will create the 2nd Floor walls using the **Wall** command and editing tools including **Copy** and **Mirror**.

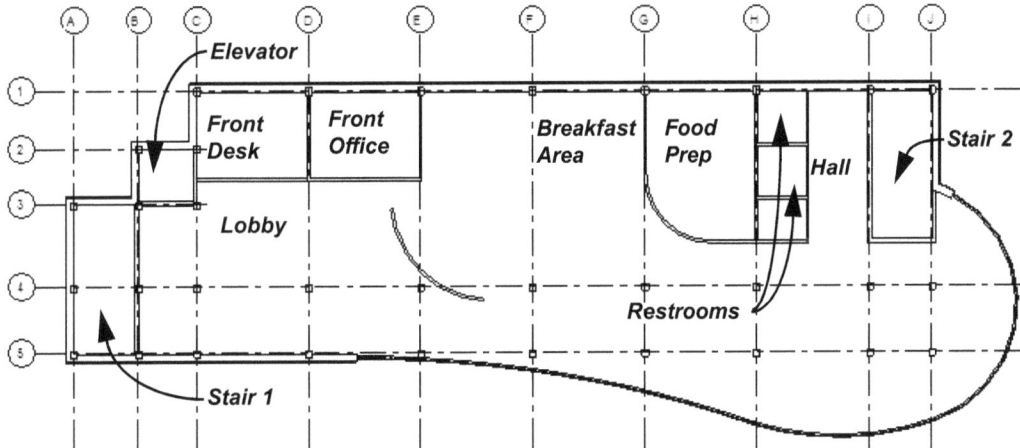

Figure 4–27

Task 1 - Add and align the stair and elevator walls.

1. Open the project **Modern-Hotel-Interior-Walls-M.rvt** from your class folder.

2. Open the **Floor Plans: Floor 1** view.

3. Zoom in on the stair and elevator area on the left side of the building.

4. Start the **Wall** command.

---

5. In the Options Bar and Properties, set the following options:

- Wall Type: **Basic Wall: Generic 225mm Masonry**
- Height: **Roof**
- Base Offset: **0.0**
- Top Offset:**0.0**

6. Draw the stair and elevator walls from column to column, as shown in Figure 4–28.

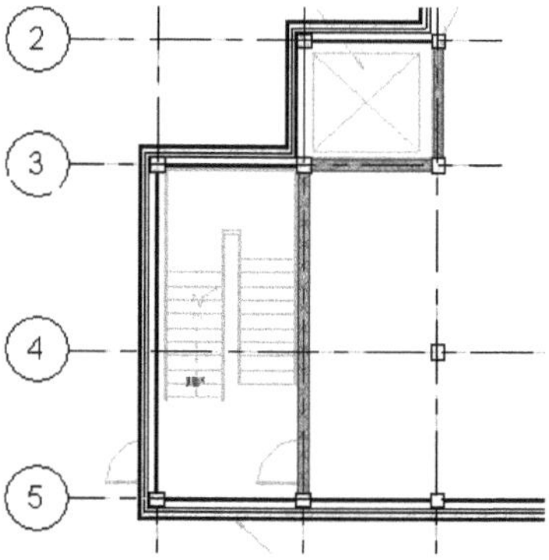

Figure 4–28

7. Return to the **Modify** command.

8. Zoom in on the elevator walls and ensure you can also display some of the related grid lines.

9. In the *Modify* tab>Modify panel, click ⬚ (Align).

10. Select the vertical **Grid C**.

11. Hover the cursor over the vertical elevator wall to display its center line (as shown in Figure 4–29), and then select it. Press <Tab> to display the center line if it is not displayed. This aligns the wall to the grid along its center line.

The alignment line defaults to the center line of the wall. If you wanted it to align to a different part of the wall, you could <Tab> to cycle through the other wall faces.

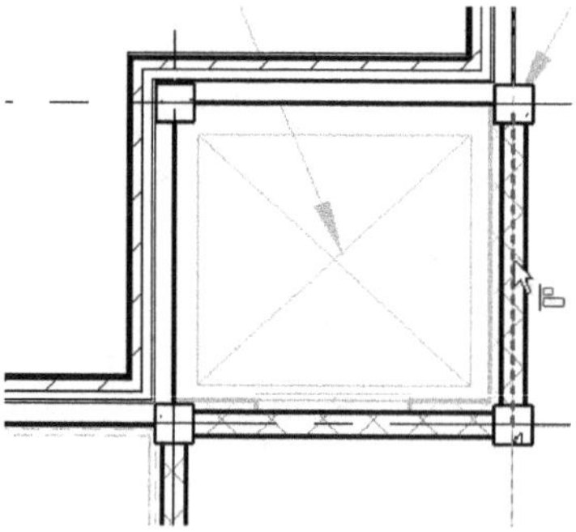

Figure 4–29

12. Click the padlock to lock the wall so that it is constrained to the grid line.

13. Repeat with the other two walls, aligning the center of the wall to the associated grid and locking the wall to the grid (Align the horizontal elevator wall to Grid 3 and the vertical stairs wall to the Grid B).

14. Return to the **Modify** command.

15. Use the drag controls on the ends of the walls to connect any of the places where the walls do not touch other walls.

16. Repeat the process of creating walls on the other stairwell. Align and lock the center line of the left concrete block wall to the grid line and the right concrete wall to the inside face of the exterior wall, as shown in Figure 4–30.

If required, before aligning, disallow the join between the interior and exterior walls. After everything is in place, you can enable the join again.

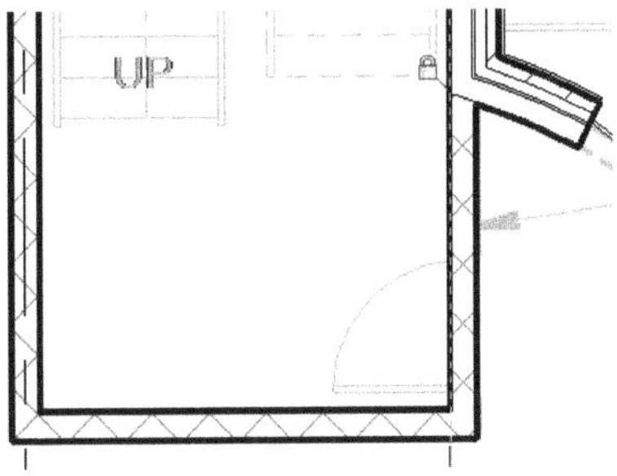

Figure 4–30

17. Zoom out to display the entire building floor plan.

18. Save the project.

Task 2 - Add the front desk and office walls.

---

1. Select the linked file. A blue rectangle enclosing the linked file with a pin in the center is displayed.

2. Right-click and select **Hide in View>Elements**. The linked file is hidden and only the elements are displayed.

3. Click (Wall) and set the following properties:

   - Wall type: **Basic Wall: Interior - 138mm Partition (1-hr)**
   - Height: **Floor 2**
   - Location Line: **Wall Centerline**
   - Top Offset: (negative) **-300mm**

Setting the Top Offset to a negative number leaves room for the floor above.

---

4. Draw the walls shown in Figure 4–31.

5. In the *Modify I Place Wall* tab>Modify panel, click ⊕ (Split Element).

6. Click the horizontal wall at the point shown in Figure 4–31.

Figure 4–31

7. Return to the **Modify** command.and select the wall on the left. Change the *Top Constraint* to **Unconnected** and the *Unconnected Height* to **1220mm**. This becomes the base for the Front Desk shelf.

8. Modify the lower wall to butt up against the taller walls, as shown in Figure 4–32.

Figure 4–32

Task 3 - Add the support room walls.

---

1. Pan over to the other stairwell and add the walls shown in Figure 4–33. Use the same wall type and properties as the other main interior walls.

In the Quick Access Toolbar, click ☰ (Thin Lines) to make the close-up easier to see.

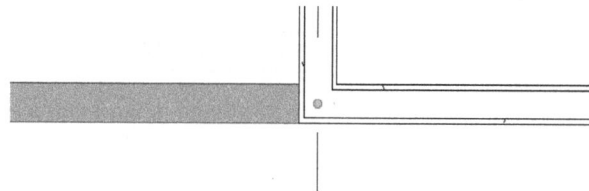

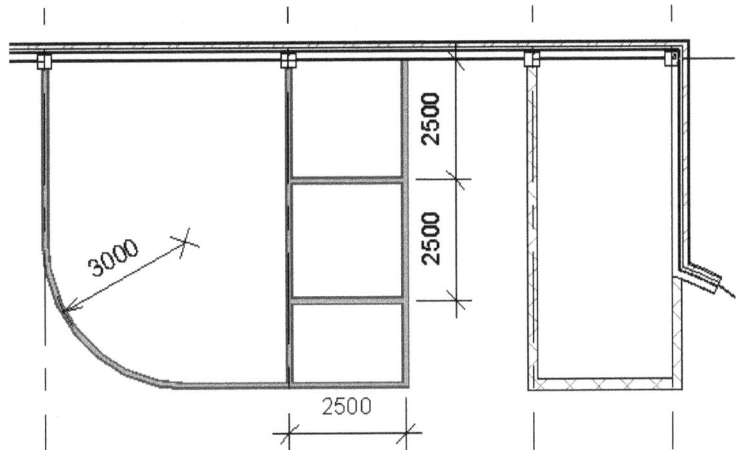

Figure 4–33

- Use 🔲 (Offset) to locate the 2500mm distance walls after you have drawn some of the others.

- Use 🔲 (Align) to match up the front face of the lower wall with the front face of the stairwell wall.

- To create the arc wall, add two straight walls first. Click

  🔲 (Fillet Arc), set the *Fillet radius* to **3000mm**, and select the two walls to create the arc at the corner.

- Use 🔲 (Trim/Extend to Corner), 🔲 (Trim/Extend

  Single), and 🔲 (Trim/Extend Multiple) as required to get the walls in place.

2. Zoom out and add a **2500mm** high curved wall to separate the Lobby from the Breakfast area, as shown in Figure 4–34.

The exact size and location does not matter, but ensure there is enough room for people to get by on both sides.

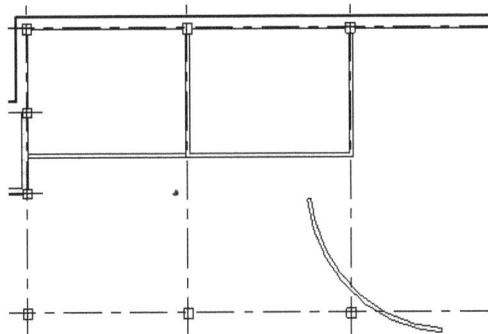

Figure 4–34

3. Zoom out and save the project.

Task 4 - Add typical guest floor walls.

1. Open the **Floor Plans: Floor 2** view. The view displays the walls created in the project, the linked drawing of the second floor, and the underlay of the Floor 1.

2. In Properties, change the *Underlay* to **None** to hide the underlay of Floor 1.

The linked drawing has been hidden in the view for clarity.

3. Add walls for the guest rooms, as shown in Figure 4–35, using the wall type **Interior - 138mm Partition (1-hr)** with a *Height* of **Floor 3** and a *Top Offset* of (negative) **-300mm**.

   • Align and lock the center of the vertical walls to the grids.

   • Ignore all of the door openings.

   • You can use (Copy) and (Mirror) to duplicate the walls once you have drawn one guest room layout.

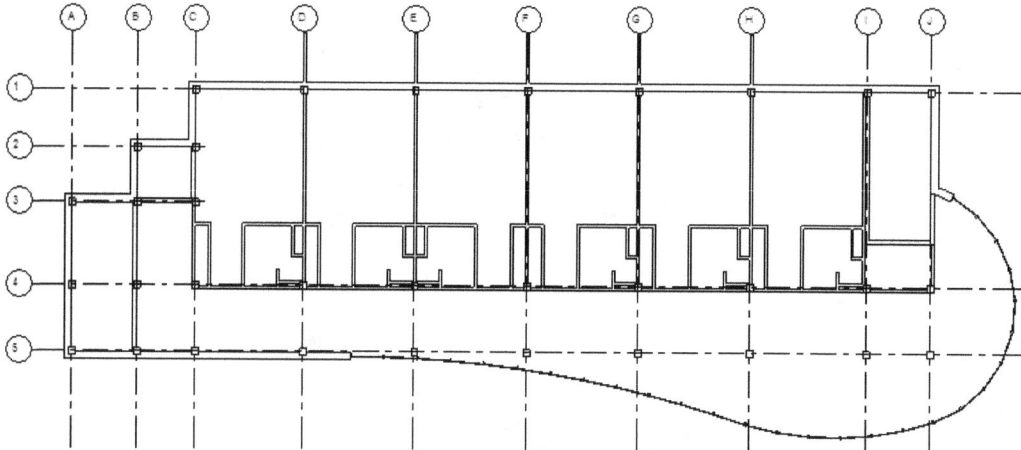

Figure 4–35

4. Return to **Floor Plans: Floor 1** view.

5. Save the project.

Chapter Review Questions

1. Where do you specify the height of a wall before you start drawing it? (Select all that apply.)

   a. In the *Modify | Place Wall* tab.

   b. In the Options Bar.

   c. In Properties Palette.

   d. In the Quick Access Toolbar.

2. Some walls are made from multiple layers of materials, such as brick, block, and drywall, as shown on the bottom in Figure 4–36. If the hatching for these materials is not displayed (as shown at the top in Figure 4–36), how do you change this?

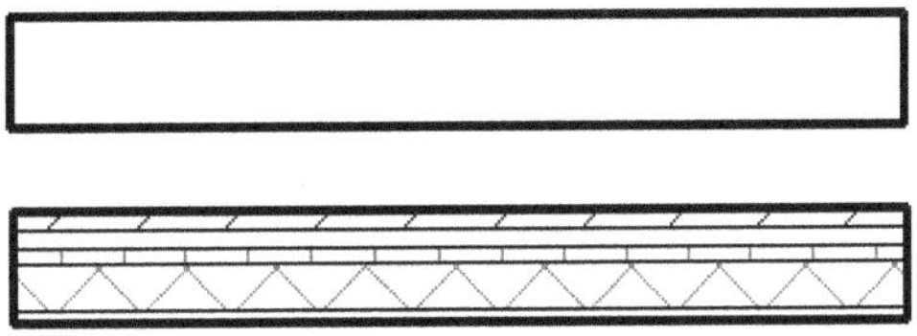

Figure 4–36

   a. Set the *Visual Style* to **Realistic**.

   b. Set the *Detail Level* to **Medium**.

   c. Set the *View Scale* to be higher.

   d. Set the *Phase* to **New**.

3. Which of the following tools allows you to change a wall from one made out of studs and brick, to one made out of concrete?

   a. Properties

   b. Change Wall

   c. Type Selector

   d. Edit Wall

4. Match the names for the following controls with the numbers shown in Figure 4–37.

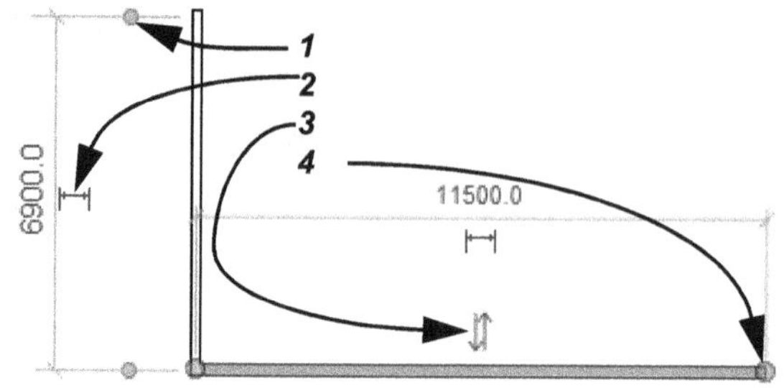

Figure 4–37

Control	Number
Drag wall end	
Flip	
Move witness line	
Make this temporary dimension permanent	

5. What is the difference between the column surround and the associated walls to the left and right shown in Figure 4–38? (Select all that apply.)

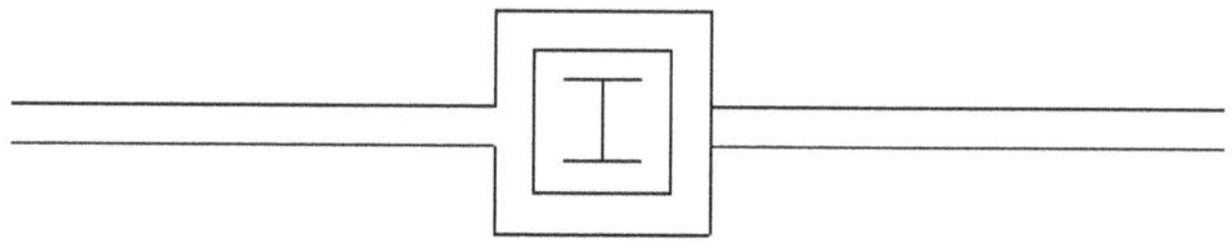

Figure 4–38

a. The column surround and wall on the left are made with the same wall type, while the wall type on the left is different.

b. The wall on the right has been joined together with the column surround, while the wall on the left was set to **Disallow Join**.

c. The wall on the left was trimmed against the column surround.

d. The wall on the right was extended to the column surround.

6. Which of the following would be true if you changed the top constraint of a wall to a level? (Select all that apply.)

   a. All walls of that type would also change height.

   b. Only that wall would change height.

   c. If you changed the height of the level, the wall height would change as well.

Command Summary

Button	Command	Location
	Detail Level: Coarse	• **View Control Bar**
	Detail Level: Fine	• **View Control Bar**
	Detail Level: Medium	• **View Control Bar**
	Edit Type/ Type Properties	• **Ribbon:** Modify tab>Properties panel • **Properties palette:** Edit Type
	Match Type	• **Ribbon:** Modify tab>Clipboard panel • **Shortcut:** \<M> and \<A>
	Properties	• **Ribbon:** Modify tab>Properties panel • **Shortcut:** \<P> and \<P>
N/A	**Type Selector**	• **Properties palette** • **Ribbon:** Modify tab (optional) • **Quick Access Toolbar** (optional)
	Wall	• **Ribbon:** Architecture tab>Build panel
	Wall Opening	• **Ribbon:** Architecture tab>Opening panel

Chapter 5

Working with Doors and Windows

In this chapter you learn how to insert doors and windows. You learn how to load and use door and window types as well as how to create additional sizes.

This chapter contains the following topics:

- **Inserting Doors and Windows**
- **Loading Door and Window Types from the Library**
- **Creating Additional Door and Window Sizes**

5.1 Inserting Doors and Windows

Autodesk Certification Topics & Objectives

Pro.   User

Elements
* Edit doors   ✓
* Edit windows   ✓

Learning Objectives

* Insert doors and windows in walls.
* Modify door and window locations.
* Set door and window properties.

Doors and windows in the Autodesk® Revit® software are designed to be hosted by walls. You can use alignment lines and temporary dimensions to help place the openings exactly where you need them in the walls, as shown in Figure 5–1.

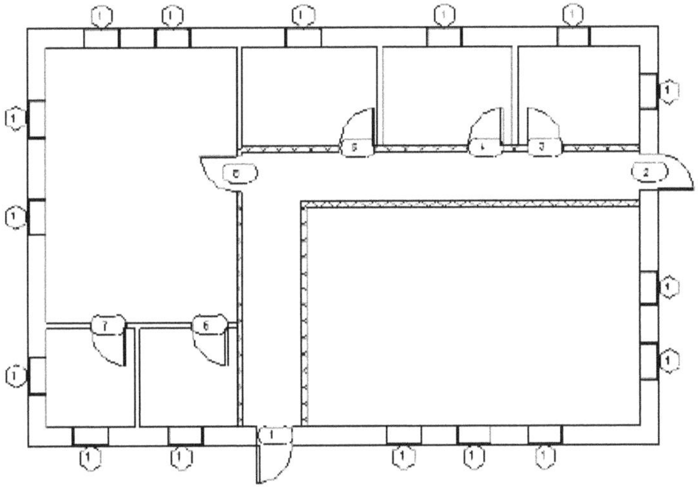

Figure 5–1

A variety of door and window types are included with the software's templates. However, you can also create your own custom types. Tags can be included automatically as you insert the door or window, or you can add them later as you build on the project.

- Additional door and window types are available in the Library or online at Autodesk® Seek.

- You can use the shortcut by pressing <S> and pressing <M> to place openings directly at the midpoint of wall segments.

How To: Add a Door or Window

1. In the *Architecture* tab>Build panel, click (Door) or

    (Window). You can also press <D> and then press <R> for the shortcut for the **Door** command, or press <W> and then press <N> for the shortcut for the **Window** command.
2. In the Type Selector, select the type of door or window, as shown in Figure 5–2.

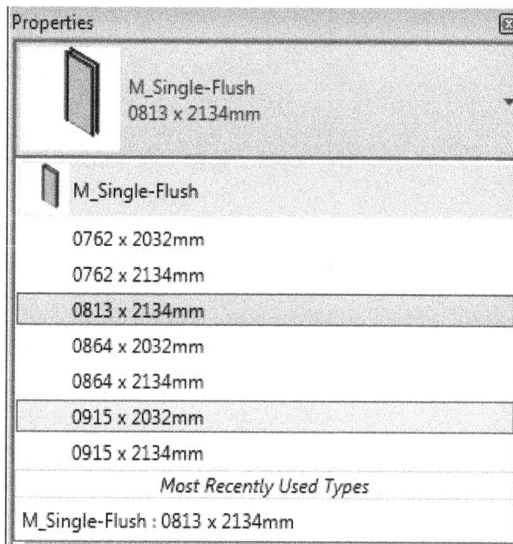

Figure 5–2

3. If the door or window type that you want is not listed, in the

    Modify | Place Door tab>Mode panel, click (Load Family), to load additional types from the Library.

4. To insert a tag with each door or window, verify that (Tag on Placement) is toggled on.
5. In the Options Bar, specify the tag options, as shown in Figure 5–3.

Figure 5–3

6. Select the wall to place the door or window. You can use the alignment lines and temporary dimensions to help position it.
7. Add another door or window or return to the **Modify** command to finish.

- While placing the door or window, you can adjust the element using temporary dimensions and the flip arrows to change the swing and hinge locations, as shown in Figure 5–4. With windows, you can flip the interior and exterior using the same technique.

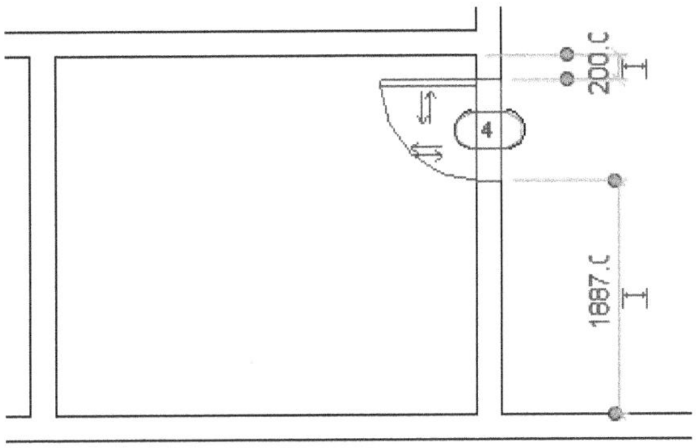

Figure 5–4

- If including window tags, select a point close to the outside of the wall when inserting the window so that the tag is placed on the outside.

- Other tag options in the Options Bar include **Horizontal** and **Vertical** text placement and Tags... , which opens the Loaded Tags dialog box. This dialog box contains a list of the tags loaded in the project. You can also load other tags here. If you want a tag to have a leader, select the **Leader** option and specify its length.

Modifying Doors and Windows

Doors and windows can be modified in many of the same ways as walls. In Figure 5–5, one window is changed to a different type and size using the Type Selector, a window is moved using temporary dimensions, and the door and one window are flipped using controls. Tags are also moved with a control.

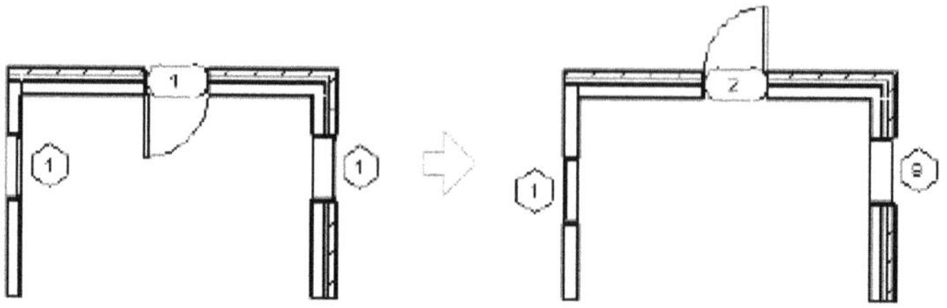

Figure 5–5

Modifying Door and Window Properties

The door or window types control most of their properties. To change the property information, you change the type in the Type Selector. You can also change Instance Parameters (such as **Level**, **Sill Height**, and materials), as shown in Figure 5–6, that impact the specific door or window in the associated schedule.

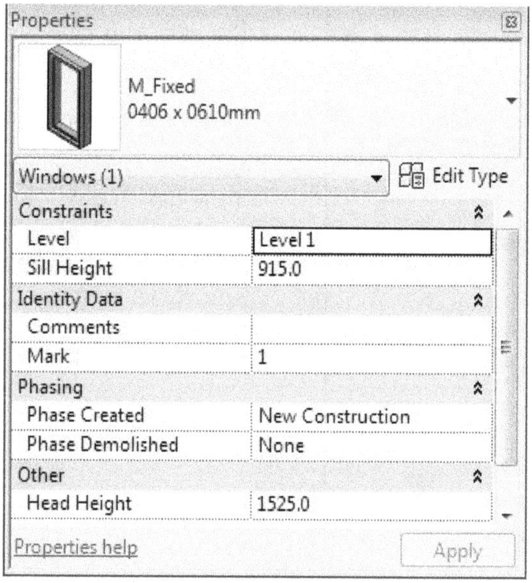

Figure 5–6

Temporary Dimensions with Doors and Windows

Temporary dimensions measure to the edge of the door or window and to the edge of the closest wall or opening (default), as shown in Figure 5–7.

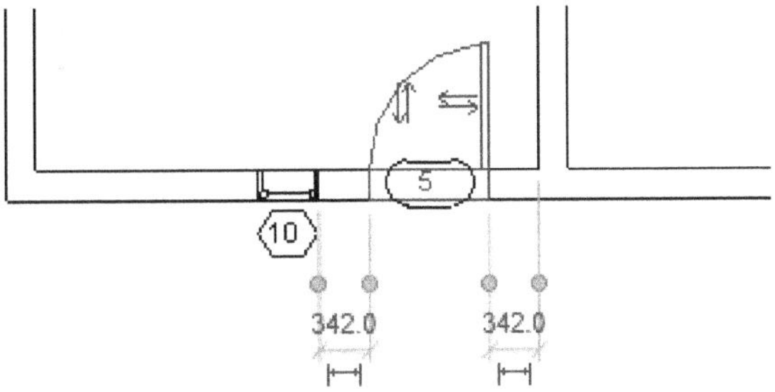

Figure 5–7

- Click the **Move Witness Line** control to toggle through the measurement reference options. The line snaps to the inside, center, and outside of the reference element.

- Once the witness line is toggled to a new location, the software remembers that location as long as the current session of the Autodesk Revit software is active.

Controls for Doors and Windows

Controls for doors and windows include **Flip the instance** *facing* and **Flip the instance** *hand*, as shown on the left in Figure 5–8.

- To move a door or window tag, select the tag. A control displays, as shown on the right in Figure 5–8, enabling you to drag it to a new location.

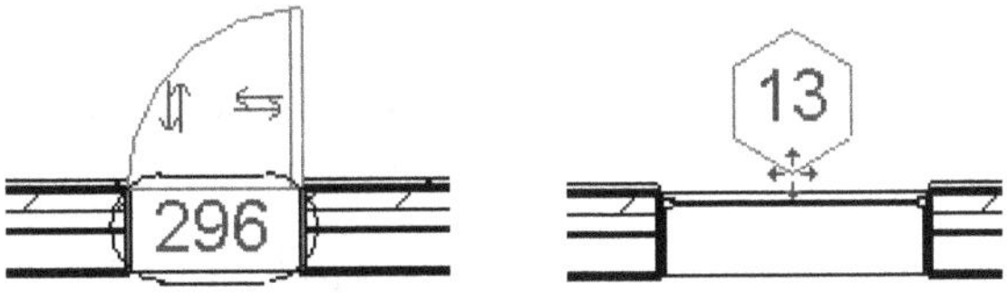

Figure 5–8

Hint: Copying Elements to Levels

The standard Windows commands ✂ (Cut or <Ctrl>+<X>),

▭ (Copy To Clipboard or <Ctrl>+<C>), and ▭ (Paste From Clipboard or <Ctrl>+<V>) work in the Autodesk Revit software just as they do in other Windows-compatible software. They are available in the *Modify* tab>Clipboard panel, but not in the right-click menu.

In the software, you can also paste elements aligned to various views or levels, as shown in Figure 5–9.

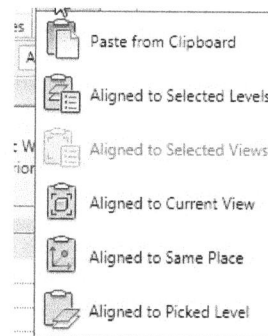

Figure 5–9

Aligned to Selected Levels: Opens a dialog box where you can select the level to which you want to copy. This enables you to copy items on one level and paste them to the same location on another level (e.g., windows in a high-rise building).

Aligned to Selected Views: Copies view-specific elements (such as text or dimensions) into a view that you select in a dialog box. Only the Floor Plan or Reflected Ceiling Plan views are available.

Aligned to Current View: Pastes elements copied in one view to the same location in another view.

Aligned to Same Place: Pastes elements to the same location in the same view.

Aligned to Picked Level: Pastes elements to the level you select in an elevation or section view.

Practice 5a

Insert Doors and Windows

✅ **Learning Objectives**

- Add doors and windows with tags.
- Use controls and temporary dimensions to place doors and windows.
- Copy windows to multiple levels.

Estimated time for completion: 15 minutes

In this practice you will add doors and windows to a model, as shown for Floor 1 in Figure 5–10. You will use controls, temporary dimensions, and dimensions set to equal to place the doors and windows.

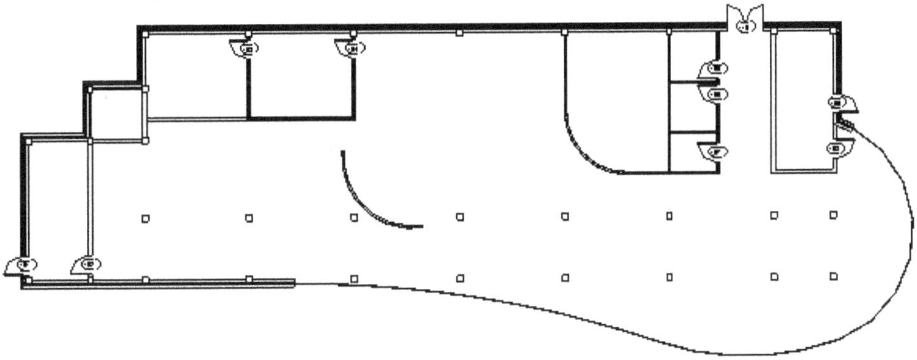

Figure 5–10

Task 1 - Add doors.

1. Open the project **Modern-Hotel-Doors-M.rvt** from your class folder.

2. Working in the **Floor Plans: Floor 1** view, select one of the grid lines. Right-click and select **Hide in view>Category** to turn off all of the grid lines.

3. In the *Architecture* tab>Build panel, click 🚪 (Door).

4. In the Type Selector, select **M_Single-Flush: 0915 x 2134mm**

5. In the *Modify | Place Door* tab>Tag panel, verify that 🏷️ (Tag on Placement) is on.

6. Place the door near the lower left corner of the building, as shown in Figure 5–11. Use the flip arrows to make it swing in the right direction and use temporary dimensions to place it to the correct location on the wall. Click on the tag and change the number to **101**.

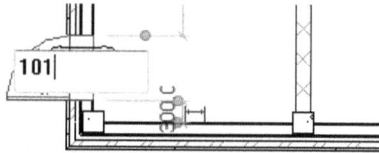

Figure 5–11

7. Continue adding single flush doors in the project, similar to the locations shown in Figure 5–12. Use the same door type. The tag number automatically increments.

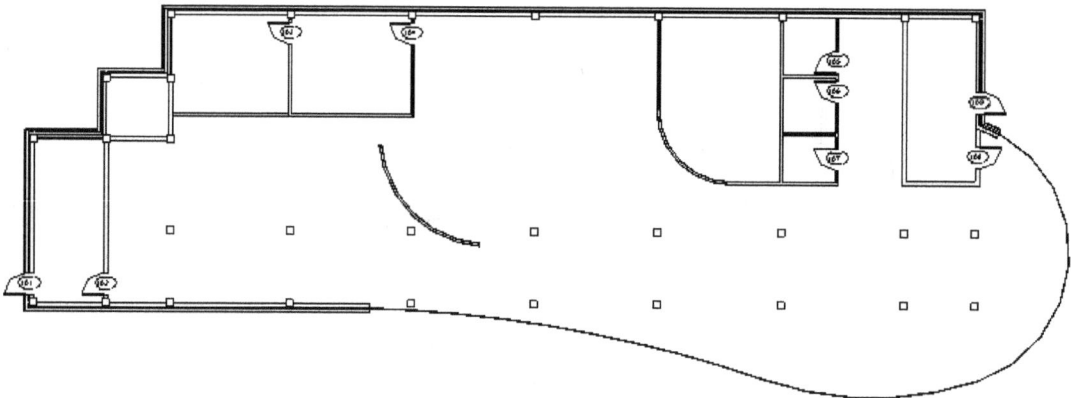

Figure 5–12

8. Click ⬚ (Modify) and select the two sets of stairwell doors (two doors on the left side and two doors on the right side of the building).

   • If you select multiple categories, use ▽ (Filter) to help select only the doors.

9. In the Type Selector, select **M_Single-Flush Vision: 0915 x 2032mm**.

10. Zoom in on the upper right corner of the building, in the area of the stairwell and hallway.

11. Click (Door) and in the Type Selector, select **M_Double-Glass 1: 1830 x 2134mm**.

12. Place the door at the end of the hall. At this point the location does not need to be exact as you are going to modify the placement in the following steps.

13. In the Quick Access Toolbar, click (Aligned Dimension). Note that by starting another command, you automatically end the previous command.)

Press <Tab> to cycle through the reference points.

14. For the dimension locations select the inside of the left wall, the center of the door, and in the inside of the right wall, as shown on the left in Figure 5–13. Click to place the dimension.

15. Click the **EQ** control. The door is centered evenly between the two walls, as shown on the right in Figure 5–13. Lock the padlocks. This keeps the door centered on the interior of the walls even if the location of the walls change.

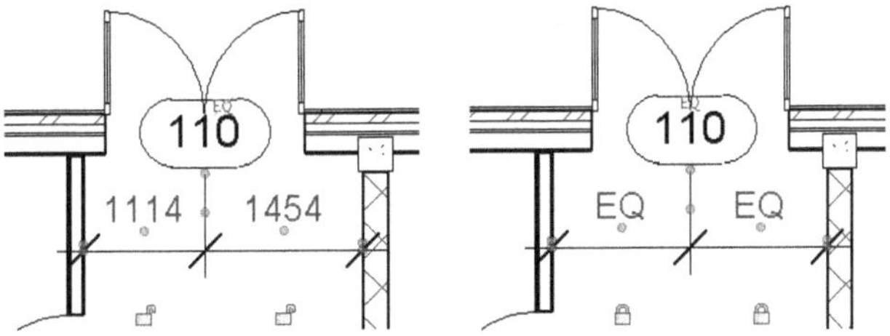

Figure 5–13

16. Delete the dimension. An alert displays, as shown in Figure 5–14. In this case, you want the dimensions constrained to be equal. Click [OK].

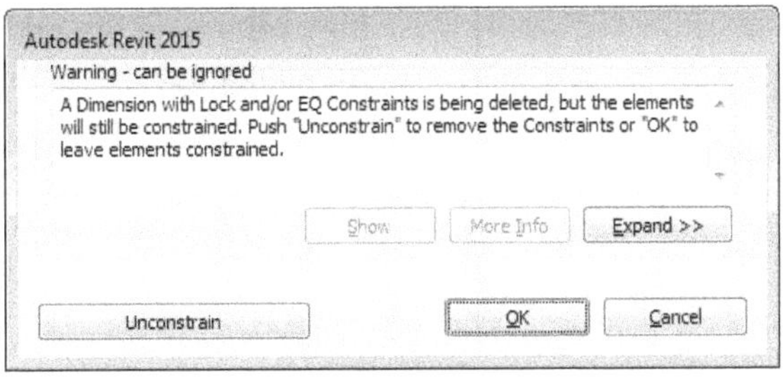

Figure 5–14

17. Zoom out to see the full floor plan.

18. Save the project.

Task 2 - Add and copy windows.

1. Open the **Floor Plans: Floor 2** view.

2. The linked CAD file is still displayed in this view. Select it and in the Status Bar click ⌖ (Temporary Hide/Isolate)>**Hide Element**. Leave the grids displayed, as they enable you to place the windows correctly.

3. In the *Architecture* tab>Build panel, click ▦ (Window).

4. In the *Modify | Place Window* tab>Tag panel, verify that ⌖ (Tag on Placement) is turned on.

5. In the Type Selector, select **Casement 3x3 with Trim: 1220 x 1220mm**.

6. Add four windows along the lower exterior wall, as shown in Figure 5–15. The exact location is not important right now.

Figure 5–15

7. Click ⌖ (Modify) and select the window closest to the stair. Move the witness lines of the temporary dimensions so that they reference the grid line and the center of the window. Set the dimension to 1400mm. as shown in Figure 5–16

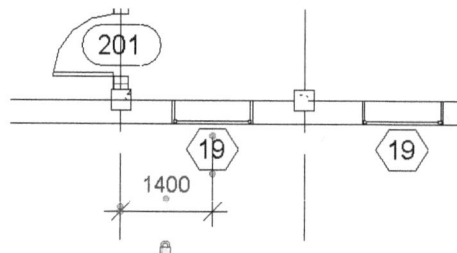

Figure 5–16

8. In the Quick Access Toolbar or in the *Annotate* tab>
Dimension panel, click ✎ (Aligned Dimension). Dimension from the grid to the center of the window and lock the dimension in place, as shown in Figure 5–17.

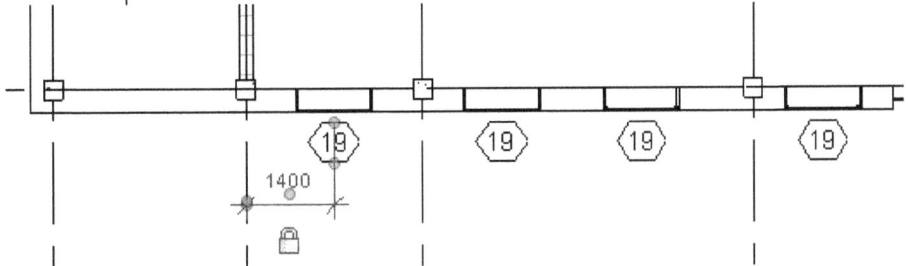

Figure 5–17

9. With the ✎ (Aligned Dimension) still active, dimension from center to center of the windows. Click the **EQ** control and lock the padlocks, as shown in Figure 5–18.

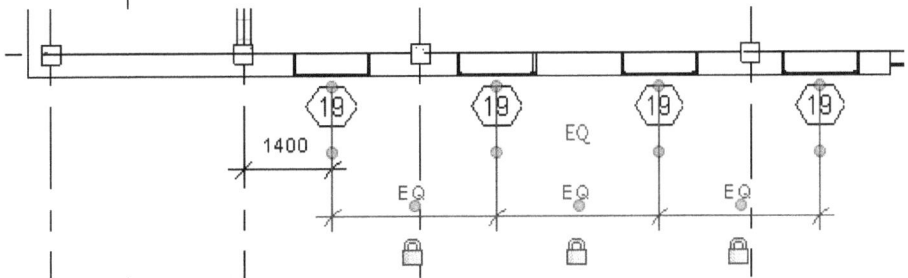

Figure 5–18

10. Delete the dimensions, but keep the constraints.

11. Open the 3D view and verify that the front of the building where the windows are located is displayed.

12. Select all four windows by holding down <Ctrl> and selecting each one.

13. In the *Modify | Windows* tab>Clipboard panel, click 🗐 (Copy to Clipboard).

14. In the Clipboard panel, expand 🗐 (Paste) and click 🗐 (Aligned to Selected Levels).

15. In the Select Levels dialog box, select the floors between and including **Floor 3** and **Floor 8**, as shown in Figure 5–19.

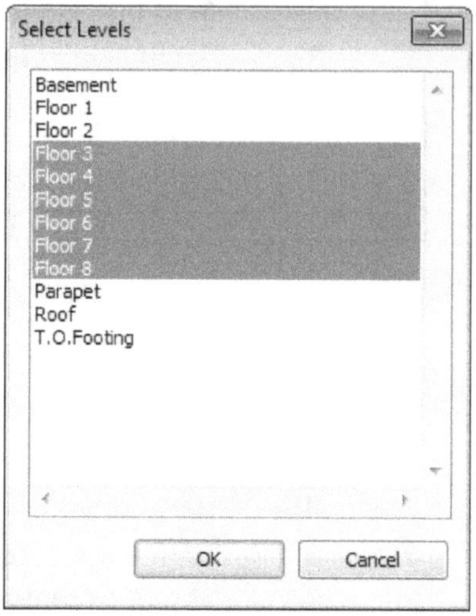

Figure 5–19

16. Click [OK]. The windows are copied up the side of the building, as shown in Figure 5–20.

Additional doors and windows will be placed using storefront curtain walls.

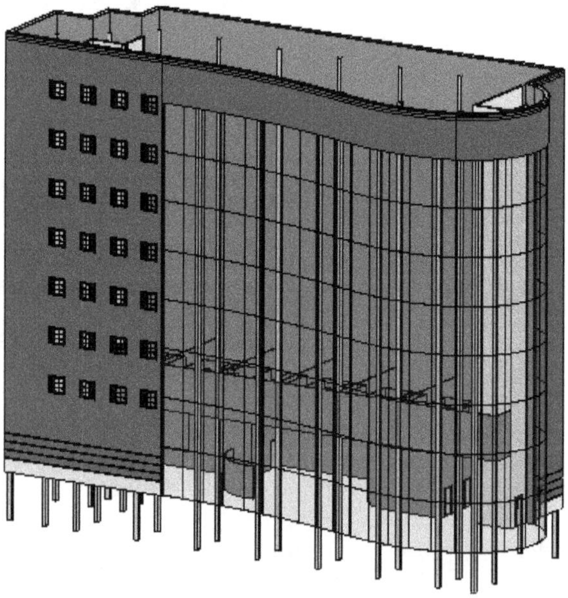

Figure 5–20

17. Save the project.

5.2 Loading Door and Window Types from the Library

Learning Objective

- Load door and window types from the library.

A variety of door and window types are available in the Autodesk Revit Library. They are grouped in *family* files with the extension RFA. For example, a door family named **Double-Panel 1.rfa** can contain several types and sizes of doors, as shown in Figure 5–21.

The process is the same for loading all types of families.

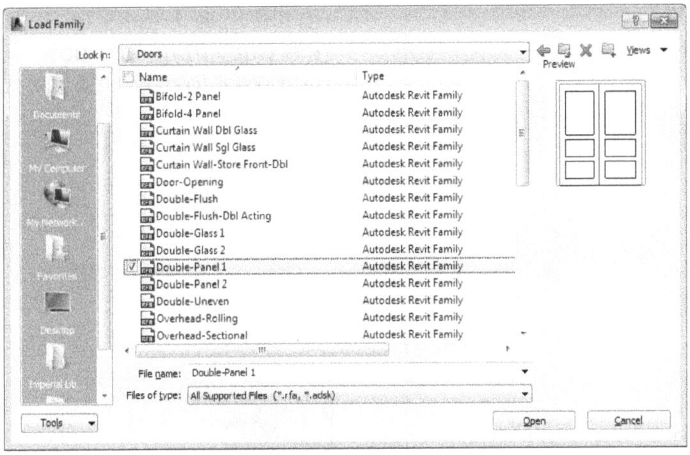

Figure 5–21

How To: Load a Family

1. Start the **Door** or **Window** command and, in the *Modify | Place [Door / Window]* tab>Mode panel or the *Insert* tab>Load from Library panel, click (Load Family).
2. In the Load Family dialog box, find the folder that contains the family you want to load and select the family.
3. Click Open .
4. Once the family is loaded, in the Type Selector, select the component you want to use.

- When you are working within a command such as **Door** or **Window**, you can only load families that are from that category of elements. For example, you cannot load window families while working in the **Door** command.

- There are several families used for openings. In the *Doors* folder: **Door-Opening.rfa** and in the *Windows* folder: **Window-Round Opening.rfa** and **Window-Square Opening.rfa**.

Hint: Transferring Project Standards

Some elements (such as wall types) are not accessible from a specific library. However, you can copy them from other projects.

1. Open the project from which you want to copy information.
2. Open the project to which you want to copy the information.

3. In the *Manage* tab>Settings panel, click 🔲 (Transfer Project Standards).
4. In the Select Items To Copy dialog box, select an option in the *Copy from* drop-down list and then select the settings you want to copy into the current file, as shown in Figure 5–22. Click ⬜ OK ⬜ .

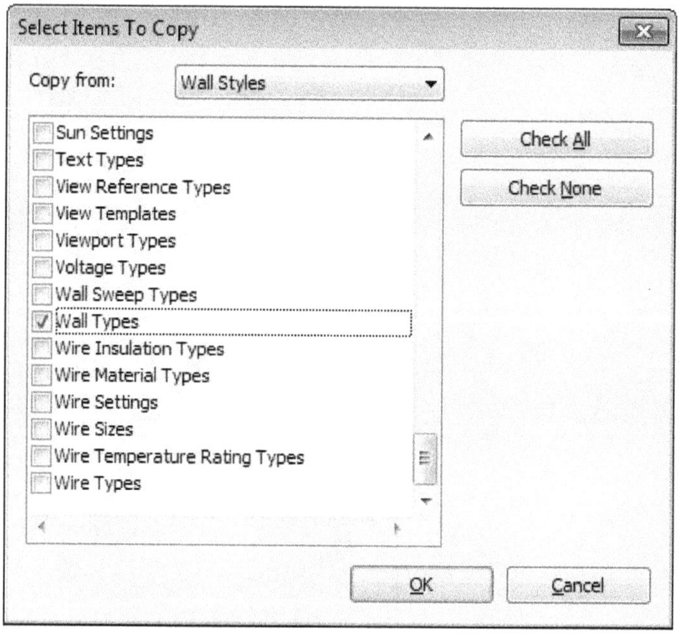

Figure 5–22

5. In the Duplicate Types dialog box, click either ⬜ Overwrite ⬜ or ⬜ New Only ⬜ to apply the settings to the current project.

5.3 Creating Additional Door and Window Sizes

Autodesk Certification Topics & Objectives

Pro.   User

Elements

* Create a new family type ✓

Learning Objective

* Duplicate door and window types and modify the sizes.

You can easily add additional sizes to existing families of doors or windows that have been loaded into a project. To do this, you create a new type of the required size based on an existing type, as shown in Figure 5–23.

You can specify materials for door and window sub-elements in the Type Properties.

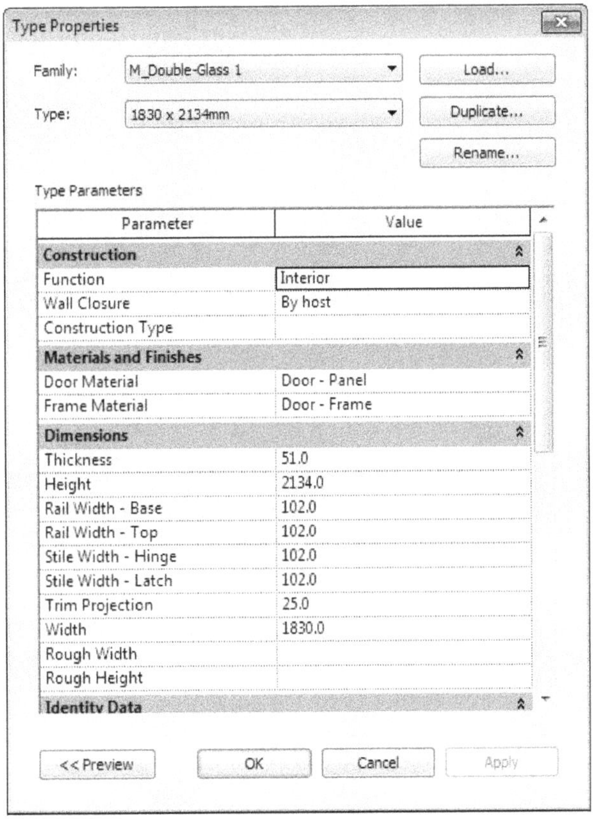

Figure 5–23

How To: Create Additional Door and Window Sizes

1. Start the **Door** or **Window** command.
2. In the Type Selector, select the type you want to modify. In Properties, click ▦ (Edit Type) or in the *Modify* tab> Properties panel, click ▦ (Type Properties).
3. In the Type Properties dialog box, click [Duplicate].
4. Type a new name for the element and click [OK].
5. In the Type Properties dialog box, change the *Height* and *Width* parameters to match the size.
6. Click [OK] to close the dialog box. The new window or door type is now available for use.

Hint: Measuring Distances

As you are working in a project, you might need to know some existing distances. Two methods can be used: **Measure Between Two References** and **Measure Along An Element**. Both are available in the Quick Access Toolbar (as shown in Figure 5–24), as well as in the *Modify* tab>Measure panel.

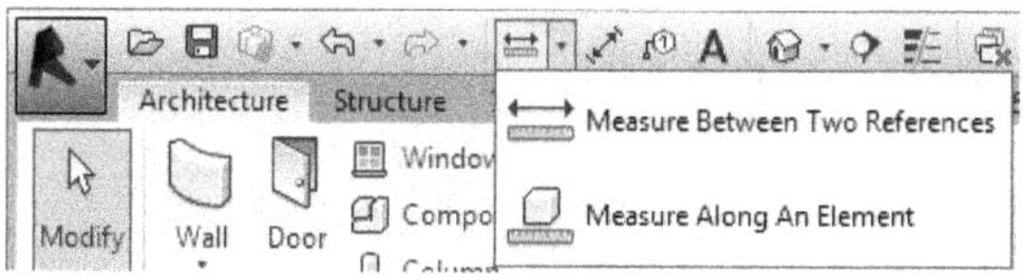

Figure 5–24

- To measure between two references, select the references, which can include any snap point, wall lines, or other references (such as door center lines).

- To measure along an element, select the element you want to measure or use <Tab> to select other elements and then click to measure along all of them, as shown in Figure 5–25.

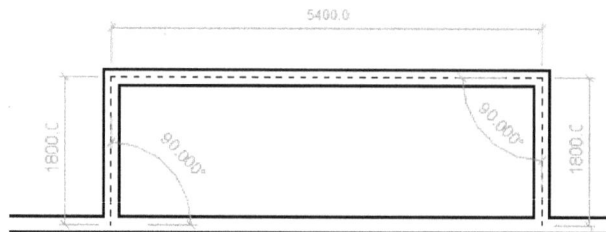

Figure 5–25

Practice 5b

Load and Create Door Types

Learning Objectives

- Load door types.
- Duplicate and modify a door type.

Estimated time for completion: 15 minutes

In this practice you will load door types, create a new door size, and add doors to the 2nd floor, as shown in Figure 5–26.

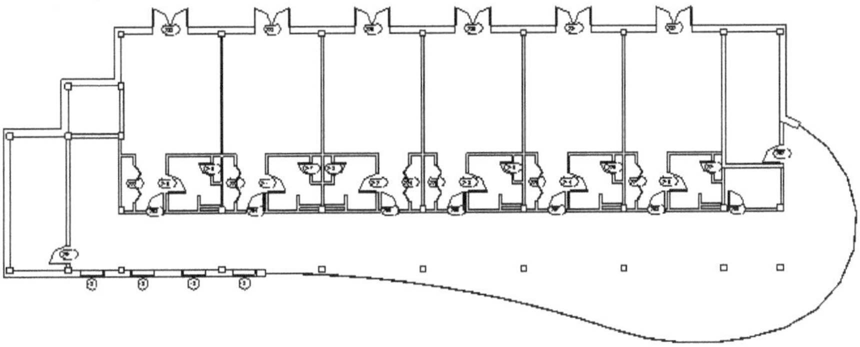

Figure 5–26

Task 1 - Load door types.

1. Open the project **Modern-Hotel-Load-M.rvt** from the class folder.

2. In the *Architecture* tab>Build panel, click (Door).

3. In the *Modify | Place Door* tab>Mode panel, click (Load Family).

To select more than one file at a time, hold down <Ctrl> as you select.

4. In the Load Family dialog box, navigate to the *Doors* folder. Select **M_Double-Flush-Dbl Acting.rfa** and

   M_Single-Panel 4.rfa and click Open .

5. In the **Floor 1** plan, zoom in on the kitchen area.

6. In the Type Selector, select **M_Double-Flush-Dlb Acting: 1830 x 2083mm**, and place an instance of it in the wall between the kitchen and dining area, as shown in Figure 5–27.

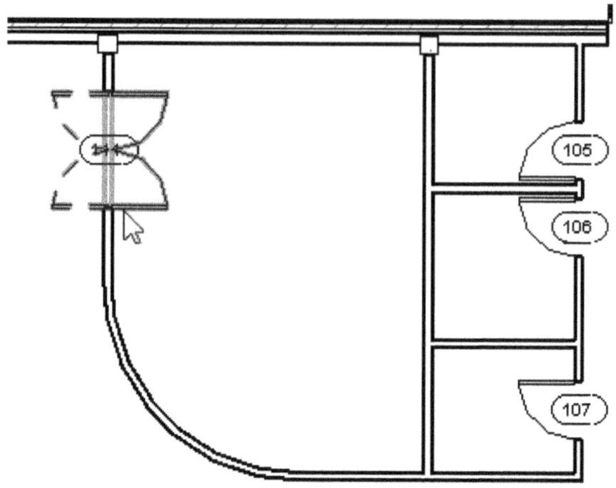

Figure 5–27

7. Zoom to the extents of the view and save the project.

Task 2 - Add doors to Floor 2.

---

1. Open the **Floor Plans: Floor 2** view.

2. To make the view easier to read, temporarily hide the grids. Leave the linked CAD file displayed to help place the doors.

3. In the *Architecture* tab>Build panel, click (Door).

4. In the Type Selector, select **M_Single-Flush-Vision: 0915 x 2032mm.**

5. Place the first door in the lower left stairwell as shown in the linked file and change the tag number to **201**.

6. Add another door of the same type to the other stairwell at the opposite end of the building.

7. Change the door type to **M_Single-Panel 4: 0915 x 2032mm** and place a door at the entrance of each of the rooms, using the CAD file as a guideline.

8. Use the same type to add doors to the bathrooms.

The door to the small closet in the guest bathroom is smaller than the existing door sizes. Therefore, you need to find out what size it is and create a new size.

9. Change the door type to **M_Single Flush: 0762 x 2032mm**.

10. In Properties, click [Edit Type] (Edit Type) or in the *Modify | Place Door* tab>Properties panel, click [Type Properties] (Type Properties).

11. In the Type Properties dialog box, click [Duplicate].

12. Enter **0620 x 2032mm** for the name and click [OK].

13. In the Type Properties dialog box, change the **Width** parameter to **620mm**.

14. Click [OK] to close the dialog box. The new door type is available for use. Add it to the small closets.

15. Continue adding other doors using different door styles (i.e., Bifold and Double-Glass). The rooms should look similar to the layout shown in Figure 5–28, though your numbering might be different.

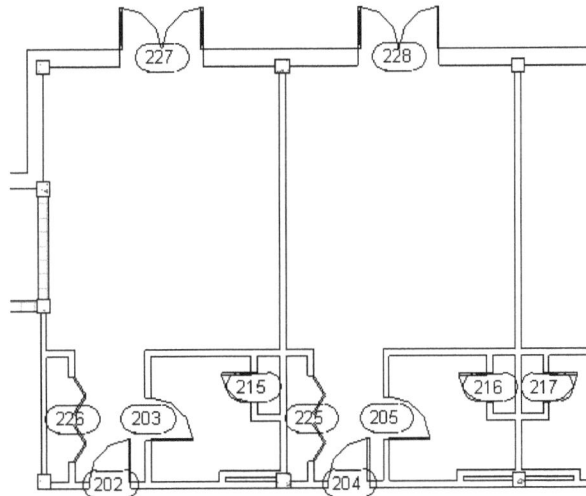

Figure 5–28

16. Select and hide the CAD file.

17. Save the project.

Chapter Review Questions

1. How do you change the swing direction of a door, as shown in Figure 5–29? (Select all that apply.)

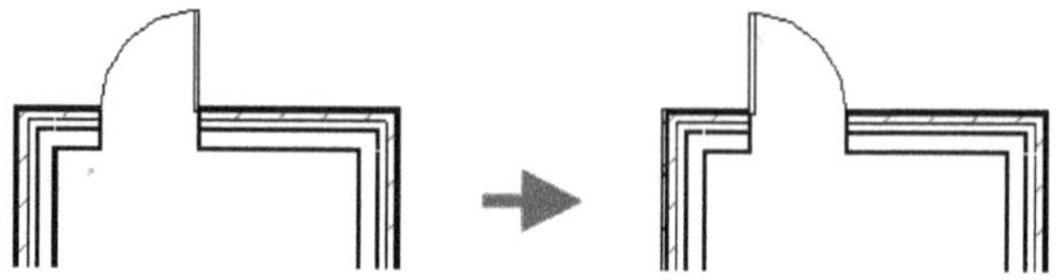

Figure 5–29

   a. When placing the door, press <Spacebar>.

   b. When placing the door, right-click and select **Change Swing**.

   c. Select an existing door and select the flip arrows.

   d. Select an existing door, right-click and select **Change Swing**.

2. How do you add additional window or door families to a project?

   a. Find the window or door family using Windows Explorer, right-click and select **Import into Revit Project**.

   b. Import them from the Window or Door Catalog.

   c. Load them from the Library.

   d. Use the Window/Door Wizard to create new families.

3. How do you include a tag with a door or window, as shown in Figure 5–30?

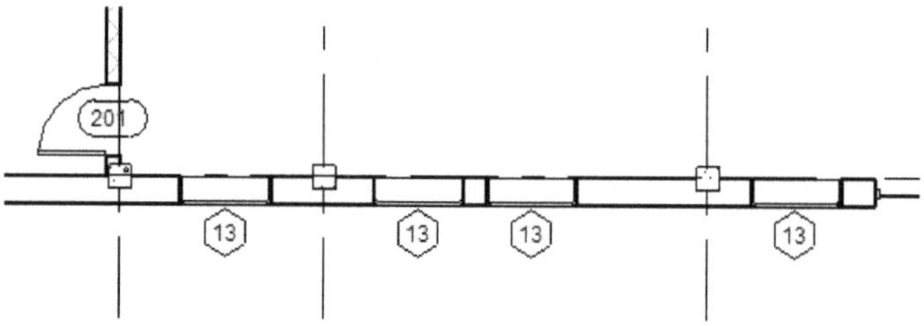

Figure 5–30

   a. Select a door or window family that includes a tag.

   b. Select the Tag box in the Options Bar before placing the door or window.

   c. Tags can only be used after placing the door or window.

   d. Select **Tag on Placement** in the contextual tab.

4. Where are the door and window sizes stored?

   a. In Properties.

   b. In Type Properties.

   c. In Door/ Window Settings.

   d. In the template file.

5. How do you create additional door or window sizes, as shown in Figure 5–31?

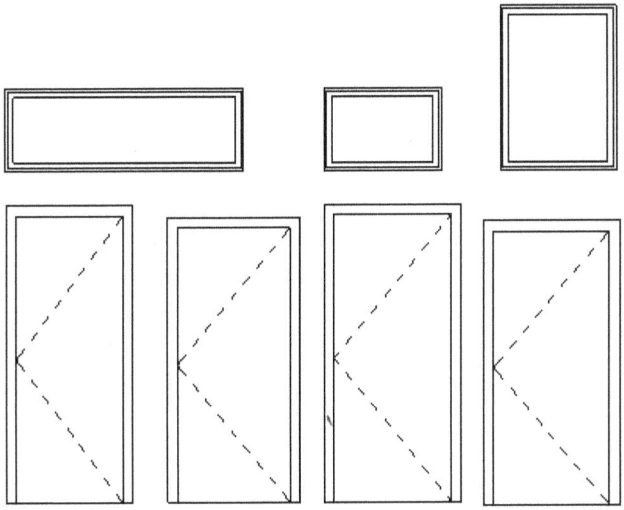

Figure 5–31

   a. Select the required door or window and use the Size Wizard to specify a new size.

   b. Select the required door or window and in Type Properties, Duplicate an existing door and modify it.

   c. Find the existing door or window family in the Project Browser, right-click and select **New Size**.

   d. Select the door or window in the view, and edit it using size controls to the required size.

Command Summary

Button	Command	Location
Clipboard		
	Copy to Clipboard	• **Ribbon:** *Modify* tab>Clipboard panel • **Shortcut:** <Ctrl>+<C>
	Cut to the Clipboard	• **Ribbon:** *Modify* tab>Clipboard panel • **Shortcut:** <Ctrl>+<X>
	Paste - Aligned to Current View	• **Ribbon:** *Modify* tab>Clipboard panel> expand Paste
	Paste - Aligned to Same Place	• **Ribbon:** *Modify* tab>Clipboard panel> expand Paste
	Paste - Aligned to Selected Levels	• **Ribbon:** *Modify* tab>Clipboard panel> expand Paste
	Paste - Aligned to Selected Views	• **Ribbon:** *Modify* tab>Clipboard panel> expand Paste
	Paste - Aligned to Picked Level	• **Ribbon:** *Modify* tab>Clipboard panel> expand Paste
	Paste from Clipboard	• **Ribbon:** *Modify* tab>Clipboard panel • **Shortcut:** <Ctrl>+<V>
Doors and Windows		
	Door	• **Ribbon:** *Architecture* tab>Build panel • **Shortcut:** <D> and <R>
	Edit Type/ Type Properties	• **Properties palette:** Edit Type • **Ribbon:** *Modify* tab>Properties panel
	Measure	• **Quick Access Toolbar** • **Ribbon:** *Modify* tab>Measure panel
	Window	• **Ribbon:** *Architecture* tab>Build panel • **Shortcut:** <W> and <N>

Chapter 6

Working with Curtain Walls

In this chapter you learn how to create curtain walls, create curtain wall types with automatic grids, apply and create curtain wall panels, and attach mullions to curtain grids.

This chapter contains the following topics:

- **Creating Curtain Walls**
- **Adding Curtain Grids**
- **Working with Curtain Wall Panels**
- **Attaching Mullions to Curtain Grids**

6.1 Creating Curtain Walls

Learning Objective

- Create curtain walls and storefronts using special wall types.

Curtain walls are non-bearing walls consisting of panels laid out in a grid pattern. They can encase an entire building like a membrane or, as shown in Figure 6–1, fill a cutout in a standard wall, often called a storefront.

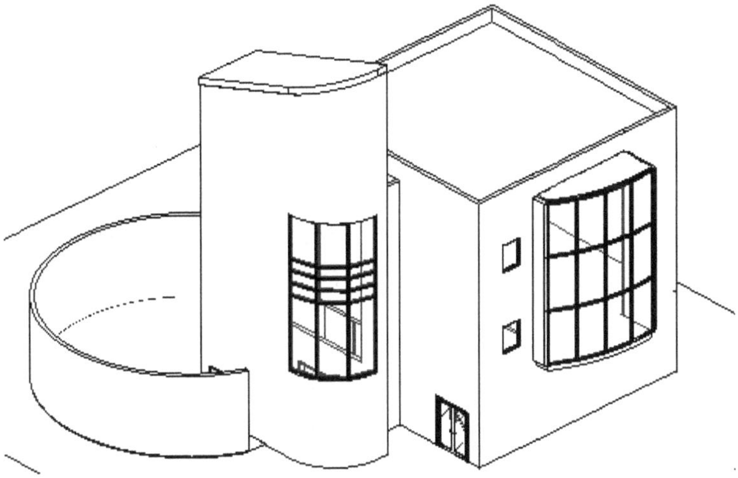

Figure 6–1

How To: Create a Curtain Wall.

1. In a plan view, draw a wall using a curtain wall type.
2. In an elevation or 3D view, add grids to the curtain wall.
3. Modify the panels of the curtain wall. Panels can be a specific material (such as glass or stone) or can incorporate doors, windows, or other wall types.
4. Add mullions to separate the panels.

The components of a curtain wall are shown in Figure 6–2.

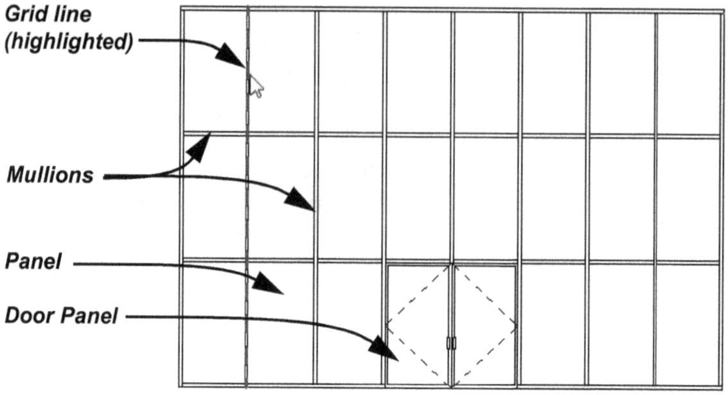

Grid line
(highlighted)

Mullions

Panel

Door Panel

Figure 6–2

- The simplest way to create a curtain wall is to use a curtain wall type with a preset uniform grid already applied to it, such as **Curtain Wall:Exterior Glazing** or **Curtain Wall: Storefront**, which come with the software, as shown in Figure 6–3.

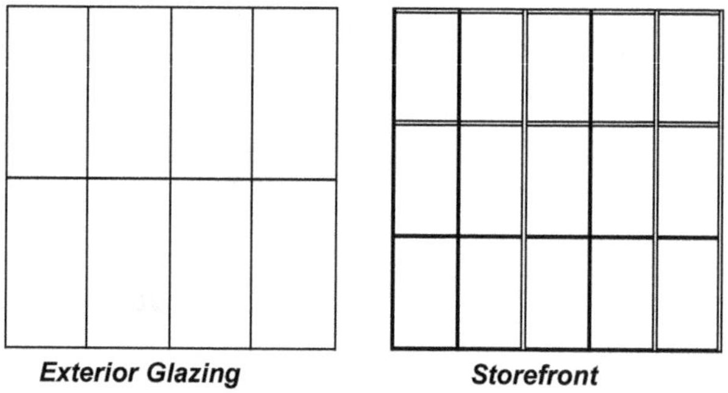

Exterior Glazing   *Storefront*

Figure 6–3

- The Autodesk® Revit® software also comes with a standard curtain wall type, **Curtain Wall 1**, that creates a single glass panel to which you can apply a grid in any pattern.

- Many curtain walls do not have a uniform pattern of exact distances between grids, as shown in Figure 6–4. Therefore, you need to create these designs directly on the curtain wall. You can start with a curtain wall type that has a basic uniform grid, if applicable.

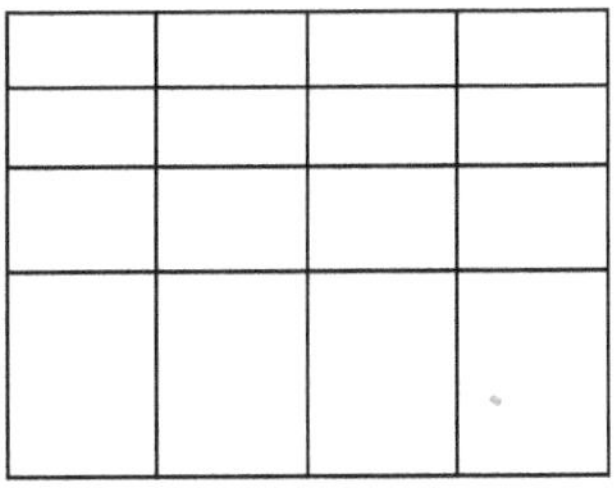

Figure 6–4

Creating Storefronts

Storefronts are a special type of curtain wall that can be embedded into other walls, as shown in Figure 6–5. They can also be used to create what looks like a complex set of windows. Some curtain wall types, such as the **Storefront** wall type, are designed to be embedded in another wall.

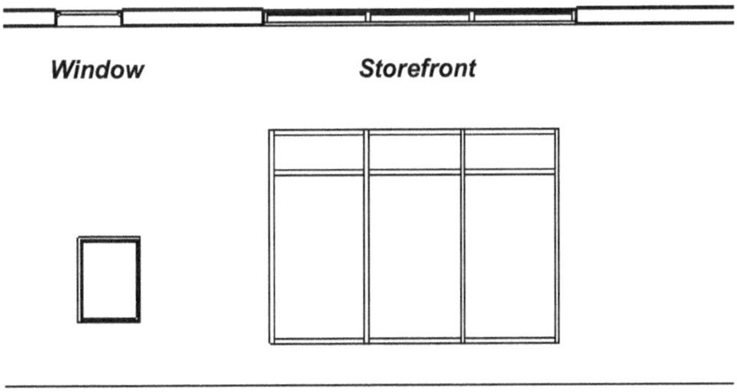

Window   *Storefront*

Figure 6–5

How To: Add a Storefront Wall in an Existing Wall

1. In the *Architecture* tab>Build panel, click ⬭ (Wall).
2. In the Type Selector, select the curtain wall type you want to use. In Properties, set the *Base Constraint, Top Constraint*, and *Offsets* as required. The height can be less than the height of the wall in which you are embedding.
3. Select a point on the existing wall, as shown in Figure 6–6.

Figure 6–6

4. Press <Tab> to cycle from the default Horizontal and Nearest snap to the dynamic dimension. Type the distance for the embedded curtain wall. The wall displays as shown in Figure 6–7.

Figure 6–7

5. Open the appropriate elevation view. Select the outside edge of the curtain wall and use the shape handles and dynamic dimensions, as shown in Figure 6–8, to place the storefront in the wall as required.

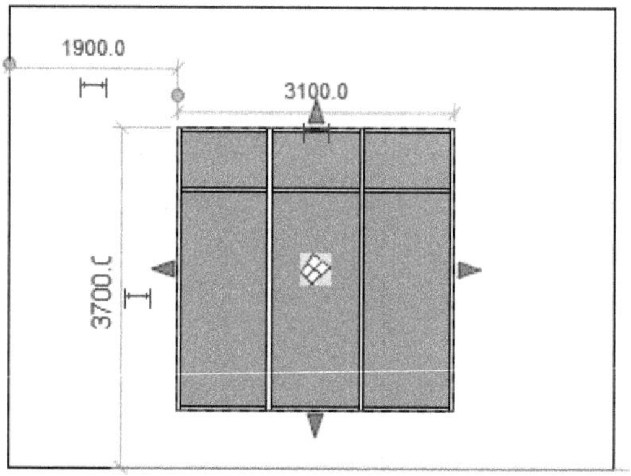

Figure 6–8

6.2 Adding Curtain Grids

Autodesk Certification Topics & Objectives

	Pro.	User

Elements

• Change elements within a curtain wall	✓	

Learning Objective

- Add and remove segments to create a curtain grid pattern.

Once you have a curtain wall in place with at least one panel, you need to separate it into multiple panels for the design. Each grid line divides a panel into two or more smaller panels, as shown in Figure 6–9.

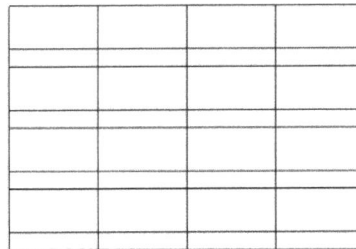

Figure 6–9

How To: Create a Curtain Grid

1. After you have drawn the base curtain wall in a plan view, switch to an elevation or 3D view.

2. In the *Architecture* tab>Build panel, click ⊞ (Curtain Grid).
3. In the *Modify | Place Curtain Grid* tab>Placement panel, select an insertion method, as described below.

╪ **(All Segments)**	Creates a grid line through the entire curtain wall height or width.
╪ **(One Segment)**	Creates a grid line between only the selection point and the next line. The entire grid line is established, but only one segment displays. You can add other segments later.

╪ **(All Except Picked)**	Creates a grid line through the entire grid and permits you to go back and remove segments of the grid line. The removed segment displays as a dashed line until you draw another grid line or start another command.

4. Move the cursor over an edge of the curtain wall or an existing grid line. Dynamic dimensions are displayed, as shown in Figure 6–10. The new grid line is perpendicular to the edge at the point you select. Click at the required location.

Figure 6–10

- Curtain grids automatically snap to the midpoint or 1/3 point of the panel. They also snap to levels, column grids, and reference planes.

- You can use (Copy) and (Array) on the curtain grid lines. This method can be the fastest way of creating grids across the length of a wall.

- You can add additional grids to curtain wall types that include grids when they are created.

Modifying Curtain Grids

Once you have placed the grid lines, they might not be exactly where you want them or overlap other lines where you do not want them to overlap. You can modify the location of lines in the grid and add or remove segments from the lines, as shown in Figure 6–11.

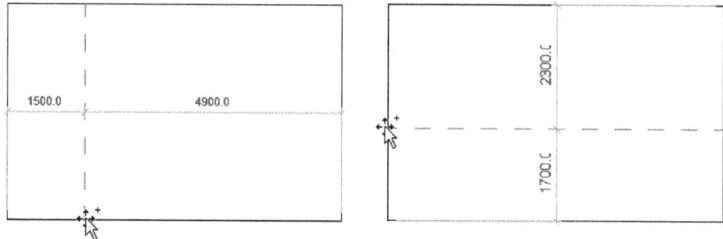

Figure 6–11

- To modify the grid, you must select a grid line, not a wall or the mullion. Press <Tab> to cycle through elements.

- To move a grid line, select it and use dynamic dimensions or ⊕ (Move).

- If you select a grid line that was created using a curtain wall type, ◎ (Push Pin) is displayed, indicating that the element is constrained. Click on the icon to enable the line to move.

How To: Add or Remove Segments of Curtain Grids

1. Select a grid line to modify.
2. In the Modify |Curtain Wall Grids tab>Curtain Grid panel, click ⊬ (Add/Remove Segments).
3. Click on the part of the grid that you want to add or remove. The line displays as dashed when you click to remove a segment, as shown in Figure 6–12. You must select grid lines one at a time with this command.

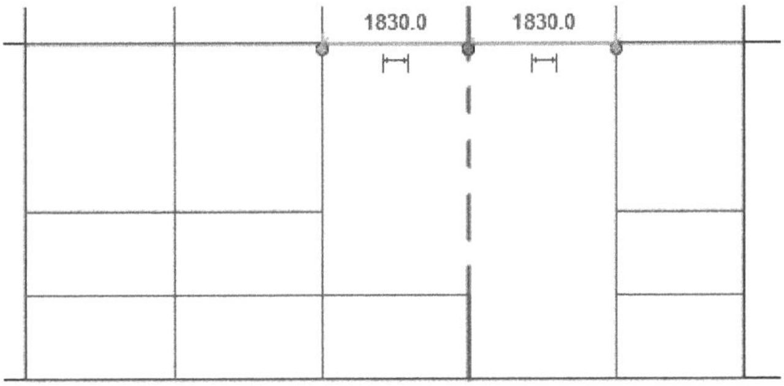

Figure 6–12

4. Click in empty space to finish the command.

- You can create non-rectangular panels by removing individual grid segments.

> **Hint: Aligning and Locking**
>
> When you use the **Align** command, you can also lock the lines together so if one moves, the other does as well. However, locking also causes the software to slow down. Therefore, be careful how much you use the **Lock** option and apply it only when you expect to make a lot of modifications.

Practice 6a

Work with Curtain Walls

Learning Objectives

- Modify the curtain wall properties so that it lines up with other elements in the model.
- Add curtain wall grid lines to match the other wall style.

Estimated time for completion: 10 minutes

In this practice you will modify a curtain wall using Properties and add grid lines. The finished elevation is shown in Figure 6–13.

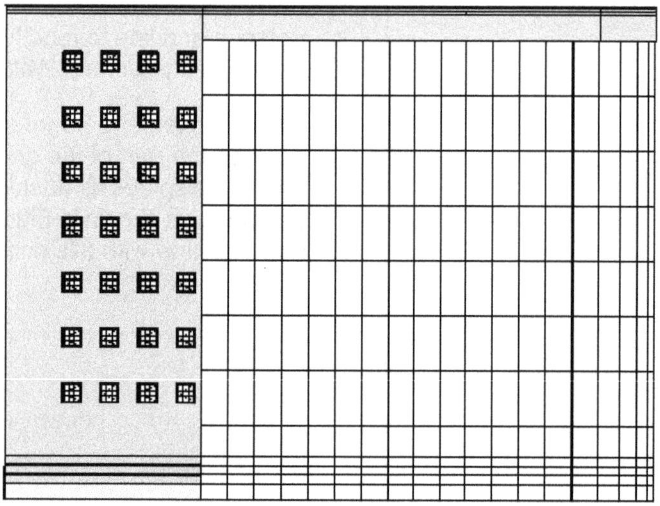

Figure 6–13

Task 1 - Modify the curtain wall.

1. Open the project **Modern-Hotel-Curtain-Walls-M.rvt** from your class folder.

2. Open the **Elevations (Building Elevation):South** view.

3. To make the view easier to understand, select one grid line, one column, and one level line. (Hold down <Ctrl> to select more than one element.) Then, right-click and select **Hide in View>Category**.

   The curtain wall grid does not match up with any of the other features, as shown in Figure 6–14.

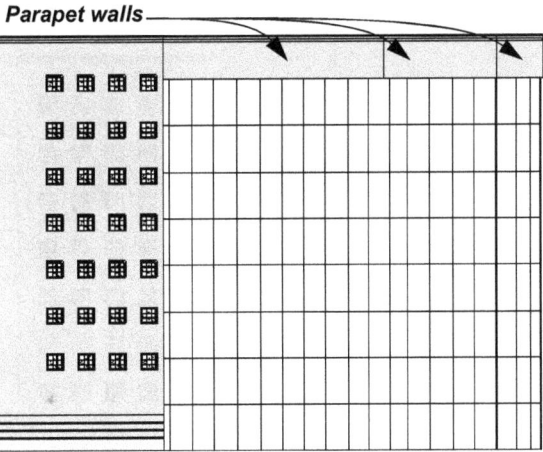

Parapet walls

Figure 6–14

4. Select the three parapet walls. In Properties, change the *Base Offset* to (negative) **-610mm** and click [Apply]. This shortens the parapet.

5. Select the three curtain walls. In Properties, change the *Top Offset* to (negative) **-610mm** and click [Apply]. This extends the curtain wall up to the parapet.

6. Change *Horizontal Offset* to **1220mm** (Offset field in the *Horizontal Grid* area), as shown in Figure 6–15.

Figure 6–15

The grid now fits better, as shown in Figure 6–16.

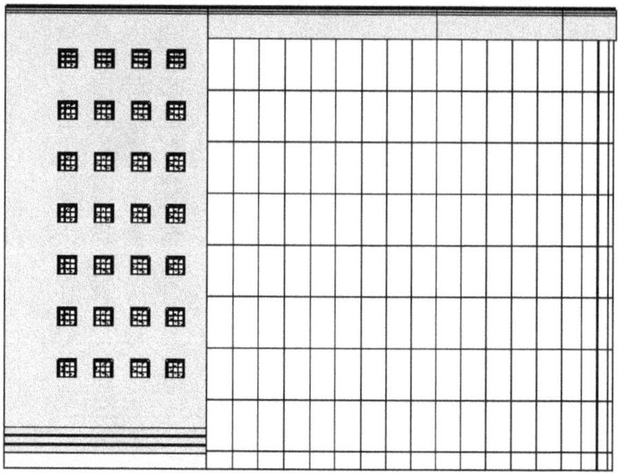

Figure 6–16

Task 2 - Add grid lines.

In this task you will add grid lines to match up with multiple lines at the bottom of the building.

1. Zoom in to the bottom edge of the building and ensure that the brick/CMU and the curtain wall is displayed. Select the grid line and unpin it, as shown in Figure 6–17.

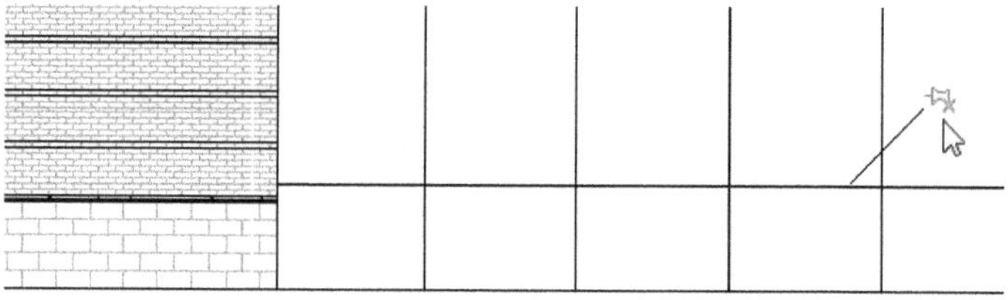

Figure 6–17

2. Use ▣ (Align) to move the curtain grid line so it matches with the top of the CMU sill, as shown in Figure 6–18.

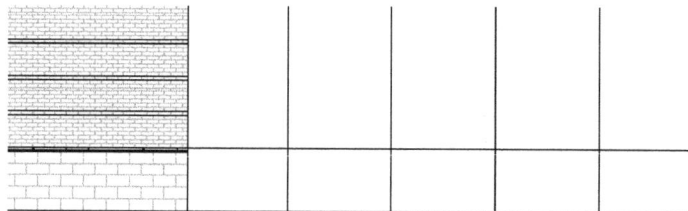

Figure 6–18

3. In the *Architecture* tab>Build panel, click ⊞ (Curtain Grid).

4. Add three grid lines aligned with the top of the reveals in the brick, as shown in Figure 6–19.

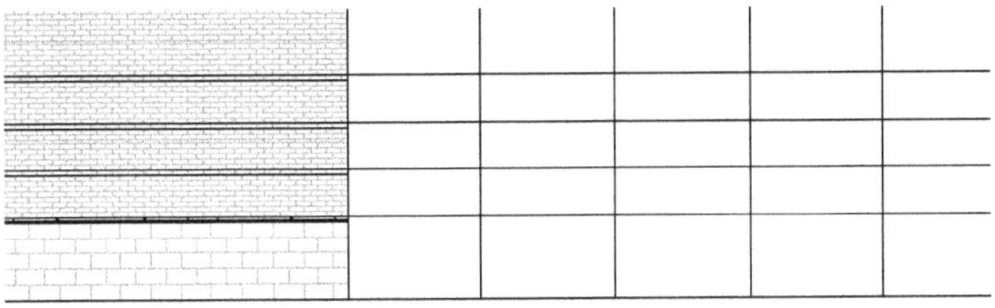

Zoom in until the heavier lines of the brick reveals are displayed.

Figure 6–19

5. Select these four curtain grid lines (hold down <Ctrl> and select each line individually) and move them down **20mm**. Ensure you drag the cursor down before entering the move value. This places them correctly for the mullions, that are added later.

6. Pan over and align and add curtain grid lines to the other two parts of the curtain wall, as shown in Figure 6–20. Ensure you unpin the existing horizontal curtain grid lines before aligning them.

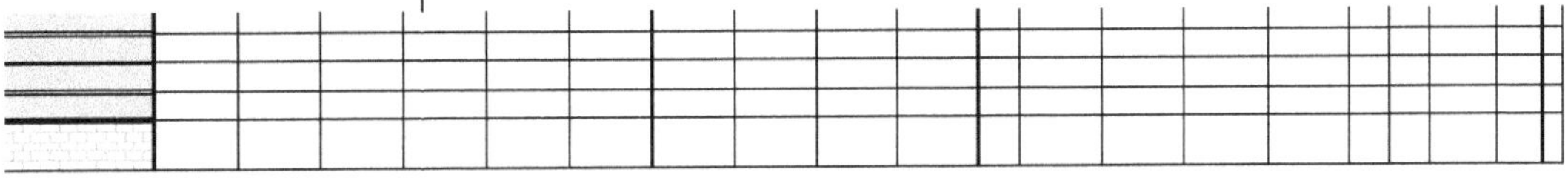

Figure 6–20

7. Zoom out until the entire front of the building is displayed.

8. Save the project.

6.3 Working with Curtain Wall Panels

Autodesk Certification Topics & Objectives

Pro.   User

Elements

- Change elements within a curtain wall   ✓

Learning Objectives

- Switch out curtain wall panels with other types, doors, or windows.
- Create a curtain wall panel type.

The default panel for a curtain wall is typically a glazed panel. As you create the curtain grid and refine the wall design, you might want to use other materials for some of the panels, as shown in Figure 6–21. You can select the existing panels and in the Type Selector, select a panel type with the material you want to use. The panel type also controls the thickness and can define a door or window for the panel.

*To select all of the panels, select the edge of the curtain wall, right-click, and select **Select Panels on Host**.*

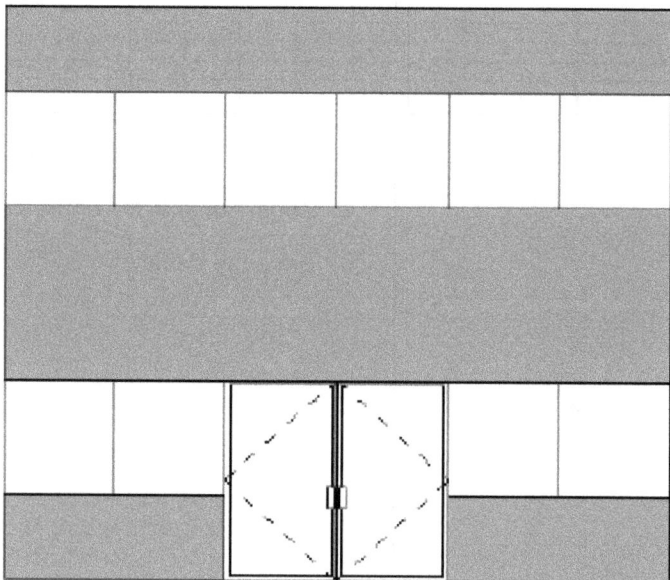

Figure 6–21

- To select a panel, move the cursor over its edge, press <Tab> until it highlights, and then click to select it. If (Push Pin) displays, it indicates that the panel is locked and that changes to the element are not permitted, as shown in Figure 6–22. Click the icon to turn off the lock and modify the panel.

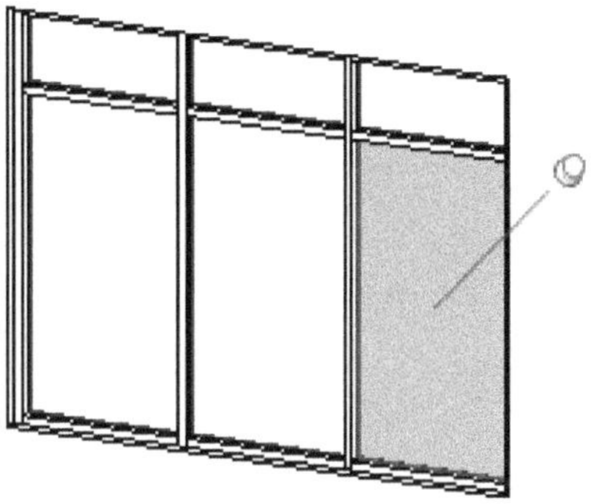

To unpin multiple panels, select them and type UP (for Unpin)

Figure 6–22

Default Panel Types

Three panel types come with the default project template:

Empty Panel	You cannot delete a panel in a curtain wall, but you can change the panel type to an empty panel.
Glazed Panel	A typical panel type with glass as its material.
Solid Panel	A panel type using a solid material. You can create variations of this type with other materials.

- You can use any other wall type (including other curtain wall types) to fill in a panel.

- Door and window panels are available through the Library. Similar to other panel types, door and window panels fill the size of the panel to which they are applied. Adjust the curtain grid for the correct sizes.

Hint: Placing Doors in Curtain Walls

You can place doors in curtain wall panels, as shown in Figure 6–23. You first need to have a door type that can be used as a curtain wall panel (the software comes with several). Then, ensure the size of the opening in the curtain wall matches the size of the door you want to use. The door type expands to fill the grid opening.

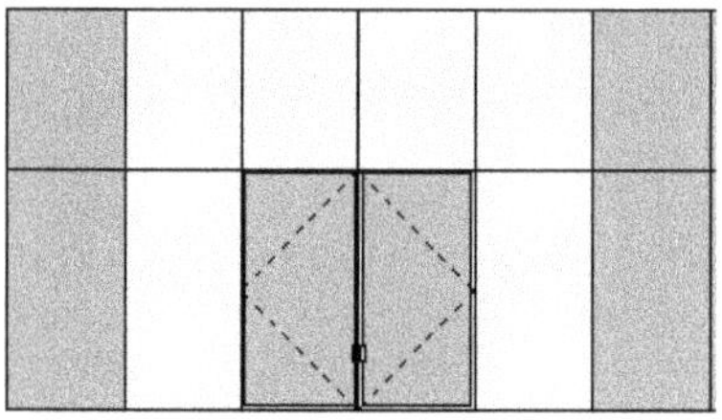

Figure 6–23

- When you tag a curtain wall panel door, you need to add the number to the tag. It does not automatically increment.

- You can also use a standard wall type as a panel. Then you can add a door into the panel using the standard **Door** command.

Creating a Curtain Wall Panel

While you can create curtain wall panels in many complex ways, a basic technique is to specify a material for a flat system panel, as shown in Figure 6–24.

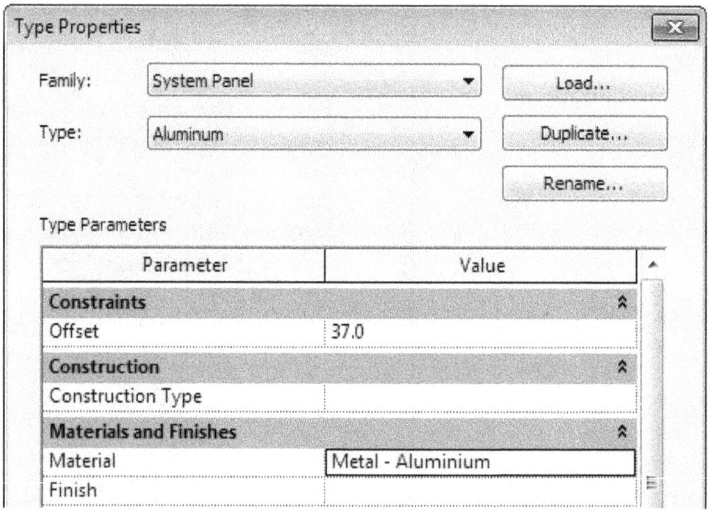

Figure 6–24

How To: Create a Curtain Wall Panel

1. Select a panel similar to the one you want to create (e.g., select a solid panel to create a new solid panel type). If it is locked, unlock it by clicking ⌾ (Push Pin).

2. In Properties, click 🔲 (Edit Type), or, in the *Modify | Curtain Panels* tab>Properties panel, click 🔲 (Type Properties).

3. In the Type Properties dialog box, click [Duplicate...] to create a copy of the existing family type.

4. Give the panel a new name that describes its purpose (e.g., **Brick** or **Aluminum**). The new name automatically includes the family name, such as **System Panel**.

5. Set the *Thickness*, *Offset*, and *Material* and any other parameters as required. Many materials are available in the Materials dialog box that opens when you click [...] (Browse) in the Materials list.

6. Click [OK] to close the dialog box and finish the panel. It is automatically applied to the panel you selected for modification.

- The *Thickness* of the material is centered on the grid if you did not specify an *Offset*. If you want the panel to be recessed in the wall, use a negative offset. If you want the panel to stand out from the wall, use a positive offset.

- Materials with patterns, such as the glass block shown in Figure 6–25, do not display the pattern when the view is zoomed out far. Zoom in to view the material.

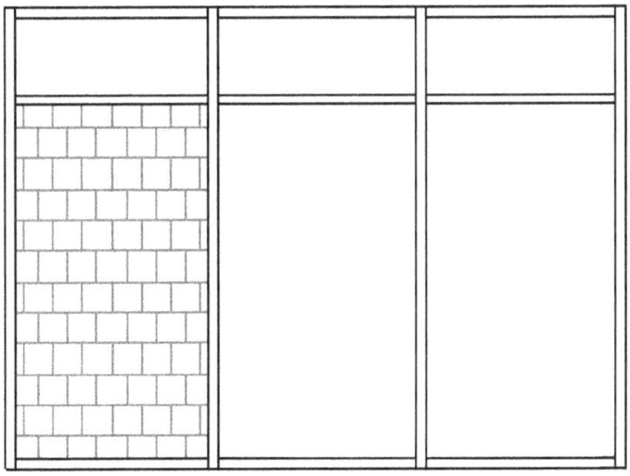

Figure 6–25

6.4 Attaching Mullions to Curtain Grids

Autodesk Certification Topics & Objectives

Pro.   User

Elements

* Change elements within a curtain wall   ✓

Learning Objectives

* Add mullions to curtain wall grids.
* Modify mullion types and intersections.

Mullions are the frameworks for curtain wall panels, as shown in Figure 6–26. They can be many sizes, shapes, and materials. Add them as the final step in your curtain wall design after you have placed the grid lines.

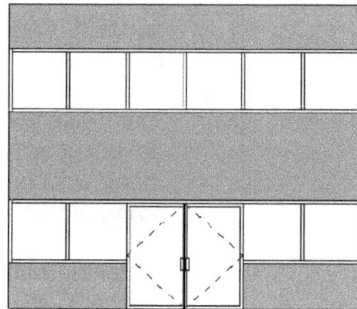

Figure 6–26

How To: Add Mullions

1. In the *Architecture* tab>Build panel, click ⊞ (Mullion).
2. In the Type Selector, select the mullion style. There are no modifiable properties when you insert a mullion.
3. In the *Modify | Place Mullion* tab>Placement panel, select a *Create Mullion on* method: ⊞ (Grid Line), ⊞ (Grid Line Segment), or ⊞ (All Grid Lines), as shown in Figure 6–27.

Mullions must be placed individually; they cannot be copied or arrayed.

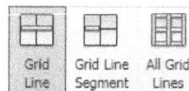

Figure 6–27

4. Select the grid line on which you want to place the mullion. If the grid line is inside a grid, the mullion is placed on the grid's center line. If it is on the edge of the wall, the mullion is placed so that its exterior is flush with the outside of the wall.

- Hold down <Shift> to place a mullion only on the selected segment.
- Hold down <Ctrl> to place the mullion on all empty grid segments (i.e., all without mullions).

- Corner mullion types are designed for the intersection of two curtain walls. They adjust to fit the angle of the intersection.

Modifying Mullions

To quickly select mullions, right-click on the edge of the curtain wall and select **Select Mullions**. The mullion options include **On Vertical Grid** or **On Horizontal Grid**, **Inner Mullions**, **Border Mullions**, or **Mullions on Host**, as shown in Figure 6–28.

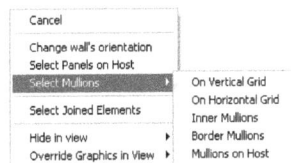

Figure 6–28

- Modify mullion styles by changing their type in the Type Selector.

- If you move a grid line, the mullion moves with it.

- If you delete a grid line, the mullion is also deleted. However, if you delete a mullion, the grid line is not deleted.

- You can change the way mullions intersect. Select the mullion to display the *Modify | Curtain Wall Mullions* tab. In the Mullion panel, click ⊤ (Make Continuous) or ⊧ (Break at Join), You can also do this directly on the mullion, as shown in Figure 6–29.

Figure 6–29

Hint: Temporary Hide/Isolate

You might want to temporarily remove elements from a view, modify the project, and then restore the elements. Instead of completely turning the elements off, you can use

🐛 (Temporary Hide/Isolate) in the View Control Bar. The Temporary Hide/Isolate status is not saved with the project.

Select the elements you want to hide (make invisible) or isolate (keep displayed while all other elements are hidden) and click

🐛 (Temporary Hide/Isolate). Select the method you want to use, as shown in Figure 6–30.

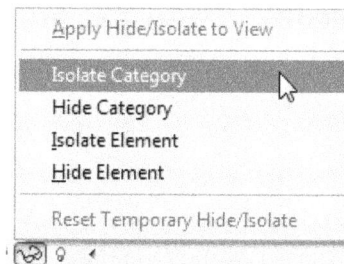

Figure 6–30

The elements or category are hidden or isolated. A cyan border displays around the view with a note in the upper left corner, as shown in Figure 6–31. It indicates that the view contains temporarily hidden or isolated elements.

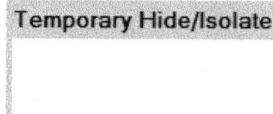

Figure 6–31

- Click 🐛 (Temporary Hide/Isolate) again and select **Reset Temporary Hide/Isolate** to restore the elements to the view.

- If you want to permanently hide the elements in the view, select **Apply Hide/Isolate to View**.

- Elements that are temporarily hidden in a view are not hidden when the view is printed.

Practice 6b

Add Mullions and Panels to Curtain Walls

Learning Objectives

- Add and modify mullions.
- Add a storefront entrance and door panel.

In this practice you will add and modify mullions, and create a storefront using a door panel. The finished elevation is shown in Figure 6–32.

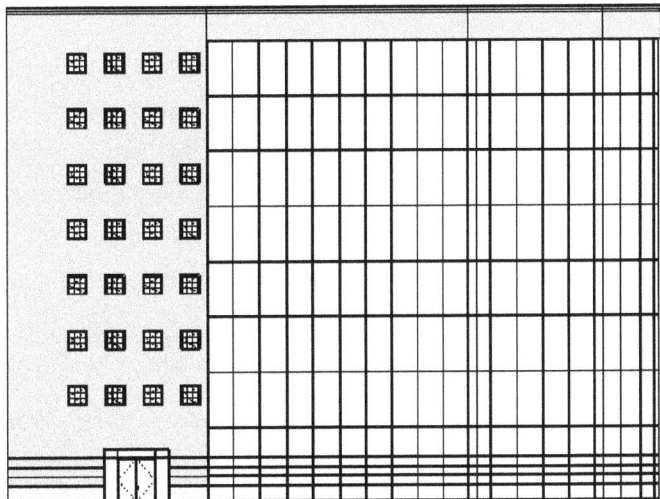

Figure 6–32

Estimated time for completion: 15 minutes

Task 1 - Add and modify mullions.

1. Open the project **Modern-Hotel-Mullions-M.rvt** in your class folder.

2. Open the **Elevations (Building Elevations): South** view, or work in the 3D view.

3. In the *Architecture* tab>Build panel, click ⊞ (Mullion).

4. In the *Modify | Place Mullion* tab>Placement panel, click ⊞ (All Grid Lines).

5. Select each of the curtain walls. Mullions are place on all of the grid lines.

6. Return to the **Modify** command.

7. At the two lines where the curtain walls meet, extra mullions are added, as shown in Figure 6–33. These are not needed and should be removed.

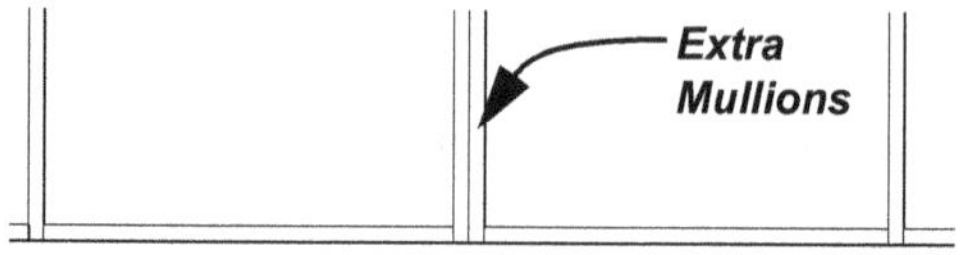

Figure 6–33

8. Select one of the mullions.

9. In the View Control Bar, click 〰 (Temporary Hide/Isolate) and select **Isolate Category**. This makes selecting the mullions you want to delete easier.

10. Delete the extra mullions by selecting one mullion, right-clicking and clicking Select Mullions>On Gridline.

11. Zoom out until all of the curtain walls are displayed.

12. Select the entire bottom row of mullions. You can use the Window selection box to select the entire row.

13. In the *Modify | Curtain Wall Mullions* tab>Mullion panel, click

    ⊥ (Make Continuous). This changes the mullion direction, as shown in Figure 6–34.

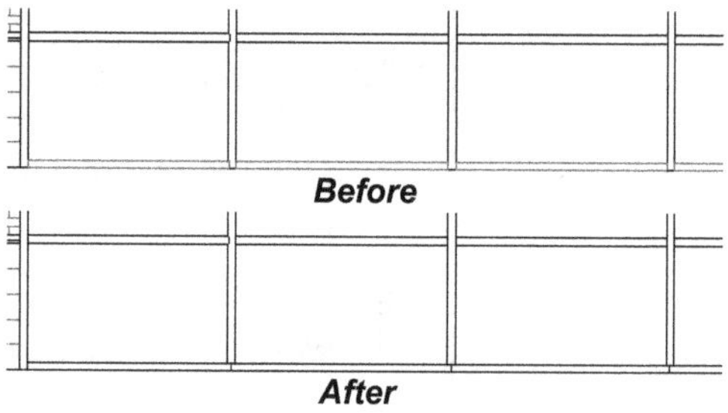

Before

After

Figure 6–34

14. Repeat with the top row of mullions.

15. In the View Control Bar, click 〰 (Temporary Hide/Isolate) and select **Reset Temporary Hide/Isolate**.

16. Save the project.

Task 2 - Add the storefront entrance.

1. Open the **Floor Plans: Floor 1** view.

2. In the *Architecture* tab>Build panel, click ⬕ (Wall).

3. In the Type Selector, select **Curtain Wall:Storefront**.

4. Set the *Base Offset* to **0**, the *Top Constraint* to **Up to level: Floor 2** and the *Top Offset* to (negative) **-1850mm**.

5. Draw the storefront within the existing wall **600mm** off the right gridline, as shown in Figure 6–35.

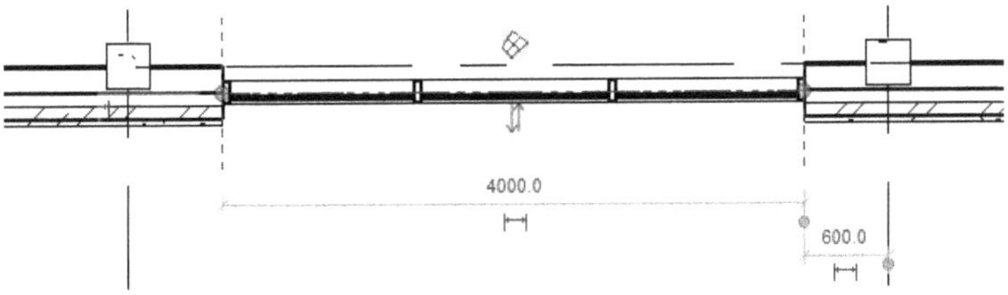

Figure 6–35

- If you draw from right to left, the exterior of the storefront is placed correctly. If you draw from left to right, you need to flip the storefront.
- If you have trouble drawing from the grid line, draw the storefront first, and then modify the location after it is placed.

6. Open the **Elevations (Building Elevation): South** view and zoom in on the storefront.

7. Window around to select the storefront. Because it was created with a preset type, all of the grids and panels are pinned, as shown on the left in Figure 6–36. Type **UP** to unpin the elements, as shown on the right in Figure 6–36.

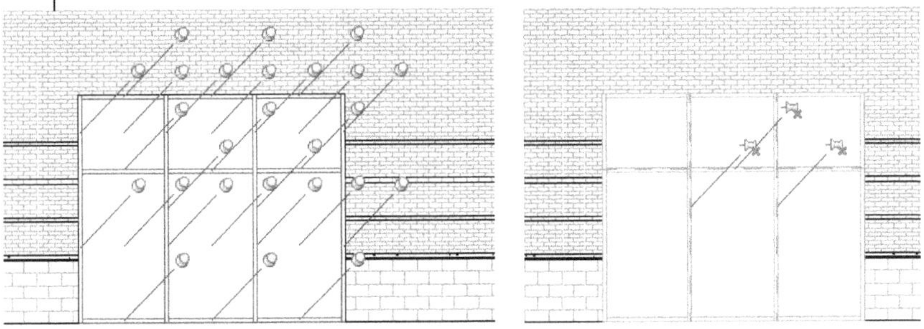

Figure 6–36

8. Modify the storefront, as shown in Figure 6–37. Align the horizontal curtain grid lines and use temporary dimensions to locate the vertical grid lines.

Ensure you are selecting curtain grid lines as you work and not the mullions. Use <Tab> to cycle through the elements.

Figure 6–37

Task 3 - Add a door in the storefront.

1. In the *Insert* tab>Load from Library panel, click ⬇ (Load Family). Use this more generic method of loading the curtain wall door family because you cannot use the **Door** command to place doors in curtain walls.

2. In the Load Family dialog box, in the *Doors* folder, select the door **M_Curtain Wall Store Front-Dbl.rfa**, as shown in Figure 6–38. Click [Open].

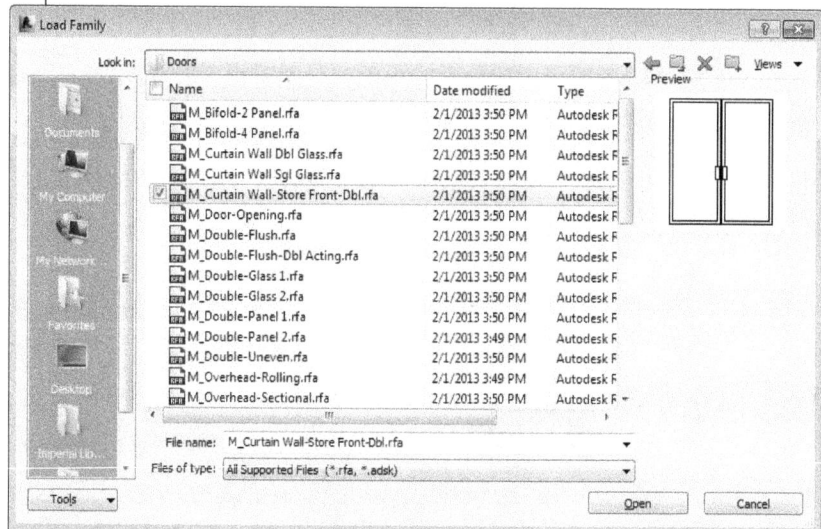

Figure 6–38

3. Select the large panel, as shown in Figure 6–39. Use <Tab> to cycle through the selections and then click to select it.

Figure 6–39

4. In the Type Selector, select **M_Curtain Wall-Store Front-Dbl: Store Front Double Door**. The panel changes to the door. Delete the mullion at the bottom of the door, as shown in Figure 6–40.

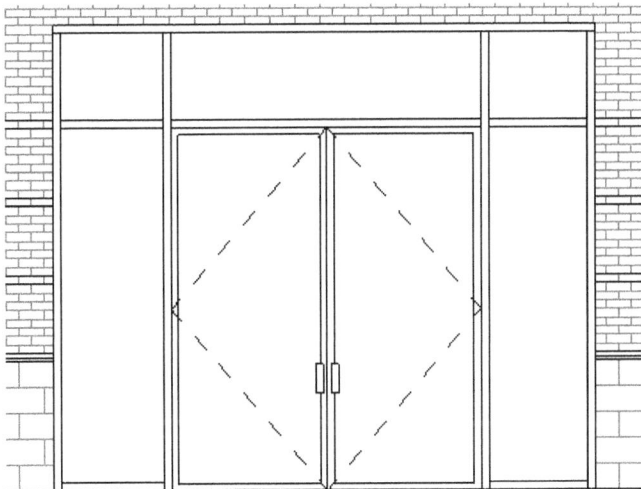

Figure 6–40

5. Zoom out until the entire front elevation is displayed.

6. View the project in 3D.

7. Save the project.

Chapter Review Questions

1. Which command do you start with to create a curtain wall?

   a. ⬜ (Wall)

   b. ▦ (Curtain Grid)

   c. ▦ (Curtain System)

2. You are placing a curtain grid and it keeps snapping to one dimension, such as the TWO-THIRDS OF CURTAIN PANEL shown in Figure 6–41, when you want it to be another. What should you do?

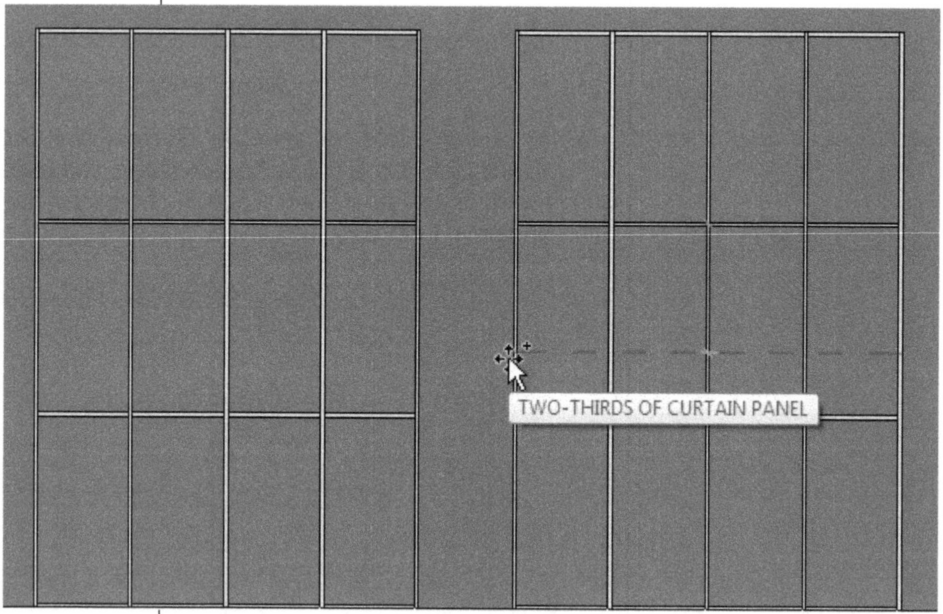

Figure 6–41

   a. Change the snap settings.

   b. Edit the Curtain Wall Type to permit manual grid placement.

   c. Use a Non-Uniform Curtain Wall Type instead of a Uniform one.

   d. Place the curtain grid anyway, select the temporary dimension, and change it to the required value.

3. How do you select one panel to modify it?

   a. Select the middle of the panel.

   b. Point to the edge of the panel and press <Tab> until it is identified.

   c. Select the curtain wall, right-click and select **Panel Select**.

   d. In the Selection Priority drop-down list, select **Curtain Panel**.

4. Once you select a panel, what can you swap it for? (Select all that apply.)

   a. Empty system panel

   b. Store Front Door

   c. Blank

   d. Wall Type

5. How do you change the way in which two mullions intersect, as shown in Figure 6–42? (Select all that apply.)

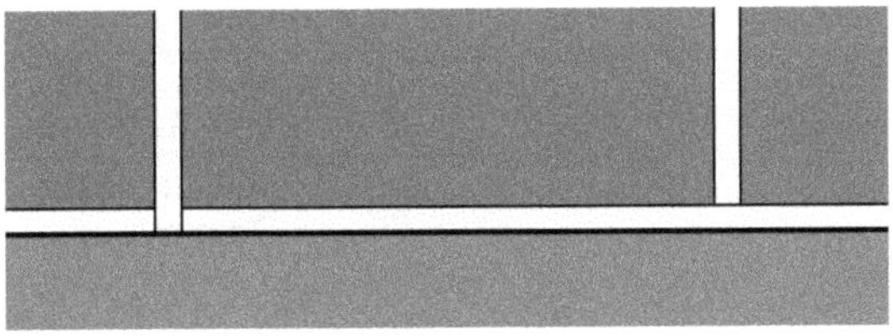

Figure 6–42

   a. Select one of the mullions, right-click and select **Toggle Intersection**.

   b. Select one of the mullions and click the **Make Continuous** or **Break at Join** icons in the contextual tab.

   c. Select one of the mullions and click the **Toggle Mullion Join** control.

   d. Select both mullions and select the **Intersect** box in the Options Bar.

Command Summary

Button	Command	Location
	Add/Remove Segments	• **Ribbon:** *Modify	Curtain Wall Grids* tab> Curtain Grid panel
	Curtain Grid	• **Ribbon:** *Architecture* tab>Build panel
	Curtain Grid: All Except Picked	• **Ribbon:** *Modify	Place Curtain Grid* tab> Placement panel
	Curtain Grid: All Segments	• **Ribbon:** *Modify	Place Curtain Grid* tab> Placement panel
	Curtain Grid: One Segment	• **Ribbon:** *Modify	Place Curtain Grid* tab> Placement panel
	Mullion	• **Ribbon:** *Architecture* tab>Build panel
	Mullion: All Grid Lines	• **Ribbon:** *Modify	Place Mullion* tab> Placement panel
	Mullion: Break at Join	• **Ribbon:** *Modify	Curtain Wall Mullions* tab>Mullion panel
	Mullion: Grid Line	• **Ribbon:** *Modify	Place Mullion* tab> Placement panel
	Mullion: Grid Line Segment	• **Ribbon:** *Modify	Place Mullion* tab> Placement panel
	Mullion: Make Continuous	• **Ribbon:** *Modify	Curtain Wall Mullions* tab>Mullion panel

Chapter 7

Working with Views

In this chapter you learn how to create duplicate views, callout views, elevations, and sections. You also learn how to setup views using underlays and view range as well as by overriding graphics in views.

This chapter contains the following topics:

- **Duplicating Views**
- **Adding Callout Views**
- **Setting the View Display**
- **Elevations and Sections**

7.1 Duplicating Views

Autodesk Certification Topics & Objectives

Pro.   User

Views

- Create a duplicate view for a plan, section, elevation, drafting view, etc.   ✓

Learning Objective

- Duplicate views so that you can modify what displays in each view.

Once you have created a model, you do not have to redraw the elements at different scales or copy them so that they can be used on more than one sheet. Instead, duplicate views and modify them to suit your needs. For example, a view or callout of the First Floor plan can be duplicated and modified to create a dimension plan, furniture plan, etc., as shown in Figure 7–1.

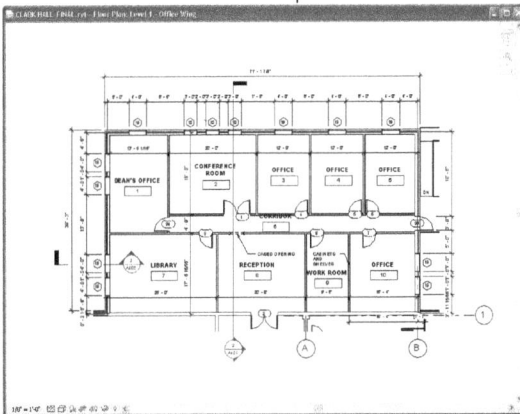

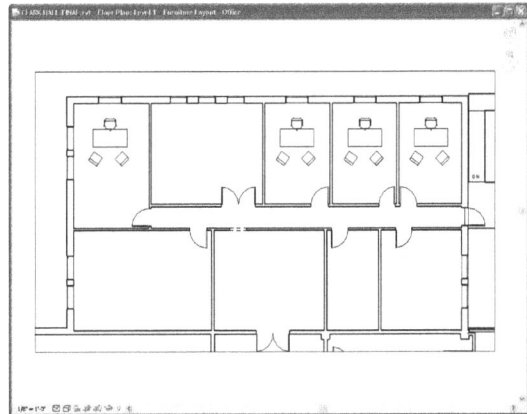

Figure 7–1

How To: Create Duplicate Views

1. Open the view you want to duplicate.
2. In the *View* tab>Create panel, expand **Duplicate View** and select the type of duplicate view you want to create, as shown in Figure 7–2.

Most types of views can be duplicated.

Figure 7–2

- Alternatively, you can right-click on a view in the Project Browser and select the type of duplicate that you want to use, as shown in Figure 7–3.

Figure 7–3

Enhanced in 2015

- When you duplicate a view, it is named after the original view name with "Copy x" appended to the end (x stands for the number of the copy).

Duplication Types

Duplicate creates a copy of the view that only includes the building elements, as shown in Figure 7–4. Annotation and detailing are not copied into the new view. Building model elements automatically change in all views, but view-specific changes made to the new view are not reflected in the original view. For example, you can duplicate a Floor Plan view, and then modify the new view to show the furniture layout. No furniture is displayed in the original view.

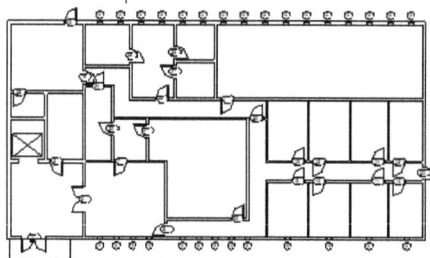
Original

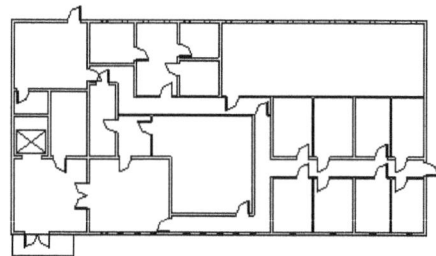
Duplicate

Figure 7–4

Duplicate with Detailing creates a copy of the view and includes all annotation and detail elements (such as tags), as shown in Figure 7–5. Any annotation or view-specific elements created in the new view are not reflected in the original view.

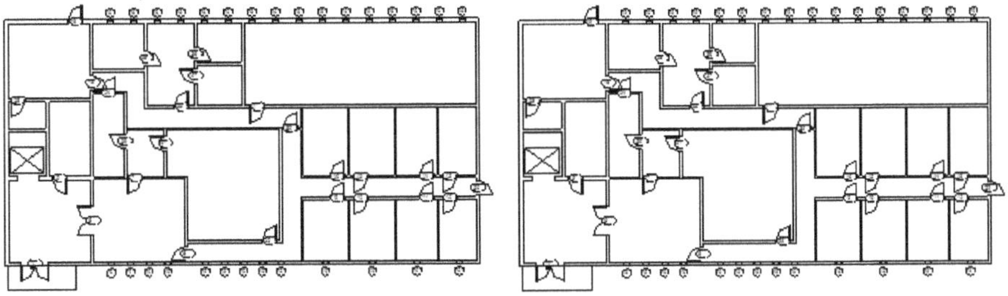

Original   *Duplicate with Detailing*

Figure 7–5

Duplicate as a Dependent creates a copy of the view and links it to the original (parent) view. View-specific changes made to the original view are also reflected in the dependent (child) view and vice-versa. Any updates to View Properties, View Display, or Visibility/Graphic Overrides display in both the original and dependent views.

Hint: Common Uses of Duplicate as a Dependent

Use dependent views when the building model is so large that you need to split the building onto separate sheets, with views that are all same scale. Having one overall view with dependent views makes viewing changes (i.e., scale or detail level) easier.

Dependent views display in the Project Browser under the top-level view, as shown in Figure 7–6.

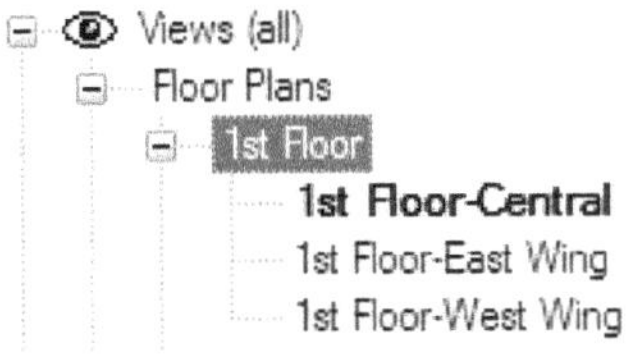

Figure 7–6

- If you need a plan displayed at a smaller scale, create a regular duplicate view, change the scale, and then create dependent views of this new view if needed.

- If you want to separate a dependent view from the original view, right-click on the dependent view and select **Convert to independent view**.

- The building model always updates in every view, but annotation elements (such as door tags, window tags, and dimensions) are view-specific.

- You can use View Properties, View Display, and Visibility/Graphic Overrides to make the duplicate view different from the original view.

*You can also press <F2> to start the **Rename** command.*

- Once you create a new view, you probably want to assign a new name to it. Right-click on the new view in the Project Browser and select **Rename**. In the Rename View dialog box, type in the new name in place of the copy, as shown in Figure 7–7.

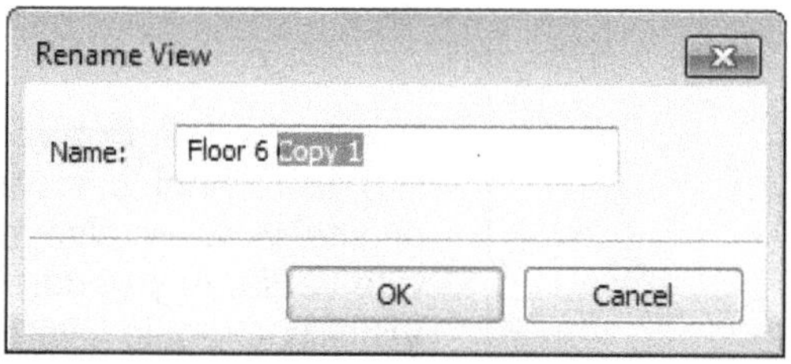

Figure 7–7

7.2 Adding Callout Views

Learning Objectives

- Create callout views for detailed plans and sections.
- Modify callout views in the main view and in the callout view including setting the Annotation Crop Region.

Callouts are details of plan, elevation, or section views. When you place a callout in a view, it automatically creates a new view clipped to the boundary of the callout, as shown in Figure 7–8. If you change the size of the callout box in the original view, it automatically updates the callout view and vice-versa. You can create rectangular or sketched callout boundaries.

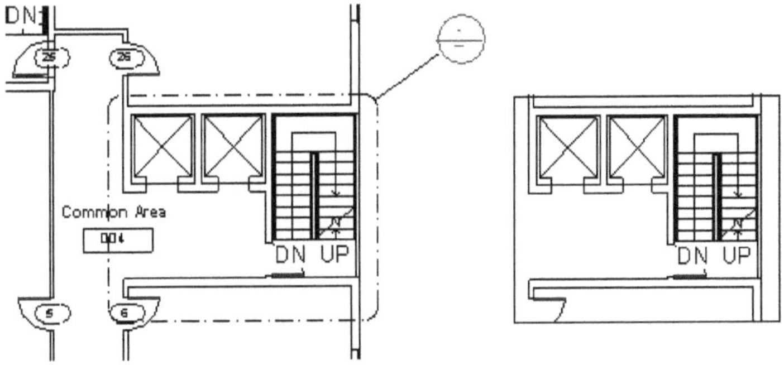

Figure 7–8

How To: Create a Rectangular Callout

1. In the *View tab>Create panel,* click $\overset{\oplus}{\circlearrowright}$ **(Callout)**.
2. Select points for two opposite corners to define the callout box around the area you want to detail.
3. Select the callout and use the shape handles to modify the location of the bubble and any other edges that might need changing.
4. In the Project Browser, rename the callout as required.

How To: Create a Sketched Callout

1. In the *View tab>Create panel,* expand ⌀ (Callout), and click
   📝 (Sketch).
2. Sketch the shape of the callout using the tools in the *Modify |
   Edit Profile* tab>Draw panel, as shown in Figure 7–9.

Figure 7–9

3. Click ✓ (Finish) to complete the boundary.
4. Select the callout and use the shape handles to modify the
   location of the bubble and any other edges that might need to
   be changed.
5. In the Project Browser, rename the callout as required.

- To open the callout view, double-click on its name in the
  Project Browser or double-click on the callout bubble (verify
  that it is not selected before you double-click on it).

- The callout bubble information automatically populates when
  you place the callout on a sheet.

Modifying Callouts

Modifying Callout Boundaries

In the original view where the callout is created, you can use the
shape handles to modify the callout boundary and bubble
location, as shown in Figure 7–10. You can also rotate the
callout box by dragging ↻ (Rotate).

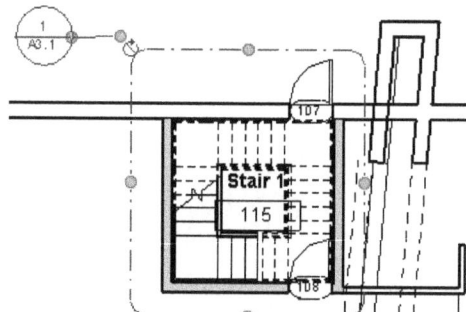

*The callout bubble
displays numbers when
the view is placed on a
sheet.*

Figure 7–10

Modifying Callout Views

In the callout view, you can modify callouts with controls and view breaks, as shown in Figure 7–11.

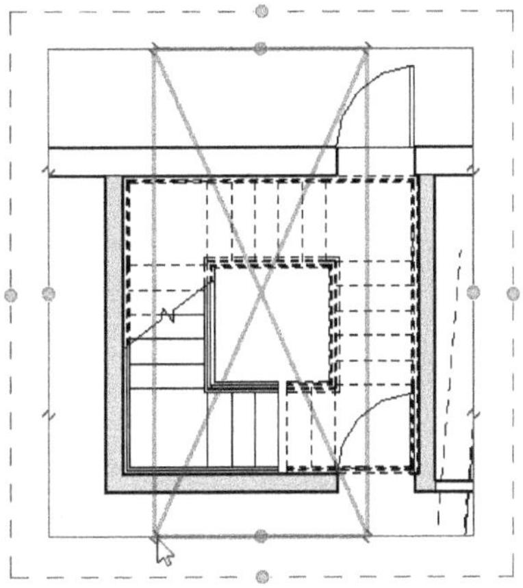

The crop region options are also available in section and elevation views.

Figure 7–11

- The crop region must be displayed if you want to modify the size of the view. In the View Control Bar, click ⬚ (Show Crop Region) if it is not displayed.

- Resize the crop region using the ○ control on each side of the region.

Breaking the crop region is typically used with sections or details.

- If you want to break the crop region, click ⤙ (Break Line) control to split the view into two regions, horizontally or vertically. Each part of the view can then be modified in size to display what is needed and be moved independently.

- The display in the callout view is controlled by the two crop regions, as shown in Figure 7–12.

  - **Model Crop Region:** Controls which model elements are displayed and how they are cropped.
  - **Annotation Crop Region:** Controls which annotation elements (such as dimensions and tags) are displayed. By default, annotation elements that are cut by the callout box are not displayed in the callout view.

- If the Annotation Crop Region is not displaying, turn it on in the Properties of the view. Scroll down to the *Extents* area and select **Annotation Crop**, as shown in Figure 7–12.

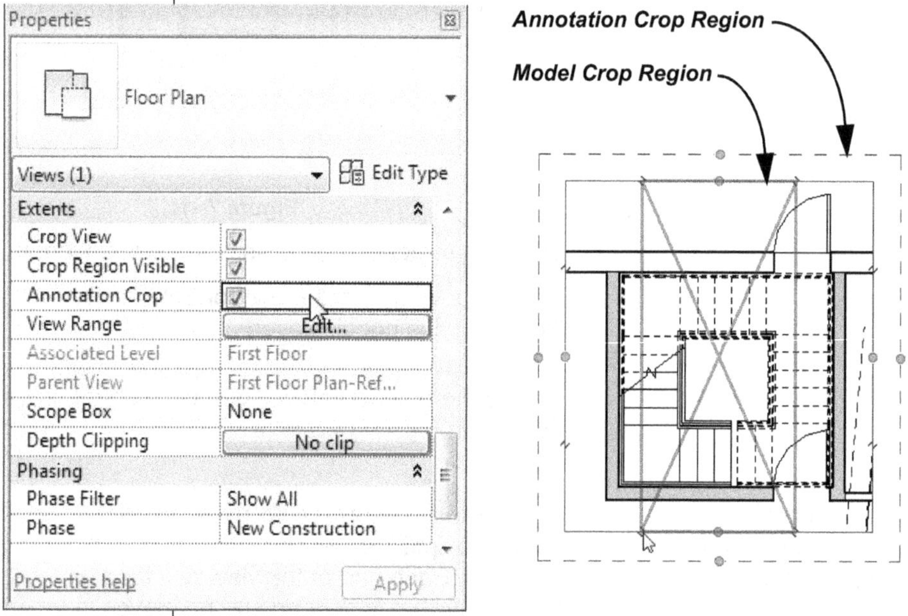

Properties

Floor Plan

Views (1)   Edit Type

Extents
Crop View   ✓
Crop Region Visible   ✓
Annotation Crop   ✓
View Range   Edit...
Associated Level   First Floor
Parent View   First Floor Plan-Ref...
Scope Box   None
Depth Clipping   No clip
Phasing
Phase Filter   Show All
Phase   New Construction

Properties help   Apply

Annotation Crop Region

Model Crop Region

Figure 7–12

- The annotation crop region remains rectangular even if the original callout boundary was created by a sketch.

- If you want to edit the crop region to reshape the boundary of the view, select the crop region and, in the *Modify | Floor Plan* tab>Mode panel, click (Edit Crop). If you want to return a modified crop region to the original rectangular configuration, click (Reset Crop).

- You can also resize the crop region and the annotation crop region using the Crop Region Size dialog box as shown in Figure 7–13. In the *Modify | Floor Plan* tab>Crop panel, click

  📐 (Size Crop) to open the dialog box.

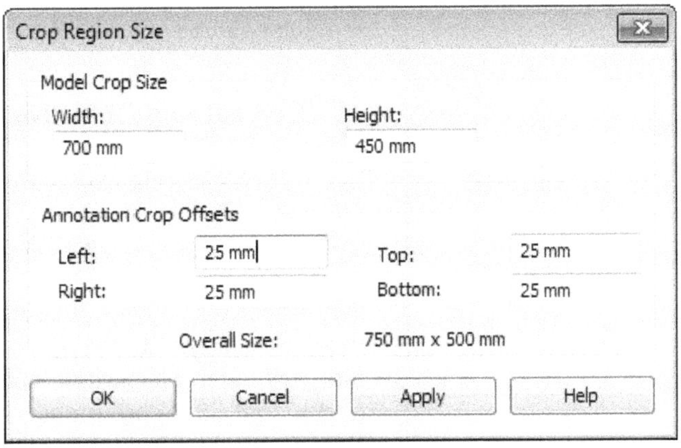

Figure 7–13

- It is a good idea to hide a crop region before placing a view on a sheet. Doing so minimizes the viewport size. In the View Control Bar, click 🔲 (Hide Crop Region).

7.3 Setting the View Display

Autodesk Certification Topics & Objectives

Pro.   User

Views

*   Control visibility ✓

Learning Objectives

*   Modify the view display so that it only displays what is needed for that view.
*   Override graphics in views for elements and categories.

Whenever you have not selected any objects, the Properties palette displays the View Properties, as shown in Figure 7–14. Many of these properties (such as the *View Scale*, *Detail Level*, and *Visual Style*) are most often changed in the View Control Bar. Several important modifications to views include setting Underlays, modifying the View Range, and overriding graphics of elements and categories.

The options in View Properties vary according to the type of view. A floor plan has some different parameters than a 3D view.

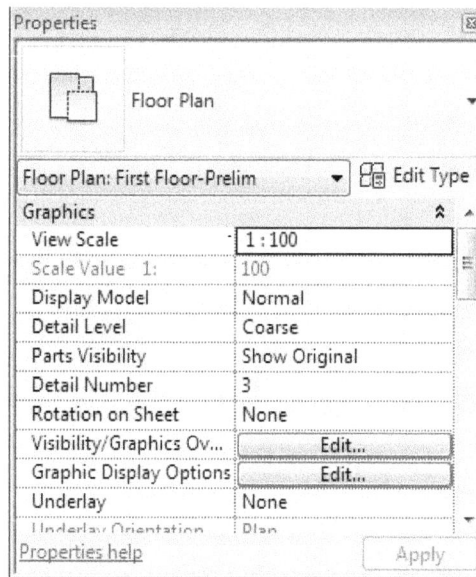

Figure 7–14

Underlays

Setting an *Underlay* (*Graphics* area in Properties) is helpful if you need to display elements on a different level, such as the basement plan shown with an underlay of the first floor plan in Figure 7–15. You can then use the elements to trace over or even copy to the current level of the view.

Underlays are only available in Floor Plan and Ceiling Plan views.

Figure 7–15

- To prevent moving elements in the underlay by mistake, in the Select panel, expand the panel title, and clear **Select underlay elements**. You can also toggle this on/off using

  (Select Underlay Elements) in the Status Bar.

View Range

The View Range sets the locations of cut planes and view depths in plans or ceiling plans as shown in a section in Figure 7–16.

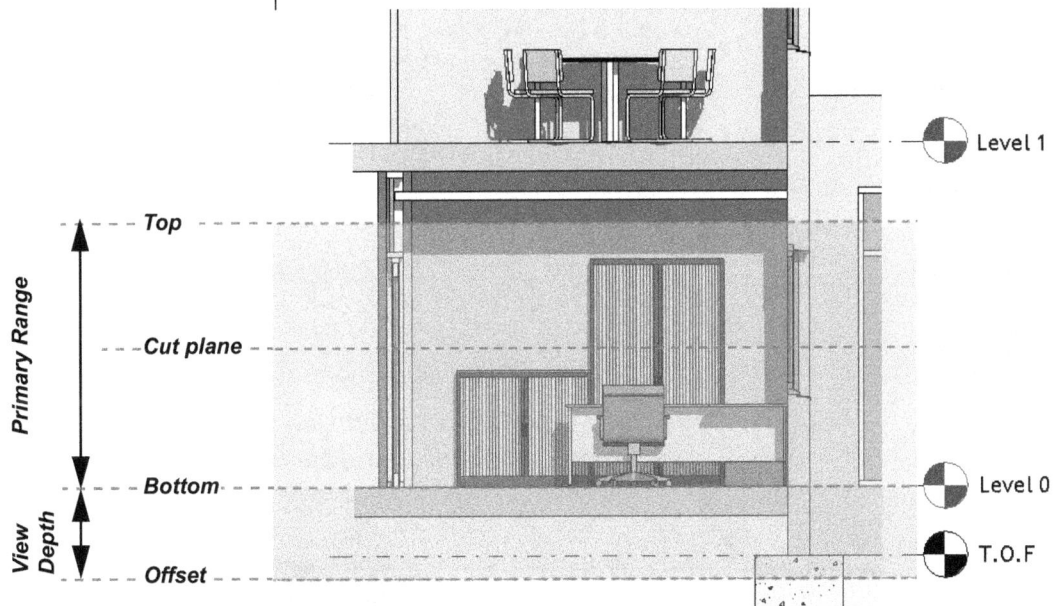

Figure 7–16

How To: Set the View Range

1. In Properties, scroll down to *View Range* and select **Edit...**.
2. In the View Range dialog box, as shown in Figure 7–17, modify the Levels and Offsets for the *Primary Range* and

   View Depth and click [OK].

If the settings used cannot be represented graphically, a warning displays stating the inconsistency.

View Range

Primary Range

Top:	Associated Level (Level 1) ▼	Offset:	2300.0
Cut plane:	Associated Level (Level 1) ▼	Offset:	1200.0
Bottom:	Associated Level (Level 1) ▼	Offset:	0.0

View Depth

Level:	Associated Level (Level 1) ▼	Offset:	0.0

[OK]   [Cancel]   [Apply]   [Help]

Figure 7–17

Hint: Adjust the Depth Clipping

The **Depth Clipping** is a viewing option which sets how sloped walls are displayed if the *View Range* is set to a limited view.

1. Open a plan view.
2. In Properties, in the *Extents* area, click the button next to *Depth Clipping*.
3. In the Depth Clipping dialog box, (shown in Figure 7–18) define where you want to display a line for clipping the view.

Depth Clipping

☑ No clip

☐ Clip without line

☐ Clip with line

[OK]   [Cancel]

Figure 7–18

- **No Clip:** Defaults to the *View Depth* setting.
- **Clip without line:** Hides the visibility of the model under the clip plane and does not display a line on the object where the plane occurs.
- **Clip with line:** Hides the visibility under the clip plane and displays a line at the clip plane.
- A similar option, **Far Clipping**, is available for section and elevation views.

Overriding Graphics in a View

If you want to change the way the graphics (such as lineweight, color, or pattern) display for elements or categories, you can override them in a view. For example, you can gray out all walls and columns in a Furniture Plan, as shown in Figure 7–19.

Figure 7–19

- Hiding or overriding by element in a dependent view impacts only that view. If you hide or override by category, it impacts the primary view and all dependent views.

How To: Override Graphics of Individual Elements

1. Select the element(s) you want to modify.
2. Right-click and select **Override Graphics in View>By Element**. The View-Specific Element Graphics dialog box opens, as shown in Figure 7–20.

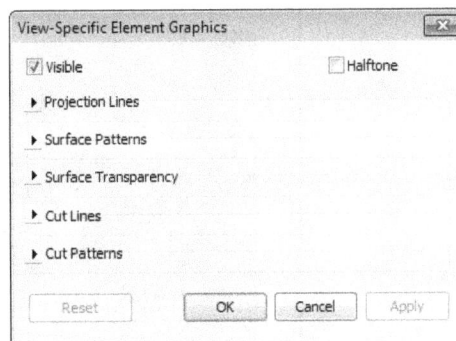

Figure 7–20

3. Select the changes you want to make and click OK.

- The options in the dialog box vary depending on the type of elements selected.

- Clearing the **Visible** option is the same as hiding elements.

- Projection Lines, Surface Patterns, Cut Lines, and Cut Patterns can change according to options, such as **Weight**, **Color**, and **Pattern**, as shown in Figure 7–21.

Figure 7–21

- You can modify the transparency of a surface by moving the Surface Transparency slider bar. For example, the transparency of the wall shown on the left in Figure 7–22 is set all the way to the right of the bar, while that of the wall on the right is set at a 33% transparency.

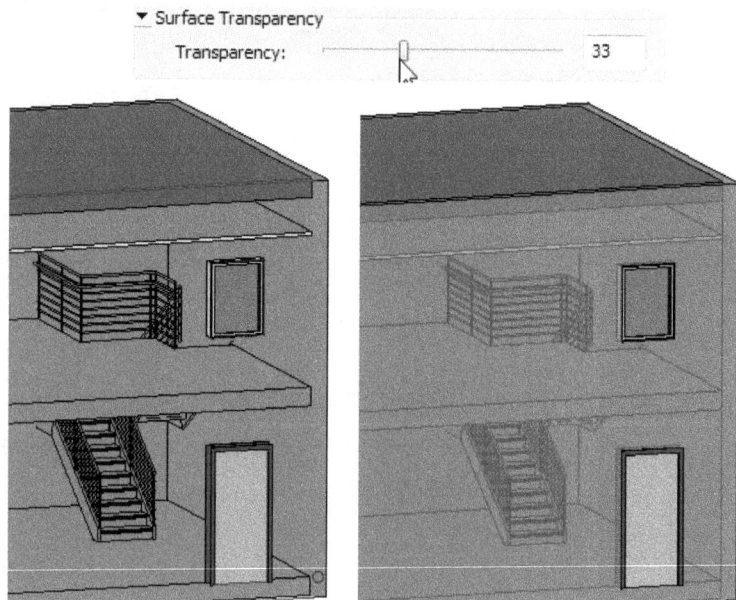

Figure 7–22

How To: Override Graphics of Entire Categories

1. Select an element in the category you want to modify.
2. Right-click and select **Override Graphics in View>By Category**.
3. In the View-Specific Category Graphics dialog box (shown in Figure 7–23), modify the options as you would modify the element graphics and click <u>OK</u>.

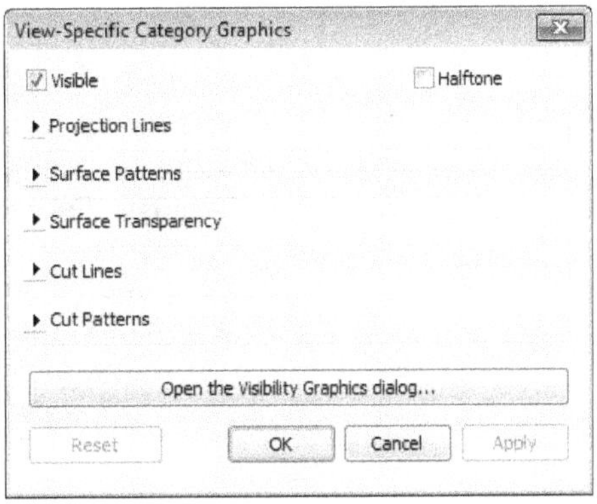

Figure 7–23

- To have more control over the categories click <u>Open the Visibility Graphics dialog...</u>. The Visibility/ Graphic Overrides dialog box opens, as shown in Figure 7–24.

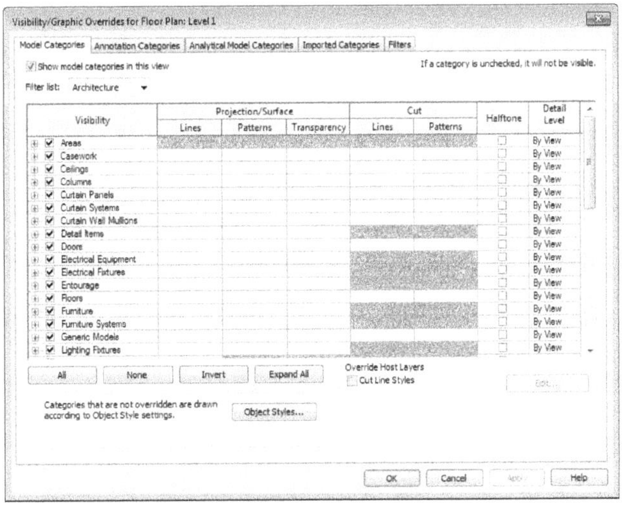

Figure 7–24

- You can also open the Visibility/Graphic Overrides dialog box without opening the View-Specific Category Graphics dialog box first. The quickest way is to use the shortcut by pressing <V> and then pressing <V> or <G>. It is also available in a view's Properties: in the *Graphics* section, beside Visibility/Graphic Overrides, click [Edit...].

For AutoCAD software users, modifying categories in this dialog box is similar to the concept of modifying layers.

- The options in the Visibility/Graphic Overrides dialog box control how every element and sub-element in the Autodesk® Revit® software is displayed per view. You can control the *Visibility, Projection/Surface for Lines, Patterns and Transparency, Cut Lines*, and *Patterns*, as well as set *Halftone*. You can also override the *Detail Level* from the default **By View** to **Coarse**, **Medium**, or **Fine**.

- Most elements contain sub-categories that can be modified by expanding the category. For example, doors consist of a panel, frame/mullion, swing, etc., each of which can be customized, as shown in Figure 7–25.

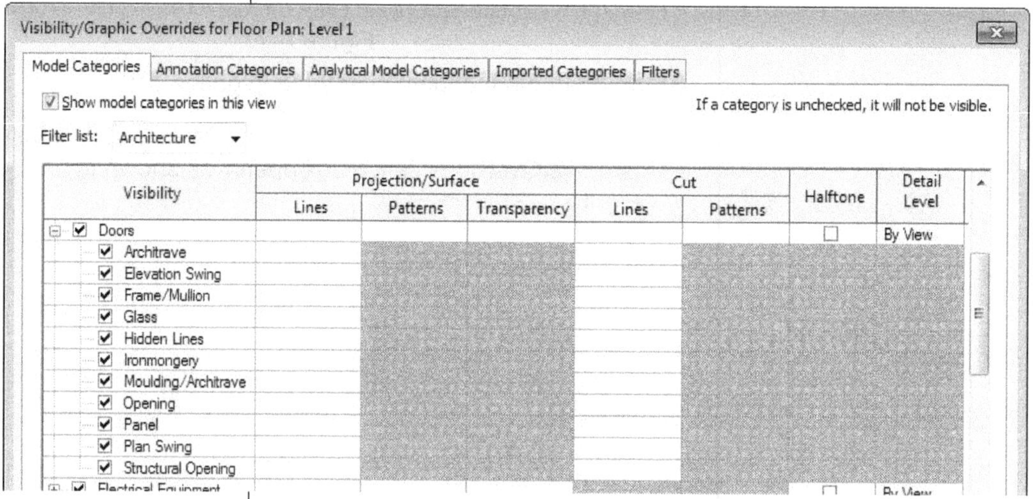

Figure 7–25

You can use filters to refine the category selection.

- The Visibility/Graphic Overrides are divided into *Model, Annotation, Analytical Model*, and *Imported* categories. If filters have been set up in the project, they are included on the *Filters* tab.

- When working with additional information or data (such as *Design Options, Linked Files*, or *Worksets*), new tabs are automatically added to the Visibility/Graphic Overrides dialog box.

Hint: Applying View Templates

A powerful way to use views effectively is to set up a view and then save it as a View Template. To apply a View Template, right-click on a view in the Project Browser and select **Apply View Template Properties....** Then, in the Apply View Template dialog box, select a *Name* in the list (as shown in Figure 7–26) and click ⬚ OK ⬚.

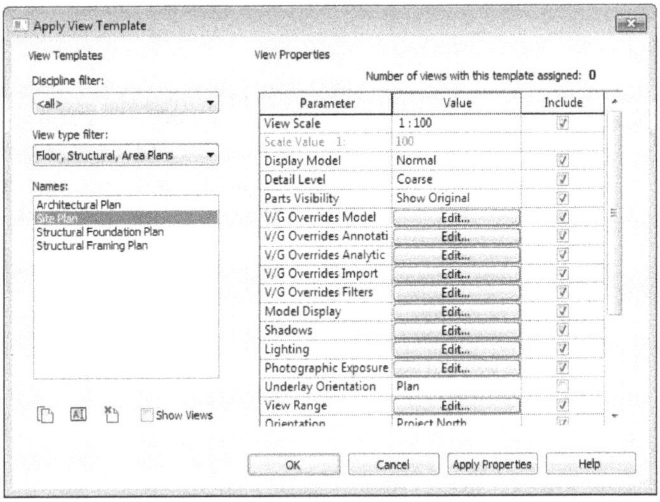

Figure 7–26

- View Templates can also be preset in the View Properties as shown in Figure 7–27.

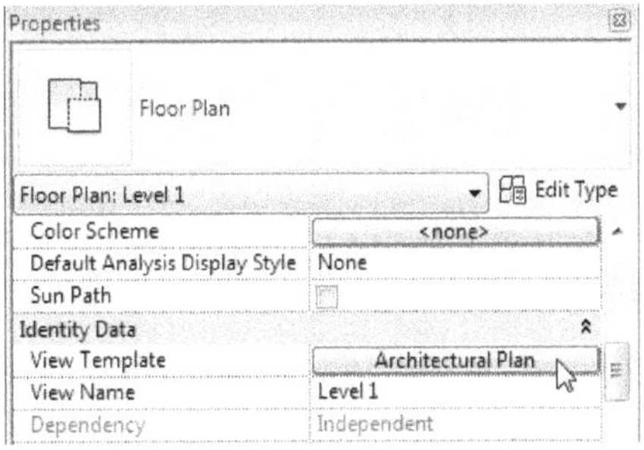

Figure 7–27

- To modify the view without long term changes, click

  ⬚ (Temporary View Properties) in the View Control Bar, enable the temporary View Properties, and select a different view template from the same menu. When finished, select **Restore View Properties**.

Practice 7a

Set Up Duplicate Views and Callouts

Learning Objectives

- Duplicate views and adjust view settings to display different parts of the building as well as different scales.
- Create callouts of a guest room and modify the visibility graphics overrides so that one displays dimensions and the other displays the furniture plan.

Estimated time for completion: 15 minutes

In this practice you will create duplicate views and set the views at different scales with different areas of the project cropped. You will also create callout views and make modifications to the visibility graphics, where furniture and other interior details can be added, as shown in Figure 7–28.

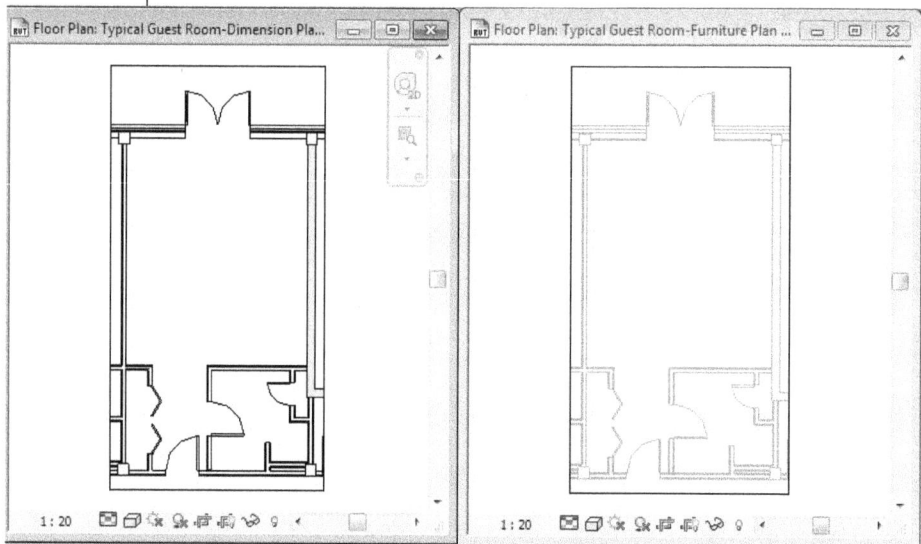

Figure 7–28

Task 1 - Duplicate views.

1. Open the project **Modern-Hotel-Views-M.rvt** from your class folder. This file contains additional elements used in this and later practices.

2. In the Project Browser, right-click on the **Floor Plans: Floor 1** view and select **Duplicate View>Duplicate with Detailing**. A copy of the view is created that includes the door tags.

3. Right-click on the new view and rename it as **Floor 1 with Pool**.

4. In the View Control Bar, change the *Scale* to **1:200**. All of the annotations become larger, as they need to plot correctly at this scale.

5. Open the **Floor Plans: Floor 1** view (the original view).

6. In the View Control Bar, click ⊞ (Show Crop Region).

7. Zoom out until the full extents of the crop region are displayed and select it, as shown in Figure 7–29.

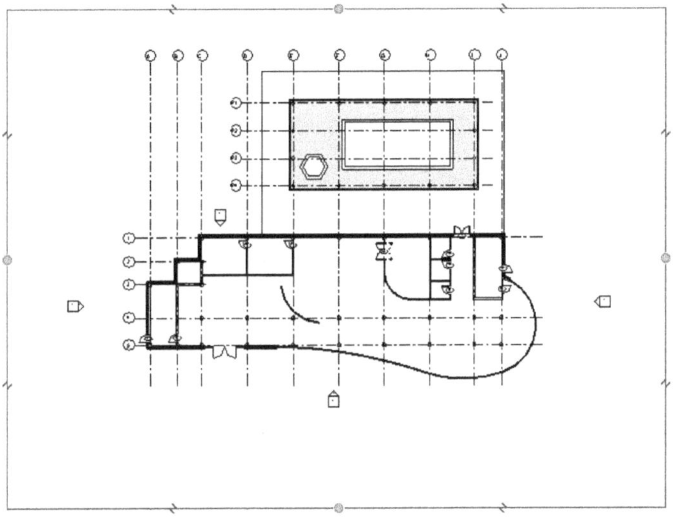

Figure 7–29

8. Drag and move the Controls (blue circles) of the crop region so that only the main building displays, as shown in Figure 7–30. The grid lines are controlled by the Annotation Crop Region, even though they are hidden.

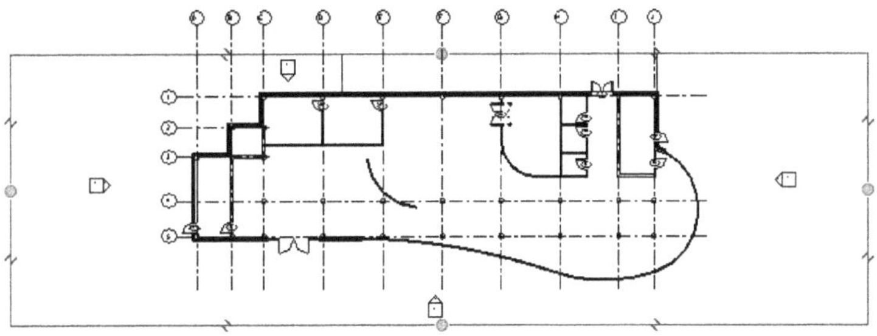

Figure 7–30

9. In the View Control Bar, click ⏹ (Hide Crop Region).

10. In the Project Browser, right-click on the **Floor Plans: Floor 2** view and select **Duplicate View>Duplicate**. This creates a new view without any annotation.

11. Rename this view to **Typical Guest Room Floor Plan**.

12. Turn on the crop region and select it.

13. In Properties, scroll down to the *Extents* area and select **Annotation Crop**. The annotation crop region is now displayed.

14. Use the top Control of the main crop region and drag it down so that it covers the pool house grids. The annotation crop region also moves with the main crop region.

15. Use the bottom Control of the main crop region and drag it up. Place it close to the building.

16. Move the annotation crop region. It can be moved separately.

17. Move the crop regions so that the elevation markers do not display and the grid bubbles are close to the main building, similar to that shown in Figure 7–31.

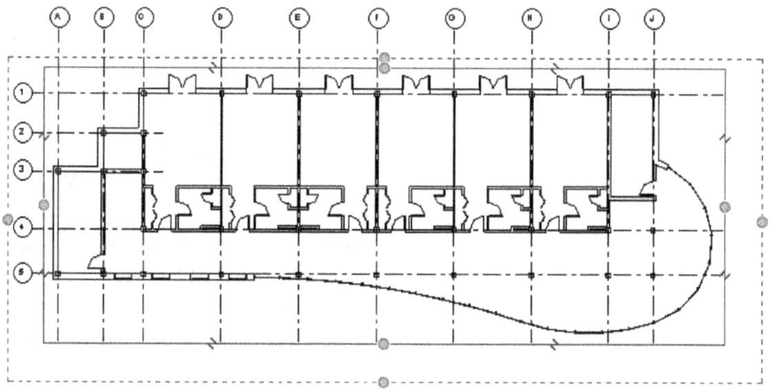

Figure 7–31

18. Turn off the crop region.

19. Select one of the grid lines, right-click and select **Hide in View>Category**.

20. Zoom out to display the entire view. (Hint: Use the shortcuts by pressing <Z> and then pressing <F> or by pressing <Z> and then pressing <E> or double-click the mouse wheel.)

21. Save the project.

Task 2 - Add callout views.

1. Continue working in the **Floor Plans: Typical Guest Room Floor Plan** view.

2. In the *View* tab>Create panel, click ⌀ (Callout).

3. Place a callout around one of the guest rooms, as shown in Figure 7–32. Using the controls, move the bubble as required. Click in empty space to release the selection.

Figure 7–32

4. Double-click on the callout view bubble. It only opens the view that is enclosed within the callout window. Rename the view to **Typical Guest Room - Dimension Plan**.

5. In Properties, change the *Underlay* to **None**.

6. Duplicate the callout view and rename it to **Typical Guest Room - Furniture Plan**. Both views should look similar to Figure 7–33.

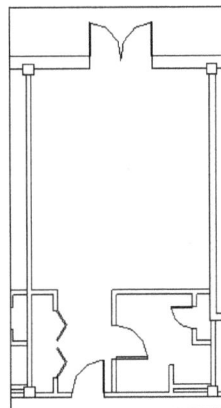

Figure 7–33

7. Open the **Floor Plans: Floor 1** view.

8. In the *View* tab>Create panel, click ⌀⊕ (Callout) and add callouts to the stairs and restrooms. Name the views as shown in Figure 7–34.

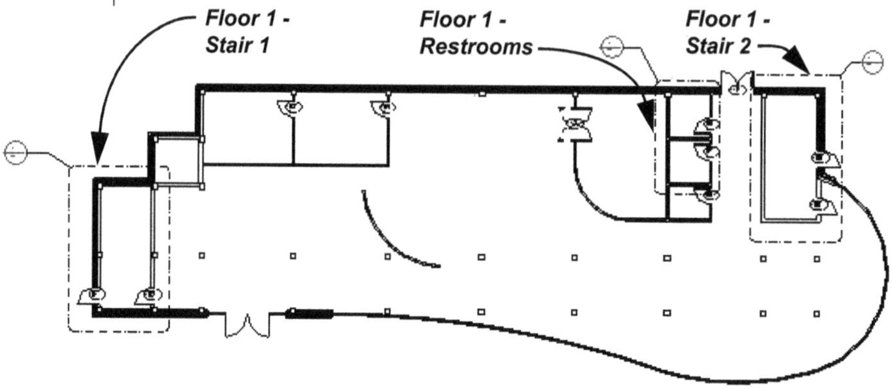

Figure 7–34

9. Save the project.

Task 3 - Override graphics in views.

1. Open the **Floor Plans: Typical Guest Room - Dimension Plan** view.

2. Press <V> twice (or press <V> and then press <G>) to open the Visibility/Graphic Overrides dialog box.

3. In the dialog box, set the *Filter list* to **Architecture** (by clearing the checkmarks for the other options except **Architecture**). In the *Visibility* column, clear **Casework**, **Furniture**, **Furniture Systems**, as shown in Figure 7–35 and **Plumbing Fixtures** (not shown).

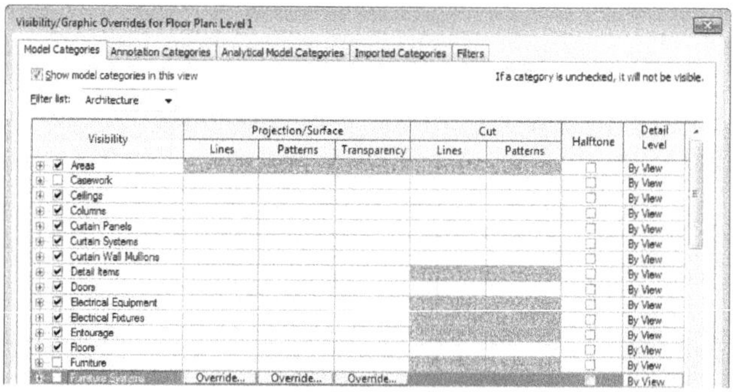

Figure 7–35

4. Click [OK]. While nothing looks different now, when furniture is placed in the model it will not display in this view.

5. Open the **Floor Plans: Typical Guest Room - Furniture Plan** view.

6. Reopen the Visibility/Graphic Overrides dialog box. Below the table, click [All] and place a checkmark in one of the *Halftone* columns. All of the elements are set to halftone.

7. Click [None] to clear all categories.

8. In the *Halftone* column, clear the **Casework**, **Furniture**, **Furniture Systems**, and **Plumbing Fixtures** categories.

9. Click [Apply] to set the changes without exiting the dialog box.

10. In the *Annotation Categories* tab, clear **Show annotation categories in this view**. No annotations elements will display in this view.

11. Click [OK] to close the dialog box. The view should display with all existing elements in halftone, as shown in Figure 7–36.

When furniture, casework, and plumbing fixtures are added, they will display in black against the other halftone elements.

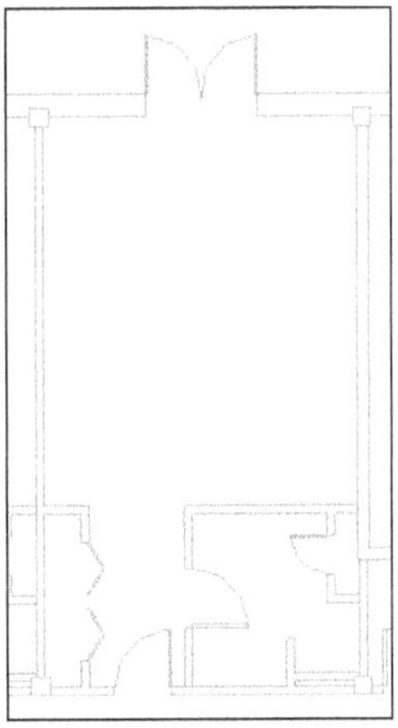

Figure 7–36

12. Save the project.

Practice 7b

Add Foundations and Footings

Learning Objectives

- Use Underlay and view range to create a foundation plan.
- Draw basement walls and add footing to the walls.

Estimated time for completion: 10 minutes

In this practice you will add foundation and footing walls under the exterior walls, as shown in Figure 7–37, and vertical circulation walls.

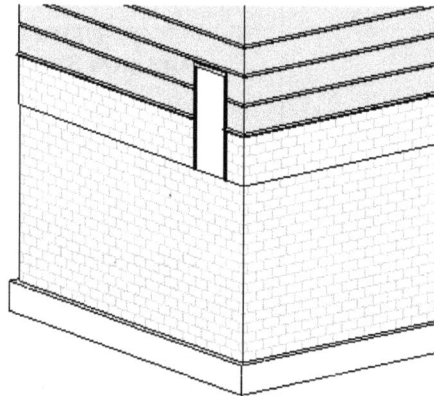

*This project uses the standard **Wall** command to draw foundations and wall footings. Additional structural tools are available.*

Figure 7–37

Task 1 - Add basement walls.

1. Open the project **Modern-Hotel-Foundations-M.rvt** from your class folder.

2. Open the **Floor Plans: T.O. Footing** view.

3. Hide the column grids.

4. In Properties, in the *Graphics* area, set the *Underlay* to **Floor 1** so that the existing walls are displayed.

Footings and foundation elements frequently are placed below the preset level of the view. Changing the View Range enables you to display these elements.

5. Scroll down to the *Extents* area and edit the *View Range*.

6. In the View Range dialog box, in the *Primary Range* area, set *Top* to **Level Above (Basement)** with an *Offset* of **2300mm**, *Cut plane Offset* to **1200mm**, and *Bottom* to **Unlimited**. In the *View Depth* area, set *Level* to **Unlimited**. Click ⬚ OK ⬚.

7. In the *Architecture* tab>Build panel, click ⬚ (Wall).

8. In Properties set the following options: (Reset the constraints if needed.)

- Wall type: **Basic Wall: Generic - 225mm Masonry**
- Location Line: **Core Centerline**
- Base Constraint: **T.O. Footing**
- Base Offset: **0.0**
- Top Constraint: **Up to Level: Floor 1**
- Top Offset: **0.0**

Hover the cursor over a wall and then press <Tab> until the center line displays.

9. In the *Modify | Place Wall* tab>Draw panel, click ✎ (Pick Lines). In the main building underlay, select the core center line of the exterior walls and curtain walls, and around the stairs and elevator to create the walls, as shown in Figure 7–38. (Hint: For the stairwell on the right side, create the inner vertical and horizontal wall and then drag the endpoint of the right exterior wall down so that it intersects with the inner horizontal wall).

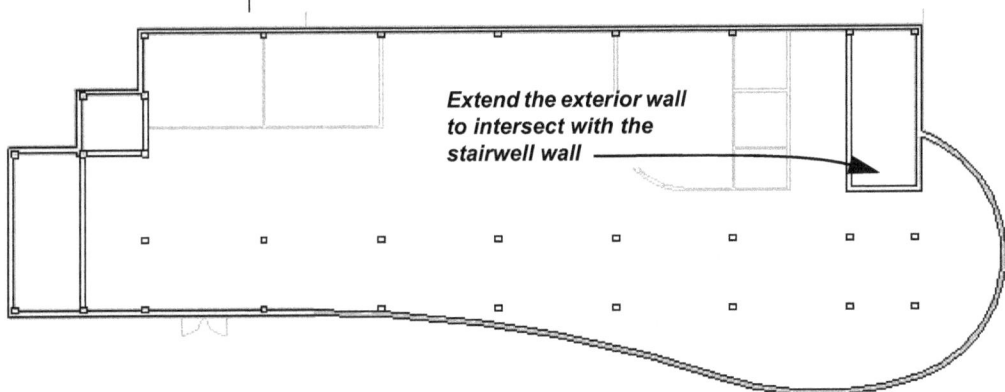

Extend the exterior wall to intersect with the stairwell wall

Figure 7–38

10. Return to the **Modify** command to complete the command.

11. In Properties, change the *Underlay* back to **None**.

Task 2 - Add footings to the walls.

1. Click 🗋 (Wall).

2. In Properties or the Options Bar, set the following options:

   - Wall type: **Basic Wall: Generic - 600mm Concrete**
   - Location Line: **Core Centerline**
   - Base Constraint: **T.O. Footing**
   - Base Offset: (negative) **-450mm**
   - Top Constraint: **Up to Level:T.O.Footing**
   - Top Offset: **0.0**

You might need to zoom in to highlight the core center line.

3. Click ✐ (Pick Line) and select the core center line of all the foundation walls. The wall footings display as shown in Figure 7–39. You add column footings later.

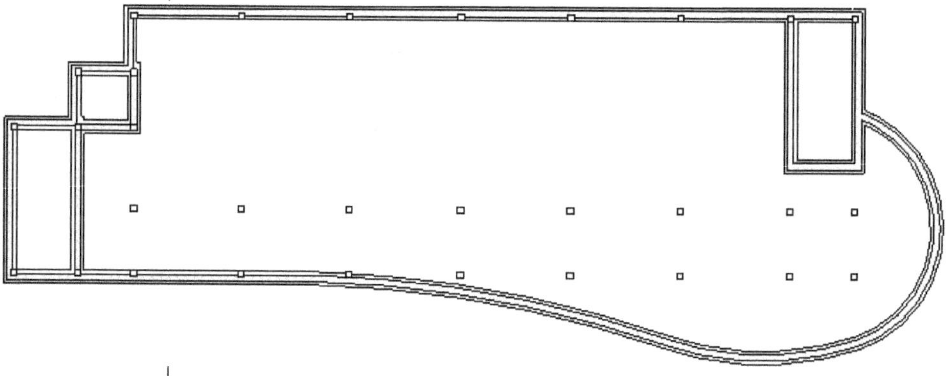

Figure 7–39

4. Save the project.

7.4 Elevations and Sections

Autodesk Certification Topics & Objectives

Pro.   User

Views

- Create section views   ✓

Learning Objectives

- Add building and interior elevations.
- Create building and wall sections.
- Modify elevation and section markers and views.

Elevations and sections are critical elements of construction documents and can assist you as you are working on a model. Any changes made in one of these views (such as the section in Figure 7–40), changes the entire model and any changes made to the project model are also displayed in the elevations and sections.

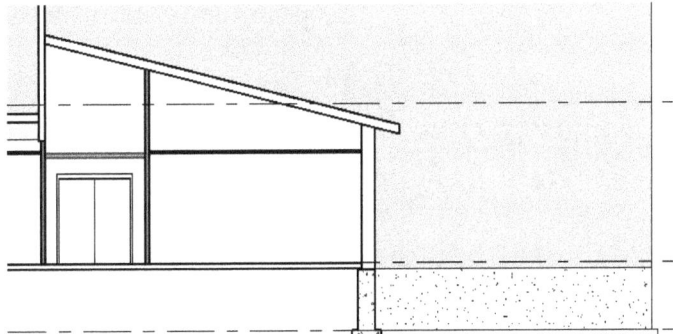

Figure 7–40

- In the Project Browser, elevations are separated by elevation type and sections are separated by section type as shown in Figure 7–41.

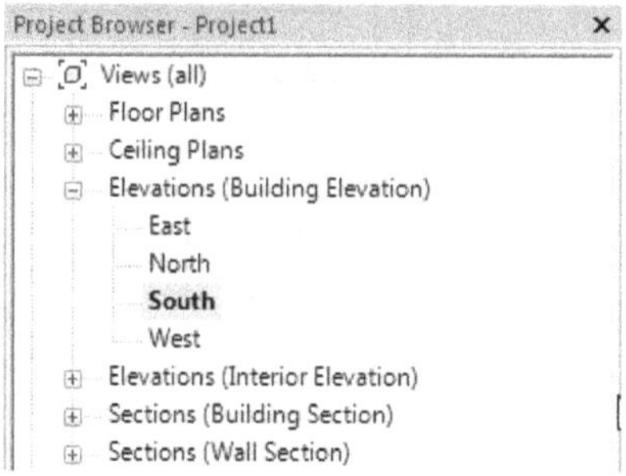

Figure 7–41

- To open an elevation or section view, double-click on the marker arrow or on its name in the Project Browser.

- To give the elevation or section a new name, right-click on it in the Project Browser and select **Rename...**

- When you add an elevation or section to a sheet, the detail number and sheet number are automatically added to the view title.

Elevations

Elevations are *face-on* views of the interiors and exteriors of a building. Four Exterior Elevation views are defined in the default template: **North**, **South**, **East**, and **West**. You can create additional building elevation views at other angles or for Interior Elevation views, such as the Kitchen elevation shown in Figure 7–42.

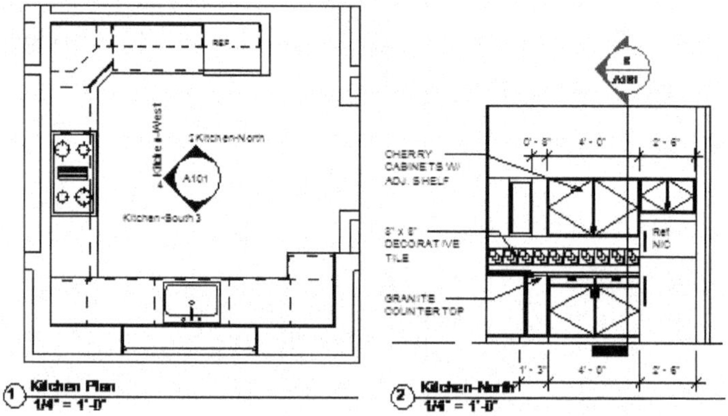

Figure 7–42

- Elevations must be created in plan views.

How To: Create an Elevation

The software remembers the last elevation type used, so you can click the top button if you want to use the same elevation command.

1. In the *View* tab>Create panel, expand ⬆ (Elevation) and click ⬆ (Elevation).
2. In the Type Selector, select the elevation type. Two options that come with the templates are **Building Elevation** and **Interior Elevation**.
3. Move the cursor near one of the walls that defines the elevation. The marker follows the angle of the wall.
4. Click to place the marker.

• The length, width, and height of an elevation are defined by the wall(s) at which the elevation marker is pointing.

Sections

Sections can be created in plan, elevation, and other section views.

Sections are slices through a model. You can create a section through an entire building, as shown in Figure 7–43, or through one wall for a detail.

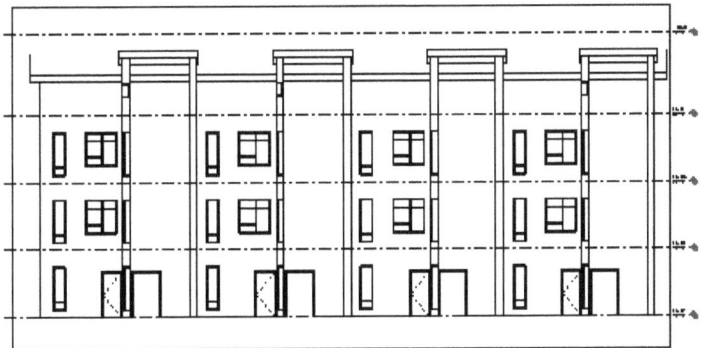

Figure 7–43

How To: Create a Section

1. In the *View* tab>Create panel or in the Quick Access Toolbar, click ◦ (Section).

2. In the Type Selector, select **Section: Building Section** or **Section: Wall Section.** If you want a section in a Drafting view select **Detail View: Detail.**
3. In the view, select a point where you want to locate the bubble and arrowhead.
4. Select the other end point that describes the section.
5. The shape controls display. You can flip the arrow and change the size of the cutting plane, as well as the location of the bubble and flag.

Hint: 3D Section Views

You can modify a 3D view to display in the section, as shown in Figure 7–44.

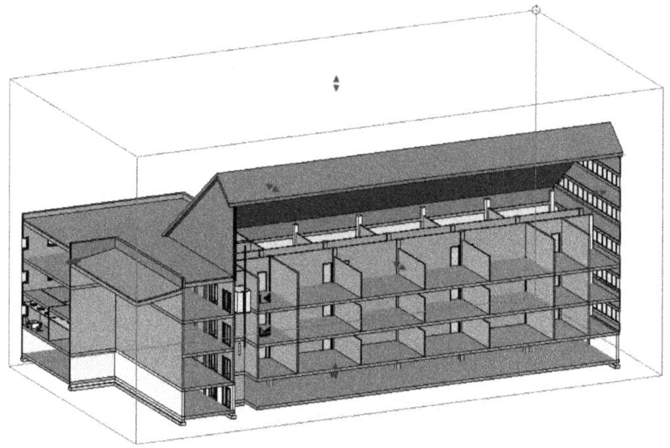

Figure 7–44

1. In a 3D view and without any elements selected, in Properties, in the *Extents* section, select **Section Box**.

2. Click [Apply], or press <Enter>, or click in the view.
3. Select **Section Box** in the 3D view and use the shape handles to modify the plane of the box.

• You can rotate the box to achieve the required cut. Select and drag the ○ (Rotate) control until the cut that you want is displayed.

Modifying Elevations and Sections

There are two parts to modifying elevations and sections, modifying the markers (as shown in Figure 7–45), and modifying the view. The markers have slightly different options, but the views have the same options.

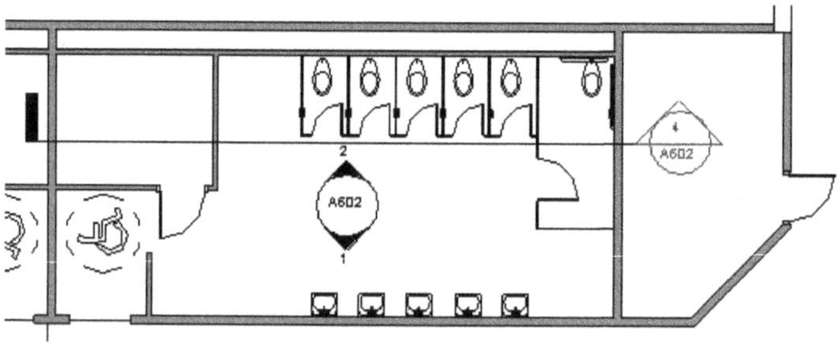

Figure 7–45

Modifying Elevation Markers

When you modify the elevation markers you can specify the length and depth of the clip plane as well as split the section line. Select the arrowhead of the elevation marker (not the circle portion) to display the clip plane. You can adjust the length of the clip planes using the round shape handles (as shown in Figure 7–46) and adjust the depth of the elevation using the

Drag control.

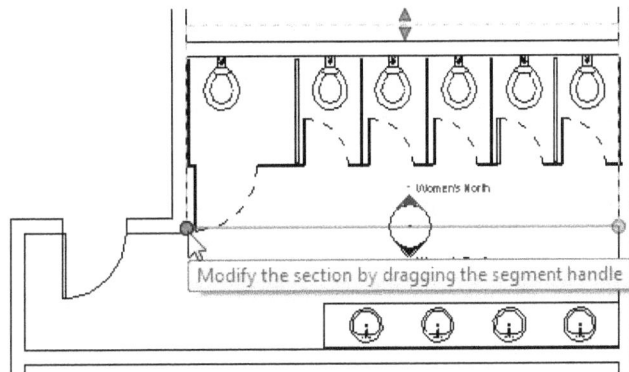

Figure 7–46

To display additional interior elevations from one marker, place an elevation marker and select the circle portion (not the arrowhead). With the elevation marker selected, place a checkmark in the directions that you want to display, as shown in Figure 7–47.

Figure 7–47

- You can also rotate the marker using ↻ (Rotate) (i.e., for a room with angled walls).

Modifying Section Markers

When you modify the section markers, you can specify the length and depth of the clip plane, flip the orientation, and create a gap as well as split the section line. Various shape handles and controls enable you to modify a section, as shown in Figure 7–48.

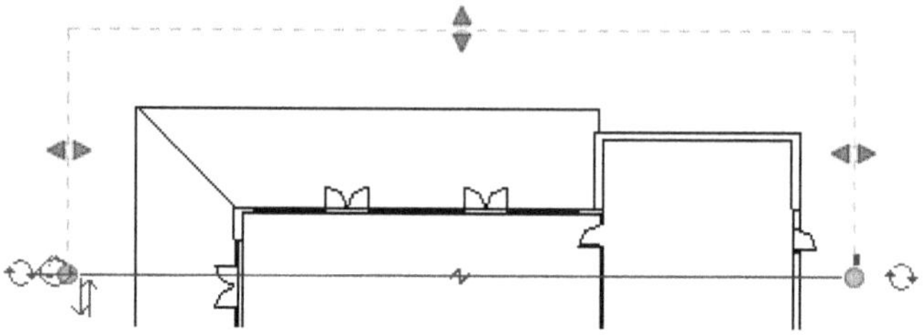

Figure 7–48

- Change the size and location of the cut plane by dragging (Arrow) on the dashed lines in or out.

- Change the location of the arrow or flag without changing the cut boundary by dragging the circular controls at either end of the section line.

- Click ⇆ (Flip) to change the direction of the arrowhead, which also flips the entire section.

- Cycle between an arrowhead, flag, or nothing on each end of the section by clicking ↻ (Cycle Section Head/Tail).

- Create gaps in section lines by clicking ⤞ (Gaps in Segments), as shown in Figure 7–49. Select it again to restore the full section cut.

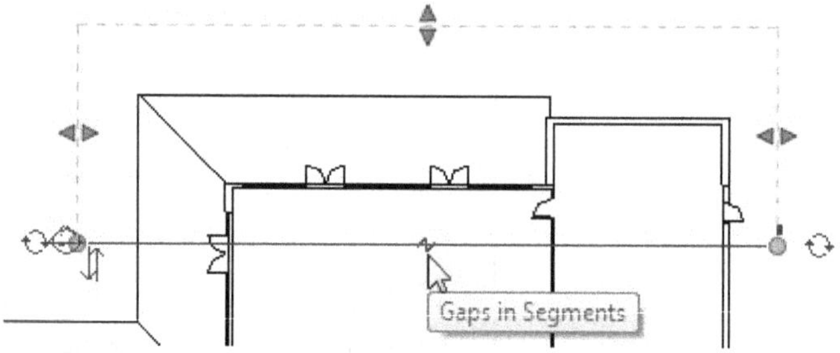

Figure 7–49

How To: Split an Elevation or Section Line

In some cases, you need to create additional jogs in an elevation or section line so that it displays the most important information along the cut, as shown for a section in Figure 7–50.

Figure 7–50

1. Select the elevation or section line you want to split.
2. In the Section panel, click (Split Segment).
3. Select the point along the line where you want to create the split, as shown in Figure 7–51.

Figure 7–51

4. Specify the location of the split line, as shown in Figure 7–52.

Figure 7–52

- If you need to adjust the location of any segment on the section line, modify it and drag the shape handles along each segment of the line, as shown in Figure 7–53.

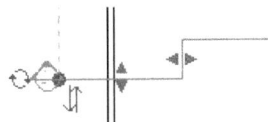

Figure 7–53

- To bring a split elevation or section line back into place, use a shape handle to drag it until it is in line with the rest of the elevation or line.

Modifying Elevation and Section Views

Modifying elevation and section views includes the same methods as the callout views, including adjusting the crop region to specify what needs to be seen. You can modify the view by dragging the segment handles and use the break controls as shown for an elevation view in Figure 7–54.

Figure 7–54

- You can also edit the crop region to reshape the boundary of the view. Select the crop region and, in the *Modify | Views* tab>Mode panel, click (Edit Crop).

- If you want to return a modified crop region to the original rectangular configuration, click (Reset Crop).

Hint: Using Thin Lines

The software automatically applies line weights to views, as shown for a section on the left in Figure 7–55. If a line weight seems heavy or obscures your work on the elements, turn off the line weights. In the Quick Access Toolbar or in the *View* tab>Graphics panel, click (Thin Lines). The lines display with the same weight, as shown on the right in Figure 7–55.

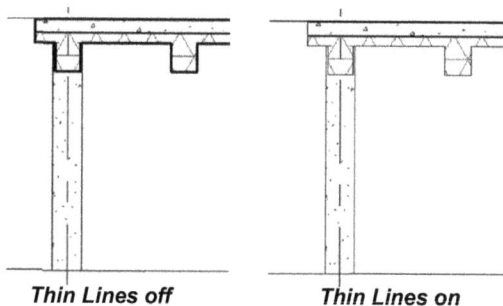

Thin Lines off   *Thin Lines on*

Figure 7–55

Practice 7c

Create Elevations and Sections

Estimated time for completion: 20 minutes

Learning Objectives

- Create exterior and interior elevations.
- Add building sections and wall sections.

In this practice you will create exterior and interior elevations. You will also add building sections, as shown in Figure 7–56, and several wall sections to the project.

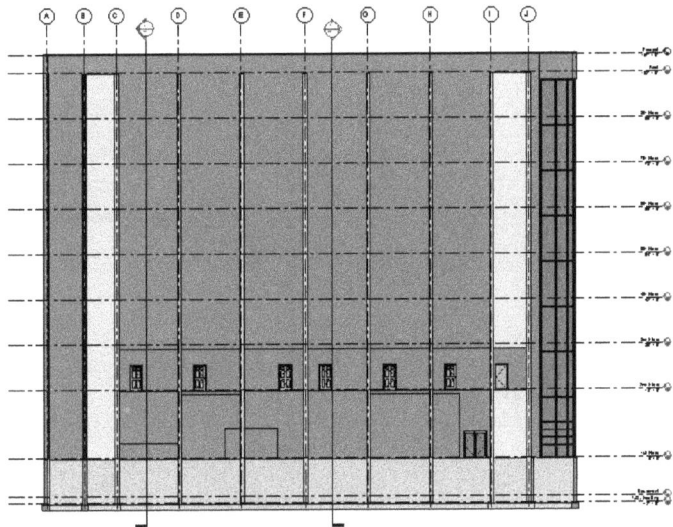

Figure 7–56

Task 1 - Add exterior elevations.

1. Open the project **Modern-Hotel-Elevations-M.rvt** from your class folder.

2. Open the **Floor Plans: Floor 1 with Pool** view.

3. In the View Control Bar, click ⬚ (Show Crop Region).

4. Ensure that there is enough space above the pool house to add an elevation mark at this scale, if not, move the crop region up.

If required, turn on the Elevation Markers using either the Visibility Graphic Overrides dialog box or Reveal Hidden Elements.

5. In the *View* tab>Create panel, expand ⬆ (Elevation) and click ⬆ (Elevation). In the Type Selector, select **Elevation: Building Elevation**.

6. Place an elevation marker outside of the pool building, as shown in Figure 7–57.

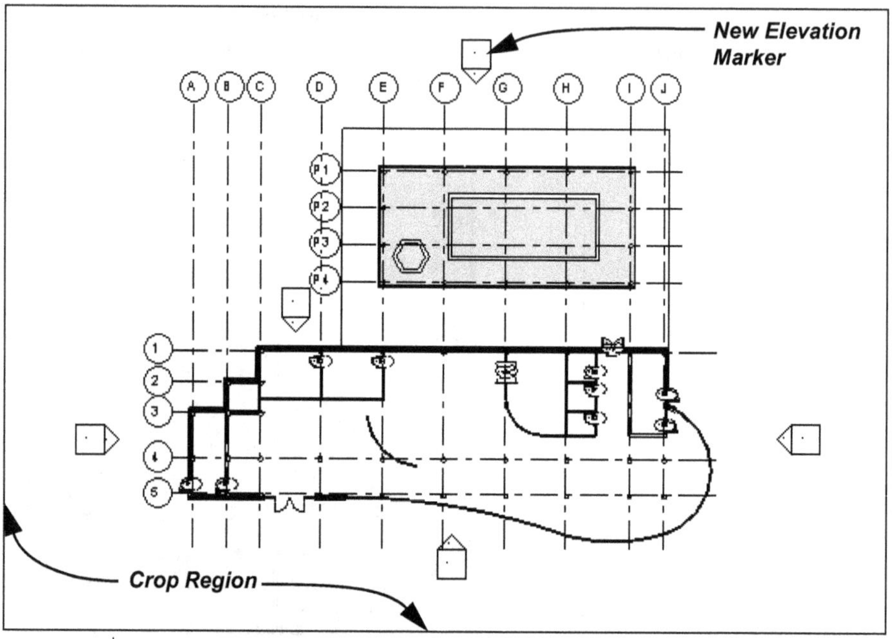

Figure 7–57

7. Return to the **Modify** command to complete the command.

8. Select the pointed side of the new elevation marker.

9. Change the length and depth of the elevation boundaries so only the poolhouse is displayed, as shown in Figure 7–58.

Grids are hidden to clarify the view.

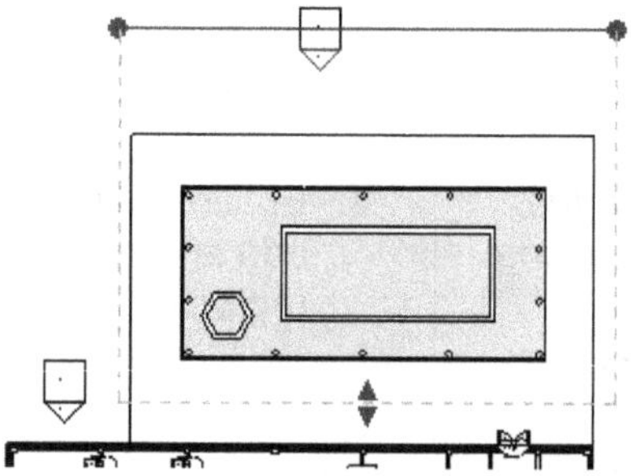

Figure 7–58

10. Double-click on the pointed side of the elevation marker to open the elevation view.

11. Change the crop region so that the height is up to **Floor 3** and the bottom is just below the floor line. Bring the sides in close to the pool building.

12. Hide the grids and levels so that the elevation is similar to that shown in Figure 7–59.

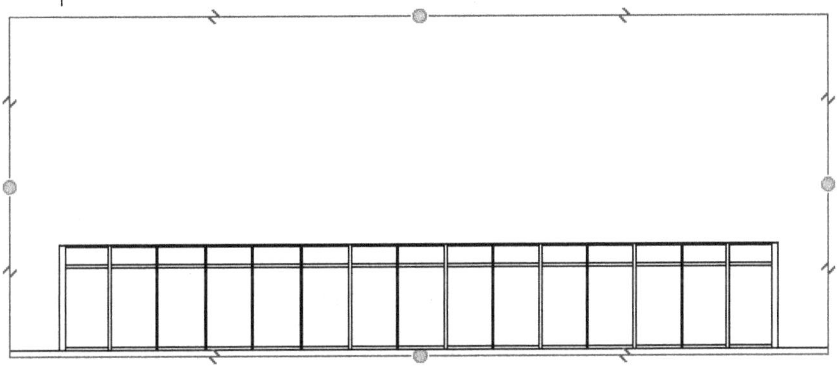

Figure 7–59

13. Turn off crop region.

In this project, North is considered the top of the project.

14. In the Project Browser, rename the elevation (Elevation 1 -a if you selected this direction first) as **Pool-North**.

15. Return to the **Floor Plans: Floor 1 with Pool** view.

16. Add elevation markers to the other sides of the poolhouse.

17. Open the new elevations. Resize and rename them as required.

18. Save the project.

Task 2 - Add interior elevations.

1. Open the **Floor Plans: Floor 1 - Restrooms** view.

2. In the *View* tab>Create panel, click 🛆 (Elevation).

3. In the Type Selector, select **Elevation: Interior Elevation**.

4. Place an elevation in one of the restrooms and then in the other restroom.

5. Return to the **Modify** command to finish.

---

6. Select the circle part of one of the elevation markers and check each of the boxes, as shown in Figure 7–60. This places an elevation in each direction.

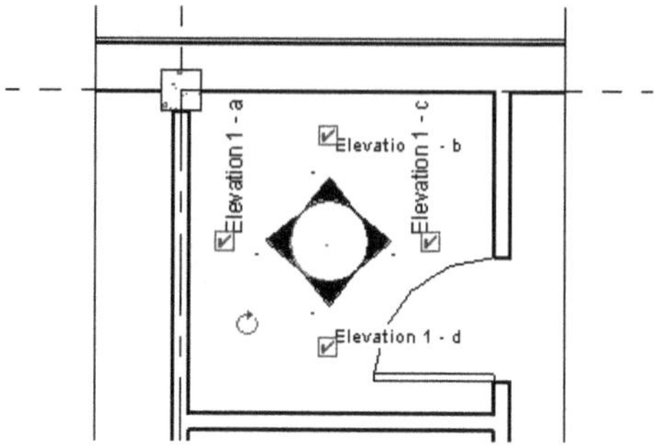

Figure 7–60

7. Repeat for the other restroom.

8. In the Project Browser, under *Elevations (Interior Elevation)*, as shown in Figure 7–61, rename the top restroom elevations as **Men's Restroom-North**, **South**, **East**, **West** and the bottom restroom elevations as **Women's Restroom-North**, **South**, **East**, **West**.

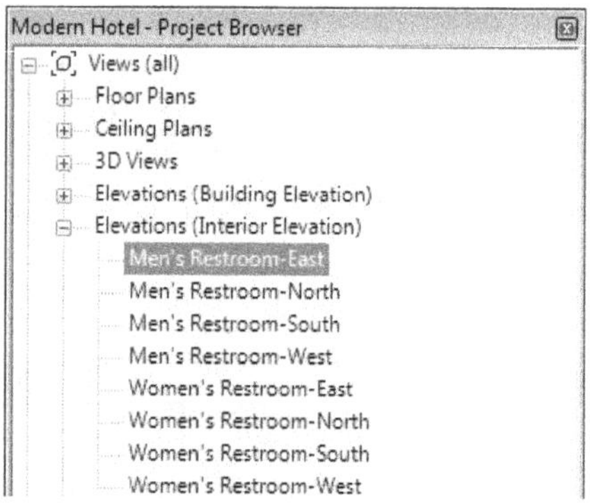

Figure 7–61

9. Open one of the elevations facing the door (**Men's Restroom-East**). The interior elevation automatically stops at the boundaries of the walls and the level above.

10. Save the project.

Task 3 - Clean up a view and add building sections.

1. Open the **Floor Plans: Floor 1** view.

2. Select all the elements around the restrooms. Use a selection window around the restrooms.

In this case you do not want to hide the entire category of elevation markers.

3. In the Status Bar or in the *Modify | Multi-Select* tab>Selection panel, click ⛢ (Filter).

4. In the Filter dialog box, clear all of the selections except **Elevations** and **Views** and click OK . Only the Interior Elevation markers in the restrooms should be selected.

5. Right-click and select **Hide in View>Elements**.

6. In the View Control Bar, click ⛶ (Do Not Crop View).

7. Move the elevation markers closer to the building.

8. In the View Control Bar, click ⛶ (Crop View).

9. In the *View* tab>Create panel, click ⛶ (Section).

10. In the Type Selector, select **Section: Building Section**.

11. Draw a horizontal section and a vertical section through the building, as shown in Figure 7–62.

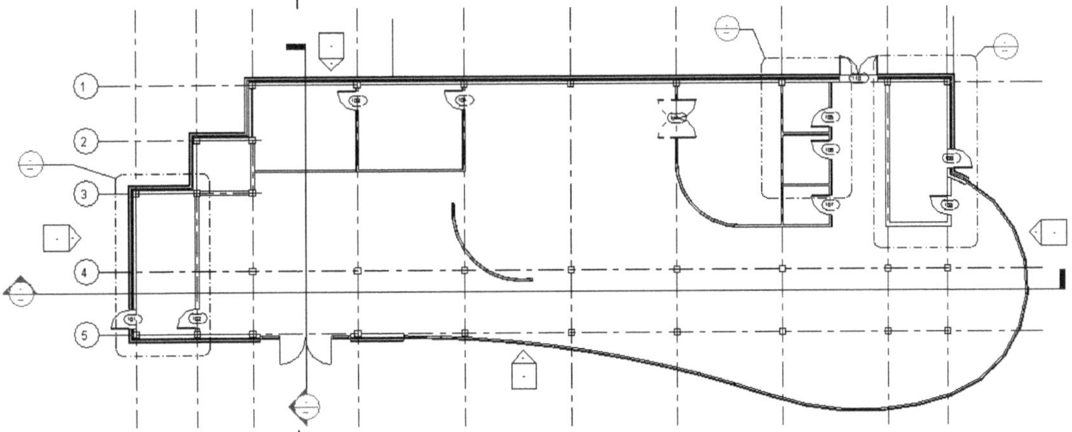

Figure 7–62

12. In the Project Browser, under *Sections*, rename them to **East-West Section** and **North-South Section**.

13. View each of the building sections.

Task 4 - Add wall sections.

You are using the
Floor 2 *view to place*
the wall sections, as you
want to ensure they go
through certain features,
such as doors and
windows.

1. Open the **Floor Plans: Floor 2** view.

2. Hide the grids if required and hide by element, any extraneous elevation markers.

3. In the *View* tab>Create panel, click ⑲ (Section). In the Type Selector, select **Section: Wall Section**.

4. Draw four wall sections, as shown in Figure 7–63. Ensure that the front wall section passes through a window and the back wall section passes through a door.

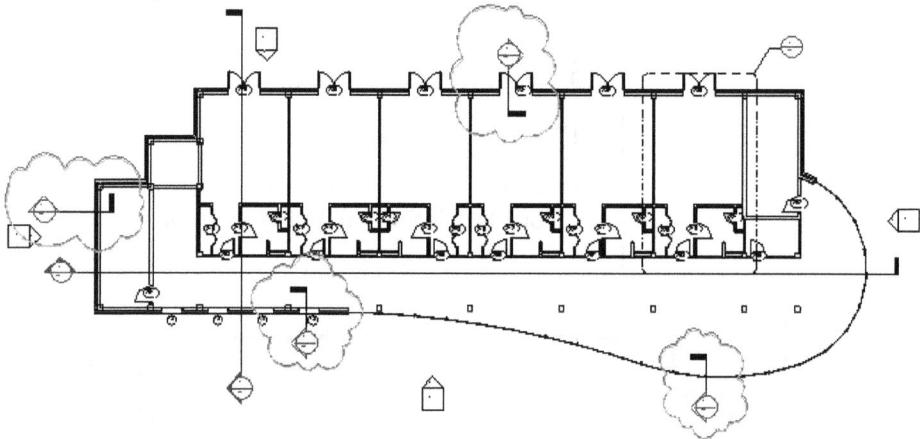

Figure 7–63

5. Move the door and window tag over so they do not interfere with the section cut.

6. View each of the wall sections.

7. Open the **Floor Plans: Floor 1** view.

8. Save the project.

Chapter Review Questions

1. Which of the following commands shown in Figure 7–64, creates a view that results in an independent view displaying the same model geometry and containing a copy of the annotation?

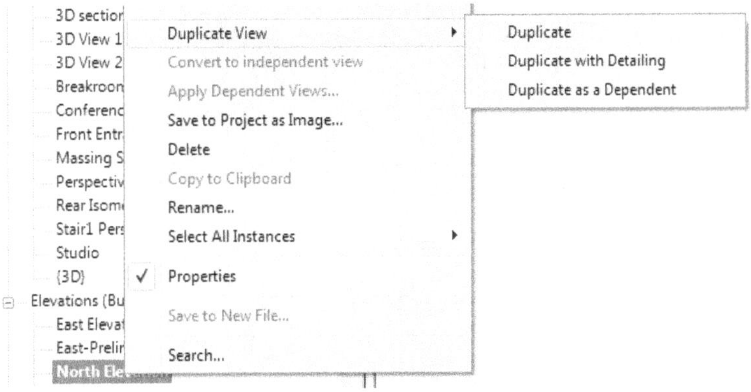

Figure 7–64

   a. Duplicate

   b. Duplicate with Detailing

   c. Duplicate as a Dependent

2. Which of the following is true about the Visibility Graphic Overrides dialog box? (Select all that apply.)

   a. Changes made in the dialog box only affect the current view.

   b. It can only be used to turn categories on and off.

   c. It can be used to turn individual elements on and off.

   d. It can be used to change the color of categories.

3. The purpose of callouts is to create a...

   a. Boundary around part of the model that needs revising, similar to a revision cloud.

   b. View of part of the model for export to the AutoCAD® software for further detailing.

   c. View of part of the model that is linked to the main view from which it is taken.

   d. 2D view of part of the model.

4. You placed dimensions in a view and some of them display and others do not (as shown on the left in Figure 7–65) but you were expecting the view to display as shown on the right in Figure 7–65. To display the missing dimensions you need to modify the...

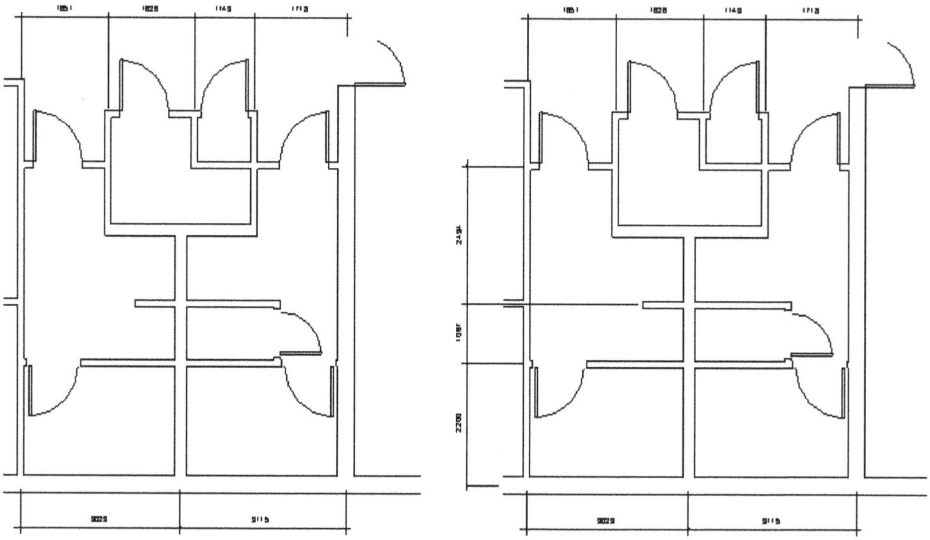

Figure 7–65

a. Dimension Settings

b. View Properties

c. Visibility Graphic Overrides

d. Annotation Crop Region

5. How do you create multiple interior elevations in one room?

a. Using the **Interior Elevation** command, place the elevation marker.

b. Using the **Elevation** command, place the first marker, select it and select the appropriate Show Arrow boxes.

c. Using the **Interior Elevation** command, place an elevation marker for each wall of the room you want to display.

d. Using the **Elevation** command, select a Multiple Elevation marker type, and place the elevation marker.

6. How do you create a jog in a building section, such as that shown in Figure 7–66?

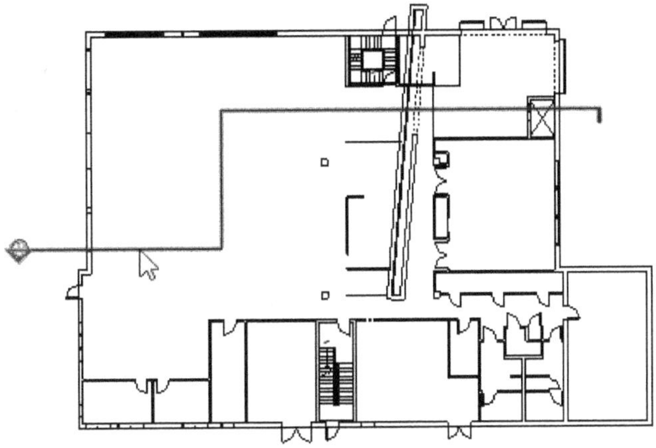

Figure 7–66

a. Use the **Split Element** tool in the *Modify* tab>Modify panel.

b. Select the building section and then click the **Split Segment** icon in the contextual tab.

c. Select the building section and click the blue control in the middle of the section line.

d. Draw two separate sections, and use the **Section Jog** tool to combine them into a jogged section.

Command Summary

Button	Command	Location
	Callout	• **Ribbon:** *View* tab>Create panel>Callout
	Crop View	• **View Control Bar** • **View Properties:** Crop View (*check*)
	Do Not Crop View	• **View Control Bar** • **View Properties:** Crop View (*clear*)
	Duplicate Views> Duplicate	• **Ribbon:** *View* tab>Create panel> Duplicate View>Duplicate View • **Right-click:** (*on a view in the Project Browser*) Duplicate View>Duplicate
	Duplicate Views> Duplicate as Dependent	• **Ribbon:** *View* tab>Create panel> Duplicate View>Duplicate as Dependent • **Right-click:** (*on a view in the Project Browser*) Duplicate View>Duplicate as Dependent
	Duplicate Views> Duplicate with Detailing	• **Ribbon:** *View* tab>Create panel> Duplicate View>Duplicate with Detailing • **Right-click:** (*on a view in the Project Browser*) Duplicate View>Duplicate with Detailing
	Edit Crop	• **Ribbon:** (*when the crop region of a callout, elevation, or section view is selected*) Modify | *Views* tab>Mode panel>Edit Crop
	Elevation	• **Ribbon:** *View* tab>Create panel> Elevation>Elevation
	Hide Crop Region	• **View Control Bar** • **View Properties:** Crop Region Visible (*clear*)
	Hide in View	• **Ribbon:** *Modify* tab>View Graphics panel>Hide>Elements *or* By Category • **Right-click:** (*when an element is selected*) Hide in View>Elements *or* Category
	Override Graphics in View	• **Ribbon:** *Modify* tab>View Graphics panel>Hide>Elements *or* By Category • **Right-click:** (*when an element is selected*) Override Graphics in View>By Element *or* By Category • **Shortcut:** (*category only*) <V> and <V>, <V> and <G>

	Reset Crop	• **Ribbon:** *(when the crop region of a callout, elevation or section view is selected)* Modify	Views tab>Mode panel>Reset Crop
	Reveal Hidden Elements	• **View Control Bar**
	Section	• **Ribbon:** *View* tab>Create panel> Section • **Quick Access Toolbar**
	Show Crop Region	• **View Control Bar** • **View Properties:** Crop Region Visible *(check)*
	Size Crop	• **Ribbon:** *(when the crop region of a callout, elevation or section view is selected)* Modify	Views tab>Mode panel>Size Crop
	Split Segment	• **Ribbon:** *(when the elevation or section marker is selected)* Modify	Views tab>Section panel>Split Segment
	Temporary Hide/Isolate	• **View Control Bar**

Chapter 8

Adding Components

In this chapter you learn about adding components in a project. You learn how to load components from the Autodesk® Revit® library and from Autodesk® Seek. You also learn how to modify component types and locations.

This chapter contains the following topics:

- **Adding Components**
- **Modifying Components**

8.1 Adding Components

Autodesk Certification Topics & Objectives

Pro.   User

Families

- Work with families   ✓   ✓

Learning Objectives

- Place stand-alone components, such as furniture, in a project.
- Load components from the Autodesk Revit library and from Autodesk Seek.

Many types of elements are added to a project using components. These can include freestanding components, such as the furniture, floor lamp, and table lamp shown in Figure 8–1. They can also include wall, ceiling, floor, roof, face and line-based components. These components must be placed on the referenced element, such as the fluorescent light fixtures in Figure 8–1.

Figure 8–1

- Several components are included in the default template, making them automatically available in new projects. You can load more components into a project or create your own as required.

- Components are located in family files with the extension RFA. For example, a component family named Desk.rfa can contain several types and sizes.

How To: Place a Component

1. In the *Architecture* tab>Build panel, click ⬚ (Place a Component), or use the shortcut by pressing <C> and then pressing <M>.
2. In the Type Selector, select the component you want to add to the project. If the component you want to use is not displayed, you can load another one.
3. In the view, select a point to place the stand-alone component.

Loading Components

If the components you are looking for are not available, you can look in the Autodesk Revit Library, which contains many options. You can also check which components your company has. As you start building a custom library, you can find vendor-specific components on Autodesk Seek.

How To: Load a Family

You can also load a family from the Modify | Place Component tab> Mode panel when placing a component.

1. In the *Insert* tab>Load from Library panel, click

   ⬚ (Load Family).
2. In the Load Family dialog box, locate the folder that contains the family or families you want to load and select them, as shown in Figure 8–2. To load more than one family at a time, hold down <Ctrl> while selecting.

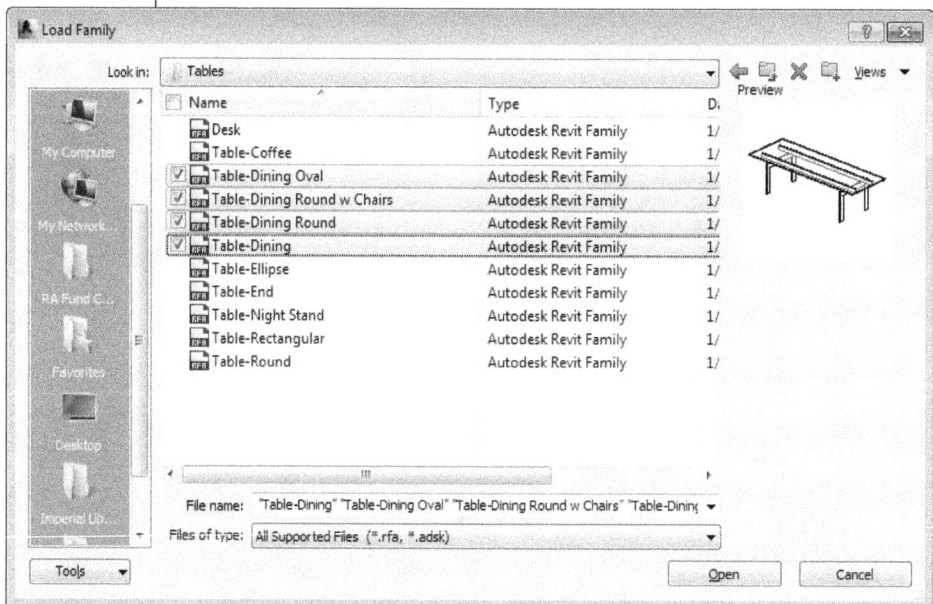

Figure 8–2

3. Click [Open] .

4. Once the family (or families) is loaded, click ⬒ (Component) and select the type you want to use from the Type Selector, as shown in Figure 8–3.

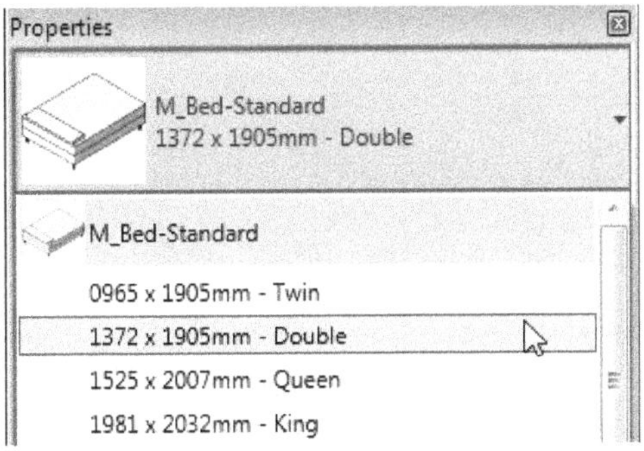

Figure 8–3

Loading from Autodesk Seek

Many components are created by manufacturers and other users that are available on-line at Autodesk Seek, as shown in Figure 8–4. You can do a search from within the software or directly on the website and access content for items as diverse as elevator doors, furniture, equipment, details, and materials.

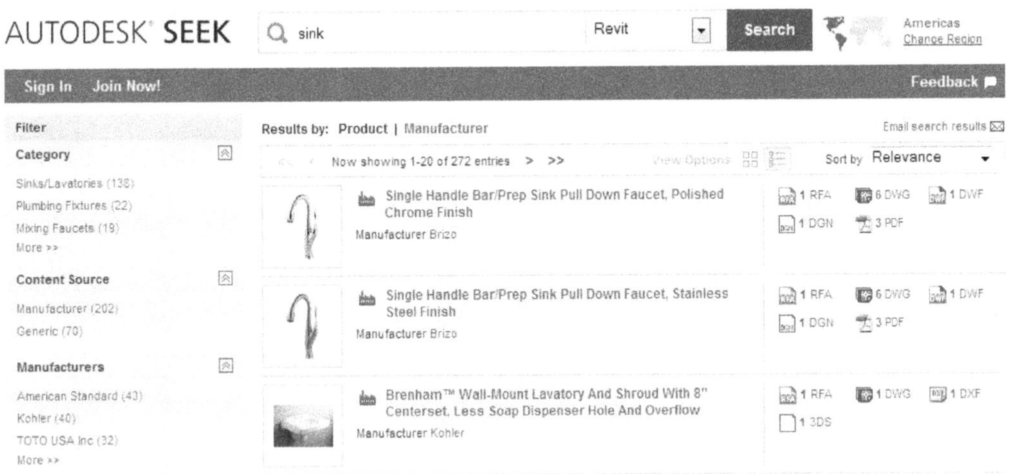

Figure 8–4

How To: Find and Load a Component from Autodesk Seek

1. In the *Insert* tab>Autodesk Seek panel, type the item you are looking for, such as elevator doors, as shown in Figure 8–5.

   Then click 🔍 (Search Seek Online).

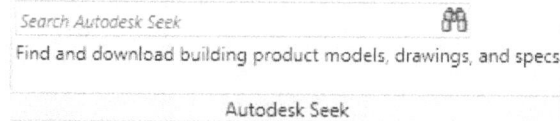

Search Autodesk Seek
Find and download building product models, drawings, and specs

Autodesk Seek

Figure 8–5

2. In the Autodesk Seek website, select the model of the component you want to use.
3. More information about that specific component displays. In the download area, as shown in Figure 8–6, select the file

   you want to use and click **Download selected**.

Figure 8–6

4. Once you accept the terms and conditions, the file is downloaded to your computer. It might automatically open in the software depending on your web browser and other settings.
5. Save the family file to the appropriate folder.
6. Use 📥 (Load Family) to bring it into the current project.

8.2 Modifying Components

Autodesk Certification Topics & Objectives

Pro.   User

Families

• Work with families   ✓   ✓

Learning Objectives

- Change component types.
- Pick a new host element or move with nearby host elements.
- Purge unused elements.

Components can be modified when they are selected by changing the type in the Type Selector. With some types, you can use controls. For example, as shown in Figure 8–7, you might have placed a task chair in a project but now you need to change it to an executive chair. You can also select a new host for a component and move components with nearby elements.

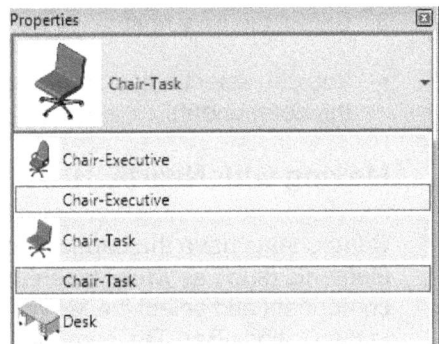

Figure 8–7

Working with Host Elements

If you need to move a component from the level on which it was inserted, you can change its host. For example, one of the desks in Figure 8–8 is floating above the floor. It was placed on Level 1 when it was inserted. You can also have components move when nearby host elements are moved.

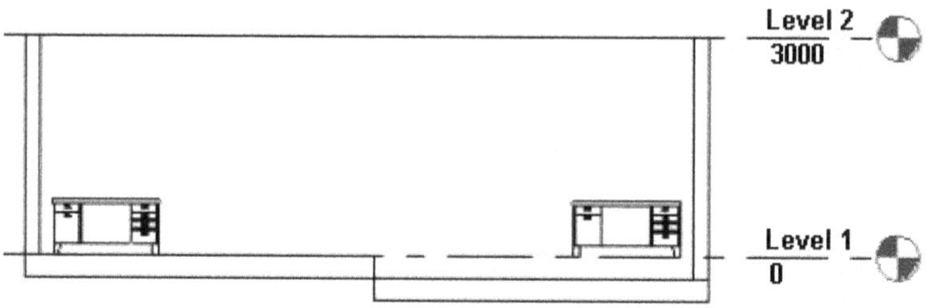

Figure 8–8

How To: Pick a New Host Element

1. Select a component.
2. In the *<component type>* contextual tab>Host panel, click

   (Pick New Host).
3. Select the new host (e.g., the floor).

- You can select a floor, surface, or level to be the new host for the components.

Moving with Nearby Host Elements

Components have the capacity to move with nearby host elements (such as walls) when they are moved. Select the component and select the **Moves With Nearby Elements** option in the Options Bar. The component is automatically assigned to the closest host elements.

For example, a desk near the corner of two walls is linked to those two walls. If you move either wall, the desk moves as well. However, you can still move the desk independently of the walls.

- You cannot specify which elements the component should be linked to; the software determines this automatically. This option only works with host elements (such as walls), not with other components.

Purging Unused Elements

You can remove unused elements from a project, including individual component types, as shown in Figure 8–9.

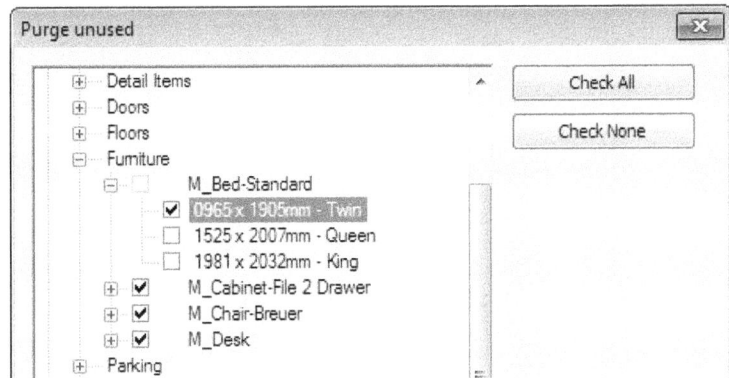

Figure 8–9

How To: Purge Unused Elements

1. In the *Manage* tab>Settings panel, click 🔲 (Purge Unused).

2. In the Purge unused dialog box, click [Check None] and select the elements you want to purge.

3. Click [OK].

• Purging unused components not only helps simplify the component list, but more importantly, reduces the project file size.

Practice 8a

Add Components

Learning Objectives

- Add furniture, casework, and planting components to a floor plan.
- Load an elevator and elevator door from Autodesk Seek and add them in the project.
- Add footings at the base of each column.

Estimated time for completion: 20 minutes

In this practice you will add furniture to the lobby of a hotel, as shown in Figure 8–10. You can follow the suggested layouts or create your own designs. You will also download components from Autodesk Seek and apply footings to columns. If you have time, add casework and equipment to the Breakfast and Preparation areas.

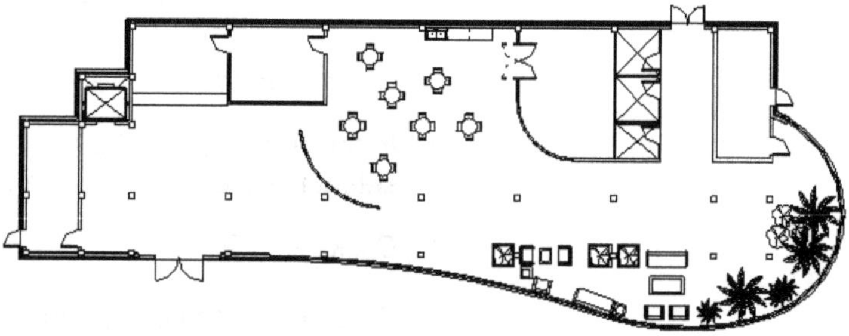

Figure 8–10

Task 1 - Add furniture to the lobby.

1. Open the project **Modern-Hotel-Components-M.rvt** from your class folder.

2. In the Project Browser, right-click on the **Floor Plans: Floor 1** view and select **Duplicate View>Duplicate**.

3. Rename the new view to **Floor 1 - Furniture Plan**.

4. Hide all annotations and grids, so that only the walls, doors, and columns are displayed.

5. In the *Architecture* tab>Build panel, expand ⬛ (Component) and click ⬛ (Place a Component).

6. In the Type Selector, review the various furniture components that are available for the project. Select **M_Chair-Corbu** and place it in the lobby area near the curved curtain walls.

7. Open the **Floor Plans: Floor 1** view. The chair displays in this view as well.

8. Open the Visibility/Graphic Overrides dialog box and toggle off the *Visibility* of **Casework, Furniture, Furniture Systems, Planting,** and **Site.** Click [OK]. The chair is no longer displayed in the Floor 1 view.

9. Return to the **Floor Plans: Floor 1 Furniture Plan**.

10. Start the **Component** command. In the *Modify | Place Component* tab>Mode panel, click (Load Family). In the *Furniture>Tables* folder, select **M_Table-Dining Round w Chairs.rfa** and open it.

11. Repeat the **Load Family** command and load the following:

    • In the *Planting* folder, **M_RPC Plant-Tropical.rfa** and **M_RPC Tree-Tropical.rfa**.
    • In the *Site>Accessories* folder, **M_Planter.rfa**.

12. Place and arrange the components as required, placing the dining tables in the breakfast area and other elements in the lobby, as shown in Figure 8–11. Place at least one plant in a planter.

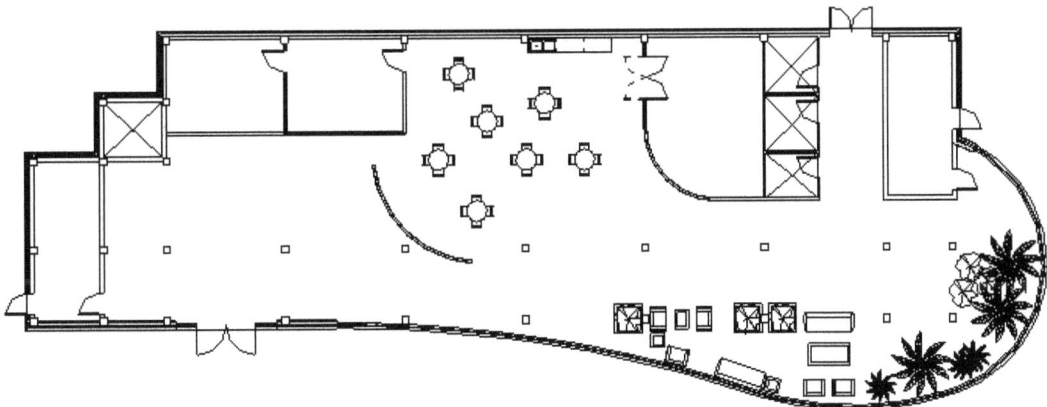

Figure 8–11

13. Zoom in on the office area near the elevator where there is a partial height wall.

Countertops are automatically set to 920mm above the level where they are placed. This wall is 1220mm high and the countertop thickness is about 40mm.

14. Start the **Component** command and load **M_Countertop-Lobby.rfa** from the *Class Library* folder in your class folder.

15. In Properties, set the *Offset* to **340mm**.

16. Place the Countertop component over the partial height wall. Modify its length using the controls on each end, as shown in Figure 8–12.

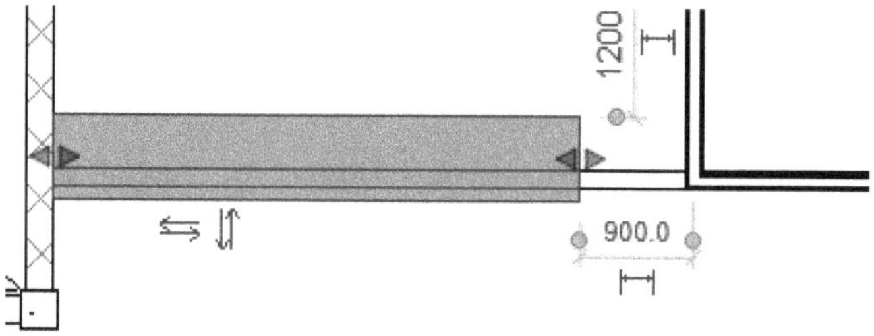

Figure 8–12

Task 2 - Add elevator components.

1. Pan over to the elevator.

2. In the *Architecture* tab>Build panel, click (Place a Component).

3. In the *Modify | Place Component* tab>Mode panel, click (Load Family).

4. In the *Class Library* folder in your class folder, open **M_Elevator-Door- Center-M.rfa** and **M_Elevator-Electoric.rfa**.

5. In the Type Selector, select **M_Elevator-Electric: 1150kg** and place it in the shaft.

6. In the Type Selector, select **M_Elevator-Door-Center: 1050 x 2100mm** and place it in the door, as shown in Figure 8–13.

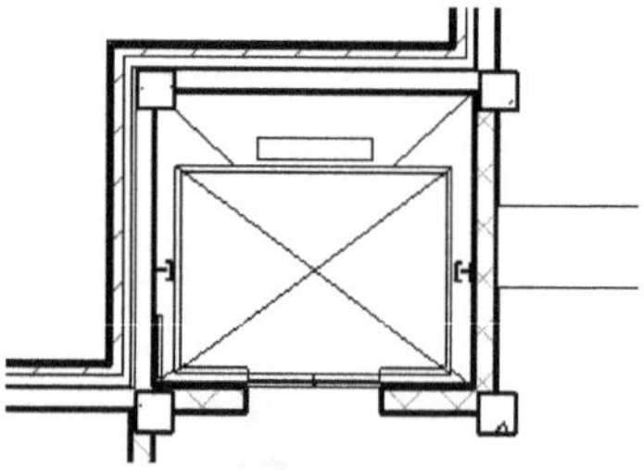

Figure 8–13

7. Select the Elevator Door component.

8. In the *Modify | Floors* tab>Clipboard panel, click ⬜ (Copy to the Clipboard).

9. In the Clipboard panel, expand ⬜ (Paste) and click

   ⬜ (Aligned to Selected Levels).

10. In the Select Levels dialog box, select **Basement** and **Floor 2** through **Floor 8**, as shown in Figure 8–14. Click

    [OK]. This copies the door to the rest of the levels.

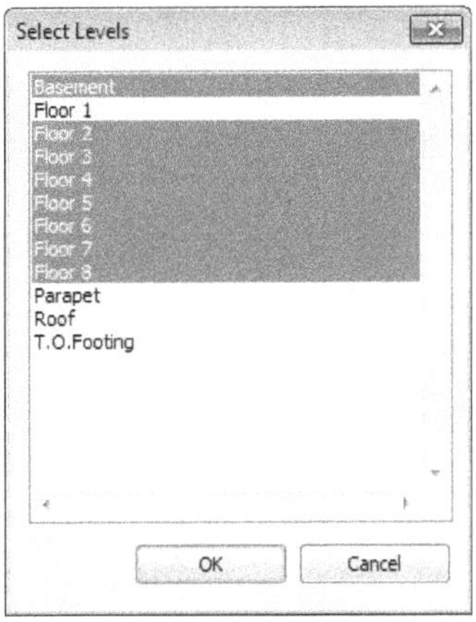

Figure 8–14

11. Save the project.

Task 3 - Add column footings.

---

1. Open the **Floor Plans: T.O. Footing** view and select everything in the view.

2. In the Status Bar (or in the *Modify | Multi-select* tab>Selection

   panel), click ▽ (Filter).

3. In the Filter dialog box, clear **Structural Columns** and click

   [OK].

4. In the Status Bar, expand ⚡ (Temporary Hide/Isolate) and select **Hide Element.** Everything except the columns should be hidden, as shown in Figure 8–15. It is now easier to identify the locations of the footings.

Figure 8–15

5. In the *Architecture* tab>Build panel, click 🗔 (Component).

6. In the *Modify | Place Component* tab>Mode panel, click 🗔 (Load Family).

7. In the *Structural Foundations* folder of the Autodesk Revit Library, select **M_Footing-Rectangular.rfa** and click

   Open .

8. In the Type Selector, select **M_Footing-Rectangular:1800 x 1200 x 450mm**. Set the *Level* to **T.O. Footing**.

9. Place a footing at each column. Once you have placed at least one footing, you can use **Copy** to add the others. Ensure that you are copying from the column midpoint, as shown in Figure 8–16.

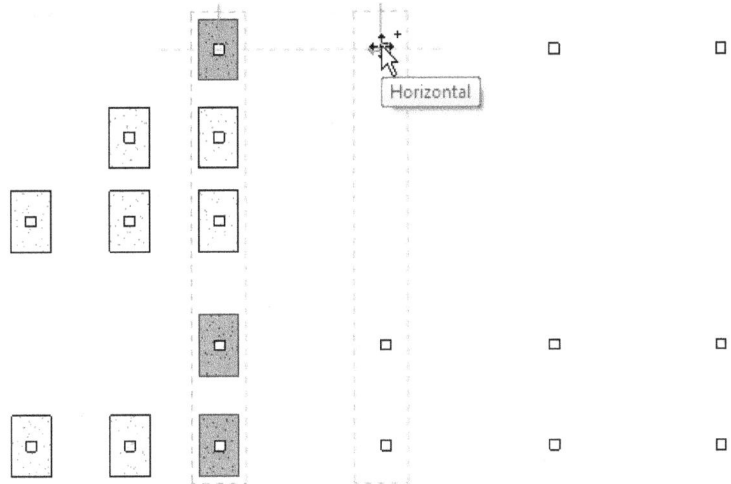

Figure 8–16

10. In the View Control Bar, click ⚬ (Temporary Hide/Isolate) and select **Reset Temporary Hide/Isolate**.

11. In Properties, edit the View Range so that the *Cut plane Offset* is **300mm**. This hides any elements that should not part of the foundation plan. as shown in Figure 8–17. (Note: the foundations are highlighted for clarity.)

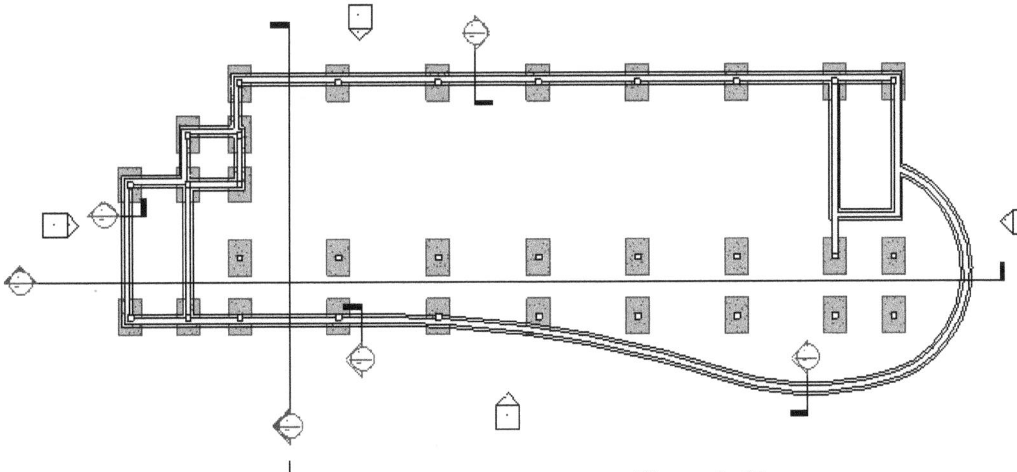

Figure 8–17

12. Save the project.

Chapter Review Questions

1. When inserting a component, you select the family that you want to use in the...

   a. Quick Access Toolbar

   b. Type Selector

   c. Options Bar

   d. Properties Palette

2. If the component you want to use is not available in the current project, where do you go to get the component? (Select all that apply.)

   a. In another project, copy the component to the clipboard and paste it into the current project.

   b. In the current project, use (Insert from File) and select the family from the list in the dialog box.

   c. In the current project, use (Load Family) and select the family from the list in the dialog box.

   d. Search Autodesk Seek for a component and download it.

3. When you use the **Moves with Nearby Elements** option, can you control which elements move with a component?

   a. Yes, select the element with which you want it to move.

   b. No, it moves with the closest wall.

4. Which of the following commands would you use if you want to move a furniture component to a floor that is lower than the level where it was original placed, as shown in Figure 8–18?

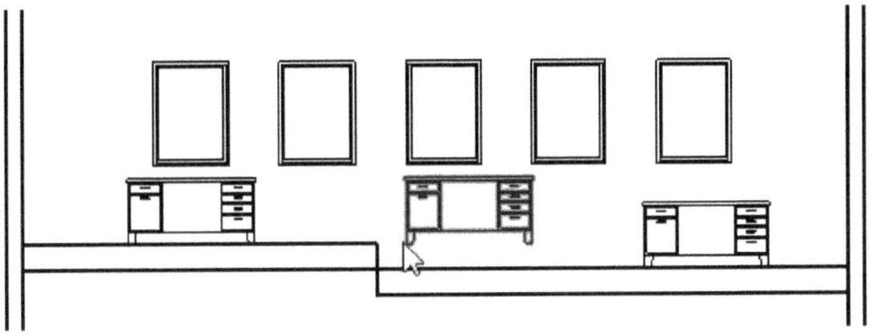

Figure 8–18

a. Use ⌖ (Level) and add a Level at the height of the lower floor.

b. Use ◿ (Ref Plane) and draw a plane aligned with the lower floor.

c. Use ▯ (Pick New Host) and select the lower floor.

d. Use ▱ (Edit Family) and change the work plane in the family so that it matches the height of the lower floor.

Command Summary

Button	Command	Location
	Load Family	• **Ribbon:** *Modify	Place Component* tab>Load panel or *Insert* tab>Load from Library panel
	Pick New Host	• **Ribbon:** *Modify	Multi-Select* or *component type* contextual tab>Host panel
	Place Component	• **Ribbon:** *Architecture* tab>Build panel> expand Component • **Shortcut:** <C> and <M>
	Purge Unused	• **Ribbon:** *Manage* tab>Settings panel
	Search Seek Online	• **Ribbon:** *Insert* tab>Autodesk Seek panel

Chapter 9

Modeling Floors

In this chapter you learn how to add a floor by creating a sketch and selecting a floor type. You also learn how to create openings in floors including openings for multilevel shafts and how to create sloped floors in one direction or in multiple directions.

This chapter contains the following topics:

- **Modeling Floors**
- **Creating Shaft Openings**
- **Creating Sloped Floors**

9.1 Modeling Floors

Autodesk Certification Topics & Objectives

Pro.   User

Modeling

- Create elements such as floors, ceilings, or roofs   ✓
- Change a generic floor/ceiling/roof to a specific type   ✓

Learning Objectives

- Add floors by sketching a boundary, setting the span direction, and drawing openings if needed.
- Modify floor properties and the floor sketch.
- Join Geometry so that intersections between walls and floors are cleaned up and display correctly.

The **Floor** command can generate any flat or sloped surface, such as floors, balconies, decks, and patios, as shown in Figure 9–1. Typically created in a plan view, the floor can be based either on bounding walls or on a sketch that you draw to define the outline. You can also change the floor type, add openings, and modify floors by editing the sketch.

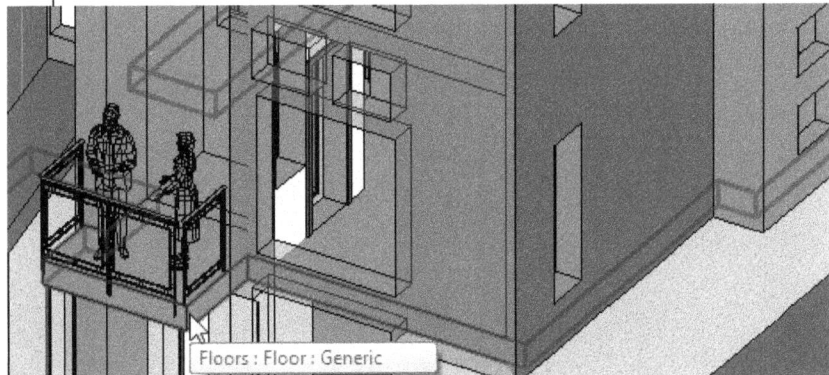

Floors : Floor : Generic

Figure 9–1

How To: Add a Floor

1. In the *Architecture* tab>Build panel, click 🗔 (Floor). You are placed in edit mode where other elements in the drawing are grayed out.
2. In the *Modify | Create Floor Boundary* tab>Draw panel, click

   ⎣ (Boundary Line).

   - Click ▨ (Pick Walls) and select the walls, setting either the inside or outside edge.

   - Click ✐ (Line) or one of the other Draw tools and draw the boundary edges.

3. Click ▨ (Slope Arrow) to define a slope for the entire floor.

4. Click ▨ (Span Direction) to modify the direction for floor spans. It comes in automatically when you place the first boundary line, as shown in Figure 9–2.

5. ⇔ (Flip) switches the inside/outside status of the boundary location if you have selected a wall, as shown in Figure 9–2.

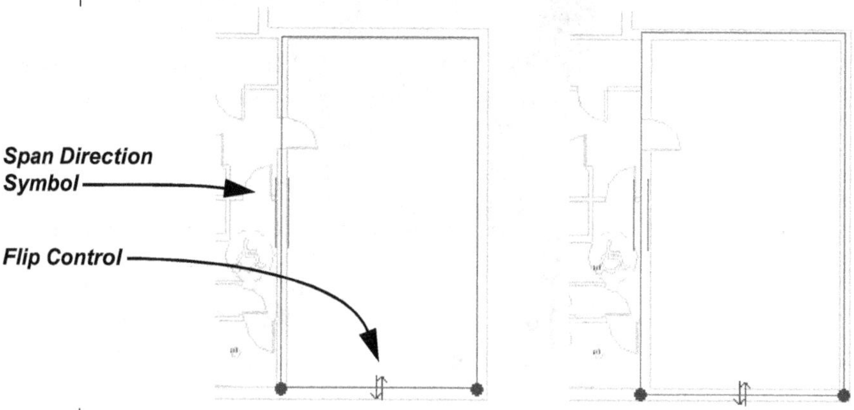

The lines in the sketch must form a closed loop. You can use tools in the Modify panel to adjust intersections.

Span Direction Symbol

Flip Control

Figure 9–2

6. Click ✔ (Finish Edit Mode) to create the floor.
7. The floor element is still selected. In the Type Selector, set the type of floor you want to use. In Properties, set any other options you might need.

   - While placing the floor boundary sketches, you can set an *Offset* in the Options Bar, which places the sketched line at a distance offset from a selected wall or sketched line.

- If you are using ⬚ (Pick Walls), the **Extend into wall (to core)** option is also available in the Options Bar. Use this if you want the floor to cut into the wall. For example, the floor would cut through the gypsum wall board and the air space but stop at a core layer such as CMU.

- If you select one of the boundary sketches, you can also set *Cantilevers* for *Concrete* or *Steel*, as shown in Figure 9–3.

| Offset: | 0.0 | ☐ Defines Slope | ☑ Extend into wall (to core) | Cantilevers : Concrete: | 0.0 | Steel: | 0.0 |

Figure 9–3

- To create an opening inside the sketch, create a separate closed loop inside the first one, as shown in Figure 9–4.

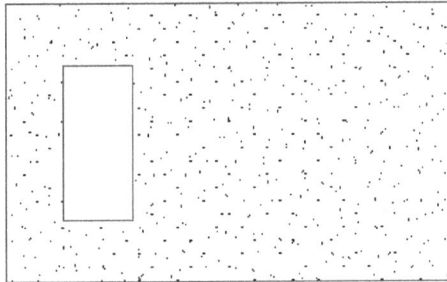

Figure 9–4

- If you create a floor on an upper level, an alert box displays prompting if you want the walls below to be attached to the underside of the floor and its level. If you have a variety of wall heights, it is better to click No and attach the walls separately.

- Another alert box might open as shown in Figure 9–5. You can automatically join the geometry or can do so at a later time.

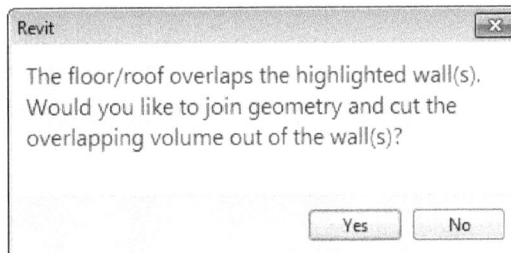

> **Revit**   ⊠
>
> The floor/roof overlaps the highlighted wall(s). Would you like to join geometry and cut the overlapping volume out of the wall(s)?
>
>   [Yes]   [No]

Figure 9–5

- Floors can be placed on top of floors. For example, a structural floor can have a finish floor of tile or carpet placed on top of it, as shown in Figure 9–6. These floors can then be scheduled separately.

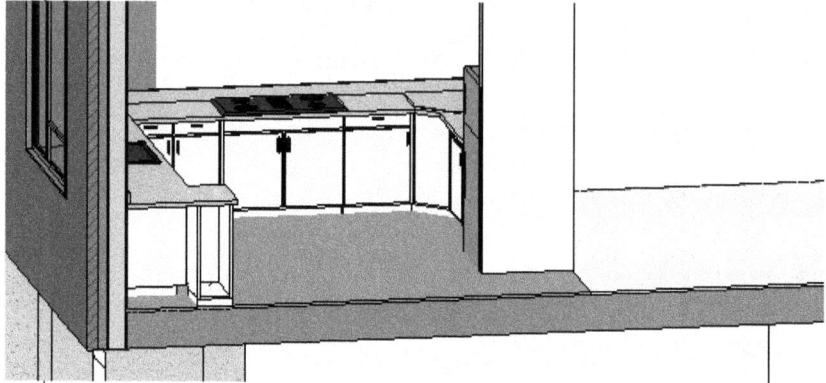

Figure 9–6

Modifying Floors

You can change a floor to a different type in the Type Selector. In Properties, you can modify parameters including the *Height Offset From Level*, as shown in Figure 9–7. When you have a floor selected, you can also edit the boundaries.

The floor type controls the thickness of a floor. To change the thickness, select a different type of floor.

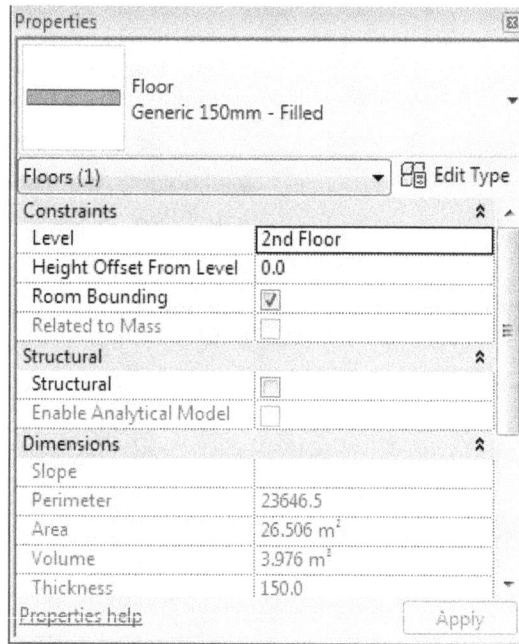

Figure 9–7

How To: Modify the Floor Sketch

1. Select a floor. You might need to highlight an element near the floor and press <Tab> until the floor type displays in the Status Bar or in a tooltip, as shown in Figure 9–8.

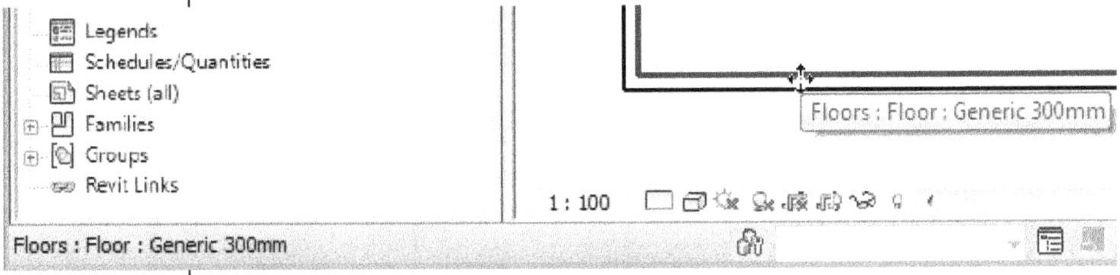

Legends
Schedules/Quantities
Sheets (all)
Families
Groups
Revit Links

Floors : Floor : Generic 300mm

1 : 100

Floors : Floor : Generic 300mm

Figure 9–8

2. In the *Modify | Floors* tab>Mode panel, click (Edit Boundary). You are placed in edit mode.
3. Modify the sketch lines by using the draw tools, controls, and the various modify tools.

4. Click (Finish Edit Mode).

• You can double-click on a floor to move directly to editing the boundary.

• Floor sketches can be edited in plan and 3D views, but not in elevations. If you try to edit in an elevation view, you are prompted to select another view in which to edit.

Hint: Selecting Floor Faces

If it is difficult to select the floor edges, toggle on the Selection Option (Select elements by face). Then can select the floor face, and not only the edges.

Joining Geometry

Join Geometry is a versatile command used to clean up intersections. The elements remain separate, but the intersections are cleaned up. It can be used with many types of elements including floors, walls, and roofs. In Figure 9–9, the wall on the left and the floor have been joined, but the wall on the right has not been joined with the floor and therefore does not display the lines that define the intersection edges.

In some cases, cutting a section (or in a 3D View, modifying the Section Box) through the objects you want to join helps to display them more clearly.

Figure 9–9

How To: Join Geometry

1. In the *Modify* tab>Geometry panel, expand ⌂ (Join) and click ⌂ (Join Geometry).
2. Select the elements to join.

- If you toggle on the **Multiple Join** option in the Options Bar, you can select several elements to join to the first selection.

- To remove the join, expand ⌂ (Join), click ⌂ (Unjoin Geometry), and select the elements to unjoin.

Practice 9a | Model Floors

Learning Objectives

- Add floors to several levels.
- Copy a floor to multiple levels.
- Create a shaft opening for the elevator.

Estimated time for completion: 30 minutes

In this practice you will create or modify floors in the Basement, first floor, and second floor of a project. You then copy the floor on the second floor to other related levels and clean up connections between the floors and wall. The second floor with balconies is shown in Figure 9–10.

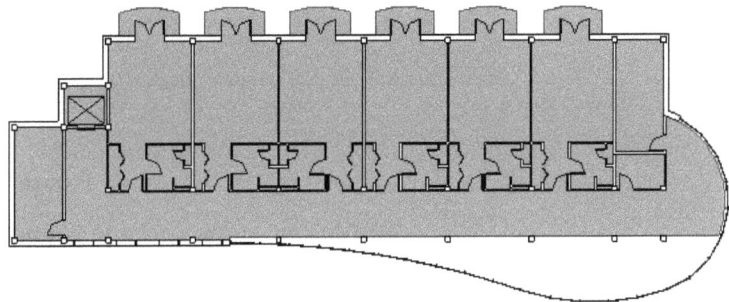

Figure 9–10

Task 1 - Add the Basement floor.

1. Open the project **Modern-Hotel-Floors-M.rvt** from your class folder.

2. Open the **Floor Plans: Basement** view.

3. In the *Architecture* tab>Build panel, click (Floor).

4. In the Type Selector, select **Floor: Insitu Concrete 225mm**.

5. In the *Modify | Create Floor Boundary* tab>Draw panel, click (Pick Walls) and select the inside face of the exterior foundation walls.

6. Click (Finish Edit Mode).

7. If an error dialog box opens, click **Continue**. Use the Modify tools to ensure that the boundary is a closed loop. (Hint: On the right side of the building, move the wall end of the stairwell up until it connects with the curved wall.)

8. Click ✓ (Finish Edit Mode) again.

9. When the alert box opens, click [Yes]. The floor pattern displays as shown in Figure 9–11.

Figure 9–11

10. Click in empty space to release the floor selection.

Press <Enter> to repeat the last command.

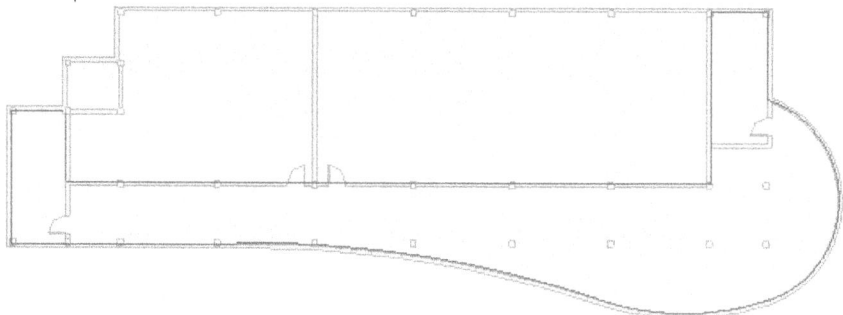

11. Start the **Floor** command again.

12. In the Type Selector, select **Floor: Tile**. In Properties, set the *Height Offset from Level* to **6mm**.

13. Draw the boundary around the stair wells and hall as shown in Figure 9–12.

Figure 9–12

14. Click ✓ (Finish Edit Mode).

15. When prompted to join overlapping geometry, click [Yes].

16. Click in empty space to release the selection and zoom in to display the different floor coverings, as shown in Figure 9–13

Figure 9–13

17. Save the project.

Task 2 - Modify a floor as a platform for the building.

1. Open the **Floor Plans**: **Floor 1 with Pool** view.

2. Hide the grid lines and the elevation markers.

3. Select the existing floor around the pool building. In the *Modify | Floors* tab>Mode panel, click (Edit Boundary).

4. Modify the boundary as shown in Figure 9–14.

Modifying the boundary of this floor creates a platform for the building.

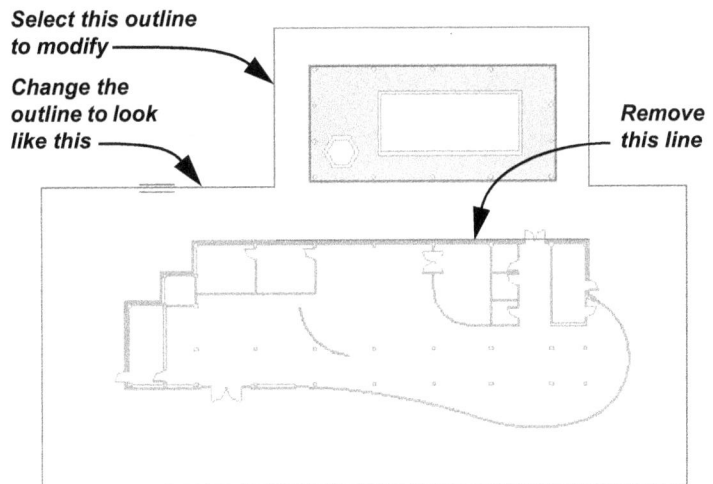

Select this outline to modify —

Change the outline to look like this —

Remove this line

Figure 9–14

5. Click (Finish Edit Mode).

6. When prompted to attach walls to the floor, click [No] .
   Some of the walls need to be attached, but not all of them.

7. Click in empty space to release the selection.

8. View the building in 3D. It now has a base to rest on.

9. Save the project.

Task 3 - Add the 2nd floor with balconies.

---

1. Open the **Floor Plans: Floor 2** view.

2. In the View Control Bar, click ⚲ (Reveal Hidden Elements).

The linked CAD file has been imported to prevent problems with the software finding the correct information for the practice.

3. Select one of the text notes in the imported CAD file.
   Right-click and select **Unhide in View>Elements**.

4. Click ⬚ (Close Reveal Hidden Elements).

Using Temporary Hide/Isolate cleans up the view temporarily as you create the floor.

5. Select any element that makes it difficult to display the outline of the floor and balcony. In the View Control Bar, click
   ⟲ (Temporary Hide/Isolate) and select **Hide Category**.

6. In the *Architecture* tab>Build panel, click ⬜ (Floor).

7. In the Type Selector, select **Floor: Generic - 300mm**.

8. In the *Modify | Create Floor Boundary* tab>Draw panel, click
   ⌐ (Boundary Line) and ▣ (Pick Walls).

9. In the Options Bar, set the *Offset* to **0.0** and select **Extend into wall (to core)**.

10. Select the main outside walls. The sketch line displays at the core of the wall, as shown in Figure 9–15. Do not select the three curved walls.

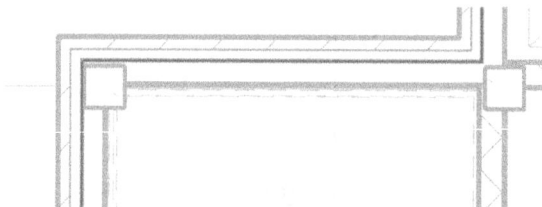

Figure 9–15

11. Change to ⚲ (Pick Lines) and select the lines of walkways in the linked CAD file. (The text notes displays as **LINE OF WALKWAYS** and points to it).

12. Use the **Draw** and **Modify** tools to fix the connections at the wall and walkway, as shown in Figure 9–16.

Figure 9–16

13. Pan over to one of the balconies.

14. Use ⚲ (Pick Lines) to draw the outline of the balcony.

15. Use drag controls to have the balcony lines meet the floor line.

16. Use ⬄ (Split Element) with **Delete Inner Segment** selected on the Options Bar, and cut the line as shown in Figure 9–17.

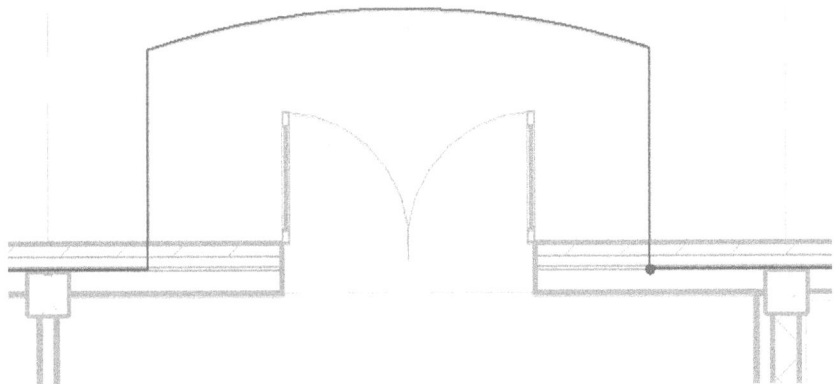

Figure 9–17

17. Start the **Modify** command and select the balcony elements.

18. Copy the elements to the other balconies and split the lines to create one continuous sketch.

19. Click ✓ (Finish Edit Sketch).

20. When the alert box shown in Figure 9–18 displays, click ⌷ Yes ⌷ to cut overlapping geometry out of the walls.

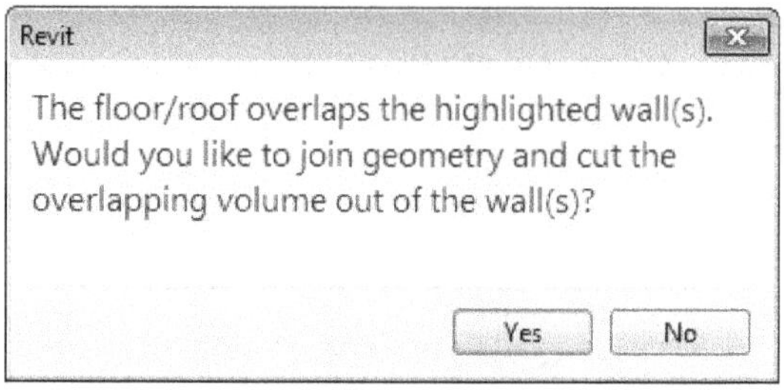

Revit
The floor/roof overlaps the highlighted wall(s). Would you like to join geometry and cut the overlapping volume out of the wall(s)?
Yes   No

Figure 9–18

21. Click in empty space to release the floor selection.

22. Hide the imported CAD file in the view.

23. In the View Control Bar, click ⌇ (Temporary/Hide Isolate) and select **Reset Temporary/Hide Isolate**. The elements you hid earlier display.

24. Save the project.

Task 4 - Copy the 2nd floor to other floors and clean up floor connections with the walls.

---

1. In the **Floor Plans: Floor 2** view, select the new floor.

2. In the *Modify | Floors* tab>Clipboard panel, click ⌷ (Copy to the Clipboard).

3. In the Clipboard panel, expand ⌷ (Paste) and click ⌷ (Aligned to Selected Levels).

4. In the Select Levels dialog box, select **Floor 3** through **Floor 8**, as shown in Figure 9–19. Click ⌷ OK ⌷.

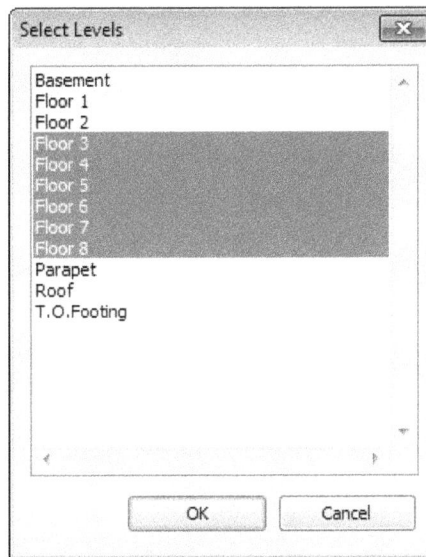

Figure 9–19

5. Open a 3D view and rotate it to display the new floors placed in the building, as shown in Figure 9–20.

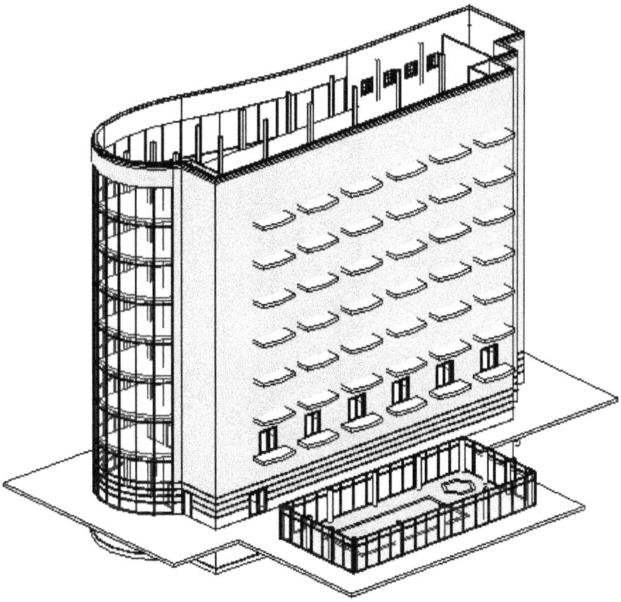

Figure 9–20

6. Return to the **Floor Plans: Floor 2** view again.

7. Select all of the interior walls and interior doors of the guest rooms as well as the exterior doors to the balcony. (Hint: You can open the floor plan of any of the floors between Floor 3 and Floor 8 to display the elements that need to be copied.)

   - Hold down <Shift> to clear the selection of anything you did not want, such as the exterior walls and the interior stairwell and elevator walls.

   - Use ￼ (Filter) to filter out items you do not want to copy, such as the columns, door tags, elevations, and views.

8. Copy the selected elements to the clipboard and paste them to the same levels as the floors.

9. Open several of the floor plan views to verify the placement of the guest room walls and doors.

10. Return to the 3D view to display the building with all of the doors and guest rooms, as shown in Figure 9–21.

Figure 9–21

11. Zoom in on the back of the building. The floor slabs that extend to the balconies are not joined with the walls and therefore do not display a line across the connection between the wall and balcony, as shown in Figure 9–22. Zoom out to display all of the floors.

Figure 9–22

12. In the *Modify* tab>Geometry panel, expand (Join) and click (Join Geometry). In the Options Bar, select **Multiple Join**.

13. Select the back exterior wall and then select each floor with a balcony to join the wall and floors, as shown in Figure 9–23. Floor 2 is already joined and does not need to be selected.

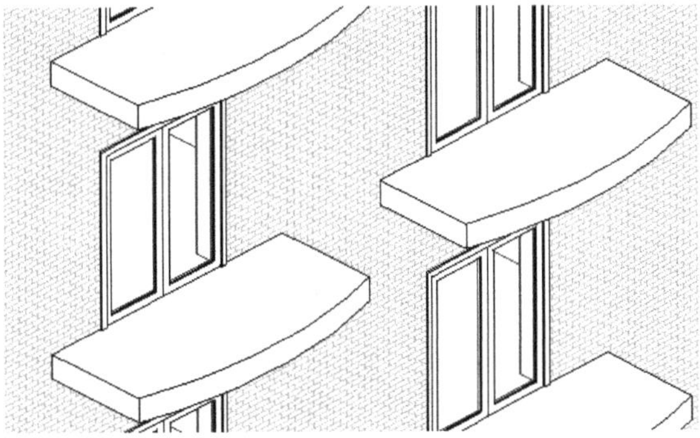

Figure 9–23

14. Zoom out to see the entire building.

15. Save the project.

9.2 Creating Shaft Openings

Learning Objective

- Add a shaft opening that cuts through multiple floors.

Openings can be added to floors (as well as roofs and ceilings) by drawing a closed sketch within the existing sketch. When you have elevator shafts or other floor openings that span more than one floor, you can create a Shaft Opening, as shown in plan and 3D in Figure 9–24.

Shaft Openings only cut floors, roofs, and ceilings. They do not cut walls, beams, or other objects.

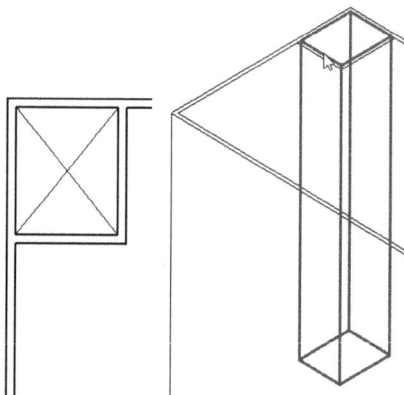

Figure 9–24

How To: Add a Shaft Opening

1. In the *Architecture* tab>Opening panel, click ▣▪▣ (Shaft).
2. In the *Modify | Create Shaft Opening Sketch* tab>Draw panel, click ⌐ (Boundary Line) and draw a line to define the opening.
3. In the Draw panel, click 🗗 (Symbolic Line) and add lines that show the opening symbol in plan view.
4. In Properties, set the *Base Constraint* and *Top Constraint* as well as the *Base Offset* and *Top Offset*.
5. Click ✓ (Finish Edit Mode) to create the opening.

- A Shaft Opening element can include symbolic lines that repeat on each level, displaying the shaft in a plan view.

- Shafts are a separate element from the floor, roof, ceiling, or wall, and can be deleted without selecting a host element.

9.3 Creating Sloped Floors

Learning Objectives

- Slope a floor in one direction.
- Create multiple slopes in a floor for drainage.

These tools also work with roofs and structural slabs.

Floors can have slopes applied to them. Slope arrows are added in the sketch of the floor. There are two main types of slopes: slopes added to the entire floor and slopes added to a sketch line in the floor. After the floor is created, you can add multiple drainage points and cause the floor to warp toward them.

How To: Slope a Floor in One Direction

To make a floor slope in one direction, you place a *slope arrow* in the sketch of the floor, as shown in Figure 9–25. The direction and properties of the arrow control the slope.

The slope arrow only displays while Sketch mode is active.

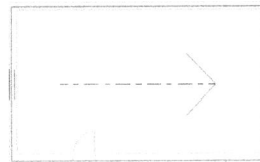

Figure 9–25

1. Select the floor you want to slope. In the *Modify | Floors* tab> Mode panel, click (Edit Boundary).
2. In the *Modify | Floors>Edit Boundary* tab>Draw panel, click (Slope Arrow).
3. Select two points to define the arrow. The first point is the tail and the second is the head. The tail and head locations are points at which you can specify heights. The direction of the arrow determines the orientation of the slope.
4. In Properties, specify the *Level* and *Offset* at the *Tail* and *Head*, as shown in Figure 9–26.

Constraints	☆
Specify	Height at Tail
Level at Tail	Default
Height Offset at Tail	300.0
Level at Head	Default
Height Offset at Head	0.0

Figure 9–26

Creating Multiple Slopes for Drainage

Restrooms, labs, garages, and other rooms often need to have floors that slope towards drains, as shown in Figure 9–27. In addition, all flat roofs are not actually flat, but also slope towards drains. Several tools provide ways of creating points for the drain locations, as well as creating lines to define how the slope is going to drain.

Figure 9–27

- These tools work with floors, roofs, and structural floors.

How To: Create Multiple Slopes for Drainage

1. Select the required flat floor, roof, or slab.
2. In the *Modify | Floors* tab>Shape Editing panel, as shown in Figure 9–28, select the tools that you want to use to define the slopes.

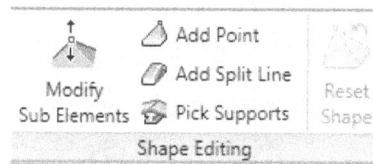

Figure 9–28

Add Point: Specify the location of the low or high points on the surface. In the Options Bar, set the *Elevation* as shown in . By default, the elevation is relative to the top of the surface. Clear the **Relative** option if you want to use the project elevation.

displays when you place the point. Slope lines are automatically added from the corners of the surface to the point.

🖉	**Add Split Line:** Define smaller areas on the surface when you place more than one drain. Depending on the size of the area you are working with, you might want to create these before you add the drains. Select the **Chain** option if you want to draw more than one connected segment.
🖐	**Pick Supports:** Select structural beams that define the split lines.
⤒	**Modify Sub-Elements:** Change the elevation of edges and points and change the location of points. You can also move points using shape handles without clicking ⤒ (Modify Sub-Elements), as shown in . Press <Tab> to cycle through the options to reach the element you want to modify. 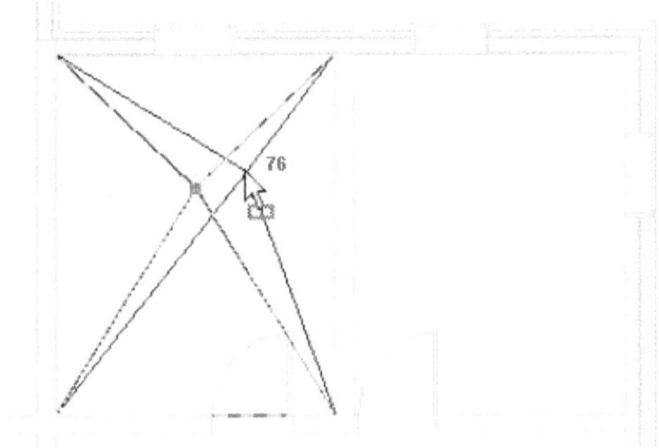

- If you want to remove the slopes from a surface, click
  🖐 (Reset Shape).

- Floors, roofs, and slabs use styles set to a constant thickness (where the entire element slopes) or to a variable thickness (where only the top layer slopes), as shown in Figure 9–29.

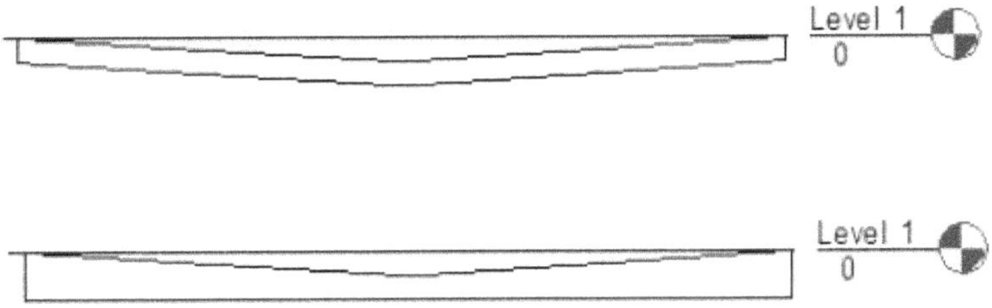

Figure 9–29

Practice 9b

Estimated time for completion: 15 minutes

Add an Elevator Shaft and Slope Floors to Floor Drains

Learning Objectives

- Create a shaft opening for the elevator.
- Slope floors in restrooms and janitors closet.

In this practice you will add a shaft opening for the elevator, as shown on the left in Figure 9–30. You will also slope floors for drainage using the Shape Editing tools, as shown on the right in Figure 9–30.

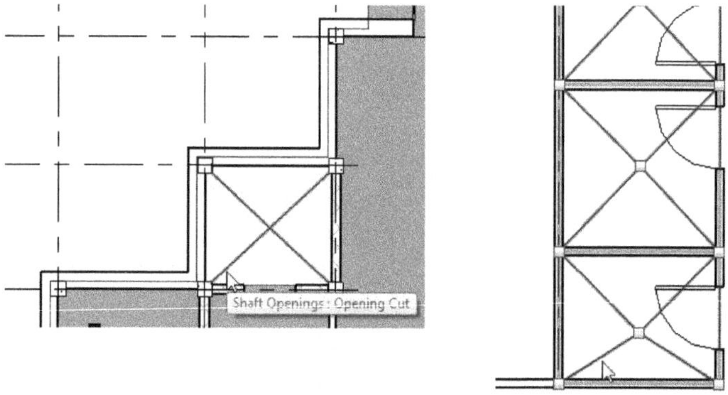

Shaft Openings : Opening Cut

Figure 9–30

Task 1 - Create a shaft opening.

1. Open the project **Modern-Hotel-Shaft-M.rvt** from the class folder.

2. Open the **Floor Plans: Floor 1** view and zoom in to the elevator area.

3. In the *Architecture* tab>Opening panel, click ⊞ (Shaft).

4. In the *Modify | Create Shaft Opening Sketch* tab>Draw panel, verify that ⌐ (Boundary Line) is selected.

5. Use ▣ (Pick Walls) to create the boundary. Then use the Draw and Modify tools to cut out the columns from the sketch, as shown in Figure 9–31.

6. In the Draw panel, click 🗖 (Symbolic Line) and draw two lines crossing the opening, as shown in Figure 9–31.

Figure 9–31

7. In Properties, change the *Base Constraint* to **Floor 1**, the *Base Offset* to (negative) **-300mm**, and the *Top Constraint* to **Up to Level:Roof**.

8. Click 🗸 (Finish Edit Mode).

9. Open the **Floor Plans: Floor 2** view.

10. In the View Control Bar, change the *Visual Style* to 🗖 (Consistent Colors) to display the opening.

11. Return the *Visual Style* to 🗖 (Hidden Line).

12. Open the 3D view and rotate it to display the shaft as it goes through all of the floors, as shown in Figure 9–32.

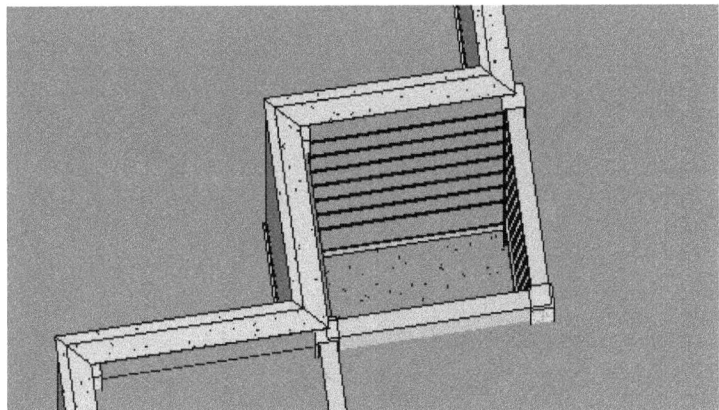

Figure 9–32

13. Open a couple other full floor plan views. The symbolic lines display in all views.

14. Return to the **Floor Plans: Floor 1** view.

15. Zoom out to display the entire view if needed.

16. In the Quick Access Toolbar, click (Close Hidden Windows).

17. Save the project.

Task 2 - Slope floors for drainage.

1. Open the **Floor Plans: Floor 1 Restrooms** view.

2. Expand the size of the crop region so the janitor's closet below is also included in the plan.

3. Select one of the elevation markers and hide the category.

4. You are not able to select the floor in this view, but you can select it in another view and then return to this view to modify it. Open the **Floor Plans: Floor 1 with Pool** view.

5. Select the floor.

6. Press <Ctrl>+<Tab> to switch back to the **Floor Plans: Floor 1 Restrooms** view. The floor is still selected and you can make changes to the floor.

7. In the *Modify | Floors* tab>Shape Editing panel, click ✐ (Add Split Line). Draw the lines, as shown in Figure 9–33.

*Use the **Chain** option and draw all of the outside edges first.*

Figure 9–33

8. In the Shape Editing panel, click ✐ (Add Point). In the Options Bar, set the *Elevation* to (negative) **-15mm**. Place a point in the center of each room, as shown for one of them in Figure 9–34.

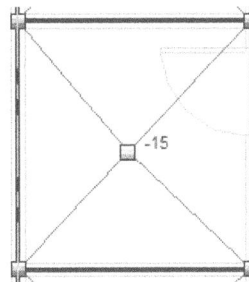

Figure 9–34

9. End the command.

10. Zoom out and save the project.

Chapter Review Questions

1. When creating a floor the boundary sketch must be...

   a. Open

   b. Closed

   c. It does not matter.

2. How do you change the thickness of a floor, such as those shown in Figure 9–35?

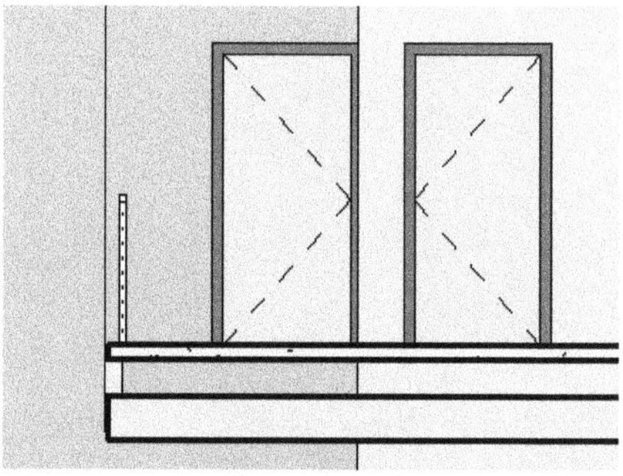

   Figure 9–35

   a. In the Type Selector, change the Floor Type.

   b. In the Options Bar, change the Floor Thickness.

   c. In Properties, change the Floor Thickness.

   d. In the contextual ribbon, change the Offset.

3. Which of the following Opening commands cuts an opening in multiple floors at the same time?

   a. **By Face**

   b. **Shaft**

   c. **Wall**

   d. **Vertical**

4. When creating a sloped floor, ◿ (Add Point) places a point at...

   a. The end of the floor where you want the slope to end.

   b. The end of the floor where you want the slope to begin.

   c. A point where several slopes converge.

   d. A point where two slopes converge.

Command Summary

Button	Command	Location
	Add Point	• **Ribbon:** *Modify	Floors* tab>Shape Editing panel>Add Point
	Add Split Line	• **Ribbon:** *Modify	Floors* tab>Shape Editing panel>Add Split Line
	Floor	• **Ribbon:** *Architecture* tab>Build panel>Floor
	Modify Sub Elements	• **Ribbon:** *Modify	Floors* tab>Shape Editing panel>Modify Sub Elements
	Pick Supports	• **Ribbon:** *Modify	Floors* tab>Shape Editing panel>Pick Supports
	Reset Shape	• **Ribbon:** *Modify	Floors* tab>Shape Editing panel>Reset Shape
	Shaft	• **Ribbon:** *Architecture* tab>Opening panel>Shaft

Chapter 10

Modeling Ceilings

In this chapter you learn how to create ceilings automatically and by sketching a ceiling boundary. You learn how to modify the boundary and move or rotate the ceiling grid within the boundary. You also learn how to create ceiling soffits and add ceiling fixtures.

This chapter contains the following topics:

- **Modeling Ceilings**
- **Adding Ceiling Fixtures**
- **Creating Ceiling Soffits**

10.1 Modeling Ceilings

Autodesk Certification Topics & Objectives

Pro.   User

Modeling

- Create elements such as floors, ceilings, or roofs ✓
- Change a generic floor/ceiling/roof to a specific type ✓

Learning Objectives

- Add automatic and sketched ceilings.
- Modify ceiling boundaries and grid locations.

Adding ceilings to Autodesk® Revit® models is a straightforward process. Ceiling grids are typically added to areas bounded by walls and are centered in the space; these are the defaults when you use the **Ceiling** command. However, you can also sketch custom ceilings when needed. The ceiling grid and any fixtures you attach to it display in reflected ceiling plans, as shown in Figure 10–1, as well as in sections and 3D views.

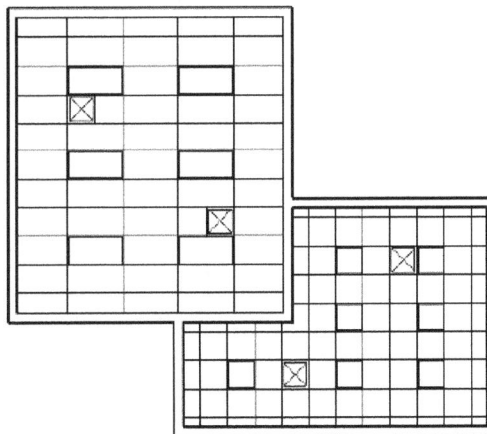

Figure 10–1

*If you do not want a level to have a ceiling plan, you can right-click on its name in the Project Browser and select **Delete**.*

- Ceiling plans are typically created by default when you add a level with a view, as shown in Figure 10–2.

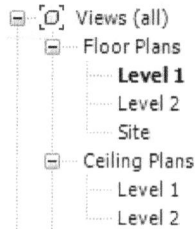

Figure 10–2

How To: Create an Automatic Boundary Ceiling

1. Switch to the appropriate Ceiling Plan view.

2. In the *Architecture* tab>Build panel, click 📧 (Ceiling).
3. In the Type Selector, select the ceiling type. In Properties, set the *Height Offset from Level*.
4. In the *Modify | Place Ceiling* tab>Ceiling panel, verify that

   📧 (Automatic Ceiling) is selected. Click inside a room to create a ceiling, as shown in Figure 10–3.

Figure 10–3

5. Continue adding ceiling grids to other rooms, as required.

- When you start the **Ceiling** command, you are placed in Auto-Ceiling mode. This mode identifies the boundaries of enclosed areas by highlighting them as you hover the cursor over them. When you click, a ceiling is created within that boundary.

Hint: Room Bounding Status

Elements (such as walls, floors, ceilings, and roofs) have a *Room Bounding* parameter that is set in Properties. In most cases, this is turned on by default, as these elements typically define areas and volumes.

The **Automatic Ceiling** tool uses this parameter to identify walls that set the outline of a ceiling. If you turn off this parameter for a wall (such as a partial height wall), the **Automatic Ceiling** tool ignores the wall.

Ceilings can also be Room Bounding. This is for volume calculations.

Sketching Ceilings

You might only want to add a ceiling to part of a room, or have two different ceiling types at separate levels, as shown in Figure 10–4. In these cases, you need to sketch a ceiling.

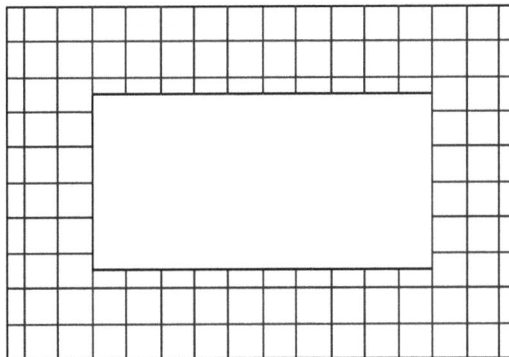

Figure 10–4

How To: Sketch a Ceiling

1. In the *Architecture* tab>Build panel, click  (Ceiling).
2. In the *Modify | Place Ceiling* tab>Ceiling panel, click

    (Sketch Ceiling).

3. In the Draw panel, click ✓ (Line) or  (Pick Walls) and define a closed loop for the ceiling boundary, similar to sketching a floor boundary.

4. Click ✓ (Finish Edit Mode) to create the ceiling.

- To include a hole in a ceiling, draw the hole as part of the sketch. The hole must be a closed loop completely inside the ceiling boundary.

- In the *Architecture* tab>Opening panel, you can also use

   (Opening By Face),   (Shaft Opening) or   (Vertical Opening) to cut a hole in a ceiling that is separate from the sketch.

Hint: Selecting Ceiling Faces

If it is difficult to select the ceiling without the grids, you can

toggle on the Selection Option   (Select elements by face). Then you can select the ceiling face, and not only the edges. If you double-click on the ceiling face (or a grid line) the Edit Boundary options are displayed.

Modifying Ceilings

You can modify the ceiling type and properties, as well as edit the boundary and position the grid lines, as shown in Figure 10–5.

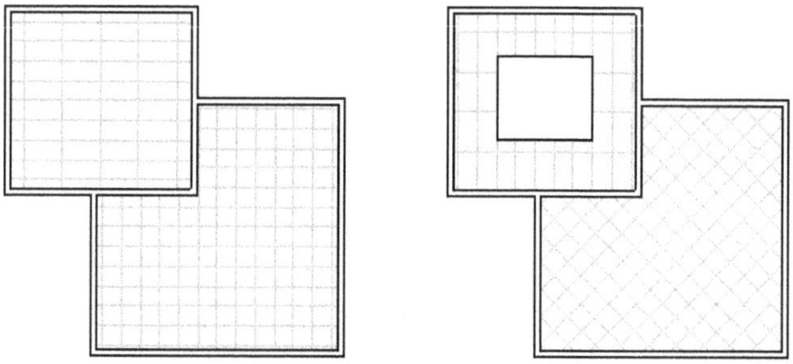

Figure 10–5

How To: Modify a Ceiling Boundary

1. Hover the cursor over a grid line or an edge of the ceiling and press <Tab> until the boundary displays. Click to select it.
2. In the *Modify |Ceilings* tab>Mode panel, click

    (Edit Boundary).
3. Modify the boundary as required by drawing additional lines or using the Modify tools.

How To: Move a Ceiling Grid

1. Select a grid line in the ceiling that you want to modify.

2. In the *Modify | Ceilings* tab>Modify panel, click ⊕ (Move).
3. Move the cursor to one side and type a distance, such as **600mm** or **300mm**.

How To: Rotate a Ceiling Grid

1. Select a grid line in the ceiling that you want to modify.

2. In the *Modify | Ceilings* tab>Modify panel, click ↻ (Rotate).

3. In the Options Bar, type an *Angle* or use ↻ (Rotate) to visually select the angle.

• The standard rectangular acoustical tile ceiling type might be oriented horizontally. To make it vertical, select a grid line and use ↻ (Rotate) to rotate it 90 degrees.

10.2 Adding Ceiling Fixtures

Learning Objective

- Add ceiling fixture components.

Several groups of components are commonly used with ceilings: lighting fixtures, mechanical equipment (for registers and diffusers), and specialty equipment (such as exit signs or sprinklers), as shown in Figure 10–6.

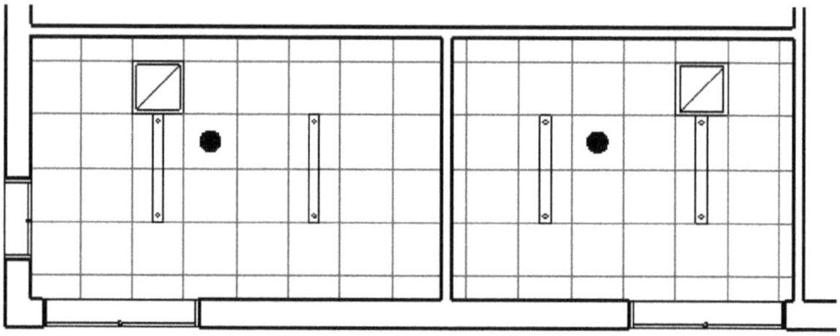

Figure 10–6

After placing a component, press the <Spacebar> to rotate it in 90-degree increments.

- Use (Component) to place ceiling fixtures in the ceiling view.

- The Autodesk Revit Library contains a variety of light fixtures and mechanical ceiling fixtures. You can also download fixtures from Autodesk Seek.

- Some light fixtures are wall-based, instead of ceiling-based, and need to be placed on a wall in a floor plan view. These include items such as sconces.

- When you delete a ceiling, the associated components (such as light fixtures) are also deleted.

- Components come in based on their center point and respond to the nearby walls, not to the ceiling grid. Therefore, you need to place an instance of the component and then move it to the correct location on the grid. You can then use **Copy** to place additional instances on the grid.

- A variety of light fixtures that come with the software include types that specify the voltage of the lamp, as shown in Figure 10–7.

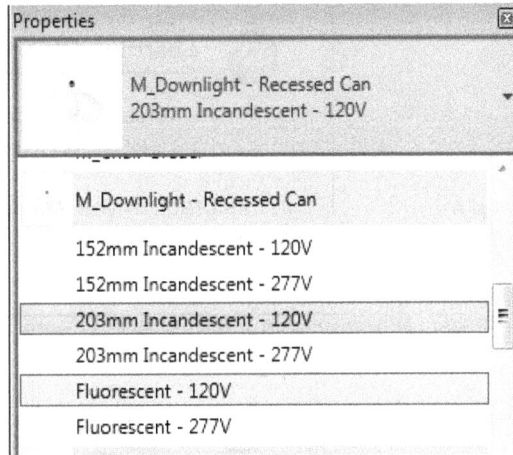

Figure 10–7

- These light fixtures can also display the light source, as shown in the section in Figure 10–8. To display the light source, in the Visibility/Graphic Overrides dialog box, *in the Model Categories* tab, expand **Lighting Fixtures** and select **Light Source,** as shown on the left in Figure 10–8

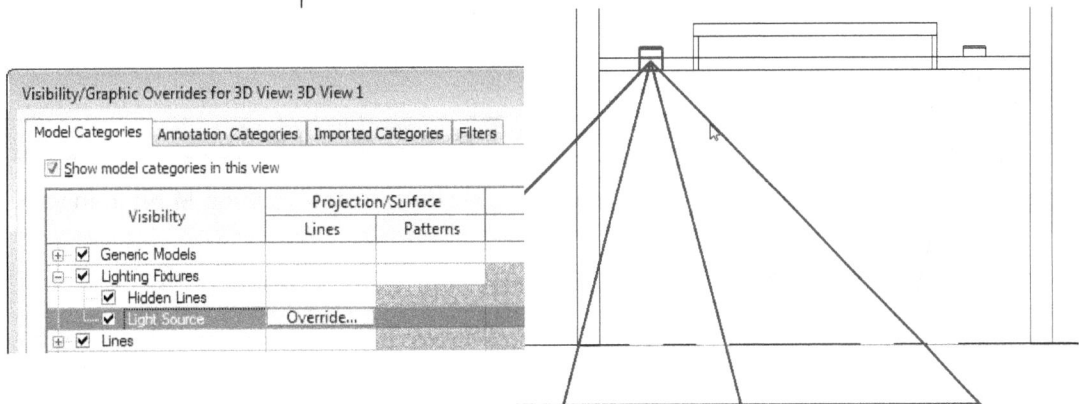

Figure 10–8

- The light sources display their true strength in renderings.

Practice 10a | Model Ceilings and Add Ceiling Fixtures

Learning Objectives

- Create automatic ceilings with grids.
- Add ceiling components.

Estimated time for completion: 15 minutes

In this practice you will add ceilings and ceiling components to a reflected ceiling plan, as shown in Figure 10–9.

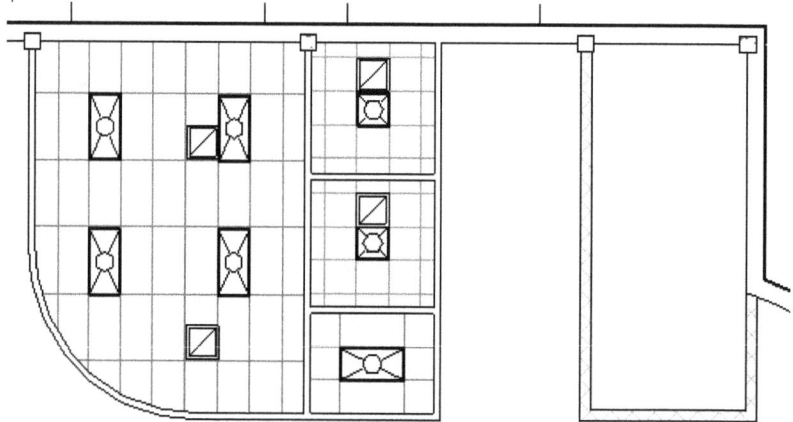

Figure 10–9

Task 1 - Create ceilings with ceiling grids.

1. Open the drawing **Modern-Hotel-Ceilings-M.rvt** from your class folder.

2. Open the **Ceiling Plans: Floor 1** view.

   - To clarify the drawing, you might want to hide the grids, elevations, and sections categories. A quick way to do this is to select one of each element and then use the **Visibility Hide** shortcut by pressing <V> and then pressing <H>.

3. In the *Architecture* tab>Build panel, click (Ceiling).

4. In the Type Selector, verify that **Compound Ceiling: 600 x 1200mm Grid** is selected.

5. Click inside the four support rooms, as shown in Figure 10–10.

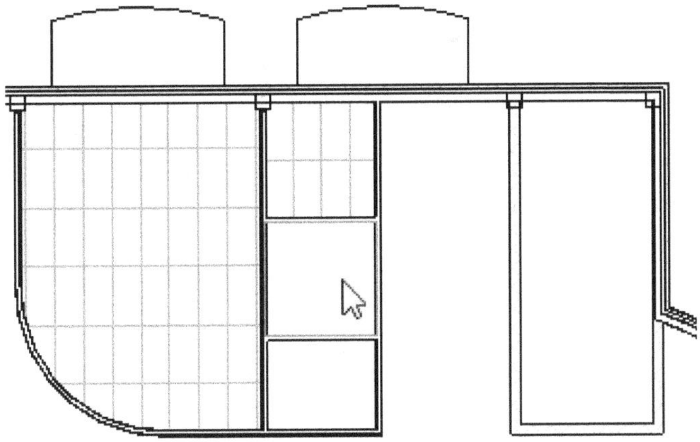

Figure 10–10

Hold down <Ctrl> to select more than one element.

6. Start the **Modify** command and select one grid line in each restroom. In the Type Selector, select **Compound Ceiling: 600 x 600mm Grid**. In Properties, set the *Height Offset from Level* to **2800mm**.

Task 2 - Add ceiling components.

1. In the *Architecture* tab>Build panel, click (Component).

2. In the Mode panel, click (Load Family) and load the following components from the associated folders:

Lighting>Architectural>Internal:

- **M_Downlight Recessed Can.rfa**
- **M_Troffer Light 2x2 Parabolic.rfa**
- **M_Troffer Light 2x4 Parabolic.rfa**

Mechanical>Architectural>Air-Side Components>Air Terminals:

- **M_Square Return Register.rfa**
- **M_Square Supply Diffuser.rfa**

3. Add the ceiling fixtures, as shown in Figure 10–11.

- Select a grid line and use **Move** to modify the grid to suit the location of the fixtures.
- Select a light fixture and place it on the grid. Press <Esc> and select the light fixture. Press <Spacebar> to rotate the light 90 degrees.
- Use snaps or **Align** to place it exactly on the grid.
- Copy it to the other locations.
- Place square return registers in each room.

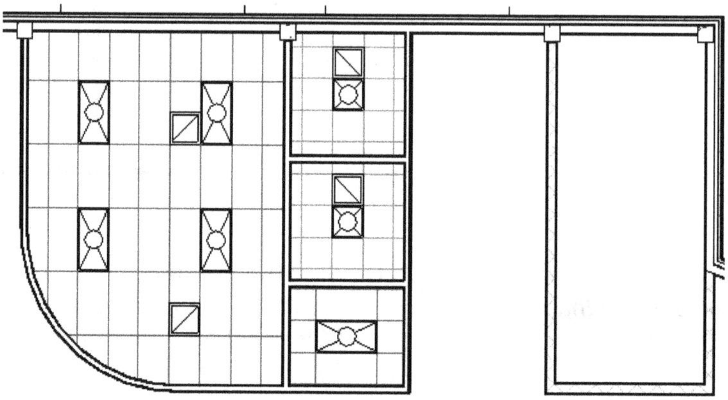

Figure 10–11

4. Save the project.

10.3 Creating Ceiling Soffits

Learning Objective

- Add soffit walls to ceilings.

Ceiling soffits are parts of a ceiling that have been lowered, as shown in Figure 10–12, or that connect two ceilings of different heights. Creating a ceiling soffit takes two steps. First, you create a ceiling, and then you draw walls using a soffit wall type.

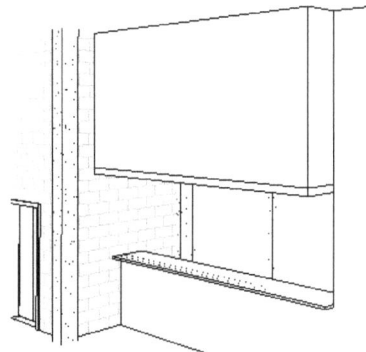

Figure 10–12

How To: Create a Ceiling with a Soffit

1. Open a ceiling plan.

2. In the *Architecture* tab>Build panel, click (Ceiling).

3. In the Type Selector, select the ceiling type. In Properties, set the *Height Offset from Level*.

4. In the *Modify | Place Ceiling* tab>Ceiling panel, click

   (Sketch Ceiling).

5. Draw the soffit design, such as the example shown in Figure 10–13.

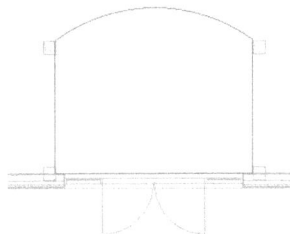

Figure 10–13

6. Click ✔ (Finish Edit Mode) when you have finished drawing the ceiling sketch.

7. In *Architecture* tab>Build panel, click ⌓ (Wall) to create the soffit wall.

8. In the Type Selector, select a soffit wall type. In Properties, set the *Base Offset* from the floor and set the *Top Constraint/Unconnected Height* as required to establish the height of the soffit, as shown in Figure 10–14. Click Apply.

Sometimes this is easier to do by extending or trimming elements in a section view.

Figure 10–14

9. In the *Modify | Place Wall* tab>Draw panel, click ⬩ (Pick Lines). Select the edges of the ceiling to create the walls, as shown in Figure 10–15.

*If the wall is on the outside of the ceiling, flip it using the Flip control and create the rest of the walls using the opposite **Location Line** option.*

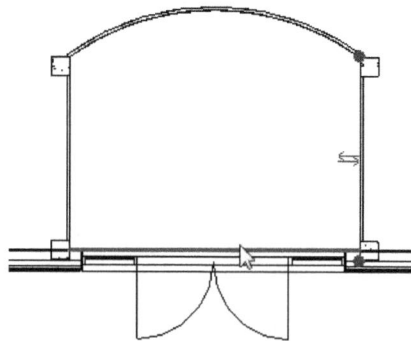

Figure 10–15

10. Display the ceiling in 3D to verify that it is displayed correctly.

Practice 10b | Create Ceiling Soffits

Learning Objective

- Create ceiling soffits.

Estimated time for completion: 15 minutes

In this practice you will sketch a ceiling, add fixtures, and create a soffit wall in the hall, as shown in Figure 10–16. Optionally, you will also add a recessed ceiling and soffit to the breakfast area.

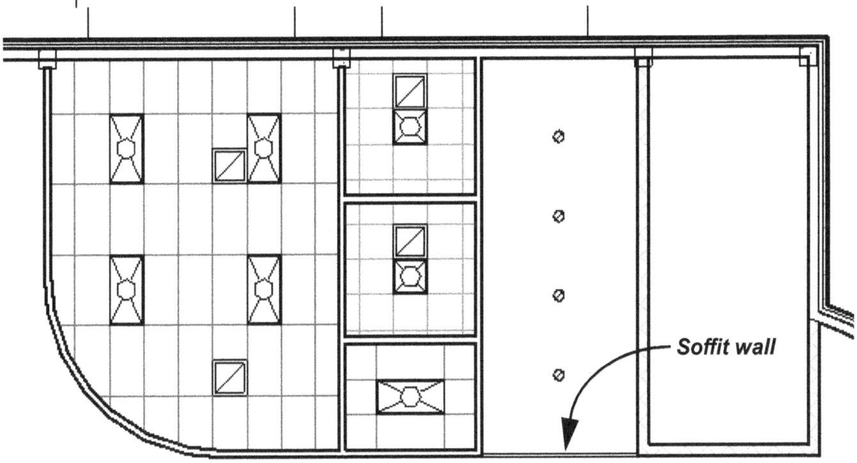

— *Soffit wall*

Figure 10–16

Task 1 - Sketch a ceiling.

1. Open the drawing **Modern-Hotel-Soffits-M.rvt** from your class folder.

2. Open the **Ceiling Plans: Floor 1** view and zoom in on the hallway by the restrooms.

3. In the *Architecture* tab> Build panel, click (Ceiling).

4. In the Type Selector, select **Compound Ceiling: Plain** and in Properties, set the *Height Offset from Level* to **3000mm**.

5. In the *Modify | Place Ceiling* tab>Ceiling panel, click

   (Sketch Ceiling) and draw sketch lines, as shown in Figure 10–17 in the hallway.

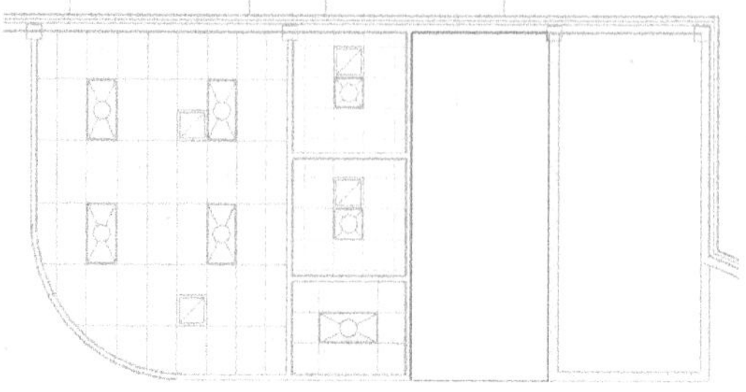

Figure 10–17

6. Click   (Finish Edit Mode).

7. Add a line of four **M_Downlight - Recessed Can** components down the hallway, set at an elevation of

   3000mm. Use   (Aligned Dimension) with the **EQ** control to space them equally in the hallway.

8. Save the project.

Task 2 - Add a soffit.

---

1. Open the **Sections (Building Section): East-West Section** view and zoom in on the hallway area shown in Figure 10–18.

The area above the ceiling is open to the next floor. A soffit wall should be placed here.

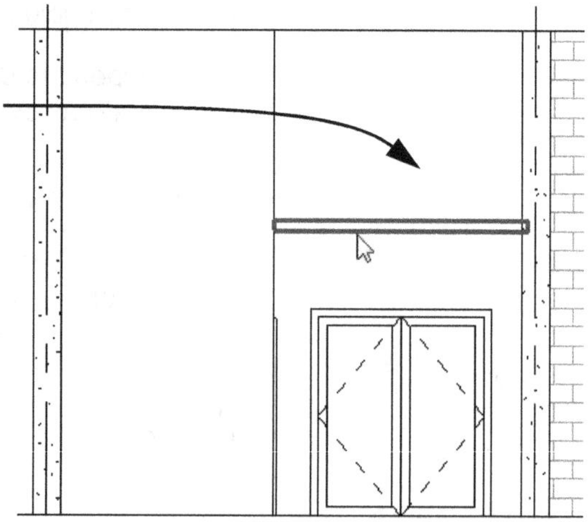

Figure 10–18

2. Return to the **Ceiling Plans: Floor 1** view.

3. Click (Wall). In the Type Selector, select **Basic Wall: Interior - 79mm Partition (1hr)**.

4. In Properties, set the *Location Line* to **Finish Face: Interior**, the *Base Offset* to **3000mm**, and the *Top Constraint* to **Up to level: Floor 2** with a *Top Offset* of (negative) **-300mm.**

5. Draw the wall across the face of the ceiling, as shown in Figure 10–19.

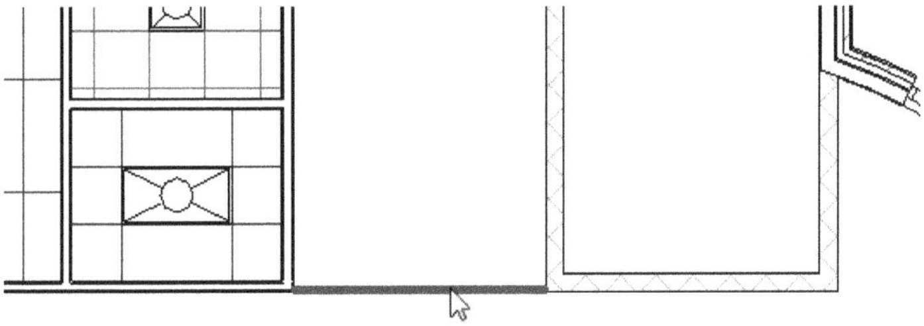

Figure 10–19

6. Open the **Floor Plans: Floor 1** view and create a camera view looking at the new ceiling and soffit, as shown in

   Figure 10–20. (Hint: Expand (Default 3D View) and click

   (Camera). Place the camera away from the hallway and point the target in the direction of the new ceiling and soffit).

Several elements were hidden to make this view more readable.

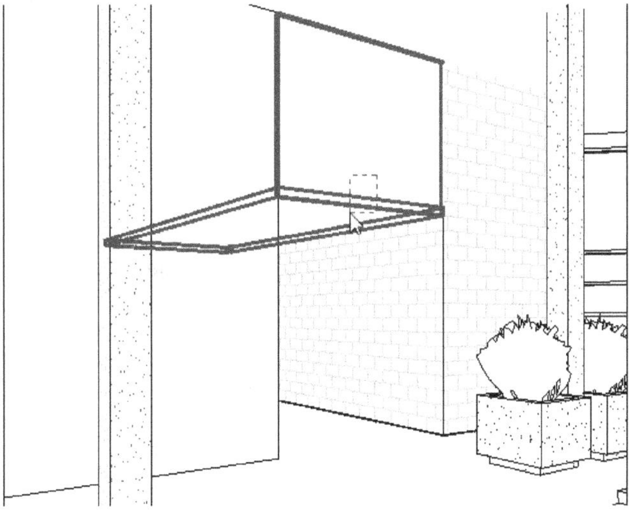

Figure 10–20

7. Save the project.

Task 3 - Add a recessed ceiling (optional).

1. In the **Ceiling Plans: Floor 1** view, pan over to the breakfast area.

2. Click (Ceiling) and click (Sketch Ceiling).

3. Create a ceiling, similar to the one shown in Figure 10–21, that has an opening in the center.

*If you have difficulty selecting the center of the curved wall, type **SC** and then select the curved wall. This snaps to the center point of the arc.*

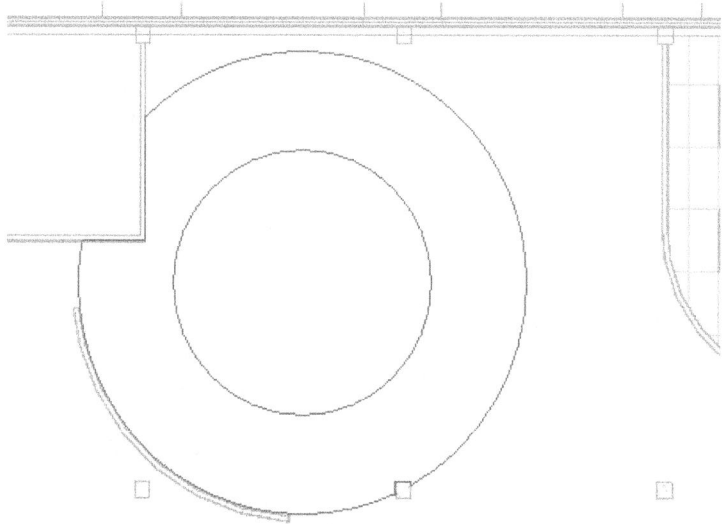

Figure 10–21

4. Click (Finish Edit Mode). The ceiling is still selected.

5. In the Type Selector, select **Compound Ceiling: Plain** and in Properties, set the *Height Offset from Level* to **3000mm**.

6. Click (Wall). In the type Selector, select **Basic Wall: Interior - 79mm Partition (1hr)** with the following parameters:

   - Location Line: **Finish Face: Interior**
   - Base Constraint: **Floor 1**
   - Base Offset: **3000mm**
   - Top Constraint: **Up to level: Floor 1**
   - Top Offset: **3600mm**

7. In the *Modify | Place Wall* tab>Draw panel, click ✒ (Pick Lines) and select the inside hole of the ceiling, as shown in Figure 10–22.

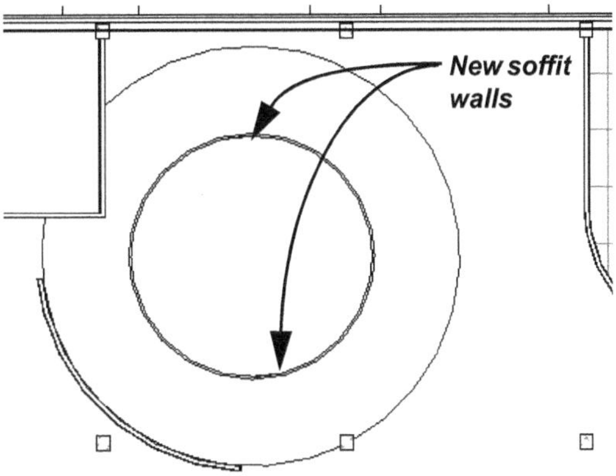

New soffit walls

Figure 10–22

8. Click 🗔 (Ceiling) again and use 🗐 (Sketch Ceiling) to draw a ceiling inside the open area. Use 🗔 (Pick Walls) to select the soffit walls.

9. Click ✔ (Finish Edit Mode).

10. In the Type Selector, select **Compound Ceiling: Plain** and in Properties, set the *Height Offset from Level* to **3600mm**.

11. Open the **Floor Plans: Floor 1** view and create a camera view looking toward the Breakfast area, as shown in Figure 10–23.

*Use **Hide in View> Elements** to turn off obstructing elements.*

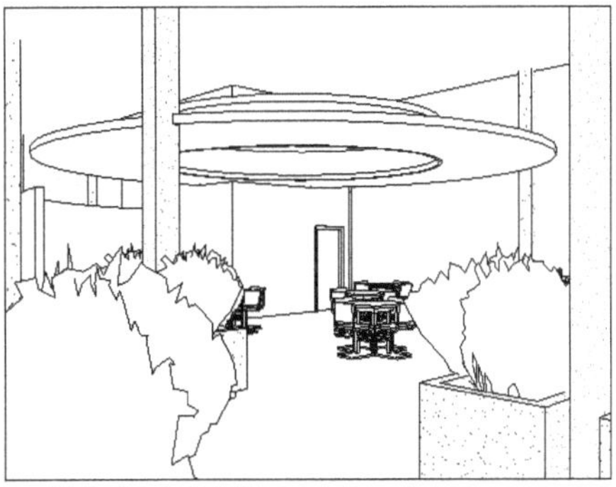

Figure 10–23

12. Save the project.

Chapter Review Questions

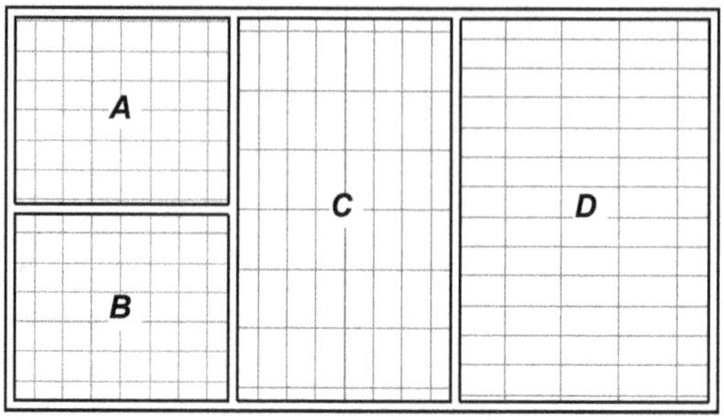

Figure 10–24

1. For the rooms labeled A and B in Figure 10–24, which command do you use to change the position of the ceiling grid?

    a. ⊟ (Align)

    b. ✥ (Move)

    c. ↻ (Rotate)

    d. ⟳ (Copy)

2. For the rooms labeled C and D in Figure 10–24, which command do you use to change the direction of the grids?

    a. ⊟ (Align)

    b. ✥ (Move)

    c. ↻ (Rotate)

    d. ⟳ (Copy)

3. Which of the following component types can be hosted by ceiling elements? (Select all that apply.)

    a. Mechanical Diffusers and Returns

    b. Lighting fixtures

    c. Curtain Grids

    d. Columns

4. Which of the following commands or options would you use to create a ceiling with a soffit around the edges?

    a. Use ⬚ (Automatic Ceiling) twice, setting the ceiling height appropriately for the main ceiling and the soffit ceiling.

    b. Use ⬚ (Sketch Ceiling) and sketch a boundary the size of the main ceiling. Start the command again and sketch a boundary the size of the soffit ceiling.

    c. Use ⬚ (Offset), set the distance to the width of the soffit, and select the ceiling edge.

    d. Use ⬚ (Move) and move the ceiling over the width of the soffit.

5. Which of the following commands can you use to get a light fixture fitted exactly in a ceiling grid as shown in Figure 10–25? (Select all that apply.)

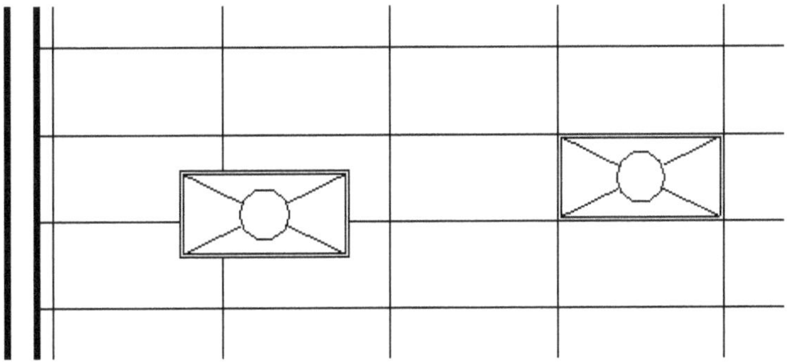

Figure 10–25

    a. ⬚ (Trim/Extend to Corner)

    b. ⬚ (Align)

    c. ⬚ (Join)

    d. ⬚ (Move)

Command Summary

Button	Command	Location
	Ceiling	• **Ribbon:** *Architecture* tab>Build panel
	Place a Component	• **Ribbon:** *Architecture* tab>Build panel

Chapter 11

Modeling Roofs

In this chapter you learn how to create roofs using two methods: by footprint and by extrusion. You learn how to use reference planes and work planes and how to clean up wall and roof intersections.

This chapter contains the following topics:

- **Modeling Roofs**
- **Creating Roofs by Footprint**
- **Reference Planes and Work Planes**
- **Creating Roofs by Extrusion**
- **Cleaning Up Wall and Roof Intersections**

11.1 Modeling Roofs

Learning Objective

- Show the difference between creating roofs by footprint and by extrusion.

The Autodesk® Revit® software provides two main ways of creating roofs:

- **Footprint:** Created in a floor plan view by defining the area to be covered.

- **Extrusion:** Created in an elevation or section by defining a profile sketch.

The footprint method can generate most common roof types, including flat, shed, gable, and hip roofs. The extrusion method is needed for an odd-shaped roof or a roof with two slopes on the same face. For example, in Figure 11–1, the front and back roofs were created by a footprint, with one slope to produce a shed roof. The center roof was created by drawing a sketch with two slopes and then extruding it.

Figure 11–1

- Other roof options, found in the Roof drop-down list, include **Roof by Face**, which is used with Massing elements, **Roof Soffit**, which connects the edge of the roof to the wall, **Fascia**, which places a flat board on the outside edge of the roof and **Gutter**, which adds a gutter on the edge of the roof.

11.2 Creating Roofs by Footprint

Autodesk Certification Topics & Objectives

Pro.   User

Modeling

	Pro.	User
• Create elements such as floors, ceilings, or roofs	✓	
• Change a generic floor/ceiling/roof to a specific type	✓	

Learning Objective

- Add roofs using the Footprint method.

To create a flat roof, or any basic single-sloped roofs (hip, shed, or gable), start with a plan view and define a sketch or "footprint" around the area that you want the roof to cover, as shown in Figure 11–2. You can then specify the slope for each edge.

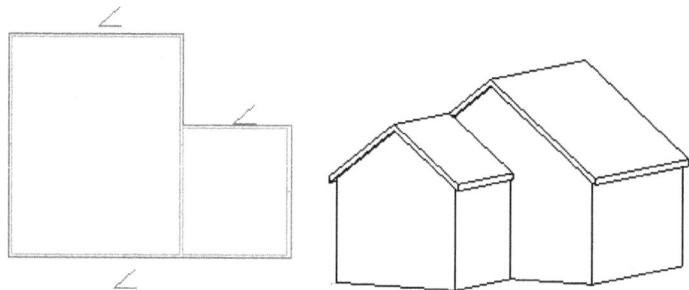

Figure 11–2

You control the type of roof by specifying which edge(s) define the slope. For example, if only one edge defines the slope, the result is a shed roof. If two opposing edges of a rectangular area define the slope, the result is a gable roof. You can also use arcs in your sketch to define the slope.

How To: Add a Roof by Footprint

1. Open a plan view at the roof level of the building.

2. In the *Architecture* tab> Build panel, expand ⬚ (Roof) and click ⬚ (Roof by Footprint).

3. In the *Modify | Create Roof Footprint* tab>Draw panel, click ⬚ (Pick Walls) or ⟋ (Line) or any other Draw tool to create the roof footprint.

4. In the Options Bar, select the **Defines slope** option if you want the edge to define the slope, and enter a value in the *Overhang* field, as shown in Figure 11–3. The **Extend to wall core** option sets the overhang from the core of the wall, rather than from the exterior.

☐ Defines slope | Overhang: 0.0 | ☐ Extend to wall core

Figure 11–3

5. Select the outside edges of the walls or draw the sketch lines as required, setting the options for each segment. The lines must form a closed boundary that does not overlap. You can use the commands in the Modify panel, such as ⇥ (Trim), to modify the lines as required.

6. Return to the **Modify** command.

7. Select each edge and in Properties, change the *Slope* and *Overhang* as required, as shown in Figure 11–4. The slope is defined as a distance over 12".

You can also change the slope of each section of the roof by modifying the slope control and modify the overhang by changing the temporary dimensions.

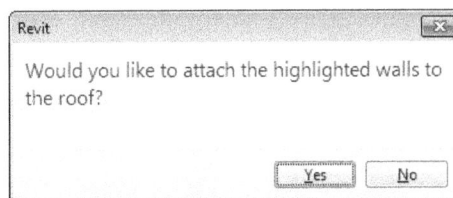

Slope control

30.00°

Constraints		☆
Defines Roof Slope	✓	
Overhang	610.0	
Plate Offset From Base	0.0	
Extend into wall (to core)	☐	
Dimensions		☆
Slope	30.00°	
Length	6906.0	

610.0

Temporary Dimensions for overhang

Figure 11–4

8. Click ✓ (Finish Edit Mode).

9. An alert box might open, as shown in Figure 11–5. You can attach the highlighted walls to the roof now or later.

Revit

Would you like to attach the highlighted walls to the roof?

Yes | No

Figure 11–5

10. The roof is still selected and you can set the options for the entire roof in Properties. These include the roof type, *Base Offset from Level*, *Rafter Cut*, and *Cutoff Level* options.

- Attaching walls to the roof extends them up to the roof, including the gable edges, as shown in Figure 11–6. You can also do this later.

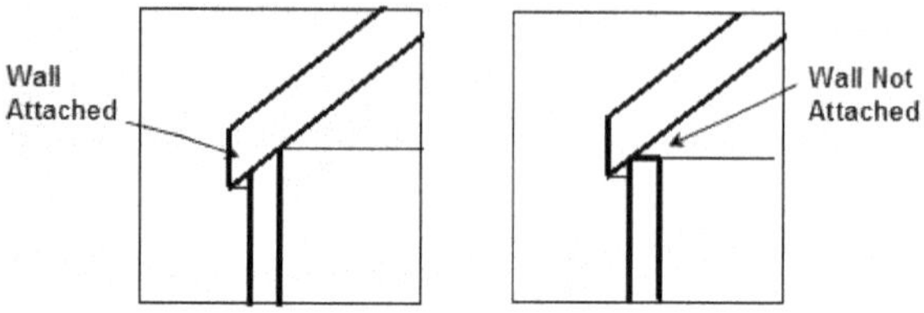

Figure 11–6

- In Sketch mode, roof edges that define the slope are marked with an angle (∠) symbol. A flat roof does not have edges set to define a slope.

- Double-click on the edge of the roof to move into **Edit Footprint** mode. If **Select Elements by Face** is on, you can click anywhere on the face of the roof to select it.

Hint: Setting Up a Roof Plan

When creating a roof, it is a good idea to set up a roof plan view by adding a level where the bottom of the roof should be located. If there are roofs at different heights, you can create a level for each location.

Most plan views are typically cut at 900mm to 1220mm above the bottom of the level, as shown in Figure 11–7. However, this does not work with pitched roofs, whose structures can reach 6000mm high or more. To change the height of the area shown in the roof plan, you need to change the *View Range* in View Properties.

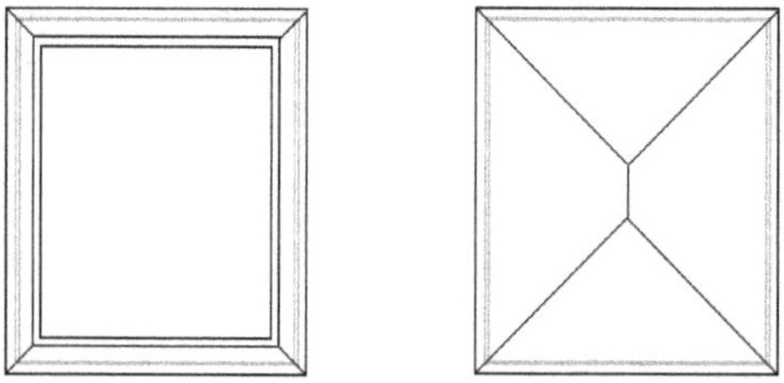

View Range Cut Plane   *View Range Cut Plane*
@ 1220mm   *@ 9000mm*

Figure 11–7

Practice 11a

Create Roofs by Footprint

Estimated time for completion: 25 minutes

Learning Objectives

- Create a flat roof on the main hotel building.
- Create a roof plan view.
- Add a complex flat and sloped roof to the poolhouse.

In this practice you will create a flat roof on the main part of the hotel, and flat and sloped roofs over the poolhouse, as shown in Figure 11–8.

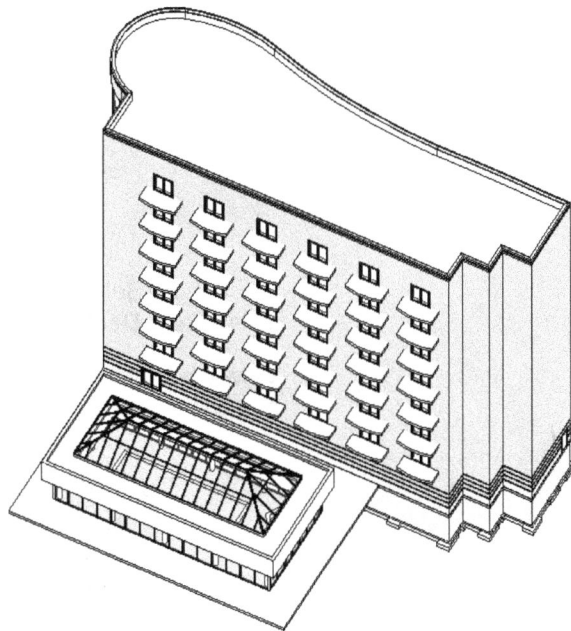

Figure 11–8

Task 1 - Create a flat roof.

1. Open **Modern-Hotel-Roof-Footprint-M.rvt** from your class folder.

2. Open the **Floor Plans: Roof** view and set the *Underlay* to **None**.

3. Hide the grid lines and section and elevation markers.

4. In the *Architecture* tab>Build panel, expand (Roof) and click (Roof by Footprint).
5. In the Options Bar, clear the **Defines slope** option.
6. In the *Modify | Create Roof Footprint* tab>Draw panel, click (Pick Walls) and select the inside of the walls around the building, as shown in Figure 11–9.

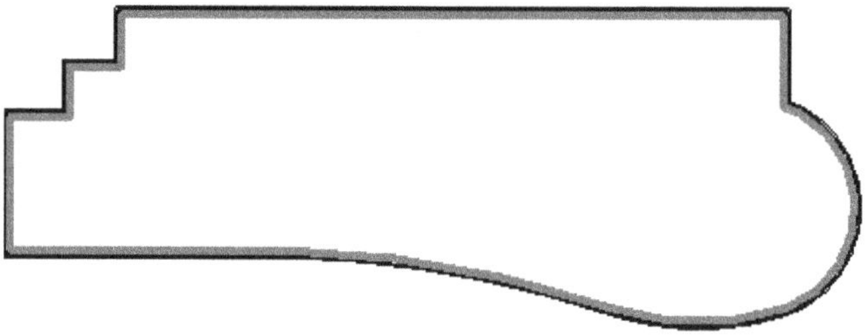

Figure 11–9

7. Click (Finish Edit Mode).
8. In the Type Selector, select **Basic Roof: Steel Bar Joist-Steel Deck - EPDM Membrane**
9. View the building in 3D to display the roof applied below the parapet wall, as shown in Figure 11–10.

Figure 11–10

10. Save the project.

Task 2 - Create a roof plan.

Hold down <Shift> and the mouse wheel to rotate in 3D view.

1. Rotate the 3D view until the poolhouse at the back of the building displays. It does not yet have a roof, but several features are in place, including the parapet walls and roof soffit, as shown in Figure 11–11.

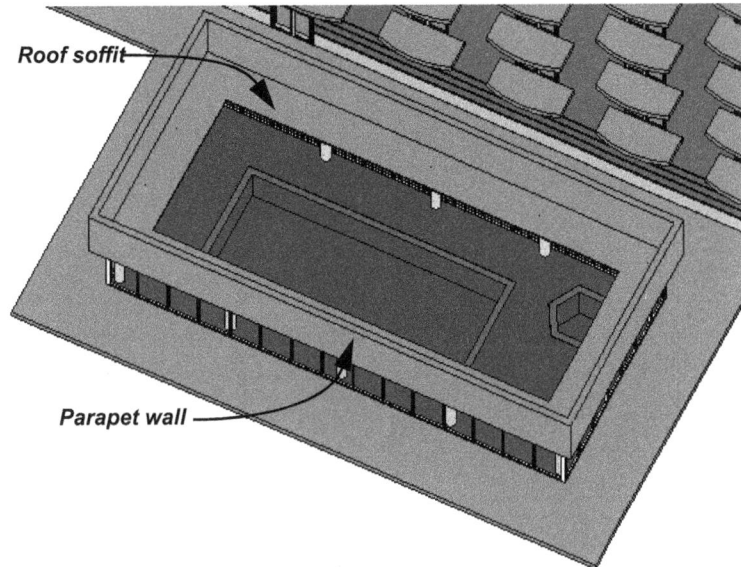

Figure 11–11

2. Duplicate (without detailing) a copy of the **Floor Plans: Floor 2** view and rename it as **Roof - Poolhouse**.

3. Verify that this view is open.

4. In Properties, edit the *View Range* and set it up as shown in Figure 11–12. Then click [OK].

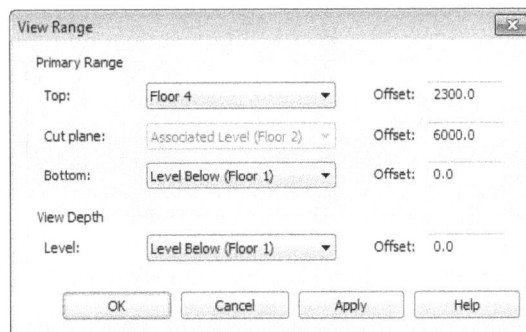

Figure 11–12

5. Expand the crop region to display the pool area and then modify it so that only the poolhouse displays, as shown in Figure 11–13. Hide any other elements as required.

Figure 11–13

6. Hide the crop region.

Task 3 - Create roofs on the poolhouse.

1. In the *Architecture* tab>Build panel, click ⬚ (Roof). The software remembers the most recently used command of **Roof by Footprint**.

2. In the Options Bar, verify that the **Defines slope** option is cleared and there is no overhang.

3. In the *Modify | Create Roof Footprint* tab>Draw panel, click ⬚ (Pick Walls) and select the inside of the parapet walls.

   Use ⬚ (Pick Lines) and select the soffit opening, as shown in Figure 11–14. This creates a flat roof with an opening in it.

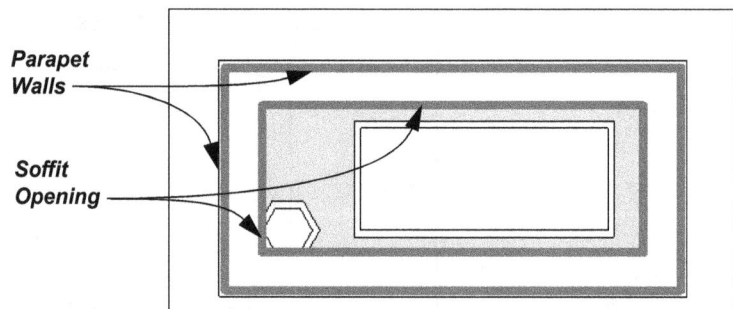

Figure 11–14

4. Click ⬚ (Finish Edit Mode.)

5. With the roof still selected, in Properties, set the *Base Level* to **Floor 2** and the *Base Offset from Level* to (negative) **-600mm**.

6. Click in the view to release the roof.

7. Click ⬡ (Wall).

8. In Properties, set the following parameters:

   - Wall Type: **Basic Wall: Exterior - EIFS on Mtl.Stud**
   - Location Line: **Finish Face: Interior**
   - Base Constraint: **Floor 2**
   - Base Offset: (negative) **-200mm**
   - Top Constraint: **Unconnected**
   - Unconnected Height: **250mm**

9. Draw this short wall around the opening, as shown in Figure 11–15.

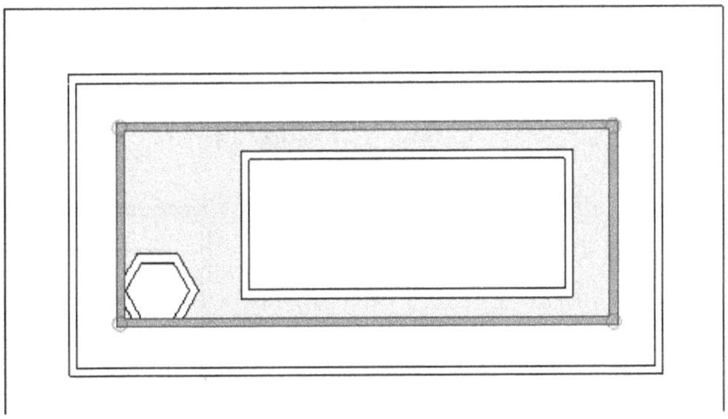

Figure 11–15

10. Click ⬒ (Roof by Footprint).

11. In the Options Bar, select the **Defines slope** option.

12. Use ⬚ (Pick Walls) and select the outside of the new walls you just created, as shown in Figure 11–16.

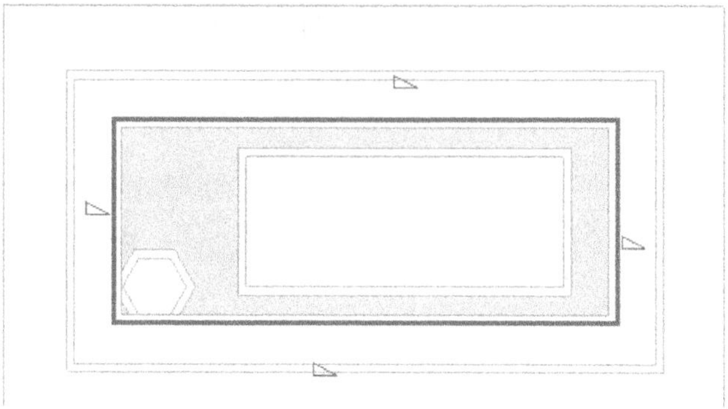

Figure 11–16

13. Click ✓ (Finish Edit Mode). In the Message dialog box, click ⬚ No to not attach any walls to the roof.

14. In the Type Selector, select **Sloped Glazing: Pool Roof** and verify that the *Base Level* is **Floor 2**. In the *Grid 1* area, set the *Justification* to **Center**. The new roof displays as shown in Figure 11–17.

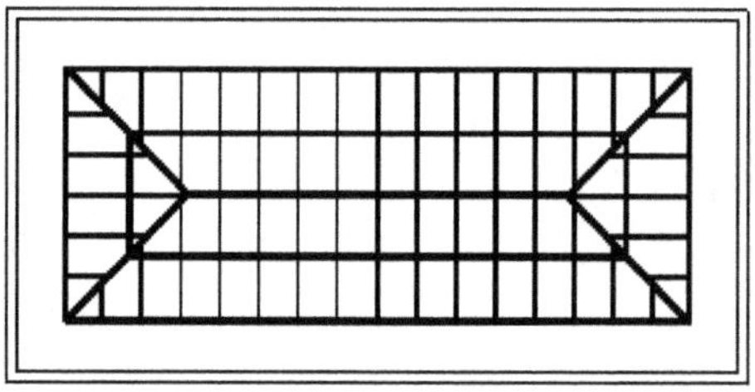

Figure 11–17

15. View the entire model in 3D.

16. Save the project.

Task 4 - Apply slopes to the main flat roof (optional).

If time permits, select the flat roof on the main hotel and use the Shape Editing tools on the *Modify | Floors* tab to add appropriate drainage slopes.

11.3 Reference Planes and Work Planes

Learning Objectives

- Sketch reference planes to help you draw and align elements.
- Set Work Planes as the surface on which elements are drawn.

Sketching Reference Planes

As you develop designs in the Autodesk Revit software, you might occasionally need additional temporary lines to help define certain locations. For example, you can draw *reference planes* (the dashed lines) when drawing extruded roof sketches or any other sketched elements, as shown in Figure 11–18. You can snap to reference planes and they display in associated views.

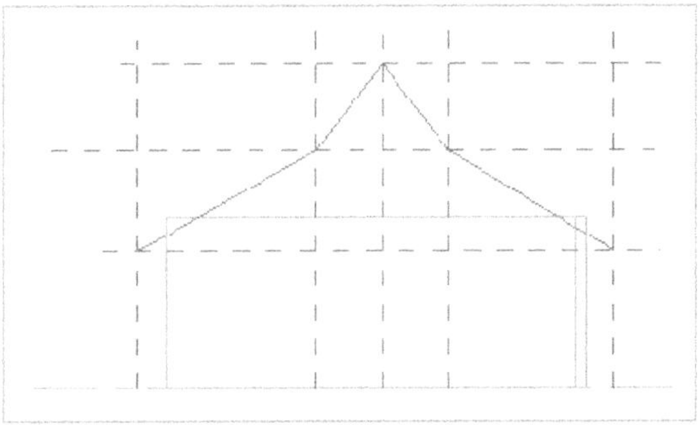

Figure 11–18

How To: Sketch with Reference Planes

1. In the *Architecture* tab>Work Plane panel, click ✏️ (Ref Plane).
2. In the *Modify | Place Reference Plane* tab>Draw panel, click
   ╱ (Line) or ⟋ (Pick Lines) and create the reference planes.

- Once you have created the reference planes, use them to draw sketch lines to create roofs and/or other sketched elements.

- If you create reference planes while working in a sketch (e.g., an extruded roof), the reference planes display only in Sketch mode.

- You can name reference planes. This is useful if you want to specify a work plane which would otherwise not be displayed in a view (i.e., extruded roofs). Select the reference plane and, in Properties, in the *Identity Data* area, type a *Name*, as shown in Figure 11–19.

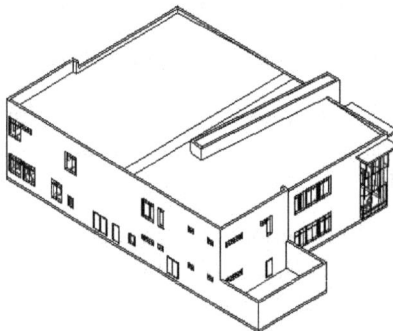

Figure 11–19

Establishing a Work Plane

In some processes, such as creating a Roof by Extrusion, you are prompted to specify a Work Plane. A Work Plane is the surface you draw on or extrude from.

- When you are in a plan view, the Work Plane is automatically parallel to the ground.

- When you are in an Elevation or 3D view, you need to specify the Work Plane before you start sketching any type of element.

- If you created a reference plane and named it, that plane is available in the *Name* drop-down list in the Work Plane dialog box.

- In the *Architecture* tab>Work Plane panel, click (Viewer) to open the Workplane Viewer. It displays a plan or section view in a separate window based on the current work plane, as shown in Figure 11–20.

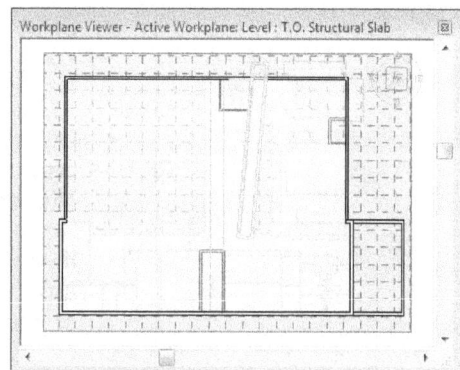

Figure 11–20

How To: Select a Work Plane

1. Start a command that requires a work plane or, in the

   Architecture tab>Work Plane panel, click 🔲 (Set).
2. In the Work Plane dialog box, select one of the options.
   - **Name:** Select an existing level, grid, or reference plane,

     as shown in Figure 11–21, and click ▭ OK ▭ .

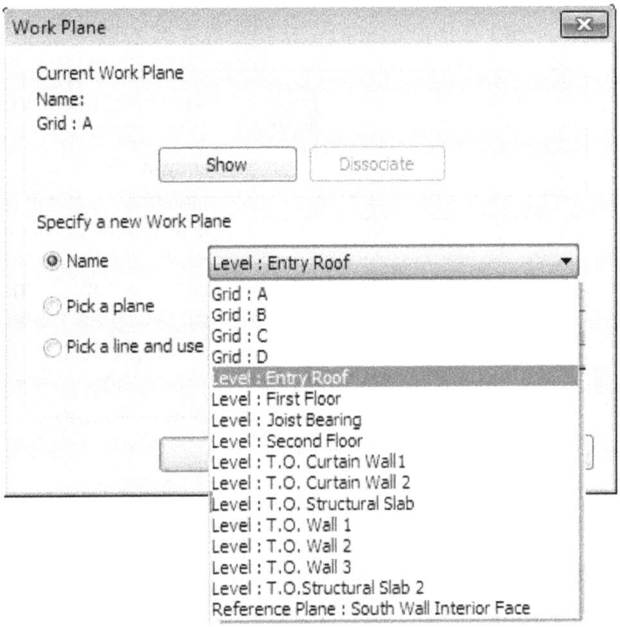

Figure 11–21

   - **Pick a plane:** After clicking ▭ OK ▭ , select a plane in
     the view, such as a wall face. To select it, move the cursor
     over the edge of the wall to highlight it and press <Tab>
     until the entire wall plane is selected. Click to complete
     the process.
   - **Pick a line and use the work plane it was sketched in:**

     After clicking ▭ OK ▭ , select a model line such as a
     room separation line.

11.4 Creating Roofs by Extrusion

Autodesk Certification Topics & Objectives

	Pro.	User

Modeling

	Pro.	User
• Create elements such as floors, ceilings, or roofs	✓	
• Change a generic floor/ceiling/roof to a specific type	✓	

Learning Objectives

- Draw a sketch for an extruded roof.
- Modify an extruded roof by setting the start and end of the extrusion and changing the plan profile of the roof.

For more complex roof forms, you might need to create an extruded roof, such as the slightly curved roof shown in Figure 11–22. Extruded roofs are based on a sketch of the roof profile in an elevation or section view. The profile is extruded between a start and end point.

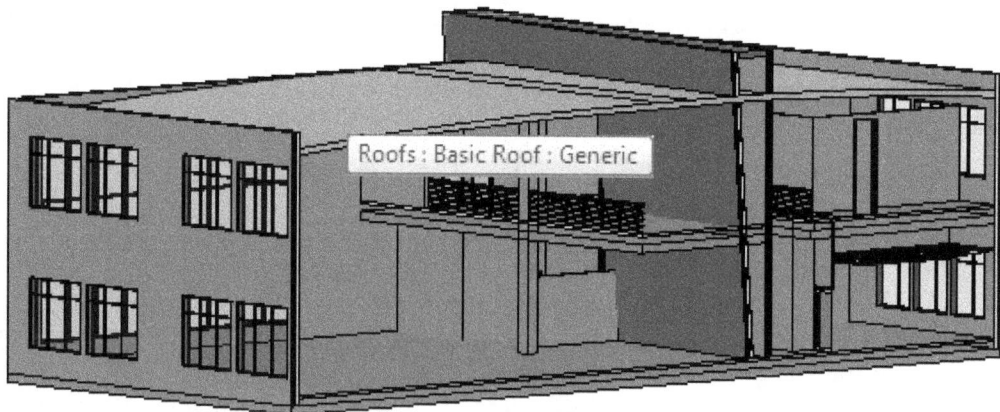

Roofs : Basic Roof : Generic

Figure 11–22

How To: Create an Extruded Roof

1. Open an elevation or a section view.

2. In the *Architecture* tab>Build panel, expand (Roof) and click (Roof by Extrusion).

3. In the Work Plane dialog box, select a method or a Name for the Work Plane on which you want to sketch the roof profile, and click [OK].

- The Go To View dialog box opens if you are not in a view in which the sketch can be created. Select one of the views and click [Open View].

4. In the Roof Reference Level and Offset dialog box, select the base *Level* for the roof, as shown in Figure 11–23. You can also specify an *Offset* from the selected level.

By default, this level is set to the highest one in the project.

Roof Reference Level and Offset	☒
Level:	Roof ▼
Offset:	0.0
	OK Cancel

Figure 11–23

5. In the *Modify | Create Extrusion Roof Profile* tab>Work Plane panel, use 🖉 (Ref Plane) to draw any reference planes that could help you create the roof profile.
6. In the Draw panel, use the Draw tools to create the profile, as shown on the left in Figure 11–24.

Sketch only the shape of the roof in profile, not the thickness. Thickness (determined by the roof type) is added below the profile sketch line when the roof is created.

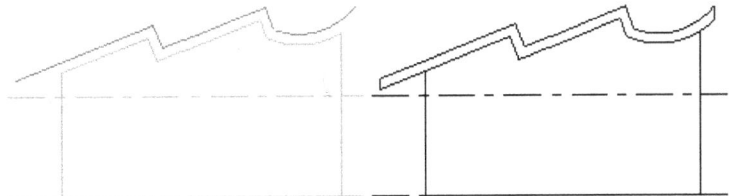

Figure 11–24

7. In Properties, set the *Extrusion Start* and *End*.

8. Click ✔ (Finish Edit Mode).
9. In the Type Selector, select the roof type. In Properties, make any other modifications to the parameters as required.

- View the roof and ensure it is in the right place.

- Use 🗖 (Align) to line up the roof edges with other elements

- Double-click on the edge of the roof to switch to Edit Profile mode. If **Select Elements by Face** is on you can click anywhere on the face of the roof to select it.

- If you are in a plan view, editing the profile opens the Go To View dialog box. Select a view in which you can edit the profile and select **Open View**.

- In a 3D view, you can use controls and temporary dimensions to modify the start and end of the extrusion, as shown in Figure 11–25. Alternatively, you can modify the information in Properties.

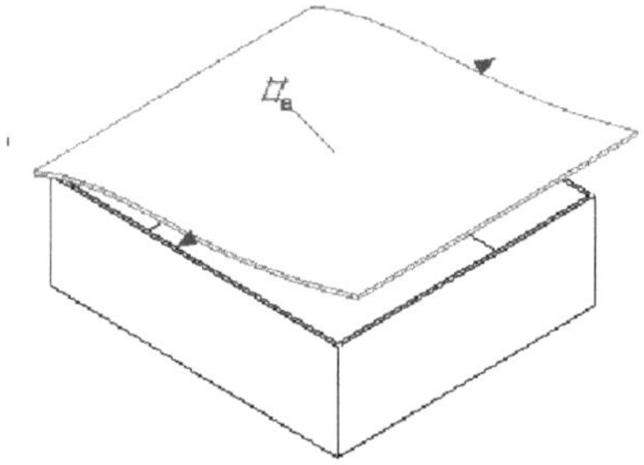

Figure 11–25

How To: Modify the Plan View of an Extruded Roof

1. Open a plan view where the entire roof displays.
2. Select the roof.

3. In the *Modify | Roofs* tab>Opening panel, click [icon] (Vertical).
4. In the *Modify | Create Extrusion Roof Profile* tab>Draw panel, use the tools to create a closed loop. The loop can be entirely inside the roof or touching the roof boundaries.

5. Click [icon] (Finish Edit Mode). The extruded view now has a cutout, as shown in Figure 11–26.

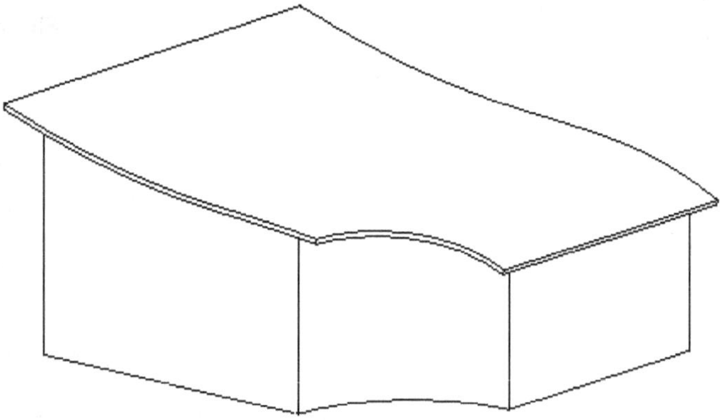

Figure 11–26

11.5 Cleaning Up Wall and Roof Intersections

Autodesk Certification Topics & Objectives

Pro.   User

Modeling

- Attach walls to a roof or ceiling   ✓

Learning Objectives

- Attach walls to roofs so that they fill in any open spaces between the two.
- Join geometry between the roofs, walls, and other roofs to clean up the intersections where they touch.
- Join roofs to tall walls or other roofs, even if they are not already touching.

The connections between walls and roofs can become very complex, as shown in Figure 11–27. A number of commands can help you edit walls or roofs to clean up the intersections. These include **Attach**, **Join Geometry**, and **Join/Unjoin Roof**.

Figure 11–27

Attaching Walls to Roofs

If you did not attach walls to a roof when you created the roof, you can come back at a later point and do this with **Attach Top/Base**, as shown in Figure 11–28.

Figure 11–28

- **Attach Top/Base** can be used with walls against sloping floors or topographic site features.

How To: Attach Walls to Roofs

1. Select the wall(s) you want to attach to the roof.

2. In the *Modify | Walls* tab>Modify Wall panel, click (Attach Top/Base). Verify that *Attach Wall* is set to **Top**, as shown in Figure 11–29.

Attach Wall: ⊙ Top ○ Base

Figure 11–29

3. Select the roof. The walls are trimmed or extended to the roofline.

Joining Geometry

Where roofs overlap walls or other roofs, you can use **Join Geometry** to clean up the intersections. The elements remain separate, but the intersections are cleaned up. In Figure 11–30, the slanted roof was joined to the parapet wall (in front) and to the flat roof. In this case, joining adds the lines that define the intersection edges.

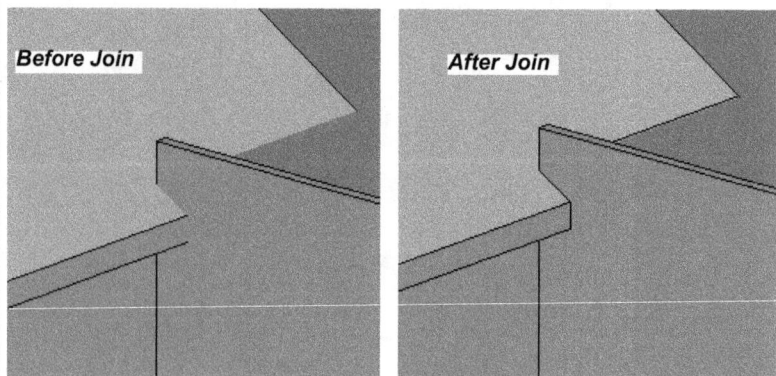

Figure 11–30

How To: Join Geometry

1. In the *Modify* tab>Geometry panel, expand ⬡ (Join) and click ⬡ (Join Geometry).
2. In the Options Bar, select **Multiple Join** to select several elements to join to the first selection.
3. Select the elements to join.

- To remove the join, expand ⬡ (Join), click ⬡ (Unjoin Geometry), and select the elements to unjoin.

Joining Roofs

When you want to join an extruded roof to another roof, or a wall face that is taller than the roof, you can use the **Join/Unjoin Roof** command, as shown in Figure 11–31.

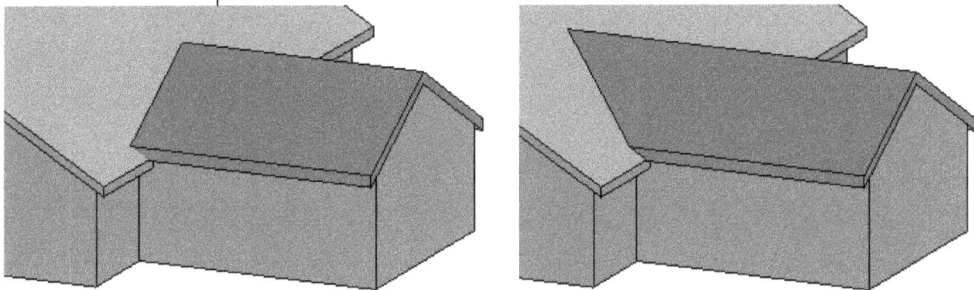

Figure 11–31

How To: Use Join/Unjoin Roof

1. In the *Modify* tab>Geometry panel, click ⬡ (Join/Unjoin Roof).
2. Select one of the roof edges.
3. Select the other roof or the wall.

Practice 11b | Create Roofs by Extrusion

Learning Objective

- Create an extruded roof and modify the plan profile of the roof.

Estimated time for completion: 20 minutes

In this practice you will create an extruded roof to cover the main entrance of the building and modify it to cover the side entrance as well, as shown in Figure 11–32.

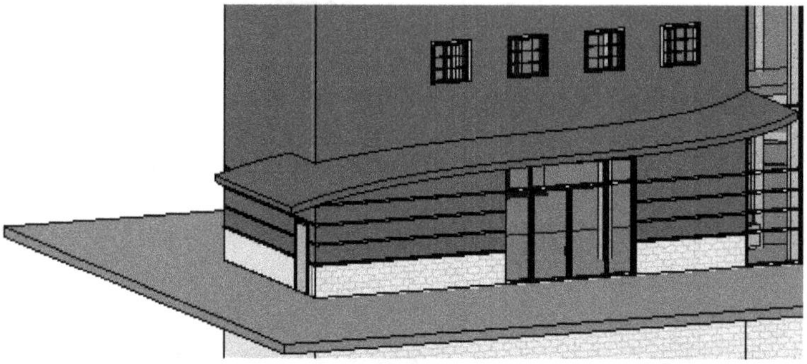

Figure 11–32

Task 1 - Create a roof by extrusion.

1. Open **Modern-Hotel-Roof-Extruded-M.rvt** from your class folder.

2. Open the **Elevations (Building Elevation): South** view.

3. Zoom in on the area around the front entrance.

4. In the *Architecture* tab>Build panel, expand (Roof) and click (Roof by Extrusion).

5. In the Work Plane dialog box, verify that **Pick a plane** is selected, and click OK .

6. Select the front face of the wall.

7. In the Roof Reference Level and Offset dialog box, set the *Level* to **Floor 2** and click OK . A reference plane is set at this level and the drawing is grayed out.

8. Sketch the profile of a roof over the front of the building that does not go above the Floor 2 reference plane. It should extend beyond the building to the left but finish at the end of the brick wall on the right. The example shown in Figure 11–33 was created using (Spline).

Figure 11–33

9. In Properties, set the *Extrusion End* to (negative) **-1850mm**.

10. Click (Finish Edit Mode).

11. In the Type Selector, select **Basic Roof: Generic - 125mm**.

12. View the new roof in 3D. It is mostly inside the building at this point.

Task 2 - Modify the extruded roof.

1. Open the **Floor Plans: Site** view. This view displays the entire building in plan including all of the roofs.

2. Hide the grid lines and elevation markers by category.

3. Select the Entrance roof and using controls, move the roof outward so that the length is **3500mm**, as shown in Figure 11–34.

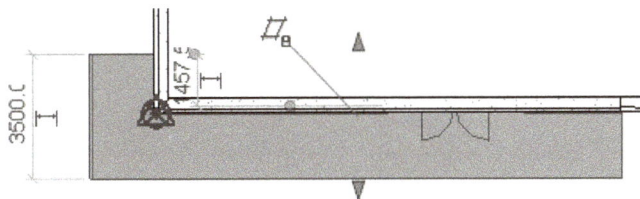

Figure 11–34

4. In the *Modify | Roofs* tab>Opening panel, click ⬛ (Vertical).

5. Create a rectangular cutout of the roof for the portion that passes through the building, as shown in Figure 11–35.

Figure 11–35

6. Click ✓ (Finish Edit Mode).

7. View the modified roof in 3D. It now wraps around the side of the building to cover the side entrance, as shown in Figure 11–36.

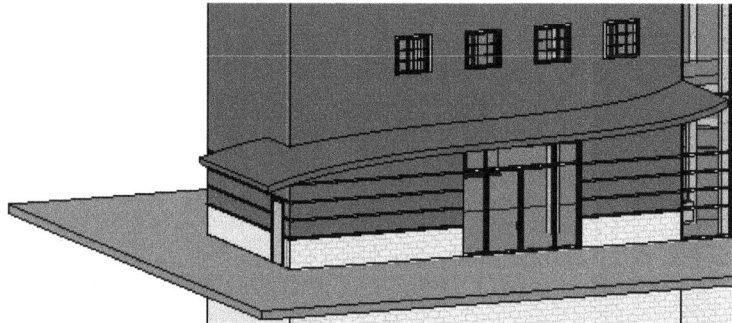

Figure 11–36

8. Save the project.

Chapter Review Questions

1. To create a roof sloping in one direction only (as shown on the front of the building in Figure 11–37), you would create a roof...

Figure 11–37

   a. By extrusion and rotate the roof to the correct angle.

   b. By footprint and specify the slope along two parallel sides.

   c. By extrusion and use the Slope Arrow to define the overall slope of the roof.

   d. By footprint and use the **Shape Editing** tools to create the slope.

2. To create a flat roof, which of the following commands would you use to draw a sketch of the boundary of the roof and to set its thickness?

   a. **Roof by Footprint** with the thickness set by the roof type.

   b. **Roof by Extrusion** with the thickness extruded from the sketch.

3. Which of the following methods makes a wall touch the underside of a roof?

   a. Select the wall and use ⬚ (Attach Top/Base).

   b. Select the roof and use ⬚ (Attach Top/Base).

   c. Select the wall and edit the profile.

   d. Select the roof and use the **By Face** option.

4. Which roof type and view should you use to create a curved roof as shown in Figure 11–38?

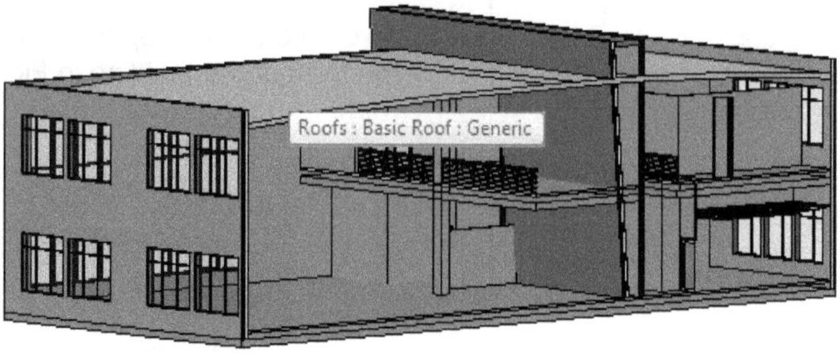

Roofs : Basic Roof : Generic

Figure 11–38

a. Roof by Footprint, Plan View

b. Roof by Footprint, Elevation or Section view

c. Roof by Extrusion, Plan View

d. Roof by Extrusion, Elevation or Section view

5. You can name Reference Planes.

a. True

b. False

Command Summary

Button	Command	Location
	Attach Top/Base	• **Ribbon:** *Modify	Walls* tab>Modify Wall panel
	Join>Join Geometry	• **Ribbon:** *Modify* tab>Geometry panel>Join>Join Geometry
	Join>Unjoin Geometry	• **Ribbon:** *Modify* tab>Geometry panel>Join>Unjoin Geometry
	Join/Unjoin Roof	• **Ribbon:** *Modify* tab>Geometry panel>Join/Unjoin Roof
	Ref Plane	• **Ribbon:** *Architecture* tab>Work Plane panel>Ref Plane
	Roof>Roof by Extrusion	• **Ribbon:** *Architecture* tab>Build panel>Roof list>Roof by Extrusion
	Roof>Roof by Footprint	• **Ribbon:** *Architecture* tab>Build panel>Roof list>Roof by Footprint
	Set Work Plane	• **Ribbon:** *Architecture* tab>Work Plane panel>Set

Chapter 12

Vertical Circulation

In this chapter you learn how to create and edit component stairs, involving runs, landings, and supports. You learn how to add railings and modify handrails and top rails. You also learn how to sketch and edit custom stair designs, and how to create ramps.

This chapter contains the following topics:

- **Creating Component Stairs**
- **Modifying Component Stairs**
- **Working with Railings**
- **Sketching Custom Stairs**
- **Creating Ramps**

12.1 Creating Component Stairs

Autodesk Certification Topics & Objectives

	Pro.	User
Modeling		
• Create a stair with a landing	✓	✓
Families		
• Assess review warnings in Revit	✓	

Learning Objective

- Create component-based stairs with runs, landings, and supports.

As with other Autodesk® Revit® elements, stairs are *smart* parametric elements. With just a few clicks, you can create stairs of varying heights and designs, complete with railings. Stairs can be created by assembling stair components (as shown in Figure 12–1), or by sketching a custom layout.

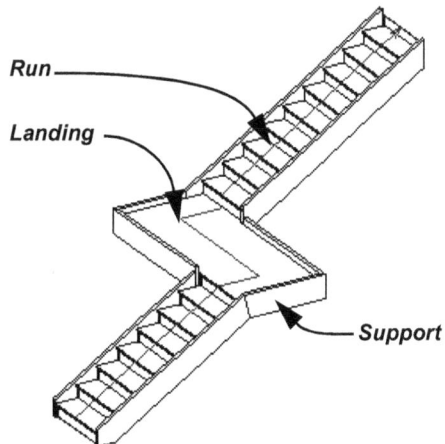

Figure 12–1

- Railings can be added within the **Stair** command. They display after you complete the stair.

When creating component-based stairs, there are three parts of a stair that can be assembled, as shown in Figure 12–1:

- **Runs:** The actual stair tread and riser elements. These include straight runs which can be combined for multi-landing stairs, spiral stairs and L-shaped and U-shaped Winders. Custom stair runs can also be created by sketching.

- **Landings:** The platform between runs. These are typically created automatically and then modified if required.

- **Supports:** The stringer or carriage that structurally holds the stair elements. These can be created automatically or you can pick the edges where you want the different types to go. These can be placed on either side of the stairs or in the center of the stairs.

- Each component of the stair is independent but also in relationship to the other components. For example, if steps are removed from one run they are added to connected runs to maintain the overall height, as shown in Figure 12–2.

Figure 12–2

- Stair components can overlap other components, as shown in Figure 12–3. You can also add multiple runs to the same landing.

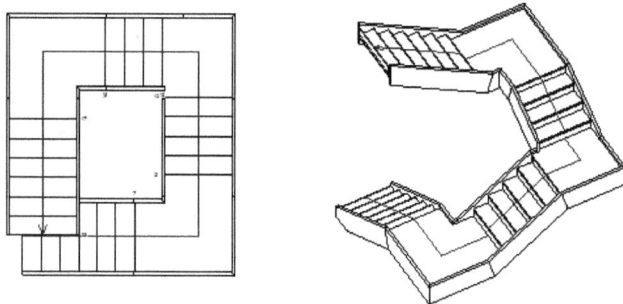

Figure 12–3

- Stair components can be individually tagged and scheduled.

- You can select and edit each of the components while you are in edit mode or after the stair has been created.

Hint: Stairs and Views

When creating stairs you can work in either plan or 3D views. It can help to have the plan view and a 3D view open and tiled side by side. Only open the views in which you want to work and press <W> and then press <T> to use the shortcut.

Creating Runs

As you create a component stair the first thing that you place is the runs. Six different methods are available in the Components panel, as shown in Figure 12–4.

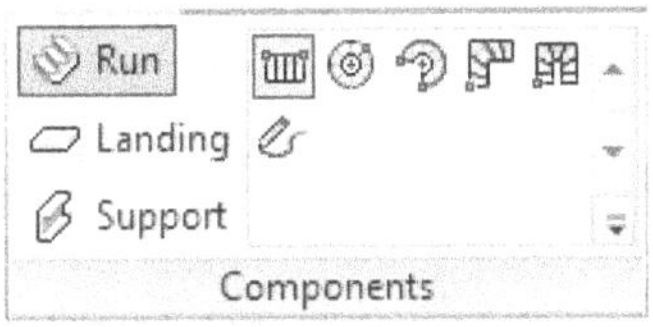

Figure 12–4

	Straight	Draws a straight run by selecting the start and end points of the run.
	Full-Step Spiral	Draws a spiral run based on a start point and radius.
	Center-Ends Spiral	Draws a spiral run based on a center point, start point, and end point.
	L-Shape Winder	Draws an L-shaped winder based on the lower end.
	U-Shape Winder	Draws a U-shaped winder based on the lower end.
	Sketch	Opens additional tools where you can sketch stair boundary and risers individually.

- Component stairs can include a mix of the different types of runs.

How To: Create a Component-based Stair with Straight Runs

The stair type can impact all of the other settings. Therefore, it is important to select it first.

1. In the *Architecture* tab>Circulation panel, click ✍ (Stair by Component).
2. In the Type Selector, select the stair type, as shown in Figure 12–5.

Figure 12–5

3. In Properties (shown in Figure 12–6), set the parameters for the *Base Level* and *Top Level*, and any other information that is needed.

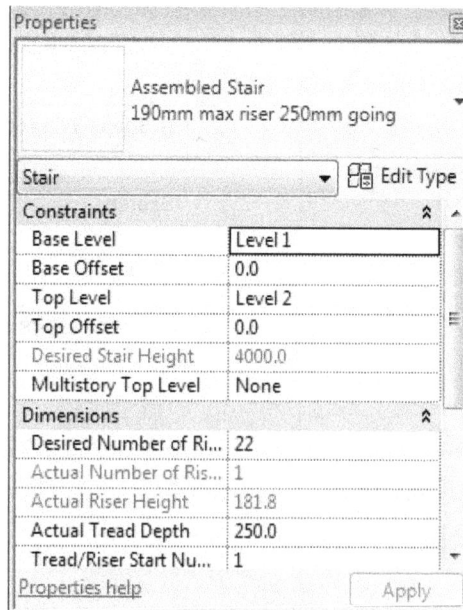

Multistory Top Level enables you to create multiple runs of stairs based on Levels. The levels need to be the same height for this to work.

Figure 12–6

4. In the *Modify | Create Stairs* tab>Tools panel, click

   ▣ (Railing), select a railing type in the Railings dialog box as shown in Figure 12–7, and specify whether the *Position* is

   on the **Treads** or **Stringer**. Click [OK].

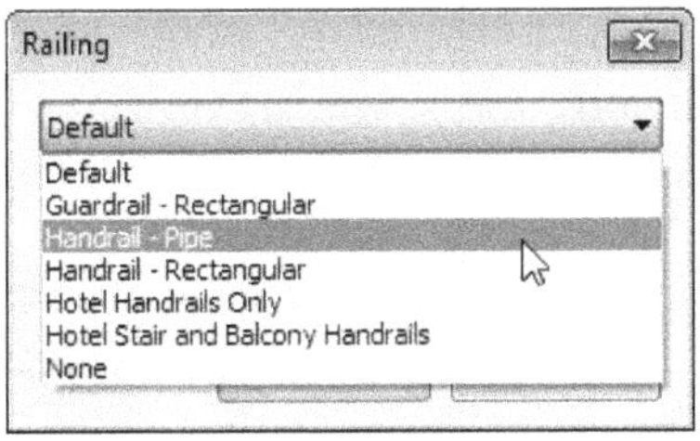

Railings can also be added and modified after the stair has been placed.

Figure 12–7

5. In the *Modify | Create Stair* tab>Components panel, click

   ✍ (Run) and then click ▥ (Straight).

6. In the Options Bar (shown in Figure 12–8), specify the following options:

   • **Location Line:** Select **Exterior Support: Left**, **Run: Left**, **Run: Center**, **Run: Right**, or **Exterior Support: Right**.

   • **Offset:** Specify a distance from the Location Line. This is typically used if you are following an existing wall but do not need to have the stairs directly against them.

   • **Actual Run Width:** Specify the width of the stair run (not including the supports).

   • **Automatic Landing:** Creates landings between stair runs (recommended).

| Location Line: Run: Center ▼ | Offset: 0.0 | Actual Run Width: 1000.0 | ☑ Automatic Landing |

Figure 12–8

7. Click on the screen to select a start point for the run. A box displays, indicating the stair orientation and the number of risers created and remaining, as shown in Figure 12–9.

Figure 12–9

- For straight stairs of a single run, select a second point anywhere outside the box to create the run.
- For multi-landing or u-shaped stairs, select a second point inside the box for the length of the first run. Then select a start point and an end point for the next run. Landings can be created automatically between runs.

8. Click ✓ (Finish Edit Mode) to create the stairs, complete with railings.

*If you are creating a complex stair pattern, sketch reference planes first while in the **Stairs** command to help you select the start and end points of each run.*

If the stair is going in the wrong direction, click

(Flip) in the Modify | Create Stair tab>Tools panel.

Creating Other Types of Runs

While most stairs are created using straight runs there are times when you need to create specialty runs, such as spirals and winders.

How To: Create a Full-Step Spiral Run

1. Start the **Stair** command and set up the Properties as required.

2. In the Components panel, click ⚙ (Full-Step Spiral).
3. Select the center point of the spiral.
4. Select (or type) the radius of the spiral. The run is created as shown in Figure 12–10.

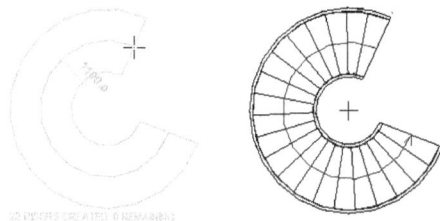

Figure 12–10

How To: Create a Center-Ends Spiral Run

1. Start the **Stair** command and set up the Properties as required.

2. In the Components panel, click ⟳ (Center-Ends Spiral).
3. Select the center of the spiral.
4. Select (or type) the radius of the spiral.
5. Drag the cursor to display the number of risers as shown on the right in Figure 12–11.

You can create spiral stairs with landings with this option.

Figure 12–11

How To: Create Winder-based stairs.

1. Start the **Stair** command and set up the Properties as required.

2. In the Components panel, click ◫ (L-Shaped Winder) or

   ▦ (U-Shaped Winder).
3. Click a start point to place the overall stair.
4. Select the stair and use the arrow controls to modify the length as shown in Figure 12–12.

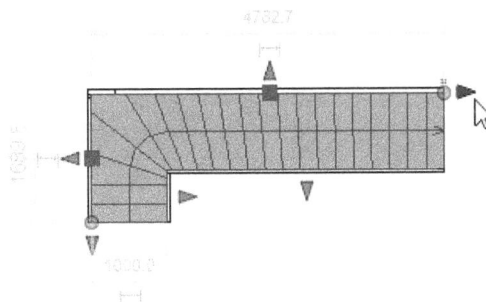

Figure 12–12

Hint: Trouble Shooting

When working with stairs and other elements, Warnings (such as the one shown in Figure 12–13), display when something is wrong, but you can keep on working. In many cases you can close the dialog box and fix the issue or wait and do it later.

Warning
Stair top end exceeds or cannot reach the top elevation of the stair. Add/remove risers at the top end or change top elevation settings in Stair instance properties.

Figure 12–13

Sometimes Errors display where you must take action. These force you to stop and fix the situation.

When you select an element for which there has been a warning ⚠ (Show Related Warnings) displays in the Ribbon. It opens a dialog box in which you can review the warning(s) related to the selected element. You can also display a list of all of the warnings in the project by clicking 🔳 (Review Warnings) in the *Manage* tab>Inquiry panel.

Creating Landings

If you are creating a straight or spiral run you can select **Automatic Landing** to automatically create landings between any breaks in runs This is the best method, and is used in most cases. There are options to **Pick Two Runs** or **Create Sketch** as shown in Figure 12–14. You can connect runs with a landing if the start level and end level of the runs are at the same height.

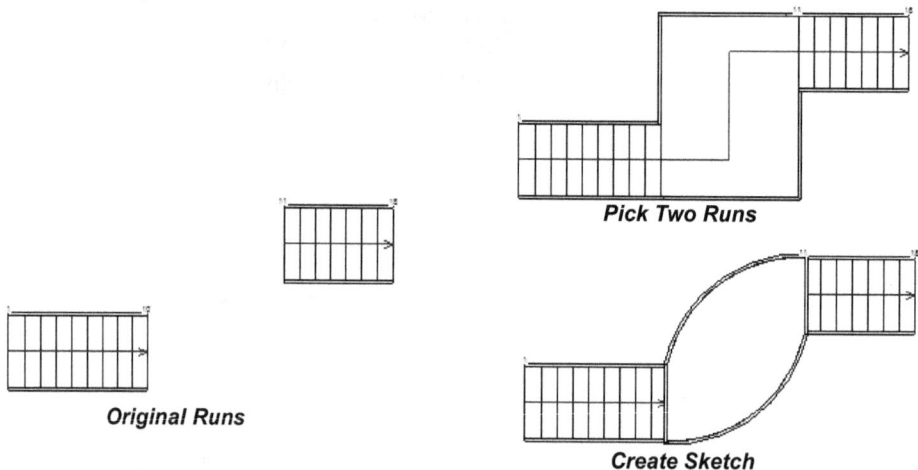

Pick Two Runs

Original Runs

Create Sketch

Figure 12–14

- When you use **Pick Two Runs** the landing is automatically placed at the right height.

- When you sketch a landing, you need to place it at the correct height. In most cases it is easier to automatically place a landing and then convert it to a sketch that you can then modify.

How To: Create a Landing by Picking Two Runs

1. Draw the runs without landings.
2. In the *Modify | Create Stair* tab>Components panel, click

   ▱ (Landing) and then click 🖼 (Pick Two Runs).
3. Select the top of the first run and then the bottom of the second run. They must be at the same height.
4. Finish the stair assembly as required.

Adding Supports

Stair supports are included in the stair type if required. However, you might want to delete them and add them later. This only works if the stair type has supports that are specified in the Type properties.

How To: Create Stair Support Components

1. If there are no supports, in the *Modify | Create Stair* tab>

   Components panel, click ✐ (Support) and then click

   ⇗ (Pick Edges).
2. Select the edge on which you want to place the support. Hover over the first support and press <Tab> if you have more than one connected edge on which you want to place the supports.
3. Finish the stair assembly as required.

12.2 Modifying Component Stairs

Learning Objectives

- Modify the runs and landings of component stairs using properties and controls.
- Convert stair components to sketches to create custom shapes.

Stairs created by the **Stair by Component** command can be modified in a variety of ways. For example, in Figure 12–15 a straight stair with a landing has been modified to make one run wider than the other and the landing wider than both runs, creating a balcony. The landing has been further customized by changing it to a sketch and creating a curved feature.

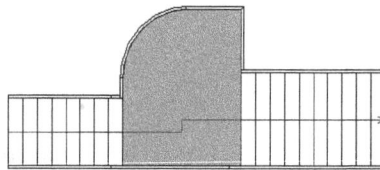

Figure 12–15

- Modifying stair components can be done when you first create the stair or later when you edit a stair.

Editing Component Stairs

When working with a finished stair assembly, you can modify the properties of the stair and select the **Flip Stairs Up Direction** control, as shown on the left in Figure 12–16. You can also hover over the stair and press <Tab> to cycle through and select the components of the stair, such as the run shown on the right in Figure 12–16. You can do limited modifications at this point. For more powerful modification tools, edit the stair assembly.

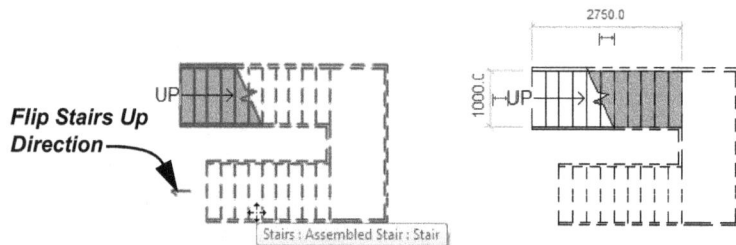

Figure 12–16

How To: Edit Component Stairs

These steps assume you have selected a component-based stair rather than a sketch-based stair.

1. Select a stair. In the *Modify | Stairs* tab>Edit panel, click

   (Edit Stairs). Alternatively, you can double-click on the stair to launch Create Stair mode.

2. All of the tools used to create stairs are available in the *Modify | Create Stair* tab as shown in Figure 12–17.

Figure 12–17

3. You can also modify the individual components using temporary dimensions and shape handles as shown in Figure 12–18. Numerous snaps and alignment lines are also available as you modify the components.

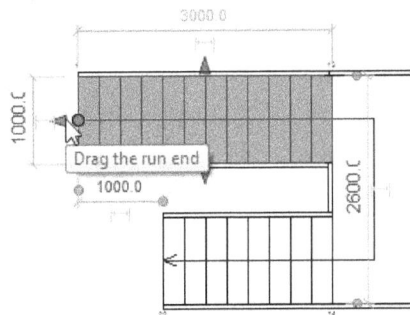

Figure 12–18

- The arrow shape handle at the end of a run lengthens or shortens the run and modifies the other run so that the overall number of steps stays consistent and retains the start and end level.

- The circle shape handle at the end of a run lengthens or shortens the run, does not modify any other runs, but changes the start and end level.

- The arrow shape handle on the sides of the runs or landings can be used to modify the width.

- You can use temporary dimensions for the run width and connections to other elements, but not for run lengths. Use the shape handles instead.

4. When you have finished modifying the stair, click

   (Finish Edit Mode).

Converting Components to Sketches

If you want to customize a run or landing with more options you can convert it into a sketch and modify the outline of the sketch as shown for a curved landing in Figure 12–19.

Figure 12–19

How To: Customize a Stair Component by Turning it into a Sketch

1. Select a stair created using the **Stair by Component** command.

2. In the *Modify | Stairs* tab>Edit panel, click (Edit Stairs).
3. Select the run or landing that you want to customize.

4. In the Tools panel, click (Convert to sketch-based). Doing so turns the component into a custom sketched element.

5. In the Tools panel, click (Edit Sketch).
6. In the *Modify | Create Stair>Sketch Landing (or Run)* tab>

   Draw panel, click (Boundary) and use the **Draw** tools to modify the boundary of the landing (or run) as shown in Figure 12–20.

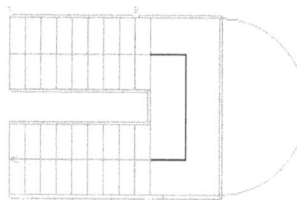

Figure 12–20

7. Click (Finish Edit Mode) to complete the sketch and again to finish the full stair editing.

This is the easiest way to create a custom landing. Have it placed automatically and then change it to a sketch and edit the sketch.

Practice 12a

Estimated time for completion: 25 minutes

Create Component Stairs

Learning Objectives

- Create a set of component stairs.
- Cut out floors where stairs penetrate them.

In this practice you will create stairs, including multi-story stairs, as shown in Figure 12–21. You will also modify the floors for stair openings.

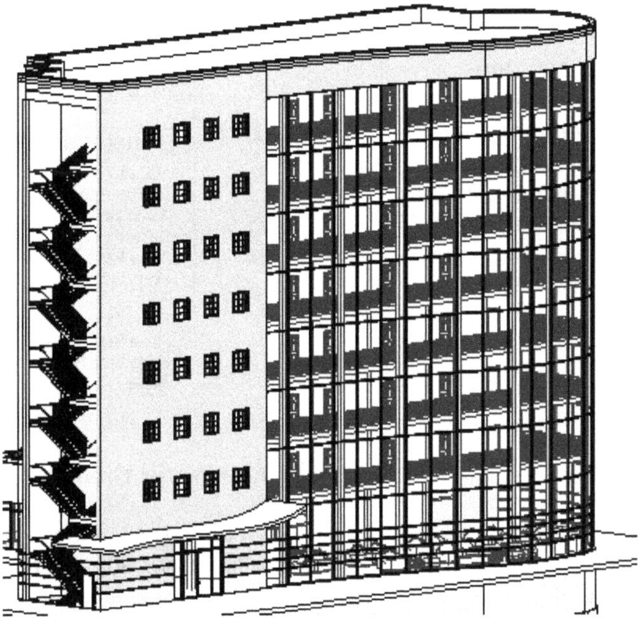

Figure 12–21

Task 1 - Create the stairs on the first floor.

1. Open the project **Modern-Hotel-Stairs-M.rvt** from your class folder.

2. Open the **Floor Plans**: **Floor 1 - Stair 1** view. This is a callout from the main floor plan.

3. Hide the grid lines, sections, and crop region.

4. In the *Architecture* tab>Circulation panel, click 🖑 (Stair).

5. In Properties, set or verify the following parameters:

    *   Stair Type: **Assembled Stair: Hotel Stairs**
    *   Base Level: **Floor 1**
    *   Top Level: **Floor 2**
    *   Base Offset: **0.0**
    *   Top Offset: **0.0**

6. In the *Modify | Create Stair* tab>Tools panel, click

    (Railing). In the Railings dialog box, select **Hotel Stair Guardrail-Floor 1**, as shown in Figure 12–22. Verify that the

    Position is set to **Treads** and click ⬚ OK ⬚.

The Guardrails are different for the upper floors. Therefore, there are two different stair guardrail styles.

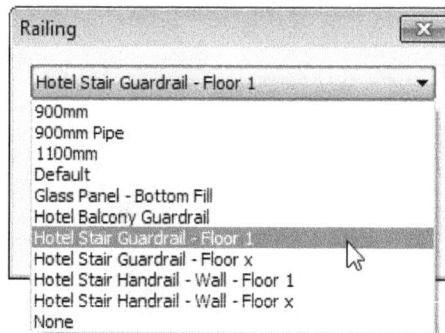

Figure 12–22

7. In the *Modify | Create Stair* tab>Work Plane panel, click

    (Ref Plane). Draw a horizontal reference plane **1200mm** from the inner edge of the top wall of the stairwell, as shown in Figure 12–23. Click ⬚ (Modify).

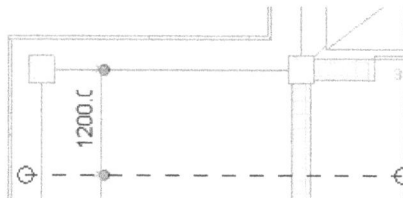

Figure 12–23

8. In the *Modify | Create Stair* tab>Components panel, click

    (Run).

9. In the Options Bar, set the *Location Line* to **Run: Left**, set *Offset* to **0.0**, the *Actual Run Width* to **1200mm**, and select **Automatic Landing**.

10. Pick the start point of the first run on the wall close to the door, as shown in Figure 12–24. The exact location is not important at this point. Pick a second point near the reference plane.

11. Pick the start point for the second run at the intersection of the wall and reference plane as shown in Figure 12–24. Pick the second point past the ghost image of the completed number of stairs.

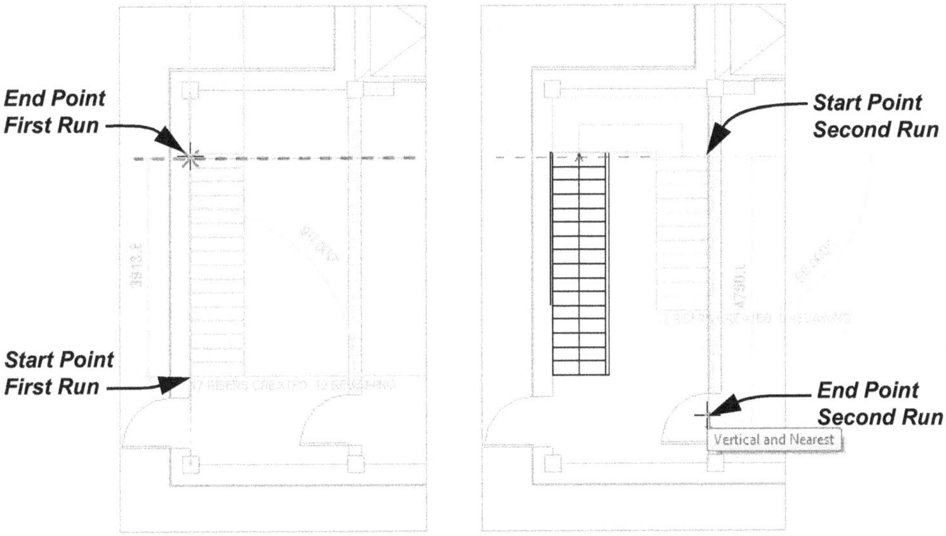

End Point First Run

Start Point First Run

Start Point Second Run

End Point Second Run

Vertical and Nearest

Figure 12–24

12. The run on the left wall might not be in the right place. Select the run and click ✛ (Move). Select a point on the top riser and then on the reference plane as shown in Figure 12–25.

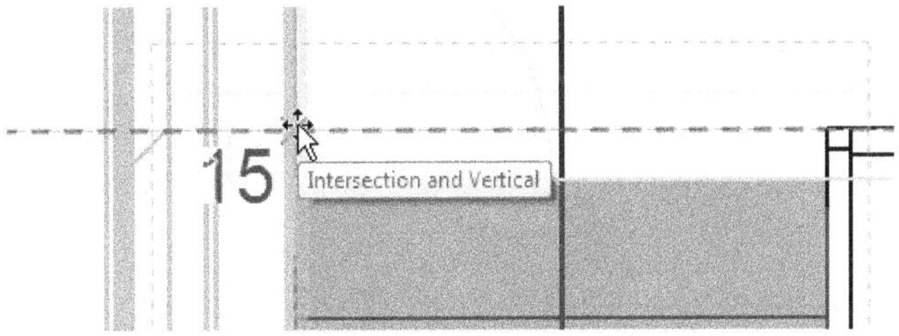

15 Intersection and Vertical

Figure 12–25

13. Depending on how you drew the runs you might also need to modify the run lengths. The left should have 1 to 16 steps and the right should have steps 17 to 31. Select the stairs on the left and use the arrow shape handle at the base of the stairs, to change the number of stairs as required.

14. Click ✓ (Finish Edit Mode).

15. Save the project.

Task 2 - Create the Upper Floor stairs.

---

1. Open the **Floor Plans: Floor 2** view and zoom in on the left stairwell. You should see the **DN** annotation and part of the stairs from the level below.

2. Use **Temporary/Hide** to clean up the view to have it display more clearly.

3. Click 🖐 (Stair).

All of the floor heights are the same between the 2nd and 8th floors, so you can create a multistory stair.

4. In Properties, verify that the *Base Level* is set to **Floor 2** and the *Top Level* is set to **Floor 3** and set the *Multistory Top Level* to **Floor 8**. Note the *Desired Number of Risers*, as shown in Figure 12–26. This number is much smaller because the height between Floor 2 and Floor 3 is less than the height between Floor 1 and Floor 2.

Properties		✕
	Assembled Stair Hotel Stairs	▾
Stair	▾	🔲 Edit Type
Constraints		≫ ▴
Base Level	Floor 2	
Base Offset	0.0	
Top Level	Floor 3	
Top Offset	0.0	≣
Desired Stair Height	3650.0	
Multistory Top Level	Floor 8	
Dimensions		≫
Desired Number of Ris...	20	
Actual Number of Risers	1	
Actual Riser Height	182.5	
Actual Tread Depth	250.0	
Tread/Riser Start Num...	1	▾
Properties help		Apply

Figure 12–26

5. In the *Modify | Create Stair* tab> Tools panel, click

   (Railing). In the Railing dialog box, set the *Railing Type* to **Hotel Stair Guardrail-Floor X**. Click OK.

6. In the Work Plane panel, click (Reference Plane) and add a horizontal reference plane **1200mm** from the inner side of back wall. Click (Modify).

7. Add the stair runs as in Task 1, modifying the runs as required to display stairs 1 to 11 on the left and 12 to 21 on the right as shown in Figure 12–27.

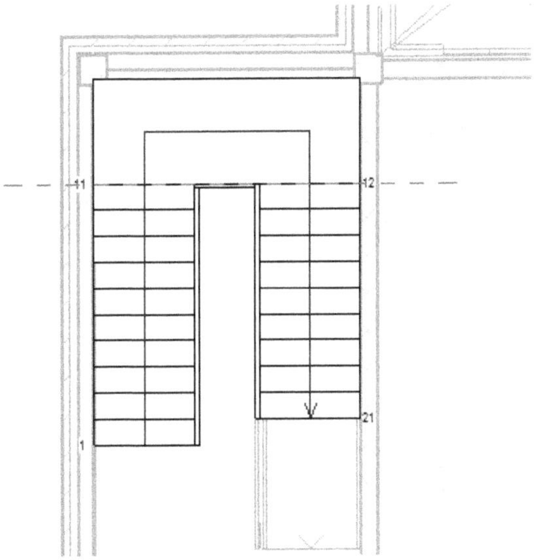

Figure 12–27

8. Click (Finish Edit Mode).

9. To see the stairs on all of the floors, open the **Sections (Building Section): East-West Section** and set the Visual Style to ⬛ (Consistent Colors), as shown in Figure 12–28.

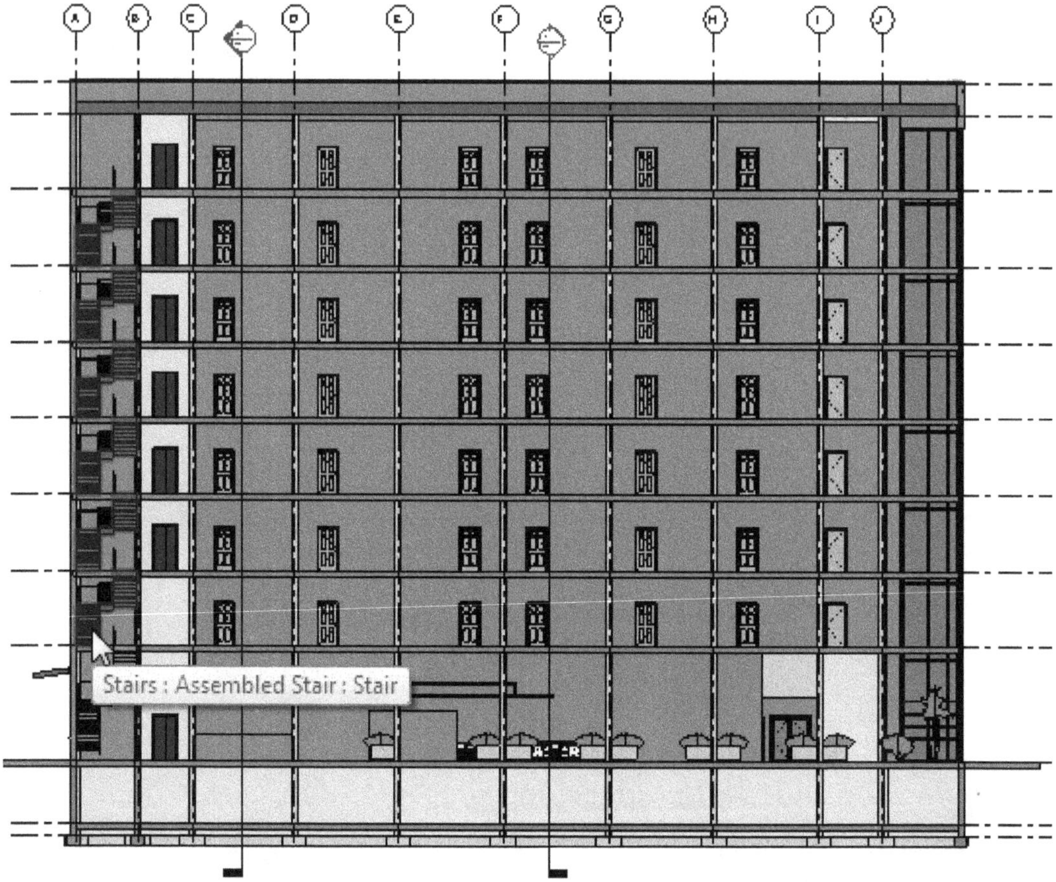

Stairs : Assembled Stair : Stair

Figure 12–28

10. If you have time at the end of the practice, create stairs from the Basement to Floor 1 and save the project.

Task 3 - Modify the second floor stair openings.

1. Open the **Floor Plans: Floor 2** view.

2. Select the floor. (It is easiest to select one of the balconies.)

3. In the *Modify | Floors* tab>Mode panel, click ⬛ (Edit Boundary).

4. Modify the boundary line so that it creates an opening for the stairs, as shown in Figure 12–29.

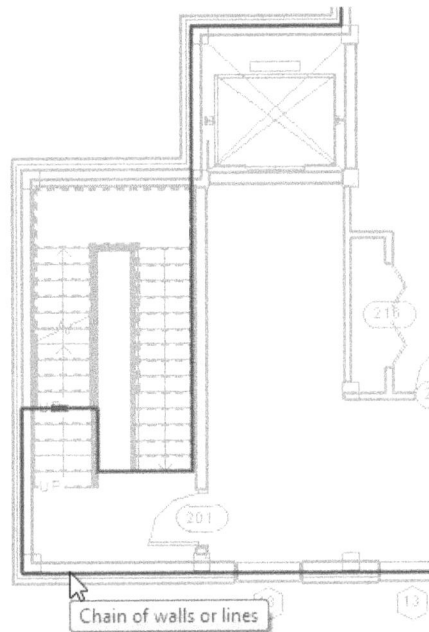

Figure 12–29

5. Click ✎ (Finish Edit Mode). Do not attach the walls to the floor.

6. Zoom out to display the entire second floor.

7. Save the project.

8. If you have time at the end of the practice, modify the floor for the Floor 1 stair opening to the Basement. Place a shaft for the Floor 3 through Floor 8. You can use a shaft here because the openings are the same on all of the floors.

9. Save the project.

12.3 Working with Railings

Autodesk Certification Topics & Objectives

Pro.   User

Modeling
- Model railings   ✓   ✓

Learning Objective

- Modify railings that were created with stairs and add railings that are not connected to stairs.

Railings are automatically created with stairs, but you can modify or delete them independently of the stair element. You can also add railings separate from the stairs and other locations, such as on a balcony, as shown in Figure 12–30.

Figure 12–30

Adding Railings

If you want to place a railing around a balcony or in the middle of wide stairs, you can create a new railing separate from the stairs, as shown in Figure 12–31. You can also add railings to existing stairs and ramps if they were not added when they were created.

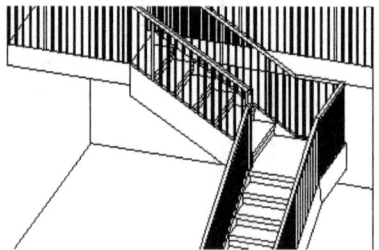

Figure 12–31

How To: Add Railings by Sketching

1. Open a plan or 3D view.
2. In the *Architecture* tab>Circulation panel, expand

    (Railing) and click (Sketch Path).

3. In the *Modify | Create Railing Path* tab>Tools panel, click

   (Pick New Host) and select the element with which the railing is associated, such as a stair or floor. (This makes the railing take on the slope of the host, and is not required if the host is flat.)

4. In the Draw panel, click (Line) and draw the lines that define the railing.

5. Click (Finish Edit Mode) to create the railing.
6. In the Type Selector, specify the railing type.

- The railing must be a single connected sketch. If it is not, you are prompted with a warning, such as that shown in

   Figure 12–32. You can use (Trim) or (Split) to clean up the railing sketch, as required.

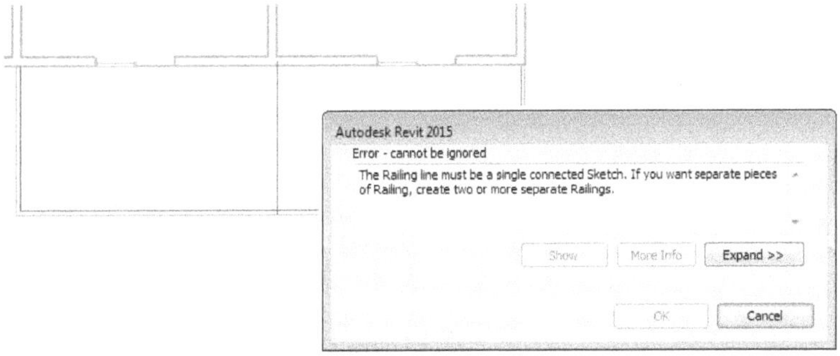

Figure 12–32

How To: Add Railings by Selecting a Host

1. In the *Architecture* tab>Circulation panel, expand

    (Railing) and click (Place on Host).
2. In the *Modify | Create Railing Place on Host* tab>Position

   panel, click (Treads) or (Stringer).
3. Select the stair or ramp where you want to add the railings.

- **Place on Host** only works if there are no railings on the stair. If you want to add an additional railing (e.g., down the middle of a wide stair) you need to sketch the railing.

Modifying Railings

Modifying railings can be as simple as changing their type in the Type Selector or as complex as creating custom railing styles. A few of the basic methods include editing the path of a railing, joining railings at different heights, and setting the extensions for the top rails as shown in Figure 12–33.

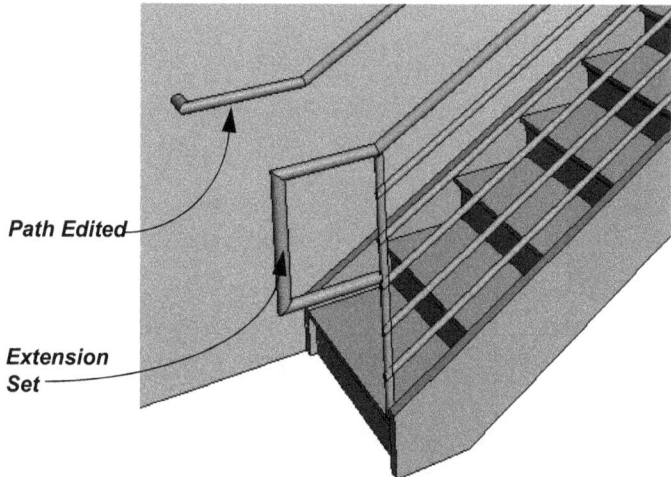

Path Edited

Extension Set

Figure 12–33

- You can delete railings separately from stairs or ramps. However, deleting a stair or ramp automatically deletes related railings.

Editing the Path of a Railing

To edit the path of a railing, in the *Modify | Railings* tab>Mode panel, click ⬜ (Edit Path) or double-click on the railing. This places you in edit mode, in which you can modify the individual lines that define the railing, as shown in Figure 12–34. You can create additional lines, but they must be connected to the existing lines.

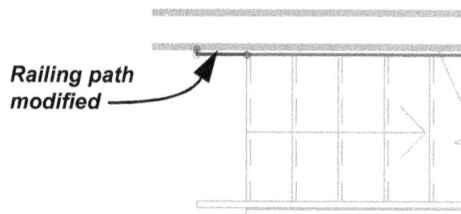

Unlike many other elements in edit mode, railings do not have to be in a closed loop.

Railing path modified

Figure 12–34

Railing Joins

If two railing segments meet in a plan, but are two different heights, you can specify how they interact. While still in edit mode, you can modify each intersection as shown in Figure 12–35.

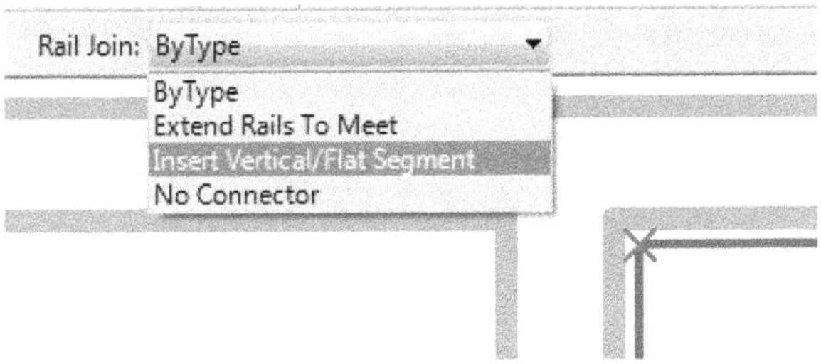

Figure 12–35

How To: Join Railings at Different Heights

1. In the *Modify | Railings>Edit Path* tab>Tools panel, click (Edit Joins).
2. Select the intersection.
3. In the Options Bar, specify the *Rail Join*, as shown in Figure 12–36. The default is **ByType**.
4. If using the default does not produce the required result, select another option in the *Rail Join* drop-down list.

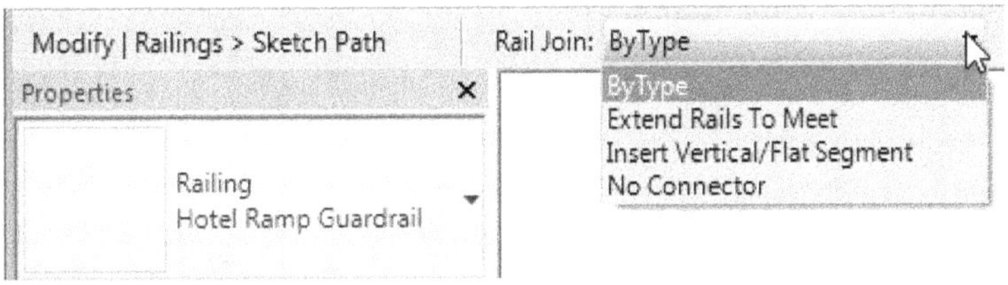

Figure 12–36

- When the *Rail Join* is set to **ByType**, this means that the method of joining the selected intersection is based on the *Angled Joins* and *Tangent Joins* parameters in the Type Properties.

Editing the Top Rail or Handrail

The top rail or handrail of railings can be modified separately from the rest of the railing. This is the first step in customizing the railing system to match many code requirements. For example, you often need to have the handrail extend from the stair as shown in Figure 12–37.

Figure 12–37

How To: Add an Extension to a Top Rail Handrail

1. In a 3D view, hover the cursor over the top rail or handrail. Press <Tab> until it is highlighted and then select it as shown in Figure 12–38.

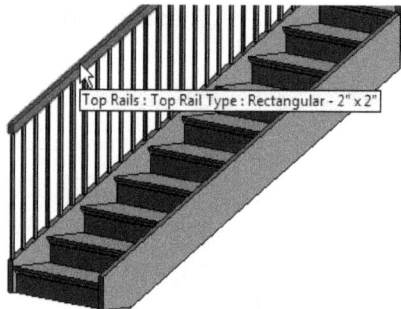

Top Rails : Top Rail Type : Rectangular - 2" x 2"

Figure 12–38

2. In the Properties dialog box, click ⊞ (Edit Type). You are editing the type properties of the Top Rail, but not the entire railing system.

3. In the Type Properties dialog box, in the *Extension (Beginning/Bottom)* area, set the *Extension Style*. The options are **None**, **Wall**, **Floor**, and **Post** as shown in Figure 12–39.

Wall   *Floor*   *Post*

Figure 12–39

4. Set the *Length* and select **Plus Tread Depth** if required by the local codes.

5. Click [Apply] to check the addition.

6. Repeat the process for the *Extension (End/Top)*.

7. Make any other changes and click [OK] to finish.

- A Termination can be added if needed. The default rectangular termination works best with the Floor Extension Style but you can also create custom ones.

Practice 12b

Modify and Add Railings

🗸 **Learning Objectives**

- Modify Railings and Rails for different floors.
- Add stand-alone railings on the balconies.

Estimated time for completion: 25 minutes

In this practice you will switch railing types and modify the type properties of a handrail type. You will also add railings to the interior (as shown in Figure 12–40), and to exterior balconies.

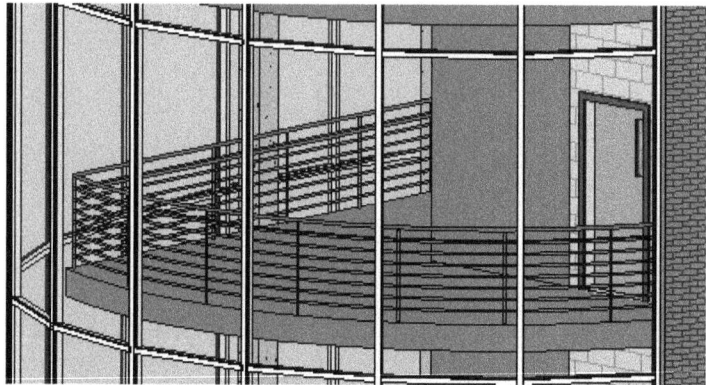

Figure 12–40

Task 1 - Modify the stairwell railings.

1. Open the project **Modern-Hotel-Railing-Ms.rvt** from your class folder.

2. Open the **Floor Plans: Floor 1 - Stair 1** view.

Use <Ctrl>+<Tab> to move between the 3D Camera view and the Floor Plan view.

3. Create a camera view looking from the door into the stairwell to display the new stairs and railings.

4. In the Project Browser, in *3D Views*, right-click on the new 3D view and rename it as **Stair 1 - Floor 1.**

5. Modify the controls as required to show the first run of the stair. and set the *Visual Style* to 🖼 (Shaded). The top rail and hand rail of the railings display a different material.

6. Select the railing that is against the wall and in the Type Selector, select **Railing: Hotel Stair Handrail-Wall-Floor 1.** The railing type changes as shown in Figure 12–41.

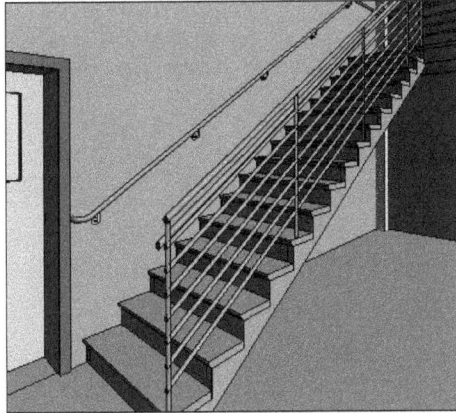

Figure 12–41

7. With the handrail still selected, in Properties set the *Tread/String Offset* to **0**. This prevents the handrail from sitting too far off the wall.

8. Open the **Floor Plans: Floor 2** view

9. Zoom in on the stairwell and select the outside railing. In the Type Selector, change the type to **Railing: Hotel Stair Handrail-Wall-Floor X** and the *Tread/Stringer Offset* to **0**.

10. Create a camera view to display the stairs and railings of the stair going up as shown in Figure 12–42. Select the railing that is partially displayed and hide it. Shade the view to display the components of the railings more clearly.

Figure 12–42

11. Rename this view as **Stair 1 - Floor 2**.

12. Click inside the camera view. In the inner guardrail, hover the cursor over the separate handrail (not the top rail). Press <Tab> so that only this handrail is highlighted and click to select it.

13. In Properties, click ⊞ (Edit Type).

14. In the Type Properties dialog box, in both the *Extension (Beginning/Bottom)* area and the *Extension (End/Top)* area, set the *Extension Style* to **Floor** and the *Length* to **300mm**.

15. In the *Terminations* area, set the *Beginning/Bottom* and *End/Top* to **Termination - Wood - Rectangular**.

16. Click [OK]. The handrail changes as shown in Figure 12–43.

The railing of the other stair is hidden in this view.

Figure 12–43

17. Open one of the other upper floor plans, as shown for Floor 5 in Figure 12–44. The stairs are in place and the guardrail handrail is modified at both ends.

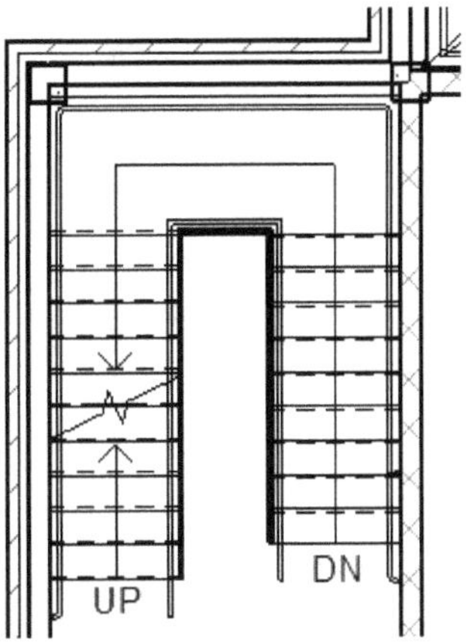

Figure 12–44

18. Open a different upper floor view. The changes to the handrails display because it is part of the multi-story stair system.

19. You can also use the **Railing** command to add a guardrail at the floor openings on the stairs.

20. Save the project.

Task 2 - Add stand-alone railings.

---

1. Open the **Floor Plans: Floor 2** view and pan and zoom over to the interior balcony (walkway line) as required.

2. In the *Architecture* tab>Circulation panel, expand

   (Railing) and click (Sketch Path).

3. In the Type Selector, select **Railing: Hotel Balcony Guardrail**.

4. Draw a sketch line that is **75mm** from the edge of the balcony floor over the lobby of the hotel, as shown in Figure 12–45. Ensure that you include the curved portion at the far end.

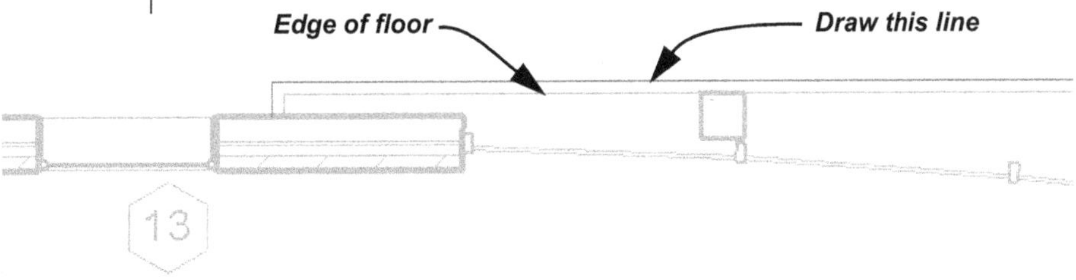

Edge of floor ——— ——— *Draw this line*

Figure 12–45

5. Click ✔ (Finish Edit Mode).

6. Zoom in on one of the outdoor balconies on the back of the building.

7. Add balcony railings, as shown in the sketch in Figure 12–46, using the same parameters as the inside balcony railing.

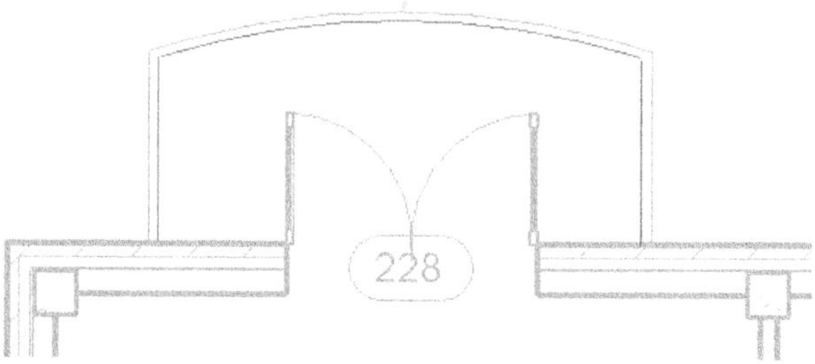

Figure 12–46

8. Click ✔ (Finish Edit Mode).

9. Copy the completed railing to the other balconies.

10. Copy all of the railings, inside and out, to the other floors.

11. Open an exterior 3D view and verify the placement of all of the railings.

12. Save the project.

12.4 Sketching Custom Stairs

Learning Objective

- Create custom stairs by sketching boundaries and risers.

To create custom stairs with irregular boundaries or risers, draw individual boundary and riser lines. For example, you can use this method to create a landscape design with multiple levels and various widths of stairs, as shown in Figure 12–47.

Figure 12–47

How To: Sketch Custom Stairs

1. Open a plan or 3D view.

2. In the *Architecture* tab>Circulation panel, expand 🖋 (Stair) and click 🗐 (Stair by Sketch).

3. In the Type Selector, select the stair type.

4. In Properties, set the *Base Level* and *Top Level*. By default, a stair height is from level to level. In many cases, a custom stair is shorter and should be set using an offset from a level as shown in Figure 12–48.

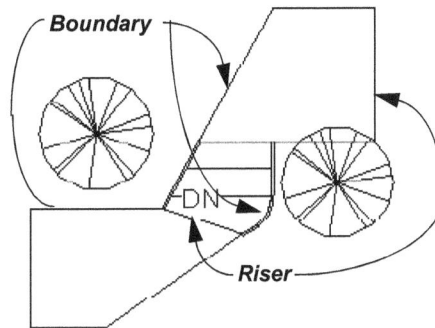

Constraints	⊗
Base Level	Level 1
Base Offset	0.0
Top Level	Level 1
Top Offset	600.0
Multistory Top Level	None

Figure 12–48

5. In the *Modify | Create Stairs Sketch* tab>Draw panel, click

   (Boundary) and draw the outline of the stairs. Do not put boundaries at the top and bottom of the stairs.

6. In the Draw panel, click (Riser) and draw the risers. The risers must touch the boundary at each end. The number of risers still needed is displayed below the sketch, as shown in Figure 12–49.

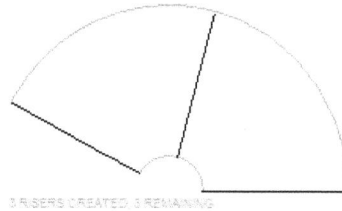

3 RISERS CREATED, 3 REMAINING

Figure 12–49

7. Click (Finish Edit Mode).

• The tools for drawing boundaries and risers are similar to those used for drawing walls.

• In edit mode, riser lines are black and boundaries are green.

• The number of risers must be appropriate for the properties of the stair type.

• You can also draw runs using the sketch tools and then modify the components of the sketch as shown in Figure 12–50. The blue line in the middle is the run length and can be modified as well. It adds or removes risers as you lengthen or shorten it.

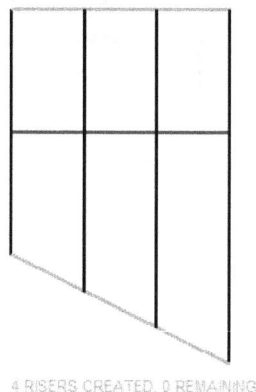

4 RISERS CREATED, 0 REMAINING

Figure 12–50

Editing Sketched Stairs

As with component stairs, you can edit stair properties and modify the type when you select a stair but you cannot select individual components. Instead, you can edit the boundary of the stairs. Using controls, you can move the *UP* text or flip the stair direction, as shown in Figure 12–51.

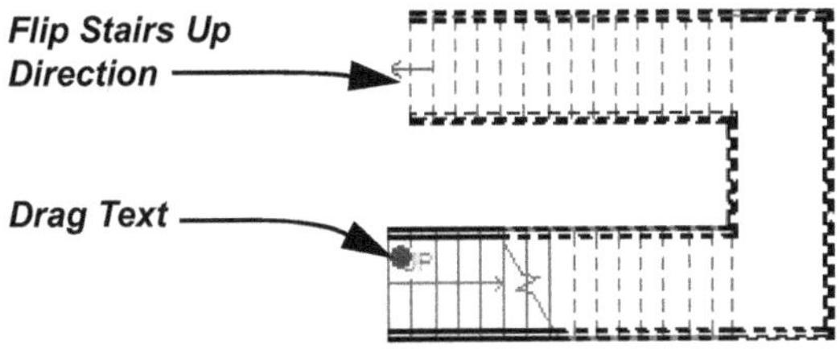

Figure 12–51

How To: Edit Sketched Stairs

1. Select the stairs (not the railings).

2. In the *Modify | Stairs* tab>Mode panel, click (Edit Sketch) and use the tools in the panels to modify the stairs.

3. Click (Finish Edit Mode) to apply the changes.

- While in edit mode, you can modify the boundary line (green), individual risers (black), and the number of risers (blue), as shown in Figure 12–52, using shape handles and dynamic dimensions.

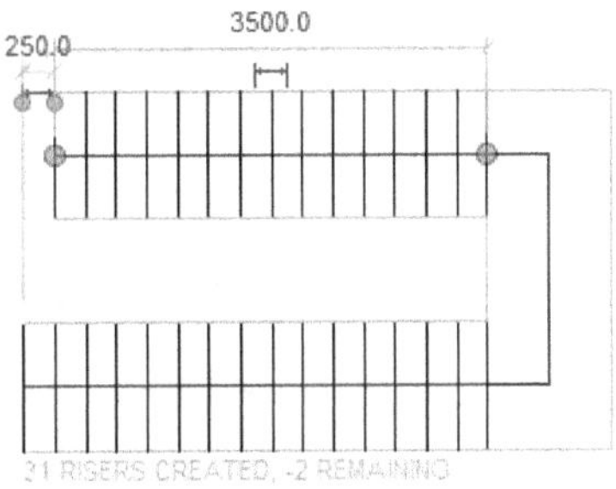

Figure 12–52

- You can also use standard editing commands, such as **Move** and **Trim** to edit the stair sketch.

12.5 Creating Ramps

Learning Objective

- Create ramps using runs or sketches.

The process of creating ramps is similar to that of creating stairs with runs and automatic landings. You can also sketch a boundary with risers at the start and end of each slope. Ramps are most often used for short vertical distances (as shown in Figure 12–53), as they require a lot of space for their runs. Check the local building codes to determine how long a run can be before a landing is required.

Figure 12–53

How To: Create a Ramp using Runs

1. In the *Architecture* tab>Circulation panel, click ⬭ (Ramp).
2. In the Type Selector, select the ramp type.
3. In the *Modify | Create Ramp Sketch* tab>Tools panel, click

   🗐 (Railing Type) and select a railing type in the Railing

   Types dialog box. Click [OK].
4. In Properties, specify the *Constraints,* especially **Base Level** and **Top Level** and their offsets as shown in Figure 12–54, and other parameters. The **Width** of the ramp is set in the *Dimensions* area.

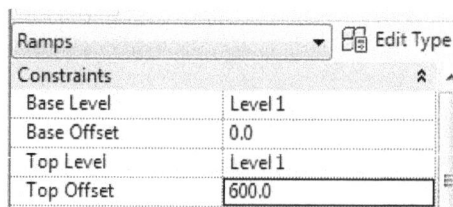

Ramps	▼ 🔲 Edit Type
Constraints	☆ ▲
Base Level	Level 1
Base Offset	0.0
Top Level	Level 1
Top Offset	600.0

Figure 12–54

5. Draw reference planes to specify the locations of the run start and end points before creating the ramp. The run is based on the centerline of the ramp.

6. In the Draw panel, click ⊞ (Run) and select a start point for the run. A preview box displays the ramp's orientation and length. Click ✓ (Line) or ⌒ (Center-end Arc) to switch between linear and curved runs.

    • For a straight ramp with a single run, select a second point anywhere outside the box to create the run.
    • For a ramp with more than one run, select a second point inside the box for the length of the first run. Select a start and an end point for the next run. Landings are automatically created between runs.

7. Click ✓ (Finish Edit Mode). The ramp (including railings) is created.

How To: Sketch a Ramp using Boundary and Riser

1. Click ⬭ (Ramp) and set up the ramp type and Properties.
2. In the *Modify | Create Ramp Sketch* tab>Draw panel, click ⌐ (Boundary).
3. Use the **Draw** tools to outline the sides (not the ends) of the ramp, as shown by the green lines in Figure 12–55.
4. In the *Modify | Create Ramp Sketch* tab>Draw panel, click ⊞ (Run).
5. Use the Draw tools to specify the ends of the slope of each ramp as shown by the black lines in Figure 12–55.

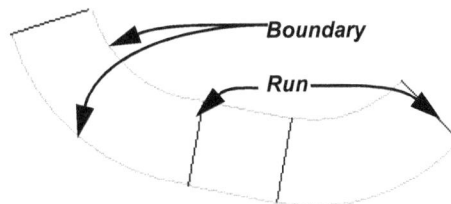

Figure 12–55

6. Click ✓ (Finish Edit Mode). The ramp (including railings) is created.

| Practice 12c | # Sketch Custom Stairs and Ramps |

Learning Objectives

- Create a custom stair using boundaries and risers.
- Add a ramp.

Estimated time for completion: 15 minutes

In this practice you will sketch a custom entrance stair and create a sketched ramp with railings, as shown in Figure 12–56.

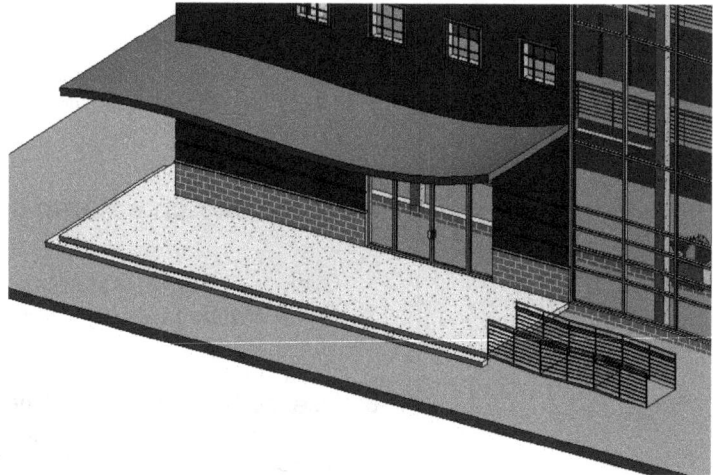

Figure 12–56

Task 1 - Create a custom entrance stair.

1. Open the project **Modern-Hotel-Ramp-M.rvt** from the class folder.

2. Open the **Floor Plans: Floor 1** view.

3. Hide the gridlines and annotations by selecting one of each and using the shortcut by pressing <V> and then pressing <H>.

4. Set the *Underlay* to **Floor 2**. This displays the outline of the entrance roof that you will use to create custom stairs.

5. In the *Architecture* tab>Circulation panel, expand (Stair), and click (Stair by Sketch).

6. In the Type Selector, select **Stair: Monolithic Stair - Hotel**.

7. In Properties, set the *Base Level* to **Floor 1,** with a *Base Offset* of (negative) **-300mm,** and set the *Top Level* to **Floor 1**, with a *Top Offset* of **0.0.**

8. In the *Modify | Create Stairs Sketch* tab>Tools panel, click

   (Railing). In the Railing dialog box, select **None** and click

   [OK] .

9. In the Draw panel, click └ (Boundary), and click ⚲ (Pick Lines). Select the ends of the roof outline, as shown in Figure 12–57.

10. Click ⁵ᵤ (Riser). Use the **Pick Lines** tool to select the other sides of the roof outline, including right up against the building.

11. With ⁵ᵤ (Riser) still selected, use the **Pick Lines** tool and set the offset to **300mm**. Offset another set of risers outside the outline, as shown in Figure 12–57.

12. Use ⫟ (Trim/Extend to Corner) to clean up the intersections.

The sketch lines have been widened for emphasis.

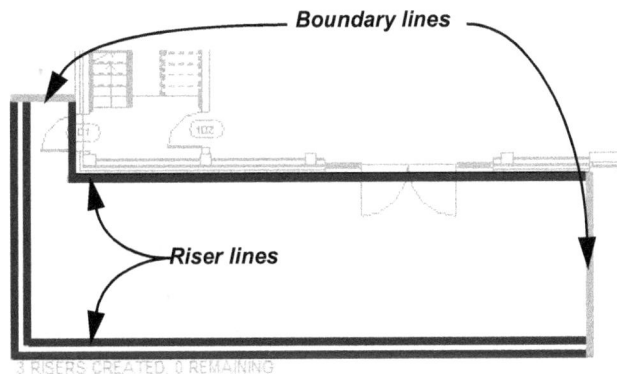

Figure 12–57

13. Click ✎ (Finish Edit Mode) to complete the stair.

14. Verify that the stairs are in the right direction. If the arrow is not pointing the same direction as that shown in Figure 12–58, click the **Flip Stairs Up Direction** control, which might be located near the main door.

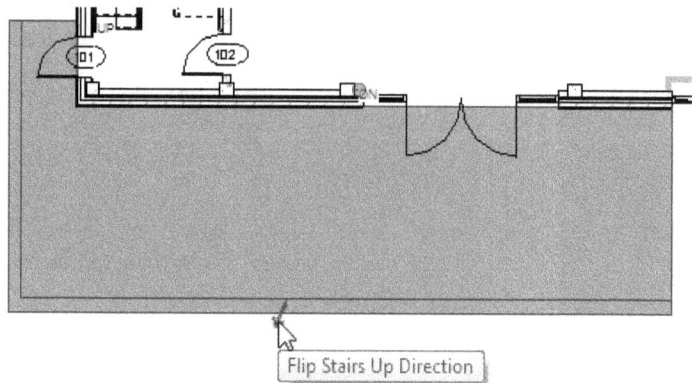

Flip Stairs Up Direction

Figure 12–58

15. There is a DN annotation that you do not need. With the stair still selected, in Properties, in the *Graphics* section clear **Down label**.

16. Set the *Underlay* to **None**.

17. View the new stairs in 3D.

18. Save the project.

Task 2 - Adding a Ramp

1. Return to the **Floor Plans: Floor 1** view.

2. In the *Architecture* tab>Circulation panel, click ⬭ (Ramp).

3. In the Type Selector, select **Ramp: Hotel Ramp**.

4. In Properties, set the *Base Level* to **Floor 1**, with a *Base Offset* of (negative) **-300mm**. Set the *Top Level* to **Floor 1**, with a *Top Offset* of **0.0**. Set the *Width* to **1800mm**.

5. In the *Modify | Create Ramp Sketch* tab>Tools panel, click ▨ (Railing), select the Railing type **Hotel Ramp Guardrail**, and click ☐ OK ☐ ..

6. In the Work Plane panel, click ◸ (Ref Plane).

7. Draw the reference planes shown in Figure 12–59.

Figure 12–59

8. Click 🔲 (Modify) to return to the *Modify | Create Ramp Sketch* tab in the ribbon.

9. In the Draw panel, click 🔲 (Run). Start the run as shown in Figure 12–60. Use the reference plane intersections to end the first run, and then draw the second run.

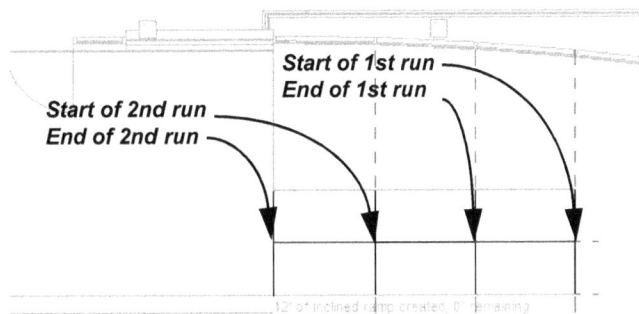

Figure 12–60

10. Click 🔲 (Finish Edit Mode).

11. The Railings need to be moved so that they are fixed on the ramp. Select both of the railings and in Properties, change the *Tread/Stringer Offset* to (negative) **-50mm**.

12. Open the 3D View and check that the ramp displays as shown in Figure 12–61.

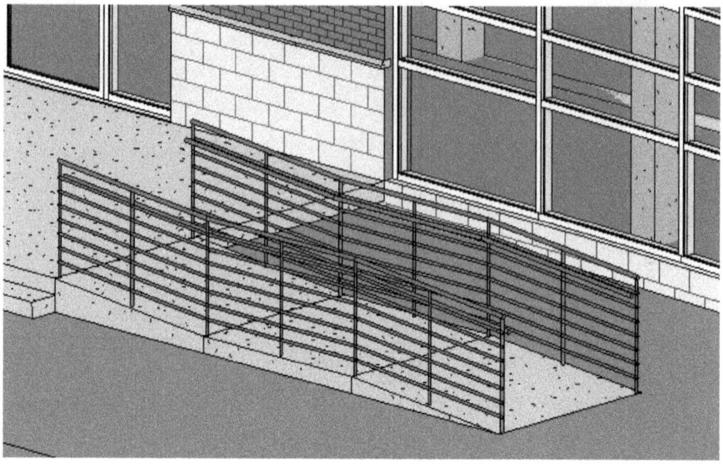

Figure 12–61

13. Zoom out and save the project.

Chapter Review Questions

1. Which of the following is NOT a stair component?

   a. Runs

   b. Landings

   c. Treads

   d. Supports

2. How do you modify a stair so that it is wider at the bottom than at the top as shown in Figure 12–62?

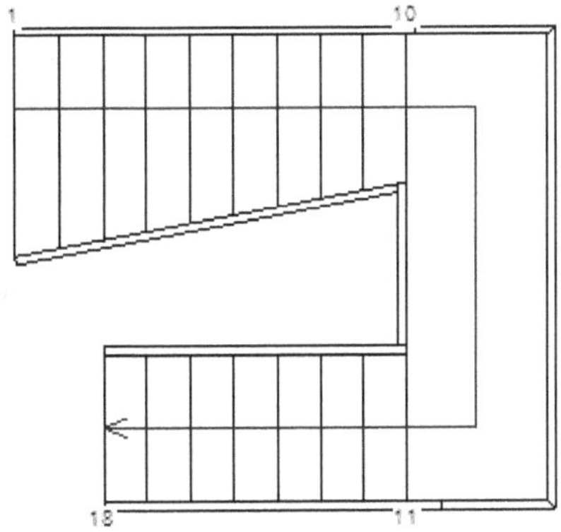

Figure 12–62

   a. Use the grips located at each corner of the stair and drag them to a new location.

   b. Convert the run to a sketch and modify the boundary and riser lines.

   c. Use <Tab> to cycle through components so that you only select the tread that you want to modify.

   d. Explode the stair into components, and then use grips to modify the stair width.

3. When do you need to use the ▦ (Railing) command? (Select all that apply.)

   a. When you want an extra railing in the middle of very wide stairs.

   b. When you create a stair or ramp.

   c. When you create railings that are not attached to stairs or ramps.

   d. When you use the **Stair by Sketch** command.

4. To draw a stair that covers multiple floors of equal height (as shown in Figure 12–63), you need to select a stair created at the bottom level of the floors and...

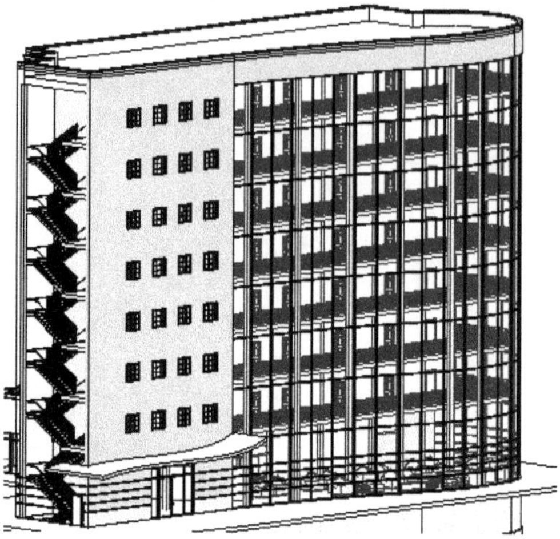

Figure 12–63

a. In Properties, select the **Multistory Top Level** from the drop-down list of levels.

b. Also select a stair created at the top level of the floors, right-click and select **Multistory Stair**.

c. Copy it to the clipboard. Then use **Paste Aligned to Selected Levels** and specify the levels where you want the stairs.

5. Which of the following elements is most helpful in specifying the start and end runs of ramps?

a. Walls

b. Stairs

c. Sketch Lines

d. Reference Planes

Command Summary

Button	Command	Location
	Boundary (Stairs by Sketch)	• **Ribbon:** *Modify	Create Stairs Sketch* tab> Draw panel
	Convert to sketch-based	• **Ribbon:** *Modify	Create Stair* tab> Tools panel
	Edit Path (Railings)	• **Ribbon:** *Modify	Railings* tab>Mode panel
	Edit Sketch	• **Ribbon:** *Modify	Create Stair* tab> Tools panel
	Edit Stairs	• **Ribbon:** *Modify	Stairs* tab>Edit panel
	Flip	• **Ribbon:** *Modify	Create Stair* tab> Tools panel
	Landing (Stair by Component)	• **Ribbon:** *Modify	Create Stair* tab> Components panel
	Pick New Host	• **Ribbon:** *Modify	Create Railing Path (Railings)* tab>Tools Panel
	Railing	• **Ribbon:** *Modify	Create Stair (Create Stairs Sketch) (Create Ramp)* tab> Tools panel
	Railing>Place on Host	• **Ribbon:** *Architecture* tab>Circulation panel>expand Railing
	Railing>Sketch Path	• **Ribbon:** *Architecture* tab>Circulation panel>expand Railing
	Riser (Stairs by Sketch)	• **Ribbon:** *Modify	Create Stairs Sketch* tab>Draw panel
	Run (Stair by Component)	• **Ribbon:** *Modify	Create Stair* tab> Components panel
	Run (Stairs by Sketch)	• **Ribbon:** *Modify	Create Stairs Sketch* tab> Draw panel
	Stair by Component	• **Ribbon:** *Architecture* tab>Circulation panel>expand Stair
	Stair by Sketch	• **Ribbon:** *Architecture* tab>Circulation panel>expand Stair
	Support (Stair by Component)	• **Ribbon:** *Modify	Create Stair* tab> Components panel

Construction Documents Phase

The third phase of this training guide continues to teach the Autodesk® Revit® tools, focusing on tools that help you to create accurate construction documents for a design.

The third phase covers the following topics:

- Creating Construction Documents

- Annotating Construction Documents

- Adding Tags and Schedules

- Creating Details

Construction Documents Phase

The third phase of this training guide continues to teach the Autodesk® Revit® tools, focusing on tools that help you to create accurate construction documents for a design.

The third phase covers the following topics:

- Creating Construction Documents

- Annotating Construction Documents

- Adding Tags and Schedules

- Creating Details

Chapter 13

Creating Construction Documents

In this chapter you learn how to setup construction documents by creating sheets with title blocks and adding views on the sheets. You also learn about printing the sheets.

This chapter contains the following topics:

- **Setting Up Sheets**
- **Placing and Modifying Views on Sheets**
- **Printing Sheets**

13.1 Setting Up Sheets

Autodesk Certification Topics & Objectives

Pro. User

Documentation

*   Create a title sheet   ✓

Learning Objectives

*   Add Sheets to the project.
*   Fill in title block information.

While you are working on a project, you should also be thinking about the working drawings that are needed to document it—that is, the printouts with details and annotation to guide construction. Any view, such as a floor plan, section, callout, or schedule, can be placed on a sheet. You can specify the scale for each view and add annotations and other detailing to the views or sheets, as shown in Figure 13–1.

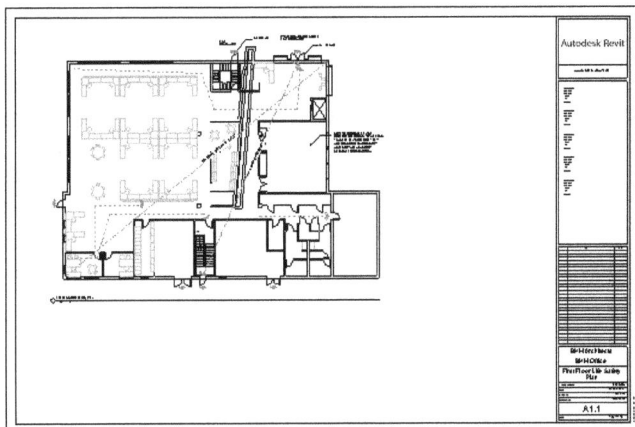

Figure 13–1

How To: Set Up Sheets

1. In the Project Browser, right-click on the *Sheets* area header and select **New Sheet...** or in the *View* tab>Sheet

    Composition panel, click ⬜ (Sheet).

Click [Load...] *to load a sheet from the Library.*

2. In the New Sheet dialog box, select a title block from the list as shown in Figure 13–2.

Figure 13–2

- If you have a preset list of placeholder sheets, you can select the one that you want to use from the list, as shown in Figure 13–3.

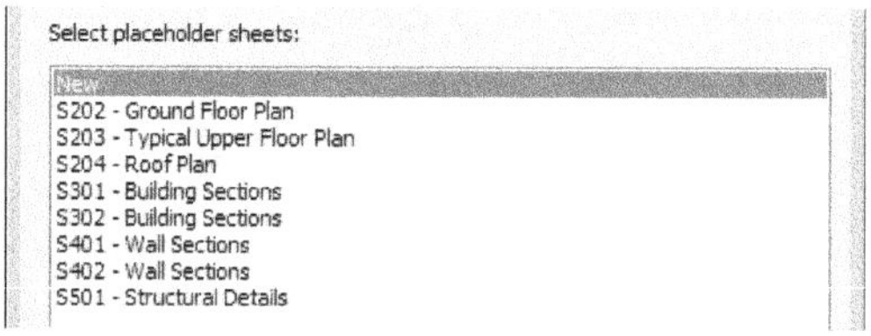

Figure 13–3

3. Click [OK]. A new sheet is created using the preferred title block.
4. Fill out the information in the title block as required.
5. Add views to the sheet by dragging and dropping them from the Project Browser onto the sheet.
6. Add any general notes or additional annotation to the sheet.

- Once created, the sheets are listed in the *Sheets (all)* area in the Project Browser.

- When you create sheets, the next sheet is incremented numerically.

- When you change the Sheet Name and/or Number in the title block, it automatically changes the name and number of the sheet in the Project Browser.

- Company templates can be created with standard sheets set up with the company (or project) title block and related views already placed on the sheet.

- You can also create placeholder sheets in a Sheet List schedule. A typical use of placeholder sheets in an architectural firm is to include the sheet names and numbers of the consultants sheets. This way they are listed in the sheet list even if they are not part of the architect's project and are not to be plotted by the architect.

- The plot stamp on the side of the sheet automatically updates according to the current date and time. The format of the display uses the regional settings of your computer.

- You can create your own title block using a template from the Autodesk® Revit® software (**Application Menu>New>Title Block**). Select the size that you want to work with and then add lines, text, labels, and imported files as required to create the title block.

Sheet (Title Block) Properties

A new sheet includes a title block. You can change the information in the title block by selecting any blue label you want to edit (Project Name, Project Number, etc.), as shown in Figure 13–4.

Figure 13–4

You can also change the title block information in Properties, as shown in Figure 13–5.

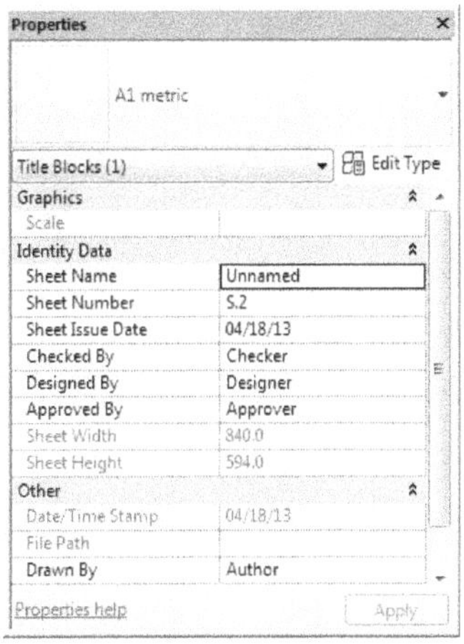

Figure 13–5

- To set the properties that apply to all of the sheets, enter the Project Properties. In the *Manage* tab>Settings panel, click

  (Project Information). In the Project Properties dialog box (as shown in Figure 13–6), add the *Project Name*, *Client*, and other project based information.

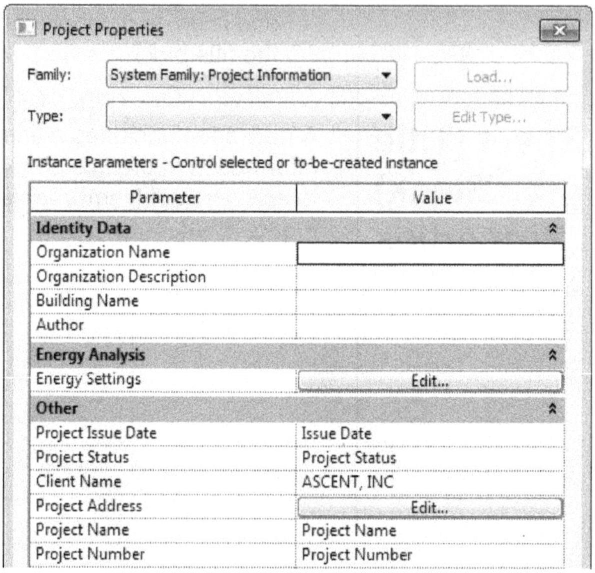

Figure 13–6

13.2 Placing and Modifying Views on Sheets

Autodesk Certification Topics & Objectives

Pro.   User

Views

* Manage view position on sheets   ✓

Learning Objectives

* Place views on sheets including using Guide Grids to help place the views.
* Modify views on sheets including moving views and view titles, removing views, and resizing views.
* Activate views on sheets to make minor changes to them.

The process of adding views to a sheet is simple. Drag and drop a view from the Project Browser onto the sheet. The new view on the sheet is displayed at the scale specified in the original view. The view title displays the name, number, and scale of the view, as shown in Figure 13–7.

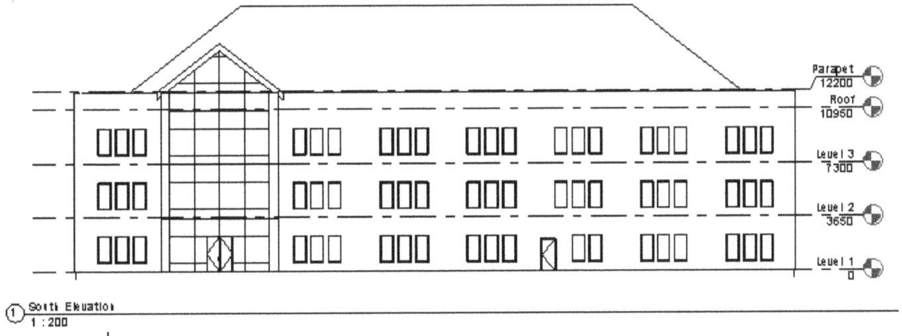

Figure 13–7

How To: Place Views on Sheets

Alignment lines from existing views display to help you place additional views.

1. Set up the view as you want it to display on the sheet, including the scale and visibility of elements.
2. Create or open the sheet where you want to place the view.
3. Select the view in the Project Browser, and drag and drop it onto the sheet.
4. The center of the view is attached to the cursor. Position the view as required, and click to place it on the sheet.

- You cannot place a view more than once on your sheets. However, you can duplicate the view and place the copy on a sheet.

- Views on a sheet are associative. They automatically update to reflect changes to the project.

- Each view on a sheet is listed under the sheet name in the Project Browser, as shown in Figure 13–8.

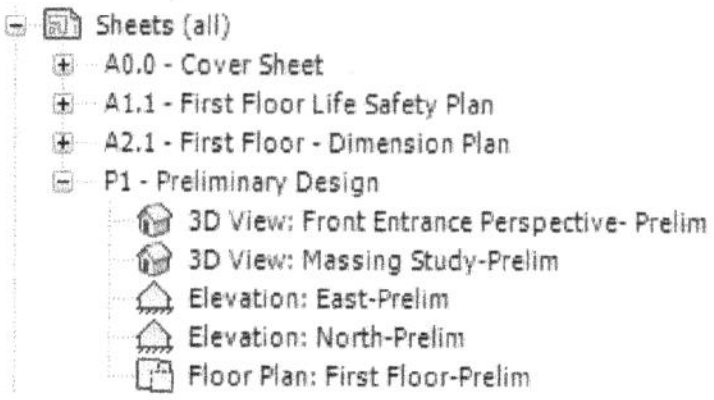

Figure 13–8

- An alternative way to place a view is to click ⬚ (View) in the Sheet Composition panel and then select the view from the list in the Views dialog box, as shown in Figure 13–9.

This method lists only those views which have not yet been placed on a sheet.

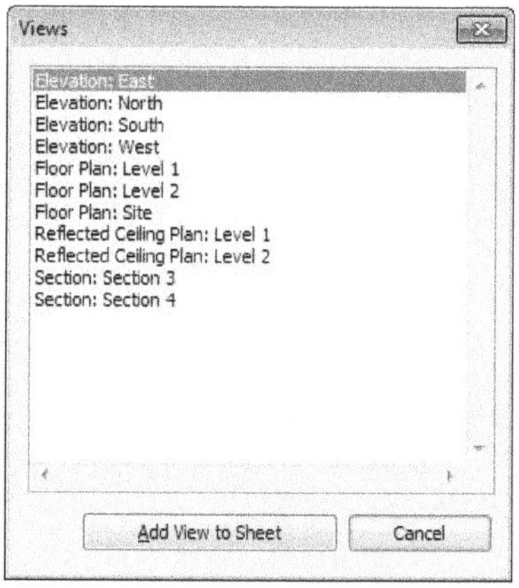

Figure 13–9

- You can change the title of a view on a sheet without changing its name in the Project Browser. In Properties, in the *Identity Data* area, type a new title for the *Title on Sheet* parameter, as shown in Figure 13–10.

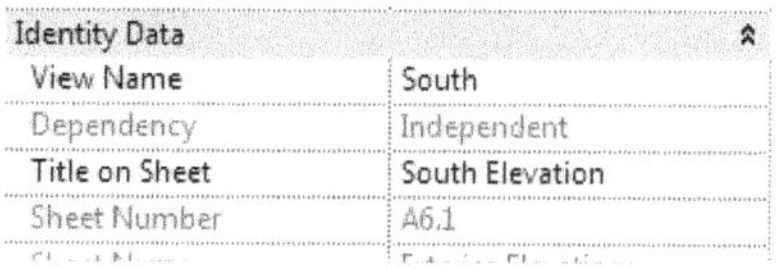

Figure 13–10

Working with Guide Grids

You can use a guide grid to help you place views on a sheet, as shown in Figure 13–11. Guide grids can be set up per sheet. You can also create different types with various grid spacings.

When moving a view to a guide grid, only orthogonal datum elements (levels and grids) and reference planes snap to the guide grid.

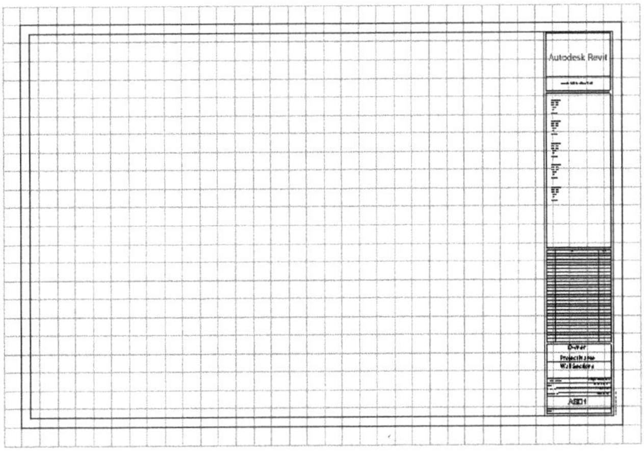

Figure 13–11

- You can move guide grids and resize them using controls.

How To: Add A Guide Grid

1. When a sheet is open, in the *View* tab>Sheet Composition panel, click ⬚ (Guide Grid).
2. In the Assign Guide Grid dialog box, select from existing guide grids (as shown in Figure 13–12), or create a new one and give it a name.

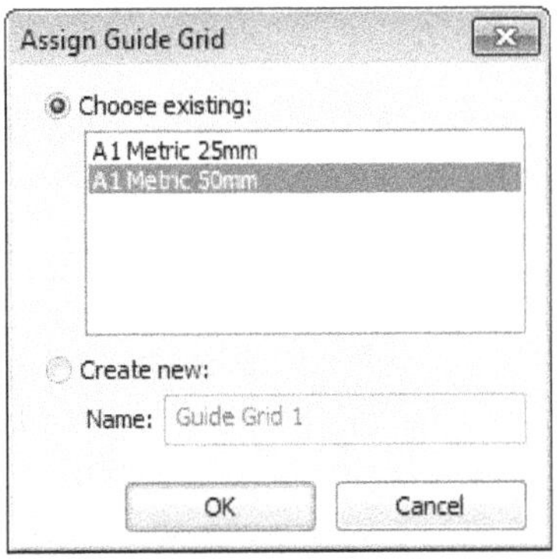

Figure 13–12

3. The guide grid displays using the specified sizing.

How To: Modify Guide Grid Sizing

1. If you create a new guide grid you need to update it to the correct size in Properties. Select the edge of the guide grid.
2. In Properties, set the *Guide Spacing*, as shown in Figure 13–13.

Properties		×
Guide Grid (1)	▼	Edit Type
Dimensions		≫
Guide Spacing	25.0000 mm	
Identity Data		≫
Name	Guide Grid 1	

Figure 13–13

Modifying Views on Sheets

Views can be modified in several ways. You can move, delete, and rotate (90 degrees) views on a sheet. The view title can also be moved independently of the view. When you change any of the view properties of a view, they automatically update on the sheet.

- To show a specific portion of a model, use a callout view or modify the crop region in the view.

Moving Views and View Titles

- To move a view on a sheet, select the edge of the viewport and drag it to a new location. The view title moves with the view.

- To move only the view title, select the title and drag it to the new location.

- To modify the length of the line under the title name, select the viewport and drag the controls, as shown in Figure 13–14.

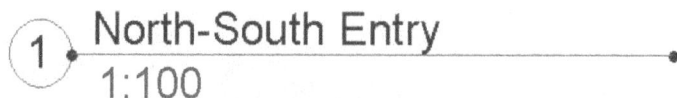

*You can also use the **Move** command or the arrow keys to move a view.*

1 North-South Entry
1:100

Figure 13–14

Deleting Views

*   To remove a view from a sheet, select it and press <Delete>. Alternatively, select the view name under the sheet in the Project Browser, right-click, and select **Remove From Sheet**.

Rotating Views

*   If you are creating a vertical sheet, you can rotate the view on the sheet by 90 degrees. Select the view and set the direction of rotation in the *Rotation on Sheet* drop-down list in the Options Bar, as shown in Figure 13–15.

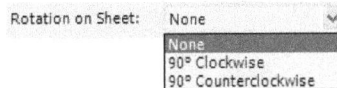

Figure 13–15

*   If a view needs to be rotated to an angle other than 90 degrees, do this before you place it on a sheet. Turn on the crop region in the view and then select the view. In the Modify panel, click ↻ (Rotate) and change the rotation. The crop region remains as is, but the elements in the view rotate.

Resizing Views on Sheets

Each view displays the extents of the model or the elements contained in the crop region. If the view does not fit on a sheet, as shown in Figure 13–16, you might need to crop the view or move the elevation markers closer to the building.

If the extents of the view change dramatically based on a scale change or a crop region, it might be easier to delete the view on the sheet and drag it over again, rather than reworking the location of the view and title on the sheet.

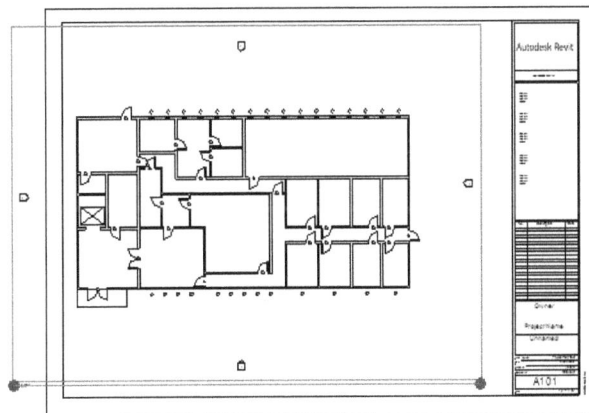

Figure 13–16

Working Inside Views

If you need to make small changes to a view while working on a sheet, you can work *through* the viewport on the model itself by activating a view.

Double-click inside the viewport to activate it or select the viewport, right-click and select **Activate View**. Alternatively, in the *Modify | Viewports* tab>Viewport panel, click ⬚ (Activate View). Only elements within the viewport are available for modification. The rest of the sheet is grayed out, as shown in Figure 13–17.

Only use this method for small changes. Significant changes should be made directly in the view.

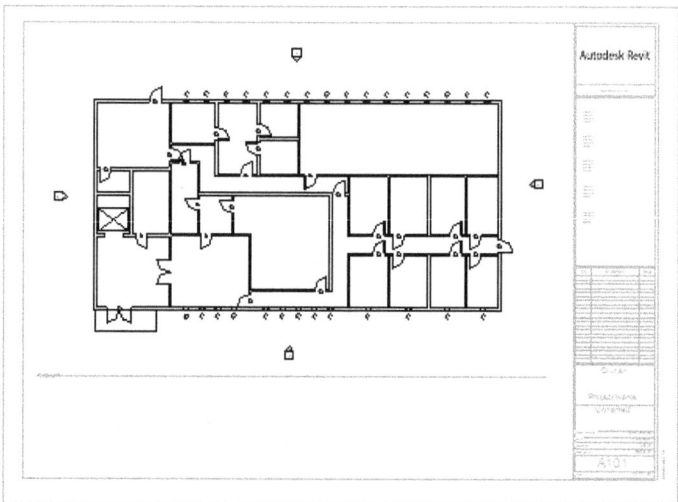

Figure 13–17

Enhanced in 2015

- To return to the sheet, double-click outside of the viewport on the sheet, or right-click and select **Deactivate View**, as shown in Figure 13–18. Alternatively, switch to the *View* tab>Sheet Composition panel, expand ⬚ (Viewports), and click ⬚ (Deactivate View).

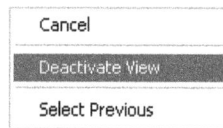

Figure 13–18

- Changes you make to elements when a view is activated also display in the original view.

Hint: Add an Image to a Sheet

Company logos are usually displayed in titleblocks to identify the design team and consultants on the project. In most cases, the logos are added directly to the titleblock family.

1. Open a titleblock. (A titleblock is a family file and has an RFA extension.)
2. In the *Insert* tab>Import panel, click ▨ (Image).
3. In the Import Image dialog box, select and open the image file. Cross-hatching lines with grips at the ends display, indicating the extents of the image as shown in Figure 13–19.

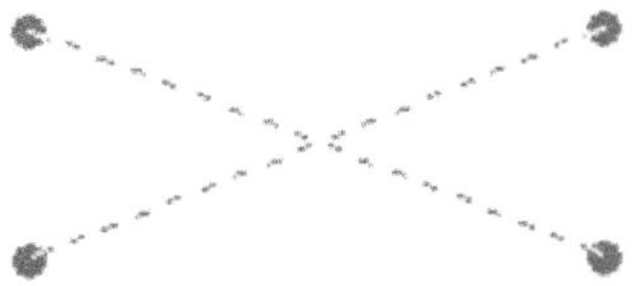

Figure 13–19

4. Place the image where you want it to be located within the titleblock.
5. The image is displayed. Pick one of the grips and extend it to modify the size of the image.

- In Properties, you can adjust the height and width and also set the *Draw Layer* to either **Background** or **Foreground**, as shown in Figure 13–20.

Dimensions	☆
Width	200.0
Height	74.1
Horizontal Scale	1.077812
Vertical Scale	1.077812
Lock Proportions	☑
Other	☆
Draw Layer	Background

Figure 13–20

- You can select more than one image at a time and move them as a group to the background or foreground.

Practice 13a | Create Construction Documents

Learning Objectives

- Set up project properties.
- Create sheets individually and use placeholder sheets.
- Modify views to prepare them to be placed on sheets.
- Place views on sheets.

Estimated time for completion: 20 minutes

In this practice you will complete the project information, add new sheets and use placeholder sheets to add sheets to the project. You will fill in title block information. You will then add views to sheets, such as the Wall Sections sheet shown in Figure 13–21. Complete as many sheets as you have time for in class.

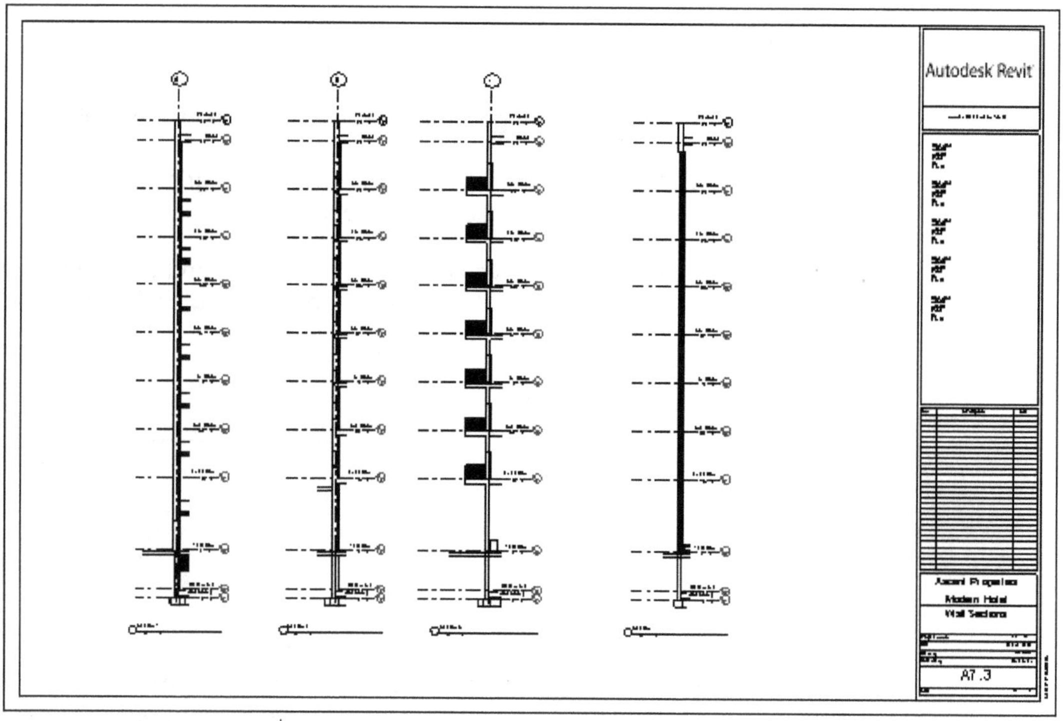

Figure 13–21

Task 1 - Complete the project information.

1. Open the project **Modern-Hotel-Sheets-M.rvt** from your class folder. This file contains some additional elements that are required for the practice.

2. In the *Manage* tab>Settings panel, click 🖳 (Project Information).

3. In the Project Properties dialog box, in the *Other* area, set the following parameters:

   • Project Issue Date: **Issue Date**
   • Project Status: **Design Development**
   • Client Name: **Ascent Properties**
   • Project Address: Click ⟨ Edit... ⟩ **- your address**
   • Project Name: **Modern Hotel**
   • Project Number: **1234-567**

4. Click ⟨ OK ⟩.

5. Save the project.

These properties are used across the entire sheet set and do not need to be entered on each sheet.

Task 2 - Create sheets.

1. In the *View* tab>Sheet Composition panel, click 🗋 (Sheet).

2. In the New Sheet dialog box, select **A1 metric**. In the *Select placeholder sheets* area, **New** is selected by default. Click ⟨ OK ⟩.

3. Zoom in on the lower right corner of the title block. The Project Properties filled out earlier are automatically added to the sheet.

4. Continue filling out the title block, as shown in Figure 13–22. Changing the sheet number and sheet name also changes the name in the Project Browser. Certain labels can be entered on a per sheet basis, such as the *Sheet Name*, *Sheet Number*, *Drawn by*, and *Checked by*. Leave the *Issue Date* as is.

*The Scale is automatically entered when a view is inserted onto a sheet. If a sheet has multiple scales, the scale reads **As Indicated**.*

Ascent Properties Modern Hotel	
Cover Sheet	
Project number	1234-567
Date	Issue Date
Drawn by	MAH
Checked by	RM
A0.0	
Scale	

4/8/2013 11:58:34 AM

Figure 13–22

5. In the Sheet Composition panel, click ⬜ (Sheet). Using the D-sized title block, create the following new sheets:

   • A2.1 - 1st Floor Plan Overall
   • A2.2 - 1st Floor Plan
   • A2.3 - 2nd-8th Floor Plan (Typical)

6. Click ⬜ (Sheet). This time, in the *Select placeholder sheets* area, select one of the placeholder sheets and click ⬜ OK .

7. In the Project Browser, expand *Sheets (all)*. Note that the selected placeholder sheet and the other sheets that you created are displayed.

8. Click ⬚ (Sheet) again. Select all of the other placeholder sheets (use <Ctrl> or <Shift> to select multiple sheets) and click [OK].

The rest of the sheets are placed in the project, as shown in Figure 13–23.

Having typical placeholder sheets created in the company template is a timesaver. Another option is having the sheets already in the template project.

```
Modern Hotel-Project Browser                    ⊠
⊟ 🔲 Sheets (all)                                 ▲
        A0.0 - Cover Sheet
        A1.1 - 1st Floor Life Safety Plan
        A1.2 - 2ndFloor Life Safety Plan
        A2.1 - 1st Floor Plan
        A2.2 - 2nd-8th Floor Plan (Typical)
        A3.1 - Enlarged Plans
        A3.2 - Enlarged Plans
        A3.3 - Enlarged Plans
        A3.4 - Enlarged Plans
        A4.1 - Reflected Ceiling Plan
        A4.2 - Reflected Ceiling Plan
        A4.3 - Reflected Ceiling Plan
        A5.1 - Roof Plan
        A5.2 - Roof Details                       ▤
        A6.1 - Exterior Elevations
        A6.2 - Exterior Elevations
        A6.3 - Exterior Elevations
        A6.4 - Exterior Elevations
        A6.5 - Exterior Elevations
        A7.1 - Building Sections
        A7.2 - Building Sections
        A7.3 - Wall Sections                      ▼
```

Figure 13–23

Task 3 - Set up and add views to sheets.

1. Duplicate (no detailing) the **Floor Plans: Floor 1** and **Floor 2** views and name them **1st Floor-Life Safety Plan** and **2nd-8th Floor-Life Safety Plan**.

2. Open the new views and do the following:

    - Hide all elements except the actual building elements.
    - Turn on the crop region and ensure it is tight up against the building.
    - Turn the crop region off.

The crop region defines the extent of the view on the sheet.

3. Open the appropriate sheet and drag and drop the corresponding Life Safety Plans onto it.

4. Rename sheet **2nd Floor Life Safety Plan** as **2nd-8th Floor Life Safety Plan**.

5. Repeat the process of adding views to sheets using the views you have available.

- Modify crop regions and hide unnecessary elements in the views, as shown in Figure 13–24. Turn off crop regions after you have modified them.

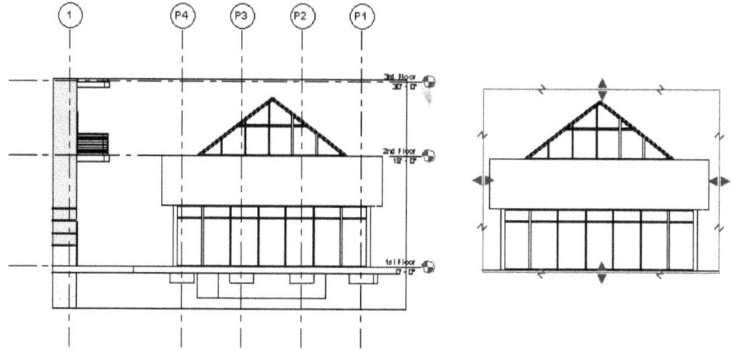

Figure 13–24

- Verify the scale of a view in Properties before placing it on a sheet.
- Use alignment lines to help place multiple views on one sheet, as shown in Figure 13–25.

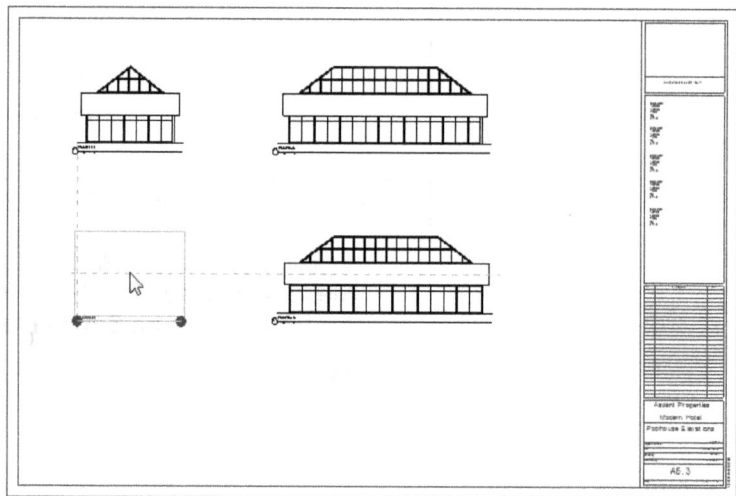

Figure 13–25

- Change the view title, if required, to more accurately describe what is on the sheet.

- To make minor changes to a view once it is on a sheet, double-click in the viewport or right-click on the view and select **Activate View**. To return to the sheet, double-click outside the viewport or right-click on the view and select **Deactivate View**.

6. Once you have added callout, section, or elevation views to sheets, switch back to the **Floor Plans: Floor 1** view. Zoom in on one of the markers. Note that it has now been automatically assigned a detail and sheet number, as shown in Figure 13–26.

Your numbers might not exactly match the numbers in the example.

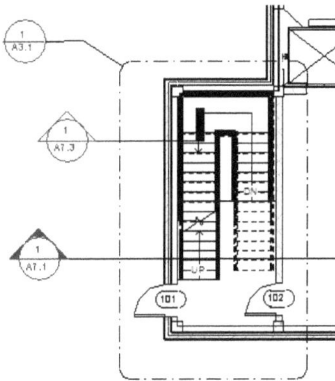

Figure 13–26

7. Save the project.

13.3 Printing Sheets

Learning Objective

*   Print sheets using the default Print dialog box.

With the **Print** command, you can print individual sheets or a list of selected sheets. You can also print an individual view or a portion of a view for check prints or presentations. The Print dialog box is shown in Figure 13–27.

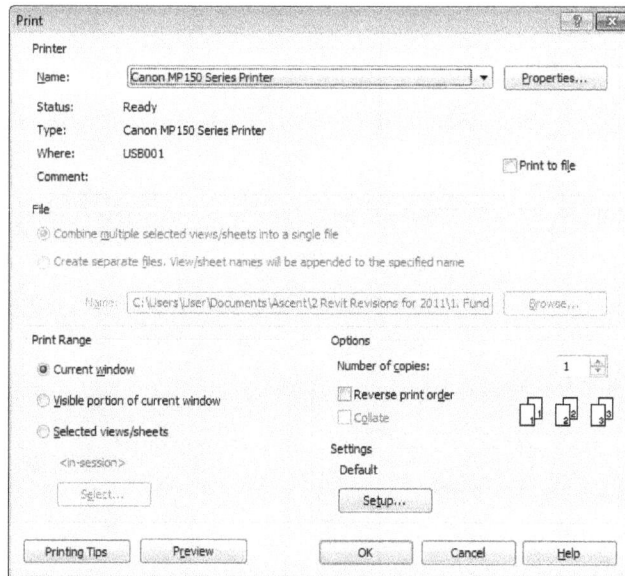

Figure 13–27

How To: Print Sheets

1. In the Application Menu, click 🖨 (Print).
2. Set the options in the Print dialog box as required. In the *Printer* area, verify the printer's *Name* and *Properties* first.
3. Click OK

Printing Options

The Print dialog box is divided into the following areas: *Printer*, *File*, *Print Range*, *Options*, and *Settings*. Modify them as required to produce the plot you want.

- [Printing Tips] opens Autodesk WikiHelp online in which you can find help with troubleshooting printing issues.

- [Preview] opens a preview of the print output so that you can see what is going to be printed.

Printer

Select from the list of available printers, as shown in Figure 13–28. Click [Properties...] to adjust the properties of the selected printer. The options vary according to the printer. Select the **Print to file** option to print to a file rather than directly to a printer. You can create .PLT or .PRN files.

If you do not have an Adobe PDF print driver installed on your system, you cannot print PDF files.

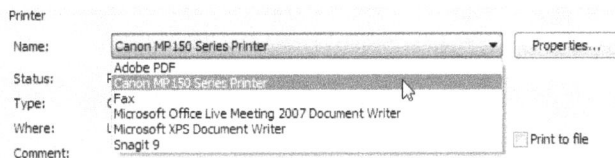

Figure 13–28

File

The *File* area is only available if the **Print to file** option has been selected in the *Printer* area. You can create one file or multiple files depending on the type of printer you are using, as shown in Figure 13–29.

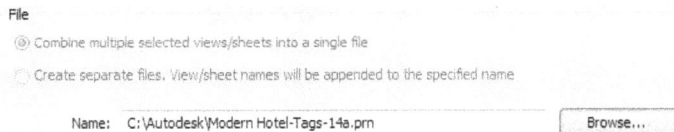

Figure 13–29

Options

If your printer supports multiple copies, you can specify the number in the *Options* area, as shown in Figure 13–30. You can also reverse the print order or collate your prints. These options are also available in the printer properties.

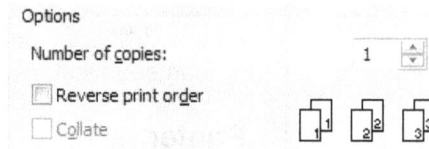

Options

Number of copies: 1

[ ] Reverse print order

[ ] Collate

Figure 13–30

Print Range

The *Print Range* area, as shown in Figure 13–31, enables you to print individual views/sheets or sets of views/sheets. The **Current window** option prints the entire current sheet or view you have open. The **Visible portion of current window** option prints only what is displayed in the current sheet or view.

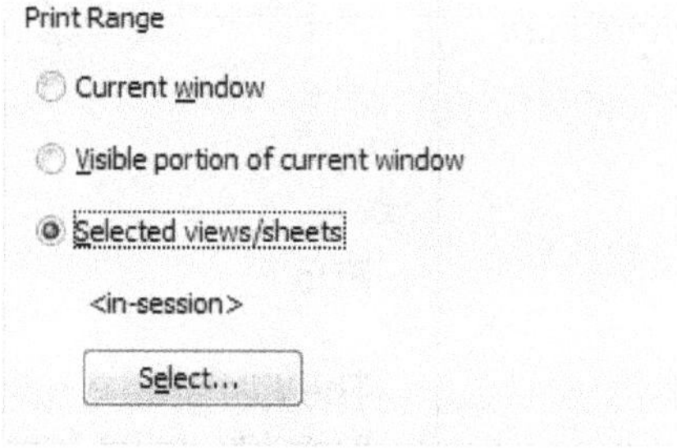

Print Range

( ) Current window

( ) Visible portion of current window

(●) Selected views/sheets

<in-session>

Select...

Figure 13–31

To print multiple sheets, select the **Selected views/sheets**

option and click  Select... to open the View/Sheet Set dialog box. Select each view or sheet to be included in the print set. You can save these sets by name so that you can more easily print the same group again.

Settings

Click [Setup...] to open the Print Setup dialog box, as shown in Figure 13–32. Here, you can specify the *Orientation* and *Zoom* settings, among others. You can also save these settings by name.

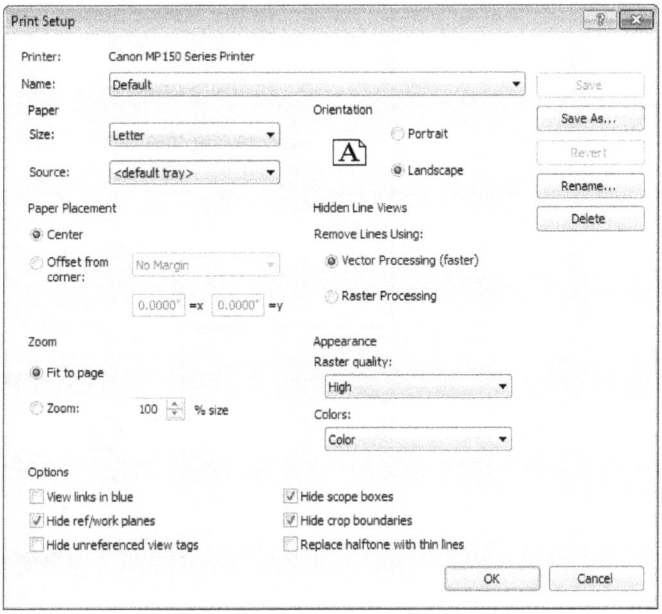

Figure 13–32

Chapter Review Questions

1. How do you specify the size of a sheet?

   a. In the Sheet Properties, specify the **Sheet Size**.

   b. In the Options Bar, specify the **Sheet Size**.

   c. In the New Sheet dialog box, select a title block to control the Sheet Size.

   d. In the Sheet view, right-click and select **Sheet Size**.

2. How is the title block information filled in as shown in Figure 13–33? (Select all that apply.)

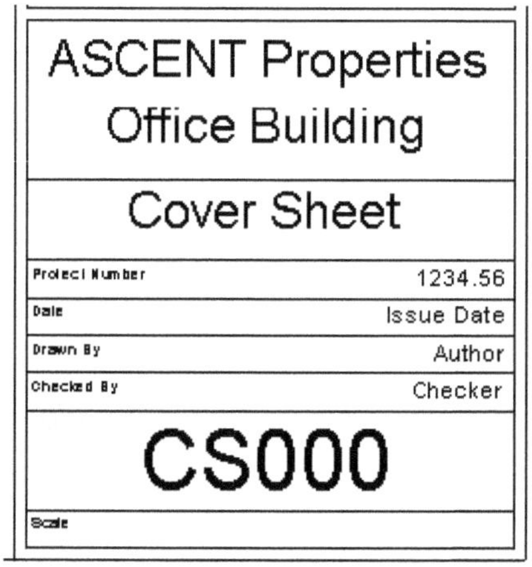

   ASCENT Properties
   Office Building

   Cover Sheet

Project Number	1234.56
Date	Issue Date
Drawn By	Author
Checked By	Checker

   CS000

   | Scale | |

   Figure 13–33

   a. Select the title block and select the label that you want to change.

   b. Select the title block and modify it in Properties.

   c. Right-click on the Sheet in the Project Browser and select **Information**.

   d. Some of the information is filled in automatically.

3. On how many sheets can a view be placed?

   a. 1

   b. 2-5

   c. 6+

   d. As many as you want.

4. Which of the following is the best method to use if the size of a view is too large for a sheet, as shown in Figure 13–34?

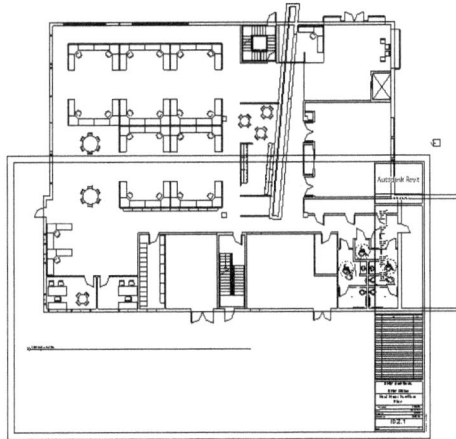

Figure 13–34

a. Delete the view, change the scale and place the view back on the sheet.

b. Activate the view and change the View Scale.

5. How do you set up a view on a sheet that only displays part of a floor plan, as shown in Figure 13–35?

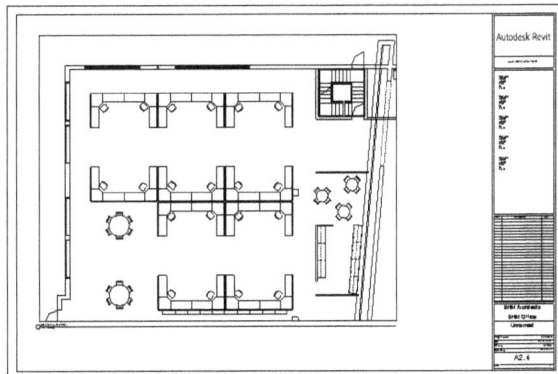

Figure 13–35

a. Drag and drop the view to the sheet and use the crop region to modify it.

b. Activate the view and rescale it.

c. Create a callout view displaying the part that you want to use and place the callout view on the sheet.

d. Open the view in the Project Browser and change the View Scale.

Command Summary

Button	Command	Location
	Activate View	• **Ribbon:** *(select the view) Modify | Viewports* tab>Viewport panel> Activate View
		• **Right-click:** *(on view)* Activate View
	Deactivate View	• **Ribbon:** *View* tab>Sheet Composition panel>expand Viewports> Deactivate View
		• **Right-click:** *(on view)* Deactivate View
	Guide Grid	• **Ribbon:** *View* tab>Sheet Composition panel>Guide Grid
		• **Properties:** *(when a sheet is selected)*
	Sheet	• **Ribbon:** *View* tab>Sheet Composition panel>Sheet
	View	• **Ribbon:** *View* tab>Sheet Composition panel>View

Chapter 14

Annotating Construction Documents

In this chapter you learn about adding dimensions and text to views used in construction documents. You learn how to add view specific detail lines and symbols to clarify design intent. You also learn how to create legends and add legend components.

This chapter contains the following topics:

- **Working with Dimensions**
- **Working With Text**
- **Adding Detail Lines and Symbols**
- **Creating Legends**

14.1 Working with Dimensions

Autodesk Certification Topics & Objectives

Pro.   User

Documentation
* Use dimension strings   ✓

Modeling
* Add dimensions   ✓

Learning Objectives

* Add a string of dimensions to walls and other elements and add dimensions to entire walls and their related elements.
* Add other dimensions, such as angular, radial, diameter, and arc length.
* Modify dimensions including the text and setting equal constraints.

You can create permanent dimensions using aligned, linear, angular, radial, and arc length dimensions. These can be individual or a string of dimensions, as shown in Figure 14–1. With aligned dimensions, you can also dimension entire walls with openings, grid lines, and/or intersecting walls.

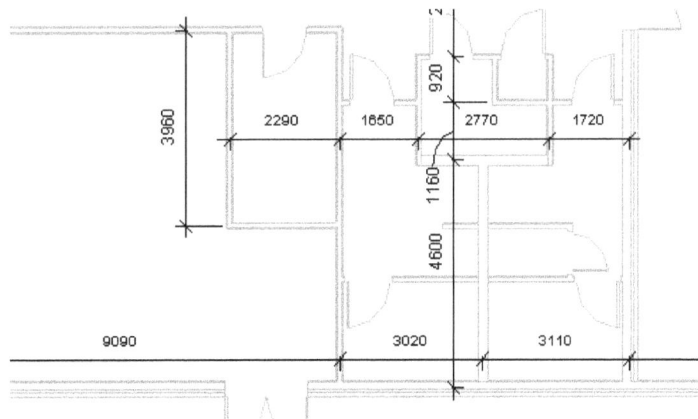

Figure 14–1

* Dimensions referencing model elements must be drawn on a model in an active view. You can dimension on sheets, but only to items drawn directly on the sheets.

* You can use permanent dimensions to modify elements. First, select the element being dimensioned and then edit the dimension value, as you would with temporary dimensions.

(Aligned) is also located in the Quick Access Toolbar.

- Dimensions are available in the *Annotate* tab>Dimension panel and the *Modify* tab>Measure panel, as shown in Figure 14–2.

Figure 14–2

- The default template includes several dimension styles for each type of dimension. It also includes different styles with different leaders when you pull the text away from the dimension line, as shown in Figure 14–3. You can also create your own dimension styles with different text sizes, fonts, and arrowheads.

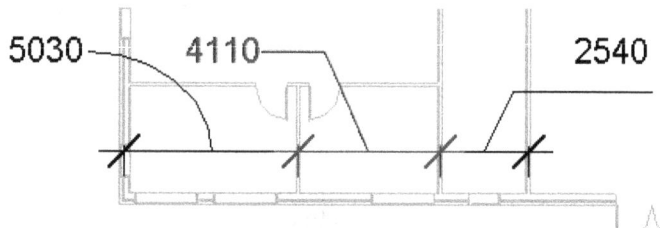

5030   4110   2540

Figure 14–3

How To: Add Dimensions for a Series of Walls

1. In the Quick Access Toolbar or *Annotate* tab>Dimensions panel, click   (Aligned) or use the shortcut by pressing <D> and then pressing <I>.
2. In the Type Selector, select the dimension type you want to use.
3. In the Options Bar, set *Pick* to **Individual References**.
4. Select from the drop-down list to define how the dimensions work with walls: **Wall centerlines**, **Wall faces**, **Center of core**, or **Faces of core**. This can be changed as you add dimensions.
5. Move the cursor over the first element you want to dimension. When it highlights, select the element. A ghost image of the dimension line displays.
6. Select the next wall to dimension, as shown in Figure 14–4.

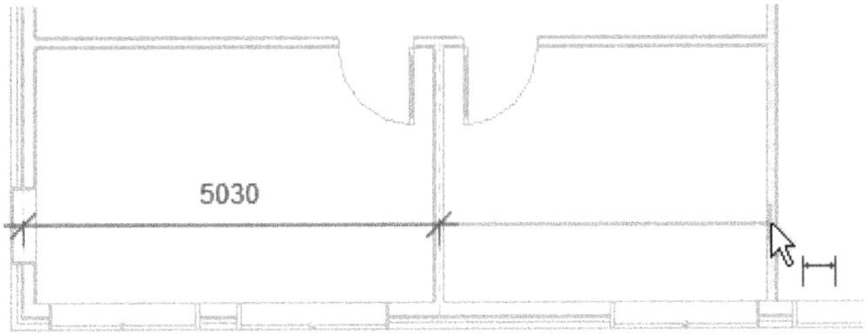

Figure 14–4

7. Continue selecting elements to dimension in a continuous line, as required.
8. After the last element to be dimensioned has been selected, move the cursor to a location for the dimension string. Click in an empty space to place it.

How To: Add Dimensions to Entire Walls

1. Click ✦ (Aligned).
2. In the Type Selector, select the dimension type.
3. In the Options Bar, select the layer of the wall to dimension from. The options are **Wall centerlines**, **Wall faces**, **Center of core**, and **Faces of core**, as shown in Figure 14–5.

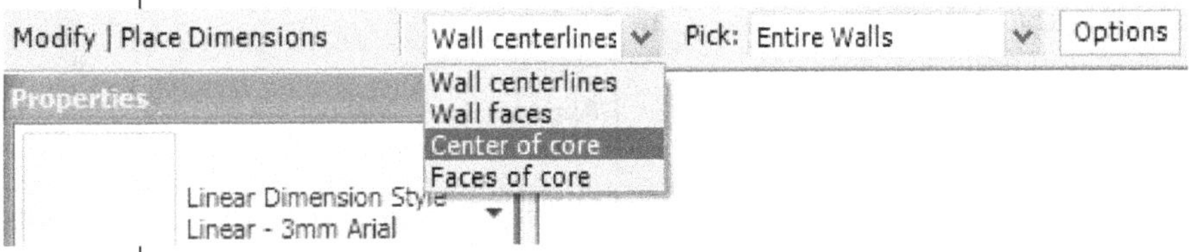

Figure 14–5

*A dimension string created with the **Entire Walls** option is one element and must be modified as one element.*

*If the **Entire Wall** option is selected without additional options, it places an overall wall dimension.*

4. In the Options Bar, set *Pick* to **Entire Walls**, and click Options . In the Auto Dimension Options dialog box, select the references you want to have automatically dimensioned, as shown in Figure 14–6.

Figure 14–6

5. Click [OK] .
6. Select the wall you want to dimension and then drag the cursor to position the dimension string. Click in empty space to place it. One continuous string of dimensions is created with the specified options, as shown in Figure 14–7.

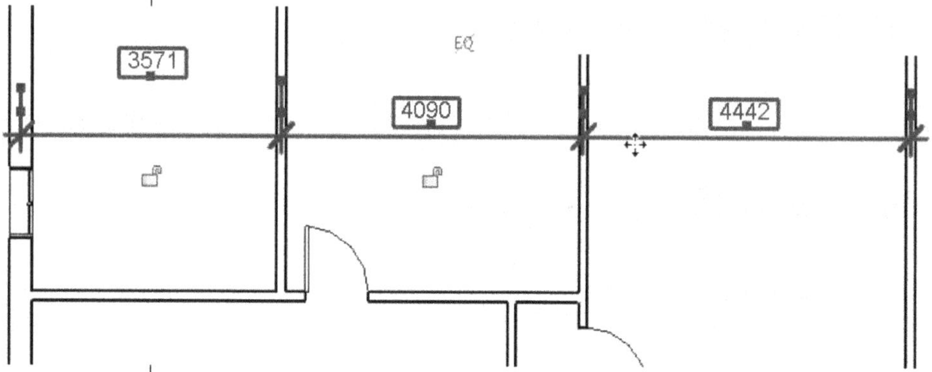

Figure 14–7

7. Select and dimension other walls as required.

How To: Add Other Types of Dimensions

*When the **Dimension** command is active, the dimension methods are also accessible in the Modify | Place Dimensions tab> Dimension panel.*

1. In the *Annotate* tab>Dimension panel, select a dimension method.

	Aligned	Most commonly used dimension type. Select individual elements or entire walls to dimension.
	Linear	Used when you need to specify certain points on elements.
	Angular	Used to dimension the angle between two elements.
	Radial	Used to dimension the radius of circular elements.
	Diameter	Used to dimension the diameter of circular elements.
	Arc Length	Used to dimension the length of the arc of circular elements.

2. In the Type Selector, select the dimension type.
3. Follow the prompts for the selected method.

Modifying Dimensions

Dimensions automatically update when you move the dimensioned elements. You can also modify the dimensions using various controls and constraints. While the dimension text is automatically updated you can still edit the dimension text, replace, or add to the dimension. There are also constraints for locking the dimension in place and to make dimensions equal.

When the **Modify** command is active and you select a dimension or dimension string, you can change several aspects of the dimension, as shown in Figure 14–8.

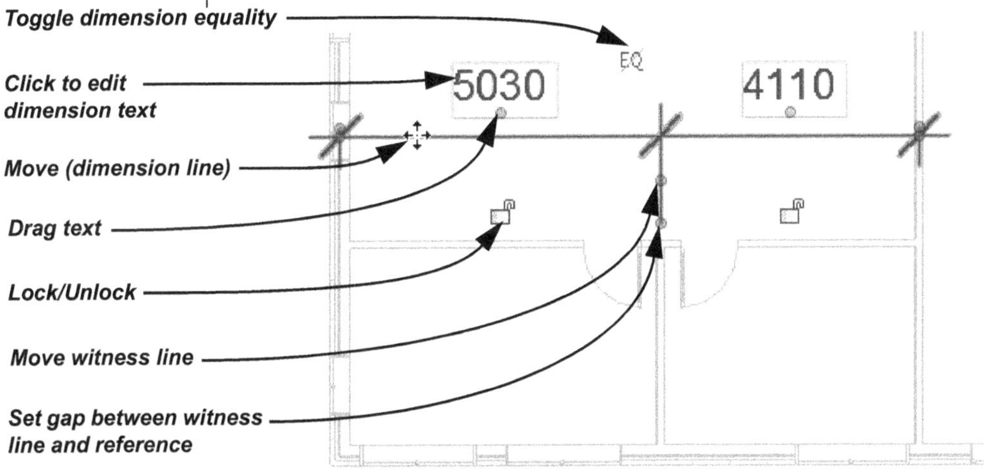

Toggle dimension equality

Click to edit dimension text

Move (dimension line)

Drag text

Lock/Unlock

Move witness line

Set gap between witness line and reference

5030   EQ   4110

Figure 14–8

Modifying the Dimension Element

- To move the dimension text, select the **Drag text** control under the text and drag it to a new location. It automatically creates a leader from the dimension line if you drag it away. The style of the leader (arc or line) depends on the dimension style.

- To move the dimension line (the line parallel to the element being dimensioned), hover the cursor over the line until

  ⟡ (Move) displays. Drag the line to a new location.

- To change the gap between the witness line and the element being dimensioned, drag the control at the end of the witness line.

Modifying the Witness Lines

- To move the witness line (the line perpendicular to the element being dimensioned) to a different element or face of a wall, use the **Move Witness Line** control in the middle of the witness line. Click repeatedly to cycle through the various options. You can also drag this control to move the witness line to a different element, or right-click on the control and select **Move Witness Line**.

- To add a witness line to a string of dimensions, select the dimension and, in the *Modify | Dimensions* tab>Witness Lines panel, click ⊢⌐ (Edit Witness Lines). Select the element(s) you want to add to the dimension. Click in space to finish.

- To delete a witness line, move the cursor over the control in the middle of the witness line, right-click, and select **Delete Witness Line**. Alternatively, you can drag the control to another existing witness line.

- To delete one dimension in a string and break the string into two separate dimensions, select the string, hover over the dimension that you want to delete, and press <Tab>. When it highlights (as shown on top in Figure 14–9), pick it and press <Delete>. The selected dimension is deleted and the dimension string is separated into two elements as shown on the bottom in Figure 14–9.

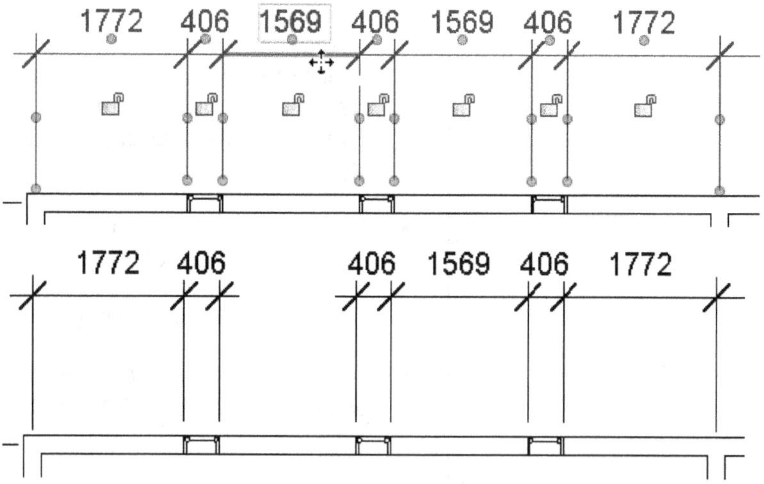

Figure 14–9

Modifying Dimension Text

The dimension text can be changed to a different value, though typically it is not recommended. Because the Autodesk® Revit® software is parametric, changing the dimension text without actually changing the elements dimensioned, can cause problems throughout the project especially if you use the project model to estimate materials or work with other disciplines. You can append the text, as shown in Figure 14–10, with prefixes and suffixes which is very useful in renovation projects.

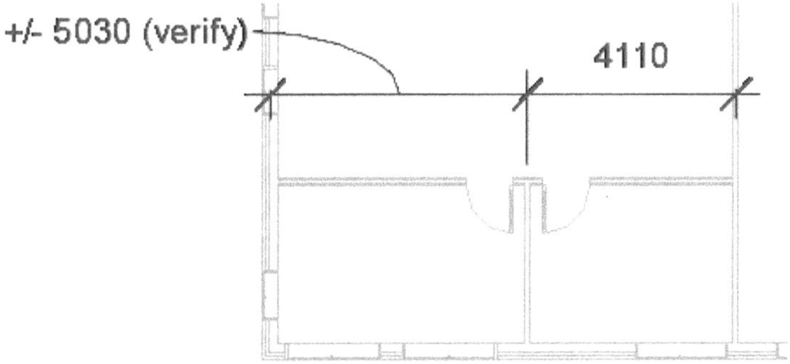

Figure 14–10

Double-click on the dimension text to open the Dimension Text dialog box, as shown in Figure 14–11, and make modifications as required.

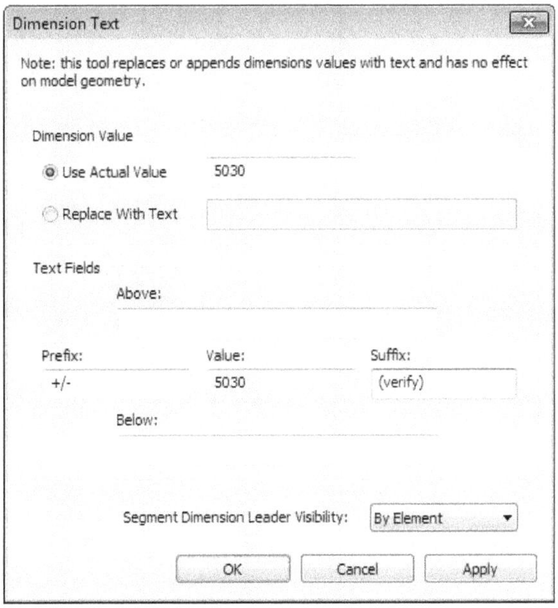

Figure 14–11

Setting Constraints

The two types of constraints that work with dimensions are locks and equal settings, as shown in Figure 14–12.

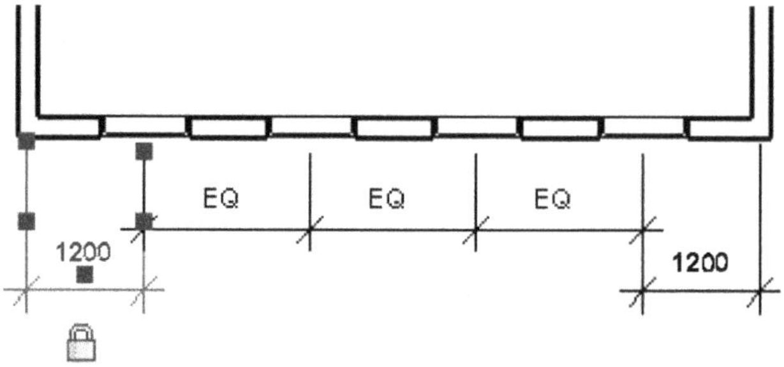

Figure 14–12

- When you lock a dimension, the value is set and you cannot make a change between it and the referenced elements. If it is unlocked, you can move it and change its value.

- For a string of dimensions, select the **EQ** symbol to constrain the elements to be at an equal distance apart. This actually moves the elements that are dimensioned.

- The equality text display can be changed in Properties as shown in Figure 14–13. The style for each of the display types is set in the dimension type.

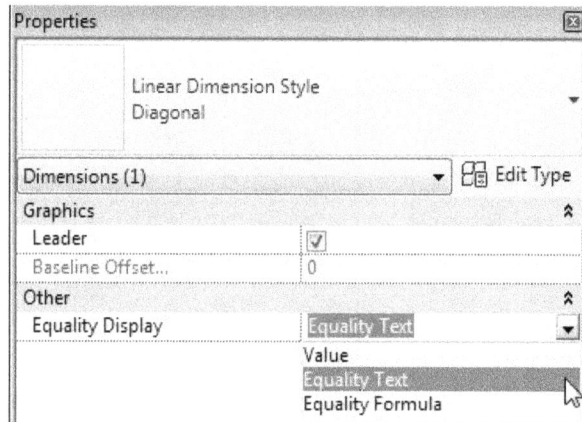

Figure 14–13

Practice 14a | Add Dimensions

Learning Objectives

- Add a string of dimensions to the column grid.
- Dimension walls using the **Entire Walls** option.
- Edit witness lines to include elements that were not automatically included in the dimensions.

Estimated time for completion: 10 minutes

In this practice you will add dimensions to a floor plan view, as shown on its sheet in Figure 14–14. Some additional elements including storefronts (curtain walls inset into a wall as a window) and windows have been added at the back of the building.

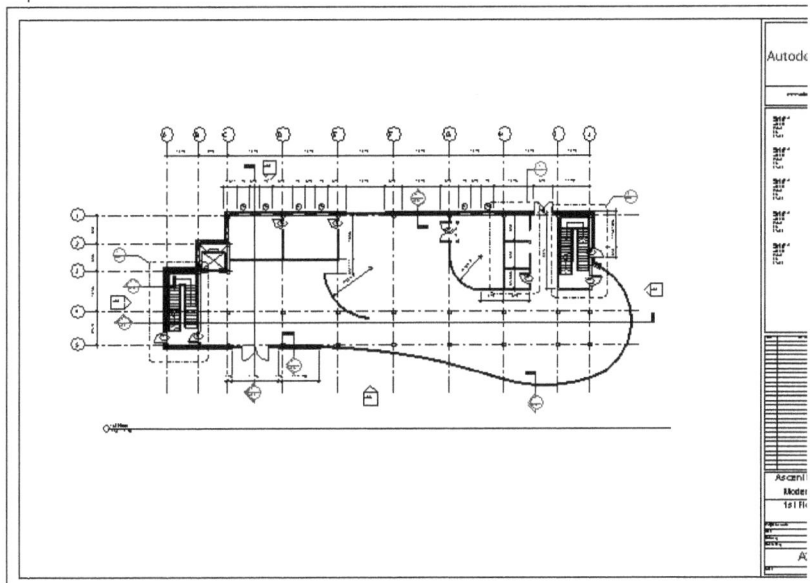

Figure 14–14

Task 1 - Add dimensions to the column grid.

1. Open the project **Modern-Hotel-Dimensions-M.rvt** from your class folder.

In this case, you do not want elements such as door and window tags to display so you can easily read the dimensions.

2. In the Project Browser, duplicate (without detailing), the **Floor Plans: Floor 1** view and rename it as **Floor 1-Dimensioned Plan**. Open the view.

3. In the View Control Bar, click 📐 (Show Crop Region).

4. In Properties, in *Extents* area, select **Annotation Crop**.

5. Select the crop region and expand the annotation crop region on each side so there is room to place dimensions.

6. Hide the crop region.

7. Move the location of the grid bubbles so that there is enough room for dimensioning.

8. In the Quick Access Toolbar, click ↗ (Aligned).

9. Dimension the column grid lines in each direction, as shown in Figure 14–15.

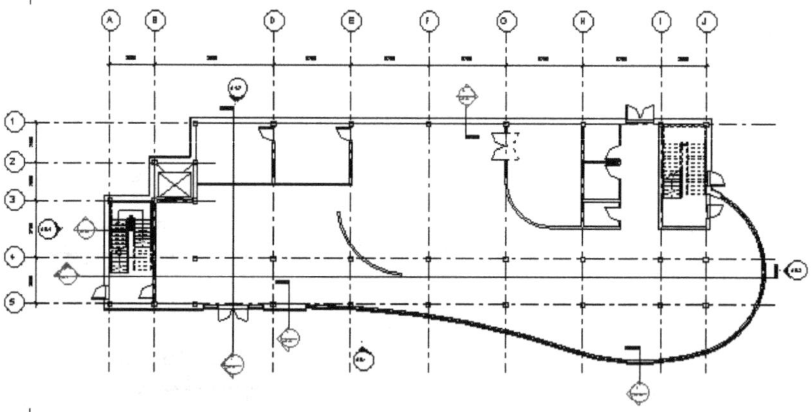

Figure 14–15

Task 2 - Dimension the exterior and interior walls.

1. Click ↗ (Aligned).

2. In the Options Bar, select **Wall faces** and set *Pick* to **Entire Walls**.

3. Click Options and set the *Openings* to **Widths**, as shown in Figure 14–16, and click OK .

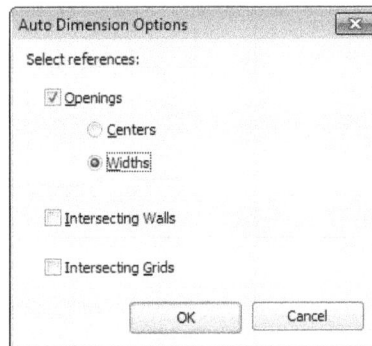

Figure 14–16

4. Select the back wall and place the dimension above it.

5. Zoom in on the upper left corner of the building. Use the **Move Witness Line** control to relocate the line from the end of the wall (as shown in Figure 14–17), to Grid Line C, the closest grid line on the right that passes through the corner column.

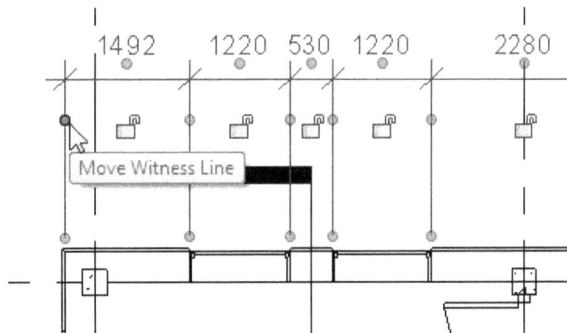

Figure 14–17

6. Return to the **Modify** command.

7. In the same wall, pan over to the right where the storefront openings are displayed. These were not dimensioned automatically.

8. Select the dimension line that you added for this wall. In the *Modify | Dimensions* tab> Witness Lines panel, click

   ⊢⊣ (Edit Witness Lines).

Move the elevation and section markers as well as the dimension line to keep the dimensions clear. You might also want to move the dimension text away from the grid lines.

9. Select the outside edges of each side of the storefront openings to add the witness lines and then click in empty space to apply the changes. The modified dimension string displays as shown in Figure 14–18.

Figure 14–18

10. Add other dimensions that are not dependent on grid lines. Modify some of the elements as required to obtain the expected dimensions. Remember the actual size/length of elements controls the dimensions.

11. Use the various dimensioning commands and methods to dimension the interior spaces, as shown in Figure 14–19. The dimensions might not be exactly as shown. You can modify the project walls to obtain the correct dimensions.

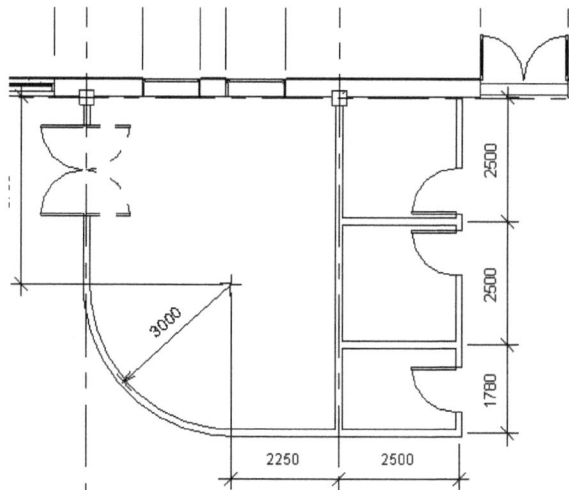

Figure 14–19

12. Save the project.

13. If time permits, dimension the **Floor Plans: Typical Guest Room - Dimension Plan** view. Make adjustments as required to the locations of the walls and doors.

14.2 Working With Text

Autodesk Certification Topics & Objectives

Pro.   User

Modeling

* Add model text to a plan   ✓

Learning Objectives

* Add text with or without leaders.
* Create Text Types using different fonts and sizes.

The **Text** command enables you to add notes to views or sheets, such as the detail shown in Figure 14–20. The same command is used to create text with or without leaders.

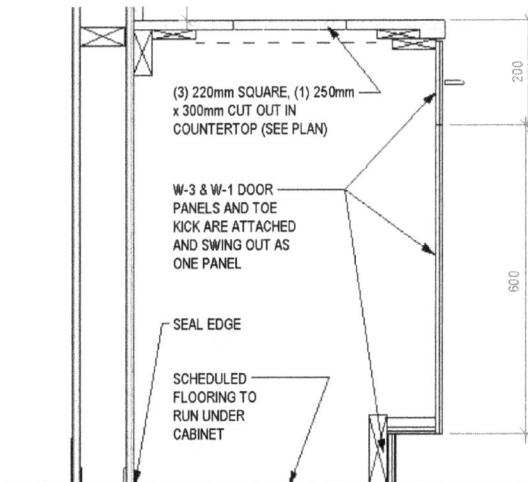

(3) 220mm SQUARE, (1) 250mm x 300mm CUT OUT IN COUNTERTOP (SEE PLAN)

W-3 & W-1 DOOR PANELS AND TOE KICK ARE ATTACHED AND SWING OUT AS ONE PANEL

SEAL EDGE

SCHEDULED FLOORING TO RUN UNDER CABINET

Figure 14–20

The text height is automatically set by the text type in conjunction with the scale of the view (as shown in Figure 14–21), using the same size text type at two different scales. Text types display at the specified height, both in the views and on the sheet.

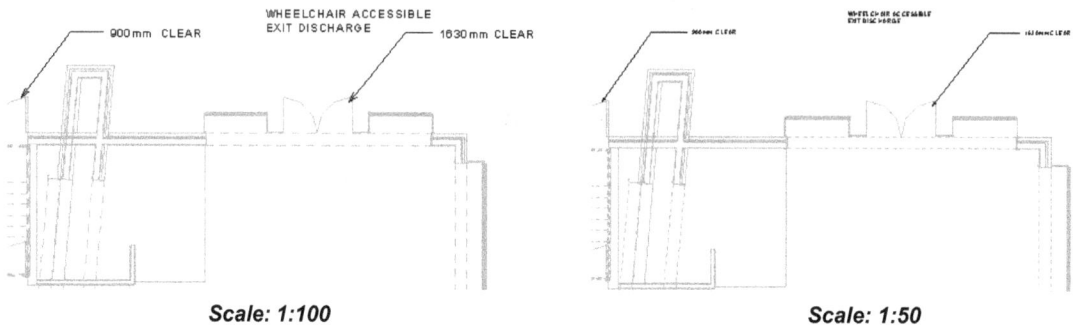

Scale: 1:100   Scale: 1:50

Figure 14–21

How To: Add Text

1. In the *Annotate* tab>Text panel, click **A** (Text).
2. In the Type Selector, set the text type.
3. In the *Modify | Place Text* tab>Format panel, select the method you want to use: **A** (No Leader), **←A** (One Segment), **⟋A** (Two Segments), or **⟍A** (Curved).
4. In the Format panel, set the justification for the text and leader, as shown in Figure 14–22.

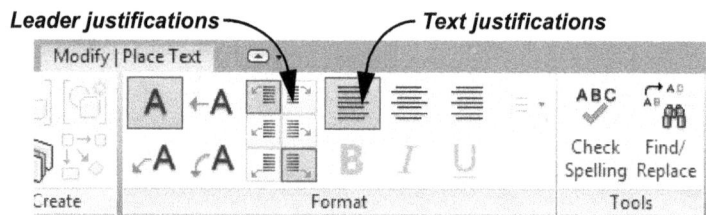

Leader justifications ————   ———— *Text justifications*

Figure 14–22

5. Select the location for the leader and text.
   - If the **No leader** option is selected, select the start point for the text and begin typing.
   - If using a leader, the first point places the arrow and you then select points for the leader. The text starts at the last leader point.
   - To set a word wrapping distance, click and drag to set the start and end points of the text.

*The **Bold**, **Italic**, and **Underline** options only apply to that instance of text. If you want a specific type of text to have this formatting, create a new text type and select the new type in the Type Selector.*

6. Type the required text. In the Format panel, as shown in Figure 14–23, you can apply bold, italic, or underlined formatting to the text, as well as set a paragraph format.

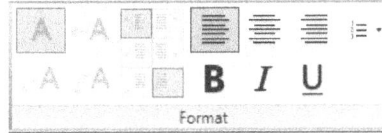

Figure 14–23

7. Click outside the text box to complete the text element.
   - Pressing <Enter> after a line of text starts a new line of text in the same text window.
8. Click in a new location to start another text element, or return to the **Modify** command to finish.

- Use the controls shown in Figure 14–24 to position, rotate, or edit the text as required.

text with a two segment leader

Figure 14–24

- You can add leaders to text when it is selected. Click the related icon in the Format panel, as shown in Figure 14–25. Use the grips to move the leader once it is placed.

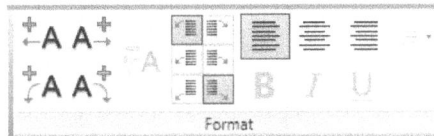

More than one leader can be applied to each side.

Figure 14–25

- Several text types are included in the default template. These can be set in the Type Selector. You can also create your own text types.

- When placing text, alignment lines help you align the text with other text elements based on the justification of the original text.

Setting the Paragraph Format

While entering text, you can set up individual lines of text using the paragraph formats shown in Figure 14–26. Change the text format option before you type the line of text. When you press <Enter> to start the next line, it continues to use the new format.

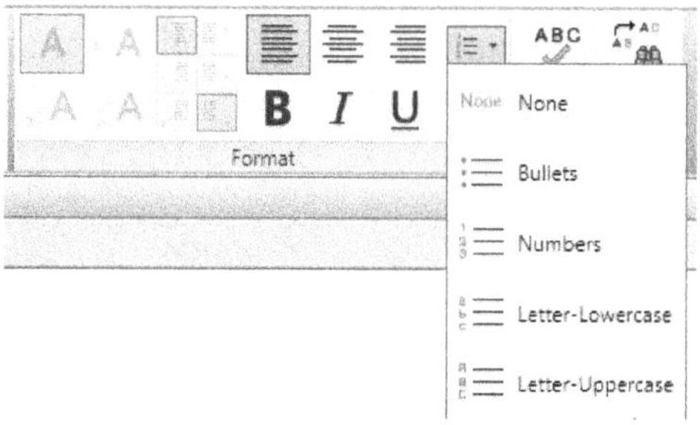

Figure 14–26

- To change a line that has already been typed, click anywhere on the line of text and change the paragraph format.

- You can also select several lines of text by dragging the cursor to highlight them and then change the paragraph format.

Hint: Model Text

Model text is different from annotation text. It is designed to create full-size text on the model itself. For example, you would use model text to create a sign on a door, as shown in Figure 14–27. One model text type, **600mm Arial**, is included with the default template. You can create other types as required.

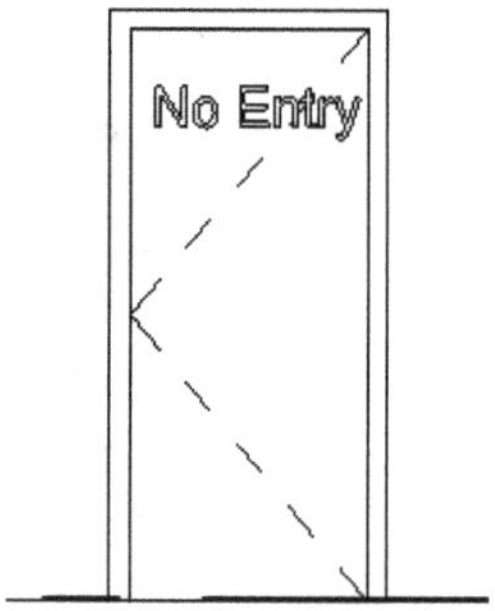

Figure 14–27

- Model text is found in the *Architecture* tab>Model panel, by clicking ⚛ (Model Text).

Spell Checking

The Spelling dialog box displays any misspelled words in context and provides several options for changing them, as shown in Figure 14–28.

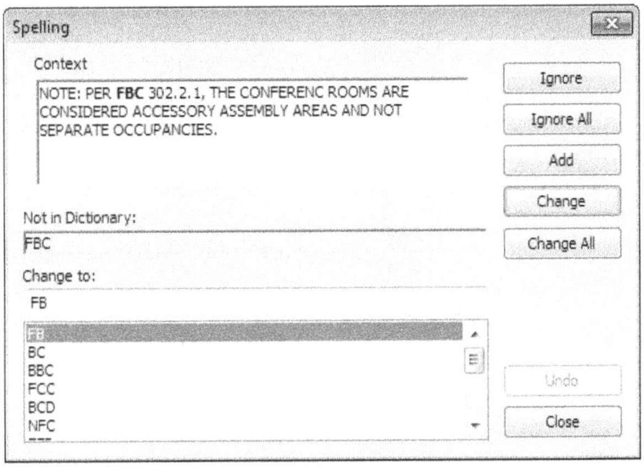

Figure 14–28

- To spell check all text in a view, in the *Annotate* tab>Text

  panel, click ^{ABC} ✓ (Spelling) or press <F7>. As with other spell checkers, you can **Ignore**, **Add**, or **Change** the word.

- You can also check the spelling in selected text. With text selected, in the *Modify | Text Notes* tab>Tools panel, click

  ^{ABC} ✓ (Spelling).

Creating Text Types

If you need new text types with a different text size or font (such as for a title or hand-lettering), you can create new ones, as shown in Figure 14–29. It is recommended that you create these in a project template so they are available in future projects.

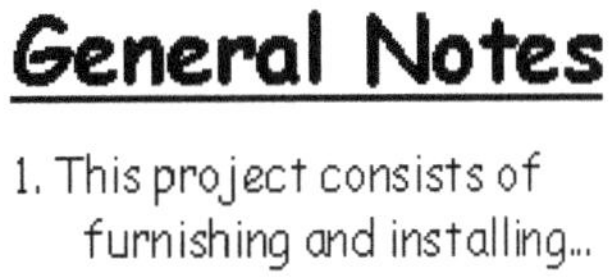

General Notes

1. This project consists of
   furnishing and installing...

Figure 14–29

- You can copy and paste text types from one project to another or use **Transfer Project Standards**.

How To: Create Text Types

1. In the *Annotate* tab>Text panel, click **A** (Text). You can also start by selecting an existing text element.

2. In Properties, click ⊞ (Edit Type).

3. In the Type Properties dialog box, click [Duplicate].

4. In the Name dialog box, type a new name and click [OK].

5. Modify the text parameters as required. The parameters are shown in Figure 14–30.

The Show Border parameter, when selected, draws a rectangle around the text.

Parameter	Value
Graphics	⟩
Color	■ Black
Line Weight	1
Background	Opaque
Show Border	☐
Leader/Border Offset	2.0320 mm
Leader Arrowhead	Arrow 30 Degree
Text	⟩
Text Font	Arial
Text Size	2.5000 mm
Tab Size	12.7000 mm
Bold	☐
Italic	☐
Underline	☐
Width Factor	1.000000

Figure 14–30

- In the *Graphics* area, click in the cell next to the **Color** parameter and select a color for the text in the Color dialog box. Typically, this remains black if you are creating working drawings. However, if you want to add color to a presentation, you can use the full range of True colors and Pantone colors.

- The **Background** parameter can be set to **Opaque** or **Transparent**. An opaque background includes a masking region that hides lines or elements beneath the text.

- In the *Text* area, the **Width Factor** parameter controls the width of the lettering, but does not affect the height. A width factor greater than **1** spreads the text out and a width factor less than **1** compresses it.

6. Click [OK] to close the Type Properties dialog box.

14.3 Adding Detail Lines and Symbols

Learning Objectives

- Draw detail lines to display non model elements.
- Add 2D annotation symbols to specific views.

While annotating views for construction documents, you might need to add lines and symbols to clarify the design intent or show information, such as the life safety plan exit information, as shown in Figure 14–31.

Detail lines and symbols are view-specific, which means that they only display in the view in which they were created.

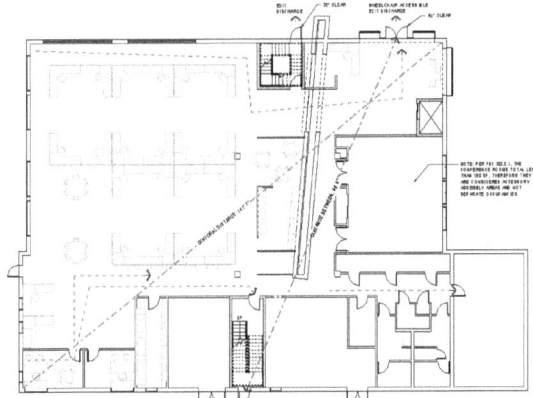

Figure 14–31

- Detail Lines and Symbols are also used to create detail views.

How To: Draw Detail Lines

1. In the *Annotation* tab>Detail panel, click ⬚ (Detail Line).
2. In the *Modify | Place Detail Lines* tab>Line Style panel, select the type of line you want to use, as shown in Figure 14–32.

You can select from a variety of line styles including thin, medium, and wide lines, center lines, and demolition, hidden, and overhead lines. You can also create your own line styles.

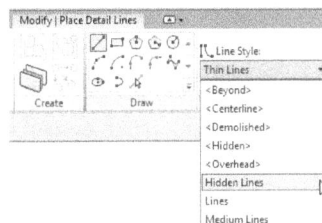

Figure 14–32

3. Use the tools in the Draw panel to create the detail lines.

Using Symbols

Symbols are 2D elements that only display in one view, while components can be in 3D and display in many views.

Many of the annotations used in architectural drawings are frequently repeated. Several of them have been saved as symbols in the Autodesk Revit software, such as the North Arrow, Center Line, and Graphic Scale annotations as shown in Figure 14–33.

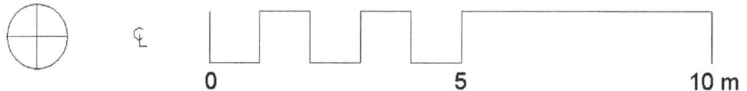

Figure 14–33

• You can also create or load custom annotation symbols.

How To: Place a Symbol

1. In the *Annotation* tab>Symbol panel, click ✛ (Symbol).
2. In the Type Selector, select the symbol you want to use.
3. In the *Modify | Place Symbol* tab>Mode panel, click

   📥 (Load Family) if you want to load other symbols.
4. In the Options Bar, as shown in Figure 14–34, set the *Number of Leaders* and select the **Rotate after placement** option if you want to rotate the symbol as you insert it.

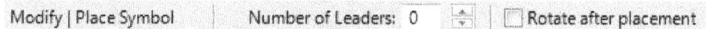

Figure 14–34

5. Place the symbol in the view. Rotate it if you selected the **Rotate after placement** option. If you specified leaders, use the controls to move them into place.

Stair Path Symbol

If a stair in a plan view does not already have a stair path (as shown in Figure 14–35), you can add one. In the *Annotate* tab>

Symbol panel, click ▦ (Stair Path) and select the stair.

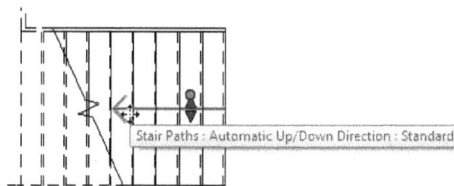

Figure 14–35

Practice 14b | Annotate Construction Documents

Learning Objectives

- Add detail lines and arrowhead symbols to indicate exit routes.
- Add text to create labels and notes.

Estimated time for completion: 30 minutes

In this practice you will create a Life Safety Plan with detail lines, symbols, and text, as shown in Figure 14–36.

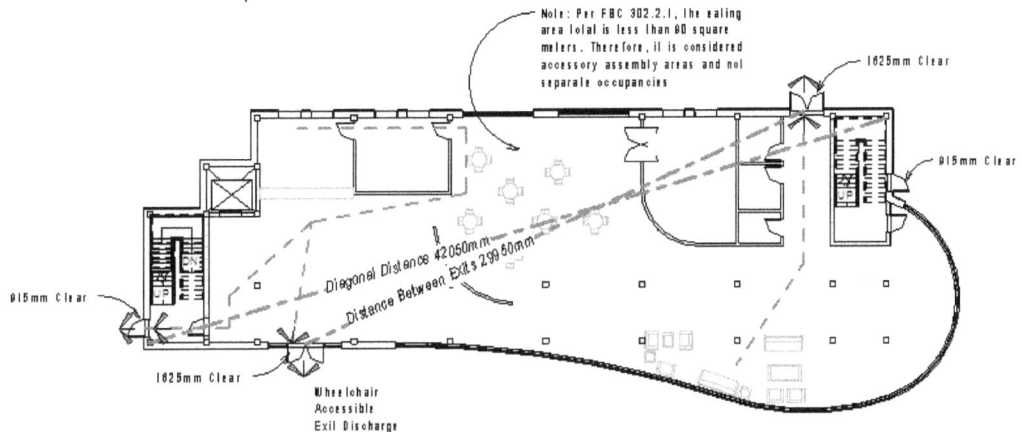

Figure 14–36

Task 1 - Create a Life Safety Plan (lines and symbols).

1. Open the project **Modern-Hotel-Annotations-M.rvt** from your class folder.

2. Open the **Floor Plans: 1st Floor Life Safety Plan** view.

3. In the View Control Bar or in Properties, change the *View Scale* to **1:200**.

4. Open the Visibility/Graphic Overrides dialog box.

5. In the *Model Categories* tab, select **Casework**, **Furniture**, and **Furniture Systems** to toggle them on. Select the **Halftone** option for each of these items as well.

6. Click OK to close the dialog box.

7. In the *Annotate* tab>Detail panel, click ⬛ (Detail Line).

8. In the *Modify | Place Detail Lines* tab>Line Style panel, set the *Line Style:* to **Life Safety Diagonal**.

9. In the Options Bar, clear the **Chain** option.

10. Draw a diagonal line from the lower left corner of the building to the upper right corner of the building, and another diagonal line from exit to exit, as shown in Figure 14–37.

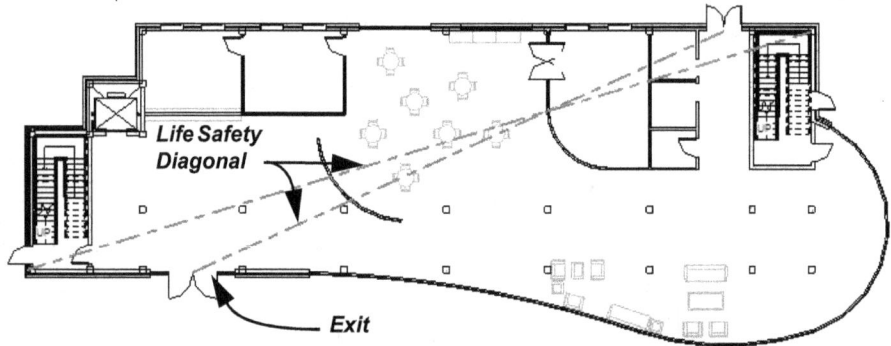

Figure 14–37

11. In the Options Bar, select the **Chain** option.

12. Using the **Life Safety Travel Distance** line type, draw the detail lines shown in Figure 14–38.

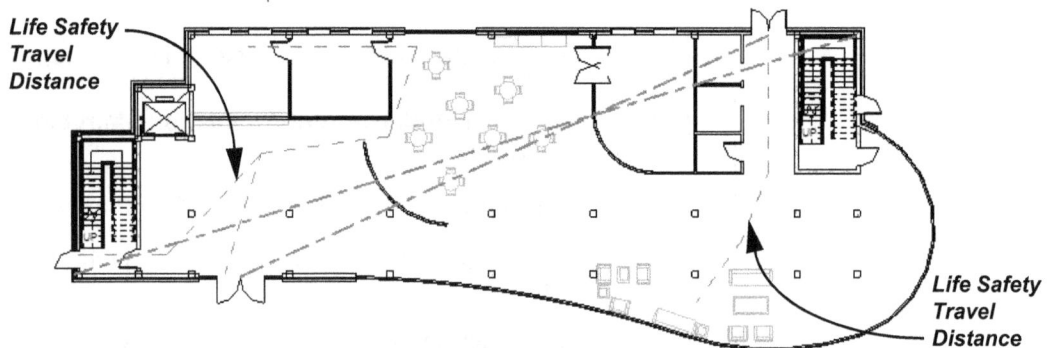

Figure 14–38

13. Zoom in on the front entrance.

14. In the *Annotate* tab>Symbol panel, click ⊕ (Symbol).

15. In the *Modify | Place Symbol* tab>Mode panel, click

    ⬇ (Load Family).

16. In your class files *Class Library* folder, select the
    Life-Safety-Line-Arrowhead.rfa symbol and click
    ⟨ Open ⟩.

Use <Spacebar> to rotate the symbol as it is placed. Highlight the end point of the line to rotate to a specific angle.

17. Insert an arrowhead at the end of each travel line and outside
    the door, as shown in Figure 14–39. Rotate them as required.

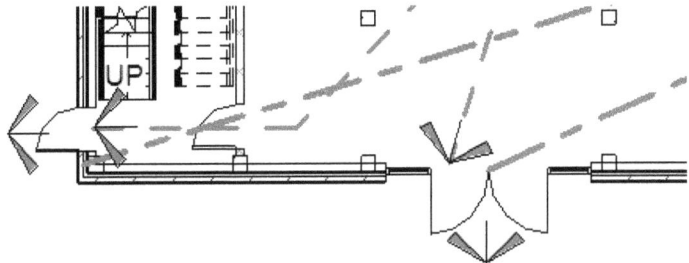

Figure 14–39

18. Add arrows to the ends of the other travel lines, pointing the
    travel direction toward the doors.

Task 2 - Create a Life Safety Plan (text).

1. In the *Annotate* tab>Text panel, click **A** (Text).

2. Create two new text types. In Properties, click ⊞ (Edit
   Type). In the Type Properties dialog box, click ⟨ Duplicate ⟩.
   For the first new text type, enter **3mm Arial Narrow** as the
   name and click ⟨ OK ⟩.

3. Set the following properties:

   • Text Font: **Arial**
   • Text Size: **3mm**
   • Width Factor: **0.9**

4. Click ⟨ OK ⟩ to save the settings and close the dialog
   box.

5. Click ⊞ (Edit Type) again to open the Type Properties dialog box. Click [Duplicate] and create another text type named **3mm Arial Narrow Italic**.

6. Select the **Italic** option and click [OK].

7. Zoom in on the front entrance and add text using the **3mm Arial Narrow** text type, as shown in Figure 14–40. Adjust the Annotation Crop Region as necessary to place the text. Add similar notes for the door sizes at the other exits.

915mm Clear

1625mm Clear

Wheelchair
Accessible
Exit Discharge

Figure 14–40

8. Add a note to the breakfast room, as shown in Figure 14–41.

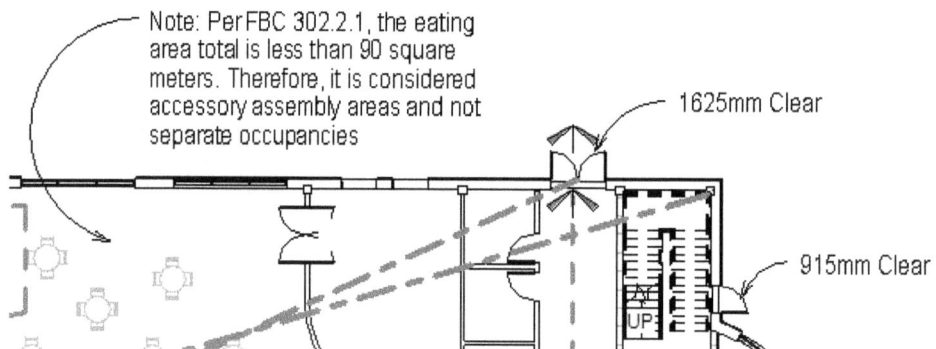

Note: Per FBC 302.2.1, the eating area total is less than 90 square meters. Therefore, it is considered accessory assembly areas and not separate occupancies

1625mm Clear

915mm Clear

Figure 14–41

9. Using the **3mm Narrow Italic** text type, add text to each diagonal distance line, as shown in Figure 14–42. Enter the text first and then click in empty space to exit the text box.

- Use the ✛ (Move) control at the start of the line of text and the ↻ (Rotate) control at the other end of the text line to get the text on top of the appropriate diagonal line. The text automatically masks the line.

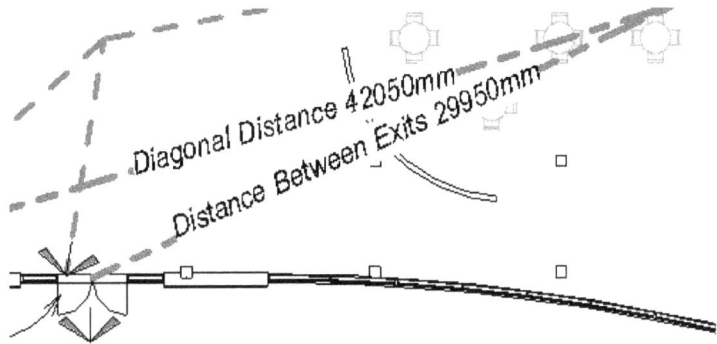

Figure 14–42

10. Save the project.

14.4 Creating Legends

Autodesk Certification Topics & Objectives

Pro.   User

Views

- Create and manage legends   ✓

Learning Objective

- Create legends in a legend view using detail lines, text, legend components, detail components, and symbols.

A legend is a separate view in which you can list the symbols used in your project and provide explanatory notes next to them. They are typically in a table format. Legends can include a list of all annotation symbols you use in your drawings, such as door, window, and wall tags, as shown in Figure 14–43, as well as a list of materials, or elevations of window types used in the project.

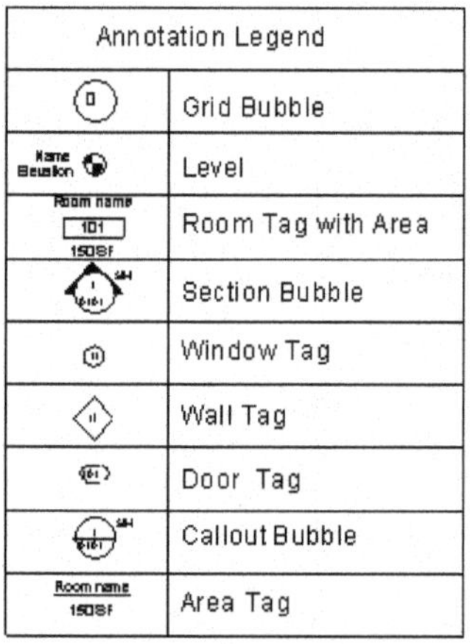

Annotation Legend	
⊙	Grid Bubble
Name Elevation ⊕	Level
Room name 101 150SF	Room Tag with Area
◆	Section Bubble
⊙	Window Tag
◇	Wall Tag
⊕	Door Tag
⊕	Callout Bubble
Room name 150SF	Area Tag

Figure 14–43

- You use ⌐ (Detail Lines) and A (Text) to create the table and explanatory notes. Once you have a legend view, you can use commands, such as ⊟ (Legend Component), ⊡ (Detail Component), and ⊕ (Symbol), to place elements in the drawing.

- Unlike other views, legend views can be attached to more than one sheet.

- You can set a legend's scale in the View Status Bar.

- Elements in legends can be dimensioned.

How To: Create a Legend

1. In the *View* tab>Create panel, expand ▦ (Legends) and

   click ▦ (Legend) or in the Project Browser, right-click on the *Legends* area title and select **New Legend**.
2. In the New Legend View dialog box, enter a name and select a scale for the legend, as shown in Figure 14–44, and click

   OK .

Figure 14–44

3. Place the components in the view first, and then sketch the outline of the table when you know the sizes. Use **Ref Planes** to line up the components.

How To: Use Legend Components

1. In the *Annotate* tab>Detail panel, expand ▱ (Component)

   and click ▦ (Legend Component).
2. In the Options Bar, select the *Family* type that you want to use, as shown in Figure 14–45. This list contains all of the elements in a drawing that can be used in a legend. For example, you might want to display the elevation of all door types used in the project.

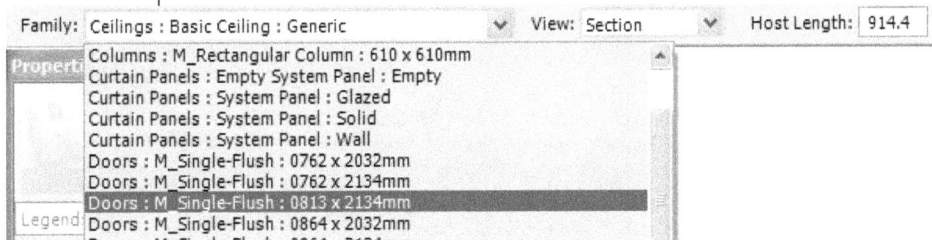

Figure 14–45

---

3. Select the *View* of the element that you want to use. For example, you might want to display the section of the floors or roofs, and the front elevation of the doors (as shown in Figure 14–46) and windows.

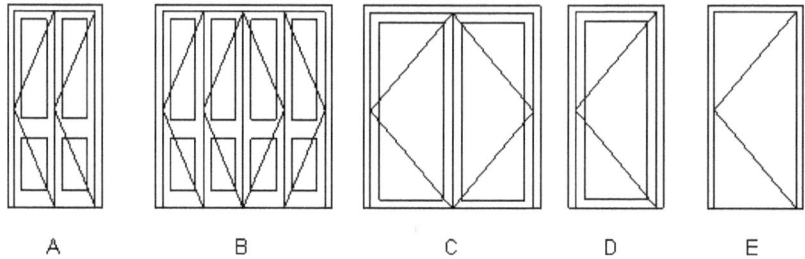

A   B   C   D   E

Door Elevations
1 : 50

Figure 14–46

4. For section elements (such as walls, floors, and roofs), type a distance for the *Host Length*.

- Elements that are full size, such as planting components or doors, come in at their full size.

Practice 14c | Create Legends

Learning Objective

- Create door and window legends using elevation legend components and text.

Estimated time for completion: 10 minutes

In this practice you will create door and window legends (as shown in Figure 14–47), create legend views, add detail components, and label doors and windows with text

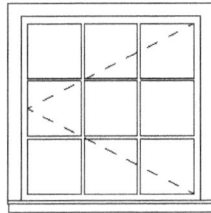

13

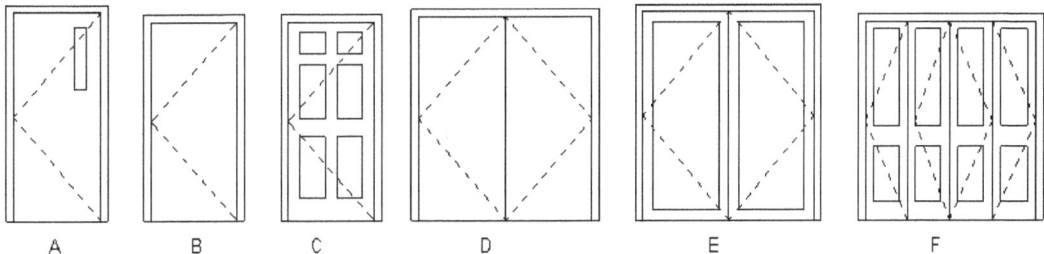

Figure 14–47

Task 1 - Add window and door legends.

1. Open the project **Modern-Hotel-Legends-M.rvt** from your class folder.

2. In the *View* tab>Create panel, expand 🔲 (Legends) and click 🔲 (Legend) to create a new Legend view.

3. Name it **Window Elevations** and set the *Scale* to **1:50**.

4. In the *Annotate* tab>Detail panel, expand 🔲 (Component) and click 🔲 (Legend Component).

5. In the Options Bar, set *Family* to **Windows : Casement 3 x 3 with Trim: 1220x1220mm** and *View* to **Elevation: Front**. Place the component in the view. The window displays, as shown in Figure 14–48.

6. In the *Annotate* tab>Text panel, click **A** (Text).

7. In the Type Selector, select **Text: 3mm Arial Narrow** and add the window number 13 under the window, as shown in Figure 14–48.

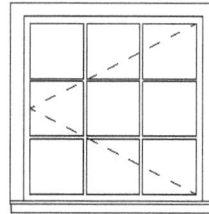

13

Figure 14–48

8. Create another Legend view. Name it **Door Elevations** and set the *Scale* to **1:50**.

9. In the Legend view, click (Legend Component) and add the elevations of the doors used in the project.

10. Label the doors as shown in Figure 14–49.

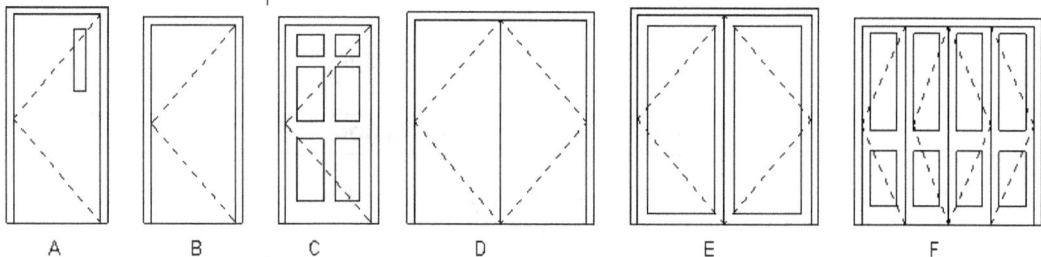

A   B   C   D   E   F

Figure 14–49

11. Save the project.

Chapter Review Questions

1. When a wall is moved (as shown in Figure 14–50), how do you update the dimension?

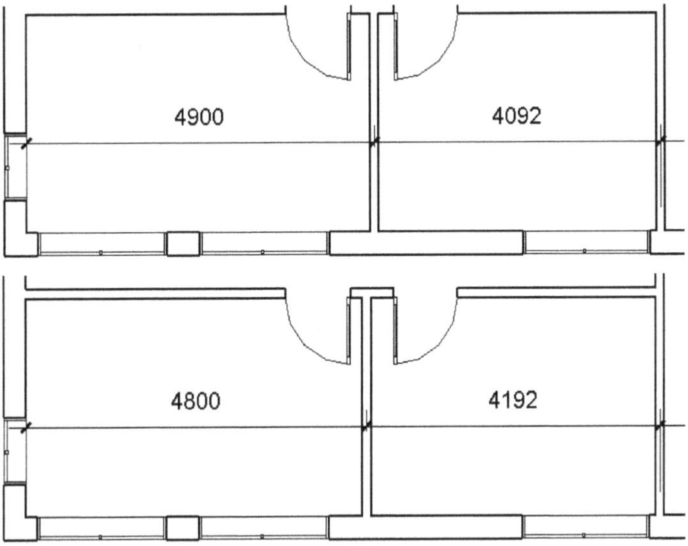

Figure 14–50

   a. Edit the dimension and move it over.

   b. Select the dimension and then click the **Update** button in the Options Bar.

   c. The dimension automatically updates.

   d. Delete the existing dimension and add a new one.

2. How do you create new text styles?

   a. Using the **Text Styles** command.

   b. Duplicate an existing type.

   c. They must be included in a template.

   d. Using the **Format Styles** command.

3. When you edit text, how many leaders can be added using the leader tools shown in Figure 14–51?

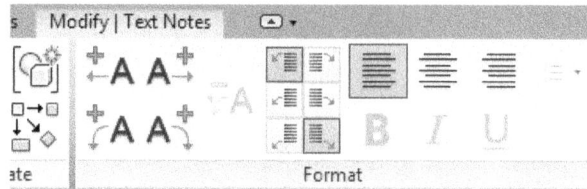

Figure 14–51

a. One

b. One on each end of the text.

c. As many as you want at each end of the text.

4. Detail Lines created in one view also display in the related view.

a. True

b. False

5. Which of the following describes the difference between a symbol and a component?

a. Symbols are 3D and only display in one view. Components are 2D and display in many views.

b. Symbols are 2D and only display in one view. Components are 3D and display in many views.

c. Symbols are 2D and display in many views. Components are 3D and only display in one view.

d. Symbols are 3D and display in many views. Components are 2D and only display in one view.

6. When creating a Legend, which of the following elements cannot be added?

a. Legend Components

b. Tags

c. Rooms

d. Symbols

Command Summary

Button	Command	Location
	Aligned (Dimension)	• **Ribbon:** *Annotate* tab>Dimension panel>Aligned or *Modify* tab>Measure panel, expanded drop-down list • **Quick Access Toolbar** • **Shortcut:** \<D\> and \<I\>
	Angular (Dimension)	• **Ribbon:** *Annotate* tab>Dimension panel>Angular or *Modify* tab> Measure panel, expanded drop-down list
	Arc Length (Dimension)	• **Ribbon:** *Annotate* tab>Dimension panel>Arc Length or *Modify* tab> Measure panel, expanded drop-down list
	Diameter (Dimension)	• **Ribbon:** *Annotate* tab> Dimension panel>Diameter or *Modify* tab> Measure panel, expanded drop-down list
	Detail Line	• **Ribbon:** *Annotate* tab>Detail panel> Detail Line • **Shortcut:** \<D\> and \<L\>
	Linear (Dimension)	• **Ribbon:** *Annotate* tab>Dimension panel>Linear or *Modify* tab>Measure panel, expanded drop-down list
	Radial (Dimension)	• **Ribbon:** *Annotate* tab>Dimension panel>Radial or *Modify* tab>Measure panel, expanded drop-down list
	Stair Path	• **Ribbon:** *Annotate* tab>Symbol panel>Stair Path
	Symbol	• **Ribbon:** *Annotate* tab>Symbol panel>Symbol
	Text	• **Ribbon:** *Annotate* tab>Text panel> Text • **Shortcut:** \<T\> and \<X\>
	Legend	• **Ribbon:** *View* tab>Create panel> expand Legends>Legend
	Legend Component	• **Ribbon:** *Annotate* tab>Detail panel> expand Component>Legend Component

Chapter 15

Adding Tags and Schedules

In this chapter you learn how to add tags to individual and multiple elements. You learn about rooms and how to add room tags. You also review schedules, how they update, and how to modify them in the schedule view and on a sheet.

This chapter contains the following topics:

- **Adding Tags**
- **Adding Rooms and Tags**
- **Working with Schedules**

15.1 Adding Tags

Autodesk Certification Topics & Objectives

Pro.   User

Documentation

- Tag elements (doors, windows, etc.) by category   ✓   ✓

Learning Objectives

- Add tags in 2D and 3D views individually or to all of the elements at the same time.
- Load tags that are needed for projects.

Tags identify elements that are listed in schedules. Door and window tags come in automatically if you use the **Tag on Placement** option when inserting the door or window. You can also add them later. Many other types of tags are available in the Autodesk® Revit® software, such as room tags and furniture tags, as shown in Figure 15–1.

There are tags for many elements, including doors, stairs, curtain panels, and plants. These tags are stored in the Annotations folder in the Library.

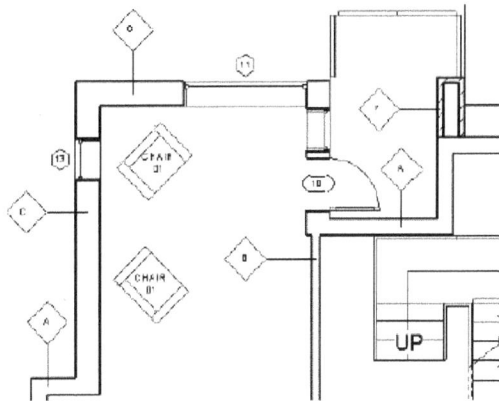

Figure 15–1

- The **Tag** command places all types of tags manually for most elements, except for a few that have separate commands.

You can place three types of tags, as follows:

- **(Tag by Category):** Tags according to the category of the element. It places door tags on doors and wall tags on walls.

- **(Multi-Category):** Tags elements belonging to multiple categories. The tags display information from parameters that they have in common.

- **(Material):** Tags that display the type of material. They are typically used in detailing.

How To: Add Tags

1. In the *Annotate* tab>Tag panel, click (Tag by Category), (Multi-Category), or (Material) depending on the type of tag you want to place.
2. In the Options Bar, set the options as required, as shown in Figure 15–2.

Figure 15–2

3. Select the element you want to tag. The appropriate tag is applied for the type of element selected. If the tag is not loaded, you are prompted to load it from the Library.

Tag Options

You can set tag options for leaders and tag rotation, as shown in Figure 15–3. You can also press the <Spacebar> to toggle the orientation while placing the tag or when modifying it.

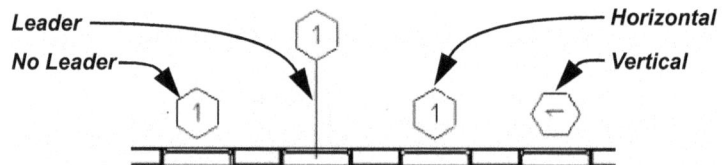

Figure 15–3

- Leaders can have an **Attached End** or a **Free End**, as shown in Figure 15–4. The attached end must be connected to the element being tagged. A free end has an additional drag control where the leader touches the element.

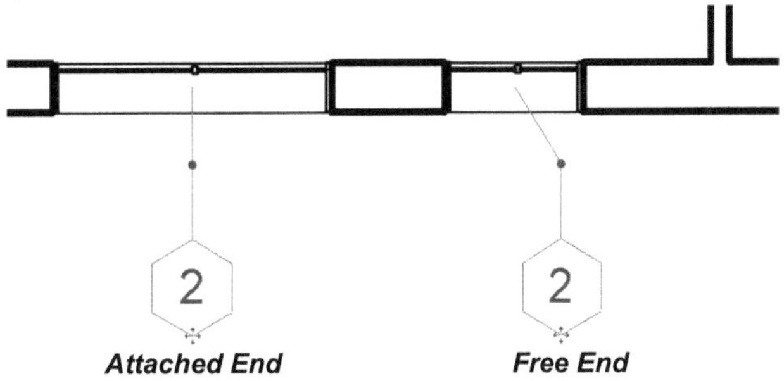

Attached End   **Free End**

Figure 15–4

- The **Length** option specifies the length of the leader in plotting units. It is grayed out if the **Leader** option is not selected or if a **Free End** leader is defined.

- If a tag is not loaded a warning box opens as shown in Figure 15–5. Click [Yes] to open the Load Family dialog box in which you can select the appropriate tag.

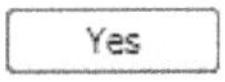

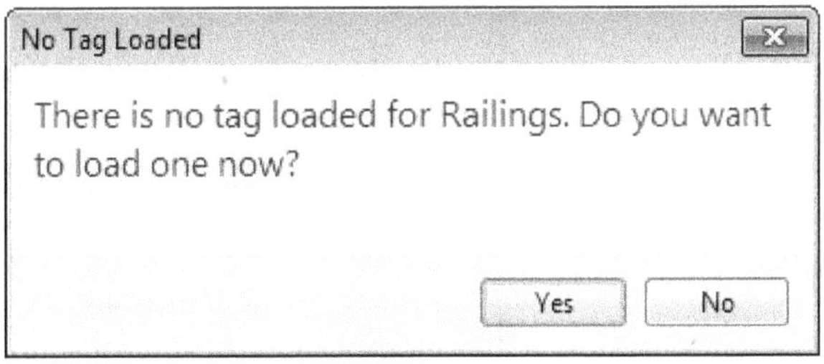

Figure 15–5

- To load tags, you can click `Tags...` in the Options Bar when a **Tag** command is active, or, in the *Annotate* tab, expand the Tag panel and click 🔌 (Loaded Tags). This opens the Tags dialog box, which displays the tags that have been loaded and load additional tags, as shown in Figure 15–6. Most tags are stored in the *Annotations* folder in the Library.

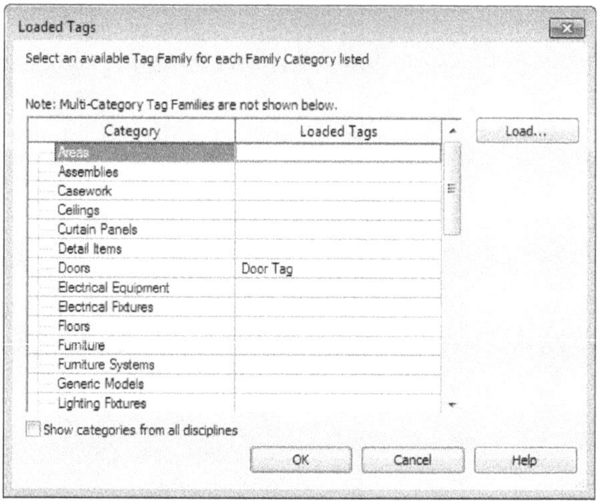

Figure 15–6

Instance vs.Type Based Tags

Doors are tagged in a numbered sequence, with each instance of the door having a separate tag number. Other elements (such as windows and walls) are tagged by type, as shown in Figure 15–7. Changing the information in one tag changes all instances of that element.

*An additional window tag (**Window Tag-Number.rfa**) is stored in the Annotations> Architectural folder in the Library. It tags windows using sequential numbers.*

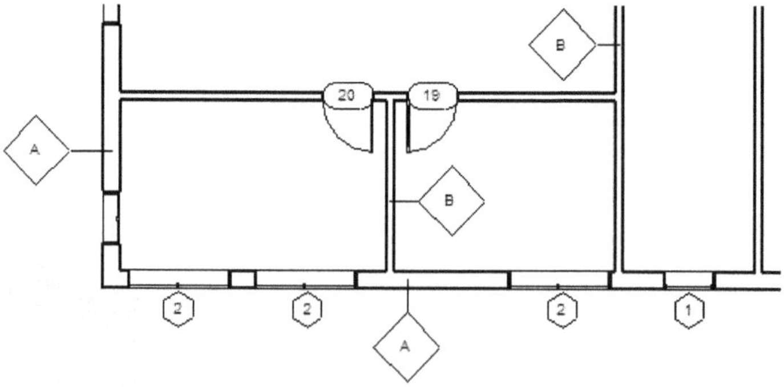

Figure 15–7

- In Properties or the Options Bar, change the *Leader* and *Orientation* of any type of tag.

- Tags can be letters or numbers, or a combination of the two.

- To modify the number of an instance tag (such as a door or room), you can double-click directly on the number in the tag and modify it. Alternatively, you can select the element (not the tag) and in Properties, in the *Identity Data* area, modify the *Mark* as shown in Figure 15–8. Only that one instance updates.

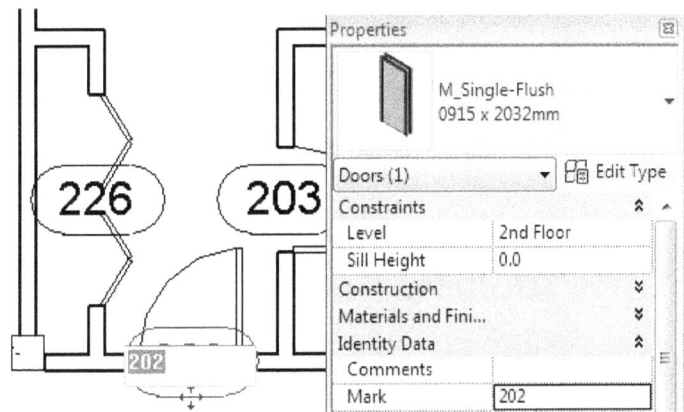

Figure 15–8

- To modify the number of a type tag (such as a window or wall), you can either click directly on the number in the tag and modify it, or select the element and, in Properties, click

  (Edit Type). In the Type Properties dialog box, in the *Identity Data* area, modify the *Type Mark*, as shown in Figure 15–9. All instances of this element then update.

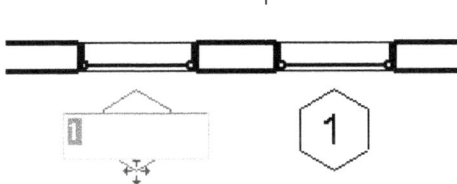

Figure 15–9

- Some tags (such as wall tags) come in empty, as shown in Figure 15–10. You can select the empty tag, click on the question mark, and type a number. Doing so changes all instances of the wall type in the project.

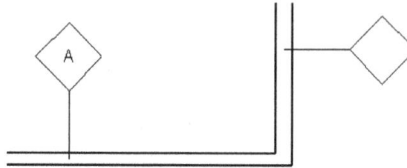

Figure 15–10

When you change a number for a type tag (such as a wall or window), an alert box opens, warning you that changing a type parameter affects other elements. If you want this tag to modify all other elements of this type, click [Yes].

Tagging in 3D Views

You can add tags (and some dimensions) to 3D views, as shown in Figure 15–11, as long as the views are locked first. You can only add tags in isometric views.

Figure 15–11

How To: Lock a 3D View

1. Open a 3D view and set it up as you want it to display.

2. In the View Control Bar, expand 🏠 (Unlocked 3D View) and click 🔒 (Save Orientation and Lock View).

- If you are using the default 3D view and it has not been saved, you are prompted to name and save the view first.

- You can modify the orientation of the view, expand 🔒 (Locked 3D View) and click 🏠 (Unlock View). This also removes any tags you have applied.

• To return to the previous locked view, expand 🏠 (Unlocked

3D View) and click 🏠 (Restore Orientation and Lock View).

Tagging Multiple Elements

If you have not applied tags to doors, windows, walls, or rooms, you can quickly tag them in a view using the **Tag All Not Tagged** command. For example, if you want to show tags in an elevation (as shown in Figure 15–12), or if you copy windows and doors in a plan view, you can tag all of the new elements at the same time.

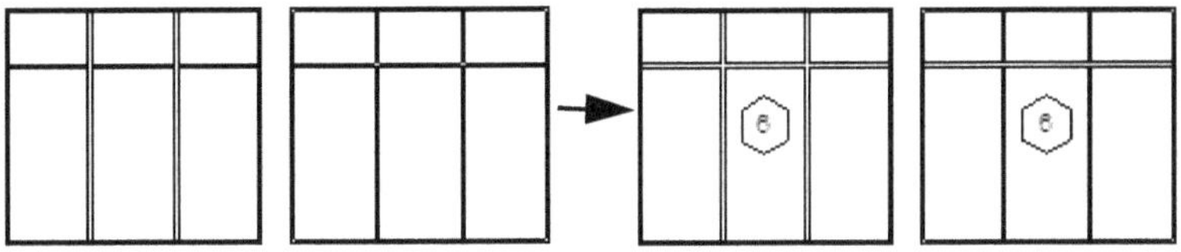

Figure 15–12

How To: Add Multiple Tags

1. In the *Annotate* tab>Tag panel, click 🏷️ (Tag All).
2. Select one or more categories that you want to tag, as shown in Figure 15–13. You can select more than one category by holding down <Shift> or <Ctrl>. Set the *Leader* and *Orientation* as required.

*To only tag some elements, select them before starting this command. In the Tag All Not Tagged dialog box, select the **Only selected objects in the current view** option.*

Figure 15–13

3. Click [Apply] to stay in the dialog box and continue

applying to other categories. Click [OK] to apply the tags and close the dialog box.

Hint: Stair and Railing Tags

Tag by Category can be used to tag the overall stair, stair runs, landings, and railings, as shown in Figure 15–14. An additional type of tag, **Stair Tread/Riser Number**, creates a sequence of numbers for each tread or riser.

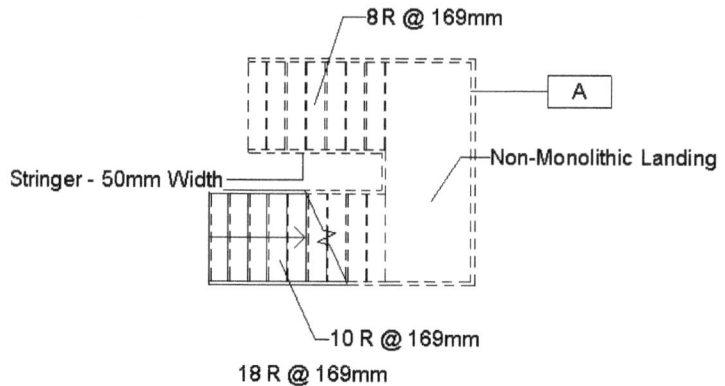

8 R @ 169mm

A

Non-Monolithic Landing

Stringer - 50mm Width

10 R @ 169mm

18 R @ 169mm

Figure 15–14

How To: Add Tread and Riser Numbers to Stairs

1. Open a plan, elevation, or section view.

2. In the *Annotate* tab>Tag panel, click ✏ (Stair Tread/Riser Number).

3. Select a reference line of a stair to place the numbers, as shown in Figure 15–15.

Runs : Monolithic Run

Figure 15–15

4. Continue selecting runs as required.

Practice 15a | Add Tags

Learning Objectives

- Add wall tags to different walls and modify the **Type Mark** parameter for each wall type.
- Use **Tag All Not Tagged** to add wall tags to the additional walls.

Estimated time for completion: 10 minutes

In this practice you will add wall tags in a floor plan and modify the Type Mark numbers for the walls. You will also tag all of the walls using **Tag All Not Tagged**, as shown in Figure 15–16.

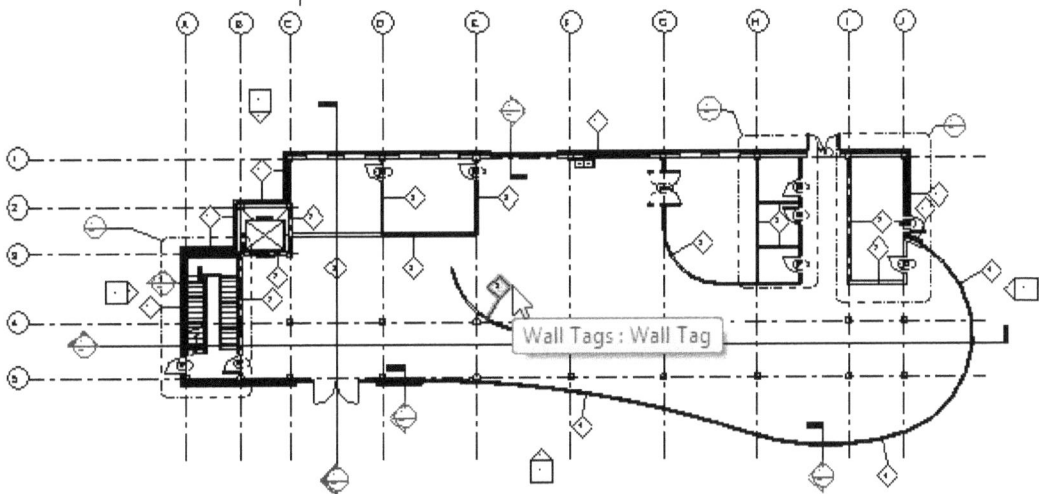

Figure 15–16

Task 1 - Add tags to a floor plan.

1. Open the project **Modern-Hotel-Tags-M.rvt** from your class folder.

2. In the **Floor Plans: Floor 1** view, zoom into the elevator and stair area near the left side of the building.

3. In the *Annotate* tab>Tag panel, click (Tag by Category). In the Options Bar, select **Leader** and verify that the **Attached End** option is selected.

Autodesk Revit 2015 Architecture Fundamentals

4. Select the exterior wall, as shown in Figure 15–17.

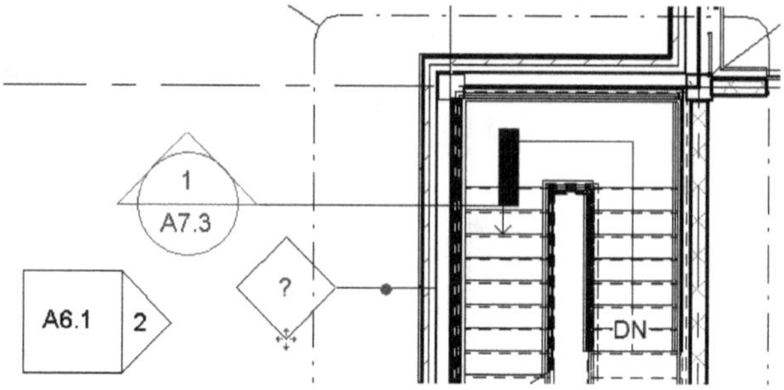

Figure 15–17

5. The tag comes in with a question mark because the wall does not have a *Type Mark* set yet. Click on the **?** in the tag and change the tag number to **1** and press <Enter>.

6. When alerted that you are changing a type parameter, click [Yes] to continue.

7. You are still in the **Tag** command. Add a tag to another exterior wall. This time, the tag number 1 comes in automatically as it is the same wall type as the first one.

8. Return to the **Modify** command.

9. Select the masonry wall dividing the stairs from the lobby.

10. In Properties, click ▥ (Edit Type).

11. In the Type Properties dialog box, in *Identity Data* area, set *Type Mark* to **2**, as shown in Figure 15–18. Click [OK].

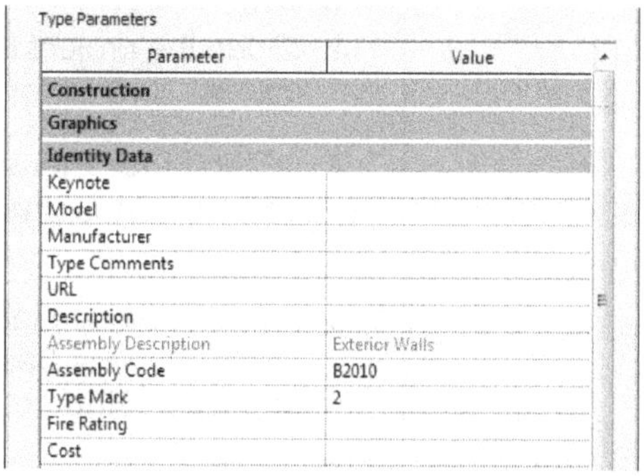

Figure 15–18

15–12   © 2014, ASCENT - Center for Technical Knowledge®

12. Select one of the interior partitions and set the *Type Mark* to **3**.

13. Use $\stackrel{\textstyle\frown}{\text{\scriptsize(1)}}$ (Tag By Category) to tag one of each of the wall types. The Type Mark displays as set in the Type Properties.

14. Zoom out to display the entire floor plan.

15. Save the project.

Task 2 - Tag all the rest of the walls and modify tag locations.

---

1. In the *Annotate* tab>Tag panel, click $\stackrel{\textstyle\frown}{\text{\scriptsize(1)}}$ (Tag All).

2. In the Tag All Not Tagged dialog box, set the *Wall Tags* category to the **12mm** tag type and select **Leader** as shown in Figure 15–19.

Tag All Not Tagged	
Select at least one Category and Tag Family to tag non-tagged objects:	

◉ All objects in current view
○ Only selected objects in current view
☐ Include elements from linked files

Category	Loaded Tags
Door Tags	M_Door Tag
Room Tags	M_Room Tag : Room Tag
Room Tags	M_Room Tag : Room Tag With Ar
Room Tags	M_Room Tag : Room Tag With Vo
Structural Framing Tags	M_Structural Framing Tag : Boxed
Structural Framing Tags	M_Structural Framing Tag : Stand
Wall Tags	M_Wall Tag : 12mm
Wall Tags	M_Wall Tag : 8mm
Window Tags	M_Window Tag

Leader
☑ Create Length: 12.7 m

Orientation:
Horizontal ▼

OK	Cancel	Apply	Help

Figure 15–19

3. Click [OK] to add wall tags where they have not already been added.

---

4. Many of the tags overlap other annotation objects. Use the controls to move the tags and/or leaders to a more visible location, as shown in Figure 15–20.

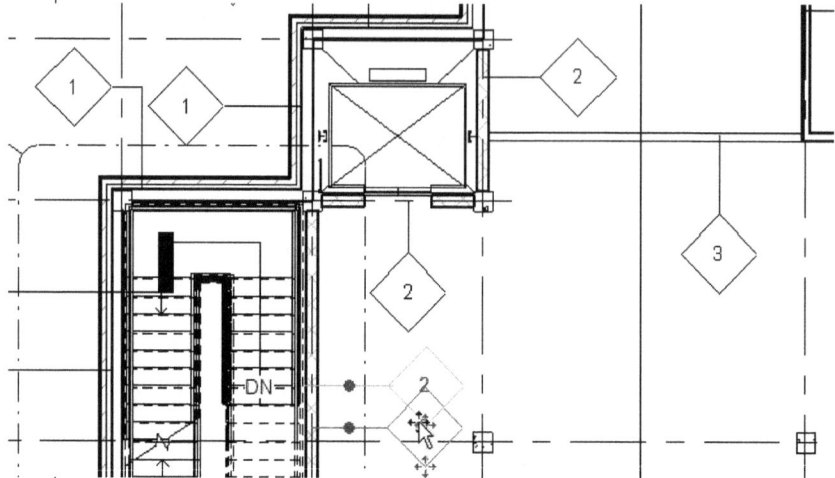

Figure 15–20

5. Update the tag for the main curtain wall to type number **4**.

6. Delete the wall tags that identify the storefront (inset) curtain walls along the back of the building and at the entrance. Delete any other wall tags you do not need to fully annotate the floor plan.

7. Save the project.

15.2 Adding Rooms and Tags

Learning Objectives

- Add room elements and room separation lines.
- Display rooms in color to indicate where they are.
- Add room tags.

Room tags are a special type of tag associated with room elements. Room elements are important for room names and numbers as well as adding room information to schedules. You can place a room element in any space bounded by walls, as shown in Figure 15–21, or by room separation lines. Room separation lines enable you to divide an open space into more rooms.

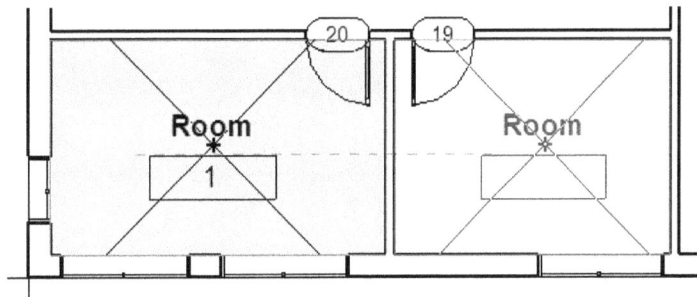

Figure 15–21

- To make the rooms display, in the Visibility/Graphic Overrides dialog box, expand **Rooms** and select **Interior Fill** and/or **Reference** as shown in Figure 15–22.

If these two options are cleared (not on), you can still select rooms by hovering the cursor over them, unless Rooms are turned off.

Figure 15–22

- **Color Fill** is used when a color scheme is applied to a view.

How To: Add Rooms

1. In the *Architecture* tab>Room & Area panel, click

   ⊠ (Room).
2. Move the cursor inside a boundary and click to place room element. If you have **Tag on Placement** active, it also places the tag at the point you selected.
3. Continue clicking inside boundaries to add other rooms.
4. Press <Esc> to finish the command.

How To: Add Room Separation Lines

1. In the *Architecture* tab>Room & Area panel, expand

   ⊠ (Room) and click ⊠ (Room Separation Line).
2. Use the Draw tools to place lines that divide the spaces.
3. After creating the room separation lines use the **Room** command to add the rooms, as shown in Figure 15–23.

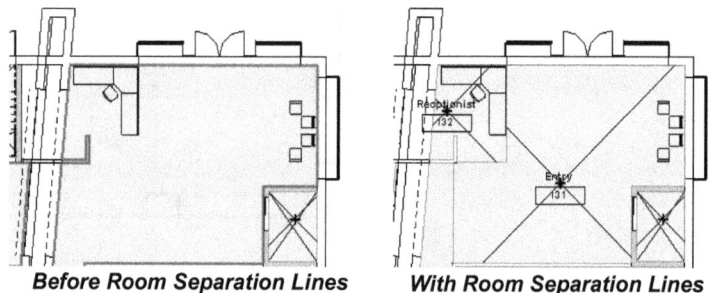

Before Room Separation Lines   **With Room Separation Lines**

Figure 15–23

Room Tags

A room tag (as shown in Figure 15–24), is placed when the room

is added if ⌐① (Tag on Placement) is toggled on in the *Modify | Place Room* tab>Tag Panel.

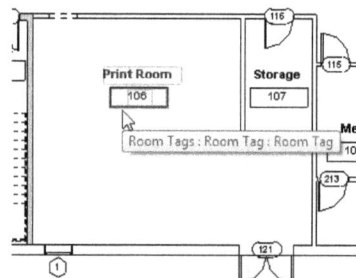

Figure 15–24

- You can also add tags to rooms after they are created. In the Architecture tab>Room & Area panel, expand ▣ (Tag) and click ▣ (Room Tag) or use ▣ (Tag All Not Tagged).

- Tags come in with the default name of *Room*. You can change the name by clicking on the tag to edit it, as shown in Figure 15–25.

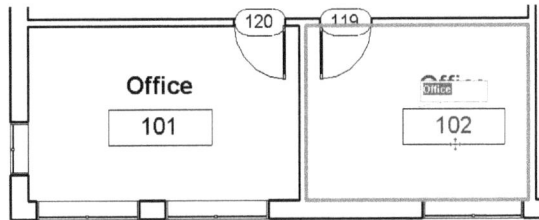

Figure 15–25

- Numbers increment automatically as you place rooms. Select the first room on a floor, change the number as required, and then select the rest of the room locations.

- To change the names of several room tags to the same name, select the room elements and change the *Name* parameter in Properties, as shown in Figure 15–26.

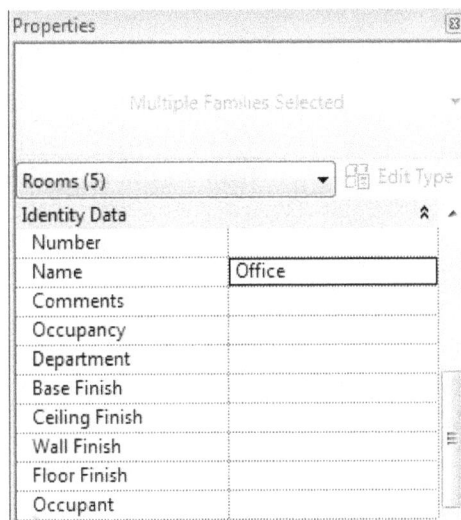

Figure 15–26

- Other information, such as finishes, can also be added in the room properties. This information is also made available to schedules.

Practice 15b

Add Rooms and Room Tags

Learning Objectives

- Set up a view that displays rooms.
- Add rooms and room separation lines.
- Add room tags to an additional view.

Estimated time for completion: 10 minutes

In this practice you will set up a view that displays rooms, add rooms to the model, change the names and numbers of rooms using tags and Properties, and add room separation lines, as shown in Figure 15–27. You will also add room tags to a view where the room elements are not displayed.

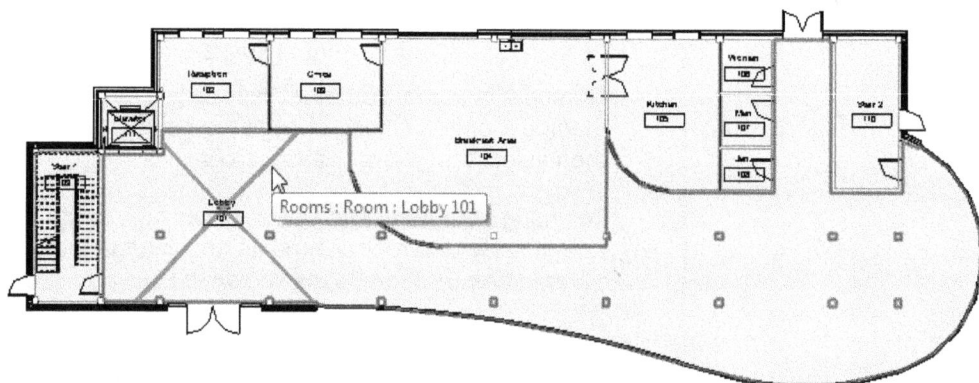

Figure 15–27

Task 1 - Set up a view that displays rooms.

1. Open the project **Modern-Hotel-Rooms-M.rvt** from the class folder.

2. In the Project Browser, right-click on the **Floor Plans: Floor 1** view and select **Duplicate View>Duplicate**.

3. Rename the new view to **Floor 1 - Rooms**.

4. Hide the gridlines and all elevation and section markers.

5. Open the Visibility/Graphic Overrides dialog box. In the *Model Categories* tab, expand **Rooms,** and select **Interior Fill**, as shown in Figure 15–28.

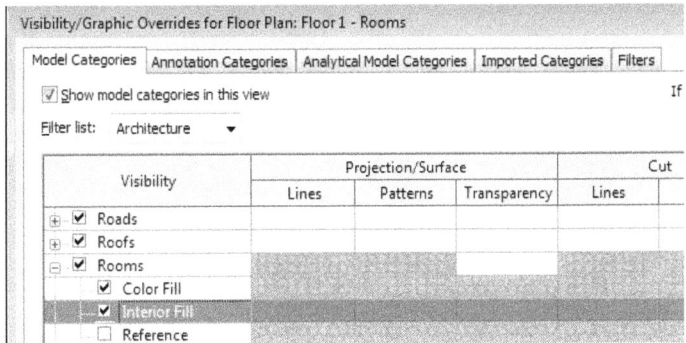

Figure 15–28

6. Nothing displays in the view as there are no rooms in the project.

7. Save the project.

Task 2 - Add rooms and room tags.

---

1. In the *Architecture* tab>Room & Area panel, click ⬚ (Tag Room). Click inside the lobby area. You cannot place the room tag because a room element is not assigned to the area.

2. In the *Architecture* tab>Room & Area panel, click ⬚ (Room) and place a room element inside the lobby area. The room tag comes in by default.

3. Return to the **Modify** command and change the name of the room and the room number, as shown in Figure 15–29. Click in empty space to finish the command.

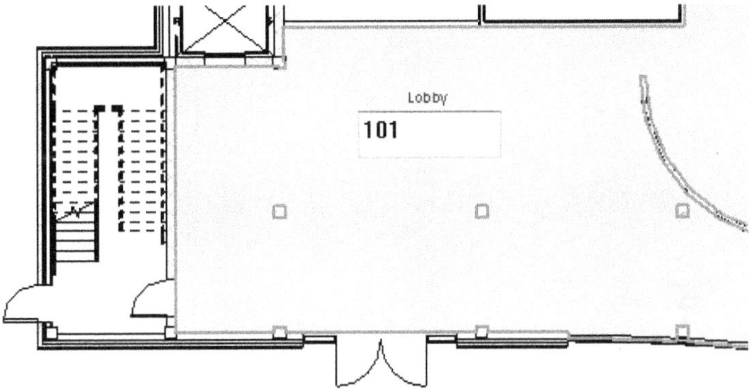

Figure 15–29

---

4. Click ⊠ (Room) again. In the *Modify I Place Room* tab, toggle off the **Tag on Placement** option. Place the room element in the check in area (the small room next to the elevator) and finish the command. Select the room element.

5. In Properties, in the *Identity Data* area, note that the *Number* is automatically set to **102**. Set the *Name* as **Reception** (as shown in Figure 15–30) and click ⌈ Apply ⌉.

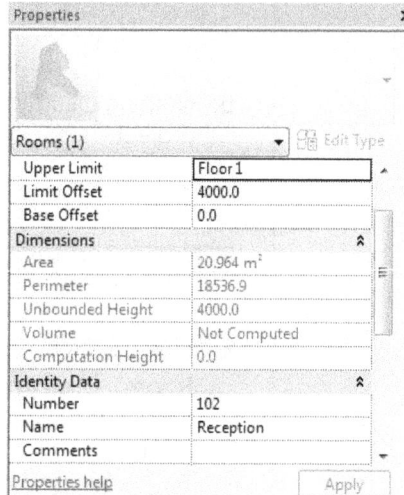

Figure 15–30

6. In the *Architecture* tab>Room & Area panel, click ⊠ (Tag Room).

7. Tag the new room and press <Esc>. The tag is displayed with the name you specified in Properties, as shown in Figure 15–31.

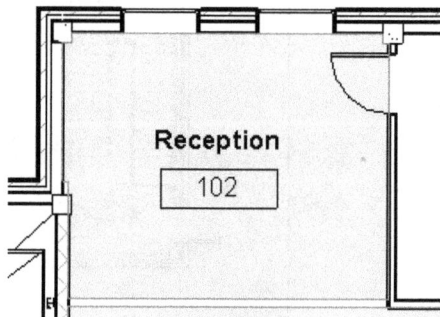

Figure 15–31

8. Add a room and tag in the room to the right of the Reception room and name it **Office**.

9. Save the project.

Task 3 - Add Room Separation Lines and additional rooms.

1. In the *Architecture* tab>Room & Area panel, click 🔲 (Room Separator).

2. Draw room separation lines to separate the breakfast area from the main lobby as shown in Figure 15–32.

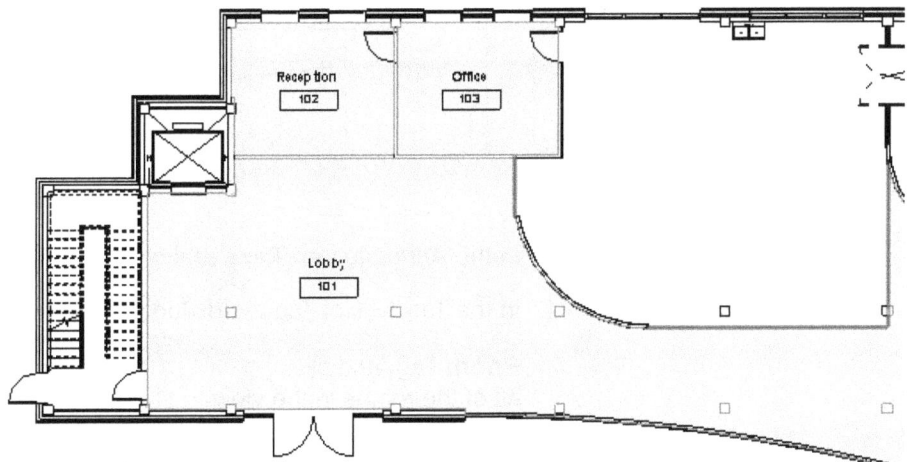

Figure 15–32

3. Using 🔲 (Room) with the **Tag on Placement** option toggled on. in Properties, in the *Name* field, type **Breakfast Area**, and then place the room in that location.

4. Continue to add room elements and room tags to the rest of the rooms on the first floor. Rename the rooms as required.

   • If a room tag is too large for the room, toggle on the **Leader** option and move the tag. If the **Leader** option is not toggled on, the tag is orphaned from the room.

5. Save the project.

Task 4 - Add Room Tags to another view.

1. Open the **Floor Plans: Floor 1** view.

2. Although you do not see the rooms in the view, you can roll the cursor over the rooms in the plan and select the room elements, as shown in Figure 15–33.

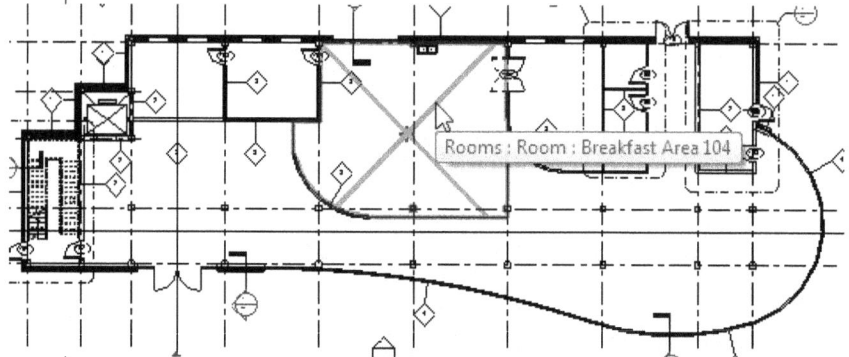

Rooms : Room : Breakfast Area 104

Figure 15–33

3. In the *Annotate* tab>Tag panel click (Tag All).

4. In the Tag All Not Tagged dialog box, select **Room Tags: Room Tag,** and click OK. Room tags are added to all of the rooms in the view.

5. Zoom in and clean up the view by moving the various tags so that they do not overlap, as shown in Figure 15–34.

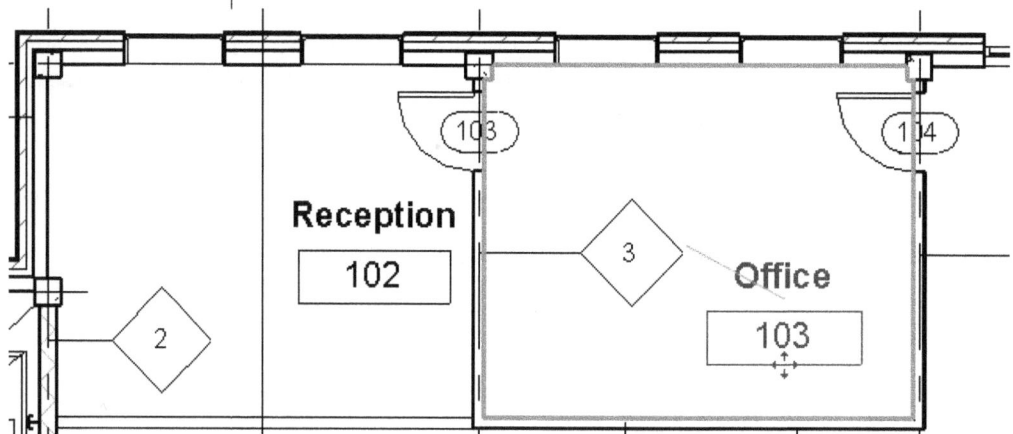

Reception
102

Office
103

Figure 15–34

6. Save the project.

15.3 Working with Schedules

Autodesk Certification Topics & Objectives

Pro.   User

Views

- Define element properties in a schedule   ✓

Learning Objectives

- Open schedules and modify schedule cells that are not filled out automatically.
- Add schedules to sheets and modify them so that they fit.
- Import schedule styles from other projects and export schedule information to a spreadsheet.

Schedules extract information from a project and display it in table form. They gather property information from doors, windows, walls, rooms, and other elements. Each schedule is stored as a separate view and can be placed on sheets, as shown in Figure 15–35. Any changes you make to the project that affect the schedules are automatically updated in both views and sheets.

Schedules are typically included in project templates. Ask your BIM Manager for more information about your company's schedules.

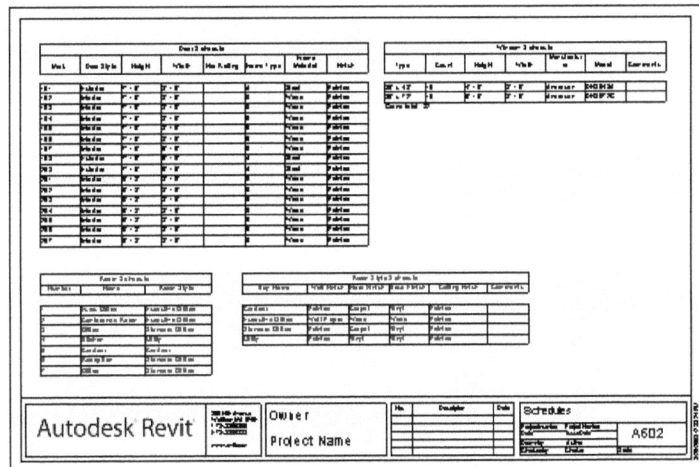

Figure 15–35

How To: Work with Schedules

1. In the Project Browser, expand the *Schedules/Quantities* area, as shown in Figure 15–36, and double-click on the schedule you want to open.

⊟ ▦ Schedules/Quantities
         Door Schedule
         Room Schedule
         Wall Schedule

Figure 15–36

2. Schedules are automatically filled out with the information stored in the property parameters of related elements that are added to the model.
3. Fill out additional information in either the schedule or Properties. Some information is per instance and some is by type.
4. Drag and drop the schedule onto a sheet.

Modifying Schedules

When you make changes to scheduled elements (such as changing the size of a door or adding a fire rating in the Type Properties), the schedule automatically updates. You can also change information in the cells of the schedule table, which automatically updates the elements in the project.

The tools in the *Modify Schedule/Quantities* tab (as shown in Figure 15–37), are used to further modify the schedule table. The available tools depend on what you have selected in the table: the title, headers, or cells. The other tools are grayed out.

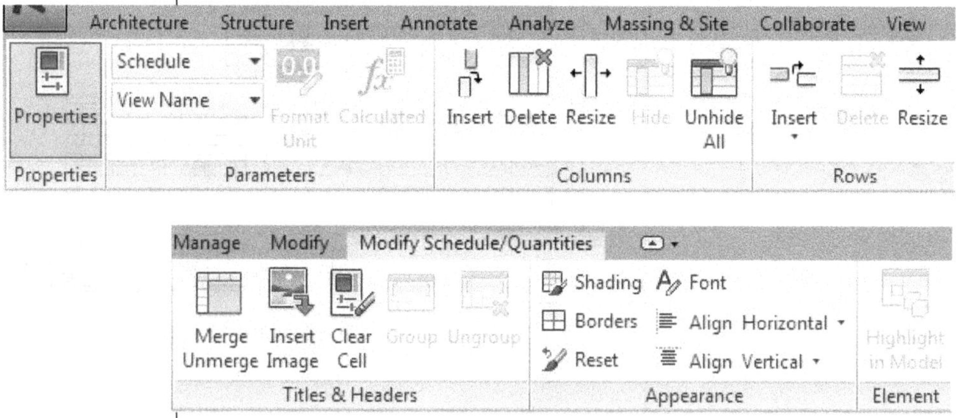

Figure 15–37

- Be careful about making changes using the Ribbon tools as you can easily alter the schedule that was created using the company or project standard.

How To: Modify Schedule Cells

1. Open the schedule view.
2. Select the cell you want to change. Some cells have drop-down lists, as shown in Figure 15–38. Others have edit fields.

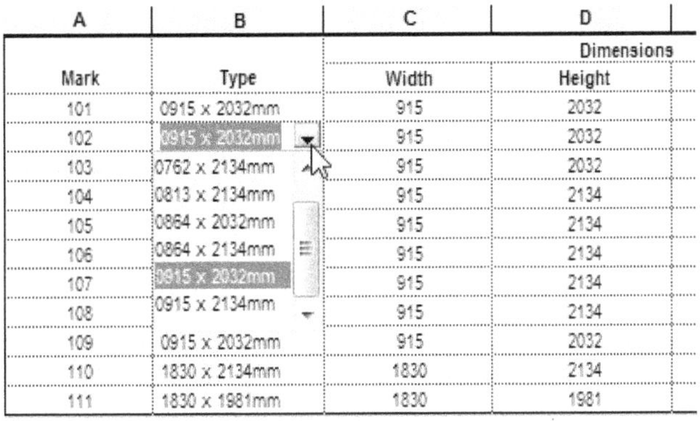

A	B	C	D
			Dimensions
Mark	Type	Width	Height
101	0915 x 2032mm	915	2032
102	0915 x 2032mm	915	2032
103	0762 x 2134mm	915	2032
104	0813 x 2134mm	915	2134
105	0864 x 2032mm	915	2134
106	0864 x 2134mm	915	2134
107	0915 x 2032mm	915	2134
108	0915 x 2134mm	915	2134
109	0915 x 2032mm	915	2032
110	1830 x 2134mm	1830	2134
111	1830 x 1981mm	1830	1981

Figure 15–38

3. Add the new information. The change is reflected in the schedule, on the sheet, and in the elements of the project.

• If you change a Type Property in the schedule, it applies to all elements of that type. If you change an Instance Property, it only applies to that instance.

• If you change a Type Property, an alert box opens as shown in Figure 15–39. Changing the schedule updates all related elements.

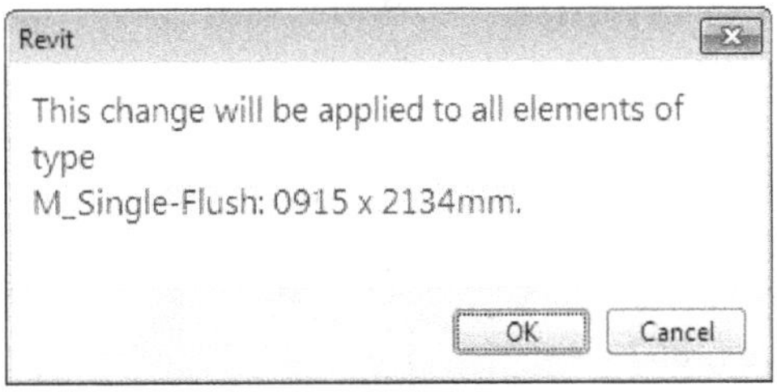

Revit

This change will be applied to all elements of type
M_Single-Flush: 0915 x 2134mm.

OK   Cancel

Figure 15–39

- When you select an element in a schedule, in the *Modify Schedule/Quantities* tab>Element panel, you can click

  (Highlight in Model). This opens a close-up view of the element with the Show Element(s) in View dialog box, as

  shown in Figure 15–40. Click [Show] to display more

  views of the element. Click [Close] to finish the command.

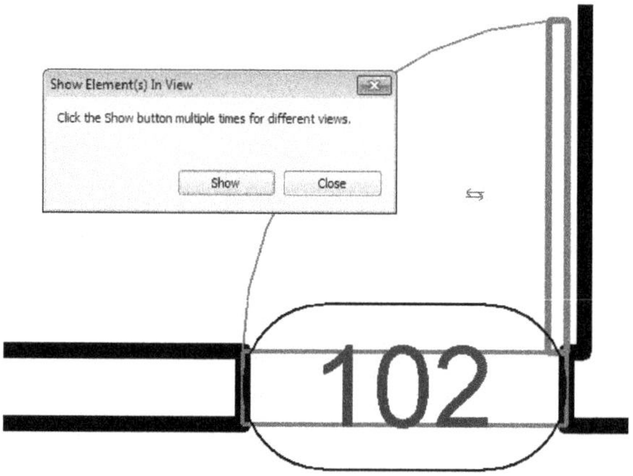

Figure 15–40

Modifying a Schedule on a Sheet

Once you have placed a schedule on a sheet, you can manipulate it to fit the information into the available space. Select the schedule to display the controls that enable you to modify it, as shown in Figure 15–41.

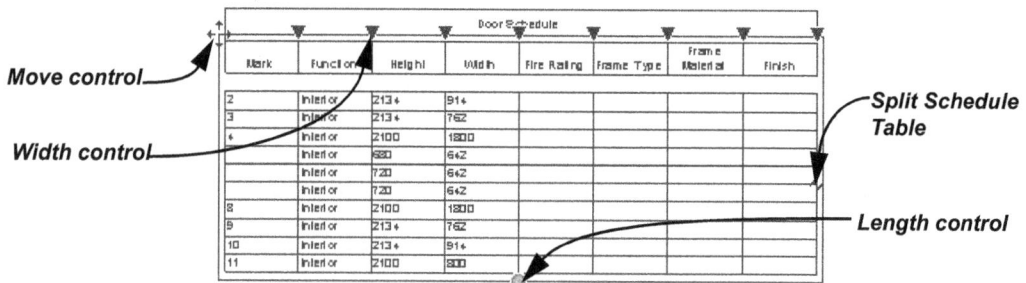

Figure 15–41

- The blue triangles modify the width of each column.

- The break mark splits the schedule into two parts.

- In each part of a split schedule, additional blue controls are displayed. The arrows in the center enable you to drag that portion of the schedule. The bottom circle on the first schedule enables you to modify the length of the schedule, which automatically impacts the other part(s) of the split, as shown in Figure 15–42.

Room Schedule		
Level	Number	Name
Not Placed	1	Room
Not Placed	2	Room
Not Placed	3	Room
First Floor	101	Office
First Floor	102	Office
First Floor	103	Studio
First Floor	104	Product Library
First Floor	105	Mech/Elec
First Floor	106	Stair 2
First Floor	107	Print Room
First Floor	108	Storage

Room Schedule		
Level	Number	Name
First Floor	109	Men
First Floor	110	Women
First Floor	111	Conference
First Floor	112	Storage
First Floor	113	Shower
First Floor	114	Chiller Enclosure Area
First Floor	115	Stair 1
Second Floor	116	Room
Second Floor	117	Room

Figure 15–42

- To unsplit a schedule, drag the Move control from the side of the schedule that you want to unsplit back to the original column.

Importing and Exporting Schedules

Schedules are views and can be copied into your project from other projects. Only the formatting information is copied; the information about individually scheduled items is not included. That information is automatically added by the project the schedule is copied into. You can also export the schedule information to be used in spreadsheets.

How To: Import Schedules

1. In the *Insert* tab>Import panel, expand 🗋 (Insert From File) and click ⬚ (Insert Views From File).
2. In the Open dialog box, locate the project file containing the schedule you want to use.

3. Select the schedules you want to import, as shown in Figure 15–43.

*If the referenced project contains many types of views, change Views: to **Show schedules and reports only**.*

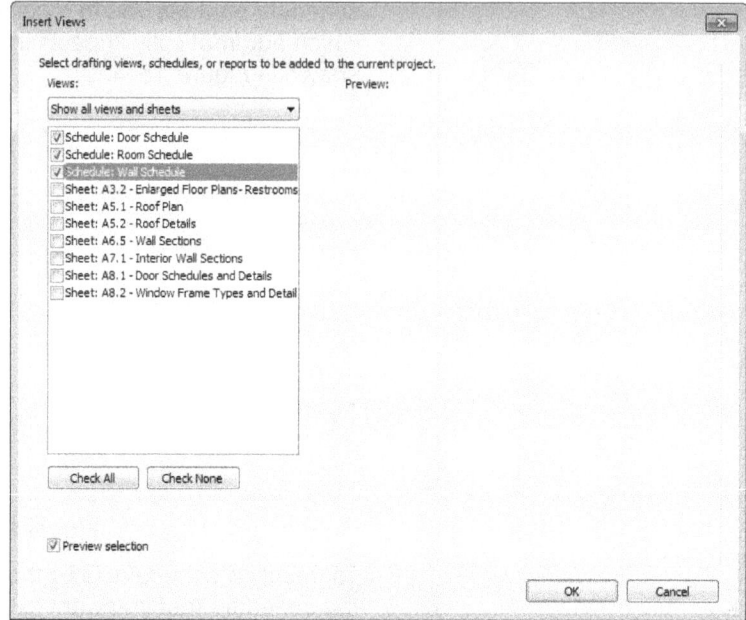

Figure 15–43

4. Click OK .

How To: Export Schedule Information

1. Switch to the schedule view that you want to export.

2. In the Application Menu, click (Export)> (Reports)> (Schedule).

3. Select a location and name for the text file in the Export Schedule dialog box and click Save .

4. In the Export Schedule dialog box, set the options in the *Schedule appearance* and *Output options* areas that best suit your spreadsheet software, as shown in Figure 15–44.

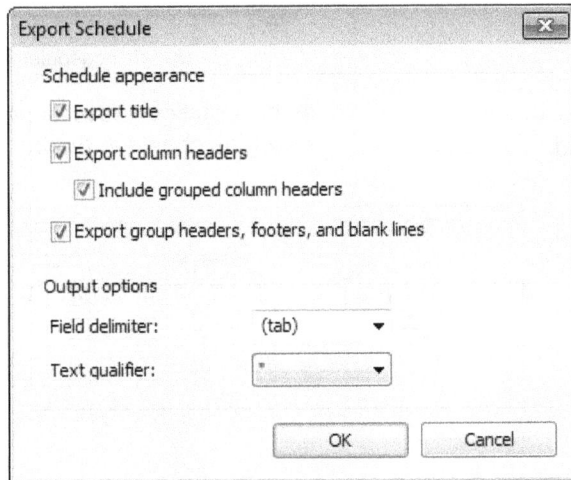

Figure 15–44

5. Click [OK]. A new text file is created that you can open in a spreadsheet, as shown in Figure 15–45.

Figure 15–45

Practice 15c

Work with Schedules

Learning Objective

- Update schedules and add schedules to sheets.

Estimated time for completion:10 minutes

In this practice you will update a schedule and place it on a sheet, as shown in Figure 15–46.

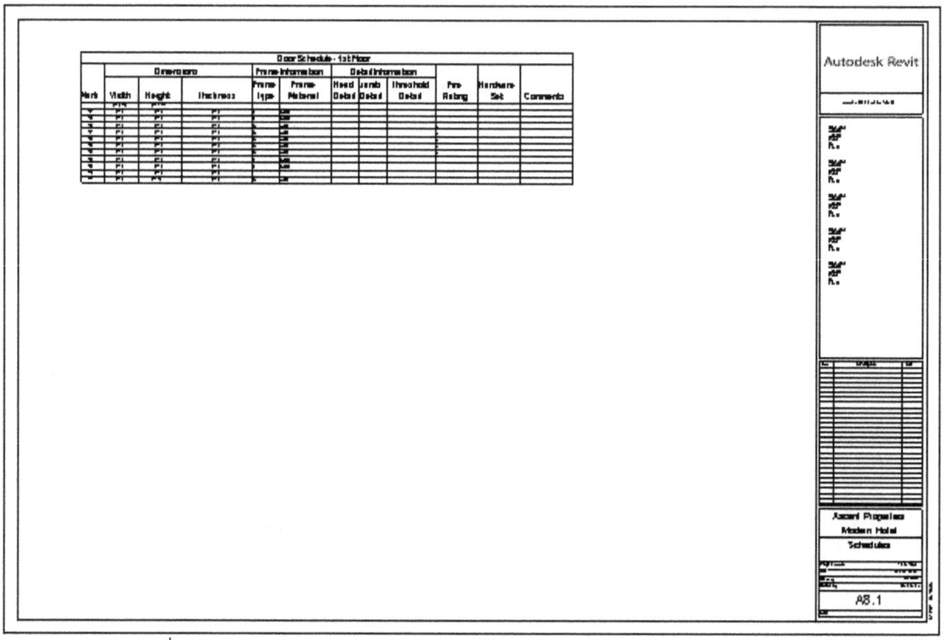

Figure 15–46

Task 1 - Fill in schedules.

1. Open the project **Modern-Hotel-Schedules-M.rvt** from the class folder.

2. In the Project Browser, expand *Schedules/Quantities*. Four schedules have been added to this project.

3. Double-click on **Door Schedule - 1st Floor** to open it. The existing doors in the project are already populated with some of the basic information included with the door, as shown in Figure 15–47.

Mark	Dimensions			Frame Information			
	Width	Height	Thickness	Frame Type	Frame Material	Head Detail	
	2350	2865					
101	915	2032	51				
102	915	2032	51				
103	915	2032	51				
104	915	2134	51				
105	915	2134	51				
106	915	2134	51				
107	915	2134	51				
108	915	2134	51				

Figure 15–47

4. The first door in the list does not have a mark associated with it. Click in the empty *Mark* cell. In the *Modify Schedules/ Quantities* tab>Element panel, click ⬚ (Highlight in Model). The front door that is part of a curtain wall displays and is highlighted, even though storefront doors are typically not included in Door Schedules. There are no other views to display. Click ⬚ Close in the Show Element(s) in View dialog box.

5. Select one of the single exterior doors other than the front door.

6. In Properties, set a *Frame Type as* **A**, *Frame Material* as **Steel**, and *Finish* as **Coated**.

7. Click ⬚ (Edit Type).

8. In the Type Properties dialog box, in the *Identity Data* area, set the *Fire Rating* to **A**.

9. Click ⬚ OK to finish.

10. Return to the Door Schedule. (Press <Ctrl>+<Tab> to switch between open windows.)

11. Note that the *Frame Type* and *Frame Material* display for one door and the matching exterior doors also have a fire rating. Use the drop-down list and change the options for the matching doors, as shown in Figure 15–48.

\<Door Schedule - 1st Floor\>

A	B	C	D	E	F	G	H	I	J
Mark	Dimensions		Thickness	Frame Information		Head Detail	Detail Information		Fire Rating
	Width	Height		Frame Type	Frame Material		Jamb Detail	Threshold Detail	
	2350	2865							
101	915	2032	51	A	Steel				A
102	915	2032	51	A					A
103	915	2032	51		Steel				A
104	915	2134	51						

Figure 15–48

12. In the Door Schedule view, specify the *Fire Rating* for some other doors in the schedule. When you change the fire rating, you are prompted to change all elements of that type. Click

    [OK] .

13. Open the **Floor Plans: Floor 1** view.

14. Select the door to the office, then right-click and select **Select All Instances>In Entire Project**.

15. Look at the Status Bar beside ▽ (Filter) and note that more doors have been selected than are in the current view.

16. In Properties, set the *Frame Type* and *Frame Material* for these doors.

17. Press <Esc> to clear the selection when you are finished.

18. Switch back to the schedule view to see the additions. Not all of the doors are showing because the schedule has been limited to the 1st floor doors.

19. Save the project.

Task 2 - Add schedules to a sheet.

---

1. In the Project Browser, right-click on Sheets (all) and select **New Sheet**. Select the D-sized title block and click

   [OK] .

2. In the Project Browser, right-click on the new sheet (which is bold) and select Rename. In the Sheet Title dialog box, set the *Number* to **A8.1** and the *Name* to **Schedules** and click

   [OK] .

3. Drag and drop the **Door Schedule - 1st Floor** view onto the sheet, as shown in Figure 15–49.

| | | | | Door Schedule - 1st Floor | | | | | | | |
| | Dimensions | | | Frame Information | | Detail Information | | | | | |
Mark	Width	Height	Thickness	Frame Type	Frame Material	Head Detail	Jamb Detail	Threshold Detail	Fire Rating	Hardware Set	Comments
	2050	2085									
01	95	2002	11	A	Steel				A		
02	95	2002	11	A	Steel				A		
03	95	2002	11	A	Steel				A		
04	95	2084	11						B		
05	95	2084	11						B		
06	95	2084	11						B		
07	95	2084	11						B		
08	95	2084	11						B		
09	95	2002	11	A	Steel				A		

Figure 15–49

4. Zoom in and use the arrows at the top to modify the width of the columns so that the titles display correctly.

5. Click in empty space on the sheet to finish placing the schedule.

6. Switch back to the **Floor Plans: Floor 1** view and select the double-swing door at the kitchen.

7. In the Type Selector, change it to a different size. In Properties, add a Frame Type, Frame Material, and Finish.

8. Return to the Door Schedule sheet. The information is automatically populated, as shown in Figure 15–50.

	Door Schedule - 1st Floor							
	Dimensions			Frame Information		Detail Informat		
Mark	Width	Height	Thickness	Frame Type	Frame Material	Head Detail	Jamb Detail	Thr
	2350	2865						
101	915	2032	51	A	Steel			
102	915	2032	51	A	Steel			
103	915	2032	51	A	Steel			
104	915	2134	51					
105	915	2134	51					
106	915	2134	51					
107	915	2134	51					
108	915	2134	51					
109	915	2032	51	A	Steel			
110	1830	2134	51					
111	1830	2083	51	B	Wood			

Figure 15–50

9. Return to the 3D view.

10. In the Quick Access Toolbar, click ⬚ (Close Hidden Windows.

11. Save the project.

Chapter Review Questions

1. Which of the following elements cannot be tagged using **Tag by Category**?

   a. Rooms

   b. Floors

   c. Walls

   d. Doors

2. What happens when you delete a door in an Autodesk Revit model, as shown in Figure 15–51?

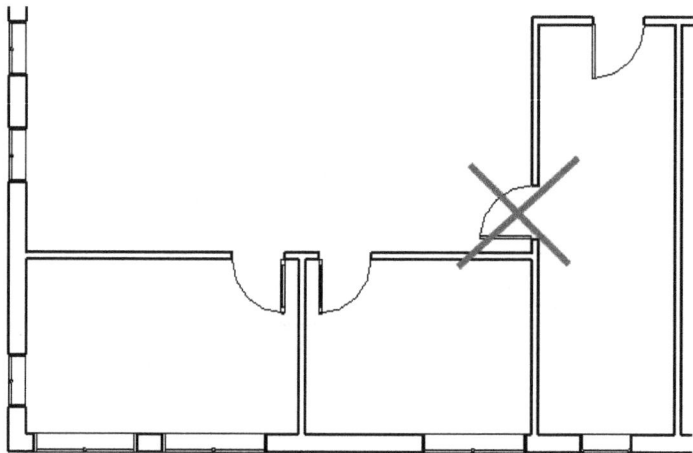

Figure 15–51

   a. You must delete the door on the drawing sheet.

   b. You must delete the door from the schedule.

   c. The door is removed from the model, but not from the schedule.

   d. The door is removed from the model and the schedule.

3. In a schedule, if you change type information (such as a Type Mark) all instances of that type update with the new information.

   a. True

   b. False

4. If you want to add rooms to a project (as shown in Figure 15–52), but they are not displayed, what do you have to do?

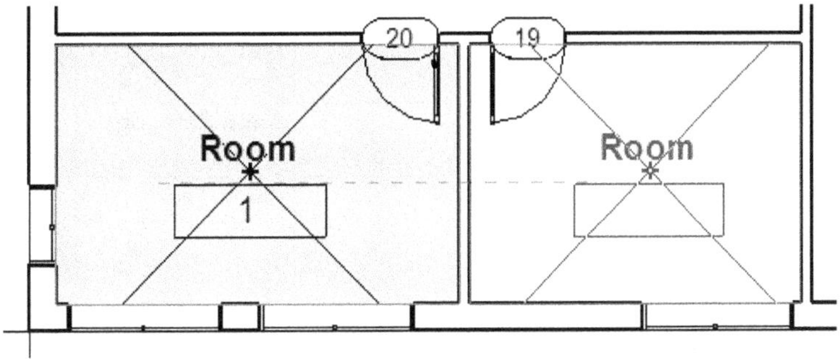

Figure 15–52

   a. Create a new Room Plan view.

   b. In the View Control Bar, turn on **Rooms**.

   c. In the Visibility/Graphic Overrides dialog box, under Rooms turn on **Interior Fill**.

   d. While the **Room** command is active, in the *Place Room* tab, verify that **Interior Fill** is selected.

5. Which of the following commands enables you to reuse a schedule from another project?

   a. **Schedules>Schedule/Quantities**

   b. **Insert from File>Insert Views from File**

   c. **Insert from File>Insert 2D Elements from File**

   d. **Import Reports>Schedule**

Command Summary

Button	Command	Location
	Material Tag	**Ribbon:** *Annotate* tab>Tag panel>Material tag
	Multi-Category	**Ribbon:** *Annotate* tab>Tag panel>Multi-Category
	Room	**Ribbon:** *Architecture* tab>Room & Area panel>Room **Shortcut:** \<R\> and \<M\>
	Room Separation Line	**Ribbon:** *Architecture* tab>Room & Area panel>expand Room>Room Separation Line
	Room Tag	**Ribbon:** *Architecture* tab>Room & Area panel>Tag>Room Tag **Shortcut:** \<R\> and \<T\>
	Stair Tread/ Riser Number	**Ribbon:** *Annotate* tab>Tag panel>Stair Tread/Riser Number
	Tag All Not Tagged	**Ribbon:** *Annotate* tab>Tag panel>Tag All
	Tag by Category	**Ribbon:** *Annotate* tab>Tag panel>Tag by Category **Shortcut:** \<T\> and \<G\>

Chapter 16

Creating Details

In this chapter you learn how to set up detail views, add detail components, and annotate details. You also learn how to use Keynotes and set up Keynote Legends.

This chapter contains the following topics:

- **Setting Up Detail Views**
- **Adding Detail Components**
- **Annotating Details**
- **Keynoting and Keynote Legends**

16.1 Setting Up Detail Views

Learning Objectives

- Create 2D drafting views in which you can draw details indicating how parts of a building fit together.
- Link callout views to drafting views so that they are referenced correctly in the construction documents.
- Save drafting views so that you can use them in other projects.

Most of the work you do in the Autodesk® Revit® software is exclusively with *smart* elements (i.e., walls, doors, floors, etc.) that interconnect and work together in the model. However, the software does not automatically display how elements should be built to fit together. For this, you need to create detail drawings, as shown in Figure 16–1. There are a variety of tools that enable you to create details, including drafting views, detail lines, special components, filled regions, and insulation.

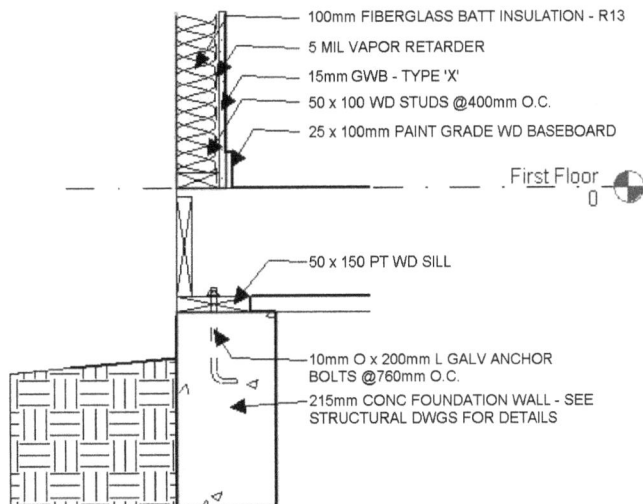

100mm FIBERGLASS BATT INSULATION - R13
5 MIL VAPOR RETARDER
15mm GWB - TYPE 'X'
50 x 100 WD STUDS @400mm O.C.
25 x 100mm PAINT GRADE WD BASEBOARD

First Floor
0

50 x 150 PT WD SILL

10mm O x 200mm L GALV ANCHOR BOLTS @760mm O.C.
215mm CONC FOUNDATION WALL - SEE STRUCTURAL DWGS FOR DETAILS

Figure 16–1

- You can use detailing tools (such as detail lines and components, filled regions, and insulation) directly in a specially created *Drafting View*, or you can work in a callout from a plan, elevation, or section view.

- Drafting views are listed in their own section in the Project Browser

How To: Create a Drafting View

1. In the *View* tab>Create panel, click 🖨 (Drafting View).
2. In the New Drafting View dialog box, enter a *Name* and set a *Scale*, as shown in Figure 16–2.

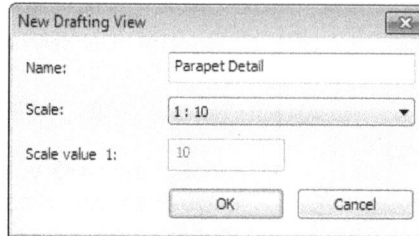

If you set the Scale to ***Custom****, you can type the Scale value. Otherwise, the Scale automatically controls the Scale value.*

New Drafting View	
Name:	Parapet Detail
Scale:	1 : 10
Scale value 1:	10
	OK Cancel

Figure 16–2

3. Click [OK]. A blank view is created with space in which you can draw.
4. Add detail lines, components, text, and dimensions as required.

Hint: Importing Details from Other CAD Software

In many cases, you might already have a set of standard details that have been used in various projects. You can reuse them in the Autodesk Revit software, even if they were created in other software, such as the AutoCAD® software. Import the detail into a new project, clean it up, and save it as a view before bringing it into your project.

1. Create a drafting view and make it active.

2. In the *Insert* tab>Import panel, click 📄 (Import CAD).
3. In the Import CAD dialog box, select the file to import. Most of the default values are what you need. You might want to change the *Layer/Level colors* to **Black and White**.

4. Click [Open].

- If you want to modify the detail, select the imported data. In the *Modify | [filename]* tab>Import Instance panel, expand 📦 (Explode) and click 📦 (Partial Explode) or 📦 (Full Explode). Click 📦 (Delete Layers) before you explode the detail. A full explode greatly increases the file size.

- Modify the detail using tools in the Modify panel. Change all the text and line styles to Autodesk Revit specific elements.

How To: Create a Detail View from a Section

1. In the Quick Access Toolbar or the *View* tab>Create panel, click ♀ (Section).
2. In the Type Selector select **Section:Detail**.
3. Draw the section detail, such as the sample shown in Figure 16–3. The marker indicates that it is a detail, rather than a section, but it is still creating a section cut.

Callouts also have a Detail View Type that can be used in the same way.

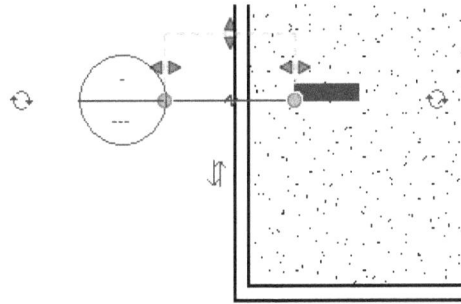

Figure 16–3

4. Open the new detail. Use the tools to draw on top of or add to the building elements.

• In this type of detail view when the building elements change, the detail changes as well, as shown in Figure 16–4.

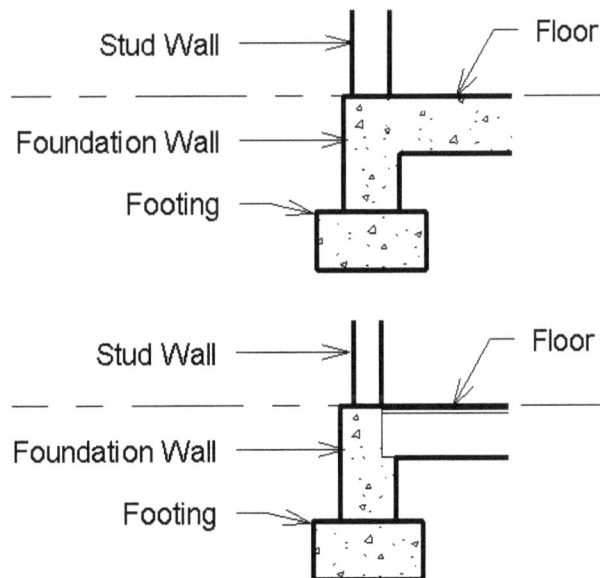

Stud Wall ⟶   ⌐ Floor

Foundation Wall ⟶

Footing ⟶

Stud Wall ⟶   ⌐ Floor

Foundation Wall ⟶

Footing ⟶

Figure 16–4

Connecting a Callout to a Drafting View

Once you have created a drafting view, you can link it to a callout in another view, as shown in Figure 16–5. For example, in a section view, you might want a callout that references a roof detail. You can reference drafting views, sections, elevations, and callouts.

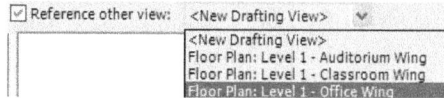

Figure 16–5

How To: Connect a Callout to a Drafting View

1. Open the view in which you want to place the callout.

2. In the *View* tab>Create panel, click ⌀ (Callout).
3. In the Options Bar, select **Reference other view**. In the drop-down list, select **<New Drafting View>** or an existing drafting view.
4. Draw the callout box around the required area and move the bubble as required.
5. When you place the associated drafting view on a sheet, the callout bubble in this view updates with the appropriate information.

- In the drop-down list, the information in parentheses displays the detail number and sheet where a callout is placed. If no information displays after the name, the existing view has not yet been placed on a sheet.

- If you select **<New Drafting View>** from the drop-down list, a new view is created in the *Drafting Views (Detail)* area in the Project Browser. You can rename it as required. The new view does not include any model elements.

Enhanced 🔍
in 2015

- You can change a referenced view to a different referenced view. Select the callout box or section line and in the Options Bar, select the new view from the list.

Saving a Drafting View

When you create a drafting view and add detail components to it, you might want to save it so that you can use it again in another project. This enables you to create a library of standard details that can be copied into a project and then modified to suit the new software.

Drafting views can be saved in two ways: save an individual drafting view to a new file or save all of the drafting views as a group in one new file.

How To: Save One Drafting View to a File

1. In the Project Browser, right-click on the drafting view you want to save and select **Save to New File...**, as shown in Figure 16–6.

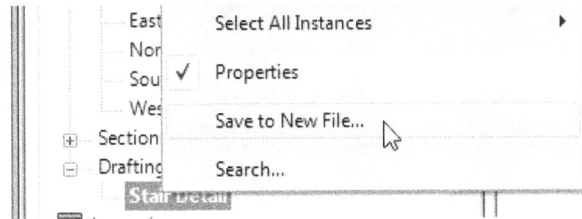

Figure 16–6

2. In the Save As dialog box, specify a name and location for the file and click [Save].

How To: Save a Group of Drafting Views to a File

You can save sheets, drafting views, model views (floor plans), schedules, and reports.

1. In the Application Menu, expand 🖫 (Save As), expand 📖 (Library), and click ◻ (View).
2. In the Save Views dialog box, in the *Views:* pane, expand the list and select **Show drafting views only**.
3. Select the drafting views that you want to save as shown in Figure 16–7.

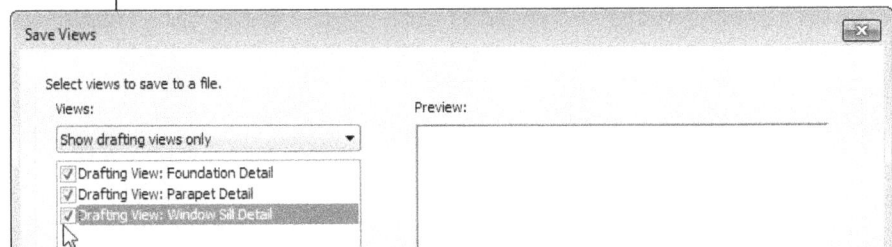

Figure 16–7

4. Click [OK].
5. In the Save As dialog box, specify a name and location for the file and click [Save].

How To: Use a Saved Drafting View in another Project

1. Open the project to which you want to add the drafting view.

2. In the *Insert* tab>Import panel, expand ⬚ (Insert from File) and click ⬚ (Insert Views from File).

3. In the Open dialog box, select the project in which you saved the detail and click [Open].

4. In the Insert Views dialog box, limit the types of views to **Show drafting views only**, as shown in Figure 16–8.

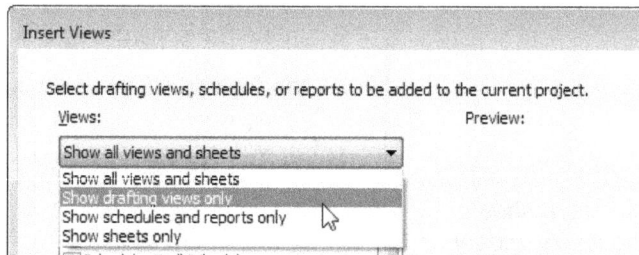

Insert Views

Select drafting views, schedules, or reports to be added to the current project.

Views: Preview:

Show all views and sheets ▼
Show all views and sheets
Show drafting views only
Show schedules and reports only
Show sheets only

Figure 16–8

5. Select the view(s) that you want to insert and click [OK].

16.2 Adding Detail Components

Autodesk Certification Topics & Objectives

Pro.   User

Documentation

- Place detail components and repeating details   ✓

Learning Objective

- Add detail components to a drafting view to create a 2D building detail.

Autodesk Revit elements. such as the casework section shown on the left in Figure 16–9, typically require additional information to ensure that they are constructed correctly. To create details such as the one shown on the right in Figure 16–9, you add detail components, detail lines, and various annotation elements. These elements are drawn in a 2D drafting view, and are not directly connected to the full model.

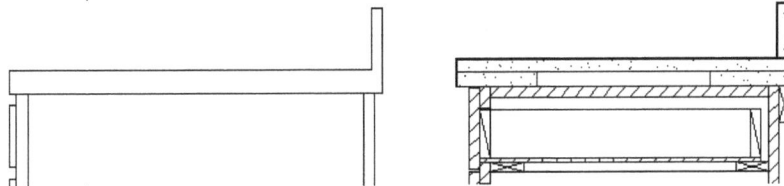

Figure 16–9

Detail Components

Detail components are 2D drawings made with detail sketch lines that are created in a detail component family. The Detail Library contains components, such as roof drains, cabinet sections, window heads, and jambs. The Library contains over 500 2D detail components organized by CSI format. An example is shown in Figure 16–10.

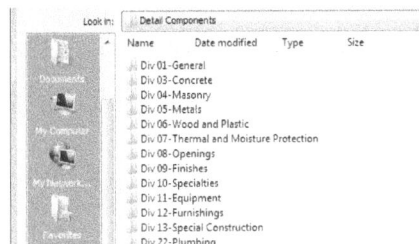

Figure 16–10

- Additional components can be created through Families.

How To: Add a Detail Component

1. In the *Annotate* tab>Detail panel, expand 🔲 (Component) and click 🔲 (Detail Component).
2. In the Type Selector, select the detail component type. You can load additional types from the Library.
3. Many detail components can be rotated as you insert them by pressing the <Spacebar>. If you know that the components do not rotate by this method, select the **Rotate after placement** option in the Options Bar, as shown in Figure 16–11.

☐ Rotate after placement

Figure 16–11

4. Place the component in the drawing. Rotate it by pressing the <Spacebar> or using the prompts if you selected the **Rotate after placement** option.

Adding Break Lines

A **Break Line** is a component. It can be found in the *Detail Components>Div 01-General* folder, and is inserted using

🔲 (Detail Component). A break line consists of a rectangular area (shown highlighted in Figure 16–12) which is used to block out elements behind it. You can modify the size of the area that is covered and change the size of the cut line using controls.

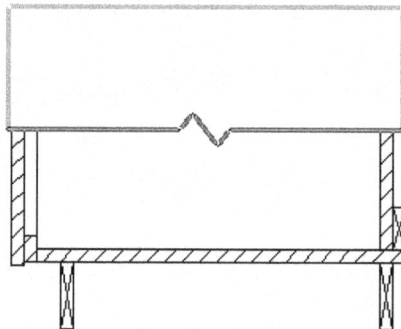

Figure 16–12

Hint: Working with the Draw Order of Details

When you select detail elements in a view, the *Modify | Detail Items* tab displays. In the Arrange panel, you can change the draw order of the elements. You can bring elements in front of other elements or place them behind elements, as shown in Figure 16–13.

Figure 16–13

- 　**(Bring to Front):** Places element in front of all other elements.

- 　**(Send to Back):** Places element behind all other elements.

- 　**(Bring Forward):** Moves element one step to the front.

- 　**(Send Backward):** Moves element one step to the back.

- You can select multiple detail elements and change the draw order of all of them in one step. If they are on different layers, they keep the relative order of the original selection.

Repeating Details

Details are often repeated, such as a brick or concrete block. Instead of having to insert a component multiple times, you can use 　(Repeating Detail Component) and draw a string of components, as shown in Figure 16–14. One repeating detail is included with the standard template. You can also create custom details.

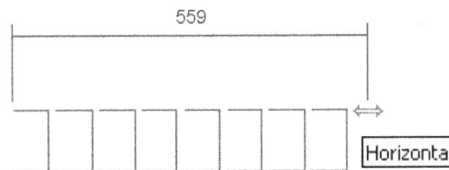

559

Horizontal

Figure 16–14

How To: Insert a Repeating Detail

1. In the *Annotate* tab>Detail panel, expand 🔲 (Component) and click ⠿ (Repeating Detail Component).
2. In the Type Selector, select the detail you want to use.
3. In the Draw panel, click ✓ (Line) or ↙ (Pick Lines). You can create details at a specified distance from the selected points or line. In the Options Bar, type a value for the *Offset*.

   - If you click ✓ (Line), select two points on the screen and the components repeat.

   - If you click ↙ (Pick Lines), select a detail line that exists in the view.

4. The components repeat as required to fit the length of the line, as shown in Figure 16–15. You can lock the components to the line.

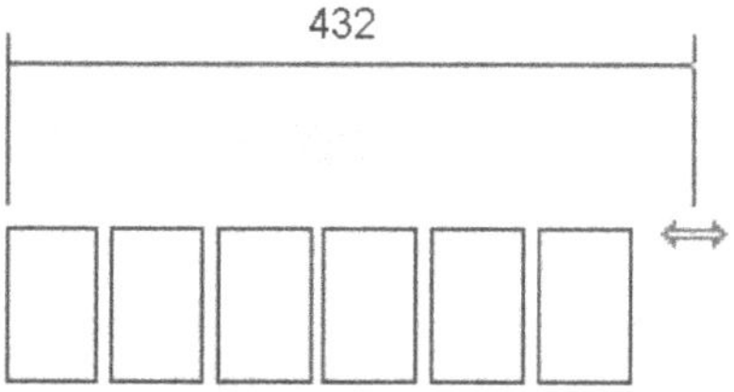

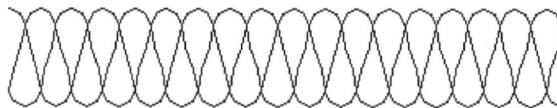

Figure 16–15

Hint: ⧖ (Insulation)

Adding batt insulation is similar to adding a repeating detail component, but instead of a series of bricks or other elements, it creates the linear batting pattern, shown in Figure 16–16.

Figure 16–16

Before you place the insulation in the drawing, specify the *Width* and other options in the Options Bar, as shown in Figure 16–17.

| Modify | Place Insulation | Width 80.0 | ☐ Chain | Offset: 0.0 | to center ⌄ |

Figure 16–17

16.3 Annotating Details

Autodesk Certification Topics & Objectives

Pro. User

Documentation

* Create and modify filled regions ✓

Learning Objective

* Use annotation tools including patterning and detail tags to annotate a 2D building detail.

After you have added components and drawn detail lines, you need to add annotations to the drawing. You can use standard annotation tools to place text notes, dimensions and symbols, as shown in Figure 16–18. You can also fill regions with a pattern and add detail tags to the region.

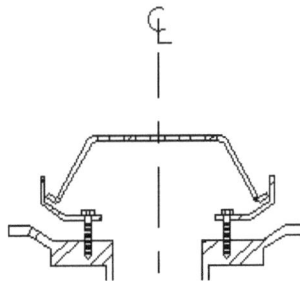

Figure 16–18

Creating Filled Regions

Many elements include material information that displays in plan and section views, while other elements need such details to be added. For example, the concrete wall shown in Figure 16–19 includes material information, while the earth to the left of the wall needs the information to be added. You add this information by creating filled regions.

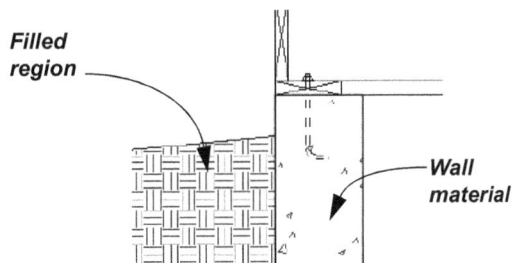

Figure 16–19

The patterns used in details are *drafting patterns*. They are scaled to the view scale and update if you modify it. You can also add full-size *model patterns*, such as a Flemish Bond brick pattern, to the surface of some elements.

- Fill patterns can be applied to all surfaces in a model. If the surface is warped, the patterns display as planar surfaces to keep the visual integrity of the geometry.

How To: Add a Filled Region

1. In the *Annotate* tab>Detail panel, expand ⬚ (Region) and click ⬚ (Filled Region).
2. In the *Modify | Create Filled Region Boundary* tab>Draw panel, click ✏ (Line) or ⚲ (Pick Lines) and outline the region (it must be a closed area).
3. In the Line Style panel, select the line type for the outside edge of the boundary.
4. Click ✔ (Finish Edit Mode).
5. In the Type Selector, select the fill type, as shown in Figure 16–20.

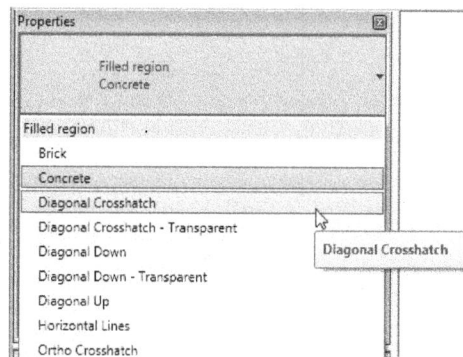

Figure 16–20

6. Click in empty space to finish.

- You can modify a region after it is added by selecting and changing the fill type in the Type Selector or by editing the sketch.

- Double-click on the filled region to edit the sketch. If you have the Selection option set to 🔲 (Select elements by face) you can select the pattern. If it is not toggled on, you need to select the edge of the filled region.

Hint: Creating a Filled Region Pattern Type

You can create a custom pattern by duplicating and editing an existing pattern type.

1. Select an existing region or create a boundary.

2. In Properties, click 🔲 (Edit Type).

3. In the Type Properties dialog box, click | Duplicate... | and name the new pattern.

4. Select a *Fill Pattern*, *Background*, *Line Weight*, and *Color*, as shown in Figure 16–21.

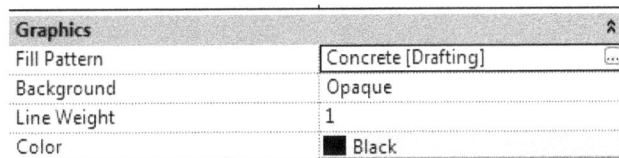

Graphics	
Fill Pattern	Concrete [Drafting]
Background	Opaque
Line Weight	1
Color	■ Black

Figure 16–21

5. Click | OK |.

• You can select from two types of Fill Patterns: **Drafting**, as shown in Figure 16–22, and **Model**. Drafting fill patterns scale to the view scale factor. Model fill patterns display full scale on the model and are not impacted by the view scale factor.

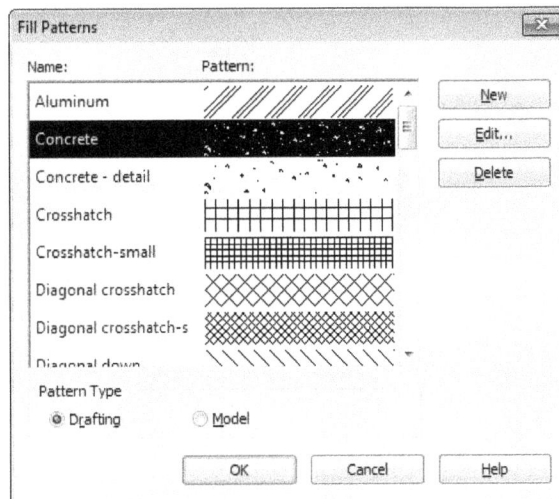

Figure 16–22

Adding Detail Tags

You can tag detail items, such as components, using (Tag By Category). This is another way of annotating your details instead of using text and leaders. When you modify the tag name, you actually change the *Type Mark* that is set in the Type Parameters for that detail, as shown in Figure 16–23. This means that if you have more than one copy of the component in your drawing, you do not have to rename it each time you place its tag.

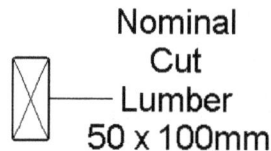

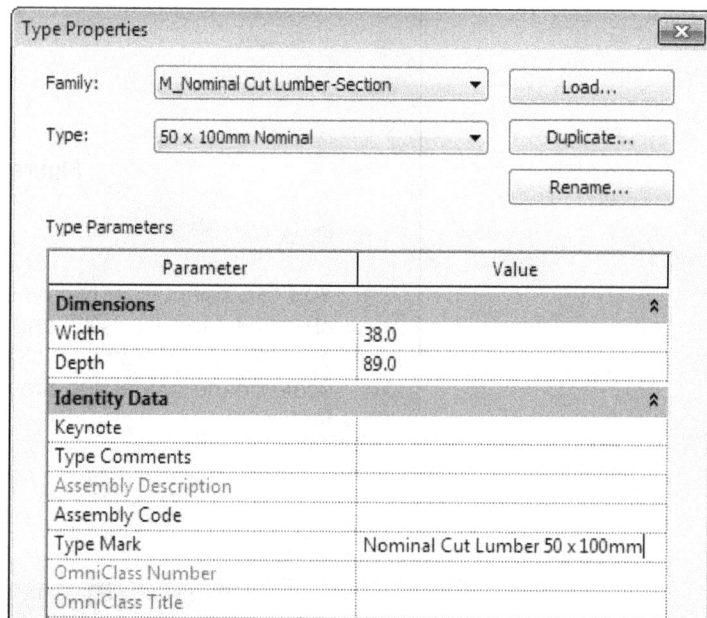

Figure 16–23

- The **Detail Item Tag.rfa** tag is located in the *Annotations* folder in the Library.

- The first time you modify a *Type Mark* for a detail, an alert box opens warning that you are changing a type rather than an instance of the element.

Hint: Multiple Dimension Options

If you are creating details that show one element with multiple dimension values, as shown in Figure 16–24, you can easily modify the dimension text.

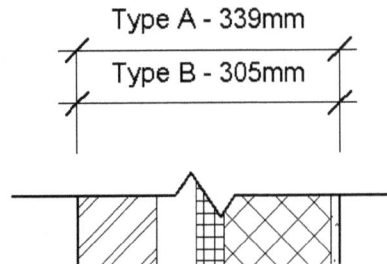

Type A - 339mm

Type B - 305mm

Figure 16–24

Select the dimension and then the dimension text. The Dimension Text dialog box opens. You can replace the text, as shown in Figure 16–25, or add text fields above or below, as well as a prefix or suffix.

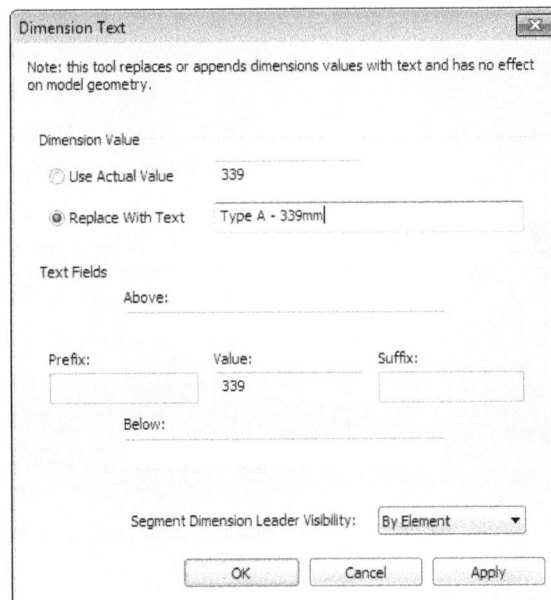

Dimension Text

Note: this tool replaces or appends dimensions values with text and has no effect on model geometry.

Dimension Value

○ Use Actual Value   339

◉ Replace With Text   Type A - 339mm|

Text Fields

Above:

Prefix:	Value:	Suffix:
	339	

Below:

Segment Dimension Leader Visibility: By Element   ▼

OK   Cancel   Apply

Figure 16–25

Practice 16a | Create a Detail Based on a CAD File

Learning Objectives

- Create a detail based on an imported CAD file. Explode it and change all of the elements to Autodesk Revit specific elements, including text and filled regions.
- Create a view of the new detail and import it into a project.

Estimated time for completion: 10 minutes

In this practice you will create a detail in a drafting view based on an existing detail created in the AutoCAD software, as shown in Figure 16–26. You will then create leaders for text and patterning using Autodesk Revit elements.

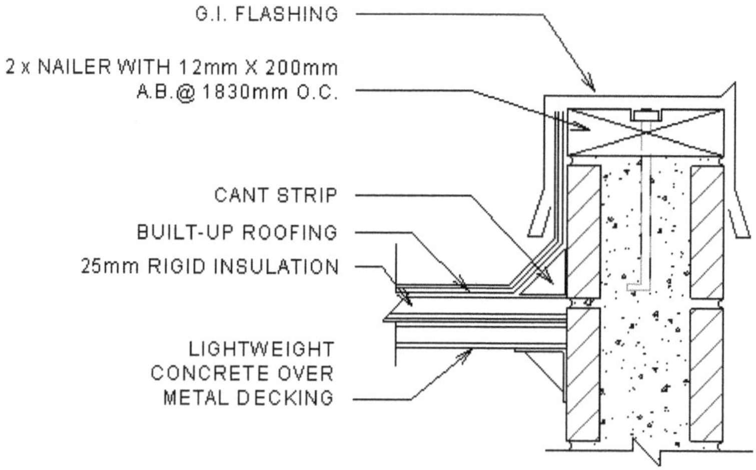

G.I. FLASHING

2 x NAILER WITH 12mm X 200mm
A.B.@ 1830mm O.C.

CANT STRIP

BUILT-UP ROOFING

25mm RIGID INSULATION

LIGHTWEIGHT
CONCRETE OVER
METAL DECKING

Figure 16–26

Task 1 - Create a detail based on an AutoCAD drawing.

1. Start a new project based on the default architectural template.

2. In the *View* tab>Create panel, click ⬛ (Drafting View).

3. In the New Drafting View dialog box, set the name and scale to the following:

   - Name: **Parapet Detail**
   - Scale: **1:10**

4. In the *Insert* tab>Import panel, click (Import CAD).

5. In the Import CAD Formats dialog box, select the AutoCAD drawing **Roof-Detail-M.dwg** from your class folder. Change the *Colors* to **Black and White** and keep the other default options, as shown in Figure 16–27.

Colors:	Black and White ▼	
Layers/Levels:	All ▼	
Import units:	Auto-Detect ▼ 1.000000	
	☑ Correct lines that are slightly off axis	

Positioning:	Auto - Center to Center ▼
Place at:	Level 1
	☑ Orient to View
	Open Cancel

Figure 16–27

6. Click [Open] to place the detail.

7. Zoom in and select the detail. It is all one element, as shown in Figure 16–28.

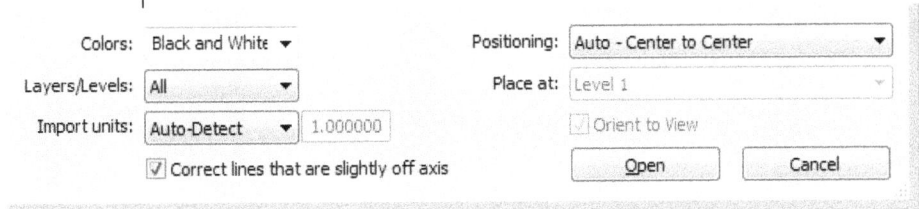

Figure 16–28

8. In the *Modify | Roof-Detail.dwg* tab>Import Instance panel, expand (Explode) and click (Full Explode). You are now able to edit individual sections of the imported detail.

9. Select all of the text, as shown in Figure 16–29.

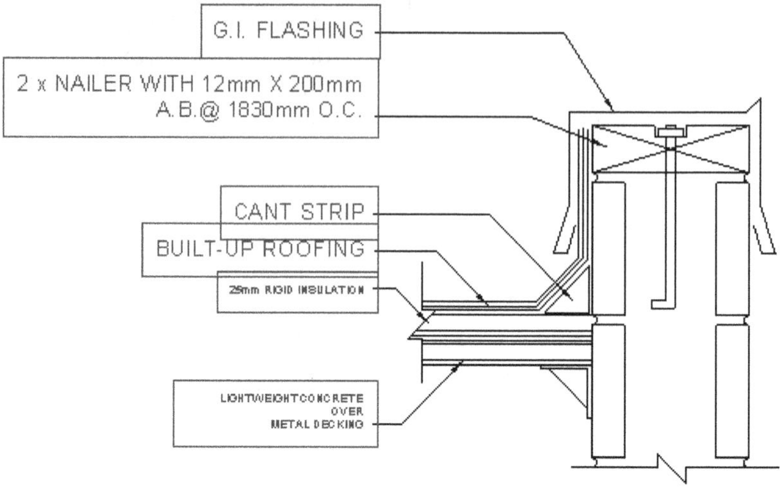

Figure 16–29

10. In the Type Selector, select **Text: 2.5mm Arial**.

11. Return to the **Modify** command and select the entire drawing (it is now all individual elements).

12. In the *Modify | Multi-Select* tab>Selection panel, click ⟟ (Filter).

These lines are referenced to AutoCAD layers names rather than Autodesk Revit Line Type names.

13. In the Filter dialog box, click [Check None] and then select **Lines (Heavy)** as shown in Figure 16–30. Click [OK].

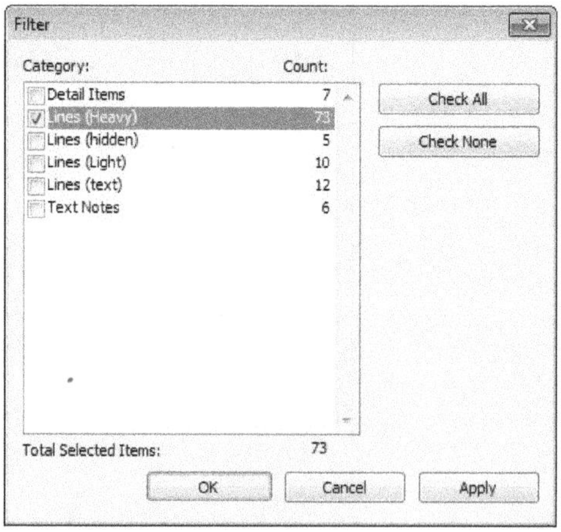

Figure 16–30

14. In the *Modify | Lines* tab>Line Style panel, change the *Line Style* to **Medium Lines**.

15. Return to the **Modify** command to finish.

16. Repeat the process with the other line types changing *Lines (hidden)* to **Hidden Lines** and *Lines (Light)* to **Thin Lines**.

Task 2 - Modify text and leaders.

1. Select everything again and use the **Filter** command to select **Lines (text)**. Delete these lines as they are not used.

2. Select one of the arrowheads that remain in the drawing. Right-click and select **Select All Instances>Visible in View**. Delete the elements.

3. Select a text element. In the *Modify | Text Notes* tab>Format panel, click A^{+} (Add Right Side Straight Leader). Modify the leader to point to the correct element, as shown in the example in Figure 16–31.

G.I. FLASHING

2 x NAILER WITH 12mm X 200mm
A.B.@ 1830mm O.C.

CANT STRIP

BUILT-UP ROOFING

Figure 16–31

4. Repeat the process of adding leaders to the text, pointing to the appropriate parts of the detail, as shown in Figure 16–32.

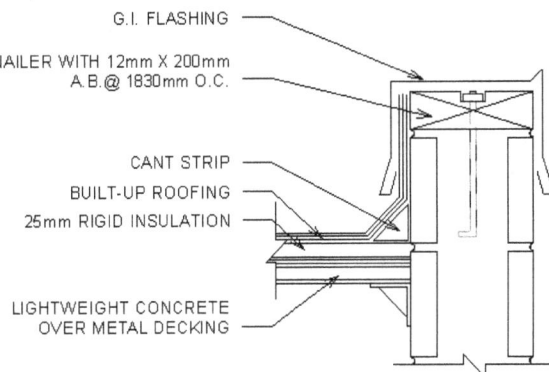

G.I. FLASHING

2 x NAILER WITH 12mm X 200mm
A.B.@ 1830mm O.C.

CANT STRIP
BUILT-UP ROOFING
25mm RIGID INSULATION

LIGHTWEIGHT CONCRETE
OVER METAL DECKING

Figure 16–32

Task 3 - Add filled regions.

1. In the *Annotate* tab>Detail panel, click ▦ (Region).

Use the <Invisible lines> type because the boundary does not need to display.

2. In the *Modify | Create Filled Region Boundary* tab>Line Style panel, set the line style to **<Invisible lines>**.

3. In the Draw panel, click ⤢ (Pick Lines) and add a box around each of the four rectangular brick sections, as shown in Figure 16–33. You can do all four areas in one sketch.

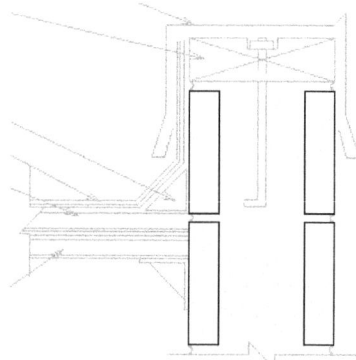

Figure 16–33

4. Click ✓ (Finish Edit Mode).

5. In the Type Selector, set the *pattern type* to **Diagonal Up** and click in empty space to clear the selection.

This area was hatched in the AutoCAD drawing. The hatching was automatically converted to a filled region when the drawing was imported into the project, but was not assigned an Autodesk Revit based pattern. AutoCAD.pat files can be imported into Autodesk Revit to be used as filled regions.

6. Select the large region between the areas that you just hatched, as shown in Figure 16–34.

Figure 16–34

7. In Properties, click ⊞ (Edit Type).

8. In the Type Properties dialog box, click [Duplicate] and name the new pattern **Concrete**.

9. In the *Value* field for the *Fill Pattern* parameter, click [...] (Browse).

10. In the Fill Patterns dialog box, in *Pattern Type* area, select **Drafting** and then select the pattern **Concrete**.

11. Click [OK] twice to create the Filled Region type and apply it to the selected boundary.

12. The detail view now consists of only Autodesk Revit elements and is safe to use in another project.

Task 4 - Create a View and Import it in to a Project.

1. In the Application Menu, expand ⬚ (Save As), expand ⬚ (Library), and select **View**.

2. In the Save Views dialog box, verify that **Drafting View: Parapet Detail** is selected, as shown in Figure 16–35 and click [OK].

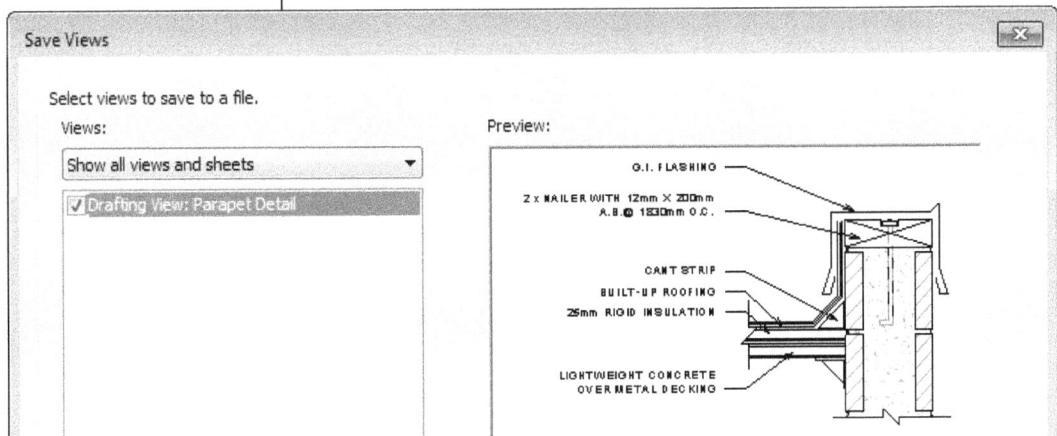

Figure 16–35

3. In the Save As dialog box, navigate to your class folder and click [Save] .

4. Close the project and do not save it.

5. Open **Modern-Hotel-Detailing-M.rvt** from your class folder.

6. In the *Insert* tab>Import panel, expand (Insert from File) and click (Insert Views from File).

7. In the Open dialog box, navigate to your class folder and open **Parapet-Detail.rvt**.

8. In the Insert Views dialog box only this view is available. Click [OK] .

9. Accept any warnings that might display about duplicate types. They do not impact the project.

10. Save the project.

16.4 Keynoting and Keynote Legends

Learning Objective

- Place keynotes on a detail and add a keynote legend that expands on the information stored in the keynote tag.

Keynotes are special kinds of tags that apply specific numbering to various elements in a detail. They can be used on all model and detail elements, as well as materials. By default, the Autodesk Revit software uses the CSI master format system of keynote designations. Using keynotes requires less room on a drawing than standard text notes, as shown in Figure 16–36. The full explanation of the note is shown in a corresponding *keynote legend* placed elsewhere in the drawing.

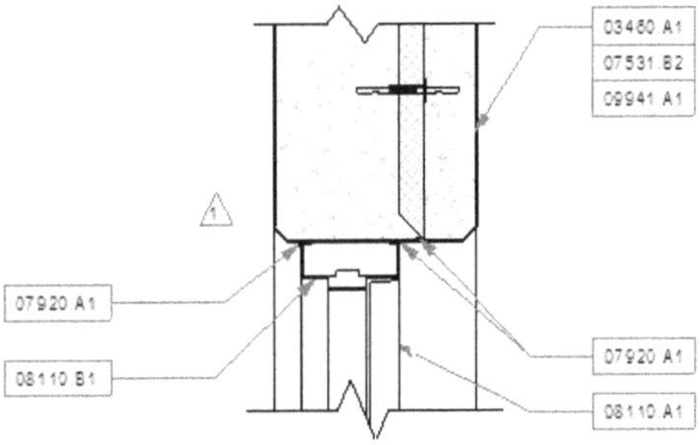

Figure 16–36

- Keynote tags are found in the Library in the *Annotations* folder and must be loaded into a project before you can apply them.

- Keynotes are stored in a keynote table (a text file), as shown in Figure 16–37. Any updates made to the keynote table are reflected in the project after it is closed and then re-opened.

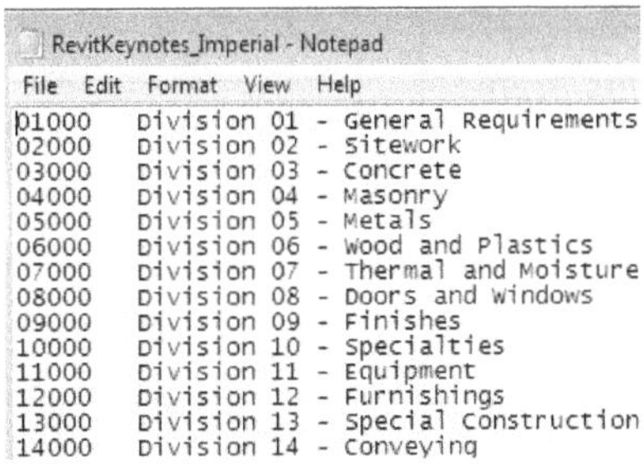

Figure 16–37

How To: Place a Keynote

1. In the *Annotate* tab>Tag panel, expand ⌐[1] (Keynote) and click ⌐[1]₀ (Element), ⌐[1]⊗ (Material), or ⌐[1]⌷ (User).

The Element keynote is used when you want to tag elements, such as a door, wall, or detail components.

The Material keynote looks for the material assigned to a component in a family or painted onto a surface using Paint. The User keynote must first be developed in a keynote table.

2. Move the cursor over the element you want to keynote and select it.
3. If an element has keynote information assigned to it, the keynote is automatically applied. If it is not assigned, the Keynotes dialog box opens, as shown in Figure 16–38.

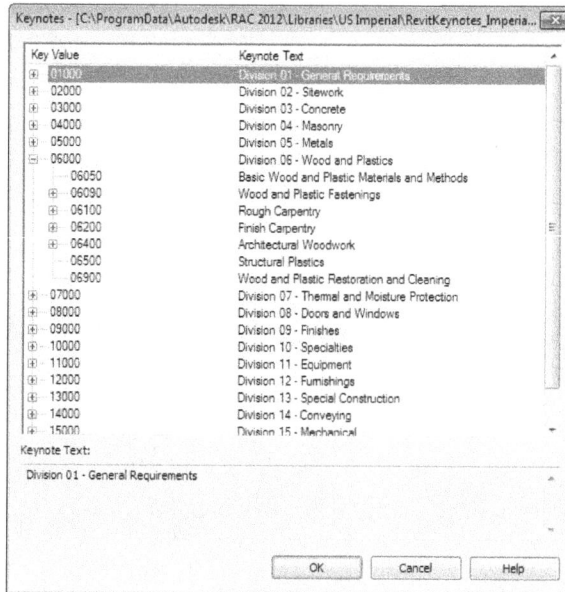

Figure 16–38

4. Select the keynote you need from the list of divisions and click [OK].

• The options for keynotes are the same as for other tags, including orientation and leaders, as shown in Figure 16–39.

The keynote remembers the leader settings from the last time it was used.

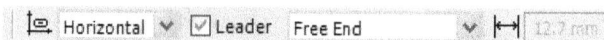

Figure 16–39

Hint: Setting the Keynote Numbering Method

Keynotes can be listed in a drawing by the full keynote number or by sheet, as shown in Figure 16–40. Only one method can be used at a time in a project, but you can change between the two methods at any time in the project.

In the *Annotate* tab>Tag panel, expand the Tag panel heading and click (Keynote Settings).

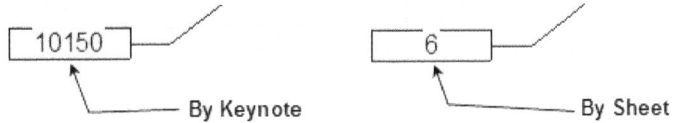

Figure 16–40

In the Keynoting Settings dialog box, you can set the *Keynote Table* and *Path Type* used for keynote information, as shown in Figure 16–41.

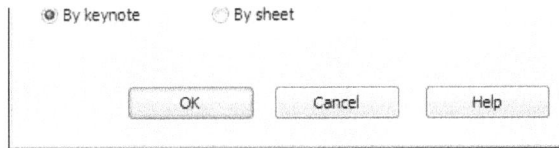

Figure 16–41

Keynote Legends

A keynote legend is different from a standard legend.

A keynote legend is a table containing the information stored in the keynote that is placed on a sheet, as shown in Figure 16–42. In the Autodesk Revit software, it is created in a similar way to schedules.

Keynote Legend	
Key Value	**Keynote Text**
04050	Basic Masonry Materials and Methods
05050	Basic Metal Materials and Methods
05100	Structural Metal Framing
08110.G1	70mm Single Rabbet HM Door Frame
08210	Wood Doors
10150	Compartments and Cubicles
12400	Furnishings and Accessories

Figure 16–42

How To: Create a Keynote Legend

1. In the *View* tab>Create panel, expand ▦ (Legends) and click ▦ (Keynote Legend).
2. Type a name in the New Keynote Legend dialog box and click [OK].
3. The Keynote Legend Properties dialog box typically only displays two scheduled fields, which are already set up for you, as shown in Figure 16–43.

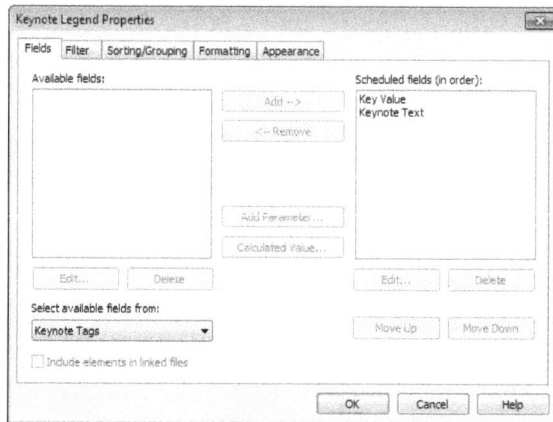

Figure 16–43

4. In the other tabs, set up the format of the table as required.

5. Click [OK] to create the keynote legend.
6. When you are ready to place a keynote legend, drag it from the Project Browser onto the sheet. You can manipulate it in the same way, similar to modifying other schedules.

- As you add keynotes to the project, they are added to the keynote legend, as shown in Figure 16–44.

Keynote Legend	
Key Value	Keynote Text
04 21 00.A	Modular Brick - 10mm Joint
04 21 00.A	Roman Brick - 10mm Joint
04 21 00.A	Titan Brick - 12mm Joint
05 12 00.A	L200x100x10

Keynote Legend	
Key Value	Keynote Text
04 21 00.A	Modular Brick - 10mm Joint
04 21 00.A	Roman Brick - 10mm Joint
04 21 00.A	Titan Brick - 12mm Joint
05 12 00.A	L200x100x10
06 01 10.A	25x200R
09 39 13.A	Ceramic Tile

Figure 16–44

- The key value in the legend displays either the keynote or the sheet number, depending on the keynote settings.

Practice 16b | Create Additional Details

![Learning Objective icon] **Learning Objective**

- Create and annotate details in the Autodesk Revit software.

In this practice you will create a window sill detail and a structural detail, and then annotate them. The following tasks are designed to be completed without detailed steps. Refer to the earlier topics and practice for assistance, as required. You can also use keynotes instead of text notes if required.

- Open the project **Modern-Hotel-Detailing-M.rvt** from your class folder as the base file for these tasks.

Task 1 - Create a window sill detail.

In this task you will create a window sill detail, as shown in Figure 16–45.

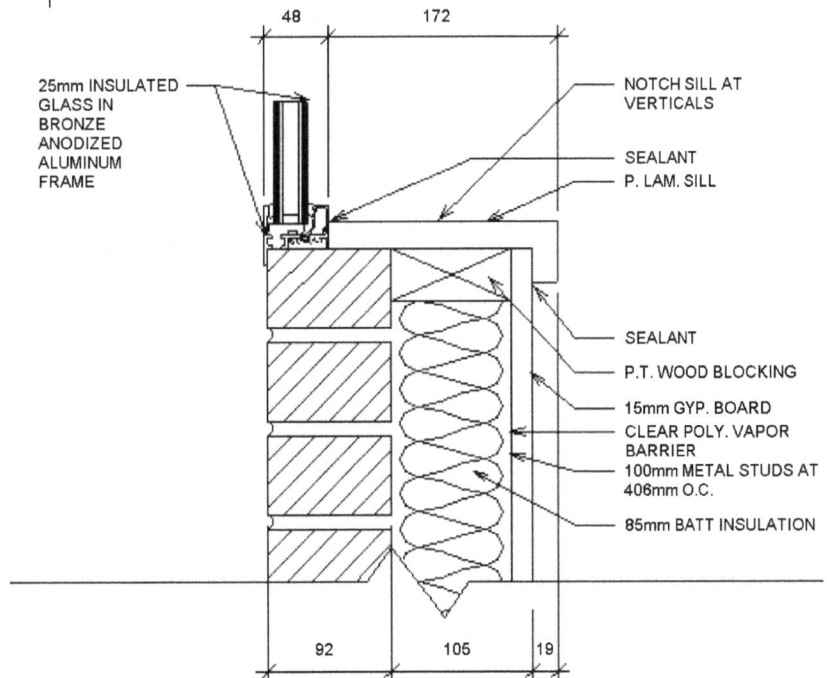

Figure 16–45

- Use detail components from the Library, detail lines, patterning, text, and dimensions to create the window sill detail.

Task 2 - Add structural detail.

In this task you will create a structural detail, as shown in Figure 16–46.

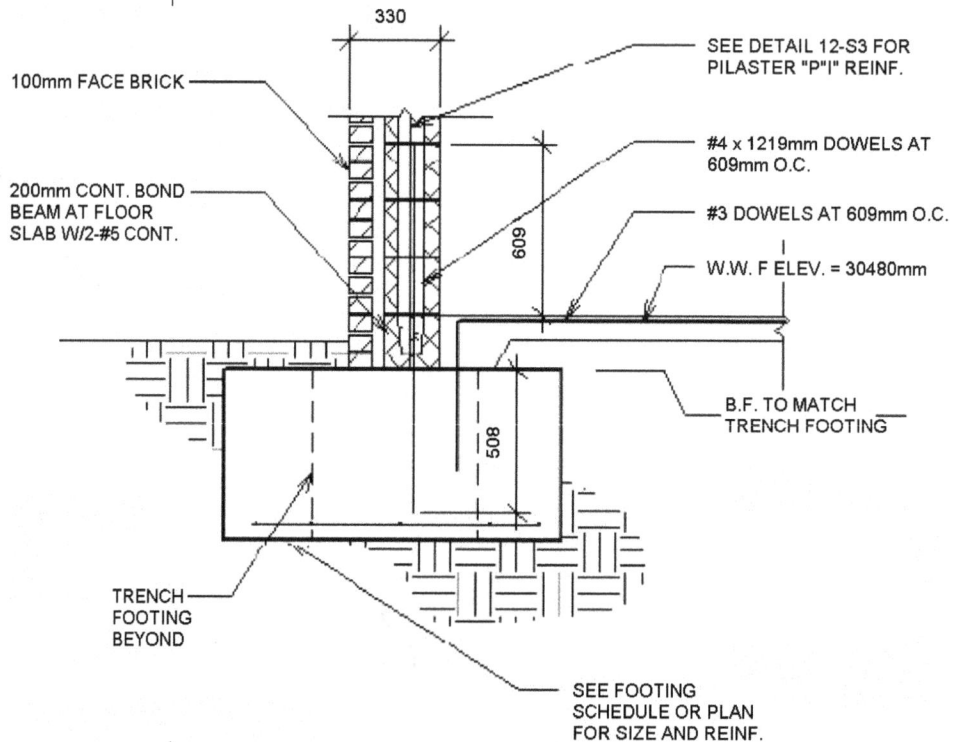

330

SEE DETAIL 12-S3 FOR
PILASTER "P"I" REINF.

100mm FACE BRICK

#4 x 1219mm DOWELS AT
609mm O.C.

200mm CONT. BOND
BEAM AT FLOOR
SLAB W/2-#5 CONT.

609

#3 DOWELS AT 609mm O.C.

W.W. F ELEV. = 30480mm

B.F. TO MATCH
TRENCH FOOTING

508

TRENCH
FOOTING
BEYOND

SEE FOOTING
SCHEDULE OR PLAN
FOR SIZE AND REINF.

Figure 16–46

- Create a new drafting view and draw the structural detail using the various sketching tools and structural detail components.

- Use the **Invisible lines** line type when you draw the lines for the fill boundary. The curved lines are made with splines.

- Create the Earth pattern type by duplicating an existing type and assigning a new drafting pattern to it.

- The brick sections are located in the *Detail Components> Division 4>Masonry>Concrete Masonry (CMU)* folder and the *Clay Masonry Units for Brick* folder.

Chapter Review Questions

1. Which of the following are ways in which you can create a detail? (Select all that apply.)

   a. Make a callout of a section and draw over it.

   b. Draw all of the elements from scratch.

   c. Import a CAD detail and modify or draw over it.

   d. Insert an existing drafting view from another file.

2. In which type of view (access shown in Figure 16–47) can you NOT add detail lines?

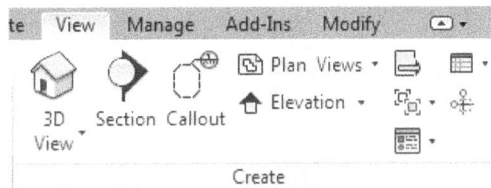

Figure 16–47

   a. Plans

   b. Elevations

   c. 3D views

   d. Legends

3. How is a detail component different from a building component?

   a. There is no difference.

   b. Detail components are made of 2D detail lines only.

   c. Detail components are made of building elements, but only display in detail views.

   d. Detail components are made of 2D and 3D elements.

4. When you draw detail lines they are...

   a. Always the same width.

   b. Vary in width according to the view.

   c. Display in all views associated with the detail.

   d. Display only in the view in which they were created.

5. Which command do you use to add a pattern (such as concrete or earth as shown in Figure 16–48) to part of a detail?

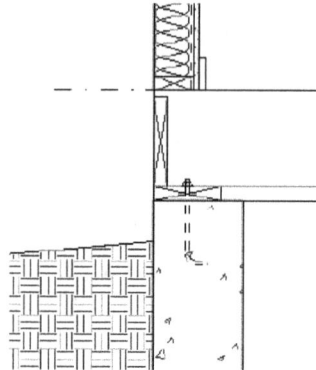

Figure 16–48

a. Region

b. Filled Region

c. Masking Region

d. Pattern Region

Command Summary

Button	Command	Location
CAD Import Tools		
	Delete Layers	• **Ribbon:** *Modify	<imported filename>* tab>Import Instance panel
	Full Explode	• **Ribbon:** *Modify	<imported filename>* tab>Import Instance panel> expand Explode
	Import CAD	• **Ribbon:** *Insert* tab>Import panel
	Partial Explode	• **Ribbon:** *Modify	<imported filename>* tab>Import Instance panel> expand Explode
Detail Tools		
	Detail Component	• **Ribbon:** *Annotate* tab>Detail panel> expand Component
	Detail Line	• **Ribbon:** *Annotate* tab>Detail panel
	Insulation	• **Ribbon:** *Annotate* tab>Detail panel
	Region	• **Ribbon:** *Annotate* tab>Detail panel
	Repeating Detail Component	• **Ribbon:** *Annotate* tab>Detail panel> expand Component
View Tools		
	Bring Forward	• **Ribbon:** *Modify	Detail Items* tab> Arrange panel
	Bring to Front	• **Ribbon:** *Modify	Detail Items* tab> Arrange panel
	Drafting View	• **Ribbon:** *View* tab>Create panel
	Insert from File: Insert Views from File	• **Ribbon:** *Insert* tab>Import panel> expand Insert from File
	Send Backward	• **Ribbon:** *Modify	Detail Items* tab> Arrange panel
	Send to Back	• **Ribbon:** *Modify	Detail Items* tab> Arrange panel

Appendix A

Introduction to Worksets

In this chapter you learn about the purpose of worksharing and the basics of using worksets including how to open a local file, work in a local file, and synchronize with a central file.

This chapter contains the following topics:

- **Introduction to Worksets**

A.1 Introduction to Worksets

Learning Objective

- Create a local file and synchronize it back to a central file.

When a project becomes too big for one person, it needs to be subdivided so that a team of people can work on it. Since Autodesk® Revit® projects include the entire building model in one file, the file needs to be separated into logical components, as shown in Figure A–1, without losing the connection to the whole. This process is called *worksharing* and the main components are worksets.

Figure A–1

When worksets are established in a project, there is one **central file** and as many **local files** as required for each person on the team to have a file, as shown in Figure A–2.

*The **central file** is created by the BIM Manager, Project Manager, or Project Lead, and is stored on a server, enabling multiple users to access it. A **local file** is a copy of the central file that is stored on your computer.*

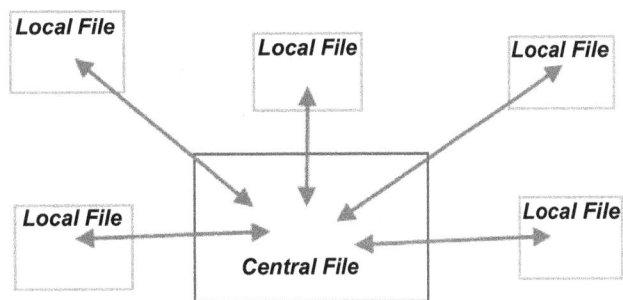

Figure A–2

- All local files are saved back to the central file, and updates to the central file are sent out to the local files. This way, all changes remain in one file, while the project, model, views, and sheets are automatically updated.

How To: Create a Local File

1. In the Application Menu or Quick Access Toolbar click

   (Open). You must use this method to be able to create a local file from the central file.
2. In the Open dialog box, navigate to the central file server location, and select the central file. Do not work in this file. Select **Create New Local**, as shown in Figure A–3.

3. Verify that this option is selected and click ⌐ Open ⌐.

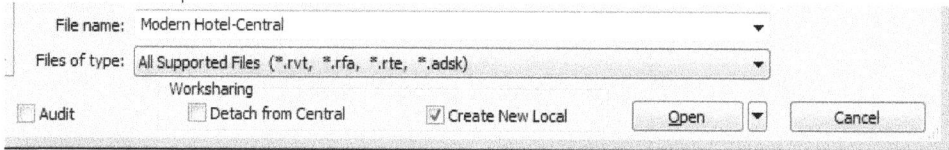

Figure A–3

User Names can be assigned in Options.

4. A copy of the project is created. It is named the same as the central file, but with your *User Name* added to the end.

5. In the Quick Access Toolbar, click ▦ (Save) to save the file using the default file name (i.e., *Central File Name-Local*.rvt).

• You can also use ▦ (Save As) and name the file according to your office's standard. It should include *Local* in the name to indicate that it is saved on your local computer, or that you are the only one working with that version of the file.

How To: Work in a Workset-Related File

1. Open your local file.
2. In the Status Bar, expand the *Active Workset* drop-down list and select a workset, as shown in Figure A–4. By setting the active workset, other people can work in the project but cannot edit elements that you add to the workset.

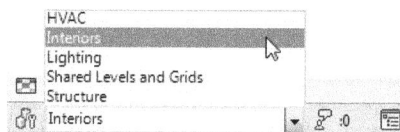

Figure A–4

3. Work on the project as required.

Saving Workset-Related Files

When you are using a workset-related file, you need to save the file locally and centrally.

- Save the local file frequently (every 15-30 minutes). In the Quick Access Toolbar, click ▣ (Save) to save the local file just as you would any other project.

- Synchronize the local file with the central file periodically (every hour or two) or after you have made major changes to the project.

Hint: Set up Notifications to Save and Synchronize

You can set up reminders to save and synchronize files to the central file in the Options dialog box, on the *General* pane, as shown in Figure A–5.

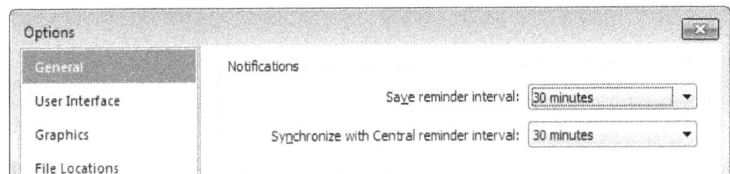

Figure A–5

Synchronizing to the Central File

There are two methods for synchronizing to the central file. They are located in the Quick Access Toolbar or the *Collaborate* tab> Synchronize panel.

Click 🗗 (Synchronize Now) to update the central file and then the local file with any changes to the central file since the last synchronization. This does not prompt you for any thing. It automatically relinquishes elements borrowed from a workset used by another person, but retains worksets used by the current person.

Click 🗗 (Synchronize and Modify Settings) to open the Synchronize with Central dialog box, as shown in Figure A–6, where you can set the location of the central file, add comments, save the file locally before and after synchronization, and set the options for relinquishing worksets and elements.

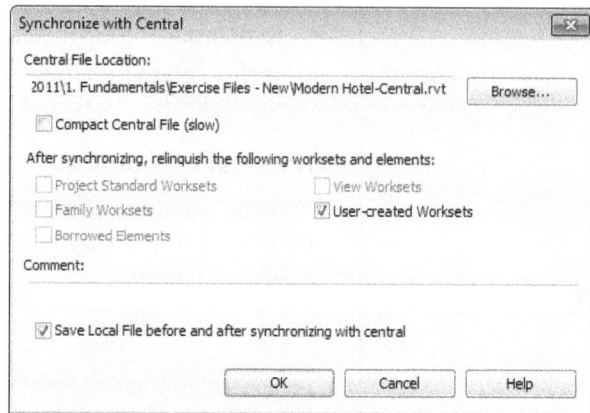

Figure A–6

- Always save the local file after you have synchronized the file with central. Changes from the central file might have been copied into your file.

- When you close a local file without saving to the central file, you are prompted with options, as shown in Figure A–7.

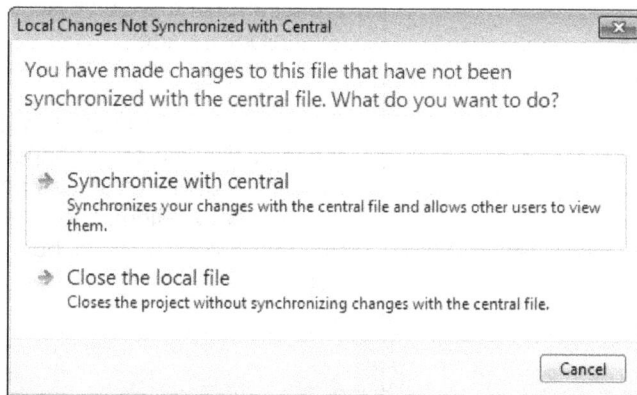

Figure A–7

Command Summary

Button	Command	Location
	Save	• **Quick Access Toolbar** • **Application Menu:** Save • **Shortcut:** <Ctrl>+<S>
	Synchronize and Modify Settings	• **Quick Access Toolbar** • **Ribbon:** *Collaborate* tab>Synchronize panel>expand Synchronize with Central
	Synchronize Now	• **Quick Access Toolbar** • **Ribbon:** *Collaborate* tab>Synchronize panel>expand Synchronize with Central

Appendix B

Additional Tools

In this appendix you learn how to reuse selection sets, add wall sweeps, create curtain wall types with automatic grids, and add dormers to roofs. You learn how to enhance views, set up and use revisions, annotate dependent views, create building component schedules. and create repeating details.

This chapter contains the following topics:

- **Reusing Selection Sets**
- **Wall Sweeps and Reveals**
- **Creating Curtain Wall Types with Automatic Grids**
- **Enhancing Views**
- **Creating Dormers**
- **Revision Tracking**
- **Annotating Dependent Views**
- **Creating Building Component Schedules**
- **Creating a Repeating Detail**

B.1 Reusing Selection Sets

Learning Objective

- Save and use selection sets of multiple building elements.

When multiple elements types are selected you can save the selection set so that it can be reused. For example, a structural column and an architectural column need to move together. Instead of picking each element, create a selection set that you can quickly access as shown in Figure B–1. You can also edit selection sets to add or remove elements from the set.

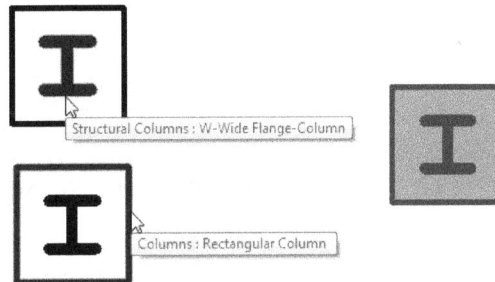

Structural Columns : W-Wide Flange-Column

Columns : Rectangular Column

Figure B–1

- Selection sets are a filter of specific elements rather than types of elements.

How To: Save Selection Sets

1. Select the elements that you want to include in the selection set.
2. In the *Modify | Multi-Select* tab>Selection panel, click ⬚ (Save).
3. In the Save Selection dialog box, type a name for the set as shown in Figure B–2, and click OK .

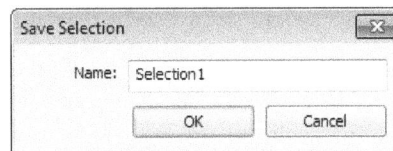

Save Selection

Name: Selection1

OK   Cancel

Figure B–2

How To: Retrieve Selection Sets

1. Select any other elements you might want to use. In the *Modify | Multi-Select* tab>Selection panel, click ⬚ (Load). Alternatively, without any other selection, in the *Manage* tab> Selection panel, click ⬚ (Load).
2. In the Retrieve Filters dialog box (shown in Figure B–3), select the set that you want to use and click [OK].

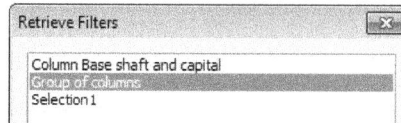

Retrieve Filters

Column Base shaft and capital
Group of columns
Selection 1

Figure B–3

3. The elements are selected and you can continue to select other elements or use the selection.

How To: Edit Selection Sets

1. If elements are selected, in the *Modify | Multi-Select* tab> Selection panel, click ⬚ (Edit). Alternatively, without any selection, in the *Manage* tab>Selection panel, click ⬚ (Edit).
2. In the Filters dialog box (shown in Figure B–4), select the set that you want to edit and click [Edit...].

Some filters in this dialog box are not selection sets but apply to categories of elements, such as the Interior filter shown in Figure B–4.

Filters

Column Base shaft and capital
Group of columns
Interior
Selection 1

New...
Edit...
Rename...
Delete

OK   Cancel   Help

Figure B–4

• If you want to modify the name of the Filter, click [Rename...].

3. The selection set elements remain black while the rest of the elements are grayed out. The *Edit Selection Set* contextual tab displays as well, as shown in Figure B–5.

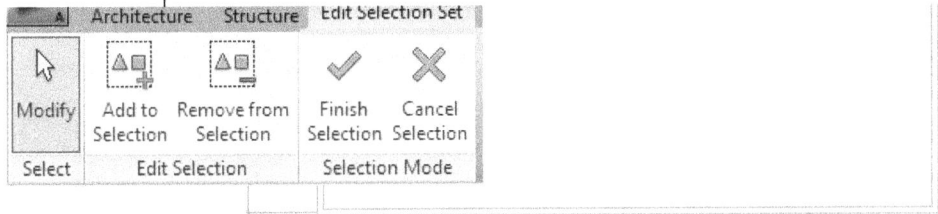

Figure B–5

4. Use ⬛ (Add to Selection) to select additional elements for the set and ⬛ (Remove from Selection) to delete elements from the set.

5. When you have finished editing, click ✓ (Finish Selection).

• In the Filters dialog box, click ⬛ OK ⬛ to finish.

B.2 Wall Sweeps and Reveals

Learning Objectives

- Add wall sweeps and reveals, roof fascias and gutters, and floor slab edges to existing elements.
- Setup sweep types using profiles.

The Autodesk Revit software includes a series of commands that enable you to modify walls, roofs, and floors by sweeping a profile along an element. For example, you can quickly add a gutter along the full length of a roof, or a curb at the edge of a floor used as a balcony, as shown in Figure B–6. The element modified by the sweep is called the host. Therefore, all of these operations are known as host sweeps.

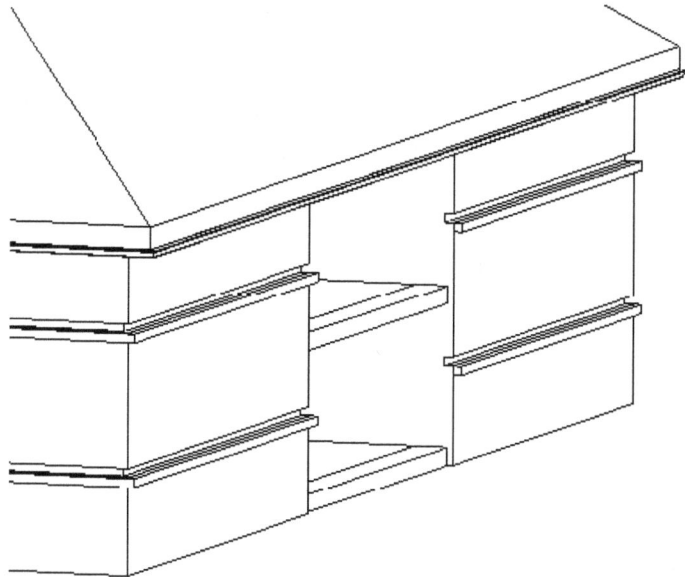

Figure B–6

- The software comes with a few standard profiles for the sweeps. You can also create your own custom profiles.

- Open a 3D view if you are working with walls. You can be in a plan or elevation view for working with roof and floor sweeps.

- There are specific commands to create wall sweeps and reveals, roof fascias and gutters, and floor slab edges. These are located by expanding the associated command in the *Architecture* tab>Build panel, as shown in Figure B–7. For walls and floors, they are also located in the *Structure* tab> Structure.

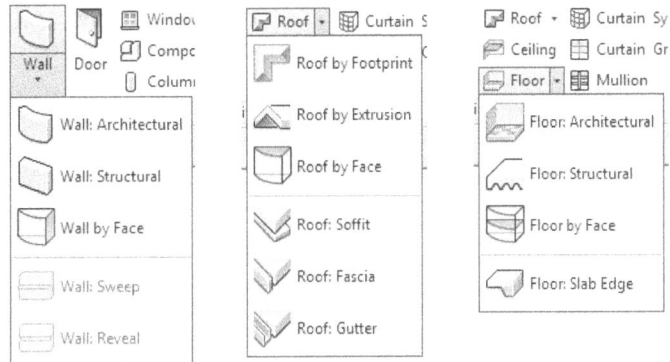

Figure B–7

- Wall Sweeps and Wall Reveals can only be applied in elevation, section, or 3D views.

How To: Use the Wall Sweep Command

The process of creating reveals, gutters, and floor slab edges is similar.

1. Open an elevation or 3D view.

2. In the *Architecture* tab>Build panel, expand ⬭ (Wall) and click ⬒ (Wall Sweep).

3. In Properties, select a Wall Sweep type. (The Wall Sweep type needs to be set up before you start the command.)

4. In the *Modify|Place Wall Sweep* tab>Placement panel, click either ⬭ (Horizontal) or ⬭ (Vertical). (This is only for walls.)

5. Move the cursor over the element where you want to add the sweep and click to place it.

6. If you are doing horizontal sweeps, continue selecting elements. The sweep is placed at the same height as the first element.

7. To change sweep styles or the height, in the Placement panel, click ⬓ (Restart Wall Sweep), or return to the **Modify** command.to finish.

To specify a precise location for the sweep element, select it after you have created it and modify the dimensions as required.

How To: Set Up Sweep Profiles

1. In the *Insert* tab>Load from Library panel, click ⬇️ (Load Family).
2. In the Load Family dialog box, select the profile you want to use (in the *Profiles* folder) or select a custom profile.
3. Start the related host sweep command. For example, if you are working with a gutter, click 〰️ (Gutter).
4. In Properties, select a Sweep type and click 🔲 Edit Type .
5. In the Type Properties dialog box, click ⬜ Duplicate... .
6. Enter a new name for the type.
7. In the Type Properties dialog box, under *Construction*, select the *Profile*. You can also apply *Constraints, Materials and Finishes*, and *Identity Data*, as shown in Figure B–8.

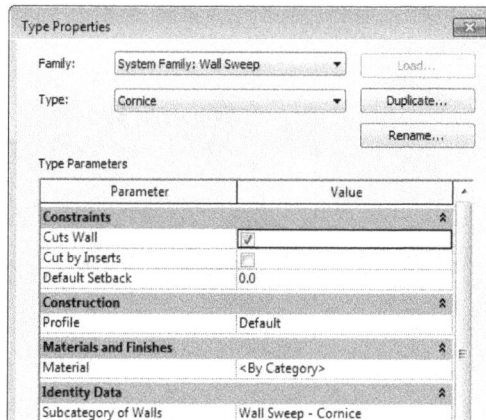

Figure B–8

8. Click ⬜ OK to close the dialog box. The new type is set to be current.

Constraints

Constraints give you more control over how the sweep works.

Cuts Wall	If selected, cuts the geometry out of the host wall where it overlaps. Turning this off might increase the performance if the project contains a large amount of sweeps.
Cut by Inserts	If selected, when doors or windows are inserted into a wall with a wall sweep, the insert cuts the sweep.
Default Setback	Specify the distance that the sweep is set back from interacting wall inserts.

B.3 Creating Curtain Wall Types with Automatic Grids

Learning Objective

- Duplicate a Curtain Wall type and set up a new type with a grid pattern.

If you have a curtain wall with a fixed distance or a fixed number of grids in the vertical or horizontal direction, you can create a curtain wall type containing this information, as shown in Figure B–9. The automatic grid lines can also be set to an angle.

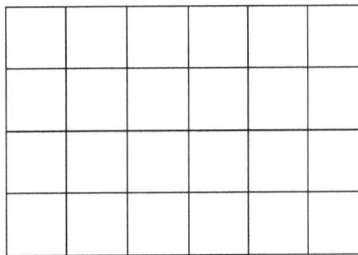

Figure B–9

How To: Create a Curtain Wall with Automatic Grids

1. In the *Architecture* tab>Build panel, click ⬚ (Wall).
2. In the Type Selector, select a curtain wall similar to the one you want to create.
3. In Properties, click ▤ (Edit Type).
4. In the Type Properties dialog box, click [Duplicate...] to create a copy of the existing family type.
5. In the Name dialog box, give the curtain wall a name that describes its purpose, as shown in Figure B–10. The new name automatically includes the family name, such as **Curtain Wall**. Therefore, you do not have to include the family name.

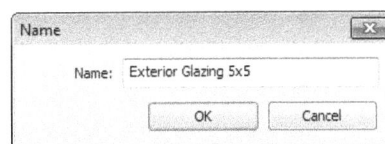

Name: Exterior Glazing 5x5

Figure B–10

6. In the Type Properties dialog box, enter information for the *Construction*, *Vertical* and *Horizontal Grid Pattern*, and *Vertical* and *Horizontal Mullions* parameters, as shown in Figure B–11.

Type Parameters apply to all instances of that type inserted into the Autodesk Revit software. This is true for all families (walls, doors, windows, etc.). Changing a Type Parameter changes all instances of that type in the project.

Parameter	Value
Construction	⌃
Function	Exterior
Automatically Embed	☑
Curtain Panel	None
Join Condition	Not Defined
Graphics	⌃
Display in Hidden Views	Edges Hidden by Other Members
Vertical Grid Pattern	⌃
Layout	Fixed Distance
Spacing	1500.0
Adjust for Mullion Size	☑
Horizontal Grid Pattern	⌃
Layout	Fixed Distance
Spacing	1500.0
Adjust for Mullion Size	☑
Vertical Mullions	⌃
Interior Type	None
Border 1 Type	None
Border 2 Type	None

Figure B–11

- Enable the *Automatically Embed* parameter if you want to use the curtain wall as a storefront.

- Set the *Curtain Panel* to the primary type you plan to use. You can modify the panels once they are in the project.

- The Grid Patterns can be set to the following:

Fixed Distance	Grids are placed a specified distance apart. Specify the size in the **Spacing** option.
Fixed Number	Grids are divided across a wall based on a specified number. The *Number* of grid lines is specified in the Instance Parameters.
Maximum Spacing	Grids are spaced evenly with the greatest distance between them specified in the **Spacing** option.
None	No grids are specified.

- The **Adjust for Mullion Size** parameter ensures that panels inserted between grid lines are equal in size. This is very important if you use a different size of mullion on the borders from the ones on the interior separations.

- Mullions can be specified in the Type Parameters for Interior and Border mullions. The vertical **Border 1** type is applied to the left of the curtain wall and **Border 2** is applied to the right. The horizontal **Border 1** type is at the bottom and **Border 2** is at the top.
- You can preapply the mullions to the grid in the type or add them later. If you are planning to use the curtain wall type as a base to create a more complex curtain wall, do not add mullions in the type because doing so makes it difficult to select the grid lines to modify them.

7. Click [OK] to close the Type Properties dialog box.
8. In Properties, set the *Vertical* and *Horizontal Grid Pattern* (including *Number* for Fixed Number, *Justification*, *Angle*, and *Offset*), as shown in Figure B–12.

The options in Properties are Instance Parameters applied to the selected instance of the type inserted into the Autodesk Revit software.

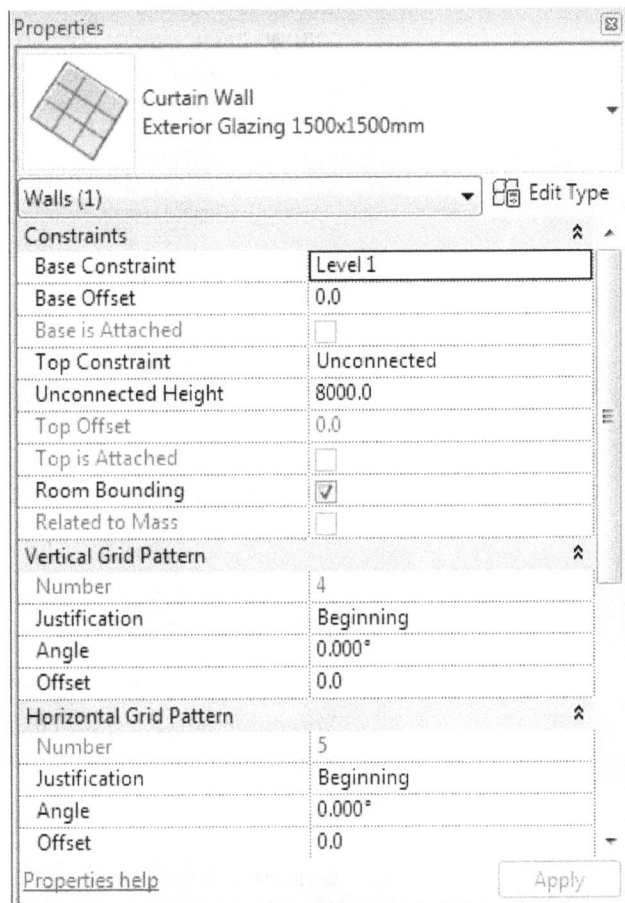

Properties

Curtain Wall
Exterior Glazing 1500x1500mm

Walls (1)　　　　　　　　　　　▼　🖳 Edit Type

Constraints		⌃
Base Constraint	Level 1	
Base Offset	0.0	
Base is Attached	☐	
Top Constraint	Unconnected	
Unconnected Height	8000.0	
Top Offset	0.0	
Top is Attached	☐	
Room Bounding	☑	
Related to Mass	☐	
Vertical Grid Pattern		⌃
Number	4	
Justification	Beginning	
Angle	0.000°	
Offset	0.0	
Horizontal Grid Pattern		⌃
Number	5	
Justification	Beginning	
Angle	0.000°	
Offset	0.0	

Properties help　　　　　　　　　　Apply

Figure B–12

B.4 Enhancing Views

Learning Objectives

- Clarify views using **Split Face** and **Paint** to add materials to parts of elevations or sections and **Linework** to change the line style or weight to emphasize elements.

- Modify elements in plan views and sections by editing the cut profile to indicate the most accurate connections and using **Join Geometry** so the elements display correctly.

When you start detailing views (such as elevations and sections), several tools can help clarify what you are trying to show. **Split Face** divides an elevation face into smaller separate faces. You can then use **Paint** to apply different materials to the faces, as shown in Figure B–13. **Linework** enables you to change the lineweight or line style of lines in a view to emphasize various components. In plan views and sections, you can use **Edit Cut Profile** and **Join Geometry** to enhance the views.

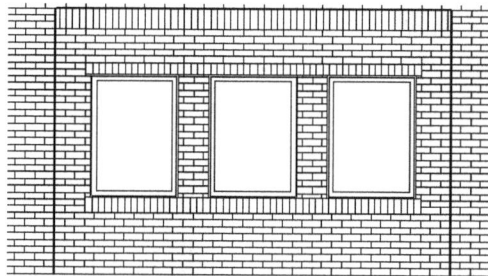

Figure B–13

- The changes made with **Split Face** and **Paint** are displayed in elevations and 3D views.

- Changes made using **Linework** are view-specific, applying only in the view in which they are made.

Hint: Changing the Host of an Element

You can change the wall that a window or door is associated with by re-hosting the element. Select the window or door and in the *Modify contextual* tab>Host panel, click (Pick New Host). Then select the new wall where you want the door or window to be located.

- This also works with other hosted and workplane-based elements.

Splitting Faces

You can split a face into separate surfaces so you can apply different materials to each part. A sketch defines the split, which must be a closed shape completely inside the face, or an open shape that touches the face edges, as shown in Figure B–14. Windows are cut out of faces automatically.

Figure B–14

How to:

How To: Create a Split Face

1. Switch to an elevation view (a 3D view works as well).

2. In the *Modify* tab>Geometry panel, click 📦 (Split Face).
3. Select the edge of the face that you want to modify. Use <Tab> as required to toggle through the available faces.
4. In the *Modify | Split Face>Create Boundary* tab>Draw panel, use the sketch tools to create a sketch as required to define the split.

5. Click ✓ (Finish Edit Mode).

*If you have **Select elements by face** toggled on you can click directly on the face.*

- To save time, use a wall style that includes the primary material you want to use on the split face. For example, if you are working with brick, set the wall to a type that has a brick face. This way, you can work with the brick courses when you are creating the split face.

- When using a material, such as brick, you can snap to the pattern and even lock the split lines to the pattern as shown in Figure B–15.

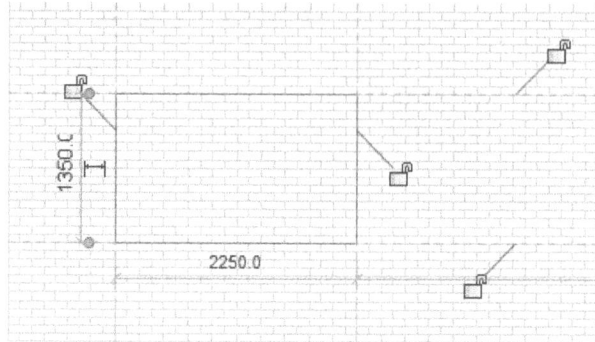

Figure B–15

- You can double-click on the edge of the split face lines to switch to Edit Boundary mode. If you double-click on the face (with **Select elements by face** toggled on) it switches to Edit Profile mode, which impacts the entire wall, not just the split face boundary.

Editing Wall Joins

Before you start working with split faces, ensure the walls are mitered, as shown in Figure B–16. By default, the walls are butted to each other. This creates a problem when you select faces. Use **Edit Wall Joins** to modify the intersections. Do not use this command if you have complex wall joins; instead, modify the length of the wall in relation to the adjoining walls.

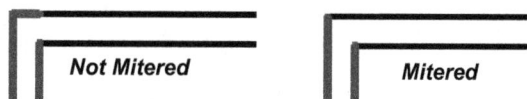

Not Mitered   *Mitered*

Figure B–16

How To: Edit a Wall Join

1. In the *Modify* tab>Geometry panel, click ⌐⌐ (Wall Joins).
2. Move the cursor over the wall join that you want to edit. There is a square box around the join.
3. Click on the join to edit it.
4. In the Options Bar, the configuration options display, as shown in Figure B–17. Select the required option.

Figure B–17

- You can select from three configurations: **Butt**, **Miter**, and **Square off**, as shown in Figure B–18. Click `Previous` and `Next` to toggle the butt or squared-off corner configurations through the various intersection options.

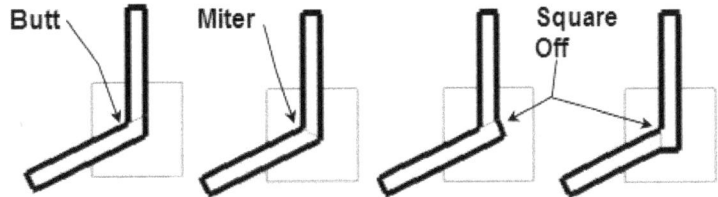

Butt   Miter   Square Off

Figure B–18

- The *Display* controls whether or not wall joins are displayed. The options are **Use View Settings** (set up in View Properties), **Clean Join**, and **Don't Clean Join**.

5. If you select the end of a wall that is not joined to another wall, you can change the option to **Allow Join** in the Options Bar, as shown in Figure B–19. Reselect the wall join to make the configurations available.

Display   ⦿ Allow Join   ◯ Disallow Join

Figure B–19

Applying Materials

Once you have a face split into sections, you can apply different materials to each part. For example, you might want a soldier course under each window on a brick wall. First, you would create the split face and then apply the new material using **Paint**, as shown in Figure B–20.

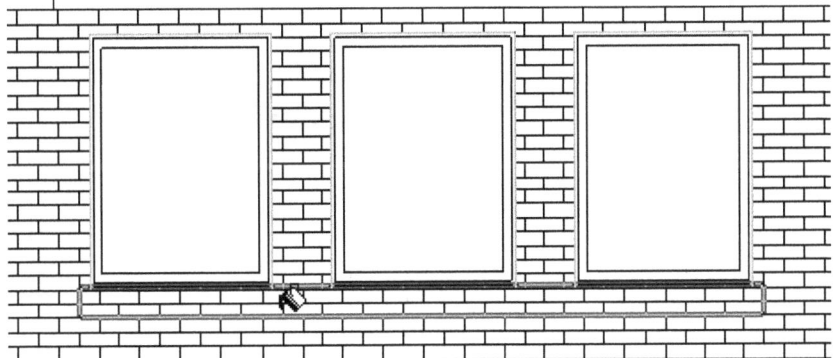

Figure B–20

How To: Apply Material with Paint

1. In the *Modify* tab>Geometry panel, click ⊘ (Paint) or type **PT**.
2. In the Material Browser, select a material. You can run a search or filter the list using specific types of materials, as shown in Figure B–21.

The browser remains open as you are applying the paint.

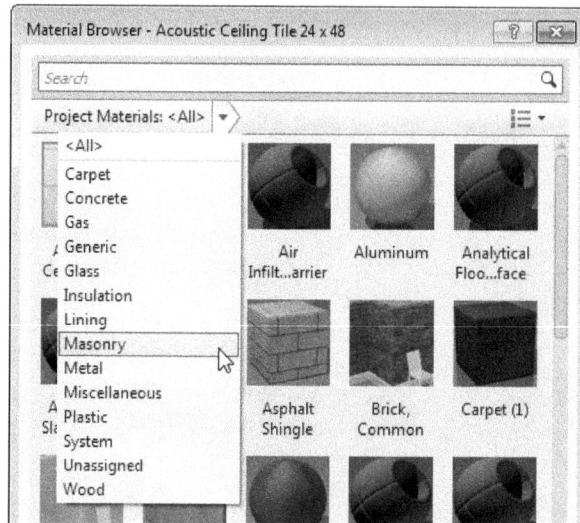

Figure B–21

3. Move the cursor over the face you want to paint. It should pre-highlight. Click on the face to apply the material.
4. Continue selecting materials and painting other faces as required.

5. In the Material Browser, click [Done] to finish the command.

• Some material patterns display as shaded when you zoom out. Zoom in to display the pattern. Other material patterns only display when you are in the 🖼 (Realistic) Visual Style.

• To change the material applied to a face, in the *Modify* tab> Geometry panel, expand ⊘ (Paint) and click ⊘ (Remove Paint). Select the face(s) from which you want to remove the material.

Adjusting Linework

To emphasize a particular line or change the look of a line in elevations and other views, modify the lines with the **Linework** command. Changes made to lines with the **Linework** command are view-specific, applying only to the view in which you make them, as shown in Figure B–22.

- The **Linework** command can be used on project edges of model elements, cut edges of model elements, edges in imported CAD files, and edges in linked Autodesk® Revit® models.

Figure B–22

How To: Adjust Linework

1. In the *Modify* tab>View panel, click (Linework) or type the shortcut **LW**.
2. In the *Modify | Linework* tab>Line Style panel, select the line style you want to use from the list.
3. Move the cursor and pre-highlight the line you want to change. You can use <Tab> to toggle through the lines as required.
4. Click on the line to change it to the new line style.
5. Click on other lines as required or return to the **Modify** command to finish.

- If the line is too long or short, you can modify the length using the controls at the end of the line.

How To: Create Line Styles

1. In the *Manage* tab>Settings panel, expand [icon] (Additional Settings) and click [icon] (Line Styles).
2. In the Line Styles dialog box, as shown in Figure B–23, in the *Modify Subcategories* area, click [New].

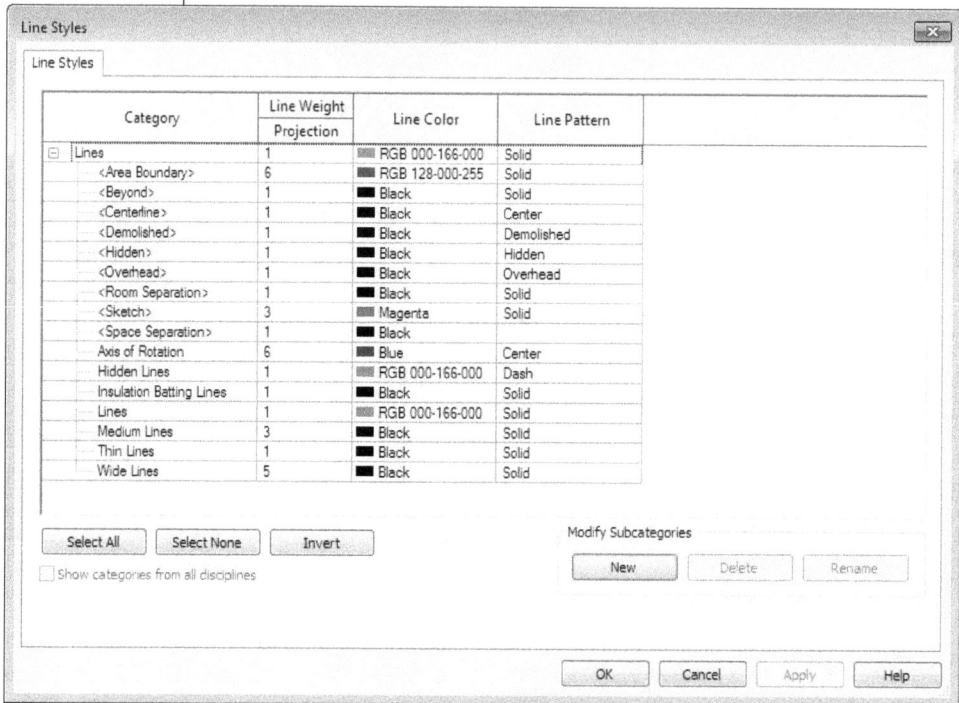

Figure B–23

3. In the New Subcategory dialog box, type a name for the new style, as shown in Figure B–24, and click [OK].

*The **Subcategory of:** option is automatically set to **Lines**.*

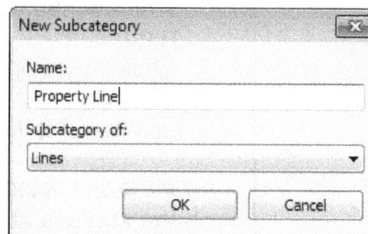

Figure B–24

4. In the Line Styles dialog box, assign the required line weight, color, and pattern to the new style.

Editing Plan and Section Profiles

*If you are working on a compound face (such as a wall with several layers of information), change the Detail Level to **Medium** or **Fine** to display the fill patterns.*

In plan and section details, you might need to modify portions of the cut to show the specific intersection of two faces, as shown in Figure B–25. This can be done using **Cut Profile**. The cut profile changes the shape of the elements at their cut plane, but does not modify their 3D information. The cut is only displayed in the view in which it is drawn.

Figure B–25

- You can modify the cut of walls, floors, and roofs.

How To: Use Cut Profile

1. In the *View* tab>Graphics panel, click ▦ (Cut Profile).
2. In the Options Bar, select to edit the **Face** or the **Boundary between faces**, as shown in Figure B–26.

Edit: ○ Face ◉ Boundary between faces

Figure B–26

3. Select the face or boundary that you want to edit.
4. In the *Modify | Create Cut Profile Sketch* tab>Draw panel, use the sketch tools to sketch a new profile, as shown in Figure B–27.

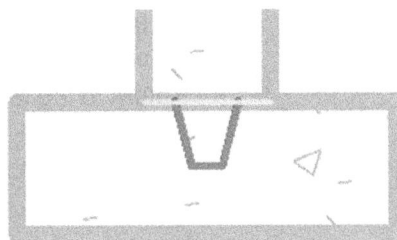

Figure B–27

5. Click ✓ (Finish Edit Mode).

- If a warning box opens, verify that the lines start and end on the same boundary line and that they do not make a closed loop or cross over each other.

Joining Cut Sections

When you are creating a section, you might want the intersections to be seamless. You can do this by *joining* the geometry. This works between walls and other walls, beams, ceilings, floors, and roofs, as shown in Figure B–28.

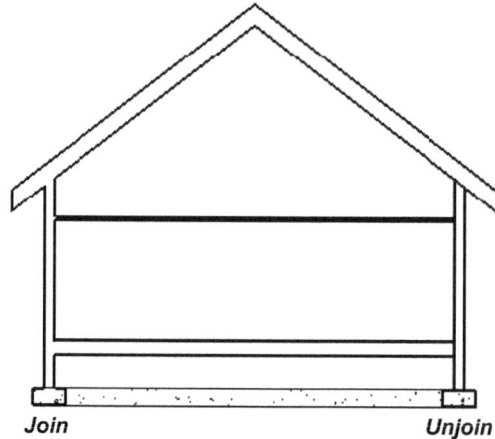

Join   Unjoin

Figure B–28

How To: Join Geometry

1. In the *Modify* tab>Geometry panel, expand ⬡ (Join) and click ⬡ (Join Geometry).
2. In the Options Bar, select the **Multiple Join** option if you want to join several elements to the first element.
3. Select the first element.
4. Select the second element.
   - If you selected the **Multiple Join** option, select additional elements.
5. Return to the **Modify** command.to finish the command.

B.5 Creating Dormers

Learning Objective

• Add dormers to roofs.

You can add two types of dormers to a project. One type of dormer cuts through the roof, as shown in Figure B–29. This dormer type has walls supporting a separate roof. You create the supporting walls and dormer roof, and then cut a hole in the roof.

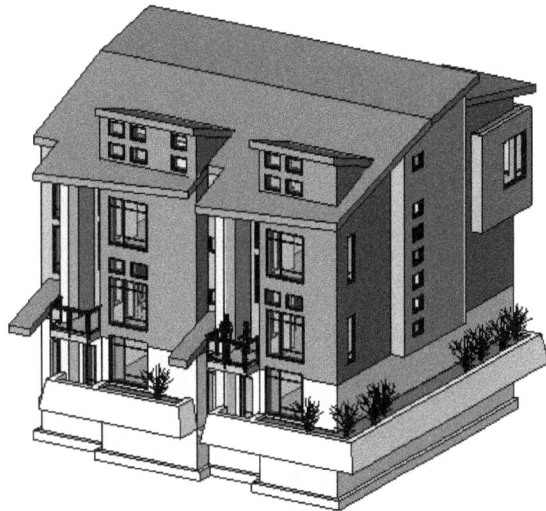

Figure B–29

The other type of dormers are part of the roof, as shown in Figure B–30. This is created by sketching the roof, modifying it, and adding slope arrows to define the additional peak.

Figure B–30

• The dormer must be added to a plane that defines a slope.

How To: Add a Dormer with Supporting Walls to a Roof

1. Draw the main roof. When it is placed correctly, create a secondary dormer roof and supporting walls, as shown in Figure B–31.

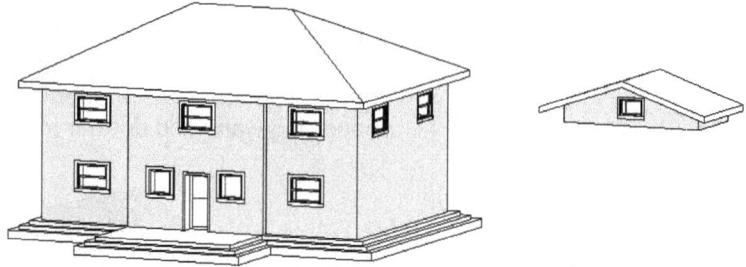

Figure B–31

2. Move the new dormer (walls and roof) into position as required.

3. In the *Modify* tab>Geometry panel, click (Join) and connect the dormer walls/roof to the existing roof.

4. In the *Architecture* tab>Openings panel, click (Dormer Opening).
5. In a roof plan view, select the main roof (the one to be cut).

6. In the *Modify | Edit Sketch* tab>Pick panel, click (Pick Roof/Wall Edges) and sketch the opening to be cut.

- The dormer opening sketch does not need to be closed.

- Clean up the roofs and roof edges as required using tools such as **Join**, **Attach Top/Base**, etc.

How To: Add A Dormer Using Slope Arrows to a Roof

1. Draw a roof. When it is placed, select the roof. In the *Modify |*

   Roofs tab>Mode panel, click (Edit Footprint) to edit the roof sketch.
2. In the *Modify | Roofs>Edit Footprint* tab>Modify panel, click

   (Split Element) to split the edge of the roof between the two points where you want the dormer to be located. Do not delete the inner segment. You can use dynamic dimensions to help locate the points to split.

3. In the Selection panel, click ⬉ (Modify) and select the new segment between the split points. In the Options Bar, clear the **Defines Slope** option for this segment.

4. In the Draw panel, click 📧 (Slope Arrow).

5. Draw a slope arrow from one end of the segment to the midpoint. Then draw a second slope arrow from the other end to the midpoint, as shown in Figure B–32.

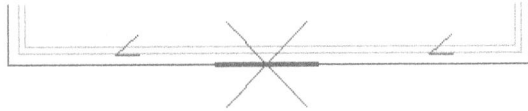

Figure B–32

6. Select the slope arrows. In Properties, specify the **Height at the Tail** or **Slope** option and type the required properties.

7. In the Mode panel, click ✓ (Finish Edit Mode).

8. View the roof in a 3D view to verify the results, as shown in Figure B–33.

Figure B–33

B.6 Revision Tracking

Learning Objectives

- Add and tag revision clouds around areas that are changed on sheets.
- Create a revision table for the project or a template.
- Issue revisions for the record.

When a set of drawings has been put into production, you need to show where changes are made. Typically, these are shown on drawing sheets using a revision cloud. Each cloud is then tagged and the number is referenced elsewhere on the sheet with the description and date, as shown in Figure B–34. The Autodesk Revit software has created a process where the numbering and description are automatically applied to the title blocks when you associate a revision cloud with the information.

Figure B–34

The information is stored in a revision table. This table can be created before or after you start adding revision clouds to the project. Once the table is created, you can modify the **Revision** parameter of the cloud to match the corresponding information.

- More than one revision cloud can be associated with a revision number.

- The title blocks that come with the Autodesk Revit software already have a revision schedule inserted into the title area. It is recommended that you also add a revision schedule to your company title block.

Revision Clouds

Revision clouds can be added before or after you create a revision table that assigns the number and value.

When you add revision clouds to a project, you also need to assign the revision to the cloud and tag the cloud, as shown in Figure B–35.

Figure B–35

How To: Add Revision Clouds

1. In the *Annotate* tab>Detail panel, click ☁ (Revision Cloud).
2. In the *Modify | Create Revision Cloud Sketch* tab>Draw panel, use the draw tools to create the cloud.
3. In the *Modify | Create Revision Cloud Sketch* tab>Mode panel, click ✓ (Finish Edit Mode).
4. In the Options Bar or Properties, expand the Revision drop-down list and select the Revision list, as shown in Figure B–36.

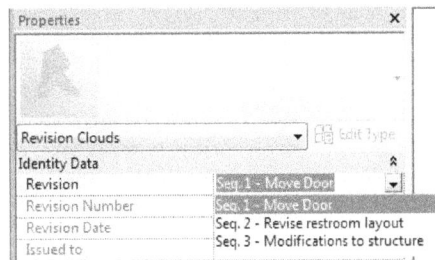

If the revision table has not be set up, you can do this at a later date.

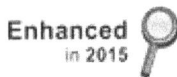

Figure B–36

5. Click in empty space to release the selection.

- The *Revision Number* and *Date* are automatically assigned according to the specifications in the revision table.

- The length of the arcs that form the revision cloud is controlled in the Sheet Issues/Revisions dialog box. It is an annotation element, and therefore is scaled according to the view scale.

- You can create an open cloud (e.g., as a tree line), as shown in Figure B–37.

Figure B–37

- You can double-click on the edge of revision cloud to switch to Edit Sketch mode and modify the size or location of the revision cloud arcs.

How to:

How To: Tag Revision Clouds

1. In the *Annotate* tab>Tag panel, click (Tag By Category).
2. Select the revision cloud to tag. A tooltip containing the revision number and revision from the cloud properties displays when you hover the cursor over the revision cloud, as shown in Figure B–38.

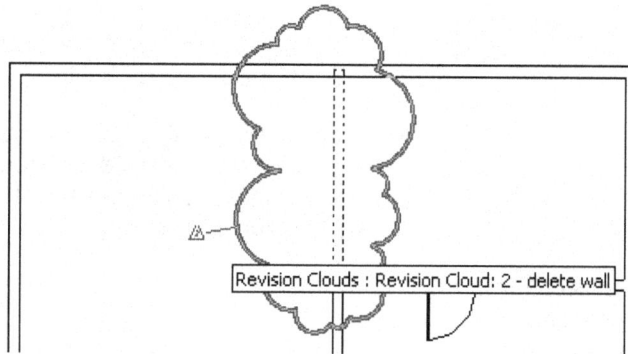

Revision Clouds : Revision Cloud: 2 - delete wall

Figure B–38

- If the revision cloud tag is not loaded, load **Revision Tag.rfa** from the *Annotations* folder in the Library.

Creating the Revision Table

As you add revisions, you need to create the table that specifies the revision tag number, revision date, and description.

- One revision is always available in a project.

- Revision clouds can be added before creating the revision table as required.

How To: Create a Revision Table

1. Open an existing project or a template,

2. In the *View* tab>Sheet Composition panel, click ⌁ (Sheet Issues/Revisions), or in the *Manage* tab>Settings panel, expand 🔧 (Additional Settings) and click ⌁ (Sheet Issues/Revisions).

3. In the Sheet Issues/Revisions dialog box, in the *Numbering* area, select **Per Project** or **Per Sheet**.

4. One revision is always set in each project and you can modify it before it is issued.

Enhanced in 2015

5. Click [Add] to add a new revision. Specify the *Numbering*, *Date*, and *Description* for the revision, as shown in Figure B–39. Do not modify the *Issued*, *Issued by*, or *Issued to* columns.

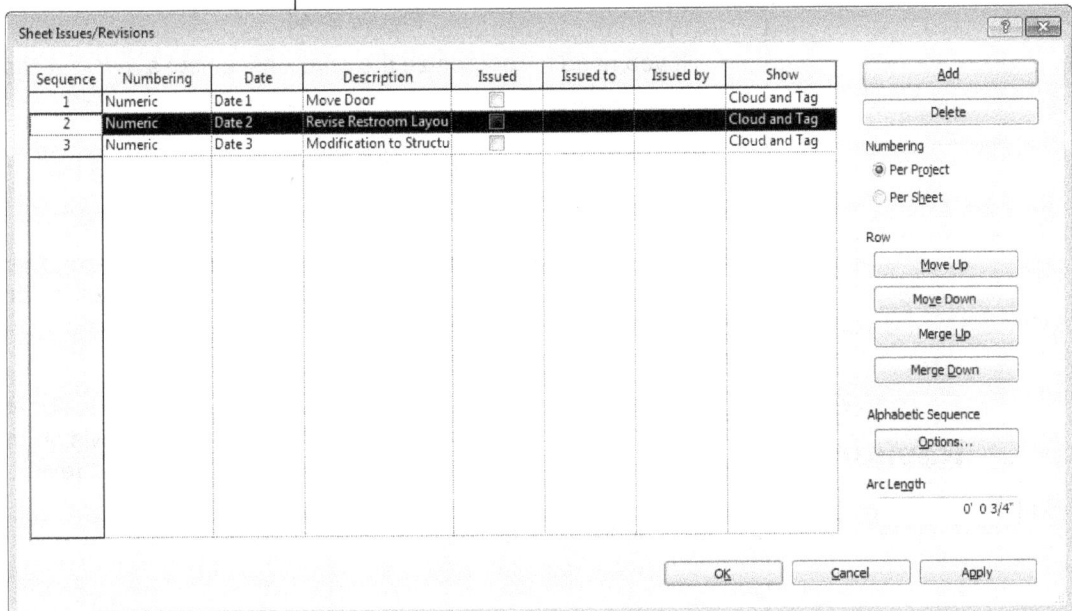

Sequence	Numbering	Date	Description	Issued	Issued to	Issued by	Show
1	Numeric	Date 1	Move Door	☐			Cloud and Tag
2	Numeric	Date 2	Revise Restroom Layou	☐			Cloud and Tag
3	Numeric	Date 3	Modification to Structu	☐			Cloud and Tag

Figure B–39

Enhanced in 2015

- You can click [Delete] to remove revision rows, if required.

6. Click [OK] when you have finished adding revisions.

- If the numbering method is set to **Per Project**, then the numbering sequence is used throughout the project. In many cases, companies prefer to use the **Per Sheet** method where the numbers are sequenced per sheet.

- If you are using **Alphabetic** numbering, click [Options...] to set the alphabetic sequence, as shown in Figure B–40.

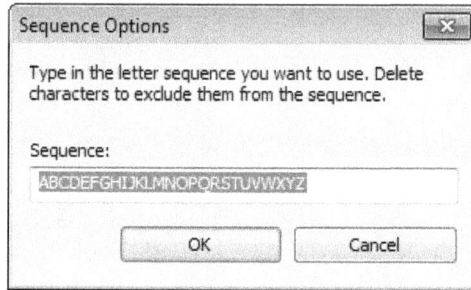

Figure B–40

- If you need to reorganize the revisions, select a row and click [Move Up] and [Move Down] or use [Merge Up] and [Merge Down] to combine the revisions into one.

- When a revision is issued, you cannot modify the information. Therefore, you should wait to issue revisions until just before printing the sheets.

Issuing Revisions

When you have completed the revisions and are ready to submit new documents to the field, you should first lock the revision for the record. This is called issuing the revision. An issued revision is noted in the tooltip of a revision cloud, as shown in Figure B–41.

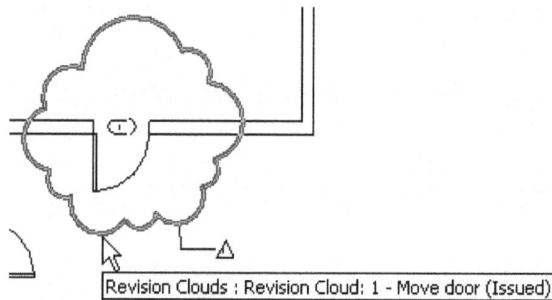

Revision Clouds : Revision Cloud: 1 - Move door (Issued)

Figure B–41

How To: Issue Revisions

1. In the Sheet Issues/Revisions dialog box, in the row for the revision that you are issuing, type a name in the *Issued to* and *Issued by* fields, as required.
2. In the same row, select the **Issued** option.
3. Continue issuing any other revisions, as required.
4. Click [OK] to finish.

- Once the **Issued** option is selected, you cannot modify that revision in the Revisions dialog box or by moving the revision cloud(s). The tooltip on the cloud(s) note that it is **Issued**.

- You can unlock the revision by clearing the **Issued** option. Unlocking enables you to modify the revision after it has been locked.

B.7 Annotating Dependent Views

Learning Objectives

- Duplicate dependent views so that a large building can be placed across several sheets.
- Add Matchlines and View References to indicate where the dependent views separate.

The **Duplicate as a Dependent** command creates a copy of the view and links it to the selected view. Changes made to the original view are also made in the dependent view and vice-versa. Use dependent views when the building model is so large you need to split the building up on separate sheets, with views that are all at the same scale. Having one overall view with dependent views makes viewing changes, such as to the scale or detail level, easier.

Dependent views display in the Project Browser under the top-level view, as shown in Figure B–42.

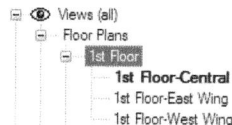

Figure B–42

How To: Duplicate Dependent Views

1. Select the view you want to use as the top-level view.
2. Right-click and select **Duplicate View>Duplicate as a Dependent**.
3. Rename the dependent views as required.

- If you want to separate a dependent view from the original view, right-click on the dependent view and select **Convert to independent view**.

Annotating Views

Annotation Crop Region and Matchlines can be used in any type of view.

When you work with a dependent view, you can use several tools to clarify and annotate the view, including **Matchlines** and **View References**, as shown in Figure B–43.

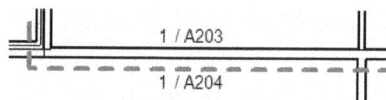

Figure B–43

How To: Add Matchlines

Matchlines are drawn in the primary view to specify where dependent views separate. They display in all related views, as shown in Figure B–44, and extend through all levels of the project by default.

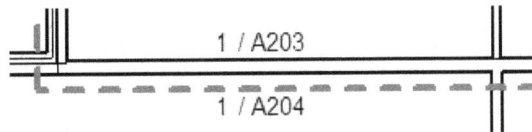

Figure B–44

1. In the *View* tab>Sheet Composition panel, click

    (Matchline).

2. In the Draw panel, click (Line) and draw the location of the matchline.

3. In the Matchline panel, click (Finish Edit Mode) when you are finished.

- To modify an existing matchline by selecting it and clicking

   (Edit Sketch) in the *Modify | Matchline* tab>Mode panel.

- In the *Manage* tab>Settings panel, click (Object Styles) to open the Object Styles dialog box. In the *Annotation Objects* tab, you can make changes to Matchline properties including color, linetype, and line weight.

How To: Add View References

View references only work with primary or dependent views.

Once you have dependent views and a matchline in place, you might want to add view references on either side of the matchline.

1. In the *View* tab>Sheet Composition panel or *Annotate* tab>

   Tag panel, click (View Reference).

2. In the Options Bar, set the *Target view*, as shown in Figure B–45.

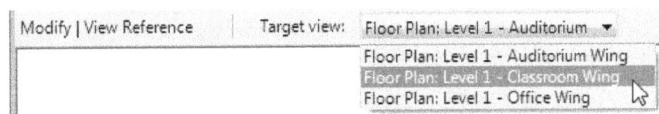

The views listed are the dependent views of the primary view in which you are working.

Figure B–45

3. Place the tag on the side of the matchline that corresponds to the target view.
4. Select another target view from the list and place the tag on the other side of the matchline.
5. The tags display as empty dashes until the views are placed onto sheets. They then update to include the detail and sheet number, as shown in Figure B–46.

```
-/ ---              1 / A102
---  ---  ---  ---  ---  ---  ---  ---
-/ ---              1 / A101
```

Figure B–46

- You can click on the view reference to open the associated view.

- If only a label named **REF** displays when you place a view reference, it means you need to load and update the tag. The **View Reference.rfa** tag is located in the *Annotations* folder. Once you have the tag loaded, in the Type Selector, select

  one of the view references and, in Properties, click 🔲 (Edit Type). Select the **View Reference** tag in the drop-down list,

  as shown in Figure B–47, and click [OK] to close the dialog box. The new tag displays.

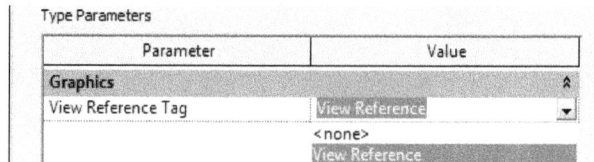

Type Parameters	
Parameter	Value
Graphics	
View Reference Tag	View Reference
	<none>
	View Reference

Figure B–47

B.8 Creating Building Component Schedules

Autodesk Certification Topics & Objectives

Pro.　User

Views

* Create a schedule and add schedule tags　　　　　　✓
* Organize and sort items in a schedule　　　　✓

Learning Objectives

* Schedule building components based on type and instance parameters of elements.
* Setup schedule tables using filters, sorting, grouping, formatting, and appearance.
* Access the Schedule Properties dialog box from the Properties palette

A Building Component schedule is a table view of the type and instance parameters of a specific element. You can specify the parameters (fields) you want to include in the schedule. All of the parameters found in the type of element you are scheduling are available to use. For example, a door schedule (as shown in Figure B–48) can include instance parameters that are automatically filled in (such as the **Height** and **Width**) and type parameters that might need to have the information assigned in the schedule or element type (such as the **Fire Rating** and **Frame**).

			<Door Schedule>			
A	B	C	D	E	F	G
Mark	Height	Width	Fire Rating	Frame Type	Frame Material	Finish
101	2032	915	A	A	Steel	Coated
102	2032	915	A	A	Steel	
103	2032	915	A	A	Steel	
104	2134	915	B			
105	2134	915	B			
106	2134	915	B			

Figure B–48

How To: Create a Building Component Schedule

1. In the *View* tab>Create panel, expand ⊞ (Schedules) and

    click 🗒 (Schedule/Quantities) or in the Project Browser, right-click on the Schedule/Quantities node and select **New Schedule/Quantities**.
2. In the New Schedule dialog box, select the type of schedule you want to create (e.g., Doors) from the *Category* list, as shown in Figure B–49.

In the Filter list drop-down list, you can specify the discipline(s) to show only the categories that you want to display.

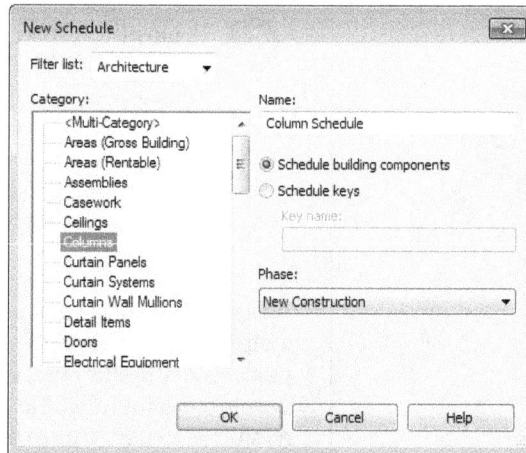

Figure B–49

3. Type a new *Name*, if the default does not suit.
4. Select **Schedule building components.**
5. Specify the *Phase* as required.
6. Click ⸢ OK ⸥.
7. Fill out the information in the Schedule Properties dialog box. This includes the information in the *Fields*, *Filter*, *Sorting/Grouping*, *Formatting*, and *Appearance* tabs.
8. Once you have entering the schedule properties, click ⸢ OK ⸥. A schedule report is created in its own view.

Schedule Properties – Fields Tab

In the *Fields* tab, you can select from a list of available fields and organize them in the order in which you want them to display in the schedule, as shown in Figure B–50.

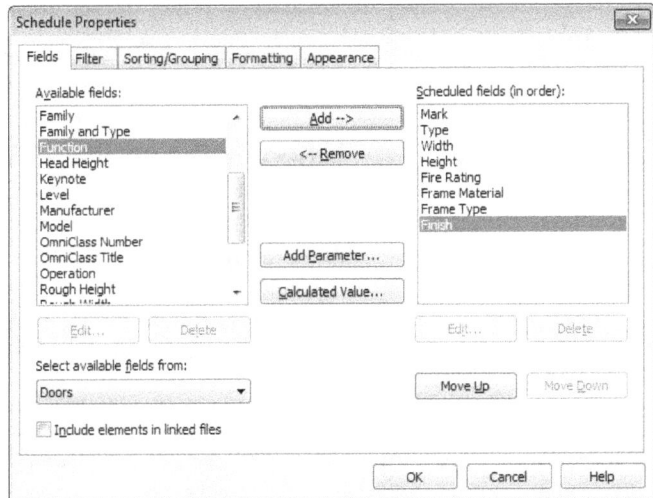

Figure B–50

How To: Fill out the Fields Tab

You can also double-click on a field to move it from the Available Fields to the Scheduled Fields list.

1. In the *Available fields* list, select one or more fields you want to add to the schedule and click [Add -->]. The field(s) are placed in the *Scheduled fields (in order)* list.
2. Continue adding fields as required. If you add one you did not want to use, select it in the *Scheduled fields* list and click [<-- Remove] to move it back to the *Available fields* list.
3. Use [Move Up] and [Move Down] to change the order of the scheduled fields.

Other Fields Tab Options

Select available fields from	Enables you to select additional category fields for the specified schedule. The available list of additional fields depends on the original category of the schedule. Typically, they include room information.
Include elements in linked files	Includes elements that are in files linked to the current project, so that their elements can be included in the schedule.

Add Parameter...	Adds a new field according to your specification. New fields can be placed by instance or by type.
Calculated Value...	Enables you to create a field that uses a formula based on other fields.
Edit...	Enables you to edit custom fields. This is grayed out if you select a standard field.
Delete	Deletes selected custom fields. This is grayed out if you select a standard field.

Schedule Properties – Filter Tab

In the *Filter* tab, you can set up filters so that only elements meeting specific criteria are included in the schedule. For example, you might only want to show information for one level, as shown in Figure B–51. You can create filters for up to eight values. All values must be satisfied for the elements to display.

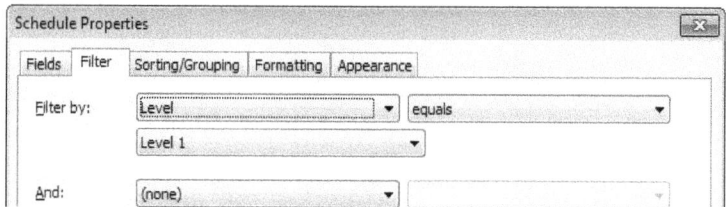

Enhanced
in 2015

Figure B–51

• The parameter you want to use as a filter must be included in the schedule. You can hide the parameter once you have completed the schedule, if required.

Filter by	Specifies the field to filter. Not all fields are available to be filtered.
Condition	Specifies the condition that must be met. This includes options such as **equal**, **not equal**, **greater than**, and **less than**.
Value	Specifies the value of the element to be filtered. You can select from a drop-down list of appropriate values. For example, if you set *Filter By* to **Level**, it displays the list of levels in the project.

Schedule Properties – Sorting/Grouping Tab

In the *Sorting/Grouping* tab, you can set how you want the information to be sorted, as shown in Figure B–52. For example, you can sort by **Mark** (number) and then **Type**.

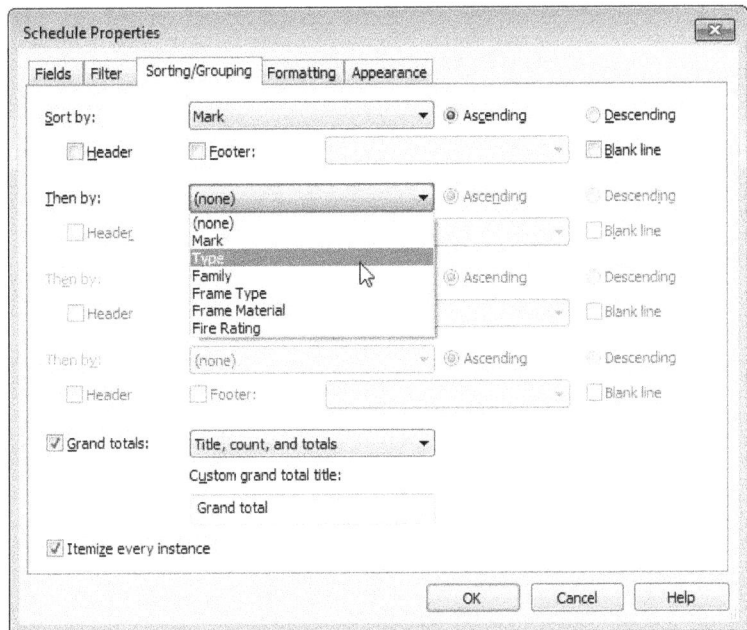

Figure B–52

Sort by	Enables you to select the field(s) you want to sort by. You can select up to four levels of sorting.
Ascending/ Descending	Sorts fields in **Ascending** or **Descending** order.
Header/Footer	Enables you to group similar information and separate it by a **Header** with a title and/or a **Footer** with quantity information.
Blank line	Adds a blank line between groups.
Grand totals	Selects which totals to display for the entire schedule. You can specify a name to display in the schedule for the Grand total.
Itemize every instance	If selected, displays each instance of the element in the schedule. If not selected, displays only one instance of each type, as shown in Figure B–53.

Enhanced
in 2015

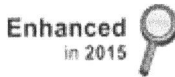

Figure B–53

Schedule Properties – Formatting Tab

In the *Formatting* tab, you can control how the headers of each field display, as shown in Figure B–54.

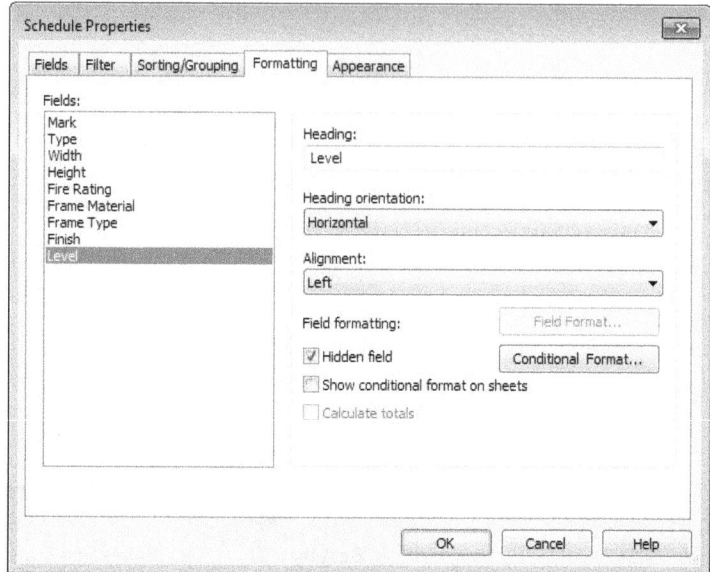

Figure B–54

Fields	Enables you to select the field for which you want to modify the formatting.
Heading	Enables you to change the heading of the field if you want it to be different from the field name. For example, you might want to replace **Mark** (a generic name) with the more specific **Door Number** in a door schedule.
Heading orientation	Enables you to set the heading on sheets to **Horizontal** or **Vertical**. This does not impact the schedule view.
Alignment	Aligns the text in rows under the heading to be **Left**, **Right**, or **Center**.
Field Format...	Sets the units format for the length, area, volume, angle, or number field. By default, this is set to use the project settings.
Conditional Format...	Sets up the schedule to display visual feedback based on the conditions listed.
Hidden field	Enables you to hide a field. For example, you might want to use a field for sorting purposes, but not have it display in the schedule. You can also modify this option in the schedule view later.

Show conditional format on sheets	Select if you want the color code set up in the Conditional Format dialog box to display on sheets.
Calculate totals	Displays the subtotals of numerical columns in a group.

Schedule Properties – Appearance Tab

In the *Appearance* tab, you can set the text style and grid options for a schedule, as shown in Figure B–55.

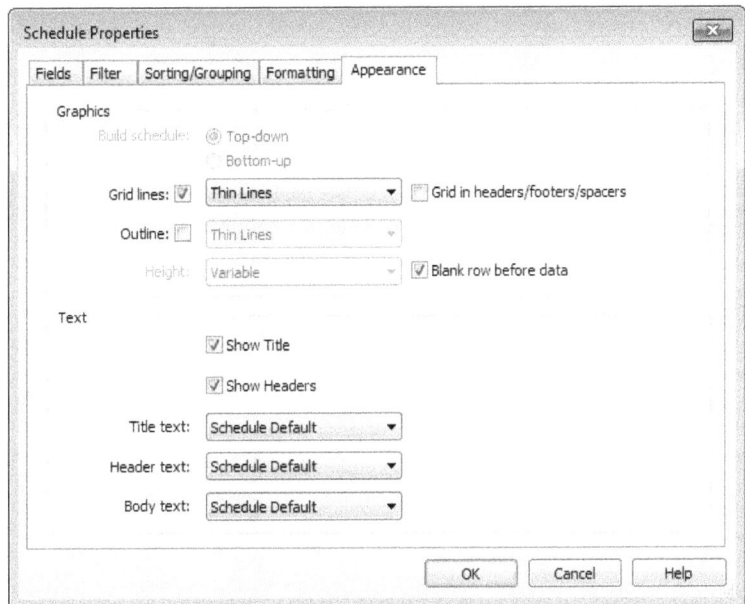

Figure B–55

Grid lines	Displays lines between each instance listed and around the outside of the schedule. Select the style of lines from the drop-down list; this controls all lines for the schedule, unless modified.
Grid in headers/footers/ spacers	Extends the vertical grid lines between the columns.
Outline	Specify a different line type for the outline of the schedule.
Blank row before data	Select this option if you want a blank row to be displayed before the data begins in the schedule.

Show Title/Show Headers	Select these options to include the text in the schedule.
Title text/Header text/Body Text	Select the text style for the title, header, and body text.

Schedule Properties

Schedule views have properties including the *View Name*, *Phases* and methods of returning to the Schedule Properties dialog box as shown in Figure B–56. In the *Other* area, select the button next to the tab that you want to open in the Schedule Properties dialog box. In the dialog box, you can switch from tab to tab and make any required changes to the overall schedule.

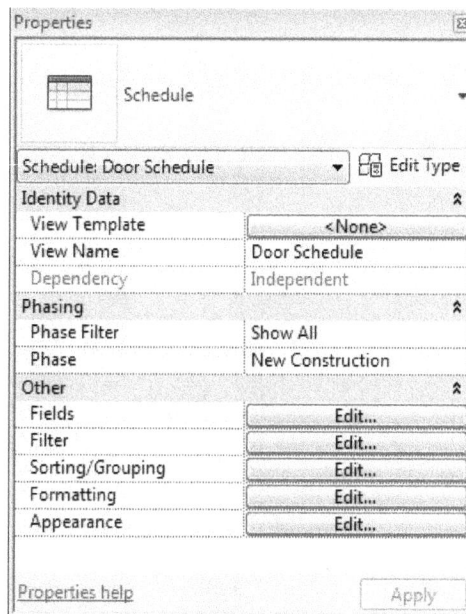

Figure B–56

B.9 Creating a Repeating Detail

Learning Objective

- Turn a detail component into a repeating detail component.

Repeating detail components are very useful when working on complex details, such as those that include a brick wall. You can also create a repeating detail using any detail component, such as the glass block shown in Figure B–57.

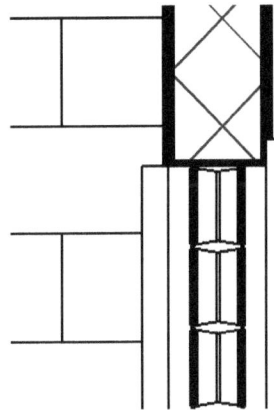

Figure B–57

How To: Create a Repeating Detail

1. Load the detail component you want to use.

2. In the *Annotate* tab>Detail panel, expand ▣ (Component) and click ▤ (Repeating Detail Component).

3. In Properties, click ▣ (Edit Type).

4. In the Type Properties dialog box, click [Duplicate]. Enter a name.

5. Set the *Detail* parameter. This is the component name.

6. Fill out the rest of the parameters, as shown in Figure B–58.

Parameter	Value
Pattern	⟨⟩
Detail	Brick - UK Standard : Running Sec
Layout	Fixed Distance
Inside	☐
Spacing	75.0
Detail Rotation	None

Figure B–58

7. Set the *Layout* to **Fill Available Space**, **Fixed Distance**, **Fixed Number**, or **Maximum Spacing**. Select the **Inside** option if you want all components to be within the specified distance or line. Leaving this option clear causes the first component to start before the first point.

8. Set the *Spacing* between components if you are using **Fixed Distance** or **Maximum Spacing**.

9. Set the *Detail Rotation* as required, and close the dialog box.

Command Summary

Button	Command	Location
Annotations		
	Matchline	• **Ribbon:** *View* tab>Sheet Composition panel
	View Reference	• **Ribbon:** *View* tab>Sheet Composition panel or *Annotate* tab>Tag panel
Curtain Walls		
N/A	**Edit Type**	• **Properties** (with a Curtain Wall type selected)
Details		
	Edit Type	• **Properties** (with a Repeating Detail element selected)
Dormers		
	Dormer	• **Ribbon:** *Architecture* tab>Opening panel
Revisions		
	Revision Cloud	• **Ribbon:** *Annotate* tab>Detail panel
	Sheet Issues/ Revisions	• **Ribbon:** *Manage* tab>Settings panel> expand Additional Settings
Schedules		
	Schedule/ Quantities	• **Ribbon:** *View* tab>Create panel> expand Schedules
Selection Sets		
	Edit Selection	• **Ribbon:** *Modify	Multi-Select* tab>Selection panel
	Load Selection	• **Ribbon:** *Modify	Multi-Select* tab>Selection panel
	Save Selection	• **Ribbon:** *Modify	Multi-Select* tab>Selection panel
Sweeps and Reveals		
	Floor: Slab Edge	• **Ribbon:** *Architecture* tab>Build panel or *Structure* tab>Structure panel> expand Floor
	Roof: Fascia	• **Ribbon:** *Architecture* tab>Build panel> expand Roof
	Roof: Gutter	• **Ribbon:** *Architecture* tab>Build panel> expand Roof

	Wall: Reveal	• **Ribbon:** *Architecture* tab>Build panel or *Structure* tab>Structure panel> expand Wall
	Wall: Sweep	• **Ribbon:** *Architecture* tab>Build panel or *Structure* tab>Structure panel> expand Wall

Views

	Cut Profile	• **Ribbon:** *View* tab>Graphics panel
	Insert Views from File	• **Ribbon:** *Insert* tab>Import panel> expand Insert from File
	Join Geometry	• **Ribbon:** *Modify* tab>Geometry panel>expand Join
	Line Styles	• **Ribbon:** *Manage* tab>Settings panel> expand Additional Settings
	Linework	• **Ribbon:** *Modify* tab>View panel • **Shortcut:** <L> and <W>
	Paint	• **Ribbon:** *Modify* tab>Geometry panel
	Pick New Host	• **Ribbon:** *Modify	varies* tab>Host panel
	Split Face	• **Ribbon:** *Modify* tab>Geometry panel
	Unjoin Geometry	• **Ribbon:** *Modify* tab>Geometry panel>expand Join
	Wall Joins	• **Ribbon:** *Modify* tab>Geometry panel

Appendix C

Autodesk Revit 2015 Certification Exam Objectives

This appendix lists the Autodesk Revit 2015 Certification Exam Objectives for both the Professional and User exams.

This appendix contains the following topics:

- **Autodesk Certified Exam Objectives**

C.1 Autodesk Certified Exam Objectives

The following table will help you to locate the exam objectives within the chapters of the *Autodesk Revit 2015 Architecture Fundamentals* training guide to help you prepare for the Autodesk Revit 2015 Certified Professional (Pro.) and Autodesk Revit 2015 Certified User exams.

Pro.	User	Exam Objectives	Training Guide & Chapter
User Interface			
	✓	Change the view scale	• **Fundamentals:** Ch. 1
	✓	Identify file types	• **Fundamentals:** Ch. 1
	✓	Identify primary parts of the User Interface (UI)	• **Fundamentals:** Ch. 1
✓	✓	Use the Project Browser	• **Fundamentals:** Ch. 1
Collaboration			
✓		Copy and monitor elements in a linked file	• **Collaboration Tools:** Ch. 2
✓		Import DWG and image files	• **Fundamentals:** Ch. 3 • **Collaboration Tools:** Ch. 3
✓		Use worksharing	• **Collaboration Tools:** Ch. 4
Documentation			
	✓	Create a title sheet	• **Fundamentals:** Ch. 13
✓		Create and modify filled regions	• **Fundamentals:** Ch. 16
✓		Place detail components and repeating details	• **Fundamentals:** Ch. 16
✓		Set the colors used in a color scheme legend	• **Conceptual Design and Visualization:** Ch. 2
✓	✓	Tag elements (doors, windows, etc.) by category	• **Fundamentals:** Ch. 15
✓		Use dimension strings	• **Fundamentals:** Ch. 14
✓		Work with phases	• **Collaboration Tools:** Ch. 1

Pro.	User	Exam Objectives	Training Guide & Chapter
Elements			
✓		Change elements within a curtain wall	• **Fundamentals:** Ch. 6
✓		Create a new family type	• **Fundamentals:** Ch. 5 • **BIM Management:** Ch. 4
✓		Create a stacked wall	• **BIM Management:** Ch. 3
	✓	Create and modify walls	• **Fundamentals:** Ch. 4
✓		Create compound walls	• **BIM Management:** Ch. 3
✓		Differentiate system and component families	• **BIM Management:** Ch. 3 and 4
	✓	Edit doors	• **Fundamentals:** Ch. 5
	✓	Edit windows	• **Fundamentals:** Ch. 5
	✓	Trim objects	• **Fundamentals:** Ch. 2
✓		Work with family Parameters	• **BIM Management:** Ch. 4
Families			
✓		Assess review warnings in Revit	• **Fundamentals:** Ch. 12
✓		Use Family creation procedures	• **BIM Management:** Ch. 4
✓	✓	Work with families	• **Fundamentals:** Ch. 8
Modeling			
	✓	Add dimensions	• **Fundamentals:** Ch. 14
	✓	Add model text to a plan	• **Fundamentals:** Ch. 14
✓		Attach walls to a roof or ceiling	• **Fundamentals:** Ch. 11
✓		Change a generic floor/ceiling/roof to a specific type	• **Fundamentals:** Ch. 9, 10, and 11
✓		Create a building pad	• **Site and Structural Design:** Ch. 1
✓	✓	Create a stair with a landing	• **Fundamentals:** Ch. 12
✓		Create elements such as floors, ceilings, or roofs	• **Fundamentals:** Ch. 9, 10, and 11
✓		Define floors for a mass	• **Conceptual Design and Visualization:** Ch. 1
✓		Edit a model element's material	• **BIM Management:** Ch. 4 and 6

Pro.	User	Exam Objectives	Training Guide & Chapter
✓		Edit room-aware families	• **BIM Management:** Ch. 4
✓		Generate a toposurface	• **Site and Structural Design:** Ch. 1
✓	✓	Model railings	• **Fundamentals:** Ch. 12
	✓	Use grids	• **Fundamentals:** Ch. 3
Views			
✓		Control visibility	• **Fundamentals:** Ch. 7
✓		Create a duplicate view for a plan, section, elevation, drafting view, etc.	• **Fundamentals:** Ch. 7
	✓	Create a schedule and add schedule tags	• **Fundamentals:** App. B
✓		Create and manage legends	• **Fundamentals:** Ch. 14
	✓	Create section views	• **Fundamentals:** Ch. 7
✓		Define element properties in a schedule	• **Fundamentals:** Ch. 15
✓		Manage view position on sheets	• **Fundamentals:** Ch. 13
✓		Organize and sort items in a schedule	• **Fundamentals:** App. B • **BIM Management:** Ch. 2
✓	✓	Use levels	• **Fundamentals:** Ch. 3

Index

www.ingramcontent.com/pod-product-compliance
Lightning Source LLC
Chambersburg PA
CBHW060939210326

41598CB00031B/4677

* 9 7 8 1 9 4 3 1 8 4 0 7 1 *